Lecture Notes in Computer Science 8519

Commenced Publication in 1973
Founding and Former Series Editors:
Gerhard Goos, Juris Hartmanis, and Jan van Leeuwen

Aaron Marcus (Ed.)

Design, User Experience, and Usability

User Experience Design for Everyday
Life Applications and Services

Third International Conference, DUXU 2014
Held as Part of HCI International 2014
Heraklion, Crete, Greece, June 22-27, 2014
Proceedings, Part III

 Springer

Volume Editor

Aaron Marcus
Aaron Marcus and Associates, Inc.
1196 Euclid Avenue, Suite 1F, Berkeley, CA 94708-1640, USA
E-mail: aaron.marcus@AMandA.com

ISSN 0302-9743   e-ISSN 1611-3349
ISBN 978-3-319-07634-8   e-ISBN 978-3-319-07635-5
DOI 10.1007/978-3-319-07635-5
Springer Cham Heidelberg New York Dordrecht London

Library of Congress Control Number: 2014939619

LNCS Sublibrary: SL 3 – Information Systems and Application, incl. Internet/Web
and HCI

Typesetting: Camera-ready by author, data conversion by Scientific Publishing Services, Chennai, India

Printed on acid-free paper

Springer is part of Springer Science+Business Media (www.springer.com)

Foreword

The 16th International Conference on Human–Computer Interaction, HCI International 2014, was held in Heraklion, Crete, Greece, during June 22–27, 2014, incorporating 14 conferences/thematic areas:

Thematic areas:

- Human–Computer Interaction
- Human Interface and the Management of Information

Affiliated conferences:

- 11th International Conference on Engineering Psychology and Cognitive Ergonomics
- 8th International Conference on Universal Access in Human–Computer Interaction
- 6th International Conference on Virtual, Augmented and Mixed Reality
- 6th International Conference on Cross-Cultural Design
- 6th International Conference on Social Computing and Social Media
- 8th International Conference on Augmented Cognition
- 5th International Conference on Digital Human Modeling and Applications in Health, Safety, Ergonomics and Risk Management
- Third International Conference on Design, User Experience and Usability
- Second International Conference on Distributed, Ambient and Pervasive Interactions
- Second International Conference on Human Aspects of Information Security, Privacy and Trust
- First International Conference on HCI in Business
- First International Conference on Learning and Collaboration Technologies

A total of 4,766 individuals from academia, research institutes, industry, and governmental agencies from 78 countries submitted contributions, and 1,476 papers and 225 posters were included in the proceedings. These papers address the latest research and development efforts and highlight the human aspects of design and use of computing systems. The papers thoroughly cover the entire field of human–computer interaction, addressing major advances in knowledge and effective use of computers in a variety of application areas.

This volume, edited by Aaron Marcus, contains papers focusing on the thematic area of Design, User Experience and Usability, addressing the following major topics:

- Design for health
- Design for reading and learning

- Design for mobility, transport and safety
- Design for rural, low literacy and developing communities
- Design for environment and sustainability
- Design for human-computer symbiosis

The remaining volumes of the HCI International 2014 proceedings are:

- Volume 1, LNCS 8510, Human–Computer Interaction: HCI Theories, Methods and Tools (Part I), edited by Masaaki Kurosu
- Volume 2, LNCS 8511, Human–Computer Interaction: Advanced Interaction Modalities and Techniques (Part II), edited by Masaaki Kurosu
- Volume 3, LNCS 8512, Human–Computer Interaction: Applications and Services (Part III), edited by Masaaki Kurosu
- Volume 4, LNCS 8513, Universal Access in Human–Computer Interaction: Design and Development Methods for Universal Access (Part I), edited by Constantine Stephanidis and Margherita Antona
- Volume 5, LNCS 8514, Universal Access in Human–Computer Interaction: Universal Access to Information and Knowledge (Part II), edited by Constantine Stephanidis and Margherita Antona
- Volume 6, LNCS 8515, Universal Access in Human–Computer Interaction: Aging and Assistive Environments (Part III), edited by Constantine Stephanidis and Margherita Antona
- Volume 7, LNCS 8516, Universal Access in Human–Computer Interaction: Design for All and Accessibility Practice (Part IV), edited by Constantine Stephanidis and Margherita Antona
- Volume 8, LNCS 8517, Design, User Experience, and Usability: Theories, Methods and Tools for Designing the User Experience (Part I), edited by Aaron Marcus
- Volume 9, LNCS 8518, Design, User Experience, and Usability: User Experience Design for Diverse Interaction Platforms and Environments (Part II), edited by Aaron Marcus
- Volume 11, LNCS 8520, Design, User Experience, and Usability: User Experience Design Practice (Part IV), edited by Aaron Marcus
- Volume 12, LNCS 8521, Human Interface and the Management of Information: Information and Knowledge Design and Evaluation (Part I), edited by Sakae Yamamoto
- Volume 13, LNCS 8522, Human Interface and the Management of Information: Information and Knowledge in Applications and Services (Part II), edited by Sakae Yamamoto
- Volume 14, LNCS 8523, Learning and Collaboration Technologies: Designing and Developing Novel Learning Experiences (Part I), edited by Panayiotis Zaphiris and Andri Ioannou
- Volume 15, LNCS 8524, Learning and Collaboration Technologies: Technology-rich Environments for Learning and Collaboration (Part II), edited by Panayiotis Zaphiris and Andri Ioannou

- Volume 16, LNCS 8525, Virtual, Augmented and Mixed Reality: Designing and Developing Virtual and Augmented Environments (Part I), edited by Randall Shumaker and Stephanie Lackey
- Volume 17, LNCS 8526, Virtual, Augmented and Mixed Reality: Applications of Virtual and Augmented Reality (Part II), edited by Randall Shumaker and Stephanie Lackey
- Volume 18, LNCS 8527, HCI in Business, edited by Fiona Fui-Hoon Nah
- Volume 19, LNCS 8528, Cross-Cultural Design, edited by P.L. Patrick Rau
- Volume 20, LNCS 8529, Digital Human Modeling and Applications in Health, Safety, Ergonomics and Risk Management, edited by Vincent G. Duffy
- Volume 21, LNCS 8530, Distributed, Ambient, and Pervasive Interactions, edited by Norbert Streitz and Panos Markopoulos
- Volume 22, LNCS 8531, Social Computing and Social Media, edited by Gabriele Meiselwitz
- Volume 23, LNAI 8532, Engineering Psychology and Cognitive Ergonomics, edited by Don Harris
- Volume 24, LNCS 8533, Human Aspects of Information Security, Privacy and Trust, edited by Theo Tryfonas and Ioannis Askoxylakis
- Volume 25, LNAI 8534, Foundations of Augmented Cognition, edited by Dylan D. Schmorrow and Cali M. Fidopiastis
- Volume 26, CCIS 434, HCI International 2014 Posters Proceedings (Part I), edited by Constantine Stephanidis
- Volume 27, CCIS 435, HCI International 2014 Posters Proceedings (Part II), edited by Constantine Stephanidis

I would like to thank the Program Chairs and the members of the Program Boards of all affiliated conferences and thematic areas, listed below, for their contribution to the highest scientific quality and the overall success of the HCI International 2014 Conference.

This conference could not have been possible without the continuous support and advice of the founding chair and conference scientific advisor, Prof. Gavriel Salvendy, as well as the dedicated work and outstanding efforts of the communications chair and editor of *HCI International News*, Dr. Abbas Moallem.

I would also like to thank for their contribution towards the smooth organization of the HCI International 2014 Conference the members of the Human–Computer Interaction Laboratory of ICS-FORTH, and in particular George Paparoulis, Maria Pitsoulaki, Maria Bouhli, and George Kapnas.

April 2014   Constantine Stephanidis
                                            General Chair, HCI International 2014

Organization

Human–Computer Interaction

Program Chair: Masaaki Kurosu, Japan

Jose Abdelnour-Nocera, UK
Sebastiano Bagnara, Italy
Simone Barbosa, Brazil
Adriana Betiol, Brazil
Simone Borsci, UK
Henry Duh, Australia
Xiaowen Fang, USA
Vicki Hanson, UK
Wonil Hwang, Korea
Minna Isomursu, Finland
Yong Gu Ji, Korea
Anirudha Joshi, India
Esther Jun, USA
Kyungdoh Kim, Korea

Heidi Krömker, Germany
Chen Ling, USA
Chang S. Nam, USA
Naoko Okuizumi, Japan
Philippe Palanque, France
Ling Rothrock, USA
Naoki Sakakibara, Japan
Dominique Scapin, France
Guangfeng Song, USA
Sanjay Tripathi, India
Chui Yin Wong, Malaysia
Toshiki Yamaoka, Japan
Kazuhiko Yamazaki, Japan
Ryoji Yoshitake, Japan

Human Interface and the Management of Information

Program Chair: Sakae Yamamoto, Japan

Alan Chan, Hong Kong
Denis A. Coelho, Portugal
Linda Elliott, USA
Shin'ichi Fukuzumi, Japan
Michitaka Hirose, Japan
Makoto Itoh, Japan
Yen-Yu Kang, Taiwan
Koji Kimita, Japan
Daiji Kobayashi, Japan

Hiroyuki Miki, Japan
Shogo Nishida, Japan
Robert Proctor, USA
Youngho Rhee, Korea
Ryosuke Saga, Japan
Katsunori Shimohara, Japan
Kim-Phuong Vu, USA
Tomio Watanabe, Japan

Engineering Psychology and Cognitive Ergonomics

Program Chair: Don Harris, UK

Guy Andre Boy, USA
Shan Fu, P.R. China
Hung-Sying Jing, Taiwan
Wen-Chin Li, Taiwan
Mark Neerincx, The Netherlands
Jan Noyes, UK
Paul Salmon, Australia

Axel Schulte, Germany
Siraj Shaikh, UK
Sarah Sharples, UK
Anthony Smoker, UK
Neville Stanton, UK
Alex Stedmon, UK
Andrew Thatcher, South Africa

Universal Access in Human–Computer Interaction

**Program Chairs: Constantine Stephanidis, Greece,
and Margherita Antona, Greece**

Julio Abascal, Spain
Gisela Susanne Bahr, USA
João Barroso, Portugal
Margrit Betke, USA
Anthony Brooks, Denmark
Christian Bühler, Germany
Stefan Carmien, Spain
Hua Dong, P.R. China
Carlos Duarte, Portugal
Pier Luigi Emiliani, Italy
Qin Gao, P.R. China
Andrina Granić, Croatia
Andreas Holzinger, Austria
Josette Jones, USA
Simeon Keates, UK

Georgios Kouroupetroglou, Greece
Patrick Langdon, UK
Barbara Leporini, Italy
Eugene Loos, The Netherlands
Ana Isabel Paraguay, Brazil
Helen Petrie, UK
Michael Pieper, Germany
Enrico Pontelli, USA
Jaime Sanchez, Chile
Alberto Sanna, Italy
Anthony Savidis, Greece
Christian Stary, Austria
Hirotada Ueda, Japan
Gerhard Weber, Germany
Harald Weber, Germany

Virtual, Augmented and Mixed Reality

**Program Chairs: Randall Shumaker, USA,
and Stephanie Lackey, USA**

Roland Blach, Germany
Sheryl Brahnam, USA
Juan Cendan, USA
Jessie Chen, USA
Panagiotis D. Kaklis, UK

Hirokazu Kato, Japan
Denis Laurendeau, Canada
Fotis Liarokapis, UK
Michael Macedonia, USA
Gordon Mair, UK

Jose San Martin, Spain
Tabitha Peck, USA
Christian Sandor, Australia

Christopher Stapleton, USA
Gregory Welch, USA

Cross-Cultural Design

Program Chair: P.L. Patrick Rau, P.R. China

Yee-Yin Choong, USA
Paul Fu, USA
Zhiyong Fu, P.R. China
Pin-Chao Liao, P.R. China
Dyi-Yih Michael Lin, Taiwan
Rungtai Lin, Taiwan
Ta-Ping (Robert) Lu, Taiwan
Liang Ma, P.R. China
Alexander Mädche, Germany

Sheau-Farn Max Liang, Taiwan
Katsuhiko Ogawa, Japan
Tom Plocher, USA
Huatong Sun, USA
Emil Tso, P.R. China
Hsiu-Ping Yueh, Taiwan
Liang (Leon) Zeng, USA
Jia Zhou, P.R. China

Online Communities and Social Media

Program Chair: Gabriele Meiselwitz, USA

Leonelo Almeida, Brazil
Chee Siang Ang, UK
Aneesha Bakharia, Australia
Ania Bobrowicz, UK
James Braman, USA
Farzin Deravi, UK
Carsten Kleiner, Germany
Niki Lambropoulos, Greece
Soo Ling Lim, UK

Anthony Norcio, USA
Portia Pusey, USA
Panote Siriaraya, UK
Stefan Stieglitz, Germany
Giovanni Vincenti, USA
Yuanqiong (Kathy) Wang, USA
June Wei, USA
Brian Wentz, USA

Augmented Cognition

**Program Chairs: Dylan D. Schmorrow, USA,
and Cali M. Fidopiastis, USA**

Ahmed Abdelkhalek, USA
Robert Atkinson, USA
Monique Beaudoin, USA
John Blitch, USA
Alenka Brown, USA

Rosario Cannavò, Italy
Joseph Cohn, USA
Andrew J. Cowell, USA
Martha Crosby, USA
Wai-Tat Fu, USA

Rodolphe Gentili, USA
Frederick Gregory, USA
Michael W. Hail, USA
Monte Hancock, USA
Fei Hu, USA
Ion Juvina, USA
Joe Keebler, USA
Philip Mangos, USA
Rao Mannepalli, USA
David Martinez, USA
Yvonne R. Masakowski, USA
Santosh Mathan, USA
Ranjeev Mittu, USA

Keith Niall, USA
Tatana Olson, USA
Debra Patton, USA
June Pilcher, USA
Robinson Pino, USA
Tiffany Poeppelman, USA
Victoria Romero, USA
Amela Sadagic, USA
Anna Skinner, USA
Ann Speed, USA
Robert Sottilare, USA
Peter Walker, USA

Digital Human Modeling and Applications in Health, Safety, Ergonomics and Risk Management

Program Chair: Vincent G. Duffy, USA

Giuseppe Andreoni, Italy
Daniel Carruth, USA
Elsbeth De Korte, The Netherlands
Afzal A. Godil, USA
Ravindra Goonetilleke, Hong Kong
Noriaki Kuwahara, Japan
Kang Li, USA
Zhizhong Li, P.R. China

Tim Marler, USA
Jianwei Niu, P.R. China
Michelle Robertson, USA
Matthias Rötting, Germany
Mao-Jiun Wang, Taiwan
Xuguang Wang, France
James Yang, USA

Design, User Experience, and Usability

Program Chair: Aaron Marcus, USA

Sisira Adikari, Australia
Claire Ancient, USA
Arne Berger, Germany
Jamie Blustein, Canada
Ana Boa-Ventura, USA
Jan Brejcha, Czech Republic
Lorenzo Cantoni, Switzerland
Marc Fabri, UK
Luciane Maria Fadel, Brazil
Tricia Flanagan, Hong Kong
Jorge Frascara, Mexico

Federico Gobbo, Italy
Emilie Gould, USA
Rüdiger Heimgärtner, Germany
Brigitte Herrmann, Germany
Steffen Hess, Germany
Nouf Khashman, Canada
Fabiola Guillermina Noël, Mexico
Francisco Rebelo, Portugal
Kerem Rızvanoğlu, Turkey
Marcelo Soares, Brazil
Carla Spinillo, Brazil

Distributed, Ambient and Pervasive Interactions

Program Chairs: Norbert Streitz, Germany, and Panos Markopoulos, The Netherlands

Juan Carlos Augusto, UK
Jose Bravo, Spain
Adrian Cheok, UK
Boris de Ruyter, The Netherlands
Anind Dey, USA
Dimitris Grammenos, Greece
Nuno Guimaraes, Portugal
Achilles Kameas, Greece
Javed Vassilis Khan, The Netherlands
Shin'ichi Konomi, Japan
Carsten Magerkurth, Switzerland

Ingrid Mulder, The Netherlands
Anton Nijholt, The Netherlands
Fabio Paternó, Italy
Carsten Röcker, Germany
Teresa Romao, Portugal
Albert Ali Salah, Turkey
Manfred Tscheligi, Austria
Reiner Wichert, Germany
Woontack Woo, Korea
Xenophon Zabulis, Greece

Human Aspects of Information Security, Privacy and Trust

Program Chairs: Theo Tryfonas, UK, and Ioannis Askoxylakis, Greece

Claudio Agostino Ardagna, Italy
Zinaida Benenson, Germany
Daniele Catteddu, Italy
Raoul Chiesa, Italy
Bryan Cline, USA
Sadie Creese, UK
Jorge Cuellar, Germany
Marc Dacier, USA
Dieter Gollmann, Germany
Kirstie Hawkey, Canada
Jaap-Henk Hoepman, The Netherlands
Cagatay Karabat, Turkey
Angelos Keromytis, USA
Ayako Komatsu, Japan
Ronald Leenes, The Netherlands
Javier Lopez, Spain
Steve Marsh, Canada

Gregorio Martinez, Spain
Emilio Mordini, Italy
Yuko Murayama, Japan
Masakatsu Nishigaki, Japan
Aljosa Pasic, Spain
Milan Petković, The Netherlands
Joachim Posegga, Germany
Jean-Jacques Quisquater, Belgium
Damien Sauveron, France
George Spanoudakis, UK
Kerry-Lynn Thomson, South Africa
Julien Touzeau, France
Theo Tryfonas, UK
João Vilela, Portugal
Claire Vishik, UK
Melanie Volkamer, Germany

HCI in Business

Program Chair: Fiona Fui-Hoon Nah, USA

Andreas Auinger, Austria
Michel Avital, Denmark
Traci Carte, USA
Hock Chuan Chan, Singapore
Constantinos Coursaris, USA
Soussan Djamasbi, USA
Brenda Eschenbrenner, USA
Nobuyuki Fukawa, USA
Khaled Hassanein, Canada
Milena Head, Canada
Susanna (Shuk Ying) Ho, Australia
Jack Zhenhui Jiang, Singapore
Jinwoo Kim, Korea
Zoonky Lee, Korea
Honglei Li, UK
Nicholas Lockwood, USA
Eleanor T. Loiacono, USA
Mei Lu, USA

Scott McCoy, USA
Brian Mennecke, USA
Robin Poston, USA
Lingyun Qiu, P.R. China
Rene Riedl, Austria
Matti Rossi, Finland
April Savoy, USA
Shu Schiller, USA
Hong Sheng, USA
Choon Ling Sia, Hong Kong
Chee-Wee Tan, Denmark
Chuan Hoo Tan, Hong Kong
Noam Tractinsky, Israel
Horst Treiblmaier, Austria
Virpi Tuunainen, Finland
Dezhi Wu, USA
I-Chin Wu, Taiwan

Learning and Collaboration Technologies

**Program Chairs: Panayiotis Zaphiris, Cyprus,
and Andri Ioannou, Cyprus**

Ruthi Aladjem, Israel
Abdulaziz Aldaej, UK
John M. Carroll, USA
Maka Eradze, Estonia
Mikhail Fominykh, Norway
Denis Gillet, Switzerland
Mustafa Murat Inceoglu, Turkey
Pernilla Josefsson, Sweden
Marie Joubert, UK
Sauli Kiviranta, Finland
Tomaž Klobučar, Slovenia
Elena Kyza, Cyprus
Maarten de Laat, The Netherlands
David Lamas, Estonia

Edmund Laugasson, Estonia
Ana Loureiro, Portugal
Katherine Maillet, France
Nadia Pantidi, UK
Antigoni Parmaxi, Cyprus
Borzoo Pourabdollahian, Italy
Janet C. Read, UK
Christophe Reffay, France
Nicos Souleles, Cyprus
Ana Luísa Torres, Portugal
Stefan Trausan-Matu, Romania
Aimilia Tzanavari, Cyprus
Johnny Yuen, Hong Kong
Carmen Zahn, Switzerland

External Reviewers

Ilia Adami, Greece
Iosif Klironomos, Greece
Maria Korozi, Greece
Vassilis Kouroumalis, Greece

Asterios Leonidis, Greece
George Margetis, Greece
Stavroula Ntoa, Greece
Nikolaos Partarakis, Greece

HCI International 2015

The 15th International Conference on Human–Computer Interaction, HCI International 2015, will be held jointly with the affiliated conferences in Los Angeles, CA, USA, in the Westin Bonaventure Hotel, August 2–7, 2015. It will cover a broad spectrum of themes related to HCI, including theoretical issues, methods, tools, processes, and case studies in HCI design, as well as novel interaction techniques, interfaces, and applications. The proceedings will be published by Springer. More information will be available on the conference website: http://www.hcii2015.org/

General Chair
Professor Constantine Stephanidis
University of Crete and ICS-FORTH
Heraklion, Crete, Greece
E-mail: cs@ics.forth.gr

Table of Contents – Part III

Design for Health

Design for Reading and Learning

Design for Mobility, Transport and Safety

Design for Rural, Low Literacy and Developing Communities

Design for Environment and Sustainability

Design for Human-Computer Symbiosis

Design for Health

User Experience in Training a Personalized Hearing System

Gabriel Aldaz[1], Tyler Haydell[1], Dafna Szafer[1], Martin Steinert[2], Larry Leifer[1]

[1] Mechanical Engineering, Stanford University
{zamfir,thaydell,dszafer,leifer}@stanford.edu

Abstract. In this paper, we introduce Awear, a context-aware hearing system comprising two state-of-the-art hearing aids, an Android smartphone, and a body-worn Streamer to wirelessly connect them. Awear aims to improve the sound quality perceived by individual hearing aid wearers by learning from their stated preferences. Users personalize, or "train," the system by performing several *listening evaluations* daily. The Awear app features two types of user-initiated listening evaluations, the A/B Test and the Self-Adjustment Screen. After a longitudinal (6-week) study in which hearing impaired participants ($n = 16$) used Awear, 10 of the participants stated a preference for training their system using the A/B Test, 3 preferred using the Self-Adjustment Screen, and 3 stated No Preference. Of the 10 who chose the A/B Test, 7 named simplicity or intuitiveness as the primary reason for this preference. We also found a strong correlation between user level of functionality and listening evaluation preference, and a supplemental interview ($n = 24$) verified this correlation. Lastly, we discuss the most important aspects of the user experience: cognitive, functional, and psychological dimensions.

Keywords: User experience, hearing aids, smartphones, personalization, mobile apps, listening evaluations.

1 Background

According to the World Health Organization, 360 million people (over 5% of the world's population) have hearing loss [17]. In the United States, hearing loss affects 34.25 million people, more than 10% of the population; surprisingly only 1 in 4 Americans with hearing loss uses hearing aids [12]. In Germany, France, and the UK, hearing aid adoption is only slightly higher, perhaps due to government incentives [10].

For those who can benefit from hearing aids, have the financial means, and are willing to take action, the first step to better hearing is often to undergo a thorough evaluation by a hearing care professional. A fundamental part of the hearing care professional's audiological assessment is to use an audiometer to generate an audiogram, a representation of the softest sounds a patient can hear at different frequencies in each ear. Another important consideration during the audiological assessment is choosing a fitting rationale. A fitting rationale is a prescriptive formula

A. Marcus (Ed.): DUXU 2014, Part III, LNCS 8519, pp. 3–14, 2014.

describing the electro-acoustical characteristics of the hearing aids in response to given inputs.

The audiogram and fitting rationale only partially address the fact that hearing loss is an individual experience. How the brain processes sensory information varies from person to person, and two people with similar audiograms and fitting rationales may experience different levels of satisfaction in the long run [5]. Therefore, most fittings require multiple office visits to fine-tune the parameters correctly.

A person wearing advanced hearing aids in their daily life benefits from the devices' real-time digital signal processing, implementing a selected fitting rationale and employing sophisticated algorithms to automatically select settings to enhance speech or suppress transient noise. Hearing aids have many automatic features, such as turning Directionality and Noise Reduction on and off, as well as classifying the current sound environment (quiet, noise, speech in noise, etc.). Nonetheless, a hearing aid has very limited sensor inputs, relying entirely on its two on-board microphones to collect information about incoming sounds. Furthermore, current adaptive algorithms in hearing aids lack the ability to improve performance over time in response to sensor inputs.

In 2007, Edwards described future hearing aids that could allow fine-tuning to be done automatically outside of the clinician's office and that would have the ability to learn, making them "intelligent." Edwards predicted a greater industry shift from uniformity of patients and universal treatment to individuality of patients and therapy [6]. While the relatively slow processing speed, small storage capabilities, and limited user interface of hearing aids have largely prevented Edwards' vision from becoming reality so far, these limitations may be overcome by regarding the smartphone as part of an intelligent hearing system.

The smartphone has the potential to revolutionize the way users interact with their hearing aids, providing unprecedented personalization and increased satisfaction levels. Smartphones provide a powerful mobile computing platform, with formidable sensing, processing, communication, and memory capabilities. While the hearing aids will continue to perform the real-time sound processing, the smartphone opens new possibilities for an additional layer of processing that takes into account factors that change on a much longer timescale – such as the user's sound environment, location, or even her intentions – known in the field of computer science as context awareness [15].

2   Related Work

Although Awear is, to our knowledge, the first context-aware hearing system, there are a number of hearing aid-related apps on the market today. These may be segmented as enabling users to interact with their hearing instruments through their smartphone, akin to a remote control, or as transforming a smartphone itself into a "personal amplification device."

2.1   Remote Controls

Today's advanced digital hearing aids can store several preset programs in their memories, each created for a different listening situation. There may be a general-purpose program, one for listening to music, and one for understanding speech in noisy environments. Program changes, along with volume control, are the primary mechanisms for users to make adjustments to improve sound quality. Presently, users may change program and volume via buttons on the hearing aids themselves, on gateway devices, or on dedicated remote controls.

ReSound [13] and Starkey [16] are two manufacturers that have launched apps that enable remote control of hearing aids via a smartphone. The ReSound Control and Starkey T2 Remote (Figure 1) have simple and straightforward interfaces that allow a user to control her device's volume and program on her smartphone. Although Control and T2 Remote do not offer any novel features, they open the door to a world of possibilities by giving users a much higher degree of convenience and discretion in controlling the settings of their hearing devices.

Fig. 1. Starkey T^2 Remote User Interface

2.2   Personal Amplification Apps

These apps use a smartphone's built-in microphone to pick up sound, amplify and adjust different qualities, and transmit the resulting sound using an off-the-shelf earpiece. Their primary advantage of these personal amplification apps is that they eliminate the need for users to purchase expensive hearing aids. However, software running on smartphones lacks the sophisticated digital signal processing of hearing aids and are often used without consulting a hearing care professional [2]. Furthermore, earpieces such as headphones and ear buds are not meant to be worn all day.

BioAid [1], created by a group at the University of Essex in England, aims to make sound amplification more accessible to those who cannot afford the steep cost of real hearing devices. The app offers six basic settings that the user can fine-tune using six additional screens. Finally, a "Noise Gate" allows the user to adjust background noise between 0-100%. This complicated interface raises the question of whether or not the average user will know how to interpret and make use of moderately technical language, or if users will ever even explore all twenty-four possible settings instead of settling for one of the presets. The same holds true for other available apps that try to mimic hearing aids without the actual devices. Apps including the SoundAMP from GingerLabs [8], HearYouNow from ExSilent [7], and others allow the user to control sound quality by adjusting the volume of individual frequencies, the volume of each ear, and even in some cases the controls for a dynamic compressor.

Fig. 2. BioAid (left) and SoundAMP (right)

3　　Awear: A Context-Aware Hearing System

3.1　Hardware

The Awear off-the-shelf hardware (Figure 3) comprises a pair of state-of-the-art hearing instruments, an Android-based smartphone, and a gateway, a body-worn device with a built-in microphone that wirelessly links the hearing aids to a mobile phone. In the future, we expect technological advances to enable direct 2-way communication between the hearing aids and the smartphone.

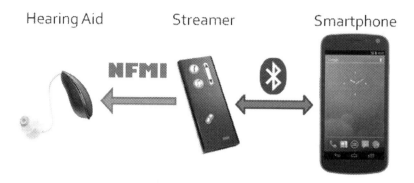

Fig. 3. Hardware components of the Awear system

3.2 User Interface

Although the Awear user interface works as a remote control – allowing the user to switch programs and change volume on the hearing instruments – its primary purpose is to solicit current user preferences for hearing aid microphone Directionality (on or off) and Noise Reduction (on or off)[1]. These interactions take place via user-initiated *listening evaluations*. There are two kinds of listening evaluations: the A/B Test and the Self-Adjustment Screen.

A/B Test. The A/B Test (Figure 4) is a standard method of comparing two variants applied here in a novel way to compare two hearing aid settings, A and B. The participant listens to both settings and gives a subjective, relative evaluation ("A is better," "B is better," or "No difference"). The settings corresponding to A (for example, "Directionality on and Noise Reduction off") and B (for example, "Directionality off and Noise Reduction off") are randomized during each evaluation.

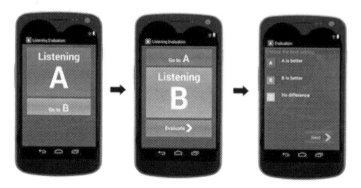

Fig. 4. A/B Test Screen Sequence

---

[1] Hearing aid microphones can be configured to pick up sounds uniformly from all directions (Directionality off) or primarily from the front (Directionality on). With Noise Reduction on, the hearing aids attempt to reduce amplification of non-speech signals while preserving the amplification of speech signals. Turning Noise Reduction off simply disables this digital signal processing step.

Self-Adjustment Screen. The self-adjustment screen (Figure 5) allows users to turn Directionality on/off and Noise Reduction on/off until they find their absolute preferred setting. Whereas the A/B test conceals the names of the settings, the Self-Adjustment Screen explicitly labels the settings, making them visible to the users.

Fig. 5. Self-Adjustment Screen (Directional Listening has just been turned on)

4   Method

Between July and December of 2013, we conducted a longitudinal (6-week) study of Awear with 16 participants (10 men, 6 women, mean age = 55.5 years) from the San Francisco Bay Area, enrolled by various private audiology clinics. All participants were at least 18 years old, had sufficient cognitive ability to successfully operate a smartphone and Awear software, and had moderate to severe hearing loss.

To understand which type of listening evaluation (A/B Test or Self-Adjustment Screen) benefited users more, we used a within-subjects study design. In the pre-interview, we asked participants about their background and demographics. Most of the data collected was self-explanatory, with the exception of "Experience" and "Functionality." Experience refers to that person's familiarity and use of computer and mobile technology. Table 1 is adapted from the typology in [9].

Table 1. User Experience Levels with Computer and Mobile Technology

Experience	Typical Assets	Typical Actions
High	Laptop Tablet Smartphone	Use computers for programming, creative work, or other advanced tasks Use mobile devices for calling, texting, information, sharing, and entertainment
Medium	Laptop Cell Phone	Use computers regularly for information, sharing, and entertainment Use mobile phones for calling and texting
Low	Desktop Cell phone	Use computer to explore internet and stay in touch with friends Use mobile phones for calling and texting
Zero	Landline phone	No online access

Functionality indicates how deeply a person delves into the features of a product. For example, a Low Functionality user may prefer to use point-and-shoot cameras, whereas a High Functionality person might want to explore the camera's technical features. Table 2 illustrates typical attitudes of these user types with regard to hearing aids.

Table 2. User Functionality Levels with Hearing Aid Technology

Functionality	Typical Assets	Typical Actions
High	Hearing aids with multiple programs and volume control	Actively change programs, use each one in its intended listening situation. Change volume several times per day
Low	Hearing aids with only one program, no volume control	Put on the hearing aids and forget *Laissez-faire* attitude

During in-situ use, participants were instructed to wear the system as often as possible during the test period of 6 weeks. Participants were instructed to do approximately 8 listening evaluations daily, especially whenever they encountered an interesting or challenging listening situation. At the conclusion of the test period, we asked the participants open-ended questions about hearing situations that they experienced and the performance of the context-aware hearing system.

In January 2014 we conducted a brief follow-up interview where we presented the two types of listening evaluations, in random order, to an additional 24 hearing impaired persons. The purpose of this interview was to confirm or refute the qualitative listening evaluation preference results of the previous study.

5   Results

The 16 participants completed a total of 3,754 listening evaluations (5.5 per person per day). At the conclusion of the test period, we asked each participant to give us his or her subjective assessment of the two types of listening evaluations: A/B Test, Self-Adjustment Screen, or No Preference. To find the key predictors of listening evaluation preference, we compared participant responses to pre-interview data (Table 3).

As Table 3 indicates, 10 participants preferred the A/B Test, 3 preferred the Self-Adjustment Screen, and 3 stated No Preference. Figure 6 lists the reasons given for choosing the A/B Test. Simplicity and intuitiveness, with 7 responses, was by far the most common response.

Table 3. Test Person Characteristics and Listening Evaluation Preference

	Attributes						
Person	Age	Gender	Years with Hearing Aids	Experience	Functionality	Smartphone Owner	Evaluation Preference
1	21	M	11	High	Low	No	AB
2	34	M	3	High	Low	Yes	AB
3	41	F	7	Medium	Low	Yes	AB
4	46	M	15	High	High	Yes	SA
5	46	M	4	Medium	High	No	SA
6	48	F	<1	Medium	Low	Yes	AB
7	51	F	<1	Medium	Low	Yes	AB
8	54	M	5	Medium	Low	Yes	NO PREF
9	54	M	<1	Low	Low	No	AB
10	61	F	<1	Medium	Low	Yes	AB
11	64	F	15	Medium	Low	Yes	AB
12	68	M	15	High	High	Yes	SA
13	73	F	<1	High	Low	Yes	AB
14	73	M	8	High	Low	Yes	NO PREF
15	76	M	23	Low	Low	No	NO PREF
16	79	M	4	Medium	Low	Yes	AB

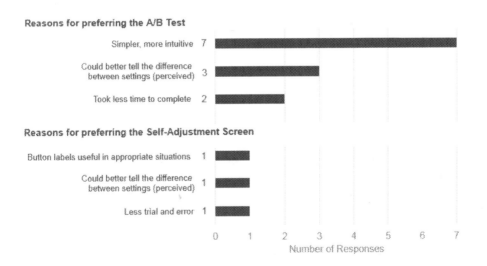

Fig. 6. Participant-given reasons for listening evaluation preference

A simple statistical analysis of the data in Table 3 indicated a strong correlation between Functionality and Listening Evaluation Preference. Of the 13 participants with Low Functionality, 10 preferred the A/B Test and 3 stated No Preference. On the other hand, all 3 participants with High Functionality preferred the Self-Adjust Screen.

Since 16 respondents was inadequate for generalizing the result of this investigation, we conducted a brief follow-up interview where we presented the two types of listening evaluations, in random order, to an additional 24 hearing impaired persons. With a sample size of to 40 (19 men, 21 women, mean age = 63 years), we computed the chi-square test for independence of each attribute with respect to listening evaluation preference.

Table 4. Chi-square test for independence p-values per user attribute

Attribute	p $(n = 16)$	p $(n = 40)$
Functionality	0.000335	0.000230
Gender	0.0561	0.254
Years of Experience with Hearing Aids	0.221	0.485
Age	0.735	0.574
Experience	0.768	0.744
Smartphone Owner	0.837	0.861

With both the small and larger sample sizes, we see that Functionality is the only attribute where the p-value is less than the significance level (0.05). Thus, we conclude that there is a relationship between Functionality and listening evaluation preference.

Overall, 23 respondents preferred the A/B Test, 10 preferred the Self-Adjustment Screen, and 7 claimed No Preference. Reasons for preferring the A/B Test were "simpler, more intuitive" (18) and "took less time to complete" (4). Reasons for preferring the Self-Adjustment Screen were "button labels useful in appropriate situations" (8) and "less trial and error" (2).

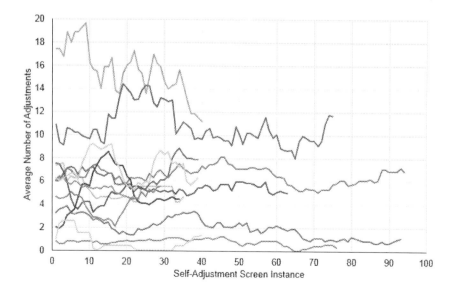

Fig. 7. Moving Average for Number of Adjustments by Participant

For the Self-Adjustment Screen, we wondered if participant engagement, measured by number of adjustments, would lessen over time. We recorded every time the participant pressed either the Directional Listening or the Noise Reduction button during a particular instance of a Self-Adjustment Screen. Figure 7 shows a running average of the number of adjustments each participant made over time. In general, we see that each participant maintained a constant level of number of adjustments. This indicates that the participants remained engaged and continued to try to find the best setting in each listening situation during the entire training phase.

6   Discussion

We conclude with a discussion of the most relevant user experience dimensions regarding training a personalized hearing system: cognitive, functional, and psychological.

Cognitive. The process of selecting participants for the longitudinal study revealed that presently there is a significant portion of the hearing impaired population for which smartphone apps are not appropriate. The average age of our study participants was 55.5 years, compared to the average age of a hearing aid user, which is around 70 years [11]. Two major exclusion criteria were low cognitive skills and Zero Experience (did not own computers or cell phones, were never online), which are more prevalent among the 80+ age group. In the follow-up interview, only 4 out of 9 (44.4%) in the 80+ age group felt hearing aid personalization could be of value, while 100% in the <80 group expressed it could be useful. However, in the future, we can expect an increasing percentage of hearing impaired people to be familiar with smartphones and apps.

To gain a better understanding of the participants' mental models [3], we asked them during the post-interview what they thought the Awear app did and how it worked. Participant 15 had the most difficulties. He had no recollection of the Self-Adjustment Screen, although the data showed that this screen did come up regularly and he did not make any adjustments. Regarding the A/B Test, he stated that, "Program A is best for speech comprehension and not bad for music. Program B is best for music listening – sounds are clearer and expanded and subtly muffled for speech." Although Settings A and B were randomized, that did not prevent Participant 15 from creating his own, very detailed mental model.

As Figure 6 illustrates, 3 of the participants who preferred the A/B Test stated that it was because they could better tell the difference between settings in the A/B Test than in the Self-Adjustment Screen. On the other hand, 1 participant who preferred the Self-Adjustment Screen claimed the opposite. The settings were inherently the same in both types of listening evaluations, but individual participants started to find patterns where perhaps none existed. Nonetheless, 14 out of 16 participants reported positive feelings of clarity, competence, and mastery of both types of listening evaluations.

Functional. All 16 participants understood the purpose of the listening evaluations and the overall app functionality. We uncovered that, of the user attributes elicited, listening evaluation preference correlated highly with the Functionality user attribute. At least in the field of hearing, one option for future apps would be a layered approach: a simple, intuitive UI (such as the A/B Test) as the default, while offering affordances for a more in-depth, technical UI (such as the Self-Adjustment Screen) that only the High Functionality users will choose to access.

Psychological. We left the choice of when they wanted to complete their listening evaluations entirely up to the participants. This participant-triggered self-reporting contrasts with the traditionally time-triggered Experience Sampling Method (ESM) used in psychology experiments [4]. Although participants averaged 5.5 listening evaluations per day – below the target of 8 per day – they did so with no reminders or further encouragement from us. Of the 21 participants who started the longitudinal study, 5 dropped out within the first few days for various reasons. The remaining 16 participants completed the 6-week study, with only 2 being asked to retain the system longer to accumulate more data. This shows the extreme level of participant motivation when involved in co-creation and personalization in an issue as fundamental to well-being as hearing.

7   Conclusion

Advances in wireless technology are quickly eliminating the need for intermediate body-worn devices such as the Streamer used in the Awear experimental setup. A new generation of Personal Sound Amplifier Products (PSAPs), which can be sold directly to consumers as electronic devices and are exempt from government regulations, connect directly to smartphones [14]. Hearing aid manufacturers are following suit. The user experience for these apps, as well as those designed by the hearing aid companies, are going to shift from simple remote control operation to incorporating increasingly sophisticated levels of personalization.

We have found that participant-triggered listening evaluations allow the user to become part of the hearing device fine-tuning process, thus leveraging to some extent the positive motivational effects of co-creation and participatory design. As customary, no single user experience design is right for every user. Designers in the arena of hearing-related apps must take into careful account the cognitive, functional, and psychological aspects of the user experience.

Acknowledgements. The authors are indebted to all personnel at Oticon A/S who supported this research, as well as the study participants. The project was funded by the Oticon Foundation.

References

1. BioAid, http://www.bioaid.org.uk
2. Coleman, M.: There's a hearing app for that. Hearing Journal 64(11), 12,14,16 (2011)
3. Craik, K.: The nature of explanation. Cambridge University Press (1943)
4. Csikszentmihalyi, M., Larson, R.: Validity and reliability of the experience-sampling method. Journal of Nervous and Mental Disease 175(9), 526–536 (1987)
5. Dalebout, S.: The Praeger Guide to Hearing and Hearing Loss: Assessment, Treatment, and Prevention. Praeger: Westport (2009)
6. Edwards, B.: The Future of Hearing Aid Technology. Trends in Amplification 11(1), 31–45 (2007)
7. ExSilent, http://www.exsilent.com
8. GingerLabs, http://www.gingerlabs.com
9. Hougaard, S., Ruf, S.: EuroTrak I: A consumer survey about hearing aids in Germany, France and the UK. Hearing Review 18(2), 12–28 (2011)
10. Horrigan, J.: The Mobile Difference, Pew Internet and American Life Project (2009)
11. Kochkin, S.: MarkeTrak VII: Hearing Loss Population Tops 31 Million People. Hearing Review 12(7), 16–29 (2005)
12. Kochkin, S.: MarkeTrak VIII: 25-year trends in the hearing health market. Hearing Review 16(11), 12–31 (2009)
13. ReSound, http://www.resound.com
14. Romano, T.: Better Hearing Through Bluetooth. New York Times (January 15, 2014)
15. Schilit, B., Adams, N., Want, R.: Context-Aware Computing Applications. In: 1st International Workshop on Mobile Computing Systems and Applications, pp. 85–90 (1994)
16. Starkey, http://www.starkey.com
17. World Health Organization Fact Sheet 300 (2013)

Developing mHealth Apps with Researchers: Multi-Stakeholder Design Considerations

Michael P. Craven[1,3], Alexandra R. Lang[2], and Jennifer L. Martin[3]

[1] The University of Nottingham, Electrical Systems & Optics Research Division,
Faculty of Engineering, University Park, Nottingham NG7 2RD, United Kingdom
michael.craven@nottingham.ac.uk
[2] The University of Nottingham, Human Factors Research Group,
University of Nottingham, University Park, Nottingham NG7 2RD, United Kingdom
alexandra.lang@nottingham.ac.uk
[3] NIHR MindTech Healthcare Technology Co-operative, The Institute of Mental Health,
Jubilee Campus, Nottingham, NG7 2TU, United Kingdom
{michael.craven,jennifer.martin}@nottingham.ac.uk

Abstract. The authors have been involved with developing a number of mHealth smartphone Apps for use in health or wellness research in collaboration with researchers, clinicians and patient groups for clinical areas including Sickle Cell Disease, Attention Deficit Hyperactivity Disorder, asthma and infertility treatment. In these types of applications, end-users self-report their symptoms and quality of life or conduct psychometric tests. Physiological data may also be captured using sensors that are internal or external to the device. Following a discussion of the multiple stakeholders that are typically involved in small scale research projects involving end-user data collection, four Apps are used as case studies to explore the issue of non-functional requirements.

Keywords: m-Health, Requirements Engineering, Software Engineering, User experience, Ethical issues in DUXU, Healthcare/Medical systems and DUXU, Management of DUXU processes, Medical/healthcare and DUXU, Mobile products and services.

1 Background

Mobile health (mHealth) applications (Apps) based on cellular phones, Smartphones and tablet computers are a rapidly growing trend in healthcare [1-3]. Healthcare researchers are increasingly turning to mobile apps for data collection as it is seen as a quick, easy way to obtain data from end-users (patients, carers or members of the public) in their everyday environment, using devices that users either own themselves or are becoming increasingly familiar with.

Apps can be used for a variety of purposes for monitoring or self-reporting of a person's health state or well-being (including performing tests) and to assist with tracking of adherence to medication use and/or treatment. They may also capture

A. Marcus (Ed.): DUXU 2014, Part III, LNCS 8519, pp. 15–24, 2014.
© Springer International Publishing Switzerland 2014

and/or process data sources from sensors that are capable of physiological measurement that are either internal to the device (accelerometer, gyroscope, camera, microphone, GPS) or external where they are carried or are worn on (or potentially in) the body or clothes or are present in the near environment [4].

However, it has been noted that Apps are often designed with little health professional involvement [5,6] and that end-user Apps are often produced from the healthcare system perspective rather than with a user-centred approach [7]. In addition, the importance of a number of other stakeholder considerations are evident, including ethical and other research governance requirements and potential for interaction with healthcare informatics infrastructure within the research institution or provider organisation(s). Some of these themes are common to other healthcare technologies or software, whereas others are the result of the mobile nature of the devices and the relatively uncontrolled environments in which they operate.

2   Multiple Stakeholders

A typical set of stakeholders for an App being developed for use in a small research project is shown in Fig. 1. This consists of four main groups: research institution and/or healthcare provider organisation, researchers, users and applications developers.

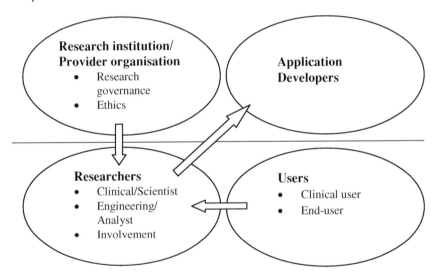

Fig. 1. Stakeholder groups in the App design process and flow of requirements

The make-up of an App development project team for a research application may include some or all of clinical/scientist, engineering/analyst and involvement researchers who will all have a role in software requirements production and also have their own requirements, not least because there is usually a tight timeline for completing the study.

In a university, for example, a research collaboration could include all three types of researcher. The goals for the researchers will be the effective testing of an App prototype for its functionality, usability and reliability in a real-world setting and to then use it to successfully capture end-user data for the study.

The clinical/scientist researcher will typically supply the App's requirements in terms of clinical or wellness outcomes (from prior knowledge or from liaison with providers) and will usually provide the study design methodology to be implemented e.g. questionnaire or psychometric test. A clinical/scientist researcher may also be a user especially at the early prototype stage or in a small study. An involvement researcher will ensure clinical user or end-user engagement throughout the process. The engineering researcher, if any, acting as a software analyst, will be responsible for producing the Apps requirements for the application developer or alternatively they may also be involved in the application development and implement the requirements themselves.

In software engineering the 'how?' of implementation is generally separated from the requirements process. However, there are some aspects of mobile development which mean that non-functional requirements [8,9] may strongly influence the choice of implementation platform and so for the application developer a number of implementation choices have to be made in parallel with the requirements process [10] e.g. What range of devices and operating systems should be supported? What device functions will be available and which are likely to be used by other applications? For mobile Apps this quickly leads to the question of whether to choose a native, web or hybrid implementation [11]. Furthermore, unless the App is standalone there is a question of server-side interfacing and interoperability across healthcare IT systems which may be prescribed or regulated though an API or interoperability toolkit. The use of Apps and sensors in a network may demand that a range of security issues be addressed in the system design [12].

Additional non-functional issues to be addressed in the development process include fully eliciting end-user & clinical/scientist user needs and fulfilling ethical and research governance requirements of the research institution or healthcare provider organisation(s). It is likely these will be addressed via the research team by liaison with clinical or end-users and with appropriate review of the proposed research by institution or provider contacts.

Ethical requirements include the practical aspects of ensuring personal data security and anonymity. Other ethical factors are privacy during the study (in particular when the App is dealing with sensitive information), burden on the patient relating to the degree of active or passive monitoring and the frequency of data collection, and impact on clinical care (e.g., potential impact on health in the course of App use due to possible stress or anxiety). Assessment of such ethical issues at an early stage of technology development is advisable. Trust in such security and privacy measures by the users and confidence in the system in general should help them offer honest and full responses, whilst early consideration of user requirements and interactions will improve the design of the research study through an improved understanding of burden, potentially leading to reduced withdrawal/drop-out rates.

User requirements include identifying all potential users and their capabilities, needs and preferences. As with Apps in general, users' physical and cognitive abilities, prior experience of using computer systems and the internet and preferences for modes of communication will all have an impact in mHealth. Also relevant are practical issues when devices are used for everyday interaction at the same time as being used for monitoring health, including text messaging and use of native phone functions such as accelerometers, alarms, microphones and cameras. Participants in research studies may rely on existing usage of these phone functions and so the mixing of their normal daily use and use for a study may conflict. We have proposed audits with the clinical population as a way of exposing these requirements [4,11] in addition to more traditional methods such as focus groups or drop-in sessions with early prototypes.

Furthermore, mHealth App users do not always keep devices turned on or charged up. For a research study this could be inconvenient or result in loss of data. However, a research instrument may also become a product and if an App is being used to monitor care it will need to be rigourously assessed for accuracy and reliability.

Constant and honest communication about requirements and expectations between researchers and App developers is essential to prevent frustration, misunderstandings, or problems when the research starts. For example, if the end-user is frustrated or has a poor experience then this may result in poor adherence or withdrawal from the study. Researchers need to be able to tell the developers what they require and in turn clinical researchers need to know the capabilities (and restrictions) of the technology so that their expectations are realistic. Developers on the other hand, will need to know about potential ethical restrictions at the outset.

This paper now draws out some of the stakeholder requirements from four case studies of App developments with researchers, all of which include one or more of the authors as the researcher(s).

3   Case Studies

3.1   Mild Asthma Self-reporting with and without Physiological Measurement

The first case study concerned persons with mild asthma. This project (described in more detail in a previous paper [4]) was a pilot study of self-reporting by means of a daily smartphone questionnaire without and then with additional twice-daily physiological measurements from a pulse oximeter and peak flow meter, to study user requirements and interactions between self-reporting and the measurement tasks.

The stakeholders in this study were University of Nottingham researchers in the Faculty of Engineering and School of Computer Science who were conducting the user requirements study and the end-users were recruited from volunteers at the university identifying themselves as having mild asthma. The application development was carried out by a graduate student.

From the researchers there was a requirement for a quick solution since the study was due to take place over 12 weeks. Since one component was a text-based questionnaire (requiring readings from peak flow meter to be entered into the questionnaire manually), it was decided to implement the study as a web App and use an inexpensive third party Android App to capture data from a Bluetooth pulse oximeter. where Android smartphones would be lent to the users by the project researchers over a period of 2 weeks, therefore it was decided to implement the study on an Android platform only.

The other main non-functional requirement prior to the study commencing was ethical. The ethics committee expressed a requirement for data security which was fulfilled by using an HTTPS connection with password protection and for analysis the data was downloaded over a secure connection to university computers, with the usual safeguards restricting access to named personnel. No user identification was collected or stored on the phone. In addition, participants were able to set a passcode to lock the phone, preventing unauthorised access during use.

From the end-user perspective a number of non-functional requirements were identified during the pilot study including convenience (e.g. inconvenience from sitting down to use the pulse oximeter), confidence in the success of data upload and dependability of the Wi-Fi, Bluetooth and battery. Another requirement was that the App should not affect the users' condition and which was not evident during the study although one participant did express the opinion that thinking about a cough may exacerbate it. On a positive note, one participant reported that using the App acted as a reminder to carry their asthma inhaler.

3.2   IVF Treatment Stress Diary

The second project concerned women undergoing in-vitro fertilisation (IVF) treatment [11]. The requirement was for ecological momentary assessment during IVF treatment using patients' own phones, allowing them to complete entries in a stress diary and respond to prompts to perform a psychological test (IPANAT [13]) in a secure manner.

The requirements were supplied by a postgraduate psychology student and their research supervisors at The University of Nottingham, School of Medicine one of whom was a Consultant Gynaecologist. They also organised patient recruitment. The requirements were produced by researchers in the Faculty of Engineering and application development was carried out by an in-house application programmer who was also a researcher on the project.

Since patients were to use their own phones, a phone survey was first carried out in which all participants were found to have access to some kind of mobile device and three-quarters of these were found to own a smartphone and use Apps [10]. Communication preferences showed a majority preference for an App to collect diary and test results and communicate them to the researchers but some participants' preferences were for other modes of communication (SMS text, voice, paper questionnaire). Furthermore, wide usage of an alarm clock function was found.

The subsequent ethics committee submission to an NHS panel for the main study raised some interesting non-functional requirements. In particular, the panel thought that text messaging for prompting could potentially compromise confidentiality and security of the data if the phone was lost. The advantage of using an App would be that data would be recorded on a secure server with password protection. Also for this particular project, the potential use of telephone conversations as a method of prompting/signalling users to carry out the ecological assessment was considered to be an unacceptable burden because this would entail contacting the patients every two days. This would also have been a burden on the researcher.

Due to the requirement for patients to use their own phones, and the fact that the survey found that most participants had either an Android phone or iPhone, it was decided to implement an App for each type of phone. The native alarm would be more acceptable for prompting since this could be turned off by the user and did not reveal the source of the prompt. Implementation of the App in Android phones used Eclipse Integrated Development Environment (IDE) with the Android Development Tools plug-in and for iPhones, Xcode was used [11].

3.3   Sickle Cell Disease Pain App

The aim of this project was to develop a valid, reliable and acceptable method of remotely monitoring blood oxygen saturation (SpO_2) for people with Sickle Cell Disease (SCD). Two data collection studies were planned. The first was a focus group study to collect subjective information from adults with SCD. The results of this were used to inform the design of the second study: a feasibility trial of a new device for home monitoring of SpO_2 using a Bluetooth pulse oximeter (using the same device as in case study 3.1) interfaced to a custom designed App (instead of the third party App in 3.1).

Stakeholders included researchers at the University of Nottingham, Faculty of Engineering including the same in-house developer as in 3.2 and the Sickle Cell Society who assisted with the recruitment of volunteers with SCD.

The aim of the feasibility trial was to test the function of the sensors to monitor variations in oxygen saturation and to gauge the acceptability of the monitoring process to the participants with SCD. Participants were given Android phones and a pulse oximeter for a period of 3 months. During this time they were be asked to take their SpO_2 readings twice a day and to record symptoms of pain and answer questions about quality of life and breathlessness several times each day, according to their location. No clinical decisions about treatment were to be made on the basis of the readings.

The requirement to include questions about symptoms of SCD in the App came from both the researcher and the users, however, this was for different reasons. Individual users wished to be able to report exactly how they were feeling in a way that was natural and meaningful to them and this varied somewhat from person to person. For the researcher, however, it was important that symptom information was collected in a standardised way that would allow comparisons to be made between users and across time.

This was resolved by a number of informal and group discussions between the researcher and potential users which aimed to discover how they talked about their symptoms with clinicians and how they talked about them with their families. The result was that validated clinical scales were used that met the requirements of the researcher but additional questions were added based on the views of the users. For example, rather than just asking about general pain, users were able to record the body area that they were experiencing pain.

Many people within the user population for this study (adults with SCD) come from disadvantaged backgrounds and a large number of potential users did not own a smartphone. As a result phones were lent to users for the duration of the study and because of budget constraints the decision was made to develop an Android app because of the lower cost of Android handsets.

Implementation of the App was in Eclipse IDE with the Android Development Tools plug-in.

3.4   Snappy App: Attention Deficit Hyperactivity Disorder Assessment App

Attention Deficit Hyperactivity Disorder (ADHD) is a neurodevelopmental syndrome that is characterised by three core symptom domains; inattention, hyperactivity and impulsivity. Given the variation in causes and behavioural consequences of ADHD, diagnosis, symptom monitoring and response to medication currently rely on subjective interpretation of information gained through clinical interview and questionnaires. Standardised measures of cognitive function offer the potential to provide a more objective measure of symptoms and response to medication, and could potentially speed up the process of treatment optimisation.

A pilot study was conducted on a non-clinical sample to establish the feasibility and validity of a smartphone application which could be appropriate for monitoring symptoms in a clinical population. The researcher preference was for users to use their own phones because of budget constraints.

The stakeholders supplying the requirements are psychology researchers in the School of Medicine and researchers in the School of Engineering who produced the requirements and these were initially implemented as a smartphone App by the same in-house application developer as for 3.2 and 3.3.

The primary aim of the pilot study is to establish whether it is feasible for end-users to conduct a continuous performance test (CPT) [14] whilst their physical activity is measured using the in-built motion sensors (accelerometer, gyroscope) [15]. This type of psychometric test involves presenting a sequence of letters (or alternatively a series of images or audio cues) and asking the user to respond when a specified target occurs e.g. by clicking a switch, or in this case via the touch screen or a button on the screen of the smartphone, whilst remaining passive to non-target stimuli.

Initially, due to time constraints, an App was developed to implement the CPT on an Android platform only. Development in Eclipse with the Android Development Tools plug-in employed a Java API to access the accelerometer and (where present) gyroscope readings, during presentations of the CPT cues. The native alarm function was used to prompt the users to take the test. However, since the test was to be conducted at a low frequency of twice a week and there had been some problems with the alarm setting function in initial tests with users, it was subsequently deemed not too burdensome to email the participants instead. At the same time the researchers also expressed a preference to widen the platform to iPhones but it was no longer possible to use the original in-house application developer.

As a result, with an extra month to make the change, it was decided to switch the implementation to a web App written in Javascript using HTML5 device motion and orientation features to access the accelerometer and gyroscope data and to dispense with the native alarm function which would not be controllable from a web client.

Server collection of the data was implemented using HTTPS. The web App was implemented by another of the Engineering researchers.

For the researchers, meaningful correlations were found in this initial study with activity data collected from the phone sensors however it was found that it was possible to collect accelerometer data from only 6 of 11 phones and just 4 phones were able to provide gyroscope orientation data [15]. This situation may improve in the future when more phones support HTML5 functions. Results from the study from the end-user point of view showed that the task was considered to be easy and not stressful, however preferences were expressed about screen background colour, font size, display of the time, and a number of usability suggestions included choice of user name, addition of a help function, further reminders (by text messaging) and a gamification function (scoring or ranking system for participants).

4   Conclusions

The results of the four case studies give some insight into the production of research-led Apps which were produced, implicitly, through a Scrum-like process [10] using a small in-house development team.

Non-functional requirements were dominated by development time from the researcher point of view and are seen to influence the implementation choice e.g. limiting it to one platform. Cost requirements also acted to limit implementation choices. Data security, privacy and concern for end-user burden dominated the requirements of the research institution ethics committees, which in turn limited implementation choices, in one case excluding text-messaging in favour of the native alarm clock for prompting the end-user (case study 3.2). Ethical challenges associated with App-based research are an ongoing issue for which theory and regulation is still catching up with current opportunities arising from the use of these technologies for research purposes.

From user feedback in case study 3.1 a number of user requirements were revealed including reliability of data collection and dependability of device networking and power. In 3.3 the App was required by end-users to produce information beyond that required by the researchers and in 3.4 there were several aesthetic and usability requirements that emerged, some of which may conflict with ethical or researcher requirements.

Device-independence is an implicit requirement that is mostly not being met and choices were made in each of the examples which acted to exclude some devices and hence also either excluded their users, or demanded that they use phones that were lent to them by the researchers. An interesting solution is a modular framework for cross-platform development, LambdaNative, devised by Petersen et al. for mHealth applications, using the Scheme (Gambit C) language, where they describe an oximeter application, a wireless monitoring and messaging device for multi-bed patient data and an anesthesia drug controller implemented as a client-server system. However, they accept that the use of Scheme will present a learning curve for engineering and the medical community personnel and that this had been the biggest challenge in their work so far (their development team consisted of four code developers on staff; one programmer, two physicists and one engineer, with diverse coding backgrounds) [16].

Requirement for the collection of sensor data from devices provides an additional challenge where it is seen from the result of 3.4 where not all phones provided motion and/or orientation data, in part due to variable support for HTML5 Javascript functions in the web App.

Due to the nature of the case studies we have not been able to explore interoperability or other informatics issues but this will involve further requirements production, in particular from provider organisation stakeholders.

Acknowledgements. The research reported in this paper was conducted by the National Institute for Health Research MindTech Healthcare Technology Co-operative (NIHR MindTech HTC) and funded by the NIHR. The views expressed are those of the author(s) and not necessarily those of the NHS, the NIHR or the Department of Health. All of the authors acknowledge additional support for this work through the Multidisciplinary Assessment of Technology for Healthcare (MATCH) programme (EPSRC Grant EP/F063822/1). MC and JM acknowledge support from MindTech. MC was involved with the asthma, IVF and ADHD (SnappyApp) projects, JM with the Sickle Cell project. The ADHD study was supported by MindTech and MATCH. The asthma diary project was supported by MATCH and a Xerox Research Centre Europe (Grenoble) donation for the support of studentships in Ubiquitous Computing within the Mixed Reality Laboratory at the University of Nottingham. The IVF project was supported by MATCH and Nurture Fertility. JM wishes to thank the Sickle Cell Society for its involvement in user testing. The authors wish to thank the other collaborators who are mentioned in the citations associated with the case studies.

References

1. World Health Organization: mHealth: New horizons for health through mobile technologies: second global survey on eHealth (2011), http://www.who.int/goe/publications/goe_mhealth_web.pdf (accessed January 28, 2014)
2. Free, C., Phillips, G., Galli, L., Watson, L., Felix, L., Edwards, P., Patel, V., Haines, A.: The effectiveness of mobile-health technology-based health behaviour change or disease management interventions for health care consumers: a systematic review. PLoS Medicine 10(1), e1001362 (2013)
3. Mosa, A.S.M.M., Yoo, I., Sheets, L.: A Systematic Review of Healthcare Applications for Smartphones. BMC Medical Informatics and Decision Making 12, 67 (2012)
4. Craven, M.P., Selvarajah, K., Miles, R., Schnädelbach, H., Massey, A., Vedhara, K., Raine-Fenning, N., Crowe, J.: User requirements for the development of Smartphone self-reporting applications in healthcare. In: Kurosu, M. (ed.) HCII/HCI 2013, Part II. LNCS, vol. 8005, pp. 36–45. Springer, Heidelberg (2013)
5. Rosser, B.A., Eccleston, C.: Smartphone applications for pain management. Journal of Telemedicine and Telecare 17(6), 307–312 (2011)
6. Buijink, A.W.G., Visser, B.J., Marshall, L.: Medical apps for smartphones: lack of evidence undermines quality and safety. Evidence Based Medicine 18(3), 90–92 (2013)

7. McCurdie, T., Taneva, S., Casselman, M., Yeung, M., McDaniel, C., Ho, W., Cafazzo, J.: mHealth Consumer Apps: The Case for User-Centered Design, AAMI Horizons, 49–56 (Fall 2012)

8. Chung, L., do Prado Leite, J.C.S.: On Non-Functional Requirements in Software Engineering. In: Borgida, A.T., Chaudhri, V.K., Giorgini, P., Yu, E.S. (eds.) Mylopoulos Festschrift. LNCS, vol. 5600, pp. 363–379. Springer, Heidelberg (2009)

9. Miller, R.E.: The Quest for Software Requirements. Maven Mark Books, Milwaukee (2009)

10. Wassermann, A.I.: Software Engineering Issues for Mobile Application Development. In: Proc. FSE/SDP Workshop on Future of Software Engineering Research (FoSER 2010), Santa Fe, New Mexico, USA, November 7-8, pp. 397–400. ACM, New York (2010)

11. Selvarajah, K., Craven, M.P., Massey, A., Crowe, J., Vedhara, K., Raine-Fenning, N.: Native Apps versus Web Apps: Which Is Best for Healthcare Applications? In: Kurosu, M. (ed.) HCII/HCI 2013, Part II. LNCS, vol. 8005, pp. 189–196. Springer, Heidelberg (2013)

12. Kumar, P., Lee, H.-J.: Security Issues in Healthcare Applications Using Wireless Medical Sensor Networks: A Survey. Sensors 12, 55–91 (2012)

13. Quirin, M., Kazén, M., Kuhl, J.: When nonsense sounds happy or helpless: The Implicit Positive and Negative Affect Test (IPANAT). J. Pers. Soc. Psychol. 97(3), 500–516 (2009)

14. van Leeuwen, T.H., Steinhausen, H.C., Overtoom, C.C., Pascual-Marqui, R.D., van't Klooster, B., Rothenberger, A., Sergeant, J.A., Brandeis, D.: The continuous performance test revisited with neuroelectric mapping: Impaired orienting in children with attention deficits. Behavioural Brain Research 94, 97–110 (1998)

15. Young, Z., Craven, M.P., Groom, M., Crowe, J.: Snappy App: a mobile continuous performance test with physical activity measurement for assessing Attention Deficit Hyperactivity Disorder. In: Kurosu, M. (ed.) Human-Computer Interaction, Part III, HCII 2014. LNCS, vol. 8512, pp. 363–373. Springer, Heidelberg (2014)

16. Petersen, C.L., Gorges, M., Dunsmuir, D., Ansermino, J.M., Dumont, G.A.: Functional Programming of mHealth Applications. In: Proc. International Conference on Functional Programming (ICFP 2013), Boston, USA, June 25-27, pp. 357–362. ACM, New York (2013)

Accessing Web Based Health Care and Resources for Mental Health: Interface Design Considerations for People Experiencing Mental Illness

Alice Good and Arunasalam Sambhanthan

School of Computing
University of Portsmouth
PO1 3AE, UK
alice.good@port.ac.uk

Abstract. A significant proportion of society experience mental illness, many of which uses the Web for advice and support relating to their illness. With a high proportion of society experiencing anxiety and depression, it is important that web designers are informed of specific requirements to ensure Websites are accessible, particularly those websites that provide support and advice for mental health. Anxiety and depression can affect cognitive functioning, which can then impact upon the accessibility of web based information. The premise of this research is to look at design elements that are most likely to cause issues for people experiencing anxiety and depression. During a focus group, people who have a diagnosis of anxiety and depression were asked to discuss difficulties they experienced when carrying out specific tasks. The results from the study show that the problems encountered can be categorized under three main themes: information retrieval; information presentation and the understanding of information.

Keywords: Web Accessibility, Guidelines, Health Care, Mental Illness, Anxiety, Depression.

1   Introduction

Across the world, a significant proportion of society experience mental illness, many of which will use the Internet. The World Health Organization states that more than 450 million people worldwide have a mental health problem. (WHO, 2010) To put the problem into perspective, both the USA and the UK report 1 in 4 people who have experienced mental illness (ONS, 2013; NIMH, 2012). Anxiety is one of the most common mental health disorders with 1 in 5 people affected (NIMH, 2012, particularly people between the ages of 40 and 59 or over 80 (ONS, 2013). When one considers the predominance of mental illness within society, particularly in terms of anxiety and depression, the issue of web accessibility for this user group should be an important consideration. To clarify, we use the term web accessibility to imply the ease with which people can access web based information, regardless of impairment

A. Marcus (Ed.): DUXU 2014, Part III, LNCS 8519, pp. 25–33, 2014.
© Springer International Publishing Switzerland 2014

or ability Thus, when designing web resources specifically for people with mental illness, web accessibility should be paramount.

1.1   Using the Web as a Resource for Self-Help in Mental Health

The Web is increasingly providing access to the provision of health care via the Web and plays a significant role in providing information on mental health. This includes a variety of resources that facilitate support and self-help, such as information sites; social networking sites; communities as well as others (Good et al, 2013; Van de belt et al., 2010). When we consider that in 2010, people in the USA spent 10 billion dollars on self-help materials (Harwood & L'Abate, 2010); it is hardly surprising that a significant number of people are increasingly also looking to the Web for self-help resources. Easy access to information and anonymity as opposed to potential stigma from using more traditional routes has certainly helped to pave the way.

1 in 5 people with a diagnosed mental health condition will use the Web to find information about mental health (Powell et al, 2007). In fact Powell at al carried out a study in 2007 that sought to investigate the extent of information seeking on mental health. The study found that 18% of Internet users had searched for information on mental health, with a higher prevalence with people who had either a history of mental health problems or who were currently experiencing psychological problems. One of the recommendations from the study was that 'there needed to be a better understanding of how individuals actually use the Internet'. (Powell et al, 2007). Given the extent to which people clearly use the Internet as a tool to manage their illnesses, it is important to ensure that the information is accessible, particularly given the effect that anxiety and depression has upon cognitive functioning.

Whilst research into designing for sensory and physical impairments has led the way with accessibility related research, it is more recently however, that there has been a drive towards focusing upon designing for people with mental illnesses (Doherty et al, 2010; Rotondi et al, 2007). When looking at accessibility design guidelines, mental health disorders tend to be categorized under cognitive impairments. However, simply designing for cognitive impairments in general presents many challenges, not least because of the range of impairments included under the label of 'cognitive' and in turn, the complex diversity of user needs arising from this 'range.

2   The Effect of Anxiety and Depression Upon Cognitive Functioning

Anxiety and depression affects cognitive functioning in many ways but what is particularly interesting is that the same issues relate to both disorders. Anxiety and depression has been shown to affect cognitive functioning in activities that relate to: learning; memory; attention and verbal ability (Papazacharias & Nardini 2012; Gualtieri & Morgan 2008; Porter at Al, 2003). Furthermore, cognitive performance can be significantly decreased up to 3 years even before depression has been diagnosed and episodic memory impairment in particular can remain after recovery from depression (Airaksinen, E et Al, 2005).   There are also a number of neurobiological studies that indicate a correlation between depression and functional changes in brain regions that relate to cognitive functioning, particularly episodic memory (Campbell at al, 2004; Frodl et al, 2002

These problems in cognitive functioning will undoubtedly impact upon the ease with which people that are experiencing anxiety and/or depression, can perceive and understand Web based information and indeed operate certain interface components. Web pages can then become inaccessible to people who are experiencing impaired cognitive functioning as a result of anxiety and/or depression. The identified user group may well already be experiencing symptoms relating to a mental health disorder prior to commencing their information seeking activity. If they encounter accessibility issues relating to the design of web pages, this could result in increased anxiety which then further impacts upon cognitive functioning.

3   Design Guidelines for Cognitive Impairments

There continues to be a drive towards making the Web inclusive; to ensure that regardless of user needs, the Web can still be accessible to all. These needs can relate to physical, sensory and cognitive deficits; both permanent and indeed temporary. Published guidelines have been available since 1999 to advise on Web accessibility for a wide range of physical and cognitive impairments (Trace Research and Development Center, 1996; World Wide Web Consortium [W3C], 1999; W3C, 2004).   Yet whilst accessibility guidelines have focused upon some cognitive impairments, there is less that relates specifically to mental illness. Given that a large number of web-based resources are designed to provide services specifically for people with mental health problems, accessibility of the information itself is paramount to ensure that regardless of disability or impairment, websites should strive for inclusiveness.

To clarify, the Web Content Accessibility Guidelines 2.0, which were developed to help designers create content that is accessible regardless of disability, have developed guidelines under 4 main principles: perceivable; understandable; operable and robust.

1. **Perceivable** - Information and user interface components must be presentable to users in ways they can perceive and not be invisible to all senses
2. **Operable** - User interface components and navigation must be operable and not require interaction that a user cannot perform
3. **Understandable** - Information and the operation of user interface must be understandable.
4. **Robust** - Content must be robust enough that it can be interpreted reliably by a wide variety of user agents, including assistive technologies. (WCAG 2.0, 2012).

Guidelines to help web designers create content that is accessible to people with disabilities or impairments are produced by the W3C Web Accessibility Initiative group. The website also provides extensive information on how people with different disabilities are able to use the Web. Disabilities or impairments are categorized as follows: *Auditory; Cognitive and neurological; Physical; Speech* and *Visual* (W3C, WAI, 2012). Within the category *'Cognitive and neurological'* are a range of disabilities that do also include *'Mental health disabilities'*, which cover mental illnesses from psychosis through to anxiety and depression. Accessibility problems with this user group are cited as:

"Difficulty focusing on information, processing information, or understanding it. In particular medication for these disorders may have side effects including blurred vision, hand tremors, and other impairment" (W3C/WAI, 2012).

3.1   W3C/WAI Guidelines for Cognitive and Neurological Impairments

The W3C/WAI does provide general guidelines for designing content that is accessible for cognitive and neurological impairments:

- Clearly structured content that facilitates overview and orientation
- Consistent labelling of forms, buttons, and other content parts
- Predictable link targets, functionality, and overall behavior
- Different ways of navigating websites, such as through a hierarchical menu or search option
- Options to suppress blinking, flickering, flashing, or otherwise distracting content
- Simpler text that is supplemented by images, graphs, and other illustrations (W3C/WAI, 2012).

Whilst there are guidelines in place that cover the general area of cognitive impairments, the premise of this paper is to look design elements that specifically cause problems for people with mental illness, but in particular, anxiety and depression. We are interested to find out whether there are general themes with the problems our targeted user group might experience and the degree of anxiety experienced. This could then help web designers to better understand the importance of accessibility for this user group and the main issues to address.

4   Understanding Accessibility Issues for People with Anxiety and Depression

It is important for our research to gain users' perspective of accessibility issues for this user group. To this extent, we wanted to carry out user centered research and talk to people who experience anxiety and depression. The aim of the research was to gain a better understanding of the accessibility issues this user group experience.

4.1   Method: Focus Group

We considered an appropriate tool for user centered research was a focus group, made up of people who have had a diagnosis of anxiety and/or depression. Two focus groups were held, each with 10 people plus a facilitator. Participants were asked to complete two tasks. The first task was locating information that advised on their condition from two websites of their choice. The rationale for this task was based upon the extent to which people use the Web to find information about mental health; 1 in 5 people (Powell et al, 2007). The second task was to find a self-help book relating to their condition, using an online shop of their choice. The rationale for this task relates to the extent to which people seek self-help books (Harwood & L'Abate, 2010). Participants were asked to write down the problems they encountered and to rate the level of anxiety that each problem caused, from 1-3, with 1 being low anxiety, 2 being moderate anxiety and 3 being assigned as a high level of anxiety.

4.2   Results

The participants identified a range of issues that caused difficulties when carrying out the tasks.

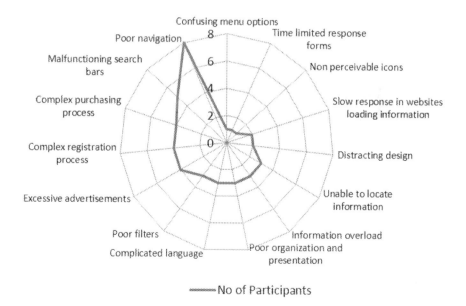

Fig. 1. Design Elements Affecting Accessibility for People with Anxiety and Depression

Furthermore, we were able to see the degree of anxiety which some design elements caused. Figure 1 shows the identified issues, along with the predominance of each issue. Poor navigation is shown to be the most commonly reported issue amongst the 20 participants, with 8 identifying it as being a significant problem. Other notable issues were: malfunctioning search bars; confusing menu options; complex purchasing process and registration process as well as excessive advertisements.

Whilst we wished to identify common accessibility problems with this user group, we were also interested as to what extent these problems caused anxiety. In figure 2, we can see that the issues that tended to cause the most anxiety related to problems with: locating information; poor navigation; malfunctioning search bars and a complex purchasing process. These results correlate with the number of participants that identified these issues as being problematic, as shown in figure 1.

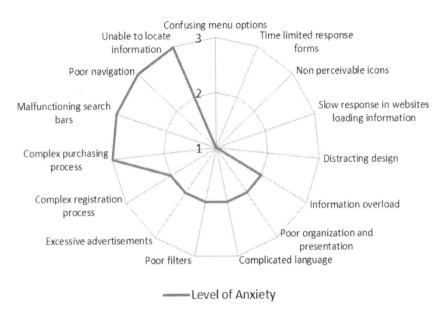

Fig. 2. Design Elements Increasing Anxiety for People with Anxiety and Depression

5   Discussion

Whilst the results from this research indicate common accessibility problems for this user group, we were interested in whether there were any identified common themes. We were able to establish three common themes from the 14 issues raised. These were notably issues with the presentation of information, understanding of information and searching of information. Table 1 shows how the issues were categorized into themes, with the associated number of participants included.

Table 1. Categorizing Design Elements Causing Accessibility Issues

Presenting Information		Understanding Information		Searching Information		Other	
Distracting design	2	Confusing menu options	1	Poor navigation	8	Time limited response forms	1
Information overload	3	Non perceivable icons	1	Unable to locate information	3	Slow response in websites loading information	2
Poor organization and presentation	3	Complicated language	3	Poor filters	3		
Excessive advertisements	4	Complex purchasing process	4	Malfunctioning search bars	5		

We can then see in figure 3, a comparison of the identified themes. Issues that relate to 'searching for information' were most prevalent.

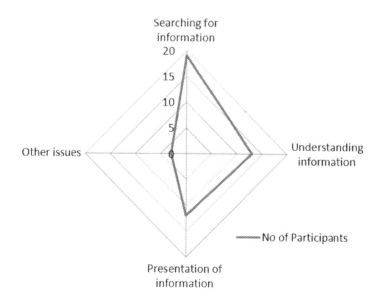

Fig. 3. Categorizing Design Elements Causing Accessibility Issues

Certainly the issue with understanding information correlates with the W3C/WAI guidelines that state people with cognitive impairments experience: *"Difficulty focusing on information, processing information, or understanding it"* (W3C/WAI, 2012). Furthermore, the guidelines for web designers provided by W3C/WAI also correlate to the general themes identified in this research, as seen in table 2.

Table 2. Correlating themes with W3C/WAI Guidelines

W3C/WAI Guideline	Identified Themes from the Research
Clearly structured content that facilitates overview and orientation	Presentation /Searching
Consistent labelling of forms etc	Presentation
Predictable link targets	Understanding / Searching
Different ways of navigating sites	Searching
Options to supress distracting content	Presentation
Simpler text	Understanding

Perhaps the most notable finding from this research is the theme of accessibility problems that cause the most anxiety for this user group, that being searching for information. In figure 2.2, we see that out of the 4 issues that cause the greatest anxiety, 3 of these relate to problems relating to searching for information. We know from the literature featured earlier in the paper that people with anxiety and depression can experience difficulties with cognitive functioning, relating to learning, memory and attention (Papazacharias & Nardini 2012; Gualtieri & Morgan 2008; Porter at Al, 2003).

Recommendations to Web designers, particularly when designing web based resources in mental health are categorized under the accessibility themes:

- **Searching for Information:** Provide intuitive navigation and ensure filters and search functions work properly.
- **Presentation of information**: Ensure information is organized well and avoid distracting design.
- **Understanding of information**: Avoid complicated language and ensure menu options and links are easy to understand.

Further to these recommendations is to advise Web designers to carry out user centred evaluation of their Web sites. These can be as simple as cognitive walkthroughs using predominant tasks, as well as more involved user testing.

This research should be considered more as an exploratory study, given the small number of participants, and therefore the results should be viewed as indicative and also as a prelude to further research into evaluating and improving accessibility to Web based mental health resources.

References

1. Airaksinen, E., Larsson, M., Forsell, Y.: Neuropsychological functions in anxiety disorders in population-based samples: evidence of episodic memory dysfunction. Journal of Psychiatric Research 39, 207–214 (2005)
2. Airaksinen, E., Larsson, M., Forsell, Y.: Low episodic memory performance as a premorbid marker of depression: evidence from a 3-year follow-up. Acta Psychiatrica Scandinavica 115(6), 458–465 (2007)

3. Campbell, S., Marriott, M., Nahmias, C., MacQueen, G.M.: Lower hippocampal volume in patients suffering from depression: a meta-analysis. Am. J. Psychiatry 161, 598–607 (2004)
4. Doherty, G., Coyle, D., Matthews, M.: Design and evaluation guidelines for mental health technologies. Interacting with Computers 22(4), 243–252 (2010)
5. Fox, S.: Health information online. The Pew Internet & American Life Project (2005), http://www.pewinternet.org/PPF/r/156/report_display.asp (retrieved)
6. Frodl, T., Meisenzahl, E.M., Zetzsche, T., et al.: Hippocampal changes in patients with a first episode of major depression. Am. J. Psychiatry 159, 1112–1118 (2002)
7. Good, A., Sambhantham, A., Panjganj, V.: Looking back at facebook content and the positive impact upon wellbeing: Exploring reminiscing as a tool for self soothing. In: Ozok, A.A., Zaphiris, P. (eds.) OCSC 2013. LNCS, vol. 8029, pp. 278–286. Springer, Heidelberg (2013)
8. Gualtieri, T., Morgan, D.: The frequency of cognitive impairment in patients with anxiety, depression, and bipolar disorder: an unaccounted source of variance in clinical trials. The Journal of Clinical Psychiatry, 69–712 (2008)
9. National Institute of Mental Health, Anxiety Disorders (2012)
10. http://www.nimh.nih.gov/statistics/1anyanx_adult.shtml
11. Office for National Statistics. Measuring National Well-being-Health 2013. Br. J. Psychiatry 189, 273–277 (2013), http://www.ons.gov.uk/ons/dcp171766_310300.pdf
12. Papazacharias, A., Nardini, M.: The Relationship Between Depression and Cognitive Deficits. Psychiatria Danubina 24(suppl. 1), 179–182 (2012)
13. Powell, J., Clarke, A.: Internet Information Seeking in Mental Health: Population Survey. In: BRJ. Psychiatry (2007)
14. Ritterband, L.A., Gonder Frederick, D.J., Cox, A.D., et al.: Internet interventions in review, in use, and into the future. Professional Psychology Research and Practice 34, 527–534 (2003)
15. Van De Belt, T.H., Engeleni, L., Berbent, S.A.A., Schoonhoven, L.: Definition of Health 2.0 and Medicine 2.0: A Systematic Review. Journal of Medical Internet Research 12(2) (2010)
16. W3C/WAI, How People with Disabilities Use the Web. W3C (2012), http://www.w3.org/WAI/intro/people-use-web/diversity#cognitive

Reading Digital Medicine Leaflets in Mobile Devices an Interactive Study Conducted in Brazil

Christopher Hammerschmidt and Carla Galvão Spinillo

Postgraduate Program in Design, Federal University of Paraná, Rua General Carneiro, 460,
8° andar, Curitiba, PR 80060-150 Brazil
chdeutschbr@yahoo.com.br, cgspin@gmail.com

Abstract. This paper describes an interaction study conducted in Brazil that aimed to investigate how people read a digital medicine leaflet in a mobile device. This insert summarizes the main typographic characteristics of Brazilian current digital leaflets. Tests were held with the participation of 20 volunteer individuals and consisted of four stages: (1) definition of participants' profile, (2) task 1: finding specific information in the digital leaflet, (3) Task 2: reading the digital leaflet in a mobile device, (4) follow-up interview. According to the results of the interaction test, there is evidence that the current structure of the digital medicine leaflets in Brazil is not designed for access via mobile devices. The findings of this study point to the need of information design guidelines for the Brazilian digital medicine leaflets, considering interactivity and navigability aspects. It is important to propose new solutions for digital leaflets and test them with people, in order to ensure the legibility and usability of these documents.

Keywords: patient information leaflets, mobile devices, usability.

1 Introduction

Medicine information leaflets are frequently regarded as documents with several problems concerning legibility and readability. Small letters, lack of attractiveness, technical language, poorly defined information hierarchy and paper transparency, among others, are examples of these deficiencies [1-5]. In contrast, the literature states that medicine leaflets play a very important role in providing information about healthcare for patients [1-3]. In order to make people become aware of the rational use of medicines and to help them getting involved in medical decision making, the PILs (patient information leaflets) are considered tools to empower patients [6-9]. Such discourse is a central point of some health policy moves in countries around Europe, US, Australia and New Zealand [2].

Legislations enacted in several countries try to address these issues, but the lack of strong evidences about how to write, design and deliver information about medicines has led to many different approaches [2]. In Brazil, since 2003 the National Health Surveillance Agency (Anvisa) regulates form and content for medicine leaflets [10], [11]. Along with regulations for the print versions of leaflets, Anvisa has also instituted the digital medicine inserts, available online on the system *Bulário Eletrônico*

A. Marcus (Ed.): DUXU 2014, Part III, LNCS 8519, pp. 34–43, 2014.

(electronic archive of medicine leaflets). This database has been released in 2005 [12] and provides free access to information leaflets for many of the medicines sold in Brazilian drugstores. There are two versions available for each leaflet: one produced to inform patients and another specifically made for health professionals. The first one must contain summarized information, written in appropriate and plain language [11]. On the other hand, leaflets intended for the use of health professionals need to present technically detailed information [7]. Distinguishing between professional and patient information leaflets is a legal obligation in Brazil since 2003, as a revision process of the national legislation about medicine leaflets [10], [13]. These changes in legislation have also been important in order to provide tools for the management of medicine leaflets produced in Brazil, creating an electronic system to that purpose called *E-Bulas* and the abovementioned archive of medicine leaflets, *Bulário Eletrônico* [12], [13], [14].

With the rise in sales of smartphones and the growing number of accesses to the web in mobile devices in Brazil, it is important to consider designing content to be accessible in such equipments. However, the current structure of *Bulário Eletrônico* demonstrates lack of concern to this statement. Patient and professional information leaflets are available as PDF files, which demand that people download them before having access to the content. Moreover, the configuration of these digital leaflets is clearly oriented for print and not for reading in electronic devices.

2   Digital Medicine Leaflets as Print Documents

Despite the efforts made by Anvisa to regulate and establish a minimum quality standard for content and form of medicine leaflets, the electronic versions of these documents are practically ignored in the Brazilian legislation. The current legal text, published in 2009 and corrected in the beginning of 2010 [11], provides guidelines to typographic aspects such as the choice of typeface, minimum body size for text setting, measure of text columns, leading – interline spacing –, text alignment, use of uppercase letters, bold, italic and underline to highlight text passages. All these specifications clearly define formatting of print documents. There is only one paragraph that describes the form of leaflets for publication in *Bulário Eletrico*, stating that these versions should not be set in more than one column of text.

Comparing the currently available digital leaflets to the literature about typography, there is evidence that many problems regarding legibility and definition of hierarchy occur in the formatting of the leaflets. Such problems include excessively lengthy lines of text, insufficient leading, tracking disorders, with altered word spacing and weak differentiation of hierarchical levels of information. Thus, the documents available on the electronic archive of medicine leaflets still show several deficiencies related to the graphic presentation of content. So, it is questionable if the problems detected can have any influence in reading the digital leaflets in mobile devices, due to the limitations in the screen size, the interaction in the touch interface, the use of zoom and pan gestures.

3   Investigating How People Read Digital Leaflets in Mobile Devices

In order to address the questions raised before about reading digital leaflets in mobile devices, an interaction test with 20 participants was conducted in Brazil. It was designed based on former research on reading strategy for print leaflets held by Fujita [15], and on the study about interaction in handheld devices by Pottes [16]. The interaction test also followed some of the guidelines for readability tests conducted in the European Union, especially regarding the number of participants [17]. Each person was asked to read a fictitious digital leaflet in an iPod Touch device, and then to engage in a follow-up interview. The leaflet prepared for this study was set in order to reproduce the most frequent typographic patterns found in Brazilian digital inserts. Therefore, the main characteristics of the document were:

- Size: A4 (210 × 297 mm);
- Margins: 28 mm (superior and left), 26 mm (inferior and right);
- Typeface: Times New Roman;
- Body size: 10 pt;
- Leading (interline spacing): 12 pt;
- Column measure: 156 mm – 109 characters per line;
- Text alignment: justified.

All results were video recorded, and participants' navigation in the digital leaflet, the use of zoom and pan gestures were assessed through screen captures.

3.1   Defining Participants' Profile

In this first part of the interaction test, participants were asked to write down in a questionnaire some information that could be used to identify their profile. This includes genre, age, level of education and also data about habits of reading patient information leaflets, opinions about quality of graphic presentation of these documents and familiarity with mobile devices.

The sample of 20 participants was selected so as to have equal numbers of male (n = 10) and female (n = 10) individuals, since this study did not consider possible discrepancies in the variable genre. Former research did not indicate the occurrence of noticeable disparities in the distribution of genre in readers of medicine leaflets [4]. Concerning age, there was no control over this variable and the sample was formed by people from the following groups: 18–25 years old (n = 13), 26–30 years old (n = 2), 31–40 years old (n = 3) and more than 50 years old (n = 2). The analysis of level of education showed that most of the participants (n = 12) were undergraduate students.

When asked about familiarity in reading patient information leaflets, participants generally rated themselves with medium or high levels (n = 12). Regarding quality in the graphic presentation of leaflets, the results point that it has been assessed as medium (n = 6) or low (n = 12). Comments justifying these opinions frequently cited the same deficiencies indicated in the literature, particularly the small letters (n = 15). Opposed to the familiarity with printed leaflets, most of the participants were unfamiliar with digital leaflets (n = 18). However, this is not due to lack of contact with electronic devices. It has been found that participants had medium or high levels of familiarity with mobile devices (n = 18).

Since not all of them declared to be accustomed to using devices such as iPod, iPhone and iPad, a brief training stage was offered to level the people who engaged in the interaction test. Participants had a small tutorial on how to use zoom and pan gestures (these last ones referred to as horizontal and vertical scrolling) to navigate through a PDF file opened in the web browser Safari for iOS on an iPod Touch. The first practical task of the interaction test started after this stage.

3.2   Task 1: Finding Specific Information in the Digital Leaflet

In this first task, participants were asked to find some pieces of information in the text of a fictitious digital leaflet prepared for the study. The questions have been formulated in order to contextualize situations in which people need to find information in leaflets, as recommended by Maat and Lentz [18]. To provide the answers, participants had to relate aspects of graphic presentation and understand the hierarchy of text elements in the digital leaflet.

When asked to find a warning, people often confused this kind of information with secondary headings (n = 5) or lists (n = 11) due to the similarity in the typographic setting. Similar findings were reached when participants had to relate a primary heading to another element in the document hierarchy. Different kinds of information, such as the main title of the leaflet (n = 3), secondary headings (n = 18) and warnings (n = 2) have been pointed as answers, along with the correct item (n = 4). Some individuals indicated more than one item as answer, so the sum of results is more than the number of participants.

To finish this task, people should find a specific section of the text and differentiate a third level heading from a warning. Because of variations in the length of these two sorts of information, the participants could tell one from the other easily, despite the resemblance in the typographic patterns of both. In this case, context of the information in the text aided people to distinguish the hierarchical structure, but the same did not occur on the first questions, when the typographic style of formatting confused the participants and led them to relate items improperly.

After this task of finding information, the individuals were requested to read the leaflet in the following step.

3.3   Task 2: Reading the Digital Leaflet in a Mobile Device

As an instruction to carry on this second task, participants were asked to read the digital leaflet naturally, as if they were in a real situation of use of that medicine. Thus, there was no need to read the whole document, only the parts they use to read. In addition, the individuals should perform this reading loud, so that their comments and the precise indication of what sections in the text they were paying attention to could be registered in audio.

The results of this phase of the interaction test revealed frequent use of pan gestures to scroll in both horizontal and vertical directions. From the 20 participants, it has been noticed that 14 used this pattern as a way to move through the text of the digital leaflet. Another important aspect observed was the orientation of the device. There was a subtle preference for the horizontal arrangement, maintained throughout the task by ten users. Among the remaining individuals, eight used the device in the vertical orientation to perform the complete reading task, whilst two other people, although having started the activity with the iPod Touch in the vertical position, opted to change it to the horizontal arrangement.

Using zoom gestures was also a recurring feature during the reading of the digital leaflet. Throughout the tests of the 20 participants, it was observed that they used gestures to zoom in content 70 times, while zoom out was used 58 times. In some cases, inaccurate gestures of panning or zooming made people involuntarily activate the text selection tool. In this situation, a magnifying glass appears to help the user select the desired passage of text. However, this feature is not intended to assist in reading and may cause some kind of discomfort to individuals. This is an event observed in 12 of the 20 interaction tests, with a total of 28 documented occurrences.

In a more detailed examination of specific aspects of the interaction test, it was found that the reading time varied greatly between users, with a minimum of 1min 53s and a maximum of 16min 20s. In average, people took approximately 7min 33s to read the leaflet. Among the 14 items in the text structure, the ones that demanded longer reading time of the participants were: *4. What should I know before using this medicine?* (2min 7s average), 8. *What kinds of harm this medicine can cause?* (1min 30s) 6. *How should I use this medicine?* (1min 13s). Fig. 1 shows the average time calculated for all 14 topics in the digital leaflet used during the reading task.

Results obtained for use of zoom (Fig. 2) reveal relevant parallels with the time that participants required in reading the leaflet. Similarly, the items on which participants used more gestures tom zoom in and out were: 8. *What kinds of harm this medicine can cause?* (zoom in: $n = 11$, zoom out: $n = 12$), *4. What should I know before using this medicine?* (zoom in: $n = 13$, zoom out: $n = 9$), *6. How should I use this medicine?* (zoom in: $n = 9$, zoom out: $n = 9$). In addition, topic *1. Why is this medication prescribed?* also presented results that stand out for the use of the zoom (zoom in: $n = 10$, zoom out: $n = 8$), although the average reading time was low (28s). This must be due to the fact that this section has a smaller length than the others previously mentioned.

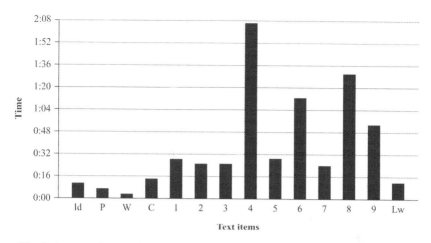

Fig. 1. Average time required by participants to read each item of the digital leaflet

Id: Medicine identification – name and active ingredient; P: Presentation; W: Warnings; C: Composition; 1: Why is this medication prescribed?; 2: How does this medicine work?; 3: When should I not use this medicine?; 4: What should I know before using this medicine?; 5: Where, how and for how long can I store this medicine?; 6: How should I use this medicine?; 7: What should I do if I forget to use this medicine?; 8: What kinds of harm this medicine can cause?; 9: What if someone uses a larger amount of this medicine than indicated?; Lw: Legal wording

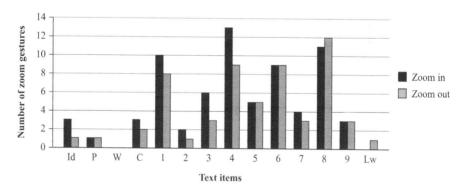

Fig. 2. Use of zoom gestures while reading each item of the digital leaflet

Id: Medicine identification – name and active ingredient; P: Presentation; W: Warnings; C: Composition; 1: Why is this medication prescribed?; 2: How does this medicine work?; 3: When should I not use this medicine?; 4: What should I know before using this medicine?; 5: Where, how and for how long can I store this medicine?; 6: How should I use this medicine?; 7: What should I do if I forget to use this medicine?; 8: What kinds of harm this medicine can cause?; 9: What if someone uses a larger amount of this medicine than indicated?; Lw: Legal wording

Concerning the exploitation of textual structure of the leaflet, it has been noticed that the items pointed out by the results obtained for average reading time and zooming were read by of most participants: item 1 (n = 17), item 4 (n = 19), item 6 (n = 20), item 8 (n = 19). These topics are part of a section entitled *Patient information*. This section attracted in general more people's attention. Information regarding the *Identification of the medicine* (items Id, P, W and C) and *Legal wording* (item Lw) were commonly dispensed by users.

The results for average time of reading and use of zoom gestures point that participants developed a more careful and detailed reading, as intended for this task, in items 1, 4, 6 and 8. Specifically in these topics, the use of horizontal scrolling was frequently observed among participants: item 1 (n = 8), item 4 (n = 11), item 6 (n = 11), item 8 (n = 12). Use of horizontal scrolling is regarded as something tedious and dull, that should be avoided [19]. Additionally, the combined use of scrolling in both horizontal and vertical directions is discouraged [20]. The need of using horizontal scrolling is due to the oversized column measure and the small letters. Therefore, readers need to zoom in so they can identify the typographic characters; in doing so, they must scroll to read a complete line of text. This demonstrates that the graphic presentation of leaflets is not meant for reading in small screens, such as those of mobile devices.

Task 2, focused on reading the digital leaflet in the iPod Touch, ended the practical stage of the interaction test. It was followed by an interview, intended to identify participants' perceptions and opinions about the previous activities.

3.4   Follow-up Interview

This interview included questions about two main themes: (1) the graphic presentation of the digital leaflet and (2) the interaction with the mobile device while reading.

Regarding the first subject, participants stated that the typeface used, Times New Roman, did not create difficulties in reading. The body size, though, has been noticed in different ways by the individuals, yielding two trends: those who considered the body size uncomfortable to read (n = 7) and those who stated it was easy to read (n = 9). Four participants were indifferent to the effects of body size in reading the leaflet. In fact, the type size displayed in the iPod Touch screen varied according to the users' preferences, since it was possible to zoom in and out. Some people preferred reducing the visualization of the document, in order to avoid horizontal scrolling. They were also asked about the text column measure, generally answering that it was too large (n = 14). Evaluations of comfort affirm that this oversized length was uncomfortable to read (n = 11). Answers for indifference (n = 5) and for comfortable reading (n = 4) due to the column measure had less occurrences. In contrast, the last aspect of typography addressed in the interview, leading, showed more positive (n = 12) evaluations than negative (n = 4) or neutral (n = 4) answers.

Opposed to what has been observed in tasks 1 and 2, participants stated they could easily distinguish the various hierarchical levels of information in the digital leaflet (n = 14). This result is similar to the answers of users about difficulties during the interaction with the mobile device. Eleven individuals did not point any problem while reading the digital leaflet, and 13 people said that the graphic presentation of the document aided them in reading the leaflet on the iPod Touch. In spite of this, participants raised some questions, such as the use of excessive scrolling, that were not considered difficulties but indicate only a partial approval of the leaflet for reading in mobile devices. So, the full positive evaluations (n = 6) were less numerous than negative (n = 7) and partially positive (n = 7) evaluations. Thus, most participants recognized some issues of the visual presentation for reading on small screens, even if such difficulties have not led them to consider this structure a hindrance to read the digital leaflet.

When asked about the situations in which they could read a digital leaflet, participants' answers revealed also details regarding the priority between the print and the digital version; in what kind of devices they would read the digital leaflet; conditions to reading this kind of document in mobile devices; situations and the main goal of reading leaflets. The number of answers in each category is presented in Table 1. It shows that the people who engaged the interaction test prioritize print leaflets.

Table 1. Classification of responses about the use of digital leaflets for the participants

Category	Participants answers	n. answers
Priority	Print leaflet	14
	Digital leaflet	5
Kind of device	Mobile devices	4
	Other electronic devices (e.g. *desktops*)	2
Conditions	Appropriate system for reading in electronic devices	4
	People need to know *Bulário Eletrônico*	1
Situations	Lack of the print leaflet	16
	Before buying the medicine	8
	During medical consultation	1
Main goal	Answer doubts about the medicine	6

Table 2. Classification of responses about the use of digital leaflets for other people, in participants' opinion

Category	Participants answers	n. answers
Priority	Print leaflet	7
	Digital leaflet	10
Kind of device	Mobile devices	9
	Other electronic devices (e.g. *desktops*)	2
Conditions	Appropriate system for reading in electronic devices	5
	People need to know *Bulário Eletrônico*	3
	Reducing number of steps to access the digital leaflet	2
Situations	Lack of the print leaflet	11
	Before buying the medicine	3
Main goal	Answer doubts about the medicine	4

When asked to project these impressions on the use of digital leaflets by other people, results were noticeably different. Participants demonstrated they think that other individuals could prioritize digital leaflets instead of the print documents. Table 2 shows the complete results obtained for this question.

To finish the follow-up interviews, participants' were asked if they thought that mobile devices are an appropriate means to read digital leaflets. Most of them stated that these devices can be used to that purpose, totaling 18 answers approving this use and only two neutral answers.

4   Conclusions and Final Considerations

According to the results of the interaction test, it is possible to assert that the current structure of the digital medicine leaflets available at the Brazilian online database for medicine leaflets is not designed for access via mobile interactive devices. The PDF file formatted as print document displayed in the small screen made not only visualizing sections of the text difficult, but also searching and finding information within the text. Thus, interaction and navigation are negatively affected by the digital leaflet structure.

The typographic variables, notably the body size and the column measure, required users to frequently use gestures to zoom and scroll in two directions, which contradicts guidelines found in the literature. Regarding the typeface used in document formatting and the interline spacing; users did not have demonstrate difficulties caused by such variables. Regarding the hierarchy of information in the digital leaflet, results show that typography in the document, instead of providing cues to participants about the structure of the text and helping them distinguish the relationship between textual elements, led to misinterpretations of how content was organized. In some cases, people pointed out the lack of distinction between hierarchical levels as a difficulty, mainly in what concerns locating information in the leaflet. For other individuals, these relationships were more satisfactory than the standard of printed leaflets, which led to positive evaluations of digital leaflet.

In conclusion, the visual presentation of the digital leaflet did not aid participants to read medicine information in the device. The document did not provide options for users to choose a comfortable setting of typographical aspects, so people have had to struggle to be able to access the desired information. The tolerance that was found in the study, in an environment with controlled conditions, may not occur in real contexts of use, especially in situations of stress. So, it is pertinent to search for alternative solutions, based on user-centered design.

The findings of this study point to the need of information design guidelines for the Brazilian digital medicine leaflets that consider interactivity and navigability aspects in order to ease reading and information searching/finding. Moreover, the structure for Brazilian digital medicine leaflets must not only be designed but tested with people to ensure their legibility as well as their usability, taking advantage of the resources available through software for mobile devices.

References

1. Silva, T., Dal-Pizzol, F., Bello, C.M., Mengue, S.S., Schenkel, E.P.: Bulas de medicamentos e a informação adequada ao paciente. Revista de Saúde Pública 34(2), 184–189 (2000)
2. Raynor, D.: Consumer medicines information: an international perspective. Chronic*ill 7, 7–11 (2003)
3. Närhi, U.: Drug information for consumers and patients: a review of the research. National Agency for Medicines, Helsinki (2006)
4. Paula, C.S., Costa, C.K., Miguel, M.D., Zanin, S.M.W., Spinillo, C.G.: Análise crítica de bulas sob a perspectiva do usuário de medicamentos. Visão Acadêmica 10(2), 123–133 (2009)
5. Spinillo, C.G., Padovani, S., Lanzoni, C.: Ergonomia informacional em bulas de medicamentos e na tarefa de uso: um estudo sobre fármaco em suspensão oral. Ação Ergonômica 5(1), 2–10 (2010)
6. Payne, S.A.: Balancing information needs: dilemmas in producing patient information leaflets. Health Informatics Journal 8, 174–179 (2002)
7. Volpato, L.F., Martins, L.C., Mialhe, F.L.: Bulas de medicamentos e profissionais de saúde: ajudam ou complicam a compreensão dos usuários? Rev. Ciênc Farm Básica Apl. 30(3), 309–314 (2009)
8. Dixon-Woods, M.: Writing wrongs? An analysis of published discourses about the use of patient information leaflets. Social Science & Medicine 52(9), 1417–1432 (2001)
9. Coulter, A.: After Bristol: putting patients at the centre. BMJ 324, 648–651 (2002)
10. Brazil. National Health Surveillance Agency. Resolução de Diretoria Colegiada n. 140. Diário Oficial da União, Brasília, 185. Section 1, pp. 53–54 (2003)
11. Brazil. National Health Surveillance Agency. Resolução de Diretoria Colegiada n. 47. Diário Oficial da União, Brasília, 12. Section 1, pp. 36–41 (2010)
12. Caldeira, T.R., Neves, E.R.Z., Perini, E.: Evolução histórica das bulas de medicamentos no Brasil. Cad. Saúde Pública 24(4), 737–743 (2008)
13. Melo, G.: Interview: Gilvania de Melo [2008]. Interviewer: S. Padovani. InfoDesign 5(3), 62–64 (2008)
14. Neves, E.R.Z., Caldeira, T.R., Melo, G., Murasaki, R.T.: Projeto Bulas: Informação sobre medicamentos on-line. In: Proceedings ...Brazilian Conference on Health Informatics, Florianópolis, vol. 10, SBIS, São Paulo (2006)
15. Fujita, P.T.L.: Análise da apresentação gráfica do conteúdo textual da bula de medicamento na perspectiva de leitura do paciente em contexto de uso. Dissertation (MSc Design) – Federal University of Paraná (2009)
16. Pottes, A.: Animação Multimídia de Instrução (AMI) visualizada em Dispositivo de Interação Móvel (DIM): um estudo exploratório acerca da influência da flexibilidade de interação sobre a visualização da informação e a realização da tarefa. Dissertation (MSc Design) – Federal University of Paraná (2012)
17. Andriesen, S.: Readability Testing of PILs – A New 'Must'. EPC: European Pharmaceutical Contractor, pp. 42–44 (Autumn 2006)
18. Maat, H.P., Lentz, L.: Improving the usability of patient information leaflets. Patient Educ. Couns. 80(1), 113–119 (2009)
19. United States. Department of Health and Human Services. U.S. General Services Administration. Research-based web design and usability guidelines. HHS, GSA, Washington, DC (2006)
20. W3C. Mobile web best practices (2007), http://www.w3.org/2007/02/mwbp_flic_cards.pdf

Visual Design in Healthcare for Low-Literate Users – A Case Study of Healthcare Leaflets for New Immigrants in Taiwan

Yah-Ling Hung[1] and Catherine Stones[2]

[1] School of Design, University of Leeds, UK
Dept. of Communication Arts, Fu Jen Catholic University, Taiwan
030872@mail.fju.edu.tw
[2] School of Design, University of Leeds, UK
c.m.stones@leeds.ac.uk

Abstract. Healthcare material is an effective communication platform to offer an innovative professional care system which provides a more accurate, accessible and applicable educational platform for patients in a diversified society. However, immigrant populations are vulnerable to serious health disparities, and language barriers may further exacerbate their limited health literacy in accessing health information. Recent studies indicate that visual design might service as a powerful mean for the delivery of health information because vivid information combined with visual elements seems to affect both affective and cognitive processes to maximize comprehension. Yet, ways to identify the visual factors of healthcare material that best affect low-literate users to learn is a question that remains unanswered. The purpose of this study is to identify the visual factors of healthcare leaflet that affect low-literate users' satisfaction, thus establishing guidelines for designing visual healthcare materials for low-literate users. The study was implemented in three stages, the first of which reviewed existing literature to survey current strategies to evaluate visual design in healthcare for low-literate users. Secondly, 36 appropriate leaflets from existing health educational materials in Taiwan were collected and analyzed. Thirdly, semi-structured interviews were conducted with 10 Vietnamese participants who were new immigrants with a low level of education in Taiwan. The results showed that the factors of healthcare material that affect low-literate users' satisfaction range from creative ideas, design layout of cover, design layout of index, typeface design, color design, pictorial illustrations to realistic photos and cultural factors. A checking list for designing visual healthcare materials for low-literate users was also listed. Successful health communication depends on the health information properly coded by the providers and correctly decoded by the consumers. The findings of this study are expected to be valuable, not only for the providers and consumers of health information, but also for the designers of healthcare material.

Keywords: Visual Design, Health literacy, Healthcare Material.

A. Marcus (Ed.): DUXU 2014, Part III, LNCS 8519, pp. 44–55, 2014.
© Springer International Publishing Switzerland 2014

1   Introduction

At present, rapidly shifting immigration trends pose a real challenge for health care. Kreps & Sparks (2008) indicate that immigrants often have significant language and health literacy difficulties, which are further exacerbated by cultural barriers and economic challenges to accessing and making sense of the relevant health information. Recent research suggests that good health educational materials can help to reduce the literacy barrier and enhance health outcome, because they can help modify attitudes, shape positive behaviours, and improve patients' self-prevention (Andersen et al., 2008; Atkinson, 2009). However, the majority of health educational materials are constructed for well-educated users rather than those with low literacy skills, numbers of new immigrants are forced to seek health information in a non-native language and navigate significant culture barriers.

Recent studies indicate that visual design might service as a powerful mean for the delivery of health information because vivid information combined with visual elements seems to affect both affective and cognitive processes to maximize comprehension. For example, Rajwan & Kim (2010) indicate that the use of visual attributes, images, information graphics, diagrams, and animations to convey and absorb information can provide techniques and tools to help patients gain situational awareness of medical information. Simplifying large data sets and accelerating communication may aid users' decisions more quickly. Furthermore, Choi & Bakken (2010) point out that using concrete and realistic pictures and pictographs with clear captions will maximise the benefit of visuals. Future designs of low-literacy interfaces should include a careful selection of icons and visual images, since these are more realistic than abstracts, and closely resemble the intended meaning of the visuals. At this time, visual appeal plays an important role in bridging the gap between the information provider and the consumer. Yet, ways to identify the visual factors of healthcare material that best affect low-literate users to learn is a question that remains unanswered.

Printed health education resources have been identified as being one of the most influential media for improving the quality of healthcare. Patients can bring them home and reread them to remind themselves of key points if they are too shy to ask in the clinic (Harvey, et al., 2000). However, racks of health information brochures in clinics are still ignored by patients and these account for much of the government's annual budget for health promotion (Kreuter et al., 2010). The purpose of this study is to identify the visual factors of healthcare leaflet that affect low-literate users' satisfaction, thus establishing guidelines for designing visual healthcare materials for low-literate users. Considering the issues of concern above, the primary research objectives of this study are described below:

- To survey current strategies to evaluate visual design in healthcare for low-literate users.
- To identify the visual factors of healthcare material which affect users' satisfaction
- To establish guidelines for designing visual healthcare materials for low-literate users

2   Theoretical Backgrounds

2.1   Developments and Assessment of Healthcare Leaflets

Leaflets are probably the most popular educational materials, because they are relatively inexpensive to create and easy to carry. However, they provide no feedback only one-way communication and are nor tailored for specific audience. The factors of leaflets to appeal to users to pick up or cause them to give up reading health information are varied. Frederikson & Bull (1995) investigated whether or not the impact of leaflets really encouraged patients to adopt a more thoughtful and prepared approach toward consulting their doctor. The results showed that there were clear differences between the control and experimental groups in terms of the proportion of consultations being perceived as containing good, average and poor communication. However, the sample size was relatively small and the use of a single doctor seriously limited the generalisability of the findings. Moreover, Steele et al. (2011) developed and evaluated health information leaflets to promote public awareness of the link between lifestyle and cancer. They made use of feedback from the general public, healthcare practitioners and design professionals by means of focus groups, questionnaires and semi-structured interviews to design newly-developed leaflets. Therefore, they conducted usability surveys and awareness tests to compare the attractiveness and effectiveness of the newly-developed leaflets and existing standard leaflets. The result showed that both of the leaflets increased awareness of the link between lifestyle and cancer but participants expected the healthcare leaflets could be more usable as well as legible and comprehensible.

Do healthcare leaflets have a similar impact on low-literate users in terms of promoting the acquisition of knowledge and changing attitudes? Kripalani et al. (2007) conducted a randomised controlled trial to explore the difficulties and needs of low-literate patient in healthcare materials. The results showed that almost all the patients declare that it was difficult to understand prescription drug labels and other medication instructions and considered an illustrated medication schedule might be a useful and easily understood tool to assist with medication management. Moreover, Shaw et al. (2009) recruited 321 patients at an in-patient cardiology unit to examine the readability of healthcare leaflet. The findings showed that 22% of the patients interviewed were found to have a low level of literacy. Many of them felt that the health information on the leaflets should be written in plain language. Apparently, there is a broad gap between patients and leaflets, because most of the existing educational leaflets do not consider both internal content and external presentation.

2.2   Visual Appeal in Healthcare

Recent studies indicate that visual appeal might service as a powerful mean for the delivery of health information. For example, Doak et al. (1996) investigated whether a message showed with visuals and graphics is better than a message showed with sound. The results showed that the memory systems in the brain favour visual storage and visual presentations have been shown to be 43 per cent more persuasive than unaided presentations. Furthermore, Brotherstone et al. (2006) explored the effectiveness of visual illustrations in improving people's understanding of the preventive aim of Flexible Sigmoidoscopy (FS) screening. They recruited 318 older people to attend FS screening and randomly allocated them to receive written information alone, or written information plus illustrations. The findings confirmed that pictorial illustrations resulted in significantly better understanding.

Low-literate users may have different preferences from high-literate users in terms of visualisation, what are the underlying factors of visual design that need to be considered for users with lower literacy? Choi & Bakken (2010) indicate that using concrete and realistic pictures and pictographs with clear captions will maximise the benefit of visuals. Nevertheless, one emerging theme is simplicity in design, content, and technical features. They also suggest that future designs of low-literate interfaces should include a careful selection of icons and visual images, since these were more realistic than abstracts, and closely resemble the intended meaning of the visuals. In addition, Rajwan & Kim (2010) indicate following perspectives to make use of visualisation to support patient-provider health communication, which includes physical and biological aspects of the participants; language, literacy, numeracy, and graphicacy encoding and decoding; shared mental models and common ground; concordance in the understanding by the participants. They also suggest some consideration for supporting patient cognition regarding medical decisions, such as the patient's ability to use visualisation techniques and tools, the patient's ability to perceive, encode and decode information as it is presented, the patient's ability to interpret visualised information in a way that is correct and consistent with care goals, and the patient's ability to make decisions based on interpreted data in an informed fashion.

2.3   Visual Factors of Healthcare Media

What are the visual factors of healthcare media that might affect users' satisfaction? Frascara (2004) indicates that 'graphic design' as a term is more descriptive and appropriate than 'visual communication', because it encompasses various creative aspects related to the following issues: perceptual message, cultural recognition, source collection, publication organisation, aesthetic styles, broadcasting media, technical quality, and written and spoken language. Arntson (2003) also suggests that designers should apply the following principles of visual perception to practice visual communication: information perception, a dynamic balance, good gestalt, usage of text types, layout styles, illustration and photography in design, advertising design, and designing with colour. Ambrose & Harris (2009) stress that graphic design is a multidisciplinary process that draws on many creative sources, including industrialisation, technology, typography, consumerism, identity and branding, social responsibility, modernism and post-modernism, nostalgia and rhetoric, semiotics, and the vernacular. Dabner (2010) points out that the fundamental components of graphic design are positive and negative space, form and space, symmetry & asymmetry, basic principles of layout, style of layout, pace and contrast, size and format, coordination and identity, and photography and illustration. When taking a comprehensive view of the above scholars' opinions, it would appear that the fundamental components of graphic design within healthcare materials cover diverse disciplines ranging from message presentation to aesthetic styles, technical quality, typography design, layout arrangement, colour contrast, cultural recognition, advertising strategy and photography and illustration.

In terms of creative ideas, although advertising strategies involve a constant search for a new and innovative way to express sales appeal, there are also some creative formats that have worked over the years; for example, creative strategies that involve straightforward demonstration, comparison, scene from everyday life, humour, and celebrity may attract attention, stimulate interest, and foster audiences' positive mood (Altstiel & Grow, 2010; Moriarty et al, 2012; Fill, 2013). In terms of layout design, a good arrangement of graphic elements, such as headlines, sub-headings, pictures, branding, etc. will achieve a smooth flow of information and eye movement for maximum effectiveness or impact. A visual structure of repetition, rhythm, pattern, series, sequence, balance, symmetry, and movement are probably the most common layout arrangements (Frascara, 2004); In terms of typography design, a typeface has aesthetically powerful impacts and is varied in colour, form, and spacing. It is better to use a suitable font size to improve the readability of the content and different styles and forms of typeface to better organise the content better and make it easier to understand (Ambrose & Harris, 2009; Dabner, 2010). In terms of colour scheme, it is crucial for designers to remember that bright colours are excellent for attracting attention; contrast value is the key to legibility. The psychology of colour may evoke emotional feeling, and the symbolic meanings of colours provoke an immediate association with synesthesia. (Dabner, 2010; Sherin, 2012); In terms of illustrations, these are many ways to visually represent an idea, object, person, or place can be used to evoke audiences', but the picture has to be well-composed, with a fashionable concept, designed in a good tonal range, and matching the aims of the title (Dabner, 2010; Sherin, 2012). In terms of the cultural issue, how can the gap of cross-cultural communication be bridged in order to appropriately deliver the desired message to the audience? Liquori (2011) indicates that designers need to consider a wide range of features, such as language, symbol, image, colours, and navigational ways of reading. Since each culture has its own unique way of constructing sentences, sharing icons, matching images, associating colours and navigating reading. All the aforementioned concerns about graphic design will be integrated into further semi-structured interviews to provide a holistic framework.

3   Methodology

In order to identify the visual factors of healthcare media that affect low-literate users' satisfaction, semi-structured interviews were conducted with 10 Vietnamese participants who were new immigrants with a low level of education in Taiwan. Based on the orientation of the data collection, in-depth interviews can be classified in a variety of ways including formal, less formal and informal; structured, semi-structured and unstructured; focused or non-directive; and informant interviews versus respondent interviews. However, semi-structured interviews are more suitable for obtaining people's opinions; furthermore, they guarantee good coverage and enable the interviewer to probe for answers (Drever,2003). Successful semi-structured interviews require much more advanced preparation and investigation than fully structured interviews, as well as more discipline and more creativity during the actual interviews, and more time for analysing and interpreting the results (Wengraf, 2001). Therefore, the method of semi-structured interview was chosen for this study. The main questions for the semi-structured interviews were planned in advance to create the overall structure and what was said during interviews was recorded to be analysed and interpreted later.

These interviews were conducted separately to avoid individual participants' statements affecting others' opinions. These interviews were also processed accompanied by a Vietnamese interpreter to reduce their stress and create a safe environment for these low-literate participants. During the face-to-face interviews, some common graphic terms were interpreted to help them to express the factors that affected their satisfaction. All the predicted answers were listed in a questionnaire format to ensure that the responses of the interviewees followed the structure of questionnaire, while all the unpredictable answers were recorded in an open text box. The duration of each interview was an hour and interview data was recorded either by hand-written notes or by audiotaping. The audiotaped data from entire interviews was transcribed and used as data to analyse the evaluation process. After searching the leaflets related to health education in Taiwan, some inappropriate issues were discarded, while some appropriate issues were retained to be applied to this research. 36 pictures from existing health educational materials in Taiwan were collected and divided into 8 categories based on the above-mentioned issues. Each category was presented with four test pictures and several corresponding interview questions, as follows: What do you see in these pictures? What do they mean to you? What emotions do you feel as you look at this? Which are your favourite pictures? Why are them your favourite? Which are your dislike pictures? What are your reasons for disliking?

4 Discussions and Suggestion

The findings from this study that contribute to new knowledge about visual designing in healthcare for low-literate immigrants are described below.

4.1 Creative Ideas

The participants considered some specific factors of creative ideas that help low-literate audiences to learn best, the first of which was the concept of being straightforward; for example, a breastfeeding photo to convey the message of the advantage of breastfeeding or an anti-smoking icon to convey the message of anti-smoking. Most of the participants mentioned that they preferred if when designers informed them of the main theme directly rather than describing a long story in detail, whereas a few of them mentioned that the idea of straightforward showed superficial creativity in design. Some of the participants pointed out that ridiculous humour may have a negative educational effect, such as using a bespectacled boy in a photo to promote the prevention of myopia. The third creative idea was the celebrity endorsement; for example, a slogan presented by an idol, a politician, or a movie star could enhance the credibility of health promotional media. However, the celebrity should be familiar to the target audience and not show a commercial intention. The fourth creative idea was conveying a cultural message using specific symbols. Most of the participants indicated that they felt being respected by local people by seeing the scenes of Vietnamese culture adopted in educational material, whereas some who had just arrived in Taiwan felt that emphasizing the Vietnamese image was discriminatory. In addition, all the participants pointed out that the idea of shock or metaphor should be avoided because they did not like the use of religion or illness to show the desire for behavioural change neither did they like the use of text under the table or the use of images beyond their understanding.

4.2   Design Layout of Cover

Most of the participants agreed that a layout containing the subjects in high contrast and the background in low contrast highlighted the theme because they did not want to spend too much time distinguishing the subject from the background. The second scheme of design layout of cover was symmetrical arrangement, and some of the participants mentioned that they would like to see a balanced design with a symmetrical arrangement of the subjects rather than a rhythmic design with the subjects spontaneously arranged. The third issue involved plenty of empty white space adopted in the layout, the majority of participants mentioned that they expect a limited content presented on a layout that contains the appropriate amount of white space, but they couldn't stand for a tiny subject shown in a wide white layout; All of the participants declared that a rhythmic composition could stimulate them to stop and read the message on the layout, because an irregular arrangement with small pictures on the layout could cause an unstable composition and further result in visual disorder. In addition, some of the participants claimed that they did not like the use of hi-tech techniques to show the creative idea; for example, an overlapping presentation combined with pictures and text created by Photoshop, because they could not distinguish the text on the upper layer from the image on the lower layer.

4.3   Design Layout of Content

Most of the participants mentioned that they preferred divided sections rather than the complete information because of their low level of patience. The second issue of was scheme with one topic per page. The majority of the participants pointed out that they didn't like the idea of too much information on the same page and several themes presented at the same time. Some of the participants pointed out that the theme was clearer when the subject was placed in the middle. The third issue was the scheme of bullet points. Most of the participants stressed that they preferred numbering rather than bullet points because it was easier to recognize. The fourth issue was the scheme of one picture per paragraph. Most of the participants said they preferred that every question is accompanied by an interpretive photo, and the illustrations were placed near the relevant text. In addition, some of them declared that they preferred the text were arranged in a row rather than the text was actively placed around a picture because they could not find the beginning and ending of the content. Some of the participants pointed out that the advertising should be clearly distinguishable from the editorial content. They would not pick up any educational material that looked like a general flyer.

4.4   Typeface Design

Most of the participants indicated that for typeface design, they would like to see the title, heading, subheading, and context presented in a variety of styles. However, some of them mentioned it would be better to use no more than two kinds of typefaces for the context, because graphic typography is incomprehensible and abstract. The second issue was the use of a suitable font size. The majority of the participants agreed with the use of a large text size to increase legibility, whereas a few of them suggested that a smaller font size, i.e. 12 points, would leave more space for the text, because they wanted to see sufficient information rather than it being limited. Moreover, some of the participants indicated that they expected a large font size, bright colour, and clear title rather than a small, dull and blurry title because they wanted to determine whether or not the specific theme met their needs at first glance. The third issue was the use of artistic headings and corresponding monochrome text. Some of the participants stressed that a monochrome text with a simple style was easy to read, but it sometimes looked boring, whereas coloured text with an artistic style was difficult for recognising the text but sometimes looked versatile. Therefore, a title with an artistic style accompanied by body text with a simple style would be the best typeface scheme; on the contrary, all the participants declared that they preferred the use of underlined text rather than the use of graphic devices to highlight key messages. Designers should not presume that highlighting is a useful method to help readers to find the key terms in an article.

4.5   Colour Scheme

Some specific factors of colour scheme were considered by the participants, the first of which was using bright colours & familiar ad colours, and most of the participants mentioned that they preferred a highly contrasting design to generate an active feeling and a well-known advertisement colours makes them remember the content at first glance; however, a few of the participants declared that the use of fancy colours could generates a vulgar feeling, whereas others thought that that drawing attention to the advertisement may cause negative effect. The second scheme was the use of monochrome colours. Some of the participants believed that the use of monochrome colours made the content look comfortable and valuable because of a natural associate, whereas others thought that a dull colour scheme made them feel excluded because of a blur associate. The third scheme was using colour for different genders; for example, warm colours are always regarded as being feminine colours, whereas cold colours are always regarded as being masculine colours. Therefore, pink and orange colours are used to promote women's health, while blue and green colours are used to promote men's health. Most of the participants stressed that they were eager to pick up healthcare materials related to men's health, because their husband were general older and needed home cares. On the contrary, all the participants declared that they disliked the scheme of using ethnic colours to stimulate them to fight for their identity, because they don't not know which colours can represent Vietnam.

4.6   Pictorial Illustrations

The majority of the participants mentioned that they preferred artists to make use of watercolours to sketch the natural world, whereas a few of them thought that the outline of subjects illustrated by watercolours was too vague to be recognised. The second factor of illustration was line drawing. Some of the participants declared that the use of line drawing gives an impression of professionalism and is convincing, whereas others thought that the use of contour line drawing shows that the designer was in a hurry to finish it. The third factor of illustration was photography, and some of the participants indicated that they preferred realistic photos to serve as visual aids to deliver healthcare information written in unfamiliar terms or complex phrases, but they can't accept a stranger's photograph or a photo that tell a miserable story. The fourth factor of illustration was cute cartoons. Some of the participants showed their interest in digital cartoons because of their cute characters, whereas others mentioned that the use of cartoons was not very convincing because they were fake. In addition, some of the participants stressed that they expected an interesting topic to be accompanied by a beautiful drawing rather than a sloppy design accompanied by monotonous pictures because nobody wants to go home with an ill-designed leaflet to prepare the necessary healthcare.

4.7   Realistic Photos

Some specific factors of realistic photos were considered by the participants, the first of which was a scene from everyday life. All the participants agreed that the use of innocent children's faces and warm family scenes make health educational material more welcoming, but they prefer to see familiar faces and scenes in pictures since this makes them feel safe. Besides, most of the participants indicated that they would love to see a scene of three generations to depict endless happiness, but the people should be healthy and beautiful to represent a positive vision. The second factor of realistic photos was using of specialization. Most of the participants preferred the use of a photo of a doctor to represent professionalism, whereas others thought that professional medical photo made them feel that the content of the article was hard to read and even reminded them that they couldn't understand what the doctor says in the clinic. The third factor of realistic photos was using symptoms of a disease, and some of the participants mentioned that the photos of symptoms which could help them to recognise the disease were useful, whereas some of them couldn't accept the use of detailed symptoms of diseases which made them feel uncomfortable. On the contrary, the majority of the participants declared that the application of general medical equipment and supplies should be avoided, because they didn't like unrelated photos only used for decorative purposes, but with no connection to the subject. They felt cheated if they depended on the photo to decide whether to read the text or not. In addition, some participants pointed out that they didn't want to see indecent photos that embarrassed them, for example, clear photos of breastfeeding, lovers kissing, or naked bodies.

4.8   Cultural Factors

Some specific cultural factors were considered by the participants, the first of which was adopting the factor of a hometown landscape, and the majority of the participants agreed that a familiar scene would remind immigrants of their origin, but the character of hometown landscape must be prominent to represent Vietnam. The second scheme was adopting the factor of hometown festivals. Some of the participants claimed that they would love to see specific props, costumes, dances and festive activities to give the impression of a family reunion, but the activities should be famous nationwide. The third scheme was adopting the factor of living habits. Some of the participants preferred to show off their delicious home-made meal to represent their uniqueness; whereas others were afraid they would be overlooked if such simple ingredients were used to represent Vietnam. However, most of the participants declare that they couldn't accept a description of a lower standard of living which made them feel being discriminated. On the contrary, the adoption of the religious references was abandoned by the participants because most of them didn't have religious beliefs and didn't like the use of serious religion to represent the relaxed lifestyle in Vietnam.

The woman varied many issues, some of which were contradictory. This shows design is not an exact science and designs need to do bespeak testing. However, despite a low sample number, the rich discussion that occurred allows us to recommend the following guidelines:

Table 1. A checking list for visual low-literate healthcare materials

Creative Idea - Suggest	Creative Idea - Avoid
• Using the concept of straightforward • Using the concept of humour • Using the concept of celebrity • Using the concept of culture	• Avoid using the idea of intimidation • Avoid using the idea of metaphor • Avoid using idea of infamous celebrity • Avoid using imitation advertising scheme
Layout Design - Suggest	**Layout Design - Avoid**
• Using plenty of empty white space • Using symmetrical arrangement • Using the scheme of bullet points • Using the scheme of segmentation • Using the scheme of one topic per page • Using the scheme of illustration of subtitle commentary	• Avoid using rhythmic composition • Avoid using unbalance composition • Avoiding using tiny subjects shown in a wide white layout • Avoid using the scheme of full layout

Table 1. (*continued*)

Typeface Design - Suggest	Typeface Design - Avoid
• Use of an eye-catching title • Use of suitable font size • Use of a variety of styles of typeface • Use of artistic headings and corresponding monochrome text	• Avoid using of graphic devices to highlight key messages • Avoid using monochrome text for whole section • Avoid using same style for title and content
Colour Design - Suggest	**Colour Design - Avoid**
• Using bright colours • Using familiar ad colours • Using colour for different genders • Using contrasting scheme	• Avoid using ethnic colours • Avoid using scheme of low contrasting • Avoid using scheme of similar colours for subjects and background
Illustration Design - Suggest	**Illustration Design - Avoid**
• Applied with watercolour • Applied with line drawing • Applied with photography • Applied with the subject of three generations	• Avoid applying fake cartoon • Avoid applying negative vision. • Avoid applying line drawing in draft
Photo Design - Suggest	**Photo Design - Avoid**
• Using everyday life • Using photo of a doctor • Using symptoms of a disease	• Avoid using intimidating photos • Avoid using indecent photos • Avoid using detailed photos of diseases and treatment • Avoid using photos unrelated to the theme
Cultural Design - Suggest	**Cultural Design - Avoid**
• Adopting the factor of hometown landscape • Adopting the factor of hometown festivals • Adopting the factor of living habits	• Avoid adopting the factor of religion • Avoid adopting unfamiliar living style • Avoid adopting the factor of a lower standard of living

References

1. Altstiel, T., Grow, J.: Advertising creative: strategy, copy + design, 2nd edn. SAGE, London (2010)
2. Ambrose, G., Harris, P.: The Fundamentals of Graphic Design. AVA Academia, Lausanne (2009)
3. Andersen, P., Andersen, S., Youngblood, E., Colmenares, E.: Health education kiosk for low-literacy patients served by community-based clinics. In: Proceedings of the 2008 IEEE International Symposium on Technology and Society, pp. 1–9 (2008)
4. Arntson, A.E.: Graphic design basics, 4th edn. Wadsworth, Belmont (2003)
5. Atkinson, N.L., Saperstein, S.L., Pleis, J.: Using the internet for health-related activities: findings from a national probability sample. J. Med. Internet Res. 11(1), e4 (2009)
6. Brotherstone, H., Miles, A., Robb, K.A., Atkin, W., Wardle, J.: The impact of illustrations on public understanding of the aim of cancer screening. Patient Education and Counselling 63(3), 328–335 (2006)

7. Choi, J., Bakken, S.: Web-based education for low-literate parents in Neonatal Intensive Care Unit: Development of a website and heuristic evaluation and usability testing. International Journal of Medical Informatics 79(8), 565–575 (2010)
8. Dabner, D., Calvert, S., Casey, A.: Graphic design school: the principles and practices of graphic design, 4th edn. John Wiley & Sons, Hoboken (2010)
9. Doak, C., Doak, L., Root, J.: Teaching Patients with Low Literacy Skills, 2nd edn. Lippincott, Philadelphia (1996)
10. Drever, E.: Using semi-structured interviews in small-scale research: a teacher's guide, Rev. edn. Scottish Council for Research in Education, Glasgow (2003)
11. Fill, C., Hughes, G., De Francesco, S.: Advertising: strategy, creativity and media. Pearson (2013)
12. Frascara, J.: Communication design: principles, methods, and practice. Allworth Press, New York (2004)
13. Frederikson, L.G., Bull, P.E.: Evaluation of a patient education leaflet designed to improve communication in medical consultations. Patient Education and Counseling 25(1), 51–57 (1995)
14. Harvey, H.D., Fleming, F., Cregan, K., Latimer, E.: The health promotion implications of knowledge and attitude of employees in relation to health and safety leaflets. International Journal of Environmental Health Research 10(4), 315–329 (2000)
15. Johnson, R.L., Saha, S., Arbelaez, J.J., Beach, M.C., Cooper, L.A.: Racial and ethnic differences in patient perceptions of bias and cultural competence in health Care. J. Gen. Intern. Med. 19, 101–110 (2004)
16. Kreps, G.L., Sparks, L.: Meeting the health literacy needs of immigrant populations. Patient Education and Counselling 71(3), 328–332 (2008)
17. Kreuter, M., Strecher, V., Glassman, B.: One Size Does Not Fit All: The Case for Tailoring Print Materials. In: Krep, G.L. (ed.) Health Communication. Health Communication and Health Promotion, vol. 2, pp. 151–168. SAGE Publications Ltd., London (2010)
18. Kripalani, S., Robertson, R., Love-Ghaffari, M.H., Henderson, L.E., Praska, J., Strawder, A., Katz, M.G., Jacobson, T.A.: Development of an illustrated medication schedule as a low-literacy patient education tool. Patient Education and Counselling 66(3), 368–377 (2007)
19. Liquori, E.: Construct a Framework for a Cross-Cultural Design, Web Design (October 2011), http://www.instantshift.com
20. Moriarty, S., Mitchell, N., Wells, W.: Advertising & IMC: principles & practice. Global, 9th edn. Pearson, Boston (2012)
21. Rajwan, Y.G., Kim, G.R.: Medical information visualization conceptual model for patient-physician health communication. In: Proceedings of the 1st ACM International Health Informatics Symposium, pp. 512–516 (2010)
22. Shaw, A., Ibrahim, S., Reid, F., Ussher, M., Rowlands, G.: Patients' perspectives of the doctor–patient relationship and information giving across a range of literacy levels. Patient Education and Counselling 75(1), 114–120 (2009)
23. Steele, M., Dow, L., Baxter, G.: Promoting public awareness of the links between lifestyle and cancer: A controlled study of the usability of health information leaflets. International Journal of Medical Informatics 80(12), 214–229 (2011)
24. Wengraf, T.: Qualitative research interviewing: biographic narrative methods and semi-structured methods. SAGE, London (2001)

Enhanced Hospital Information System by Cloud Computing: SHEFA'A

Lamiaa Fattouh Ibrahim[1,2], Suzan Sadek[1], Shahd Hakeem[1], Lana Al-Sabban[1], Asmaa Ibrahim Mohammed Ahmed [1], and Alaa Hassan Al-Sayed[1]

[1] Department of Information Technology
Faculty of Computing and Information Technology King Abdulaziz University
[2] Institute of Statistical Studies and Research, Cairo University
B.P. 42808 Zip Code 21551- Girl Section, Jeddah, Saudi Arabia
lfibrahim@kau.edu.sa, sadek.suzan@yahoo.com

Abstract. Information Technology is an important part of the healthcare environment. Accuracy and integrity of the information in any hospital system is necessary. Then, this information has to be up-to-date as well to achieve continuous quality improvement in any organization and particularly in a complex area like healthcare. Therefore, diverse information systems must be integrated across the healthcare enterprise. The main objective of this research is to develop a framework for the exchange of patients records located in different hospitals in Saudi Arabia, adding insurance and prescriptions information along with the patient's record to facilitate the insurance process and to automate the medicine prescription process that is currently manual in most hospitals. The proposed framework aims to improve the regular ways of obtaining patients medical records separated in each hospital. For instance, if a particular patient has different medical records in different hospitals visited by that patient, our architecture focuses on the method by which data should be searched and retrieved efficiently from a database on the cloud from different hospitals by preprocessing the data in current hospital's and saving them in the database that resides on the cloud. Our system design is based on cloud computing service oriented architecture. Some of the information included in these medical records is: medical history, prescribed medications and allergies, immunization status, laboratory and test results, radiology images, personal stats like age and weight, diagnoses, order tests and appointments. All of these records are identified by the national ID of the patient. these systems will be utilized by web services asp.net based framework, the doctor will use his/her ID and password to enter the system for security and then enter the patient's ID to send a request for that patient's record that will be sent back to the doctor, the record will be up-to-date since the last visit of the patient to any hospital in Saudi Arabia. The main aim of this study is to provide a data exchange model of patients records, it is used to decrease the time and cost of patients, and help doctors to get up-to-date and accurate information of patients from the records from any hospital in Saudi Arabia. By using e-Patient medical records and Mirth Connect program which use HEALTH LEVEL 7 (HL7) protocol. HL7 protocol is a standard information format of healthcare for data exchange. We provide a single, complete automated patient medical record to give a better

A. Marcus (Ed.): DUXU 2014, Part III, LNCS 8519, pp. 56–62, 2014.

patient care that avoids medical mistakes due to lack of information and unavailability of medical records.

Keywords: patient medical records, Cloud Computing, HL7, healthcare.

1   Introduction

The need for patient's medical accurate and up-to-date information each time a patient visits a different hospital increased the need for rapid patient medical data exchange. Healthcare organizations use different applications and infrastructures which always need to be updated as a result of the fast growth of healthcare services [2]. The variances in the ways of how these organizations maintain their operations, like patients medical records may result in the difficulties of accessing these data. This paper research studies the implementation of cloud computing in healthcare organizations in order for doctors to have an easy way to access patient's medical data from a browser or mobile.

The objective of this project is to provide the patient with comfort and facilitate the process of transfers between hospitals to get radiations or other required data, taking into account the reliability and availability of the required information quickly in times of need under the privacy.

Better patient care could be provided by avoiding medical mistakes due to lack of information that results of unavailability of the medical record. There would be single, complete and up-to-date e-patient medical records other than only fragmented ones. Communications between all types of doctors would be enhanced, whether they worked on a single treatment for a patient, over many treatments, or over the lifetime of a patient. There would be a single place to permanently store environmental conditions and diseases for an individual that can provide greater emphasis on an individual's preventive care and diseases could be prevented before they occur. Public health agencies can be more quickly informed about public health problems. Facilitate the long process of insurance and make the process of medicine prescription easy and automated.   Some amount of money can be saved.

We will create a web application for hospitals, to unify and facilitate the exchange of patient information for different healthcare systems to have complete and accurate e-patient medical records, along with other services for insurance and pharmacy prescriptions.

Target Users

1. Doctors: doctors in any hospital have a full access to e-patient medical records in the web application.
2. Receptionist: receptionists have partial access to the e-patient medical record; they can create a new e-patient medical record or search for the patient's record if it already exists along with payment and insurance information.
3. Nurses: nurses have partial access to the e-patient medical record; nurses can search for the patient and fill in the examination information for the patient necessary before the doctor examines the patient.

4. Pharmacist: pharmacists have partial access to the e-patient medical record, to make it easy to access the prescription prescribed by the doctor to the particular patient.
5. Insurance-employee: insurance-employees have partial access to the e-patient medical record, to access the necessary patient information to have accurate information about the patient's health to determine the necessary insurance level for the patient.

In section 2 discusses methodology. In section 3, the SHEFA'A package is introduced. The paper conclusion is presented in section 4.

2   Methodology

As explained in our system, In case some hospitals don't want to exchange their current legacy system as it was purchased with millions, and they want to have access to SHEFA'A to benefit the complete set of patients' records, and on the other hand we need the data processed in a specific hospital to be transferred to our storage. As a result different data formats from different hospitals will need to be transferred to our central storage; the problem is that data from different hospitals will have different formats. So in order to get the data, for example, previous patients' information from any hospital to SHEFA'A, we should put the data in a unified format, and send it as a message to SHEFA'A's central storage in that format. This study proposed the use of Health Level Seven International (HL7) which is widely being adopted by health care institutions in several nation-wide EMR implementations [2]. HL7 creates standards for the exchange, management, and integration of health care information system which enable interoperability of messages and documents in standardized way which also bring efficient communication among different users that assist in sharing health care information which makes the integration feasible [3]. Using HL7 we can transfer data without worrying about the current structure of the data. We can use Mirth application in SHEFA'A server in the cloud, in which we can connect to the database's hospitals and get their information dynamically. This open source solution gives us the ability to get the previous data from the database and also whenever there's an update in the database it will be automatically upload it in the cloud database which will leads into synchronized database in the cloud [4].

Mirth Connects template driven approach to creating interfaces allows you to specify the type of message your will be receiving or sending, and then create your mappings and transformations.

Mirth Connect supports numerous transfer protocols used across the healthcare industry and for SHEFA'A we choose HL7 [5] Protocol as the type of sending messages between our system and others healthcare systems.

3   SHEFA'A Concept, Model, and Structure

Only an integrated model of EMR can lead to the health care service quality improvement by strengthen the users' role in managing their own medical care [6]. The use of integrated EMR system will enable data sharing, analysis tools, and infrastructure that can speed up many research, especially in health care services, by enabling new insights and enhancing efficiency [7]. Figure 1 shows an overview of SHEFA'A system as a model. We divided our system into three separate levels that it could accommodate each hospital with its own needs with different kinds of services and different ranges of requirements.

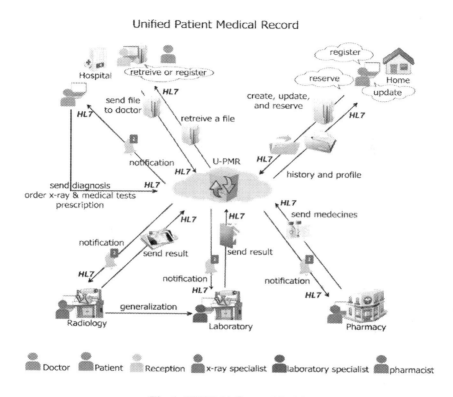

Fig. 1. SHEFA'A System Model

3.1   The Work Flow

Flowchart is a simple schematic mapping tool that shows the sequence of actions within a process. Below is a four-step flow chart diagram for SHEFA'A system.

Step 1: Search Patient or Create a New Account

At the begging the patient can create his account at home or at hospital's reception. The receptionist can search the patient record in the system by using pat SSN.

If it was exist, the receptionist can view the patient history and all information that he need. He can create a new visit by confirming the reservation.

If it was not exist in the system, he/she can create a new account for the patient and fill all required information and confirm the reservation.

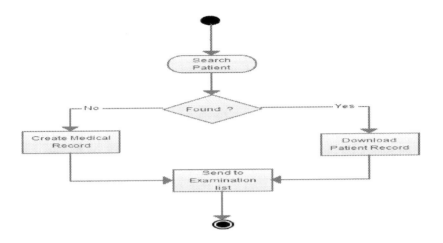

Fig. 2. Search patient or create a new account flow chart

Step 2: Patient Diagnosis

If step 1 is done that means the patient reservation is confirmed and the doctor can see the patient record in the patient diagnostic list. After all the initial examination and diagnostic comment done, the doctor can decide if the patient needs an order to create e-prescription for sending it to the pharmacy. Then, this visit with all the details will be updated in the patient history.

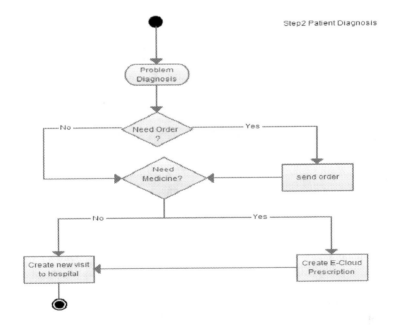

Fig. 3. Step 2: Patient Diagnosis flow chart

Step 3: e-Cloud Outpatient Order

If step 2 is done, the doctor can review patient's order result to add any diagnosis updates or create another e-prescription by clicking Patient Waiting Order Result List. Then, all the updates will be stored in the patient history.

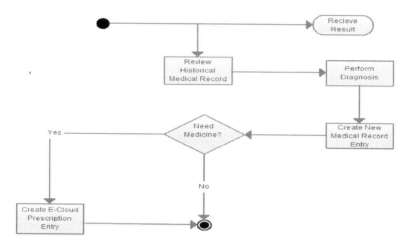

Fig. 4. Step3: e-Cloud Outpatient Order flow chart

Step 4: e-Cloud Prescription Process

At the pharmacy, the pharmacist looking up, for patient prescription if the medicines available in the pharmacy. If it is valid, the pharmacist can update the prescription if needs any editing and then all the changes will saved in the patient history.

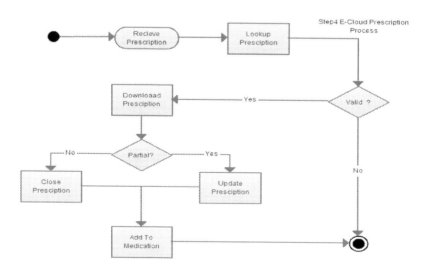

Fig. 5. Step4: e-Cloud Prescription Process flow chart

4   Conclusion and Future Work

In this work, we provide a data exchange model of patient's records in HL7 standard, to decrease the time and cost of patients, and help doctors to get up-to-date and accurate information of patients from the records from any hospital in Saudi Arabia and can be accessed and edited by authorized users from anywhere. our architecture focuses on the method by which data should be searched and retrieved efficiently from a database on the cloud from different hospitals by preprocessing the data in current hospital's and saving them in the database that resides on the cloud. Our system design is based on cloud computing service oriented architecture.

Finally, we have on mind plans to improve our system and reach our future goals. So, we intend to make our system more reactive with patient by making a mobile application contains all services plus the urgent numbers depends on the chosen country by the user. Farther more, improving the existing notifications service by sending notifications to the patient account about any update in his record like completed lab results and sending a notification to remind the patient about his appointments. For critical situations, we intend to add features such as the finger print and eye print as a replacement of SSN to find the medical record of the patient. Also, globalizing SHEFA'A system, so patients records can be accessed from anywhere around the world in case a patient has medical emergency or just wants to be diagnosed by a doctor from another country.

References

1. Kim, K.: Clinical Data Standards in Health Care: Five Case Studies. Issue brief. California Health Care Foundation (July 2005), http://www.chcf.org/~/media/MEDIA%20LIBRARY%20Files/PDF/C/PDF%20ClinicalDataStandardsInHealthCare.pdf
2. Shakir, A.-M., Cardenas, D., Datta, G., Mittra, D., Basu, A., Verma, R.: Design and Development of Standards (HL7 V3) Based Enterprise Architecture for Public Health Programs Integration at the Country of Los Angeles. International Journal of Health Care Information Systems and Informatics, 53–56 (2007)
3. Zhang, L., Xu, X.: A Community Public Health System Design based on HL7 Criterions. Computer and Information Science, 148–151 (2011)
4. Varlamis, I.: A Flexible Model for the Delivery of Multi-facet Information in Patient–centric Healthcare Information Systems
5. http://www.ejeta.org/specialMay07-issue/ejeta-special-07may-3.pdf
6. Cloud Computing: Building a New Foundation for Healthcare. Tech. IBM (February 2011), https://www-05.ibm.com/de/healthcare/literature/cloud-new-foundation-for-hv.pdf
7. Detmer, D., Bloomrosen, M., Raymond, B., Tang, P.: Integrated Personal Health Records: Transformative Tools for Consumer-Centric. BMC Medical Informatics and Decision Making, 45 (2008)
8. Nelson, E.K., Piehler, B., Eckels, J., Rauch, A., Bellew, M., Hussey, P., Ramsay, S., Nathe, C., Lum, K., Krouse, K., Stearns, D., Connoly, B., Skillman, T., Igra, M.: LabKey Server: An open source platform for scientific data integration, analysis and collaboration. BMC Bioinformatics, 71 (2011)

Exploring Possibilities of Designing Virtual Personal Health Coach in Relation to Gender Differences

Hakan Kuru[1] and Armagan Kuru[2]

[1] Middle East Technical University, Physical Education and Sports, Turkey
[2] Middle East Technical University , UTEST Product Usability Unit, Turkey
{coachhakan,k.armagan}@gmail.com

Abstract. Nowadays, technology affects our quality of life in various ways. One necessary aspect of using technology as a tool is to achieve optimal health, in other words, to make health focused decisions about everything in life. Different applications of technology now enable people to track their activity or food intake through applications, web-sites or mobile products. Now, the challenge is to interpret and use large sums of available data in order to improve people's wellbeing and promote health. In order to understand the possible approaches to promoting health, a study was designed with an aim of understanding what people would expect from a virtual personal health coach and whether there is a difference by gender on priorities. The paper makes conclusions of the possibilities of designing according to the different needs and expectations of women and men from a virtual health coach.

Keywords: Health promotion, virtual health coach, personal technologies.

1 Introduction

Today, technology has a vital role in people's lives, as it affects their lives in many areas by making them learn and share information [1, 2]. One necessary aspect of using technology as a tool is to help people to take health-focused decisions to achieve optimal health. Several applications and personal products have been designed with an aim of making people healthier or keeping their health status stable. Each system focuses on a specific kind of problem and increases the possibility of avoiding serious illnesses such as cancer or heart diseases, by collecting data from the user and analyzing it to help them make conscious decisions about their health. However, the current systems serve for several specific dimensions of health promotion; but the systems that cover the all the other dimensions of health promotion is required for a holistic approach. This paper, first explores the current state in using technology to improve wellbeing. Then a user study in which people were asked about their priorities from a possible virtual health coach for wellbeing is explained with analysis and synthesis. The paper further discusses the importance of HCI in maintaining a holistic approach in wellness research.

A. Marcus (Ed.): DUXU 2014, Part III, LNCS 8519, pp. 63–71, 2014.
© Springer International Publishing Switzerland 2014

2   Using Technology to Improve Wellness

For this paper, it is important for HCI researchers to know that, in literature wellness has strong relation with people's optimum health to sustain their quality of life [3]. Wellness is a continuous, multidimensional and active state, which is geared towards balancing one's physical, emotional, social, intellectual and spiritual wellbeing in order to enhance one's life quality [4-8]. In several references, wellness has been defined with six dimensions [4, 6, 8-13], including *physical wellness* which is related to physical health and participation of physical activities; *emotional wellness* which is about being comfortable with one's emotions; *social wellness* which is about people's positive feelings about self and the environment; *intellectual wellness* which is about thinking critically about issues and making decisions and also finding solutions; and *spiritual wellness* which is about finding the meaning of life and creating tolerance to other beliefs.

"Being well" can be defined as being in a continuum of average of all the listed dimensions. Health is mostly considered wellness as not being ill or having no disease, but The World Health Organization defines health as a state of complete physical, mental and social wellbeing and not merely the absence of disease of infirmity [3]. On the other hand, wellness term is used interchangeably with health, [12] as both contain similar issues such as, physical, emotional, spiritual and social. It is possible to state that all the issues are related to the quality of life. In relation to these, the terms "wellbeing", "wellness" and "health" have been widely used by human computer interaction researchers, however they are used interchangeably in the holistic approaches [9, 14]. Preventive approaches are stated to decrease the rate of unhealthy life and decrease the treatment expenditures for governments with an aim of keeping people's quality of life at a certain level and this connects preventive approached to wellness research [15]. In that sense, wellness has gained great interest and has become the focus of several researches that try to combine technology and wellness.

The developments in technology, now, enable people to use mobile products for wellness purposes in any context. Several applications and personal products have been designed in order to make people healthier. Each system increases the possibility of avoiding serious illnesses such as cancer or heart diseases, by collecting data from the user and analyzing it to help people make decisions [16]. Informatics systems are now being used for capturing older adults wellness [17]. Innovative technologies are also being used for health coaching to increase people's health state and helping them to life healthy [18]. In another example, statistical inference algorithms are used to assess the level of stress by using mobile phones [19]. In addition, people can prefer online support about their nutrition behavior to gain knowledge and counselling such as DietAdvise [19]. There are also approaches that specifically focus on measuring physical activity and giving virtual feedback [20-24]. As an example, Bodymedia, is a system that includes biometric sensors and measure different physical parameters to measure physical activity [25]. Personal technologies [26], including smart phones and tablets [23], can also be used as a possible technology for improving wellbeing that are now able to track physical activities [27], nutritional intakes gaining a great potential to be developed and keeping people out of hospitals [28].

Still, it is argued that technology may not be a sole media to improve wellbeing, but it requires any systems that keep doctors, nutritionists and physicians in contact to develop integrated methods and technologies for increasing the health and wellness state of people [27, 29]. For instance, when a technology pushes the user to do more physical activity, can create serious heart problems if the user already has one. That's why, the issue should not be considered on the bases of single dimension only, but instead it should try to cover all possible problems. A large amount of data can been collected with different technologies, but currently the challenge is to interpret and use all these large sums of available data in order to improve people's wellbeing properly. Therefore, this study aims to find users' expectations from a virtual health coach which aims to fulfill all areas of health for an individual by understanding their needs in their daily life.

3   Methodology

A study was designed with an aim of understanding what people would expect from a virtual health coach, specifically how they would like to be supported, and whether there is a difference between priorities of women and men. In this paper, gender difference was specifically explored, as in several wellness related studies, significant difference was observed between men and women in relation to their wellness perceptions [30-32].

3.1   Instrument and Participants

For the study, six health promotion behaviors [13] were used as the possible support dimensions. For each dimension, one visual card was designed and printed on 10cmx10cm cardboards (Fig. 1). It should be noted that these cards were designed to support the interviews with visual materials. In total, 40 participants (20 women and 20 men) were interviewed, ages ranging from 25-35.

3.2   Data Collection Procedure

Each participant was interviewed either in the participants' or researchers' offices. The participant was first introduced the health promotion support dimensions through the visual cards and was asked to rank the importance of the support that would come from a virtual health coach. Following that, the participant was asked to talk about the reasons why the support is important. Specifically, participant was asked the reasons behind that ranking, why the support dimension is important or not important, whether there is any dimension-related problem that they would like to solve through virtual health coach and if any, how they would like to interact with the virtual health coach.

A typical session lasted between 35-45 minutes and all the interviews were voice recorded with permission.

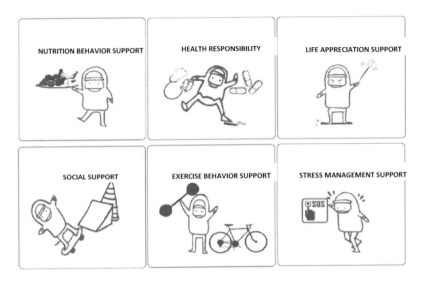

Fig. 1. Visual Cards

3.3   Data Analysis

To analyze data, the voice records were transcribed first. For qualitative data, initial open coding was done with a small set of data [33]. With these initial codes, a glossary of terms was built to reach at consistent analysis at the end. The final glossary of terms was used for data analysis of all the interviews. Participants' rank ordering of dimensions were analyzed, first in general and then in relation to gender. This was done by adding up all the rankings of participants. Finally, details of rank ordering results were interpreted in relation to findings gathered from the interviews.

4   Findings

The general rank ordering results show that, participants need *nutrition behavior* support more than other supports (Fig. 2). Following that, *health responsibility* support and *exercise behavior* support are ranked at the same importance level. *Stress management* support is at 4th place; and *social* support and *life appreciation* support are at 5th and the 6th place in the overall ranking (Fig. 2). On the other hand, gender-related rank ordering results shows that *exercise behavior* support is in the 1st place for women participants, but is in 3rd place for the men; while *nutrition behavior* support is in the 2nd place for both genders (Fig. 3). A striking result is achieved in *health responsibility* support, as the men ranked it on the 1st place, as women believed it was the 4th most important among the support behaviors.

Fig. 2. General Ranking of Support Dimensions

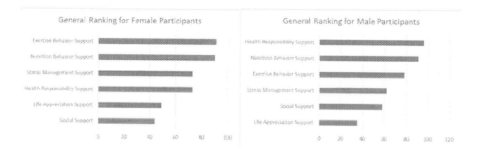

Fig. 3. Gender-Related Ranking of Support Dimensions

Not surprisingly, the results show that the main reason why people need a virtual **nutrition behavior support** is their desire to *promote health status*. Participants stated that, they cannot change their nutrition behavior as they are either unable to motivate themselves to change it or unable to be conscious about nutrition behavior. Participants stated that nutrition behavior should be supported with exercise and health responsibility feedbacks to maintain their holistic wellness. While the reasons do not differ, the design solutions differ for women and men; women prefer only *visual tips* on healthy nutrition behavior and healthy receipts, while men prefer *visual prescriptive personal nutrition information* that might come from a smart mobile technology. In addition, men prefer *audio motivational stimulus* on healthy nutrition behavior and have *reminder-type intrusive stimulus* while women do not.

In relation, participants want health responsibility support to prevent health status by them, to change their health responsibility behavior, and to be conscious about health responsibilities. The number of comments was similar for each need, but the possible design solutions differ for women and men. For instance, women prefer a personal check-up system by a mobile device; report of vital signals, log of menstrual cycle, medical tips on a visual platform especially from computer at work. On the other hand, men prefer to monitor their vital signals by a mobile device which they can carry everywhere. Men also prefer solutions about gathering information about health responsibility behaviors such as health responsibility tips and reminder from a mobile platform in an intrusive way. It was interesting that women prefer visual stimulus about unhealthy behaviors such as nutritional information on credit card bill or barcode, while men prefer audio personal healthy tips that alerts them when they are alone, like driving car.

Results show that, people need exercise behavior support to promote physical wellbeing and they expect to be motivated for physical activity and exercise, and to manage body weight. It was interesting that men stated that they cannot motivate themselves to keep regular exercise, while women participants cannot motivate themselves to exercise actually. It was also interesting that women stated that their lack of motivation for physical activity is mainly because their constantly changing psychological state, while men related their lack of motivation to their lack of knowledge on exercise. Still, custom databases and to-the-point tips on exercise with reminding features are preferred by both men and women. They also prefer to have custom visual database and intrusive stimulus from virtual health coach on managing body weight. On the other hand, while men stated that monitoring their physical activity and exercise can increase their level of motivation, women did not mention about that possibility.

The agreed reason upon why people need a virtual stress management support was unsurprisingly to overcome stress with the reasons of people's inability to manage stress level and to solve problems. There was no apparent difference between women and men apart from women' inability to solve daily problems. In the design solutions, both women and men prefer visual plans about time and work and also for daily activities. In addition, men preferred audio and visual relaxing stimulus when stress level is critical. Some of the women suggested building a smartphone application to help them about selecting dress in the mornings. For stress support, women just prefer to manage their emotional status such as overcoming stress, while men prefer to be physically active and also to overcome stress.

Desiring to manage emotional status is the reason of why people need a virtual **social support** through which they can promote their emotional status with social activities. Mostly, people need social support for managing emotional status by getting social suggestions to *realize positive side of life* and to be *motivated for social plans*. Both women and men prefer prescriptive personal suggestions for possible social activities on a visual platform. The other reason of need for a virtual social support is surprisingly to be physically active. Mostly men expected social support about the shared physical activity plans of friends so that they can socialize with friends during exercise or they can make physical activity plan with friends.

Life appreciation support was listed as the least important support in comparison to other needs. Still, the major need for this support was *to realize positive side of life* and *to appreciate life* so as to realize their daily achievements. Both men and women stated to have a report of daily achievements. In addition, men expect to have tips on how to appreciate their life. Alternatively, women stated that a stimulus to boost their emotional status can work well for life appreciation such as a song or prompts.

5   Discussion

We believe that with our findings, a virtual health coach can be designed that covers all dimensions of health promotion behaviors, focusing mainly on the top three important dimensions; nutrition behavior, health responsibility behavior and exercise behavior and supporting stress management, social and life appreciation behaviors. The results of the study showed that people can need a virtual health coach with several reasons; they can use it to *prevent or change* an undesired behavior or situation; *manage* a situation that is encountered or *promote* a desirable behavior or situation (Fig. 4).

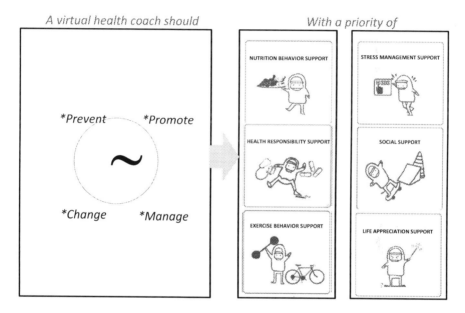

Fig. 4. Summary of the Findings

While the problems faced do not differ much between men and women, design solutions differ substantially. While women users require instant and specific solutions for a current situation, men participants require solutions that can affect their habits in the long run. The virtual system should work as an intelligent personalized system that create awareness and lead people to health choices or practical solutions, such as advising a healthy meal serving place instead of a fast-food restaurant. Design solutions, mostly clustered to be intrusive to be a motivation source for both women and men. We suggest that, the systems would work better when they are designed by considering the gender differences. Prescriptive solutions, like instant exercise suggestions for women or like personal workout plan for men users, with an additional feedback on their movement technique can work for all users that also use visual and audio feedback.

6   Concluding Remarks

Our study showed that women and men have similar needs from virtual health supports and facing similar problems in related to health promotion behaviors. On the other hand, expected design solutions vary for women and men users. We believe that, in building-up new health promotion systems, applications, or implementations designers can consider our findings and relate their design solution to user expectations in relation to gender differences.

References

1. Hassenzahl, M., Tractinsky, N.: User experience - a research agenda. Behaviour & Information Technology 25(2), 91–97 (2006)
2. McCarthy, J., Wright, P.: Technology as experience. MIT Press, USA (2004)
3. Jonas, S.: What are Health and Wellness? AMAA Journal 23(1), 10–11 (2010)
4. Corbin, C.B., Pangrazi, R.P.: Toward a Uniform Definition of Wellness: A Commentary. President's Council on Physical Fitness and Sports Research Digest (2001)
5. Corbin, C.B., Pangrazi, R.P., Franks, B.D.: Definitions: Health, Fitness, and Physical Activity. President's Council on Physical Fitness and Sports Research Digest (2000)
6. Adams, T.: The Power of Perceptions: Measuring Wellness in a Globally Acceptable, Philosophically Consistent Way, Wellness Management (2003)
7. Diener, E., Wirtz, D., Biswas-Diener, R., Tov, W., Kim-Prieto, C., Choi, D.-W., Oishi, S.: New measures of well-being. Springer (2009)
8. Jonas, S.: The wellness process for healthy living: A mental tool for facilitating progress through the stages of change. AMAA Journal, Health Care Industry (2005)
9. Hettler, B.: Six Dimensions of Wellness Model (1976)
10. Miller, G.D., Foster, L.T.: Critical synthesis of wellness literature. University of Victoria, Faculty of Human and Social Development & Department of Geography (2010)
11. Chen, M.Y., Wang, E.K., Yang, R.J., Liou, Y.M.: Adolescent health promotion scale: development and psychometric testing. Public Health Nursing 20(2), 104–110 (2003)
12. Van Rensburg, C.J., Surujlal, J., Dhurup, M.: Exploring wellness practices and barriers: A qualitative study of university student-athletes. African Journal for Physical, Health Education, Recreation & Dance 17(2), 248–265 (2011)
13. Chen, M., Wang, E.K., Yang, R., Liou, Y.: Adolescent Health Promotion Scale: development and psychometric testing. Public Health Nursing 20(2), 104–110 (2003)
14. Monroe, M.: what is wellness? IDEA Fitness Journal 3(8), 103–106 (2006)
15. Williams, L.C., Day, B.T.: Medical Cost Savings for Web-Based Wellness Program Participants From Employers Engaged in Health Promotion Activities. American Journal of Health Promotion 25(4), 272–280 (2011)
16. Ahtinen, A., Mattila, E., Väätänen, A., Hynninen, L., Salminen, J., Koskinen, E., Laine, K.: User Experiences of Mobile Wellness Applications in Health Promotion: User Study of Wellness Diary, Mobile Coach and Self Relax. In: Proceedings of the PERVASIVEHEALTH. 3rd International Conference on Pervasive Computing Technologies for Healthcare, IEEE (2009)
17. Demiris, G., Thompson, H.J., Reeder, B., Wilamowska, K., Zaslavsky, O.: Using informatics to capture older adults' wellness. International Journal of Medical Informatics 82(11), e232–e241 (2013)

18. Milner, C.: Changing the Way We AGE. Fitness Business Canada 14(2), 24–29 (2013)
19. Jae-Hyoung, C., Hyuk-Sang, K., Hun-Sung, K., Jeong-Ah, O., Kun-Ho, Y.: Effects on diabetes management of a health-care provider mediated, remote coaching system via a PDA-type glucometer and the Internet. Journal of Telemedicine & Telecare 17(7), 365–370 (2011)
20. Arteaga, S.M., Kudeki, M., Woodworth, A., Kurniawan, S.: Mobile system to motivate teenagers' physical activity. In: Proceedings of the 9th International Conference on Interaction Design and Children, Barcelona, Spain. ACM (2010)
21. Berkovsky, S., Coombe, M., Helmer, R.: Activity interface for physical activity motivating games. In: Proceedings of the 15th International Conference on Intelligent User Interfaces, Hong Kong, China. ACM (2010)
22. Consolvo, S., Klasnja, P., McDonald, D.W., Landay, J.A.: Goal-setting considerations for persuasive technologies that encourage physical activity. In: Proceedings of the 4th International Conference on Persuasive Technology, Claremont, California. ACM (2009)
23. Fujiki, Y.: iPhone as a physical activity measurement platform. In: Proceedings of the 28th International Conference Extended Abstracts on Human Factors in Computing Systems, Atlanta, Georgia, USA. ACM (2010)
24. Fujiki, Y., Kazakos, K., Puri, C., Buddharaju, P., Pavlidis, I., Levine, J.: NEAT-o-Games: blending physical activity and fun in the daily routine. Comput. Entertain. 6(2), 1–22 (2008)
25. Welk, G.J., McClain, J.J., Eisenmann, J.C., Wickel, E.E.: Field Validation of the MTI Actigraph and BodyMedia Armband Monitor Using the IDEEA Monitor. Obesity 15(4), 918–928 (2007)
26. Li, I., Dey, A.K., Forlizzi, J.: Using Context to Reveal Factors that Affect Physical Activity. ACM Trans. Comput.-Hum. Interact. 19(1), 21 (2012)
27. Kuru, A., Erbuğ, Ç., Tümer, M.: Creating Awareness Through Personal Informatics Systems: User Expectations Analysis. Tasarım+ Kuram 9(16), 58–70 (2013)
28. Franks, B.D., Wood, R.H.: Use of technology in health-related fitness programs. Quest (00336297) 49(3), 315–321 (1997)
29. Davis, R.G.: Fitness and Wellness Industry Game Changers: A Window Into the Next 30 Years. IDEA Fitness Journal 10(1), 32–40 (2013)
30. Rayle, A.D.: Adolescent gender differences in mattering and wellness. Journal of Adolescence 28(6), 753–763 (2005)
31. Crose, R., Nicholas, D.R., Gobble, D.C., Frank, B.: Gender and Wellness: A Multidimensional Systems Model for Counseling. Journal of Counseling & Development 71(2), 149–156 (1992)
32. Roothman, B., Kirsten, D.K., Wissing, M.P.: Gender Differences in Aspects of Psychological Well-Being. South African Journal of Psychology 33(4), 212–218 (2003)
33. Krippendorff, K.: Content Analysis: An introduction to Its Methodology. Sage Publications, Inc., USA (2004)

Wayfinding in Hospital: A Case Study

Laura Bezerra Martins and Hugo Fernando Vasconcelos de Melo

Federal University of Pernambuco (UFPE), Brazil
{bmartins.laura,hfernandovm}@gmail.com

Abstract. The purpose of this study is to understand how the human displacement in large buildings takes place and suggest solutions to improve its flow. The type of installation to be focused on is the hospital environment. For case study, we took as example a hospital based in Recife, capital of Pernambuco - Brazil. The importance of this research lies in the fact that it opened new horizons for the study of accessibility, bringing together areas of management and design, which are often treated in an isolated manner, but actually complement each other in order to reach an overall result for the various users of this type of system.

Keywords: Wayfinding, Design, Ergonomics and Usability, Healthcare.

1   Introduction

Space is essential for the survival of human beings and it is through it that man creates environments to fulfill ones tasks. In order to carry out activities there will always be a space built with specific functions. One of man's main tasks is the act of moving between spaces, which consists of moving from one point of origin to a destination. This act of displacement is considered the basic unit to perform almost all human activities, that is, the functional basis of a built environment is to facilitate orientation and mobility between sectors. Clear access to built environments is a basic requirement of every architectural design [1].

The influence of the environment in the way people carry out their activities, shows the importance of evaluating the quality of built environments that are increasingly inefficient for user performance [1]. We live today in a more complex and saturated world. Therefore, we are forced to live in areas where boundaries are difficult to be discerned. To detect the specific characteristics and nature of the environment allows for the creation of communication systems that improve human interactions [2].

According to modernity with its new technologies has brought about profound changes in the way of conceiving space. The built environment should now be thought to accommodate a greater diversity of people and perform different activities [1]. In light of such developments, people start to travel longer distances in shorter periods. However, their spatial skills are insufficient for locomotion in spaces of high complexity without support from systems thought to adapt the environment for everyday activities.

A. Marcus (Ed.): DUXU 2014, Part III, LNCS 8519, pp. 72–82, 2014.
© Springer International Publishing Switzerland 2014

It is understood that the act of signaling is a multidisciplinary study, that plans the space globally, i.e., it goes beyond the use of graphic language in built environments and is above all the act of planning space with dynamism, to facilitate the flow of people in a safe, natural and orientated way [3]. An example of a complex space with high variety of services and movement of people is the hospital, where it is of complex nature and presupposes certain urgency in the flow of patients and staff. It is this background that the current study focuses on, analyzing specifically a hospital based in Recife, capital of Pernambuco - Brazil. This hospital is a nonprofit organization designed to provide eye care services to the population using public health system. Its current building is used in a disorderly manner. It consists of adaptations and extensions of several houses in the region, forming an improper complex for the activity that is proposed.

To conduct the case study, this work is based on complementary theoretical references that represent a series of recommendations that will bring to the environment not only agility in moving and task performance, but will also give the environment larger personality. It is known, however, that the use of wayfinding as main reference is the best way to minimize weaknesses and find solutions forhigh complexity and great population flow locations.

The use of señalética of Costa [2], as a theoretical reference, comes after the flow issues and spatial organization are well studied and will serve as an additional signaling system. According to O'Neil cited in Ribeiro [1], in installations with wayfinding issues, the use of graphics system serves to compensate the complexity of the design and those who perform the route gain speed. Finally, informational ergonomics is used as support both for wayfinding studies and for studies of graphic signage.

The aim of this study is, in addition to point out the major flaws of flows and sectorization in hospitals, to generate unified method recommendations based on principles of Wayfinding, Señalética and Informational Ergonomics, in order to minimize disruption caused by environments without architectural planning and make them able to facilitate the tasks that each user will have to find their own destiny within a building.

2   Methods and Techniques

2.1   Wayfinding

The theoretical basis for the unification of methods aimed at improving the spatial organization and the flow of users within built environments is wayfinding that has as its object of study the dynamic relationship of human behavior with the space, resulting in drawing up a plan of action in which three processes are involved: decision making, implementation of the decision and information processing [1]. The process of wayfinding is a dynamic relationship which involves the individual, one's personal skills and the environment in which one is inserted. Thus, wayfinding is a process of behavior, design and operation.

Behavior is the external manifestation of the processes of perception and cognition related to the skills and experience of each person, i.e., involves the individual and the person's ability to interpret space and from that take decisions based on the information gathered in the environment. Spatial navigation requires capacity of perception, interpretation, memorization and spatial skills from the user, thus the subject is capable of building the mental map of the given environment [1].

Design involves the elements and organization of the built environment such as the system of architectural information that studies the morphology of the building. In order to facilitate the morphological definition of a building, Arthur and Passini cited in Ribeiro [1] distinguish three phases to define wayfinding layout: identification of spatial units; grouping of these units in zones; and, finally, sectorization no these areas and the connection between them.

Another aspect of design concerns the way the room is decorated, i.e., the information system of objects, which are the spatial elements that reveal the identity of the environment and the function of each sector [1]. The information system of objects consists of geometry, colors, lighting and finishing, as well as the furnishings and equipment that make up the space [1]. The purpose of implementation of object information system goes beyond the generation of comfort and enhances the informational matter in the environment.

A final aspect of the design is the information system that, according to [1], is everything that complements the environments in which previous systems do not address the issues of wayfinding. These systems can be graphic in nature (use of signaling signs, displays, maps and brochures), sonorous (whistles or sirens), verbal (interpersonal communication) or tactile (signaling through textures on floors and walls and Braille used on maps, signs and brochures).

The transaction relates to administrative decisions that managers tend to make in the built environment, which will affect the way space is considered and, consequently, affect positively or negatively the behavior of users in the system. They are: the choices of terminology in graphic signage, the way employees are trained to receive and inform users, the deployment of anticipated information when there are changes in the sectors and maintenance of the imaging signal system.

2.2   Señalética

Señalética is a discipline that collaborates with engineering, architecture, environment and ergonomics, under the graphic design vector, responding to the needs of information and orientation caused by the contemporary phenomenon of mobility, which is the movement of different groups of people able to generate new situations and difficulties in environment navigation [3].

The concept of señalética is divided into three systems of language (linguistic, iconic and chromatic) which, although they relate to form the graphical signaling system, contain expressions that should be studied in detail for the creation of a cohesive system, integrated with the identity of the studied area and always taking into account the studies of informational ergonomics.

2.3   Informational Ergonomics

The discipline is interested in improving the human interface of workspaces and its objects, taking into account how the environment acts in the performance of people in their workplace and during the work break [4].

In this study, fundamental concepts will be used of what is known as Informational Ergonomics, based on studies of legibility and comprehensibility of texts and images, however, regarding the signaling of constructed environments, informational ergonomics can cover not only what relates to graphic design issues, but also the layout issues of the environment and the types of flows they generate, in addition to studying human behavior when connected to these factors [5].

In terms of environmental design in wayfinding, the main contribution of informational ergonomics is to add surveys concerning zoning and recording the movements of users in the location to define dislocation problems, thus indicating possible solutions in improving the flow of people in the building.

3   Results and Discussion

3.1   Mapping of the System

The System User. Through institution database research and on-site observations, information from users of this health system was obtained. Because this is a charity hospital, it can be said that the majority of the patients are public health system users, so those without financial means to pay a private health insurance or treatment and who already attend the hospital long enough need to develop a cognitive map of the environment.

Given the previous matter, it was noted that the attendance regarding age varies between children, adults and seniors; however, with a slight advantage for the elderly, since the main vision problems in need of surgery occur at this stage of life. The increased demand from children occurs due to the existence of a program focused on the rehabilitation of this public. It was also found a great demand for routine and urgent medical appointments, both with patients varying in terms of age and physical condition. With regard to education, we observed a lot of people with problems of functional illiteracy and again, in this matter, the elderly are the ones with the most difficulties. In terms of physical impairment, motor and visual were the most noticeable types. Again, it was found that the elderly public accounts for most cases of disabled people seeking care.

Based on this survey, it is necessary to think of a wayfinding system focused on comfort, with simple morphology for users to be able, during the visits, to create a cognitive map of the location. In terms of graphical signaling, one must think about panels that favor the elderly, children and disabled users, i.e. panels with effective printing and contrasts, besides the use of good graphic resources, since the location is used by children and persons with low reading proficiency.

The Architectural Information System. The layout of a facility shall be defined by identifying the spatial units so they can be grouped by zones, and these shall be organized and close to each other according to the similarities in needs and demand from users [1]. The environments are grouped by areas having common characteristics and, in turn, the zones should be differentiated from each other.

The areas should be grouped according to the homogeneity of services, facilities, functions and even types of users. The zoning of an installation should always be done by taking as basis the main areas, i.e., the most important and most sought after, followed by their sub-areas and so on, always following a hierarchy of importance or demand [1].

Evaluating the layout of the hospital blueprint (Figure 1), it is possible to identify that the sectorization of its current headquarters is made in an arbitrary manner and that even if an environment that grew without planning, zoning could be done correctly, taking into account space limitations.

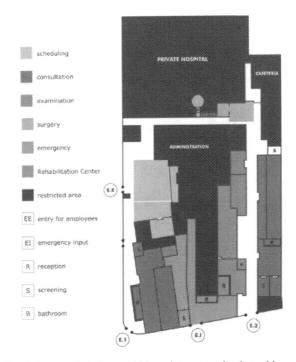

Fig. 1. layout of the hospital blueprint – sectorization arbitrary

Even without solving the chronic wayfinding problems of the current headquarters the institution first because it is a structure that was not born to house a hospital, second because the demand for services has surpassed all limits of the physical space, it is possible to indicate a simple sectorization and more integrated into the environment, as long as there are changes in the layout of the building, which should be held in a multidisciplinary way between architects, decorators, designers, ergonomists and administrators.

After mapping the environment sectors, it is necessary to trace the flow of user movement because this movement record will identify the dilemmas of environment areas, i.e., the places where bifurcations in the flow of movement occur. Based on the informations of the movement registration on the floor plan, it is also possible to set the existing activity flowcharts in the hospital, and its type of morphology.

As can be seen in the representation of the movement flow below (Figure 2), in order to navigate between sectors, users and hospital staff are required to perform unnecessary tasks to go from a given starting point to a destination. People with different needs within the facility stumble confusedly, without knowing where to go and therefore depend, for the most part, on the verbal assistance of staff and volunteers.

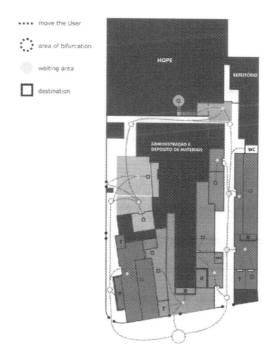

Fig. 2. representation of the movement flow below - unnecessary tasks

In view of the flow movement analysis it is possible to say that all dilemma points and sectors of the institution can be linked together, creating an interconnected system. This does not follow any organized route and the circulation paths are sinuous and defined on the basis of pre-existing barriers in areas that were annexed as the headquarters expanded. In this type of movement organizational pattern is random, there is no structural order and its information structure can only be performed using reference points and anchor points at intersections, because hierarchical order among the sectors is nonexistent.

The Information System of Objects. Environmental aesthetics is one of the strongest subjective components within a health institution and directly influences staff, patients and visitors [7]. The correct combination of hospital sectors, associated with the right choice of color, lighting and texture, makes the healthcare environment less stressful, and serves to reinforce the cognitive map of each visitor at the facility [1].

The health institution studied flees from all aesthetic rules applied to hospitals, but not in a positive way. While healthcare environments have mostly white walls as the main color and blinding lighting, the hospital analyzed has as main tone gray color followed by blue, considered the standard color of the institution, and brown, present in much of the furniture. The lighting, especially in the corridors, is precarious (see Figure 3). Not being enough the fact of it being a narrow place with dim lighting, to further aggravate the difficulties of movement, the sectors consist of cool colors poorly differentiated from each other and that, instead of increasing the lighting and giving the idea of expansion, they retract and absorb the little lighting existing in the building. Being a monotonous environment, the psychological result of misuse of colors are boredom, fatigue, drowsiness, unwillingness, decreased attention and, consequently, the disorientation.

Fig. 3. The lighting is precarious in the corridors

The System of Additional Information. The main system of additional information to the institution is the verbal system, i.e., personal communication of staff and volunteers with patients and visitors. Through field studies, it could be noted that this is the only system that really works, especially among users who visit the institution for the first time and older people who have the greatest difficulties to build cognitive maps. The institution users are approached by volunteers at the entrance, which is the beginning of the process. Instead of people seeking the reception, they are welcomed because the physical structure of the current building no longer absorbs the daily demand of patients, i.e., to prevent that a patient spend a lot of time in the wrong line or waiting for a service that will not work that day, volunteers are ready to report availability for treatment and directing people entering the wrong traffic flows.

Despite being an institution with a focus on visual impairment, there is no tactile signage to minimize possible embarrassment to the blind and visually impaired. There is a notorious lack of use of graphical signs, starting by the visual identity which is reduced to a logo without manual standardization, implementation and use restrictions. The existent graphical signs are facades and location plaques (Figure 4), placed without the slightest concern for the image of the hospital, so important in the study of señalética approached by Costa (1992).

Fig. 4. The existent graphical signs are facades and location plaques

The Operational System. Based on field research and interviews with hospital workers, it was possible to find the following administrative restrictions which can lead to problems in the implementation of a future wayfinding system [1]: lack of knowledge or interest in the technical standards dealing with organization quality management; lack of understanding the relationship between ease of navigation in the environment and quality of the services; ignorance of real importance for a designer to work with architects during the new building development, which is already in planning progress. Another limitation arising from administration is that they think that a signaling system is reduced only to the creation of direction and location support.

However, a wayfinding system covers issues that deal even with how an institution manages its spaces and services. For example, always looking to improve the infrastructure system and make a regular maintenance of the environment, and seek greater efficiency in service flow. The control over decisions on layout and ambiance of the facilities is in the hands of management and without the involvement of a multidisciplinary team. The result is poor sector division, many employees are unaware of the environments subjacent to their workplaces, and do not understand how the process of care within the hospital works. As a result, workers are unprepared to provide adequate information to system users, the forms for scheduling of appointments, exams or surgeries do not provide sufficient information for patients to find their destinations on days when attendances are marked.

As one can see from the moment the administration restrictions for each wayfinding subsystem are understood, and thereupon adjusted, the professionals involved in designing a new wayfinding system have greater dominance in applying the new project, which according to Carpman and Grant [1] should solve the existing problems and prevent new ones. For a project focused on studies of wayfinding to have wide success, it is necessary that the administration understands its physical environment as dynamic, that is, able to avoid further issues arising from possible structural changes or extensions.

3.2   Recommendations

Bearing in mind that the analyzed institution is to plan a new building, it is necessary to suggest, before the design of the new building, a type of movement system that takes into account the most sought after areas for their users. With respect to morphology and zoning, the most appropriate thing for the types of services offered by the institution would be a system of hierarchical central circulation, where the pattern of organization is through a network. In this case, users of the system come into contact first with the most popular environments, and these determine the next steps to reach the most important sectors of the building. The two most sought after areas within the hospital would be the general reception area, which does not exist in the current circulation system, and the emergency.

There is also need for a circulation system for employees that connects the restricted areas adequately to public areas, focused on the mobility of patients. In this case, it is necessary to understand how worker sand health professionals should flow within the system. Only a multidisciplinary study involving architects, designers and administrators of the hospital is able to reach a circulation system that is born already predicting future extensions and modifications, since an architectural system such as the system of hospitals, is dynamic and should be expanded over time, according to the birth of new specialties, sectors and technologies. From a well resolved circulation system, it is possible to start the design of the floor plan having in mind a structural pattern that takes into account the priority needs of users, so that they reach their destinations in a safe and more agile way.

Regarding the information system of objects, it is necessary to bear in mind the their aesthetic integration to harmonize and thereby help the users in designing the cognitive map of the building. In the hospital environment there should be two kinds of lighting, natural and artificial [7]. Some studies, according to Hood and Brink [7], show that the use of natural lighting benefits the health of people who spend many hours of the day indoors, and brings economy to the institution. The natural lighting is crucial tool for connecting the hospital building with nature, assisting in the circadian system. However, in the case of this institution that is focused on eye care, there has to be caution with the excess of natural light in the environment so no problems are cause to patients with serious ocular sensitivity.

On the use of color and knowing that most of the guidelines for its use in design is based on pre-established cultural beliefs and that there are no universal guidelines for such use in hospital environments, due to the complexity of groups that use this type of environment, especially those focused on public health, Young cited in Hood and Brink [7], conclude that the definition of color for environments is subject to a number of approaches that should work jointly and they will always vary according to installation type and work carried out in the area. The choice of colors to compose the environments of a hospital building must conform to the design principles that take into account the best degree of reflection, culture, local behavior and representative visual identity of the institution. These aspects should be arranged so that they make the best composition of lighting, surroundings and graphic signage chromaticism.

Regarding the proper use of the furniture when they are well selected, they can enhance spatial orientation of those inserted into the system as well as improve the populational flow, providing support, comfort, safety and promoting the correct interaction between visitors and employees [7]. In terms of the current case study, it is suggested that furniture use be considered so that it is appropriate in terms of comfort to the types of users in the institution. The color coordination should follow the principles of color research that should be used in the environment, i.e., in addition to providing comfort, furniture should work on strengthening user's cognitive map.

For the additional information system, the main suggestion is around the use of appropriate informational graphics systems in the new layout and objects aesthetic to be applied to the analyzed hospital environment. The system of graphic signs must respect principles of hierarchy and suggested information in the work of Joan Costa [2] Directional signs should have three to four information and messages neatly listed according to the degree of importance or demand for each sector, giving particular emphasis to primary information, ie, the name of the entry sector. The planning for the sub-sectors should be given following the order of distance of each destination. On the use of color in panels, one should always seek the contrast, i.e. the colors for each of the main sectors of the hospital should be quite different from each other so there is no orientation confusion among users of the system. Another important question regarding the use of colors is to avoid a large number of shades, answering only to the key sectors, because a large number of chromatic signs disrupt the recognition of sectors, especially for people with visual impairments.

Regarding the use of pictograms, as this study analyzes a big hospital with public health insurance, the proposition is to work the historically accepted style, the silhouettes technique produced by AIGA and applied in the research of the program "Hablamos Juntos" in partnership with the SEGD [8]. Regarding the use of maps, it would be interesting to work with them like infographics. Infographics combines images and words harmoniously, making the information in the panels contain a story for the user with beginning, middle and end [6]. The proposal to use Infographics refers to the journalistic work, since the current study goes further, suggesting that this type of approach be used not only in so-called general location maps or part of a signaling system, but also in newsletters that should be printed to educate users, causing them to become accustomed to the system of pictograms and to the movement flow logic of the institution being discussed.

Regarding other systems of additional information, it is required the use of a tactile system on floors for the visually impaired, where the textures on floors should be able to guide passersby not only to the maps with Braille communication, as well as to the main destinations within the facility. About the additional verbal system, it is necessary, in accordance with the operating system, proper training on the flow dynamics of the hospital for all staff and volunteers, so that they become part of the system helping to guide patients and visitors. This training can be done from the process flow diagram, which shows all steps of the users in the search for appropriate services within the building.

4   Conclusions

With the current research it can be concluded that to effectively work a signaling system is to go beyond the graphics system. One must work together with other disciplines beyond the ambit of graphic design. This set of disciplines addressed in harmony is called Wayfinding, which means to know where you are, know your destination and walk up to it, always having in mind evidence that the route taken is correct, without going through unnecessary procedures, Environments where the architecture favors navigation cause people to improve their cognitive skills.

An environmental project focusing on wayfinding promotes not only physical and mental health of users, but also the financial health of the institution, because it is implicit that employee productivity problems are associated with navigation issues, since they often waste time guiding patients instead of performing their tasks.

Finally, it is concluded that this case study is a rich example of how not to use health environments, as they contain errors ranging from the use of space to employee training, encompassing flaws in all subsystems of wayfinding. Therefore, it is important to demonstrate that healthcare environments should be designed by multidisciplinary teams in order to minimize future errors.

References

1. Ribeiro, L.G.: O Onde estou? Para onde vou? Ergonomia do ambiente construído: Wayfinding e Aeroportos. 120 f. Dissertação (Doutorado em Design) – Pontifícia Universidade Católica do Rio de Janeiro, Rio de Janeiro (2009)
2. Costa, J.: Señalética. Enciclopedia del Deseño. Barcelona (1992)
3. Velho, A.L.O.L.: O Design de Sinalização no Brasil: A introdução de novos conceitos de 1970 a 2000. 92 f. Dissertação (Mestrado em Design) – Pontifícia Universidade Católica do Rio de Janeiro, Rio de Janeiro (2007)
4. Cruz, F.R.F.D.: Estudo das relações entre as linguagens pictóricas e verbais: sistemas de sinalização de edificações. 31 f. Monografia (graduação) - Universidade Federal de Pernambuco, Recife (1999)
5. Moraes, A., Mont'alvão, C.: Ergonomia: Conceitos e Aplicações. iUsEr, Rio de Janeiro (2003)
6. George-Palilones, J.: Graphics Reporting: information graphics for print, web and broadcast. Focal Press is an imprint of Elsevier, Oxford (2006)
7. Lahood, S., Brink, M.V.: Aesthetics and New Product Development. In: McCullough, C. (ed.) Evidence-Based Design: For Healthcare Facilities, pp. 19–44. Sigma ThetaTau International, Indianapolis (2010)
8. Project Hablamos juntos, http://www.hablamosjuntos.org

Health Care Professionals *vs* Other Professionals: Do They Have Different Perceptions about Health Care Waste and Dangerous Products Pictograms? Some Findings Using a Digital Device in Field Survey

Cláudia Renata Mont'Alvão

Laboratory of Ergodesign and Usability of Interfaces LEUI,
Pontifical Catholic University of Rio de Janeiro PUC-Rio,
Rua Marquês de São Vicente, n 225, Gávea, Rio de Janeiro, RJ - Brazil - 22453-900
cmontalvao@puc-rio

Abstract. This paper presents a part of a wider research about GHS symbols comprehensibility. Here, a field survey was conducted using a digital device, instead of traditional platform – printed paper. Participants were health care professionals and other professionals and a comparison among the results about these groups is presented and discussed.

Keywords: symbols, comprehensibility testing, ergonomics.

1 Context

Comprehensibility of symbols used worldwide is a wide area for research.. Once these symbols must be comprehensible and understandable for all individuals, different tests according American National Standard Institute's Criteria for Safety Symbols (ANSI Z535.3, 2011) have to be conducted. In this paper, GHS - Globally Harmonized System of Classification and Labelling of Chemicals Symbols are studied.

The system called "Globally Harmonized System of Classification and Labelling of Chemicals (GHS)", addresses classification of chemicals by types of hazard and proposes harmonized hazard communication elements, including labels and safety data sheets. It aims at ensuring that information on physical hazards and toxicity from chemicals be available in order to enhance the protection of human health and the environment during the handling, transport and use of these chemicals. The GHS also provides a basis for harmonization of rules and regulations on chemicals at national, regional and worldwide level, an important factor also for trade facilitation (UNECE, 2013).

Hesse et al (2010) confirm that "sweeping globalization over the past several decades can be viewed as a double-edge sword. On the one hand, it has given rise to unparalleled economic growth and opportunity as products and services are increasingly freely traded among many different countries throughout the world".

A. Marcus (Ed.): DUXU 2014, Part III, LNCS 8519, pp. 83–90, 2014.

As presented by Kalsher & MontAlvão (2010) "one goal of existing research on this topic has been to determine how people assign blame for injuries sustained through the use of or exposure to consumer products and how various entities associated with either the production or use of consumer products view responsibility for safety."

These authors also argue that because contextual information shapes perceptions and attributions, this suggests that decision makers in a legal context (e.g., jurors, judges) may attribute responsibility for accidents on the basis of the amount and type of information accessible to them.

This paper gives a continuity of a research considering cross cultural aspects in this context, as presented in Hesse et al. (2010), when an experiment was conducted with 312 non-student participants; comprising a U.S. and   Brazilian samples. Now, a new experiment was conducted, considering health care professionals and other professionals/non-students participants.

The objective in this research – and the idea of including the health care professionals - began with the ideas of health communication and its implications on patients, teams and risk management. Once GHS symbols affect everyone, does health care professionals must be more aware of them? Their perception about how others will understand information can be more accurate? This research tried to find some answers for these questions.

2   Method

2.1   Participants

A total of 60 participants (30 males and 30 females) were recruited (M = 35.6 years; SD = 11,6). Samples from two population pools were collected: 30 were health care professionals (12 males and 18 females) and 30 comprised other professionals (14 men and 16 women).

Considering both samples, the average age of participants was 36.5 (SD = 11.3) and 36.6 (SD = 12.0), respectively, as shown in Table 1. It´s important to point out that the sample "other professionals" comprises the all kind of subjects, that aren´t students,   but that don´t work in health care area.

Table 1. General demographic data

Sample	Sample	Age (*M*)	Std deviation (*SD*)
Health professionals	30	36,5	36,6
Other professionals	30	11,3	12,0
Total	60	-	-

2.2   Procedures and Materials

As suggested by United Nations (Annex 6, Comprehensibility testing methodology, UNECE, 2013), questionnaires and experimental tests can be conducted to evaluate signal words, colors and size of GHS pictograms, as well the comprehension of hazard symbols.

First step consisted on fulfill an informed consent. Just after that, participants were answered a general interview, about demographic and other data as a basis for analysis as age, gender, occupancy and if they have some familiarity with some of these two groups of symbols: pictographs used in Brazil to identify health care waste and GHS pictographs.

Just after the general interview, volunteers were asked to evaluate, using the comprehension estimation procedure (ANSI Z535.3, 2011), five pictographs used in Brazil to identify health care waste and eleven GHS pictographs. In this phase a digital device in this field survey.

All tested symbols are shown in Figures 1 and 2. Is important to mention that in both groups of symbols there are one pictograph that is used represent 2 distinct products. Considering the group of symbols to identify health care waste, the same pictograph is used to represent *Biological waste* and *Perforating-cutting* waste.

When considering the groups of symbols to identify GHS pictographs, we have 2 repetitions: the same pictograph is used to represent *Carcinogens* and *Reproductive toxicity*, and *Flammables* and *Pyrophoric liquids*.

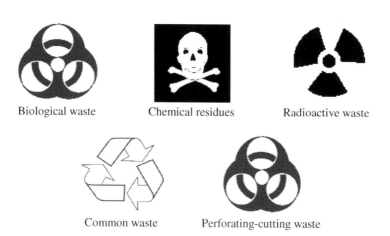

Biological waste   Chemical residues   Radioactive waste

Common waste   Perforating-cutting waste

Fig. 1. Five pictographs used in Brazil to identify health care waste, tested in this research

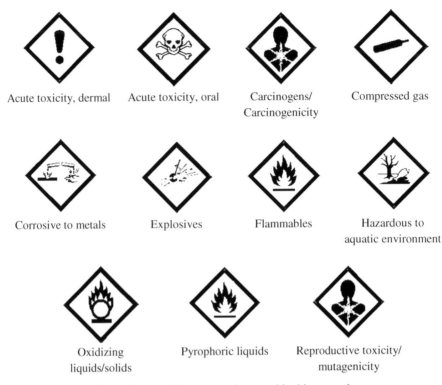

Acute toxicity, dermal   Acute toxicity, oral   Carcinogens/   Compressed gas
                                                    Carcinogenicity

Corrosive to metals   Explosives   Flammables   Hazardous to
                                                                      aquatic environment

Oxidizing   Pyrophoric liquids   Reproductive toxicity/
liquids/solids   mutagenicity

Fig. 2. Eleven GHS pictographs, tested in this research

It´s important to say that health care professionals are familiar to health waste pictographs, even all volunteers answered that aren´t directly involved with health care waste.

For each pictogram, with a subtitle with its description and after provided with the context in which each of the pictograph would likely be seen, participants were asked to estimate in their perspective, the percentage of people in Brazil who would comprehend its intended meaning. All of them were presented in black and white to avoid interferences related to color usage.

According to Hesse et al (2010) the comprehension estimation procedure is beneficial because it is less expensive and time consuming than the open-ended procedure.

3   Some Results

Symbols and pictograms are considered acceptable if 85% of the study participants are able to understand its meaning with no more than 5% critical confusions, according to criteria outlined in the American National Standard Institute's Criteria for Safety Symbols (ANSI Z535.3, 2011).

First, considering the evaluation of health care professionals and other professionals about health care waste symbols, it is possible to highlight a huge difference. If for health care professionals just 3 in 5 symbols meet ANSI acceptance, on the other hand ,for other professionals, none of them are acceptable. It is also important to note (as shown in Table 2), a high std. deviation - around 10%. Surprisingly, the symbol with highest acceptance for both groups of subjects was the *Radioactive waste* when it was expected that the one used for *Common waste* - that can be easily found in packages and trash cans - could achieve a better acceptance.

Table 2. Results for health-care professionals (N= 30) and other professionals (N= 30) for health care waste symbols

Category	Health professionals		Other professionals	
	Mean	*(Std Dev)*	*Mean*	*(Std Dev)*
Biological waste	86,00	10,37	27,87	11,04
Chemical residues	83,00	09,79	24,77	09,31
Common waste	83,67	10,50	26,63	04,48
Perforating-cutting waste	85,17	10,21	23,40	09,26
Radioactive waste	87,50	07,04	42,63	08,90

But results of both samples show a unity among GHS symbols acceptance, as shown in Table 3.

Table 3. Results for health-care professionals (N= 30) and other professionals (N= 30) for GHS symbols

Category	Health professionals		Other professionals	
	Mean	*(Std Dev)*	*Mean*	*(Std Dev)*
Acute toxicity, dermal	33,10	15,17	36,30	15,17
Acute toxicity, oral	51,10	14,53	56,40	15,62
Carcinogens/ Carcinogenicity	27,50	11,94	30,80	14,41
Compressed gas	19,20	15,28	23,60	14,61
Corrosive to metals	33,70	16,65	36,80	11,94
Explosives	56,70	21,46	60,10	17,82
Flammables	61,90	14,79	67,00	19,65
Hazardous to aquatic environment	41,80	15,23	48,30	15,62
Oxidizing liquids/solids	9,10	7,67	19,10	14,79
Pyrophoric liquids	25,90	12,32	29,50	14,00
Reproductive toxicity/ mutagenicity	11,80	13,20	15,30	14,32

It´s also interesting compare these results with the ones obtained in a previous research and presented in Kalsher & Mont'Alvão (2010). In this previous survey, 87 subjects answered about the comprehensibility of GHS pictograms using the same testing methodology.

It's possible to notice that non-health care professionals have similar perception about comprehensibility of GHS pictograms, as shown in Table 4.

Another important thing to comment about these two samples is about standard deviation. In 2010, in this wider sample, it´s possible to notice a higher std. deviation in results. But when comparing the standard error in both samples, they are almost the same. It can indicate that maybe the perception of subjects, in this 3-years period, changed.

Table 4. Results for non-health-care professionals (in 2013, N= 30) and other professionals (in 2010, N= 87) for GHS symbols

Category	Other professionals (in 2013)			Subjects (in 2010)		
	Mean	Std Dev	St. Error	Mean	Std Dev	St. Error
Acute toxity, dermal	36,30	15,17	2,77	34,70	31,25	3,35
Acute toxity, oral	56,40	15,62	2,85	53,00	39,08	4,19
Carcinogens/ Carcinogenicity	30,80	14,41	2,63	31,00	28,17	3,02
Compressed gas	23,60	14,61	2,67	21,50	24,44	2,62
Corrosive to metals	36,80	11,94	2,18	34,30	32,93	3,53
Explosives	60,10	17,82	3,25	58,60	31,34	3,36
Flammables	67,00	19,65	3,59	65,50	31,71	3,40
Hazardous to aquatic environment	48,30	15,62	2,85	46,70	34,32	3,68
Oxidizing liquids/solids	19,10	14,79	2,70	22,40	26,58	2,85
Pyrophoric liquids	29,50	14,00	2,56	27,10	28,17	3,02
Reproductive toxicity/ mutagenicity	15,30	14,32	2,61	14,50	25,74	2,76

About the health care waste pictograms, they are considered highly more acceptable for other professionals than for health care professionals.

Considering this scenario, in 2013, the symbol that presented the worst evaluation for health professionals sample was the category Oxidizing liquids/solids, that scored 9,70% (S.D.=7,67) while for non-health professionals was the one used to represent the category Reproductive toxicity/ mutagenicity , that score 15,30% (S.D. = 14,32).

On the other hand, the best evaluation was for the symbol that represents the category Flammables for both health-professionals (Mean = 61,90; S.D.=14,79) and for non-health professionals (Mean = 67,00; S.D. = 19,65). All these 3 symbols are shown in Figures 3, 4 and 5.

Oxidizing liquids/solids   *Reproductive toxicity/ mutagenicity*   *Flammables*

Fig. 3. 4. and 5. Worst and best scored GHS symbols for the studied sample. Fig. 3 (on the left) category *Oxidizing liquids/solids*, Fig. 4 (in the middle), category *Reproductive toxicity/ mutagenicity*, Fig. 5 (on the right), category *Flammables*.

4   Final Comments

Just 3 health care waste symbols met the ANSI Z535.3 criteria for correct comprehension (i.e., infectious waste, chemical waste, radioactive waste, common waste, perforating - cutting waste) when considering 85% comprehension criteria in health care professionals' sample. But when observing data from other professionals sample, all results were below 50% of comprehensibility.

But when considering results for the eleven GHS pictograms, none of categories met ANSI Z535.3 criteria in both the health care and non-health care professionals samples.

As a final comment, the idea that health care professionals are more sensitive about other people perception wasn´t confirmed. In all results, other professionals sample was more "optimistic" about general population comprehensibility. Their perception isn´t more accurate, even considering health care waste symbols.

Another important thing to mention is related to the use of a digital device while testing. When comparing to printed paper, there are no significant differences. Digital device allows better visualization once the quality of the image is better than the printed one.

5   Next Steps and Future Research

These results lead us to another questions and discussions, for example, to better understand the way that these international symbols are tested and used. It is necessary to "learn" what a symbols means, or it should be "understandable" for everyone? Do the cultural aspects are considered when they are designed? All forms of application in chemical industry (printed in paper, in adhesive, digital) are used when tested?

Pointing out some aspects that weren´t considered in this work, new questions arise as how health care professionals communicate with their patients? And how can we evaluate patient's safety communication in our scenario today? These questions lead us to future researches.

A comparison between the results using the digital device and the traditional way (using paper) for comprehensibility testing are the aim for future paper.

Acknowledgments. Author take this opportunity to express her deep regards to Brazilian National Council for Scientific and Technological Development– CNPq that supported this research.

References

1. ABIQUIM, Associação Brasileira da Indústria Química (2005). Departamento de Assuntos Técnicos. A868q O que é o GHS? Sistema harmonizado globalmente para a classificação e rotulagem de produtos químicos, 69 p. ABIQUIM/DETEC, Paulo (2005)
2. American National Standard Institute. ANSI Z535.3-2011: Criteria for safety symbols. National Electrical Manufacturers Association, Washington, DC (2011)
3. Hesse, R.G., Steele, N.H., Kalsher, M.J., Mont'Alvao, C.: Evaluating Hazard Symbols for the Globally Harmonized System (GHS) for Hazard Communication. Proceedings of the Human Factors and Ergonomics Society 54, 1832–1836 (2010)
4. Kalsher, M.J., Mont'Alvão, C.: Communicating Risk in a Global Economy: Emerging Issues Associated with the Globally Harmonized System (GHS) for Labeling Hazardous Chemicals. In: Proceedings of 10° ERGODESIGN, pp. 1–17. PUC-Rio, Rio de Janeiro (2010)
5. UNECE, United Nations Economic Commission for Europe. GHS Globally Harmonized System for Labeling Hazardous Chemicals for Hazard Communication, 5th revised edn. New York and Geneva, United Nations, 529 p. (2013)

"How am I Doing?" - Personifying Health through Animated Characters

Andreas Schmeil and Suzanne Suggs

Università della Svizzera italiana (USI), Lugano, Switzerland
{andreas.schmeil,suzanne.suggs}@usi.ch

Abstract. In this paper we present an experimental study that investigates the effects of a Virtual Representation of Health (VRH) – an online virtual character that personifies an individual's health. Testing four different variations of the VRH, we aimed to understand which variation yields the strongest overall positive effect on triggering health behavior change. The results from data collected from 512 participants in three countries indicate that all tested variations can have a positive impact on health behavior change, and show that the 'richest' VRH variation, a virtual character that models health behavior using animations, juxtaposed by an animated personification of a possible future health, has the strongest overall positive effect, compared to the other tested variations.

Keywords: Health, behavior change, personification, VRH, 3D, animated characters, virtual representation, visual communication.

1 Background and Related Work

Tailored health behavior-change communication strategies aim to persuade individuals to change what they are doing and adopt a new behavior. Tailoring aims to maximize personal connections with each individual, thereby increasing the relevance, credibility, and receptivity of the communication [15]. Tailored behavior-change strategies can come in many forms, ranging from interpersonal communication between a doctor and a patient, to customized messages delivered through print, Web, or mobile apps. Tailored health communication generally has larger positive effects on health behavior change outcomes compared to other types of health communication, including greater levels of nutrition improvement and physical activity levels [11], [4], [7]. As predicted by the Elaboration Likelihood Model [14], tailored communication recipients report greater message relevance including better recall, sharing with friends and family, and more satisfaction with it than with non-tailored communication [17].

To date, the vast majority of tailored health communication studies have tested messages. In most cases these are textual/verbal messages that are sometimes presented through a video narrative or accompanied with tailored graphics to complement the text. Numerous papers published in the last decade report tests of

A. Marcus (Ed.): DUXU 2014, Part III, LNCS 8519, pp. 91–102, 2014.
© Springer International Publishing Switzerland 2014

web-based behavior change programs, demonstrating that such programs can help people improve their health-related behaviors, have high reach, and can be cost effective [18], [8].

Visual communication has enormous potential to motivate individuals, to teach skills, and to increase self-efficacy. Numerous studies have shown the supremacy of pictures over text or verbal messages, an effect that was named Pictorial Superiority Effect [10]. The effect can be explained by dual coding theory: verbal and information is encoded in different ways in the human brain, with the visual encoding being more direct, thus more effective [13]. Pictures have shown to play an important role in health communication (see [6] for a review), and animation may work even better than pictures (see [20]). There is also a recent body of research exploring different promising effects of avatars on (health) behavior [3]. Thus, we hypothesize that tailoring communication through animated visuals, to be more precise, animated virtual characters, may be as efficacious as message tailoring, if not more efficacious.

Behavioral economics research demonstrates that visualizations of future selves are effective at serving as triggers to save money [9], [5]. A similar strategy may work in promoting physical activity and nutrition behaviors. These behaviors are directly associated with body weight and prevention of non-communicable diseases. Like with retirement savings, investing in these behaviors today has long term consequences or benefits that are not seen immediately. Thus, showing a person the future status if they continue to behave the way they do, may serve as that trigger to change.

This study presents a novel approach to tailoring behavior change communication. It aimed to provide online users with an engaging experience designed to serve as a "trigger" [2] or "cue to action" [16] to change their health behavior. The center piece of this experience was an animated character that personified the user's health.

In contrast to related studies that have investigated the effects of animated characters in virtual reality lab settings (e.g. [3]), this study looks at the effects that animated virtual characters accessed through a web browser have on an individual's health behavior. The Internet has shown to be a valuable medium for the promotion of health behavior change [19], and recent Web technology standards like the Web Graphics Library (WebGL) allow for animated and interactive visualizations, including the display of custom virtual characters. These online visualizations can be accessed using a common web browser and can reach a far larger user base than a virtual reality laboratory; this is of great value both for research but also for putting a system on the market. We thus believe an online virtual character has merit and call the new approach the Virtual Representation of Health (VRH), which fits in with the related definitions of Virtual Representation of Self (VRS) and of Others (VRO) [1].

2   Study Objective

The objective of our study was to test the effects of distinct user experiences on an individual's motivation and intention for health behavior change. These experiences consisted of an exposure to a virtual character – a Virtual Representation of their Health (VRH) – that represented the health status of the individual, and modeled their health behavior or showed a possible future status of their health. The virtual character was tailored to each study participant, based on data they provided in a questionnaire just before viewing the VRH. The study was designed to measure and analyze the effects of four variations of a VRH on the motivation and intention of the user to change their eating and/or physical activity (PA) behaviors. We also wanted to understand if people appreciated this type of health communication and would like to return to the tool for ongoing support (triggers) for making and sustaining behavior change.

The following section presents how we use the information provided by a participant to tailor the VRH to their specifics – in other words, how the VRH personifies their health.

3   Personifying Health

The design of the virtual character we use as a VRH was informed by a pre-study where 172 individuals randomly) selected from the same population as the sample of the study presented in this paper described the physical, visible characteristics of health, with the aim of understanding "what health looks like". Participants were also asked about the visual characteristics of a person that does not look healthy. Participants were asked to describe these characteristics and then choose the two most illustrative characteristics for each health status (health and non-healthy). Table 1 shows an overview of the results: it presents the physical characteristics that the participants named as the first or second best visual characteristic to describe a healthy/non-healthy looking person. The characteristics most frequently mentioned for both a healthy and a non-healthy person, relate to fitness, energy level, and agility, but also to skin color (i.e., complexity) and diverse skin issues.

With the design of our VRH and its variations we cover most of the top characteristics reported by the sample, as highlighted in Table 1. The personal characteristics used to tailor the VRH to an individual include height and weight, the calculated Body-Mass Index (BMI), past 7 day nutrition behavior, and past 7 day physical activity behavior. In order to personify the individual's health, the VRH is designed to be variable for body shapes, body animations and poses, and skin texture.

The body shape of the VRH is tailored to healthy weight, overweight, or obese weight, based on the body mass index (BMI) of an individual (see Figure 1).

Poses and animations are tailored on three levels of physical activity of an individual, including a sedentary, a moderate, and a very active level (see Figure 2). The sedentary version shows the VRH seated, slowly standing up, and sitting back down. For the moderate PA level the VRH performs an easy workout (i.e., stretches, bend, twists), for the high PA level a hard workout (i.e., jumps, pushups, bends, twists).

The skin texture is tailored to show healthy-looking skin, average skin, and unhealthy-looking skin. The skin textures were exaggerated in order for differences to be noticeable between animated characters. The unhealthy skin texture includes darker patches on the skin, wrinkles, bags under the eyes, and also slightly red eyes (see Figure 3).

Table 1. Overview of the results of the pre-study "What does health look like?" The characteristics covered by our VRH variations (i.e., body shape, poses/animations, skin complexity, skin/eye issues) are highlighted

Physical characteristics that best describe a healthy-looking person	n	%	Physical characteristics that best describe a *not* healthy-looking person	n	%
Fit	68	22.2%	Lacking energy	61	20.3%
Happy	55	18.0%	Tired	56	18.6%
Energetic	54	17.6%	Shortness of breath	40	13.3%
Healthy skin color	31	10.1%	Moving slowly	30	10.0%
Strong	29	9.5%	Pale skin color	29	9.6%
Dynamic	28	9.2%	Bags under the eyes	16	5.3%
Agile	21	6.9%	Poor/bad balance	14	4.7%
Good posture	12	3.9%	Bad posture	12	4.0%
Other	8	2.6%	Not flexible	12	4.0%
			Skin problems	11	3.7%
			Swollen hands or feet	7	2.3%
			Other	7	2.3%
			Red eyes	6	2.0%

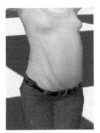

Fig. 1. Illustration of the healthy (left), overweight (center), and obese (right) versions of the (female) VRH

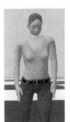

Fig. 2. Illustration of sedentary (first left), moderate (second left), and very active (third left) levels of physical activity. The VRH further personified moderate and high physical activity levels without animation using rather closed or open stances (first and second right).

Fig. 3. Illustration of the healthy (left), average (center), and unhealthy (right) variations of the skin of the VRH, for both gender versions

4   Experiment Design and Hypotheses

We developed a controlled experiment with four conditions, in order to compare four types of Virtual Representations of Health. The VRH was implemented using WebGL (Web Graphics Library) and can be accessed through a modern web browser on a common webpage. The experimental conditions were designed as follows:

1. a VRH that is tailored solely on current health status; *a non-animated virtual character*
2. a VRH that is tailored on current health status juxtaposed with a second VRH that personifies possible future health status; *two virtual characters, one present and one future, in still poses*
3. a VRH that is tailored on current health status while also modeling current health behavior; *an animated virtual character*
4. a VRH that is tailored on current health status while also modeling current health behavior, juxtaposed with a second VRH that personifies possible future changes in health status; *two animated, one present and one future, virtual characters*

With this experiment, we aimed at understanding the differing effects of the four variations of exposure a VRH, leading to four significantly different experiences for the participant. Thus, a control group without any exposure to a VRH was not needed to answer our research question.

We hypothesized that the experience of viewing one's VRH that both models current health behavior through animations and personifies changes in future health status through juxtaposition, that is, condition 4, has the greatest positive effect on motivation, intention (H1). We based this main hypothesis on the sub-hypotheses that (H1a) viewing a juxtaposition of a present VRH and a VRH representing a possible future health has a more positive effect on motivation and intention than viewing only one VRH, and that (H1b) viewing a VRH that models current health behavior using animations has a more positive effect on motivation and intention than viewing still versions of a VRH.

Further, we expected participants in experimental condition 4 to be more motivated, and have a higher intention to, return to the VRH tool than those in any other experimental condition (H2).

The theoretical foundations for the study include B.J. Fogg's Behavior Change Model and Petty and Cacioppo's Elaboration Likelihood Model [2], [14]. We hypothesized that the experience of seeing a virtual representation of the own health status now and in the future, will serve as a trigger to change. To control for the other variables in the Fogg model, (ability and motivation), participants were recruited based on being motivated and able to improve nutrition and physical activity behaviors. The study is further based on the assumption that the more tailored (i.e., relevant) the trigger is, the more likely a person is to change [14], [15].

Experimental conditions 1 and 2 (shown in Figure 4) used still poses. For tailoring on the physical activity level of a participant the VRH was displayed in either a closed pose (personifying a low level of physical activity), an average pose (for a moderate level of activity), or an open stance (representing a high level of agility).

Fig. 4. Experimental conditions 1 (left) and 2 (right)

Experimental conditions 3 and 4 (shown in Figure 5) used repeating animations instead of still poses. For tailoring on the physical activity level of a participant the VRH was displayed in either a slow movement (i.e., getting up slowly from a sitting position; personifying a low level of physical activity), a moderate speed movement (for a moderate level of activity), or a fast, agile animation (showing the VRH perform a complete workout; representing a high level of agility).

Fig. 5. Experimental conditions 3 (left) and 4 (right)

5   Methods

An online experiment was used to examine the differing effects of the four user experiences. The study participants were recruited through an online recruitment agency and came from three European countries (German, Great Britain and Poland). Eligibility criteria included being motivated to improving health behavior, being able to improve eating and physical activity behaviors, the use of a modern web browser supporting WebGL (to be able to view the VRH in the browser), and the ability to complete questionnaires in English. The study was approved by the local ethics commission.

Before the exposure to the VRH, participants completed a pre-test, in which they were asked to enter their age, gender, email, education level, country of origin and residency, height, and weight. They were asked to indicate on 7-point Likert scales how many days a week they currently engaged in physical activity and followed a healthy diet, as well as how motivated they were, and how much intention they had to engage in healthy behaviors (PA and eating) in the week to follow. After the pre-survey questionnaires which in average took about seven minutes to complete, they were shown their tailored VRH.

After viewing their VRH (for in average just over one minute), participants were again asked about their motivation and intention to engage in a health (PA and nutrition) behaviors in the week to come.

Immediately post exposure to the VRH, participants completed a post-test, where they were again asked to indicate how motivated they were, and how much they intended, to engage in healthy behaviors in the week to follow.

Outcome variables included motivation to engage in more PA, intention to engage in more PA, motivation to engage in a healthier diet, and intention to engage in a healthier diet. Each behavior was asked in reference to the coming week (e.g., motivation to engage in a healthier diet in the coming week). Further, we measured motivation and intention to access the VRH tool again.

6   Results

A total of 293 men and 219 women (N=512) from three European countries participated in this study (n=186, Germany; n=177, Poland; n=149, UK). The mean age was of 33 years. Probably due to the eligibility criteria, the sample was more inclined to healthier weight than the European average: only 39% were overweight or obese; in Europe, more than 52.6% of the adult population report to be overweight or obese [12].

We conducted t-tests for data analysis. Significant positive changes were seen in motivation to be more physically active for participants in all conditions (see the means comparison illustrated in the left chart in Figure 6). Condition 4 showed the most positive and most significant effects overall. The pre-post change of intention to be more physically active in the week to follow was highest for condition 2, and significant only for conditions 2 to 4 (see the means comparison illustrated in the right chart in Figure 6). For significance levels refer to Table 2 below.

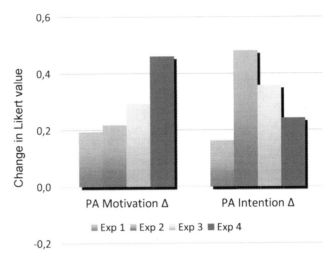

Fig. 6. Means comparison of the change (pre-/post-exposure) in motivation (left) and intention (right) to engage in more physical activity

Pre-post changes in motivation to improve nutrition behavior were significant only for participants in condition 4. The pre-post changes in intention to improve nutrition behavior, all conditions showed significant and positive changes, while condition 4 showed the largest change (see the means comparisons illustrated in Figure 7; for statistical significance levels refer to Table 2 below).

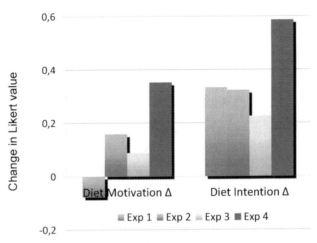

Fig. 7. Means comparison of the change (pre-/post-exposure) in motivation (left) and intention (right) to engage in a healthier diet (i.e., better nutrition)

Table 2. Overview of the outcome measures including statistical significance levels (+ = positive effect, - = negative effect; * = p<.05, ** = p<.01, *** = p<.001, n.s. = not significant)

Outcome measures	Experimental conditions			
	1. Still pose	2. Still pose & personifying future	3. Modeling health behavior	4. Modeling & personifying future
Physical activity				
Change in motivation to improve PA behavior	+* (p=.05)	+* (p=.02)	+** (p=.004)	+*** (p=.001)
Change in intention to improve PA behavior	+ n.s. (p=.113)	+*** (p=.001)	+*** (p=.001)	+* (p=.048)
Nutrition				
Change in motivation to improve nutrition behavior	- n.s. (p=.251)	+ n.s. (p=.085)	+ n.s. (p=.389)	+*** (p=.001)
Change in intention to improve nutrition behavior	+*** (p=.001)	+*** (p=.001)	+* (p=.022)	+*** (p=.001)

We measured a high level of motivation to revisit the tool with a 7-point Likert scale; the mean values are reprinted in Figure 8. No significant differences in motivation or intention between groups could be determined.

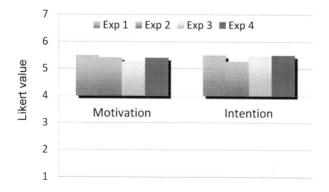

Fig. 8. Mean values of the motivation and intention to return to the VRH tool. The bars are based on Likert level 4 as it is the medium value between "totally motivated to return" (7) and "not at all motivated to return" (1).

7   Discussion

These results confirm our hypothesis that the experience of viewing one's VRH that both models current health behavior through animations and personifies changes in future health status through juxtaposition (H1), that is, condition 4, serves as the overall strongest trigger to change, when compared to using still poses instead of animations or to personifying only the current health. This is especially true for eating behavior. Thus, looking into the 'mirror of the future' has potential to be that trigger or cue to take action needed by those interested and able to change their health behavior.

As the related sub-hypotheses H1a and H1b are concerned, neither could be confirmed by the results. While all outcome measures except 'change in intention to improve nutrition behavior' yielded a result that we had expected (i.e., 4 > 1, 2 > 1, 3 > 1), only one measure each could confirm H1a and H1b, respectively. H1a was partly confirmed only for the nutrition motivation measure, where conditions 2 and 4 yielded stronger effects than the other conditions. H1b on the other hand was partly confirmed only for the PA motivation measure, where conditions 3 and 4 yielded stronger effects than the other conditions.

Our hypothesis H2 could not be confirmed by the data – the analysis did not show any significant difference in motivation or intention to return to the VRH tool between the experimental conditions.

Being aware that the sub-conditions H1a H1b were mutually exclusive to begin with, we also attribute the mixed results concerning H1a and H1b partly to the fact that the conditions were not separated clear enough in this first experiment with an online VRH. Future experiments could be set up using fewer experimental conditions and directly juxtapose even more similar variations of the VRH. This way each effect can be better attributed to a single design element. It might also be cleaner to clearly separate the health behaviors physical activity and nutrition, and conduct distinct experiments for each, with the aim of better singling out what type of VRH – and what design factors – may be beneficial to the motivation or intention to change that particular behavior.

In order to base this new research strand, it would be of value to empirically investigate also what value a VRH has as compared to non-visual communication strategies, or to visual representations of health that are not based on a virtual character. Numerous questions still exist about how to provide the most relevant, action-prompting communication to prompt health behavior change. This study serves as a first step in such research looking at an online, visual representation of an individual's health. We know that the VRH can serve as a self-reported trigger to intend to change and it increases motivation. The next step is to build on this first evidence and conduct a study with longer-term assessments that measures behavior. Ideally, these assessments include objective measures of health status and behavior, both possible through some of the modern monitoring and tracking devices (also: wearable tech) we have seen presented for example at this year's Consumer Electronics Show (CES) in Las Vegas. More research is also warranted to examine the extent of tailoring needed to maximize benefits. In terms of user experience, further study of the effects of frequency and dose of each exposure and to what extent people identify with the VRH will be beneficial. Further, bringing in the social element, that is showing a person their own VRH and as it compares with others' may further improve the efficacy for some individuals.

8   Conclusion

The study demonstrates that non-verbal communication, in the form of animations and virtual characters can be an effective approach in behavior change communication. It shows that displaying current and future health status has motivational impact on current physical activity behaviors. In terms of nutrition, the future self may not be so critical. Much more research is warranted, including investigation into other individual factors that may be important, such as personality, motivations, and goals. Future research in this area should look more into investigating possibilities of engaging experiences as triggers and calls-to-action on smartphones and other pervasive devices, also taking into account the social factor.

Acknowledgement. This study was funded by Merck & Co., Inc. In particular we thank Per Andersen, Alan Lowenstein, John Schreiber, Zachary Pinner, Jasdip Kaur, and Ralph Daniel for their collaboration on the study.

References

1. Bailenson, J.N., Blascovich, J., Guadagno, R.E.: Self-representations in immersive virtual environments. Journal of Applied Social Psychology 38(11), 2673–2690 (2008)
2. Fogg, B.J.: A Behavior Model for Persuasive Design (2010), http://www.bjfogg.com/fbm_files/page4_1.pdf (retrieved on December 7, 2013)
3. Fox, J., Bailenson, J.N., Binney, J.: Virtual experiences, physical behaviors: The effect of presence on imitation of an eating avatar. Presence: Teleoperators & Virtual Environments 18(4), 294–303 (2009)
4. Hawkins, R.P., Kreuter, M., Resnicow, K., Fishbein, M., Dijkstra, A.: Understanding tailoring in communicating about health. Health Education Research 23, 454–466 (2008)
5. Hershfield, H.E., Goldstein, D.G., Sharpe, W.F., Fox, J., Yeykelis, L., Carstensen, L.L., Bailenson, J.N.: Increasing saving behavior through age-progressed renderings of the future self. Journal of Marketing Research 48, 23–37 (2011)
6. Houts, P.S., Doak, C.C., Doak, L.G., Loscalzo, M.J.: The role of pictures in improving health communication: a review of research on attention, comprehension, recall, and adherence. Patient Educ. Couns. 61(2), 173–190 (2006)
7. Krebs, P., Prochaska, J.O., Rossi, J.: A meta-analysis of computer-tailored interventions for health behavior change. Preventive Medicine, 214–221 (2010)
8. Lustria, M.L.A., Cortese, J., Noar, S.M., Glueckauf, R.L.: Computer-tailored health interventions delivered over the Web: review and analysis of key components. Patient Education and Counseling 74(2), 156–173 (2009)
9. Murphy, S.: Your Avatar, Your Guide: Seeing a digital doppelgänger can change your mind—for better or worse. Scientific American (2011)

10. Nelson, D.L., Reed, V.S., Walling, J.R.: Journal of Experimental Psychology: Human Learning and Memory 2(5), 523–528 (1976)
11. Noar, S.M., Benac, C.N., Harris, M.S.: Does Tailoring Matter? Meta-Analytic Review of Tailored Print Health Behavior Change Interventions. Psychological Bulletin 133(4), 673–693 (2007)
12. OECD, Health at a Glance: Europe 2013: Overweight and Obesity among adults (2013), http://www.oecd.org/els/health-systems/Health-at-a-Glance-2013.pdf (retrieved)
13. Paivio, A.: Mental representations: a dual coding approach. Oxford University Press, Oxford (1986)
14. Petty, R.E., Cacioppo, J.T.: Attitudes and persuasion: Classic and contemporary approaches. William C. Brown, Dubuque (1981)
15. Rimer, B., Kreuter, M.: Advancing Tailored Health Communication: A Persuasion and Message Effects Perspective. Journal of Communication 56, S184–S201 (2006)
16. Rosenstock, I.: Historical Origins of the Health Belief Model. Health Education Monographs 2(4) (1974)
17. Spittaels, H., Bourdeaudhuij, I.D., Brug, J., Vandelanotte, C.: Effectiveness of an online computer-tailored physical activity intervention in a real-life setting. Health Education Research 22(3), 385–396 (2007)
18. Wantland, D.J., Portillo, C.J., Holzemer, W.L., Slaughter, R., McGhee, E.M.: The effectiveness of Web-based vs. non-Web-based interventions: a meta-analysis of behavioral change outcomes. Journal of Medical Internet Research 6(4) (2004)
19. Webb, T.L., Joseph, J., Yardley, L., Michie, S.: Using the Internet to Promote Health Behavior Change: A Systematic Review and Meta-analysis of the Impact of Theoretical Basis, Use of Behavior Change Techniques, and Mode of Delivery on Efficacy. Journal of Medical Internet Research 12(1) (2010)
20. Yoo, C.Y., Kim, K., Stout, P.A.: Assessing the Effects of Animation in Online Banner Advertising: Hierarchy of Effects Model. Journal of Interactive Advertising 4(2), 49–60 (2004)

SPARK: Personalized Parkinson Disease Interventions through Synergy between a Smartphone and a Smartwatch

Vinod Sharma[1], Kunal Mankodiya[3], Fernando De La Torre[4], Ada Zhang[4],
Neal Ryan[1], Thanh G.N. Ton[5], Rajeev Gandhi[3], and Samay Jain[2]

[1] Dept. of Psychiatry, University of Pittsburgh, Pittsburgh, USA
[2] Dept. of Neurology, University of Pittsburgh, Pittsburgh, USA
[3] Dept. of Electrical & Computer Engineering, Carnegie Mellon University, Pittsburgh, USA
[4] Robotics Institute, Carnegie Mellon University, Pittsburgh, USA
[5] Dept. of Neurology, University of Washington, Seattle, Washington, USA
vks3@pitt.edu, kunalm@cmu.edu, jains@upmc.edu

Abstract. Parkinson disease (PD) is a neurodegenerative disorder afflicting more than 1 million aging Americans, incurring $23 billion in annual medical costs in the U.S. alone. Approximately 90% Parkinson patients undergoing treatment have mobility related problems related to medication which prevent them doing their activities of daily living. Efficient management of PD requires complex medication regimens specifically titrated to individuals' needs. These personalized regimens are difficult to maintain for the patient and difficult to prescribe for a physician in the few minutes available during office visits. Diverging from current form of laboratory-ridden wearable sensor technologies, we have developed SPARK, a framework that leverages a synergistic combination of Smartphone and Smartwatch in monitoring multidimensional symptoms – such as facial tremors, dysfunctional speech, limb dyskinesia, and gait abnormalities. In addition, SPARK allows physicians to conduct effective tele-interventions on PD patients when they are in non-clinical settings (e.g., at home or work). Initial case series that use SPARK framework show promising results of monitoring multidimensional PD symptoms and provide a glimpse of its potential use in real-world, personalized PD interventions.

Keywords: mHealth, Smartphone, Parkinson Disease, Pervasive Healthcare, Personalized Health, Telemedicine.

1 Introduction

Parkinson disease (PD) is the second most common neurodegenerative disorder, affecting 4 million people worldwide with over 9 million PD cases being projected by 2030 [1]. Incurring $23 billion in annual medical costs in the U.S. alone and with projected increases as our population ages, there is an urgent need to improve lives and reduce costs for those afflicted with PD [2]. Currently, two major issues- complex and medication regimens and incapability of patients for frequent clinic visits hinder

A. Marcus (Ed.): DUXU 2014, Part III, LNCS 8519, pp. 103–114, 2014.
© Springer International Publishing Switzerland 2014

making substantial progress in improving treatments for patients with PD. A primary challenge of PD treatment is that PD progresses uniquely in each individual. A reliable, unobtrusive, quantitative tool for evaluating multidimensional disease progression such as dyskinesia, freezing of gait, disability with activities of daily life (ADL) in individuals with PD holds a great value both for clinical assessments and personalized treatments. We have designed SPARK, a Smartphone/Smartwatch system for Parkinson disease. Overarching goals of SPARK are to:

- Personalize PD management through intelligent sensing elements;
- Tele-monitor disease progression in PD patients in their day-to-day environments;
- Collect clinically relevant data to understand ADL affected by PD

In this paper we present the modular framework of the SPARK that is built on the advances in clinical practice, wearable technologies, mobile computing, machine learning, and pervasive healthcare. We present the advantages of the SPARK in comparison to research by other groups working on similar problems. We present three layers of SPARK architecture, enabling personalized patient-centered care for PD. We also provide initial results of in-lab pilot studies that used the SPARK framework to monitor multidimensional symptoms of control subjects. We conclude this paper with a summary of the presented work and a brief discussion on some challenges that are present in applicability of the SPARK framework.

2   Background and Related Work

2.1   Unified Parkinson Disease Rating Scale (UPDRS)

Unified Parkinson's Disease Rating Scale (UPDRS) that was originally introduced in 1987 [3] is now the most commonly used measure of PD progression [4]. Table 1 provides a complete list of UPDRS tests; with some of them require observations made by patients or caregivers while the rest of them need physicians to evaluate patients in clinics. The tests involve measurement of symptoms spanning from motors functions to activities of daily life to psychiatric health. Due to lack of longitudinal information of PD patients when they are in home settings, it makes it challenging for physicians to; 1) understand personalized issues of patients that occur on daily basis and; 2) make informed decisions on therapeutic or medication interventions.

2.2   Survey on the Use of Wearable Technology in PD Interventions

There are several reports of objectively monitoring movements in PD. Approaches include wearable accelerometers, gyroscopes, electromyography, doppler ultrasound, magnetic motion trackers, digital drawings, pressure-sensitive foot insoles, and passive infrared sensors placed in home [6-8].   Accelerometers (often with gyroscopes) have monitored motor aspects of PD including walking, freezing of gait, balance, falls, bradykinesia, dyskinesia and tremor [6].

Table 1. List of tests involved in evaluating PD patients with UPDRS (adopted from [5])

Part	Domain	Item ("Y" – potential use of SPARK)	Observer (Location)
I	Mentation, behavior and mood	1. Intellectual impairment 2. Thought disorder 3. Depression 4. Motivational/Initiative	Patient/ Caregiver (home)
II	Activities of Daily Life (ADL)	5. Speech (Y) 6. Salivation 7. Swallowing 8. Handwriting (Y) 9. Cutting food and handling utensils (Y) 10. Dressing (Y) 11. Hygiene 12. Turning in bed (Y) 13. Falling (Y) 14. Freezing when walking (Y) 15. Walking (Y) 16. Tremor (Y) 17. Sensory complaints related to PD	Patient / Caregiver (home)
III	Motor examination	18. Speech (Y) 19. Facial Expression (Y) 20. Tremor at rest (Y) 21. Action or postural tremor of hands (Y) 22. Rigidity 23. Finger taps (Y) 24. Hand movements (Y) 25. Rapid altering movement of hands (Y) 26. Leg agility (Y) 27. Arising from chair (Y) 28. Posture (Y) 29. Gait (Y) 30. Postural stability (Y) 31. Body bradykinesia & hypokinesia (Y)	Physician / Clinician (clinic)

IV	Complications of therapy	A. Diskinesias
		  32. Duration of dyskinesia (Y)
		  33. Disability associated with dyskinesia (Y)
		  34. Painful dyskinesia
		  35. Presence of early morning dystonia (Y)
		B. Clinical fluctuations
		  36. Are "OFF" periods predictable? (Y)
		  37. Are "OFF" periods unpredictable? (Y)
		  38. Do "OFF" periods come on suddenly? (Y)
		  39. What portion of day is the patient "OFF"? (Y)
		C. Other complications
		  40. Symptoms such as anorexia, nausea, or vomiting
		  41. Sleep quality (Y)
		  42. Symptomatic orthostasis
			Physician / Clinician (clinic)

Of the studies in Table 2, the six highlighted studies achieved ~90% or higher accuracy in detecting movements of interest. Four of these studies demonstrate a personalized approach in placing sensors on the most affected side instead of placing sensors on the same body parts in all patients. The other two studies [9, 10] personalized their approach further by incorporating subject-specific characteristics in analyses. Keijsers et al. [9] noted that several variables were better at classifying PD movements in patients without tremor compared to those with tremor. Moore [10, 11] monitored freezing of gait, a phenomenon when gait is halted and the patient's feet are "stuck to the ground." Using the same threshold for all patients with a Freeze Index (derived from spectral analyses), 75% of gait freezes were detected. This improved to 89% when the threshold was calibrated for each subject. Together, these studies demonstrate that a personalize approach to monitoring movement performs better than a "one size fits all" approach. Our research group (Das et al. [11]) has designed machine learning approaches which can build the person specific disease progression models and reliably (more than 90% accuracy) predict "ON" and "OFF" medication state.

3   SPARK: Smartphone/Smartwatch System in PD Interventions

Currently no wearable technology is at disposal of neurologists and clinicians to effortlessly monitor PD progression when patients are in naturalistic settings. Physicians demand deployable technologies that offer longitudinal monitoring for PD interventions in non-clinical settings:

1. Passive monitoring: This is the unobtrusive collection of data without any interruption of routine behavior of PD patient. Data collection occurs in the background of day-to-day activities. For patients, passive monitoring provides a way to be monitored without interrupting routine activities or relying on abilities that may be impaired (e.g. cognition, mobility) or thinking about "being sick."
2. Active Monitoring: Active monitoring requires patients to interact with mobile screen for collecting contextual data – such as speech, facial tremors, medication intake, mood, pain, and so forth – that are experiential samples of PD progression. In contrast to passive monitoring, active monitoring allows patients to be more engaged and proactive in managing their health.

3.1   Smartwatch/Smartphone System

Recently, mobile health (mHealth) has emerged as a promising field in treating patients with advanced mobile phones (Smartphones) since smartphones come with inbuilt sensors and computing and communication resources that allow to track individual's course-grain geo-tagged activity unobtrusively.

Table 2. Selected studies leveraging wearable accelerometers to monitor PD movements

Contribution group	Sensor type and placement	Intervention Interest	Setting (task)	Accuracy results
Bonato [12]	ACC(8): two on each arm; one on each thigh; right shin and sternum + 8 EMG's	"OFF" state, "ON" state, dyskinesias	Lab	3 clusters of data corresponding to "ON", "OFF" and dyskinesias
Keijsers [13]	ACC(6): both upper arms, both upper legs, wrist at most affected side, and sternum.	Dyskinesias	Lab simulated home environment	> 93% accurate in whether or not dyskinesia present
Keijsers [9]		"OFF" state "ON" state		58-97% sensitivity, 70-97% specificity for detecting ON/OFF
Moore [10]	Combined ACC+gyro(1): worn just above ankle	Stride length	Lab/home	100% agreement between Stride length and video observation
Moore [11]		Freezing of gait	Lab	78% -89% of freezes detected
Bächlin [15]	ACC (3): above ankle, above knee, waist	Freezing of gait	Lab	73.1% sensitivity 81.6% specificity
Patel [16]	ACC (8): 2 per limb	Selected tasks from UPDRS	Lab (UPDRS)	2.2-3.4% error in UPDRS score
Patel [17]			Lab (UPDRS)	Within 0.5 points on UPDRS scale of 0-4.
Zabaleta[18]	Combined ACC+gyro(6): 3 on each leg	Freezing of Gait	Lab	51.1-82.7% of freezing episodes correctly detected
Weiss[19]	ACC (1): on waist	Gait Variability	Lab & home	Gait variability was larger in PD
Griffiths[20]	ACC (1): on wrist of most affected side	Bradykinesia, Dyskinesia	Lab	Modest agreement with UPDRS
Tsipouras [7]	6 sets of ACC+gyro: one on each limb+waist	Dyskinesia	Lab	~84% Accuracy
Mera[22]	ACC+gyro (1): on finger	Bradykinesia & tremor	Home (UPDRS)	Medication response detected
Zwartjes[23]	Combined ACC+ gyro(4): trunk, wrist, thigh and foot of most affected side	Tremor, bradykinesia, hypokinesia	Lab (UPDRS) tasks and daily tasks	Overall 98.9% accuracy
Das[11] 2 PD patients	ACC (5): wrists, ankles, waist	Subject specific motor signs	Regular daily activities	>90% accuracy

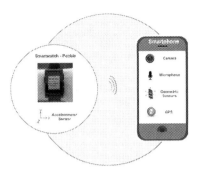

Fig. 1. Smartphone with built-in sensors and body sensor network device & Smartwatch with accelerometer

In the SPARK framework we exploit both a smartphone and a smartwatch to establish an mobile health (mHealth) system for active and passive monitoring of PD patients. Active monitoring is offered by a mobile Parkinson disease rating scale (mPDRS) designed by our research group. Passive monitoring is performed by collecting accelerometer data from a Pebble watch worn on the affected limb. In Section 4, we describe role of SPARK's elements including their functionality and applicability.

3.2   mPDRS: Mobile PDRS for Personalized PD Interventions

Most investigations of monitoring movements in PD utilize wearable sensors. Other aspects of PD symptoms such as facial expression, speech quality and components of ADL (listed in Table 1) are overlooked in monitoring PD progression, although they hold great clinical significance in improving treatment and life quality of PD patients [23, 24]. Harnessing the power of SPARK framework, we have built a mobile version of UPDRS – the mPDRS (mobile PDRS) – to objectively monitor PD severity in remote as well as clinical settings. In other words, mPDRS is an effort to conduct a subset of UPDRS tests through the Pebble watch and smartphone. The subset of tests is selected in the way that multidimensional symptoms manifested in various forms such as motor movements, speech, facial tremors, gaiting functions, and disabilities in performing ADL are considered to offer clinicians varieties of clinical data for improving treatment outcomes.

4   SPARK Framework

The overarching goal of SPARK framework is to monitor clinically relevant multidimensional data – such as facial tremors, dysfunctional speech, periods of dyskinesia, and instances of freezing of gait – from smartphones and smartwatches that are carried by the patients remotely. As shown in Figure 1 and Figure 2, SPARK is three-layered framework, enabling collection of sensor data from a synergistically functional system consisted of a smartphone and a smartwatch. Each layer in SPARK is designed such that physicians can define personalized interventions for each PD patient.

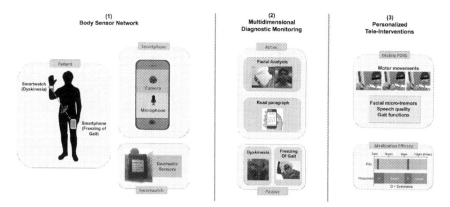

Fig. 2. Three-layered Framework of SPARK for personalized PD interventions

4.1   Body Sensor Network (Layer 1)

Body sensor network (BSN), also referred to as wireless body area network (WLAN), is a collection of wearable computing and sensing devices, communicating with one another to provide contextual awareness to end-users in various application domains. In SPARK, BSN consists of a smartphone and a smartwatch as a network of sensing devices. A smartwatch worn on the patient's wrist records accelerometer data that are streamed to smartphone.

Smartphone-Smartwatch Communication. We used the Pebble watch data logging API [25], enabling the data transfer from Pebble to smartphone. Pebble can create multiple time-stamped logs that are queued and then transferred at set intervals when a Bluetooth connection with smartphone is available. In order to reduce energy consumption and battery usage, Pebble batches up data and sends it over to the smartphone periodically.

Clinically-smart Data Management Layer. We aim to design a clinically-smart data management layer (CsDML) that segregates clinically relevant data from background noise on smartphones and makes the system more efficient in terms of energy and data transmission. The targeted CsDML is based upon on-line learning algorithms that incorporate event-driven adaptive sensor sampling and also allow forming context-awareness personalized to individual needs.

4.2   Multidimensional Diagnostic Monitoring (Layer 2)

This second layer of SPARK comprises data storage, analysis, and visualization layers implemented in a private SPARK cloud. The SPARK cloud stores data from subjects and runs machine learning algorithms to classify the symptom severity. In this layer, machine learning algorithms are aimed at looking at features of PD symptoms in the following ways:

1. Facial tremors: UPDRS test no. 19 involves physicians to score facial tremors through visual observation. In this part of SPARK technology, we attempt to automate this process through smartphone. PD patients are prompted to watch a short slideshow on their smartphones. While they watch the slideshow, the front camera of the smartphone records their facial video. The recorded face videos are then uploaded to the SPARK cloud for further clinical analysis. We have developed computer vision algorithms [27] to clinically score facial tremors in the recorded videos.
2. Speech quality: UPDRS test no. 18 asks PD patients to read a short paragraph and hence, physicians can score their speech functions. Similarly, SPARK adopts this step by allowing patients to read a paragraph displayed on their smartphone screens while the built-in microphone of the smartphone records their voice.
3. Motor tremors: There are many UPDRS tests that require physicians to score motor tremors of PD patients when they pay in-clinic visits. SPARK offers to collect patient's motor data through active or passive monitoring. In order to personalize PD monitoring and treatment, SPARK facilitates physicians to place the Pebble smartwatch on most affected limbs of their patients.

4.3   Personalized Interventions

SPARK will provide recommendations to physicians for medication changes. As shown in Figure 3, we will use an individualized conditioned hidden Markov model for predicting ON (when movement is good and medication is working) and OFF states (when movement is bad and medication is not working). Predicted OFF states will be used to recommend medication adjustments.

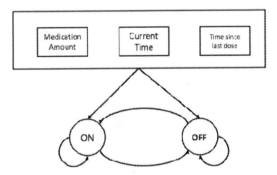

Fig. 3. Conditioned Hidden Markov Model for predicting ON/OFF states to generate recommendations for medication changes and minimizing OFF. Additional factors may be added.

5   Pilot Trials with the SPARK Framework

We conducted focus group studies on 5 control subjects. The studies were performed in laboratory settings to collect the experimental data through the SPARK framework. In the studies, we collected multidimensional data of subjects using the smartphone/smartwatch framework.

5.1   Facial Tremors

A cardinal feature of PD is diminished facial expression ("masked facies") and therefore, it is crucial for physicians to look at the pattern of masked facies of their patients when they are remotely located. We have designed a smartphone app – FaceEngage [27] that uses the front facing camera to record facial videos while the participant watches a 2-min slideshow of emotionally neutral images (Figure 4). We have also developed computer vision techniques to process face videos to detect attributes of interest such as blinking rate and parted lips instances which serve as good indicators for scoring masked facies [27].

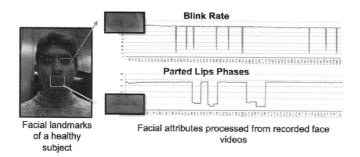

Facial landmarks
of a healthy
subject

Facial attributes processed from recorded face
videos

Fig. 4. Facial analysis of healthy individuals with emphasis on monitoring facial attributes associated with PD

5.2   Speech Analysis

Speech impairments have been associated with PD, and voice deteriorates with PD progression. Speech signals are an ideal choice for the remote monitoring of the Parkinson symptoms because they are easy to obtain, there is no special skill or instrumentation required, and they are noninvasive in nature. In the SPARK framework we propose to use active and passive speech monitoring of PD patients and use features of speech impairment – such as reading duration, pitch, jitter and shimmer – to monitor the progression of PD.

5.3   Active Monitoring of Movements

In active monitoring PD patients will be asked to perform the motor movements described in the mPDRS scale. These motor movements include wearing the smartwatch on a limb. Typical movements in mPDRS include finger tapping, opening and closing of hand, finger pointing, pronation and supination, foot tapping, walking, and getting up from a seat while hands crossed. Figure 5 shows the typical profile of a 3 axis accelerometer data from a subject performing the mPDRS scale. It is clear from the figure that each maneuver in the mPDRS carries a specific signature easily identifiable in raw accelerometer data.

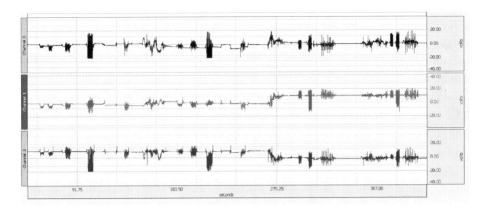

Fig. 5. 20 movements captured on accelerometers of the smartphone while a participant strapped the smartphone sequentially on wrists and then ankles (one location at a time) during mUPDRS trials

6   Conclusions and Future Work

We have presented a novel framework for personalizing the management of PD. SPARK uses smartphones and smartwatches to track symptom severity in real world situations and assess how medications affect symptoms. SPARK provides ways to measure speech and facial expressions/features, which are crucial for the understanding of PD severity. We are pilot-testing the current framework with the PD patients and evaluating the usefulness of this framework for all the stakeholders (patients, clinicians, caregivers, and family members).

While the SPARK framework is encouraging, there are inherent limitations of the usefulness of SPARK in PD interventions. Our project is focused solely on the motor features of PD and does not incorporate medication side effects or non-motor features (e.g., psychiatric disturbances, sleep problems, autonomic dysfunction, cognitive issues). We plan to incorporate non-motor features and side effects into personalized predictive models in the future. Despite our effort to maximize compatibility, there will be PD patients that will not be able to use SPARK due to their inability to adopt new technologies such as smartphones. Further, sensor misplacement, patient log errors, device malfunction, loss of data, and limitations of algorithms are challenges we may encounter.

Acknowledgements. We are very thankful to all of our study participants for their support in collecting experimental data.

References

1. Dorsey, E.R., Constantinescu, R., Thompson, J.P., Biglan, K.M., Holloway, R.G., Kieburtz, K., Marshall, F.J., Ravina, B.M., Schifitto, G., Siderowf, A., Tanner, C.M.: Projected number of people with Parkinson disease in the most populous nations, 2005 through 2030. Neurology 68, 384–386 (2007)

2. Weintraub, D., Comella, C,L., Horn, S.: Parkinson's disease–Part 1: Pathophysiology, symptoms, burden, diagnosis, and assessment. The American Journal of Managed Care 2008;14:S40-8.
3. Fahn, S., Elton, R.L., UPDRS Development Committee: Unified Parkinson's Disease Rating Scale. In: Fahn, S., Marsden, C.D., Calne, D.B., Goldstein, M. (eds.) Recent Developments in Parkinson's Disease, pp. 153–163. Macmillan, Florham Park (1987)
4. Movement Disorder Society Task Force on Rating Scales for Parkinson's Disease. The Unified Parkinson's Disease Rating Scale (UPDRS): status and recommendations. Movement Disorders: Official Journal of the Movement Disorder Society 18(7), 738 (2003)
5. Common Data Elements, Unified Parkinson's Disease Rating Scale. National Institute of Neurological Disorders and Stroke (NINDS)
6. Maetzler, W., Domingos, J., Srulijes, K., Ferreira, J.J., Bloem, B.R.: Quantitative wearable sensors for objective assessment of Parkinson's disease. Mov. Disord. 28, 1628–1637 (2013)
7. Tsipouras, M.G., Tzallas, A.T., Fotiadis, D.I., Konitsiotis, S.: On automated assessment of Levodopa- induced dyskinesia in Parkinson's disease. In: Conference Proceedings: Annual International Conference of the IEEE Engineering in Medicine and Biology Society Conference, pp. 2679–2682 (2011)
8. Pavel, P., Hayes, T., Tsay, I., Erdogmus, D., Paul, A., Larimer, N., Jimison, H., Nutt, J.: Continuous Assessment of Gait Velocity in Parkinson's Disease from Unobtrusive Measurements. In: Proceedings of the 3rd International IEEE EMBS Conference on Neural Engineering 2007, Kohala Coast, Hawaii, USA, May 2-5 (2007)
9. Keijsers, N.L.W., Horstink, M.W.I.M., Gielen, S.C.A.M.: Ambulatory motor assessment in Parkinson's disease. Movement Disord. 21, 34–44 (2006)
10. Moore, S.T., MacDougall, H.G., Ondo, W.G.: Ambulatory monitoring of freezing of gait in Parkinson's disease. Journal of Neuroscience Methods 167, 340–348 (2008)
11. Das, S., Amoedo, B., De la Torre, F., Hodgins, J.: Detecting Parkinsons' symptoms in uncontrolled home environments: a multiple instance learning approach. In: Conference Proceedings: Annual International Conference of the IEEE Engineering in Medicine and Biology Society Conference, pp. 3688–3691 (2012)
12. Bonato, P., Sherrill, D.M., Standaert, D.G., Salles, S.S., Akay, M.: Data mining techniques to detect motor fluctuations in Parkinson's disease. In: Conference Proceedings: Annual International Conference of the IEEE Engineering in Medicine and Biology Society IEEE Engineering in Medicine and Biology Society Conference, vol. 7, pp. 4766–4769 (2004)
13. Keijsers, N.L., Horstink, M.W., Gielen, S.C.: Automatic assessment of levodopa-induced dyskinesias in daily life by neural networks. Mov. Disord. 18, 70–80 (2003)
14. Moore, S.T., MacDougall, H.G., Gracies, J.M., Cohen, H.S., Ondo, W.G.: Long-term monitoring of gait in Parkinson's disease. Gait & Posture 26, 200–207 (2007)
15. Bachlin, M., Plotnik, M., Roggen, D., Giladi, N., Hausdorff, J.M., Troster, G.: A wearable system to assist walking of Parkinson's disease patients. Methods of Information in Medicine 49, 88–95 (2010)
16. Patel, S., Lorincz, K., Hughes, R., Huggins, N., Growdon, J., Standaert, D., Akay, M., Dy, J., Welsh, M., Bonato, P.: Monitoring motor fluctuations in patients with Parkinson's disease using wearable sensors. IEEE Transactions on Information Technology in Biomedicine: A Publication of the IEEE Engineering in Medicine and Biology Society 13, 864–873 (2009)

17. Patel, S., Chen, B.R., Mancinelli, C., Paganoni, S., Shih, L., Welsh, M., Dy, J., Bonato, P.: Longitudinal monitoring of patients with Parkinson's disease via wearable sensor technology in the home setting. In: Conference Proceedings: Annual International Conference of the IEEE Engineering in Medicine and Biology Society Conference 2011, pp. 1552–1555 (2011)
18. Zabaleta, H., Keller, T., Fimbel, E.: Gait analysis in frequency domain for freezing detection in patients with Parkinson's disease. Gerontechnology 7 (2008)
19. Weiss, A., Sharifi, S., Plotnik, M., van Vugt, J.P., Giladi, N., Hausdorff, J.M.: Toward automated, at-home assessment of mobility among patients with Parkinson disease, using a body-worn accelerometer. Neurorehabilitation and Neural Repair 25, 810–818 (2011)
20. Griffiths, R.I., Kotschet, K., Arfon, S., Xu, Z.M., Johnson, W., Drago, J., Evans, A., Kempster, P., Raghav, S., Horne, M.K.: Automated assessment of bradykinesia and dyskinesia in Parkinson's disease. Journal of Parkinson's Disease 2, 47–55 (2012)
21. Mera, T.O., Heldman, D.A., Espay, A.J., Payne, M., Giuffrida, J.P.: Feasibility of home-based automated Parkinson's disease motor assessment. Journal of Neuroscience Methods 203, 152–156 (2012)
22. Zwartjes, D., Heida, T., van Vugt, J., Geelen, J., Veltink, P.: Ambulatory Monitoring of Activities and Motor Symptoms in Parkinson inverted question marks Disease. IEEE Transactions on Bio-medical Engineering 57 (2010)
23. Madeley, P., Ellis, A.W., Mindham, R.H.S.: Facial expressions and Parkinson's disease. Behavioural Neurology 8(2), 115–119 (1995)
24. Howard, N., Bergmann, J.H.M., Howard, R.: Examining Everyday Speech and Motor Symptoms of Parkinson's Disea'se for Diagnosis and Progression Tracking. In: 2013 12th Mexican International Conference on Artificial Intelligence (MICAI). IEEE (2013)
25. Jankovic, J., McDermott, M., Carter, J., Gauthier, S., Goetz, C., Golbe, L., Huber, S., Koller, W., Olanow, C., Shoulson, I., et al.: Variable expression of Parkinson's disease: a base-line analysis of the DATATOP cohort. The Parkinson Study Group. Neurology 40, 1529–1534 (1990)
26. Pebble Data Logging Guide, http://developer.getpebble.com/2/guides/datalogging-guide.html (accessed on February 13, 2014)
27. Mankodiya, K., Sharma, V., Martins, R., Pande, I., Jain, S., Ryan, N., Gandhi, R.: Understanding User's Emotional Engagement to the Contents on a Smartphone Display: Psychiatric Prospective. In: 2013 IEEE 10th International Conference on and 10th International Conference on Ubiquitous Intelligence and Computing Autonomic and Trusted Computing (UIC/ATC), December 18-21, pp. 631–637 (2013)

How Do Patient Information Leaflets Aid Medicine Usage? A Proposal for Assessing Usability of Medicine Inserts

Carla Galvão Spinillo

Postgraduate Program in Design, Federal University of Paraná, Rua General Carneiro, 460,
8º andar, Curitiba, PR 80060-150 Brazil
cgspin@gmail.com

Abstract. This Patient information leaflet – PIL provides support to medicine usage. However, there is a lack of empirical evidence on the usability of PILs since most research has focused on their readability and legibility, and legal regulations worldwide have neglected their usability aspects. Considering the importance of this matter, a proposal for assessing PILs' usability is presented here, consisting of three phases: (1) task analysis diagram flow, (2) interaction test, and (3) follow-up interview, and the outputs are analyzed in a qualitative manner. To validate the usability assessment proposed, a study was conducted in Brazil with 60 participants on using medicines differing in their pharmaceutical presentation, based upon the instructions in their PILs. The results showed a direct relation between task complexity-errors; and the decision points-actions/ steps. The usability assessment aids in identifying drawbacks in the PILs design and information flow, thus, providing support to improvements towards their effectiveness in medicine usage.

Keywords: patient information leaflets, usability, assessment.

1   Introduction

Several studies have been conducted on patient information leaflets – PILs. Most of them looked at text related aspects, such as readability, legibility and typographic structure [1], [2], [3], [4], [5] and some also investigated pictorial aspects of PILs, as for instance the graphic presentation of visual instructions [6]. Despite their contributions to the communication success of PILs, the majority of these studies has not provided empirical evidence of their effectiveness on medicines usage, that is, how graphic and typographic aspects of PILs may affect the task of using/taking a medicine by a person. In this regard, research with person-centered approach might provide methods and tools to measure usability of PILs.

The concern on effectiveness communication of PILs has been driven regulations in the European Union – EU since 2005, when readability tests of PILs have been required from pharmaceutical companies to have their medicines approved. However, the EU readability tests for PILs may present limitations in assessing their communicational

A. Marcus (Ed.): DUXU 2014, Part III, LNCS 8519, pp. 115–124, 2014.

effectiveness from information design viewpoint. The tests restrict the scope of medicine usage to text comprehension, overlooking task performance and context of medicine use (from prescription to usage). Thus, regardless the contribution of readability tests to message communication, they do not actually prove PILs' efficiency in medicine usage, but how information is understood, and searched/found by medicine users [7] [8]. In this respect, it is interesting to mention a study conducted by Raynor, Knapp, Moody and Young [9] in the same year EU approved their regulation for testing PILs. The authors investigated PILs and the impact of European regulations on the use of medicine, and found that PILs were not read or noticed y several patients, and did not meet their information needs. This ratifies the importance of having PILs tested in their usability to minimally ensure their effectiveness, or at least that they would meet patients' expectations to be noticed by them. In this sense, Waarde and Spinillo [10] when discussing the development of visual information about medicines, claim that the production of PILs should follow a 'writing-designing-testing-process' and embrace all stakeholders. Moreover, they assert that legislation and guidance to develop PILs should be performance based, that is, should be based upon PILs' usability to medicine usage.

However, testing PILs is not a worldwide concern, even when limited to their readability. Countries in Latin America, Africa, Asia and still some in Europe do not require PILs testing in their regulations. Thus, the pharmaceutical companies have been marketing their medicines in those countries with no evidence on their PILs' effectiveness. The effects of lack of comprehension of information on medicine use have been observed in data on hospitalization and even death of patients reported by the press and health authorities worldwide. Taking the wrong dosage or an overdose of a medicine, adverse reactions, and taking medicines that are not suitable for use due to inappropriate storage are examples of problems that can be caused by information draw-backs in PILs. In USA, for instance, a report showed an increase of 65% in the number of hospitalizations from 1999 to 2006 as a result of medication overdose regarding pain-relief medicines, tranquilizers and sedatives [11]. As some of them are over-the-counter medicines, i.e., can be purchased without medical prescription, their PILs are the main source of information on the medicine usage. Similarly, a study conducted in Brazil by Aquino [12] reported that one third of hospitalizations were caused by misuse of medication. The impact of medication misuse on the population health safety has pushed governments to take preventive, educational and legal measures. However, medicine regulations still neglect the relevance of verifying to what extent PILs support medicine usage, as previously mentioned.

2   A Proposal for Assessing Usability of PILs

According to Rubin and Chisnell [13] usability regards how usable a product or a service is. In addition, they claim that to be so, a product or service should be useful, efficient, effective, satisfying, learnable and accessible to its users. Thus, usability regards actual interaction between an artifact and a person, and involves tasks to be performed. In general, the concept of usability is applied to product ergonomics and digital systems, within the scope of HCI – Human-Computer-Interaction. In this respect, several techniques and methods have been used by researchers and developers of products and digital systems to assess usability. Since the nineties publications have been issued on this matter, as for instance Nielsen's paper [14] presenting a list of techniques to verify usability of interfaces, followed by Dumas and Redish' book [15] presenting a guide for usability testing. However, there seems to be a lack in the literature on usability for printed artifacts. Despite the relevance of this topic, most research looks at legibility and comprehension aspects, thus, ignoring how usable printed artifacts actually are for their users. This is particularly pertinent when regards health related printed artifacts, such as PILs.

From a usability perspective, PIL is not only a pharmaceutical source for health treatment, but also an instructional document that provides patients with information on how to interact with a product (medicine). Accordingly, medicine insert is an information design artifact that mediates patient/user + medicine interaction during task performance. Thus, it empowers patients in the decision making process on health treatment. In this sense, identifying the tasks/aspects involved in a medicine usage is of prime importance to verify usability of PILs. Considering this, together with patient/user information needs to support task performance, a proposal for assessing usability of PILs is presented next, consisting of three main consecutive phases: (1) task analysis flow diagram, (2) interaction test, and (3) follow-up interview. The PIL tested can be either an existing one or a mockup of a PIL to be produced. The former is found inserted in actual medicine packages and its usability assessment would serve to produce data for academic/professional/governmental reports. This allows guidance for future improvements on the design of existing PILs, whether for the latter, the usability assessment is conducted within the PIL design process, therefore leading to improvements prior its production.

2.1 Phase 1: Task Analysis Diagram

Initially, a decision/action flow diagram is drawn to identify the actions to be taken by patients/users during task performance, decision points and conditional situations to take/use a medicine according to the information provided in the PIL. The diagram will aid researchers to be aware of possible difficulties in task performance (e.g., measuring dosage) and/or to decide on the questions to be made in the interview (e.g. how to measure dosage). This diagram is based upon Moraes and Mont'Alvão's [16], however adapted to include conditional situations that may be necessary to take/use medicines.

2.2 Phase 2: User + PIL + Medicine Interaction Test

Based upon the task analysis diagram, an interaction test is then conducted in a simulated manner to avoid risks to participants (e.g. using a syringe in a sponge). The number of participants and their characteristics are defined according to the medicine users' profile. The material for testing consists of: an actual PIL or a PIL mockup, the medicine and other material that may be necessary (e.g., sponge for simulated use of syringe). The interaction test is conducted with each participant individually and isolation. The PIL (existing or mockup) is presented to the participant, who is asked to follow the instructions provided in the PIL to use/take the medicine and to verbalize his/her actions. Participants are informed that they may consult the PIL during task performance whenever they find necessary. The data is recorded through video and audio, but written notes on task observation may be used in case participants feel comfortable with the presence of the researcher in the testing room, or if special glass room is available for this purposed. Time restriction is not posed to participants as it may be a variable to be measured. The interaction test will be over when participants consider that they finished the task, or decide to give the task up. Then, participants will be asked to engage in an interview about the task.

2.3   Phase 3: Follow-up Interview

After the interaction test, a semi-structure interview is conducted with each participant to get their reactions to the task performed, to the PIL tested, their satisfaction with User + PIL + medicine interaction, and their suggestions to improvements. A protocol with questions on these aspects is produced to guide the interviewer and to allow written notes, if necessary. The data recorded in video from the PIL's interaction testing can be used to aid in the interviewing process regarding questions on task performance (e.g., elucidate doubts, identify errors). Video and/or audio recording can be used to register participants' responses. The following table summarizes the proposed sequence of phases to assess usability of PILs. The columns present the phases and their aims; and the material employed.

Table 1. Summary of proposed sequence of phases to assess usability of PILs

Phase	Aims	Material
1. Task analysis diagram	Identify medicine usage according to PIL's information. Foreseen possible difficulties and errors in task performance.	Printed or digital support for drawing the diagram
2. User + PIL + medicine interaction test	Identify difficulties, drawbacks and errors in task performance. Identify possible weaknesses and/or omission of information in PILs when supporting task performance.	PIL Medicine (and related material)
3. Follow-up interview	Identify participants' views on/reactions to their task performance. Gather participants' suggestions to improve PILs.	Protocol with questions Video images from the interaction test

2.4   Analyzing the Data

To a proper understanding of the outcomes from the PIL usability assessment, it is necessary to discuss data in a deeper manner. Thus, qualitative analysis seems to be appropriate. In this sense, for the PIL interaction test, a human error classification for the participants' performance is proposed, considering: (1) information processing errors, (2) action errors, and (3) verification errors (regards particularities of the tasks such as dosage mistake). This classification is based on Barber and Stanton [17]; and Rasmussen [18] taxonomies for human errors, which was adapted for medicine usage mediated by PILs (Table 2).

Table 2. Classification for human errors proposed

---

1 – Information processing errors

Internal (individual repertoire)

Pi 1| Wrong/Mistaken assumption

External (insert/package/product)

Pi 2| Information was not read/searched

Pi 3| Information was incompletely read/searched

Pi 4| Wrong information searched

Pi 5| Information was searched but not found

Pi 6| Information was searched and founded but not understood

---

2 – Action errors

A 1|Task/action was not performed

A 2| Task/action was incompletely performed

A 3| Task/action was performed in wrong/inappropriate moment

A 4| Very long or very short Task/action

A 5| Task/action performed in a very little or very large amount/quantity

A 6| Task/action in wrong direction

A 7| Wrong alignment

A 8| Right task/action in wrong/mistaken object

A 9| Right task/action but in a wrong part/component of a right object

A 10| Wrong task/action in a right object

A 11| Wrong task/action in a wrong object

A 12| Selection not done

A 13| Wrong selection done

---

3 – Verification errors

V 1| Verification not done

V 2| Verification incompletely done

V 3| Verification in a wrong moment

V 4| Right verification in a wrong object

V 5| Wrong verification in right object

V 6| Wrong verification in wrong object

V 7| Verification in a very little or large amount/quantity

Afterwards, the results of task performance are compared across participants to find what errors are common among them, as well as the success or failure of the task executed. This indicates how effective the tested PIL is in using/taking a medicine.

Likewise, for the follow-up interview, responses to each question are compared across participants to identify similarities and differences in their views on the tasks performed when using/taking the medicine mediates by the PIL.

Next, a general data analysis is made by comparing the outcomes of phase 1 and 2, that is, the results of the interviews to those of the interaction test. This allows identifying trends/commonalities among the phases' results, and relations between participants' task performances and their views on the task/PIL. Then, the main drawbacks of these phases are pinpointed and placed within the task analysis diagram, taking into account their effect on the decision/action flow. This not only permits a visualization of the aspects/elements involved in the procedure of taking/using a medicine, but also make valid requirements to improve the design of a PIL possible. Finally, based on the design requirements, adjustments are made in the PIL to meet patients/users' information needs for using/taking a medicine.

Ideally, after making the adjustments in the PIL, the phases 2 and 3 should be conducted again to verify the effectiveness of the redesigned PIL to the medicine usage. Thus, interaction tests and interviews are carried out and adjustments are made so as to reach a satisfactory version for the PIL (Fig 1).

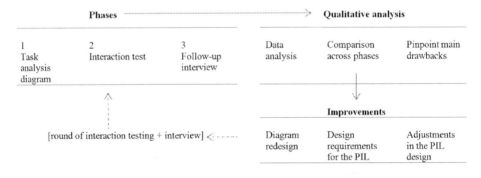

Fig. 1. Sequence of actions involved in the proposed usability assessment for PILs

3   Validating the Proposal for Assessing Usability of PILs

To validate the proposed usability assessment for PILs, a study was conducted in Brazil with 60 participants to use medicines differing in their pharmaceutical presentation: oral suspension, vaginal cream, inhaler, nasal spray and injection pen. They were equally divided into five groups according to the medicine presentation (12 participants per medicine). A task analysis diagram was drawn to each medicine according to their PILs, and decision points, steps and conditional situations were, then, identified in the medicines' procedural tasks. With this information in hand, protocols were designed considering the inputs from the diagrams to the interactions tests and follow-up interviews, which were carried out following the procedures abovementioned.

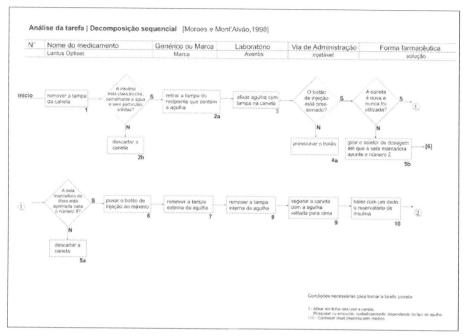

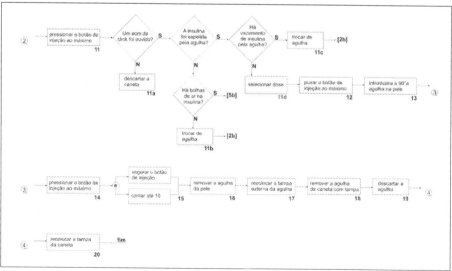

Fig. 2. Task analysis diagram for the injection pen

The results on task analysis diagrams showed that complexity of the tasks was directly proportional to the amount of decision points and actions/steps involved in the medicines' usage. Fig. 2 shows the diagram of the injection pen for taking insulin. The numbers in red (3 and 11d) refer to the conditional situations presented in the PIL on how to use the pen.

In addition, table 3 shows a comparison across the five medicines based upon the information from the diagrams produced. The columns present the number of steps/actions, the decision points and the conditions to use/take each medicine. According to their PILS, the injection pen and inhaler presented the highest number of actions (N = 20 and N = 19 respectively), whereas the vaginal cream had the lowest (N = 09). The number of decision points and conditional situations were also high for the injection pen comparing to the others. On the other hand, there was no decision point for the vaginal cream according to its PIL.

Table 3. Comparison across the five medicines

Medicine	Actions	Decision points	Conditions
(1) Inhaler	20	3	0
(2) Vaginal cream	09	0	4
(3) Injection pen	19	9	5
(4) Oral suspension	17	1	6
(5) Nasal spray	12	3	3
Total	77	16	18

Regarding the PIL + medicine interaction test, the results indicated that the more complex the task of using a medicine, the greater the number of errors made by the participants (Table 4). Information and action errors were found in all five medicine use tasks. A total of 352 were made by participants in their task performances, particularly regarding action/steps (N = 179). The injection pen showed the highest numbers in all errors categories (total of N = 162 errors), followed by the oral suspension medicine with high figures in information processing (N = 32) and action (N = 39) errors.

Table 4. Errors regarding task performances by participants

Medicine	Information Processing	Action	Verification	Total
(1) Inhaler	20	30	2	52
(2) Vaginal cream	7	13	0	20
(3) Injection pen	60	68	34	162
(4) Oral suspension	32	39	4	75
(5) Nasal spray	2	29	12	43
Total	121	179	52	352

According to these results, the PILs tested failed to support task performance since all participants did not succeed in using the medicines guided by their leaflets. This was ratified by the interview responses, in which participants attributed their difficulties in understanding information and performing the tasks to the poor quality of PILs. The outcomes of the interviews also elucidated important issues regarding the personal opinion of participants on the presentation of user instructions and on the medicines' packaging/container. For instance, difficulties in understanding and carrying out the task of using the insulin were associated to the poor design of the injection pen. Likewise, the inhaler container was criticized for not being easy to handle. Moreover, participants (N = 26) considered that use of visual instructions in the PILs tested facilitated understanding of the medicine procedures of use.

Taking into account the outcomes of the interaction testing and interviews, adjustments were made in the task analysis diagrams so as to acknowledge participants' information needs to undertake the tasks mediated by PILs. Thus, critical aspects related to the steps and decision points were marked in the medicines' task flow to support requirements for the redesign of the PILs tested, allowing improvements.

4   Final Considerations

Based upon the validation outcomes, the usability assessment proposed seems to aid in verifying effectiveness of PILs in supporting medicine usage, and may provide guidance to improve the tested PILs. However, due to its research design complexity, the PIL usability assessment should be conducted by experienced researchers who will be able to convey collected data into design requirements for PILs.

Finally, it is hoped that the PIL usability assessment phases as well as the methods and techniques proposed may serve as a starting point to the discussion on measuring effectiveness of PILs from a person-centered approach. And perhaps, such discussion may lead governmental authorities to raise awareness about the need to require PIL's usability testing from the pharmaceutical companies in the medicine regulations.

Acknowledgements. Thanks are due to Dr Stephania Padovani for her valuable contributions in the InfoBula research project of which this study is part, and to CNPq- National Council for Research and Technology, Brazil for supporting this study.

References

1. Brown, H., Ramchandani, M., Gillow, T.J., Tsaloumas, M.D.: Are patient information leaflets contributing to informed consent for cataract surgery? Journal of Med. Ethics 30, 218–220 (2004)
2. Fuchs, J., Hippius, M., Schaefer, M.: A survey of package inserts use by patients. Policy & Practice: Package Inserts, 29–31 (2005)
3. Harwood, A., Harrison, J.E.: How readable are orthodontic patient information leaflets? Journal of Orthodontics 31, 210–219 (2004)

4. Fuchs, J.: The Way Forward in Package Insert User Tests From a CRO's Perspective. Drug Information Journal 44, 119–129 (2010)
5. Gal, I., Prigat, A.: Why organizations continue to create patient information leaflets with readability and usability problems: an exploratory study. Health Education Research Theory & Practice 20(4), 485–493 (2005)
6. Spinillo, C.G., Padovani, S., Miranda, F.: Graphic and information aspects affecting the effectiveness of visual instructions in medicine inserts in Brazil. In: AHFEI – Applied Human Factors and Ergonomics Conference Proceedings of the AHFE International Conference 2008, vol. 1. USA Publishing, Louisville (2008)
7. Maat, H.P., Lentz, L.: Improving the usability of patient information leaflets. Patient Educ. Couns., 1–7 (2009), doi:10.1016/j.pec.2009.09.030
8. Andriesen, S.: Readability Testing of PILs – A New 'Must'. In: EPC, Autum pp. 42–44. Samedan Ltd. Pharmaceutical Publishers (2006)
9. Raynor, D.K., Knapp, P., Moody, A., Young, R.: Patient Information Leaflet: Impact of European regulation on safe and effective use of medicines. The Pahrmaceutical Journal 275, 606–611 (2005)
10. Waarde, K., Spinillo, C.G.: El desarrollo de información visual acerca de fármacos em Europa. In: Frascara, J. (ed.) Que és diseño De información?, pp. 167–171. Ediciones Infinito, Buenos Aires (2011)
11. Harmon, K.: Prescription drug deaths increase dramatically. Scientific American (April 6, 2010)
12. Aquino, D.S.: Por que o uso racional de medicamentos deve ser uma prioridade? Ciência & Saúde Coletiva 13(sup.), 733–736 (2008)
13. Rubin, J., Chisnell, D.: Handbook of usability testing: How to plan, design and conduct effective tests, 2nd edn. Wiley Publishing Inc., Indianapolis (2008)
14. Nielsen, J.: Usability Inspection Methods. In: Conference Companion CHI 1994, Boston, Massachusetts, USA, pp. 413–414 (April 1994)
15. Dumas, J.S., Redish, J.C.: A practical guide to usability testing. Intellect Books, Oregon (1999)
16. Moraes, A., Montalvão, C.: Ergonomia: conceitos e aplicações. Editora 2AB, Rio de Janeiro (1998)
17. Barber, C., Stanton, N.A.: Human error identification techniques applied to public technology: predictions compared with observed use. Applied Ergonomics 27(2), 119–131 (1996)
18. Rasmussen, J.: Human Error. Information Processing and human-machine interaction, pp. 140–169. North-Holland, New York (1986)

Usability Improvement of a Clinical Decision Support System

Frederick Thum[1,2], Min Soon Kim[3], Nicholas Genes[1], Laura Rivera[1],
Rosemary Beato[1], Jared Soriano[1], Joseph Kannry[4], Kevin Baumlin[1], and Ula Hwang[1]

[1] Department of Emergency Medicine, Icahn School of Medicine at Mount Sinai,
New York, NY
[2] Department of Biomedical Informatics, Columbia University, New York, NY
[3] Department of Health Management & Informatics,
University of Missouri School of Medicine, Columbia, MO
[4] Information Technology, Icahn School of Medicine at Mount Sinai, New York, NY
thumfr@gmail.com

Abstract. This paper focuses on improving the usability of an electronic health record (EHR) embedded clinical decision support system (CDSS) targeted to treat pain in elderly adults. CDSS have the potential to impact provider behavior. Optimizing CDSS-provider interaction and usability may enhance CDSS use. Five CDSS interventions were developed and deployed in test scenarios within a simulated EHR that mirrored typical Emergency Department (ED) workflow. Provider feedback was analyzed using a mixed methodology approach. The CDSS interventions were iteratively designed across three rounds of testing based upon this analysis. Iterative CDSS design led to improved provider usability and favorability scores.

Keywords: clinical decision support, CDS, clinical decision support system, CDSS, usability, emergency department, emergency medicine, human-computer-interaction, HCI, SUS, system usability scale, favorability score, mixed methodology, Healthcare IT & Predicting Adoption, Medical Error & Simulation, Patient Safety, Quality in Healthcare, , iterative design.

1   Introduction

As medical complexity and knowledge grow at a dizzying rate, medical providers rely increasingly on computer systems for support. The study of human-computer interaction in the context of healthcare delivery is essential to increase both provider satisfaction and efficiency as well as to improve patient safety and outcomes. Electronic health records (EHR) provide a mechanism to enable the delivery of healthcare; one aspect of the EHR which can impact this delivery is usability.

In the 2012 Institute of Medicine (IOM) report "Health IT and Patient Safety: Building Safer Systems for Better Care", usability of the EHR is identified as an important feature that may contribute to both improved patient safety as well as potential negative unintended consequences [1]. This report also notes that clinical decision

A. Marcus (Ed.): DUXU 2014, Part III, LNCS 8519, pp. 125–131, 2014.
© Springer International Publishing Switzerland 2014

support systems (CDSS) are an integral component of an EHR that provide suggestions to healthcare workers at the point of care. The IOM report identifies improved usability and design of CDSS as one way to maximize impact and error reduction as well as a way to limit alert fatigue [1,2,3].

In the United States, ambulatory EHR adoption has grown from 18% in 2001 to 78% in 2013 [4]. This growth can be partially attributed to various incentive ('carrot') and disincentive ('stick') programs favoring EHR adoption. The 2009 Health Information Technology for Economic and Clinical Health Act (HITECH) allowed up to US$63,750 in incentive (the 'carrot') payments per eligible provider for EHR adoption that meets certain requirements [5]. Healthcare providers who have not adopted a certified EHR by 2015 will face a 1% reduction in Medicare payments, increasing to a 3% reduction by 2018 (the 'stick'). Various other regulatory and quality improvement programs concurrently push for EHR adoption. These include Centers for Medicare and Medicaid Services' (CMS) Physician Quality Reporting System (PQRS) and Clinical Quality Measures (CQMs).

Hospital information technology (IT) and leadership such as Chief Medical Information Officers to date have largely been occupied with EHR deployment and maintenance as well as satisfaction of various regulations and metric reporting. Usability of the EHR is typically not a high priority among IT or hospital leadership given these competing factors. Further, to qualify for incentive payments under HITECH, various Meaningful Use requirements must be met, one of which is CDSS use. Usability analysis and design are not a requirement of any such regulations, and as such may receive a lower priority than deploying a non-optimized CDSS to satisfy regulations. A CDSS with poor usability may contribute to errors, rather than improve patient care and safety [1,2,3].

CDSS use is increasing as more EHRs are implemented and incentives for CDSS use are in place. CDSS are frequently utilized without regard to usability and provider feedback. Evaluation of CDSS usability within the normal provider workflow is often overlooked in the development of informatics interventions. This evaluation may help refine CDSS to reduce alert fatigue and frustration, thereby making CDSS a more valuable tool in guiding clinical care. This study sought to refine and optimize a pain care CDSS by using an iterative usability design process utilizing a test EHR environment.

2   Methods

2.1   Physical Setup

The testing scenarios were conducted in a quiet office in the Department of Emergency Medicine at the Icahn School of Medicine at Mount Sinai in New York City during daytime hours over the course of 10 weeks.

The setup of the computer and EHR reflected the setup in the clinical environment to which the test users were accustomed with the exception of the CDSS interventions being tested. The test EHR environment was Epic 2010 ASAP (Epic Systems Corp.) within XenApp (Citrix Corp.) running on a standard desktop PC platform with

Windows 7 Enterprise OS (Microsoft). User input was provided via standard 104-key keyboard and optical mouse with scroll wheel. The setup utilized a 17-inch LCD display atop which was mounted a camera for video/audio capture (Logitech Webcam Pro 9000, Logitech Corp.).

Data was recorded using screen capture and video/audio capture of participants with Morae Recorder version 3.3 software (TechSmith Corp). This allowed for later analysis of test sessions using Morae Manager as well as real-time observation of the screen/audio/video by study investigators in a nearby office using Morae Observer.

The study participant's face and audio was captured during the test sessions. A study facilitator was present in the room to direct the user to certain tasks and provide clinical context to the simulated cases. Audio of the facilitator was also captured.

2.2   Usability Testing

A group of five CDSS interventions was developed by an interdisciplinary team to address acute pain care throughout an ED visit (Table 1). Thirteen emergency physicians, all previously experienced in using the EHR, were recruited for participation.

Table 1. Description of Elderly Acute Abdominal Pain Care CDSS Interventions

CDSS Intervention	Description
Pain Score of 10 Alert	A visual pop-up graphic in the center of the EHR screen that interrupts workflow and alerts provider that patient has pain score of 10 that has not been addressed
Re-evaluate at 4 Hours Alert	A visual stimulus within the order entry screen of the EHR that alerts provider that patient has pain score of 10 that has not been re-evaluated or addressed after 4 hours
Order Set	A hyperlink that offers the provider a set of predefined analgesic treatment options for geriatric patients
HPI Reminder	A statement that appears in history of present illness documentation reminding the provider to address patient's pain
Alert at Discharge	A grayed out print button that prevents printing of discharge instructions for patients with an unaddressed pain score of 10

Users were given a $US100 incentive for their participation. Over a 10-week period, seventeen 1-hour usability sessions were conducted across three iterative rounds of testing. Users were given three patient scenarios and were asked to provide simulated clinical care using the EHR in a normal workflow.

The study facilitator provided guidance to the study participant so all tasks could be completed. The study facilitator was able to communicate real-time with the study investigators using iOS iMessage (Apple Corp.) to clarify clinically oriented questions posed by the participant. Users attention was not called to the CDSS interventions prior to the test sessions and users interacted with the CDSS interventions as they completed tasks associated with clinical care.

Patient scenarios consisted of elderly adults suffering from abdominal pain. These simulated patients were modeled as having diverticulitis, small bowel obstruction and constipation. Users utilized order entry, documentation and discharge workflows.

2.3   User Feedback

A System Usability Scale (SUS) survey (0-50 not acceptable, 50-70 marginal acceptability, 70-100 acceptable) was completed at the end of each testing session utilizing a survey function of Morae software. Following this survey, a study facilitator-led structured favorability questionnaire [scored negative (1), neutral (3), positive (5)], and open-ended narrative feedback of each CDSS intervention were completed after each session. Participants were shown pictures of each intervention as they appeared in the EHR and were asked if they would find the intervention useful or not useful and if they had any particular concerns or questions about the intervention. Users were also asked for areas of improvement for each intervention and had a time to provide open-ended feedback.

2.4   Analysis and Iterative Design

An interdisciplinary team consisting of four physicians with backgrounds in informatics, one PhD with a background in usability, one physician with a background in geriatric emergency care, one nurse/IT analyst, one IT EHR analyst and two research associates met to discuss the user provided feedback and study investigator observations. The team reviewed structured and unstructured feedback and favorability scores after each round of usability testing. The majority of this interdisciplinary team was active in the data acquisition phase of the usability studies, allowing informal real-time analysis and discussion among team members prior to formalized meetings. The team, informed by this information, triangulated discrete elements within each CDSS intervention that impacted usability, discussed which changes are feasible within the constraints of time and the EHR system, then incorporated changes to these elements in the next iteration of CDSS design.

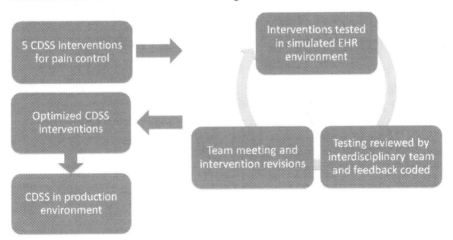

Fig. 1. Iterative design process

3   Results

Twenty-six discrete elements within the CDSS interventions were identified as impacting CDSS usability based upon expert review and testing feedback.   Of these 26 elements, 21 were prioritized and addressed in future iterations.

See Figures 1 and 2 for a representative example of the changes that occurred (e.g., reduced text, fewer required fields, and direct links to actionable items) with the intervention for managing patient-reported pain scores of 10.

Over the three testing rounds and redesigns, mean SUS scores improved from 75 to 89.   Mean favorability scores improved from 3.4 to 4.5 [scale 1 (worsened care) to 5 (improved care)].

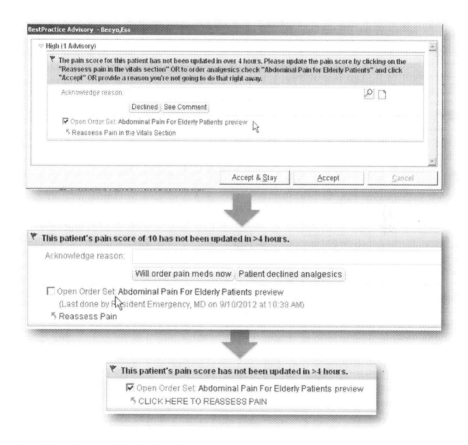

Fig. 2. Iterative usability design of one CDSS intervention over three rounds. There has been streamlining of text, clearer buttons and direct links to order sets or pain re-evaluation dialogs. A representative comment on round 1, "[this intervention] is too complex; I assumed it was an error and I ignored it", and on round 3, "[this intervention] is great, straightforward. I would want to do something about a pain score of 10".

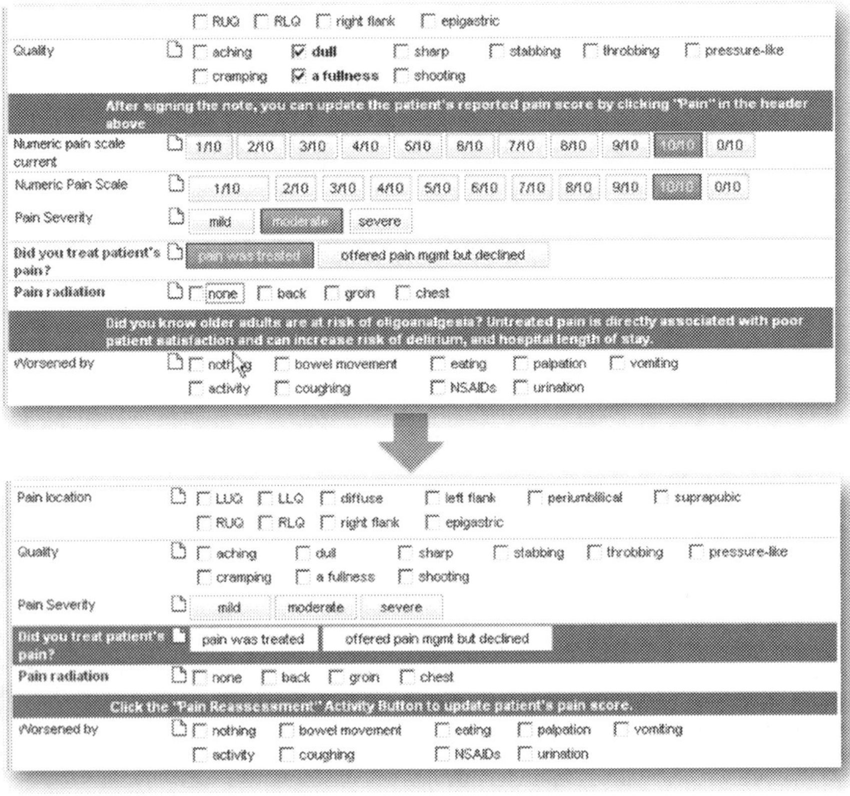

Fig. 3. Iterative usability design over two rounds of testing. Redundant pain scale buttons have been eliminated, and text prompting treatment of pain has been simplified.

4   Conclusions

This study demonstrates how an iterative design process conducted by an interdisciplinary team improves the usability and favorability of a CDSS among providers.

A close working relationship among all key stakeholders in the CDSS development was essential to rapid turnaround of the CDSS interventions. IT was informed by clinicians observing the test users, and clinicians also learned the practical constraints that IT faces. As Health IT evolves past EHR deployment and satisfaction of regulatory requirements, iterative usability design of CDSS over a short period can result in meaningful improvement of the usability of CDSS.

Improved usability may result in greater patient safety, improved provider satisfaction and more efficient workflows. This process may be utilized in other institutions to improve provider satisfaction and enhance the use of CDSS. Usability redesign prior to CDSS deployment in a production EHR environment may result in financial rewards as IT staff become less burdened with answering users questions and revising a CDSS that is already in production.

Future studies will include real-world testing of the interventions to determine provider efficiency and clinical impact.

References

1. Institute of Medicine (U.S.) and Committee on Patient Safety and Health Information Technology. Health IT and Patient Safety Building Safer Systems for Better Care. National Academies Press, Washington, D.C. (2012), http://www.nap.edu/catalog.php?record_id=13269
2. Farley, H.L., Baumlin, K.M., Hamedani, A.G., Cheung, D.S., Edwards, M.R., Fuller, D.C., Genes, N., et al.: Quality and Safety Implications of Emergency Department Information Systems. Annals of Emergency Medicine 62(4), 399–407 (2013), doi:10.1016/j.annemergmed.2013.05.019
3. Genes, N.: When Charts Cry Wolf. Emergency Physicians Monthly (March 29, 2011), http://www.epmonthly.com/features/current-features/when-charts-cry-wolf/
4. Hsiao, C.-J., Hing, E.: Use and characteristics of electronic health record systems among office-based physician practices: United States, 2001–2013. In: NCHS data brief, no 143, National Center for Health Statistics, Hyattsville (2014)
5. Getting Started - Centers for Medicare & Medicaid Services, http://www.cms.gov/Regulations-and-Guidance/Legislation/EHRIncentivePrograms/Getting_Started.html (accessed January 31, 2014)
6. Berner, E.S.: Clinical decision support systems: State of the Art. Agency for Healthcare Research and Quality, Rockville (2009)
7. Kaplan, B.: Evaluating informatics applications–clinical decision support systems literature review. Int J. Med. Inform. 64(1), 15–37 (2001)
8. Brooke, J.: SUS - A quick and dirty usability scale. In: Usability Evaluation in Industry 1996. Taylor & Francis, London (1996)

Information about Medicines for Patients in Europe: To Impede or to Empower?

Karel van der Waarde

Graphic Design - Research, Solariumlaan 15, 1982 Elewijt, Belgium
waarde@glo.be

Abstract. Information about medicines in Europe does not really fulfil its potential. For patients, it is often very hard to understand and to apply information in a specific situation. For the pharmaceutical industry, it is hard to develop (writing-designing-testing) due to strict regulations. And for the Regulatory authorities, the current situation is hard to control and check. One of the main causes is that legal-, economic-, and health-criteria are simultaneously applied to information about medicines. However, these three criteria are fundamentally different, and have proved to be unbridgeable in the last 20 years. In order to provide patients with usable information, it seems essential to develop a legal system that is not based on standardization of processes and results, but instead is based on required performances in context.

Keywords: Patient information, medicine packaging, labeling, information design.

1   Situation: Patients, Industry, and Legislation

Patients in Europe receive a substantial amount of information about their medicines. This information is supplied on packaging, in package leaflets, and on 'inner packaging' such as blister packs, tubes, or bottles. Pharmacists can add handwritten instructions and additional printed labels, and sometimes provide auxiliary letters and brochures. Especially when patients use more than one medicine, this uncoordinated information supply frequently exceeds the processing capacity of patients. The overload of visual information leads to unwanted side effects like a reduced confidence in the pharmaceutical industry ("they are just covering their backs" – see figure 1), reduced confidence in pharmacists and doctors ("they just try to give you the cheapest ones" – see figure 2) and difficult risk-benefit analyses ("it might help, but it could get worse too?" – see figure 3).

Some of the information supply is heavily regulated and controlled within a complex framework of regulations and guidelines. Other – unregulated – information is added at different stages, and this has sedimented gradually over the years into a structure that is hard to handle, difficult to read, and very hard to understand or apply. The breaking point has been reached where regulations prevent progress and hamper the supply of relevant and useful information to patients.

A. Marcus (Ed.): DUXU 2014, Part III, LNCS 8519, pp. 132–140, 2014.

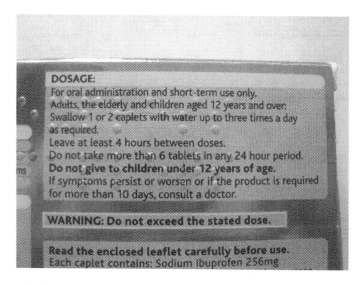

Fig. 1. Example of a detail of an outer pack. The number of warnings and the position of the warnings make it difficult for patients to follow the advice. The interpretation of the combination of 'Do not take more than 6 tablets in any 24 hour period.' and 'WARNING: Do not exceed the stated dose.' requires some mental agility. It is unclear why both are mentioned. The readability of the text is further severely reduced by the use of a highly reflective silver background, a small type size, and braille dots.

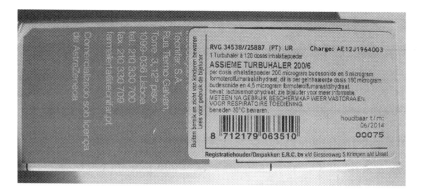

Fig. 2. Example of additional labelling. In order to maximize income, it is possible to buy medicines across Europe (parallel import). The consequence is for example that Dutch patients might receive a Portuguese package with texts in Portuguese. This is remedied by an additional sticker on the outer packing with Dutch texts. Unfortunately, this makes it very unclear who is responsible for the supply of this information. It could be the importer, the pharmacist, the Portuguese manufacturer, or the actual licence holder.

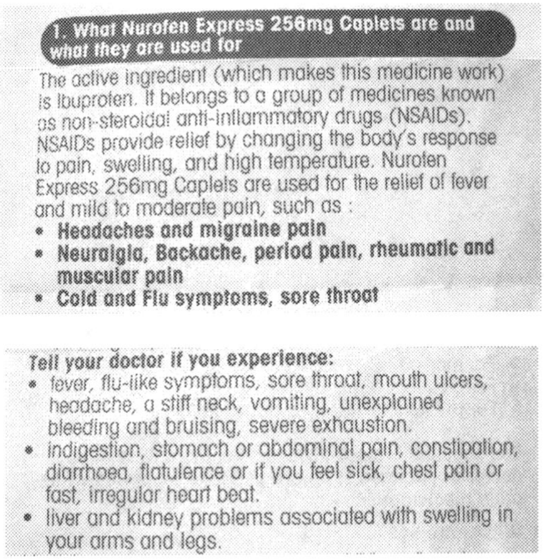

1. What Nurofen Express 256mg Caplets are and what they are used for

The active ingredient (which makes this medicine work) is Ibuprofen. It belongs to a group of medicines known as non-steroidal anti-inflammatory drugs (NSAIDs). NSAIDs provide relief by changing the body's response to pain, swelling, and high temperature. Nurofen Express 256mg Caplets are used for the relief of fever and mild to moderate pain, such as :
* **Headaches and migraine pain**
* **Neuralgia, Backache, period pain, rheumatic and muscular pain**
* **Cold and Flu symptoms, sore throat**

Tell your doctor if you experience:
* fever, flu-like symptoms, sore throat, mouth ulcers, headache, a stiff neck, vomiting, unexplained bleeding and bruising, severe exhaustion.
* indigestion, stomach or abdominal pain, constipation, diarrhoea, flatulence or if you feel sick, chest pain or fast, irregular heart beat.
* liver and kidney problems associated with swelling in your arms and legs.

Fig. 3. Package leaflet details. Top: detail of front. Bottom: Detail of the back of the same leaflet. A medicine that is used 'for the relief of fever and mild to moderate pain' (top image) might cause 'fever' and 'headaches' as side effects (bottom image). Technically, this information is likely to be correct, but it is difficult for a patient to distinguish between the 'headache before taking the tablets', and the 'headache that is caused by the tablets'.

All three examples are in conflict with the intention of the European legislation. A European Directive formulates this intention as 'information supplied to users should provide a high degree of consumer protection, in order that medicinal products may be used correctly on the basis of full and comprehensible information.'[1]. The examples are also in conflict with the actual articles in the EU-legislation which state that 'The package leaflet must be written and designed to be clear and understandable, enabling the users to act appropriately, when necessary with the help of health professionals.' [2] Most information about medicines for patients in Europe fails these criteria.

Of course this has been known for a long time, and in December 2010 a Directive mentions that 'improvements' are required. Directive 2004/84 states: 'By 1 January 2013, the Commission shall present to the European Parliament and the Council an assessment report on current shortcomings in the summary of product characteristics and the package leaflet and how they could be improved in order to better meet the needs of patients and healthcare professionals.' [3]

At the time of writing (February 2014), this report has not been published yet. The delay in the publication might be an indication of the unforseen difficulties to deal with a real 'wicked problem'.

1.1   Questions

It is clear that the information supply to patients does not always 'enable patients to take medicines correctly'. Investigations over the last years [4] point to the necessity to reframe the situation towards 'the activities of people'. It is clear that an analysis of the fundamental activities and expectations of patients is required to find out what patients really believe and need when they interpret information about their medicines. But there are two other main stakeholders. The pharmaceutical industry and the Regulatory authorities are directly involved too. Their activities and expectations, albeit very different from patients, need to be considered too.

Any legislation should therefore take account of the activities of at least three groups:

a. legislation must enable regulators to check and control. The current legislation, guidelines, and templates do not provide enough grip on the matter. Many issues remain unresolved and need to be dealt with on 'a case by case basis'. This reduces the confidence in the regulatory system because it has lead to insonsistency in decisions.

b. legislation about information about medicines must enable people to act appropriately. The aim of the legal framework is to provide patients with relevant and useful information. The contents (figure 3) and design (figure 2) leaves much to be desired, although these examples have been approved and are therefore considered to be 'appropriate'.

c. legislation must support the pharmaceutical industry to develop information, and – if required – develop innovative artefacts. The current legal framework stifles and frustrates both these activities. Although it is absolutely essential to indicate a 'minimally acceptable level', it should also be possible to excel and make progress.

And this combination of requirements of these three groups is probably the main reason that it is so difficult to develop a report about the current shortcomings. Again, this is not new. All three groups have noticed this and discussed their views. It becomes now obvious that there must be some more fundamental reasons why intervention ambitions do not reach the different environments. Two questions should be answered:

- What are the reasons that progress does not occur? Can these reasons be overcome? (section 2).
- Could a performance based design process based on thorough user experience research provide an alternative? (section 3)

1.2   Answering the Questions?

Different kinds of testing, such as usability tests, readability tests, diagnostic tests and performance tests have been performed on different types of medicines and different groups of patients. Interviews with the pharmaceutical industry have been conducted at different stages. One group of stakeholders that has only be informally interviewed are the people who work for the national and European regulatory authorities. The text below highlights some patterns from the results of these tests and interviews. Although it would be useful to analyse these results in a more formal manner, it is likely to be too timeconsuming. Changes in regulatory framework occur very often, and it is likely that a thorough analysis would become irrelevant well before it is published.

2   Patterns Preventing Change

The three main assumptions that hamper progress are related to the differences between medicines, visual information development processes, and the lack of an acceptable quality control process.

2.1   Assumption 1: Information about different Medicines Can Follow Identical Structures

The European Medicines Agency (EMA) has developed a template that must be followed [5]. The template – currently version 9 - includes information on packaging and package leaflet and is available in 24 languages. All EU-packaging and EU-package leaflets are now based on this template. There is a range of guidelines and advice that is related to the the interpretation of this template.

However, different tests show that there are substantial and relevant differences between patients. Information about medicines for health care professionals, caregivers, adults, and for the elderly might need to vary, as well as information for experienced and newly diagnosed patients. At the moment all these differences are ignored by the template: every patient receives information in the same rigid structure.

There are also fundamental differences between medicines. Patients clearly indicate that medicines for short term use, such as antibiotics, painkillers, or cough-syrups, are perceived differently from long term medicines for chronic conditions like high blood pressure or high cholesterol levels. Medicines to treat diabetes and HIV-infections are seen as yet another category. And the location, such as hospitals or at home are seen as different too. The EMA-template does not cater sufficiently for these differences.

Unfortunately, the legislation, regulations, and templates start from an assumption that 'all medicines are the same' and that it is possible to standardize all information. A comparison of the results of 'readability tests' of medicines information suggests that this assumption is incorrect.

2.2   Assumption 2: Writing, Designing, and Testing Are Simple Rule Bound Practices

The use of a standardized template [5], rigid design guidelines [6], and standardized tests [6] is very hard to apply in practice. The assumption that underlies the legislation is that 'writing, designing, testing' are three consecutive and separate activities. The pharmaceutical industry develop a written texts using the template as a starting point and adding texts in between standardized statements in a unalterable structure. This text is formatted and designed according to some suggestions in the Readability guideline in combination with corporate guidelines. The design boundaries are further set by production requirements which dictate the maximum dimensions of the packaging and the package leaflet. According to EU-legislation, it is only necessary to test the package leaflet in one language. The packaging and information in additional languages is very rarely tested.

This disjointed approach, in which there is hardly a relation between the text, the visual design, and the testing requirements results in visual information that is not really satisfying anyone.

The pharmaceutical industry keeps therefor asking three questions:

- Are we writing the correct information?
- Are we designing the correct artefacts?
- Are we testing the correct actions?

For most medicines, none of these three questions can be answered positively.

From a regulatory point of view, this disjointed approach causes severe problems too. Although it is possible to check if a text follows a template, it is not possible to check if a text really is suitable for patients. The results of the readability tests are always positive and will show that patients can find and understand the main points. Howveer, the test reports will rarely indicate any issues that patients had with the standardised texts in the template. This is because a change in the standardised template texts might not be approved and this could lead to costly delays. It is very clear that the regulatory authorities take great care to make sure that information is as good as possible. However, there is a lack of suitable tools and guidelines that would help to check the quality of a text, to assess a visual design, and to evaluate test results.

Both the pharmaceutical industry as well as the regulatory authorities struggle with the current three-step process of writing, designing, and testing. The assumption that these are easily done and easily controlled proved to be incorrect.

2.3   Assumption 3: A Digital Submission and Control System Is Not Required

In the last 20 years, the different European regulatory authorities and the pharmaceutical industry have dealt with enormous numbers of packaging, labelling, and leaflets. All packaging and leaflets have been reconsidered, modified, and are still in the process of change to conform to continuously updated legislation. Unfortunately, this process has not been set up as a system. All participants had to find the rules and processes 'while running' their normal businesses.

Although attempts have been made to automate some of the registration process, but this turns out to be very difficult. The Product Information Management (PIM) system, which would have introduced standard forms of XML into the process grounded to a halt in 2011 [7].

At the moment, combinations of Microsoft Word files (version 2003; more modern versions 2007 and 2010 cannot be accepted [8]), and pdf-files are used. This practice makes it very difficult to control different versions, to check if modifications have been implemented, and to compare different files in different languages. Both pharmaceutical industry and regulatory authorities would like to develop a more practical and less time consuming approach because they agree that the current process is vulnerable.

3   Alternative Approach: Performance Based Design

The three assumptions in the previous section show the scope of the problem, and at the same time they provide a way forward. The approach that has been used since 1992 is to gradually change and modify the legislation and guidelines. Careful, step by step, progress was made. Unfortunately, the assumptions on which the legislation was based proved to be incorrect. Furthermore, the technology changed substantially, and best practice is very different from envisaged practice. Although it might be possible to 'upgrade current legislation' by small incremental changes, it is unlikely that these fundamental conflicts will disappear.

3.1   Focus on Actions in Context

Case studies [9] show that it is possible to develop prototypes that suit particular patients in a particular context if the first two assumptions are reversed. The starting points of these prototypes is that patients and medicines differ, and that writing, designing and testing are applied in an integral 'information development process'. Practical observations, user based design, performance based outcomes are all trained in education, developed in commercial practice, and investigated in experimental research.

This approach should be used as a basis for the development of information about medicines. The consequence of this is that 'performance based measures' need to be applied to studies that investigate the effectiveness of information in specific situations. This is 'best practice' in areas like usability, service design, and experience design. The transformation of this practice into legislation about medicines might be difficult, but is is likely to result in materials that 'really enable people to act appropriately'.

3.2   Integrate Digital and Analogue Modes

Most of the information about medicines that patients receive through the approved channels is still on paper. Combinations of analogue and digital methods have rarely been introduced until now. However, at the moment, most patients do have access to digital information, and it is time that personalized information about medicines is developed and becomes available in digital formats. This needs to be always in combination with information on paper and the relation between analogue and digital paper needs to be carefully considered and tested.

This practice is already common in other consumer domains. Phone bills, tax forms, and invoicing systems already deal with a combination of digital and analogue information. For the information about medicines, it is now possible to print personalized packaging, and personalized medicines regimen. 'Fridge door reminders', reminders as apps on smartphones, instructions on paper, and personalized e-mails are now all possible. Unfortunately, they are not developed further because the current regulatory framework does not allow for these artefacts.

Apart from the digital supply of information about medicines to patients, it is also necessary to develop electronic submission systems in a way that is similarly based on best practice and user-involvement. Most pharmaceutical industries use custom made digital document management systems. Unfortunately, there is hardly any standards across these systems, and the regulatory authorities should not be forced to familiarize themselves with all these differences. In this particular situation, standardization might be a real option.

3.3   Test Legislation, Regulations, and Guidelines

Before any of the abovementioned changes is made, it is essential to conduct substantial testing. All stakeholders need to be involved to provide their criteria, and different types of tests are required. Unsufficiently tested materials will certainly waste substantial amount of time of most parties and might do more harm than good. The current regulations, templates, and guidelines quite clearly show the negative consequences.

4   Conclusion

In order to provide information about medicines that is evidence based, performance oriented and user centered it is necessary to develop a regulatory framework that supports the ambition to modify situations, and supports the control function of regulators. Four things need to be considered to achieve this:

1. Medicines differ and patients differ. Standardisation is not an effective way to provide patients with relevant and appropriate information. It is essential to start from the perspective of patients and find patterns in their expectations and needs. Performance based information should be considered as a new assumption that underlies the next legislation.

2. Patients need reliable and independent information about their medicines that is guaranteed to be 'as correct as possible'. They expect a combination of digital and analogue information. The next legislation should allow for this.

3. For both regulators and industry, it becomes essential to see writing, designing, and testing as an integrated information development process. It seems necessary to provide regulators – who must check that information is correct and unbiassed – with advice and tools how they can really control the provision of reliable information. At the same time, the pharmaceutical industry needs to be supported to develop and submit information about medicines in standardised ways. It seems necessary to develop document management systems that support both.

4. None of these suggestions should be introduced without thorough testing in different contexts. Information about medicines needs to be tested with patients, and the regulatory framework needs to be tested with regulatory authorities and pharmaceutical industries.

Ultimately, we need to support and empower patients to take medicines correctly. The legal framework, and the economical considerations should become secondary. As long as legal arguments and profits prevail, patients will have to coop with visual information about medicines that does not really fulfil its potential.

References

1. EU Directive 2001/83/EU preliminary point 40
2. EU Directive 2004/27/EU, article 63
3. EU Directive 2010/84/EU, amending article 59 of 2001/83
4. Stickdorn, M., Schneider, J.: This is Service Design Thinking. BIS Publishers, Amsterdam (2010)
5. EMA QRD-template version 9 (2013), http://www.ema.europa.eu/docs/en_GB/document_library/Template_or_form/2009/10/WC500004368.pdf
6. Readability guideline (2009), http://ec.europa.eu/health/files/eudralex/vol-2/c/2009_01_12_readability_guideline_final_en.pdf
7. http://pim.emea.europa.eu/
8. http://www.ema.europa.eu/ema/index.jsp?curl=pages/regulation/document_listing/document_listing_000134.jsp
9. Sless, D., Shrensky, R.: Writing about medicines for people. In: Usability Guidelines for Consumer Medicine Information, 3rd edn. Communication Research Institute (2006)

A Collaborative Change Experiment: Telecare as a Means for Delivery of Home Care Services

Suhas Govind Joshi and Anita Woll

Departments of Informatics, University of Oslo, Norway
{joshi,anitwo}@ifi.uio.no

Abstract. This paper presents a collaborative change experiment that introduces telecare as a means for delivery of home care service. The television is used as platform for delivery of services from the home care nurses to the elderly care recipients. Through the collaborative change experiment, we seek to address the interdependent relationship between the home care nurses and the elderly by studying the usability and user experiences on both sides of the interaction. Our work includes usability testing with the aim of optimizing the design of telecare. This paper reports findings concerning the spatial design, compensation of declined motor skills, audiovisual considerations and control mechanisms.

Keywords: usability testing, elderly, telecare, collaborative change experiment.

1   Introduction

Norwegian health authorities have designated telecare as one of several welfare technologies that can be useful in future elderly care [1]. Increased focus on community care and follow-up assistance in the home is specifically aimed at those living in care homes or those who have recently returned from hospital admission [1, 2]. It is also important to encourage the home dwellers to partake in everyday preventive rehabilitation and keep them at a level of comfort and safety that postpones the admission to care home or nursing home. The main motivation of the government is the necessity of managing scarce health resources more efficiently in order to serve a rapidly growing elderly and chronically ill population. In addition, the municipal health care sector has been through major changes during the past decades, with home care services growing in scope of human resources and service tasks [1-3]. 40 years ago, the municipalities spent 80 percent of their operating expenses on retiring and nursing homes, and barely 20 percent on home care services [1]. Today, the annual operating expenditure of approximately 70 billion NOK is almost equally divided between the home care services (160 000 recipients) and nursing homes (40 000 nursing beds) [1]. The home care service struggles with the constant expansion of service tasks and increasingly need of staffing. According to an estimate from the Directorate of Health [2], the required personnel in health and care services will increase by approximately 50 percent, equal to 60 000 positions, within 2030. This illustrates the need to study alternative ways of delivering home care services, and how services can extend to professions other than merely skilled health care workers.

A. Marcus (Ed.): DUXU 2014, Part III, LNCS 8519, pp. 141–151, 2014.
© Springer International Publishing Switzerland 2014

Although telecare in the home is not a new invention, there is limited empirical research concerning practical usability testing of telecare interface. Hence, this paper contributes to the HCI-community by adding to existing research literature with findings from our usability study aiming to optimize the design of telecare. The study is based on fieldwork at Kampen Care+, a local care home building in Oslo, as well as studies of the work practice of the home care service in the district of Gamle Oslo. Kampen Care+ consists of 87 care homes for elderly who are unable to live independently. In order to introduce telecare as a means for delivery of home care services, we have designed a collaborative change experiment consisting of five activities. The change experiment is a part of a long-term study, and set to last for a period of nine months. We are currently six months into the experiment, and this paper reports from the three first activities of the collaborative change experiment with focus on findings from the usability testing.

The paper is organized as follows. Chapter 2 presents an overview of related HCI-studies including cooperative work, older home dwellers, television interfaces and telecare. Chapter 3 describes the collaborative change experiment. Chapter 4 lists the usability test results. Chapter 5 presents findings based on results and relates these to previous work within HCI.

2   Related Work

Several prior HCI studies have reported results and findings from collaborative or interactive services where elderly people use the television from their home as a platform to receive telecare or similar services.

In [4], the authors develop and test a social television system for the elderly that encourages increased communication among the elderly in the community. Their findings suggest that design process of the social network for elderly users should use a stepwise approach where the elderly begin by interacting locally with people they already know, before expanding the design to include larger user groups.

Several articles have addressed the age-related challenges when designing for the elderly [5-8]. [9] stress the importance of user-centered interface designs for the elderly and presents a number of challenges that may have impact on the design for the elderly including cognitive, physiological and psychomotor abilities. Since the call for research concerning how to make interfaces usable for older people in [9], several authors have contributed with new knowledge, e.g. [10, 11]. Further suggestions encourage studying elderly who already master the interface in the search for compensatory strategies that may be generally applicable to this user group in order to improve the user experience. [12] also bring attention to the user needs of elderly and the design implications for HCI. Their study is based on findings from structured interviews with health professionals and elderly people. The authors express concern about technologies used for monitoring brings very little attention to the social context of the home.

[13] continues the discussion on how the design of technology can meet the needs of the elderly. They point out that previous studies, e.g. [9], mainly deal with physical, sensory and cognitive limitations that come with aging, while they

themselves believe that one should also include aspects of *"privacy, acceptability, stigma, control, trust, choice and social alienation"* (p. 614) into the design process. Specifically, they believe that privacy and trust are key elements when HCI research enters private homes and communities. They also encourage exploring the need for user interfaces that stimulate *"healthy behavior such as exercise, medication management and social interactions"* (p. 619). [14] has taken a human factor approach in their study of HCI and telecare. Their contributions of the study are three guidelines for user experience that includes users' trust, their cooperation, as well as the service aspects of telecare.

[10] have studied elderly people's problems and experiences with interactive television (iTV). The authors point out that the television has evolved from a one-way monologue into a communications platform by offering more dialogue-based services. They also argue that an iTV provides more *"complex interaction paradigm"* (p. 13) since it usually involves additional equipment such as set-top box, additional monitor and media streaming device. Based on explorative interviews of 11 participants aged 60-69 years and a survey answered by 51 participants in a bingo center, they present 10 design guidelines for user interfaces of iTV services tailored for the elderly. Their guidelines include easy navigation, one universal remote control with simplistic design, use of certain colors to achieve optimal contrast between foreground and background, scaling of subtitles, as well as removing or hiding selected iTV services.

3   Collaborative Change Experiment

We have designed a collaborative change experiment consisting of five sequential activities. Through these five activities, we aim to experiment with alternative solutions to existing routines in the delivery of home care services. Our goal is not to bring in a permanent change, but rather to explore underlying issues and gain a deeper insight that may contribute to a future permanent change. To address the inter-dependency we have designed our collaborative change experiment in such a way that it captures challenges on both sides of the service.

Two traditional task-centered user evaluations make out the key activities in our change experiment, respectively one round of usability testing and one round of diagnostic evaluation. [15] mentions that few systems are mature enough when delivered to be accepted by the intended user group, and [16] mentions that technology-enabled assistive systems that aims to cover enhanced communication should include an extensive user evaluations. Common for both of these activities is that they have been expanded from a traditional user-observer setup to a parallel experiment where we have users and observers on both sides of the service simultaneously.

In addition to these two main activities, we have supplemented the collaborative change experiment with three supporting activities that we believe helps strengthen the design process, as well as make it more coherent. Through these auxiliary activities, we (1) address some of the challenges that are not directly covered by usability testing and diagnostic evaluation, and we (2) gain important input that contribute directly towards the facilitation of the usability testing and diagnostic evaluation. Figure 1 illustrates the five activities and their order.

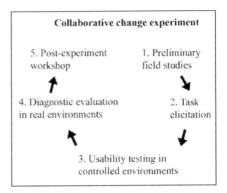

Fig. 1. Overview of the activities in the collaborative change experiment

3.1   Preliminary Field Studies

In [12], the authors present an approach to the design process where one sees past the ergonomic and purely physiological symptoms of aging, and rather focuses on addressing the actual needs of the elderly on a "higher level" (p. 674). Similar to (ibid) we wanted to approach our experiment with initial fieldwork on both sides of the service. On side of the elderly, we carried out fieldwork to get closer to the potential end-users. We wanted to immerse ourselves in the field in order to capture the social context in which we design. We also wanted to be as close to the actual use context of the technology, and as a result we did not only do interviews with them about where in the house they would prefer to have the technology placed, but we also had them invite us home and show us. They even let us move furniture and equipment around to explore different options. Furthermore, we also considered fieldwork necessary to establish confidence as it often takes time to gain acceptance in such a user group. [17] points out that it usually takes "a significant amount of time" (p. 69) to develop the local culture through which one wins their hearts and minds. By taking on the approach of [12], we simultaneously acknowledge that the elderly are individuals rather than one big homogenous group. Therefore, we demanded from ourselves that we do not overlook individual needs by generalizing the group as a whole, by rather aimed to address these individual challenges through the design. The elderly often struggle with explaining, and even understanding, their own declining functional capabilities, e.g. failing memory. Rather than having elderly non-technical people suffering from individual issues explaining challenges with the interface and interaction, we chose to look for these issues through observation.

On the other side of the interaction, the fieldwork mainly consisted of shadowing nurses during their work practice. We, along with our master students, have shadowed 30 visits into the homes of the elderly. With the exception of a few sensitive cases, we were invited along with home care nurses to watch and take notes, even though there were cases of partial nudity, heavy medication and bathroom assistance. Similar to the elderly, we do not see the home care nurses as one homogeneous group. To better understand their varying backgrounds we followed seven different home care nurses while they were delivering services, and how they experience it.

3.2   Task Elicitation

The purpose of the task elicitation was twofold. Firstly, we wanted to find representative tasks of home care nurses' work. By representative tasks, we mean tasks that (1) are often performed by nurses, preferably up to several times a day, and that (2) covers the needs of most residents in Kampen Care+. Secondly, we searched for tasks that were transferable. The home care nurses provide a range of services out of which only some are appropriate for telecare. By transferable tasks, we mean tasks that may be delivered without the physical presence of the homecare nurse, as opposed to certain tasks, e.g. helping the elderly take a shower or preparing their food, that necessarily require a physical interaction between the elderly and the home care nurse. However, transferable tasks are not guaranteed to be suited for delivery through the television. The goal of this task elicitation is only to filter out tasks that are both representative and transferable, and it is through the two activities of testing we determine which tasks better suit delivery through telecare.

Through our fieldwork, we registered difference in opinions about tasks frequency and task importance, even between nurses working within one team. The difference was mainly based on their professional responsibility as some were home care nurses and some were assistant nurses, although we also saw clear signs of difference in opinion between daytime nurses and nighttime nurses. To solve this difference of opinion we brought together representatives from all organizational units at the home care service. This gave us a forum in which all considerations could be taken, and the workshop yielded a list of tasks presented in Table 1.

Table 1. Overview of elicited tasks for the diagnostic evaluation and the usability testing

Task for diagnostic evaluation	Task for usability testing
1. Regular visit and examination of general condition	1. Answering a call
	2. Registering calls at unscheduled times
2. Help with taking medications	3. Validating text sizes and readability
	4. Zooming in on the body
3. Taking care of physical wounds	5. Testing the sound level
	6. Testing sound clarity during dialogue
4. Put on aid stockings to prevent edema	7. Simultaneous movement
	8. Testing picture clarity (color and sharpness)
	9. Panning between feet and head
5. Exercises from occupational therapists	10. Turn and move the camera
	11. Testing the light conditions

3.3   Usability Testing

The Setting. Kampen Care+ consists of 87 home care apartments, as well as 1 showroom apartment that have been dedicated to our research for testing purposes. It provides a near-real setting familiar to the participants and gives us the desired control over the environment without compromising the aspect of realism too much. The apartment is not very decorated, although we have recreated the sofa and television setting in which the interaction takes place.

The Design. The usability test is designed to include two participants at a time, one home care nurse providing a service from his office, and one elderly person receiving the service in our apartment. Both sides were equipped with 40-inch televisions and state of the art video conference wide-angle cameras. We have taken the role of observers on both side during the test and made parallel observations rather than forcing ourselves as evaluator to simulate realistic conditions and challenges. If we had chosen to either simulate one side of the interaction or conduct non-parallel observations, minor circumstantial changes could have given unfortunate bias in the measurement. Figure 2 illustrates the setup of the usability test, while Figure 3 shows photos taken during the usability testing.

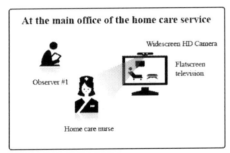

Fig. 2. Illustration of the setup of the usability test

Fig. 3. Photos taken during the usability test with the home care office on the left, and two participants from our showroom apartment on the right

Participants. We deliberately tried to avoid only including participants who were already well acquainted with various technology and different types of interfaces, even though some studies, e.g. [9], suggest making an effort to gather expert users. Very few of the residents at Kampen Care+ that would qualify to the definition given of expert users in (ibid) currently receive any home care services. For this reason, including only such elderly would yield participants that would contribute well in regards to the technical aspects, but would simultaneously lack personal knowledge of the home care services. Their statements would then not be based on personal experiences, but rather be purely analytical. As a result, we chose to prioritize the recruitment of a representative user group that mainly consisted of elderly who currently received home care services. [17] point out that the introduction of telecare requires a system able to meet the varying needs of the participants. Our selection of participants consisted of elderly with various health issues, as well as various prior experiences with technology. In regards to differences in gender, we did not make a distinct effort to recruit an equal number of men and women, despite some research, e.g. [11] referring to a "gender gap" (p. 8). Given the high average age of 83 year at Kampen Care+ the proportion of women was slightly higher in our selection. Nevertheless, we did not notice any increased anxiety or increased uncertainty related to technology even though (ibid) suggests that these traits can be prominent for elderly women interacting with technology.

At the home care service's side of the interaction, the participants were all home care nurses and assistant nurses. The experiment took place during their regular working hours in their own workplace built around their daily routines. Even though these nurses should not be regarded as one homogeneous group, the recruitment of participants was still a much more trivial affair than the recruitment of the elderly who receive the service. There is much less fluctuation in this group in terms of background and technical expertise. All participants were employable and functionally healthy people. As a result, we anticipated little observable difference in their interaction with the system.

4   Results

This chapter reports the result from the usability testing described in the previous chapter. The results are based on data gathered from eight in-depth sessions where we tested the tasks elicited for the usability testing. All eight participants were originally scheduled to test with our setup, including the television-camera solution described in the previous chapter, although two participants had to test on tablet devices due to immobility of that rendered them unable to come to our showroom apartment. Three participants wore glasses due to vision loss, one participant had reading glasses. One participant used a hearing aid. One participant said that he had a hearing loss in the sense that he heard what was said, but struggled understanding the meaning of words. The participants were asked to rate the audiovisual quality on a scale from 1 to 10, where 1 was very poor and 10 is excellent.

The participants were given brief instructions ahead of usability testing session including instruction of how to operate the remote controller. Three participants needed additional instructions along the session; however, they all manage to operate by themselves afterwards. We found no user problems with the two tasks (9) panning between feet and head and (10) turn and move the camera. Table 2 gives an overview of the user problems identified with the remaining tasks.

Table 2. Overview of tasks and the identified user problems

Task	Comment
1. Answering a call	• Poor colors contrast between the black background and the off-white foreground on the buttons. • Difficulty understanding if the button push has been registered.
2. Registering calls at unscheduled times.	• Some preferred the low-frequency alternative ringtone. • Ringtone should not be too similar to other devices. • Default ringtone is too close to sounding like a fire alarm. • Too long response time for television to turn on after incoming call has been accepted.
3. Validating text sizes and readability	• The language was unclear in some cases.
4. Zooming in on the body	• The zooming does enlarge an area, but does not result in a clearer picture.
5. Testing the sound level	• Microphones are very sensitive and thereby susceptible to interference and noise.
6. Testing sound clarity during dialogue	• Impaired sound due to room acoustics and reverberating. • Few cases of the sound appearing to be choppy.
7. Simultaneous movement	• The picture sometimes became unclear in situations with rapid movement or too much rocking back and forth. • Movement that covers and uncovers light sources may cause disturbance that requires the camera to readjust the aperture.
8. Testing picture clarity	• Unclear picture in some cases due to network issues.
11. Testing the light conditions	• Camera is too sensitive to changes in the light levels. • Different preferences on amount of light. Some preferred blurry lighting, while other disliked too strong lighting.

5   Findings

5.1   Spatial Design – Lighting and Acoustic

A key finding in our study is that when using a television in combination with a wide-angle camera that covers a larger area, it requires us to factor in spatial issues that are not prominent when interacting via a computer, tablet or mobile phone. In our case, one example of how the spatial design and arrangement affected the user experience during the video consultation was the lighting in the showroom apartment. During the usability testing, the room was lit by one single ceiling light that was placed noticeably far away from the sitting area and where the television resided. While the camera was usually able to compensate for low-light settings by increasing the exposure, the amount of light and the placement of the light source in relations to the camera became a noticeable factor. Similarly, we have observed floor or wall lamps in all the apartments we have visited at Kampen Care+, and these may easily generate too much artificial light making the picture overexposed. We stress this point because bad exposure, in either direction, may prevent the home care nurses from getting all the visual information they need, e.g. when looking for swelling or bruises.

Another aspect of spatial design is the room acoustics. One of the participants quickly pointed out that the voice reverberated in the room. When using camera-microphones designed to capture voice from distance, i.e. the distance between the television and sofa, acoustical consideration should also be taken into account. Admittedly, our showroom apartment is very primitively furnished, yet it is a significant point that even physical non-technological elements of the room such as the furniture may affect the user experience. In addition, open windows may cause noise and interference that disrupts the conversation. This was very evident in our case since the balcony and all major windows are placed adjacent to the television outlet. Similarly, for the home care nurses who were in a meeting room we also observed minor disturbances in the room, e.g. noises from ventilation.

5.2   Television Helps Compensate for Declined Motor Skills

Many user problems arise due to the inability for technology to adapt to motor challenges, which is a very prominent challenge among elderly. Several studies, e.g. [9-11], points out the importance of recognizing the physical capabilities of the elderly. By choosing a solution that is based around the television, i.e. a stationary device, we prevent the elderly from being confronted with their declined motor skills when using the system. Despite the fact that most of our participants had clear physical challenges, no one struggled interacting with the system as a result of their declined motor skills; this was not only the case for those with walkers, even our participant who was partially paralyzed and only had one functional arm was able to operate the system. We noticed no difference in the way they interacted with the system in comparison to the more functionally healthy participants. However, this still imposes strict requirements for design of the interaction mechanism, e.g. the remote control, since some challenges like rheumatism, are not automatically solved with this setup.

5.3   Audio-visual Considerations

Two participants struggled to capture high frequency sounds, which may indicate and support finding from [9] that interfaces using sound to get the user's attention will need to use lower frequency sounds for elderly users. Ringtones and other sounds used for signaling should therefore be in a lower frequency range to support age-related hearing impairment, or at least allow for individual adjustments of sound.

We also found some interesting traits in regards to visual considerations. When the home care nurse moved too much or too abruptly, the elderly quickly commented that the movement was disturbing and one even mentioned dizziness as a potential symptom. In addition, for infrastructure with bandwidth issues, too much movement might result in a choppy video transmission. The elderly preferred a minimum of motion from the home care nurse, partly due to dizziness, but also because they felt it created an unbalance where one participant was sitting and the other was vastly moving, thereby creating a disturbance in the dialogue.

It should also be possible to adjust the quality of the image, both the choice of prominent colors, as well as the sharpness of the image. This design aspect is supported by [9, 10].

5.4   Control of the Camera and Lighting

The main feedback regarding the remote control was that elderly suffering from visual impairments found it unsuitable because of its lack of contrasting colors. [10] does not address the color contrasts directly, although encourages the use of certain colors such as red, orange and yellow rather than green, blue and violet. We also found the remote adjustability of the camera to be of importance. Normally, people only have control of the camera on their own side, e.g. the ability to zoom, pan and adjust light settings, although during our usability test it became clear that both sides requested the ability to adjust not on their own side, but rather on the other. Other non-tested options include heat or motion seeking cameras, but since we are not anticipating much movement on either side of the interaction, these options may be redundant.

6   Conclusion

This paper has reported from a collaborative change experiment with focus on usability testing of telecare as means for delivery of home care services. Preliminary results from this study indicate that use of television as a platform for video consultation can compensate for many of the elderly challenges with novel interfaces accentuated through bodily and cognitive barriers. Our findings also imply the need to acknowledge spatial issues such as lightning and room acoustic.

References

1. Ministry of Education and Research, NOU 2011:11 - Innovasjon i omsorg. Ministry of Health and Care Services, Oslo (2011)
2. Directorate of Health, Velferdsteknologi. Fagrapport om implementering av velferdsteknologi i de kommunale helse – og omsorgstjenestene 2013-2020. Helsedirektoratet, Oslo (2012)
3. Ministry of Health and Care Services, Meld. St. 29 (2012-2013) - Morgendagens omsorg, Oslo (2013)
4. Miyazaki, M., Sano, M., Mitsuya, S., Sumiyoshi, H., Naemura, M., Fujii, A.: Development and field trial of a social TV system for elderly people. In: Stephanidis, C., Antona, M. (eds.) UAHCI/HCII 2013, Part II. LNCS, vol. 8010, pp. 171–180. Springer, Heidelberg (2013)
5. Carmichael, A., Newell, A.F., Morgan, M.: The efficacy of narrative video for raising awareness in ICT designers about older users' requirements. Interacting with Computers 19(5-6), 587–596 (2007)
6. O'Neill, S.A., et al.: Development of a Technology Adoption and Usage Prediction Tool for Assistive Technology for People with Dementia. Interacting with Computers 26(2), 169–176 (2014)
7. Sayago, S., Sloan, D., Blat, J.: Everyday use of computer-mediated communication tools and its evolution over time: an ethnographical study with older people. Interacting with Computers 23(5), 543–554 (2011)
8. Weiner, M.F., Rossetti, H.C., Harrah, K.: Videoconference diagnosis and management of Choctaw Indian dementia patients. Alzheimer's & Dementia 7(6), 562–566 (2011)
9. Hawthorn, D.: Possible implications of aging for interface designers. Interacting with Computers 12(5), 507–528 (2000)
10. Baunstrup, M., Larsen, L.B.: Elderly's Barriers and Requirements for Interactive TV. In: Stephanidis, C., Antona, M. (eds.) UAHCI/HCII 2013, Part II. LNCS, vol. 8010, pp. 13–22. Springer, Heidelberg (2013)
11. van de Watering, M.: The impact of computer technology on the elderly. In: Human Computer Interaction (2005)
12. Blythe, M.A., Monk, A.F., Doughty, K.: Socially dependable design: The challenge of ageing populations for HCI. Interacting with Computers 17(6), 672–689 (2005)
13. Goodman, J., Lundell, J.: HCI and the older population. Interacting with Computers 17(6), 613–620 (2005)
14. von Niman, B., et al.: User experience design guidelines for telecare services. In: Proceedings of the 8th Conference on Human-computer Interaction with Mobile Devices and Services. ACM (2006)
15. Huldtgren, A., Detweiler, C., Alers, H., Fitrianie, S., Guldemond, N.A.: Towards Community-Based Co-creation. In: Holzinger, A., Ziefle, M., Hitz, M., Debevc, M., et al. (eds.) SouthCHI 2013. LNCS, vol. 7946, pp. 585–592. Springer, Heidelberg (2013)
16. Lee, C., et al.: Integration of medication monitoring and communication technologies in designing a usability-enhanced home solution for older adults. In: 2011 International Conference on ICT Convergence (ICTC). IEEE (2011)
17. Beale, S., et al.: The initial evaluation of the Scottish telecare development program. Journal of Technology in Human Services 28(1-2), 60–73 (2010)

Design for Reading and Learning

Innovative Educational Technology
for Special Education and Usability Issues

Kursat Cagiltay[1], Filiz Cicek[1], Necdet Karasu[2], Hasan Cakir[3],
and Goknur Kaplan Akilli[1]

[1] Department of Computer Education and Instructional Technology, Faculty of Education,
Middle East Technical University, Ankara, Turkey
`{kursat,akilli,fcicek}@metu.edu.tr`
[2] Department of Special Education, Faculty of Education, Gazi University, Ankara, Turkey
`necdetkarasu@gazi.edu.tr`
[3] Department of Computer Education and Instructional Technology, Faculty of Education,
Gazi University, Ankara, Turkey
`hasanc@gazi.edu.tr`

Abstract. The purpose of this study is to introduce educational technology project, OZTEK, for special education students and present usability issues related to those developed technologies. With the OZTEK, the researchers intend to develop innovative, technology enhanced learning environments to support the education of children with such special needs and to investigate effectiveness of such learning environments.

Within the scope of the OZTEK, to provide support for special education, various instructional technologies have been developed, which are unique in terms of innovation regarding not only in Turkey but also other countries in the world. Throughout the project the following products will be developed which can either be used separately as standalone tools or together as a whole obtained by integration to each other: Interactive multimedia educational software that will detect body movements, interactive multi-touch table/board, applications and smart/interactive toys.

In this paper, the findings regarding how computer supported educational materials for special education have been developed, what kind of usability challenges were faced with, how challenges have been overcome and how those technologies are used by teachers and students are presented.

Keywords: Usability, innovative technology, technology enhanced learning environments, special needs, students with special needs.

1 Introduction

Even though the rates of special education services that children with mental disabilities benefited from have increased in recent years, the offering of effective educational services and the use of innovative instructional materials did not reach to the desired point yet. Therefore, quality of the present state of education offered

A. Marcus (Ed.): DUXU 2014, Part III, LNCS 8519, pp. 155–163, 2014.

to children with such special needs is questionable. Related to this, there is lack of information related to how instructional technology are utilized in special education.

Use of technology in education of students with disabilities has a considerable history. The literature provided evidence that several technological instruments might be used effectively in the classrooms (King-Sears & Evmenova, 2007; Hasselbring & Glaser, 2000; Alper & Raharinirina, 2006; Williams, Jamali & Nicholas, 2006). The technology not only targets teaching related to a certain content area but also might focus on limiting the difficulties caused by a disability (Hasselbring & Glasser, 2000; Lancioni & others, 2011; Lancioni et al, 2010; Kaspi-Tsahor, Heiman & Olenik-Shemesh, 2011).

The primary goal of the this project is to develop and produce technology enhanced learning programs in the light of the designated special education curriculum, for teaching basic essential and cognitive concepts. To be utilized for the education of children with special needs, OZTEK (Investigation of the teaching process of basic essential and cognitive concepts to Special education students and its effectiveness using Technology Enhanced Learning environments) has been designed and developed as interactive environments, which are consisted of content that is edited and enriched specifically for such children and of multimedia that addresses all the senses by providing audio/visual/physical and tactile interactions. Considering the cost/performance tradeoff, these technologies will be developed as to be accessible not only to schools but also to everyone including home users who own a personal computer and have an Internet access.

2   Methodology

Observation methodology, particularly nonparticipant observation, and unstructured interviews were used to collect data from the first testing process. In the process of nonparticipant observation, "researchers do not participate in the activity being observed but rather "sit on the sidelines" and watch; they are not directly involved in the situation they are observing" (Fraenkel, Wallen & Hyun, 2012, p. 446). Therefore, special education students were observed to understand usability related issues without participating the game itself. Moreover, opinion and advices of teachers for correction of the materials were taken during testing as well as interviewing with them after testing.

2.1   Research Questions of the Study

This study will be sought answers for the following question:

- What is the usability (effectiveness, efficiency and satisfaction) of the materials developed in the project by teachers?

In this study, the findings regarding how computer supported educational materials for special education have been developed, what kind of usability challenges were faced with, how challenges have been overcome and how those technologies are used by teachers and students were presented and discussed.

2.2   Participants

First of all, the prototype developed with the help of Kinect technology to improve social skills of students had revised and evaluated by an instructional technology specialist and a special education specialist at early stages of project before 2 special education teachers were interviewed about the prototype and some students were observed while they were interacting with the prototype. Additionally, before the prototype was developed, developers tested similar Kinect based games with 5 students with special needs in order to understand attitudes and abilities of the students related to usage of the games. In parallel of development of Kinect based prototype, an interactive multi-touch table/board game, which aims to help improvement of the life skills of the students, was tested with 2 students with special needs and then 3 special education teachers were interviewed in order to investigate the weaknesses of the interactive multi-touch table game and poor aspects of it. Lastly, smart/interactive toys were tested with 1 student with special needs and evaluated 1 special education teacher in order to get feedbacks in development process.

2.3   Instruments

Under the project, in order to respond to research questions, many new instructional technology products have been produced in the purpose of to support the educational process of mentally handicapped children, not only for our country but also for other countries in the world. The materials to be developed can be used integrated with each other or separately. In this projects, materials have been developing in three different areas:

Kinect-based Game. Kinect-based serious game developed to practice the process of making shopping in order to improve the students' social skills. In this digital game, there are two shelves with 5 milk cartons per half liter placed on each shelf. In the beginning of the game, the student hears an instruction: "Get a carton of milk and drop into the basket". After then, when the student put his hand on one of the milk cartons and waits for over 2 seconds, the milk carton sticks into hand. Additionally, right after leading to cart, the milk carton is dropped into cart from the hand and the sound of applause can be heard as reinforcement (see Fig. 1). All these sequential operations happen by using students' bodily movements (see Fig. 2).

Fig. 1. Kinect-based game interface

Fig. 2. A scene from the student's performance

The game was developed with Unity game engine and requires a PC, a Kinect camera and a projector or TV to run. There will be three difficulty levels in the game that enable mentally handicapped children on the different level of intellectual disability to access the game.

Interactive Multi-touch Table/board Application. A mobile application was developed in order to teach to mop floor as one of the cleaning skills in order to improve the life skills of the students (see Fig. 3 and Fig. 4). The application has certain sequential steps: Firstly, a step is shown to students in the app and then the students apply it as it was shown previously. The application was designed to be used with the help of teachers and parents so as to ensure that the students master this skill and provide implementation of the skill into everyday life without problems to be faced by students. The application was run on tablet.

Fig. 3. Interface of mopping floor application

Fig. 4. Interface of mopping floor application -2

Smart/interactive Toys Game. A game was designed with the help of smart toys to teach appropriate clothes for each season of a year. Miniature outfits were designed as much as similar how they appear on the screen and RFID sensors were placed into the outfits. When the student uses RFID reader for the game, the selected outfit appears on the screen or related instruction is given based on correct/wrong selection.

The game consists of history and game parts. Firstly, the history part of the game gives information related to chosen season of the year and the body parts that we put clothes on. Secondly, after given information in history part, the game starts and ask for the appropriate clothe for the chosen season among two presented clothes on the sides of the character (see Fig. 5 and Fig. 6). If the student is able to select correct clothe which matches with the season, the sound of applause and "thank you, I can wear a hat for sun protection" can be heard. Unless the student selects the right one, 2 different clothes continue to appear in the bubbles on both sides of the character. For wrong selection, "if I wear a thick knit beret, I can sweat and get sick" and "now look at them carefully and try again" can be heard as instructions.

Fig. 5. Seasons-themed Smart toys' Interface

Fig. 6. Seasons-themed Smart toys' Interface -2

3   Findings

In this part, the opinions of the teachers about the developed materials and the observation of the students are examined and reviewed. During the development of the materials, the materials were revised based on suggestions of subject matter experts and a specialist in instructional technology.

3.1   Findings Related to Kinect-Based Game

In overall, the first prototype of the game was found appropriate to test with the students at special education schools by the instructional technology specialist and the special education specialist because of short stories, focused and adequate illustrations, selection of products in everyday life in the game. Moreover, two special education teachers stated that visuals used in the game are suitable due to real-like representations of the actual objects. However, one of the teacher emphasized the distinctness between designs of objects in order to support obvious object detection and distinction between the objects. Addition to this, importance of videos of the stories and verbal instructions were underlined.

The findings regarding usability issues, apparently the students were able to use the materials easily, nevertheless, at the beginning of the process, the students experienced difficulties in getting used to play the game because of the lack of videos that show how to play the game. Thus, one of the teachers suggested that there can be a video that demo how to hold an object in the game. Additionally, another teacher pointed out that a user manual might be prepared for teachers in order to present what skills are taught at which stage or the contents of each level so as to increase the usability of the material.

3.2   Findings Related to Interactive Multi-touch Table/board Application

The design and flow of the game are found appropriate to use for the students with special needs by the teachers. Also, the application got attention of the students due to appearing on the tablet. However, they pointed out that the background should be more realistic and it should remind students about the place where they prepare cleaning equipment and where they would clean in real instead of using plane background in one color in order to enhance understanding of new concept and relation among the objects. Moreover, during testing process of the app, verbal instructions, quality of them (stress, tone of voice, apparentness), repetition of actions and certain distinction between the steps come out as points that should be considered for useful and effective application design for the students with special needs.

Furthermore, as findings in terms of usability issues, buttons for navigations on the screens are small and so the students have difficulties in using them. For this reason, the buttons need to be bigger. Additionally, there should be more control buttons that enable the teachers to have more supervision in game. Besides these, there should be a user manual that describes steps of the cleaning activity and present new objects and concepts to be used for this activity.

3.3   Findings Related to Smart/interactive Toys Game

The seasons-themed smart toys' game starts with a story which describes the season. According to the teacher, the story should be shorter and shouldn't be only with voice. Moreover, the objects and characteristics of seasons in the game and story should be given more obvious, clear and understandable. The clothes are given as selectable objects shouldn't mean slightly different clothes. For example, jumper-T-shirt combination is considered as good example instead of shirt-T-shirt combination. Furthermore, in this game, verbal instruction and their quality are pointed out as very important point once again. Because, verbal instructions describes every single action, they use as reinforcement and in this manner they lead students to follow steps of activities.

Furthermore, for this game, there is a need to prepare a user manual. It should have boy and girl avatars and also the RFID reader should introduce as the hand of avatars as well as identifying seasonal pictures and clothes and their explanations. The students experienced difficulties in recognizing that RFID reader refers to avatar's hand, thus the teacher suggested that RFID reader should be dressed as a hand to help the students make the connection. Moreover, the teacher stated that the miniature outfits as smart toys should represent real feeling of fabrics no matter what it is.

4   Discussion and Conclusion

The study focuses on innovative educational technology for special education and usability issues. This study aims to examine the materials developed for students with special needs in order to understand the usability of the games, students' impressions and teachers' opinions about them. Moreover, the findings related to the materials might help to improve the software developed and gain a perspective for developing similar material considering future studies.

In general, findings related the materials showed that quality of verbal instructions, size of designed objects and controls, having a user manual and real-like design are at the forefront of usable designs in special education field. For instance, if verbal instruction can be used effectively and properly, it can reduce usability issues. Because, sometimes the students were confused about what the next step is or about reinforcements due to lack of correct and sufficient verbal instructions. Teachers' verbal instructions help students stay on task (Williams, 2009) and in special education, teaching with visual reinforcement and supportive verbal instruction is considered as promising teaching approach (Davis & Florian, 2004). Thus, verbal instructions should be prepared carefully and their quality also be taken into account.

For all materials, there is a need to provide a user manual. User manual might remove some usability issues, because the user manual aims to assist teachers in effectively operating a system (Chafin, 1982). Thus, in order to help the teachers and students to use the materials effectively and efficiently, user manuals might be provided in special education as well.

Acknowledgement. This study was supported by TUBITAK under grant SOBAG 111K394.

References

1. Alper, S., Raharinirina, S.: Assistive technology for individuals with disabilities: A review and synthesis of the literature. Journal of Special Education Technology 21(2), 47–82 (2006)
2. Chafin, R.L.: User manuals: What does the user really need? In: Barlett, J., Walter, J. (eds.) Proceedings of the 1st Annual International Conference on Systems Documentation (SIGDOC 1982), pp. 36–39. ACM, New York (1982)
3. Davis, P., Florian, L.: Teaching Strategies and Approaches for Children with Special Educational Needs, A scoping study [Research Report 516]. DfES, London (2004)
4. Fraenkel, J.R., Wallen, N.E., Hyun, H.H.: How to Design and Evaluate Research in Education, 8th edn. McGraw-Hill, N.Y. (2012)
5. Hasselbring, T.S., Glaser, C.H.W.: Use of computer technology to help students with special needs. The Future of Children 10(2), 102–122 (2000)
6. Kaspi-Tsahor, D., Heiman, T., Olenik-Shemesh, D.: Assistive Technology for Students with Blindness or Visual Impairments. In: Koehler, M., Mishra, P. (eds.) Proceedings of Society for Information Technology & Teacher Education International Conference 2011, pp. 403–407 (2011)
7. King-Sears, M.E., Evmenova, A.S.: Premises, principles, and processes for integrating technology into instruction. Teaching Exceptional Children 40(1), 6–14 (2007)
8. Lancioni, G.E., O'Reilly, M.F., Singh, N., Sigafoos, J., Oliva, D., Smaldone, A., La Martire, M., Navarro, J., Spica, A., Chirico, M.: Technology-assisted programs for promoting leisure or communication engagement in two persons with pervasive motor or multiple disabilities. Disability and Rehabilitation: Assistive Technology 6(2), 108–114 (2011)
9. Lancioni, G.E., Singh, N.N., O'Reilly, M.F., Sigafoos, J., Didden, R., Pichierri, S.: Automatic Prompting and Positive Attention to Reduce Tongue Protrusion and Head Tilting by Two Adults With Severe to Profound Intellectual Disabilities. Behavior Modification 34(4), 299–309 (2010)
10. Williams, D.S.: The role of verbal and nonverbal communication between students with special needs and their teachers in middle school. Doctoral dissertation, Walden University, Minneapolis, Minnesota (2009)
11. Williams, P., Nicholas, D.: Testing the usability of information technology applications with learners with special educational needs (SEN). Journal of Research in Special Educational Needs 6(1), 31–41 (2006)

Examining the Interfaces to E-journal Articles: What Do Users Expect?

Mary C. Dyson and Elizabeth M. Jennings

Department of Typography & Graphic Communication, University of Reading, UK
M.C.Dyson@reading.ac.uk, E.M.Jennings@student.reading.ac.uk

Abstract. Researchers are increasingly relying on e-journals to access literature within their fields. The design of the interfaces to these journals is determined by the individual host or publisher and there appears to be little standardization. This exploratory study samples a set of sixteen home screens of e-journals from different disciplines and identifies common features across the set. The particular wording used to identify the features and their locations are recorded. An online survey of e-journal readers investigates where users would normally expect to locate features when first accessing a journal article. Comparison of observed and expected locations confirms inconsistencies across interfaces in terminology and locations. Mental models of the interface design do not appear to be well developed. A move toward standardization, based on some existing conventions, is desirable.

Keywords: conventions, standardization, screen layout.

1 Introduction

A primary means for researchers to gain access to academic knowledge is through e-journals. In the UK, studies adopting a fairly general perspective have looked at how academic libraries support research and teaching; how reading patterns differ across articles and books; how researchers have responded to the convenience of access to e-journals; and how this access has influenced the quantity and quality of research outcomes, e.g. [1-2]. Looking in more detail at researchers' search behaviors on publisher e-journal platforms, preferences have been found for particular routes to journal articles, e.g. gateway or third-party sites [1].

Library and Information Science approaches identify and analyze system functionality and users' search strategies, but the design of user interfaces does not fall within their scope. With the plethora of routes to journal articles, i.e. through gateways, hosts, via databases or discovery services, a researcher may encounter many different interfaces before reaching the article itself. Although functionality may be similar, publishers use different terms, and their screen layouts vary. In particular, a researcher working in an inter- or multi-disciplinary field, such as HCI or Information Design, researches topics that cross many subjects which therefore require interaction with a wide range of resources. Typically researchers wish to

A. Marcus (Ed.): DUXU 2014, Part III, LNCS 8519, pp. 164–172, 2014.

locate various items or tools, e.g. author guidelines, citation tools, past issues of a journal. Tools for interacting with the content may go beyond navigation to offer image manipulation, e.g. Elsevier's Protein Viewer.

1.1 Potential Problems

Whilst the current situation provides greater flexibility than previously, and the affordances of the interfaces are increased, the different layouts and manipulation tools may introduce inefficiencies and frustration. General Internet users have mental models for the location of various web objects, e.g. home link, navigation areas [3-4]. Violating visual conventions can leave users disoriented and hinder their performance [5]. However, if such conventions have not yet developed for e-journal articles, mental models are unlikely to exist or may be inaccurate, given the diversity of interface designs.

Current technology offers many data visualization tools that may be embedded as interactive image features. This great variety of tools and associated lack of standardization may also provide users with a more complex environment in which to diagnose and recover from technical problems. Users' inability to complete tasks frequently leads to frustration, as established by [6-8].

2 Methods of Investigation

This exploratory study develops a systematic description of a number of interface features against which users' expectations can be compared by:

- Analysing the interface designs of e-journals to determine whether they are consistent in the naming and location of specific items
- Collecting data on researchers' expectations regarding the location of common features
- Pilot work on identifying and analyzing examples of interactive image features

2.1 Analysis of Features in e-journal Interfaces

Sixteen examples of the home screens of e-journals were selected, which aimed to cover different publishers (e.g. Elsevier, Wiley, ACM, Taylor & Francis); and disciplines (e.g. HCI, Neuroscience, Design history, Chemistry, Psychology). Screen shots were overlaid with a grid of 2 inch squares to delineate areas of the screen (Fig. 1 and Fig. 2).

Features that recur on most pages were identified and their location within one or more of the cells recorded, along with the particular wording used to identify that feature. From this list of sixteen, seven features were selected for the user survey based on those which appeared to be present in most of the sample, and those that were considered relevant to users' typical activities. The wording on the survey took account of the different descriptors, i.e. alternatives were indicated. The features were

About this journal/Aims and scope; Email/article alerts; Guide or instructions for authors/submit manuscript; Help or Contact us; Login/Sign in; Name of journal probably including thumbnail (small image) of cover; Search the journal.

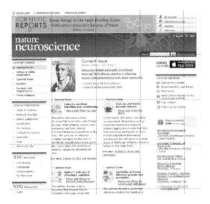

Fig. 1. Example screens with grids to divide area into 16 cells

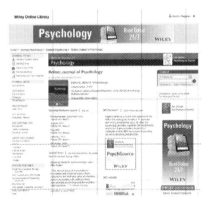

Fig. 2. Example screens with grids to divide area into 16 cells

2.2   Survey of Researchers' Expectations

An online survey was distributed to academics, research staff, and postgraduate students within the University of Reading, UK, and 53 responses were received. This asked respondents to indicate where they would normally expect to locate features when first accessing a journal article. They were provided with a 4 x 4 grid with numbered cells to locate items (Fig. 3) and could propose more than one cell per item, or more than one area. This was considered necessary to allow for respondents' uncertainty over precise locations. These questions were followed by a question on locating the *Export citation* feature, having accessed a journal article. For this question, a modified grid indicated possible areas (Fig. 4)

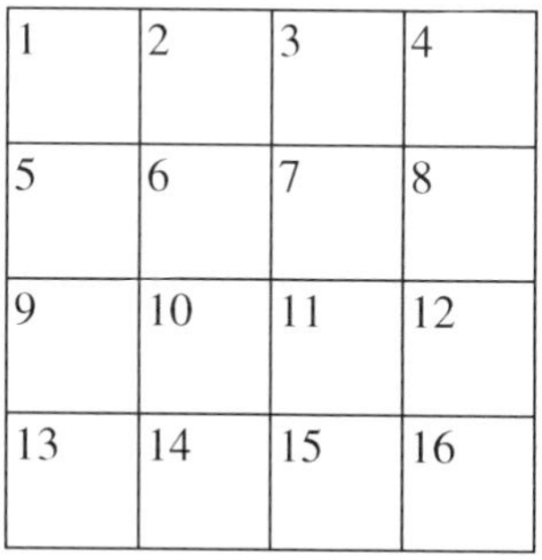

1	2	3	4
5	6	7	8
9	10	11	12
13	14	15	16

Fig. 3. Grid indicating possible locations of features

1	2	3	4
5	Article title Authors		8
9	Abstract etc.		12
13	14	15	16

Fig. 4. Grid representing first page of journal article, to indicate location of *Export citation* feature

2.3   Examples of Interactive Image Features

Two interactive image features were identified within journal articles: one employing Elsevier's Java-based Protein Viewer; [1] the second embedding a Google Earth layer to provide supplementary geospatial data to users.[2]

3   Results

The survey asked which journals respondents access most frequently, to gain an idea of the disciplines covered. Science, Social Sciences, Arts and Humanities were represented, which provides a reasonable match with the selection of examples included in the analysis (see 2.1). About two thirds of respondents reported that they typically use a desktop computer to locate articles, and the remaining third, a laptop, rather than tablets or phones. The grid could therefore be considered a reasonable representation of a typical home screen.

3.1   Observed Locations

The location of *About this journal* is heavily dependent on the publisher, and can fall in any one of 7 cells, mainly in the top area of the page. The other features are spread across fewer distinct locations. For example *Email or article alerts* are in the top right (8 out of 15 instances)[3] or the middle left (4/15); *Guide for authors* tends to be positioned on the right around the middle (7/14), but a few publishers use the middle left (4/14). The features which are more generic, i.e. there are parallels on other web

---

[1] http://dx.doi.org/10.1016/j.jmb.3009.11.045
[2] http://dx.doi.org/10.1016/j.tecto.2005.08.029
[3] Although 16 journals were included in the analysis, some did not include all of the features. The total number of possible locations may therefore be less than 16.

sites, are clustered in one area of the screen: *Login* across the top, mainly on the right (7 of the 14 at the top are on the right); *Name of journal*, top left (10/16); *Search the journal*, top right (8/15) or top left (4/15). *Help or Contact us* is mainly in the top right (8/16).

3.2   Expected Locations

Figs 5 to 11 summarize the locations indicated by respondents for each feature, with numbers indicating frequency of responses,[4] and darker shading reflecting greater agreement.[5]

The *Export citation* feature (Fig. 12) was recalled as appearing in various locations on screen. Although this feature was not included in the analysis described above, the personal frustration of the first author was the motivation for including this feature. This experience was echoed by one respondent commenting on e-journal interfaces: 'I wish they were more standardised. The hardest thing to find is the citation manager link!'

Other general comments reinforced the desire for standardization: 'It would be useful if they all have a standard layout, that is, where search article, guidelines to authors, etc. are located'. One respondent commented on who might be responsible for the problem: 'When the link to each task is not located where I expected it to be I tend to question the designer of the interface or the publisher.' This opinion runs counter to [9] who suggests that when users of information design products have difficulties, they may attribute them to their own ineptitude. This divergence may be explained by the particular user group, i.e. academics may tend not to blame themselves. There was also a negative perception of the overall interface design: 'websites are usually very cluttered'.

14	12	8	7
23	16	9	6
3	2	1	1
1	1	0	2

Fig. 5. *About this journal*

4	0	5	17
6	0	2	15
8	1	1	15
4	1	1	9

Fig. 6. *Email alerts*

1	4	6	6
8	1	0	10
13	3	2	10
10	8	8	6

Fig. 7. *Guide for authors*

---

[4] Data is reported as frequencies, rather than converting to percentages, as the frequencies enable a comparison of the strength of responses across features.

[5] Shading was applied to bands of 5 responses with 36-40 shaded black.

2	1	6	20
1	0	0	6
2	0	0	1
18	15	14	20

Fig. 8. *Help or Contact us*

4	7	11	33
7	3	4	6
1	2	2	1
0	1	0	1

Fig. 9. *Login/sign in*

32	36	18	4
7	9	4	1
1	0	0	0
2	1	0	0

Fig. 10. *Name of journal*

3	8	10	18
13	15	11	15
2	2	3	3
0	0	0	1

Fig. 11. *Search the journal*

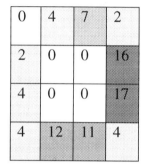

0	4	7	2
2	0	0	16
4	0	0	17
4	12	11	4

Fig. 12. *Export citation*

3.3   Comparison of Expected and Observed Locations

The most consistent responses are the expected locations of *Login/sign in* and *Name of journal*. Sites which require logins commonly place these in the top right and users expect this location [4]; e-journals are generally adopting this convention. The journal name is commonly located top left, as respondents suggest. However, a few are positioned slightly lower down, as the name of the publisher or the host takes the top left position (Fig. 13).

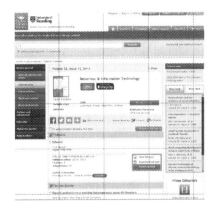

Fig. 13. Journal name is located lower as publisher's name occurs first

Help or Contact us is slightly less consistent, reflecting a spread of expected locations across the bottom of the screen, rather than on one side, and a separate location at the top right. This split was also found by [4] for their help link. The top right is the most frequent observed location, but various other positions were recorded. The lack of standardization and ambiguity in respondents' locations may be due to conflation of similar, though not necessarily identical, functions. In the analysis stage, the wording recorded included help, contact us, support, FAQ. To simplify, and allow for different terms for the same feature, the survey used the descriptors *Help or Contact us*.

The *Guide for authors/submit manuscript* shows the most variation among participants as to its expected location, even though it tends to be found in similar locations across publishers. This might be explained by the frequency with which users access this feature, in comparison with the others. Its location may be more difficult to recall if it has not been incorporated into user's mental models.

The diversity of responses in locating *Email or article alerts* may also be due to the infrequent use of this feature. Once alerts are set up using this tool, there is no need to repeat the process. Nevertheless, there is some association between the observed locations (top right and middle left) and expectations, although respondents suggest more use of the right side than was found in the sample that was analyzed.

An example of the reverse situation is *About this journal*, where observed locations are distributed across various parts of the screen but respondents are more consistent in their responses. Respondents generally expected to find this feature in the top area of the screen, more likely on the left, and below the journal name. This seems to be a logical position given the introductory nature of this feature. Users expect to find *About us* in a similar area of the screen in online shops, news portals, and company web pages [4].

The search bar can be quite wide (Fig. 12) and therefore extend over a number of cells. This is reflected in both the observed and expected locations. However, respondents positioned the feature at both the top and lower down. The lower positions may be taking account of the location of other features, such as the journal name and login, above the search tool.

3.4 Analysis of Interactive Image Features

We were unable to load the Jmol-based Protein Viewer in any web browsers available to us, which illustrated that security and other settings can impede a user's ability to access applets integrated into web publications. In contrast, the Google Earth layer functioned seamlessly and provided a more satisfactory user experience. In the next stage of our research, we intend to explore how a user's frustrating experience with one interactive image feature may influence a second, subsequent experience with another image feature.

4 Conclusions

The exploratory analysis and survey suggest that:

- Features do not share common locations across publishers' interfaces
- Where there may be only two distinct locations, these are on different sides of the screen
- There is variation in terminology
- E-journal interfaces are adopting some visual conventions from other types of web sites to locate more generic features that are shared among sites

Many users may not yet have developed a coherent mental model of the overall layout because:

- Some features are rarely used
- Inconsistency among regularly used interfaces may inhibit transfer from one journal to another
- The interfaces appear cluttered

Limitations and recommendations:

- The small scale nature of the study and the relatively crude measurement tools (i.e. coarse grids) suggest caution in deriving any firm conclusions
- There may be some constraints placed on the overall design in order to fit with the brand or template used by the publisher or host
- A move towards standardization of the terminology and location of the most common features, drawing on existing conventions where possible, would ease frustrations in interacting with the interfaces

References

1. Research Information Network: E-journals: their use, value and impact (2011),
   http://www.rin.ac.uk/our-work/communicating-and-
   disseminating-research/e-journals-their-use-value-and-impact
   (February 6, 2014)

2. Tenopir, C., Volentine, R.: UK scholarly reading and the value of library resources: Summary results of the study conducted spring 2011. JISC Collections Center for Information and Communication Studies, University of Tennessee, Knoxville, TN (2012)
3. Shaikh, A.D., Lenz, K.: Where's the search? Re-examining user expectations of web objects. Usability News 8(1) (2006), http://usabilitynews.org/wheres-the-search-re-examining-user-expectations-of-web-objects/ (February 6, 2014)
4. Roth, S.P., Schmutz, P., Pauwels, S.L., Bargas-Avila, J.A., Opwis, K.: Mental models for web objects: Where do users expect to find the most frequent objects in online shops, news portals, and company web pages? Interacting with Computers 22(2), 140–152 (2010)
5. Santa-Maria, L., Dyson, M.C.: The effect of violating visual conventions of a website on user performance and disorientation. How bad can it be? In: SIGDOC 2008, pp. 47–54 (2008)
6. Ceaparu, I., Lazar, J., Bessiere, K., Robinson, J., Shneiderman, B.: Determining causes and severity of end-user frustration. International Journal of Human-Computer Interaction 17(3), 333–335 (2004)
7. Hertzum, M.: Frustration: A common user experience. In: Hertzum, M., Hansen, M. (eds.) DHRS 2010: Proceedings of the Tenth Danish Human-Computer Interaction Research Symposium, Computer Science Research Report 132, Roskilde University, Roskilde, Denmark (2010)
8. Lazar, J., Jones, A., Shneiderman, B.: Workplace user frustration with computers: An exploratory investigation of the causes and severity. Behaviour & Information Technology 25(3), 239–251 (2006)
9. Adams, A.: Usability testing in information design. In: Zwaga, H.J.G., Boersema, T., Hoonhout, H.C.M. (eds.) Visual Information for Everyday Use, pp. 3–20. Taylor & Francis, London (1999)

The Impact of Media and Background Color on Handwriting

Chao-Yang Yang[1], Wei-Lin Hsu[2], and Ting-Yi Chou Huang[3]

[1] Department of Industrial Design, Tatung University, No.40, Sec. 3,Zhongshan N. Rd.,
Taipei City 104, Taiwan
dillon.yang@gmail.com
[2] Department of Industrial Design, Chang Gung University, 259, Wen Hua 1st Rd,
Kuei Shan, Tao-Yuan, Taiwan
sidney790711@gmail.com
[3] Department of Industrial Design, Chang Gung University, 259, Wen Hua 1st Rd,
Kuei Shan, Tao-Yuan, Taiwan
team0213@hotmail.com

Abstract. Handwriting is an important issue in Taiwan's school system, and it remains to be determined if tablet computers are a suitable medium for the development of good handwriting. The primary purpose of this study is to determine whether visual and tactile instructional strategies can be used to help students improve their handwriting performance. The study recruited 31 6th grade elementary school students to hand write a short phrase on backgrounds of various colors (white, red, yellow, green and blue), both on pen and on tablet computer. Finally, a questionnaire was administered to determine emotional associations with the various background colors. Results showed that media type does have an impact on handwriting performance, with familiar media (paper) providing better results. Descriptive statistics indicate that using a red background provided the best subjective and objective performance, and consistently produced characters of better proportional size. Red was also found to have an emotional association with excitement and triggered positive emotions among the students.

Keywords: tablet computer, color, writing, handwriting, educational strategy.

1 Introduction

1.1 Research Background and Motivation

Many studies have verified that the use of tablet computers can lead to improved learning outcomes (Hulls, 2005; McClanahan, Williams, Kennedy, & Tate, 2012). Handwriting function on tablet computers is useful for handwriting practice while simultaneously allowing users to engage in visual learning strategies. In addition, many studies have examined the use of color as a learning strategy, confirming that different colors have varying impacts on learner achievement (Arnold, 1972; Fordham

A. Marcus (Ed.): DUXU 2014, Part III, LNCS 8519, pp. 173–183, 2014.

& Hayes, 2009; Iovino, Fletcher, Breitmeyer, & Foorman, 1998). Writing is a complex process requiring a focus on visual attention and physical harmony, thus this study seeks to understand the impact of tactile and visual sensory inputs on children's handwriting. We examine differences in handwriting performance using different medium for writing instruction among elementary school children, including:

1. Explore whether medium and color have an impact on children's writing performance.
2. Analyze whether specific colors can lead to improved (or degraded) writing performance.
3. Explore whether children's emotional response to or preference for different colors has an impact on student writing.

Tablet computers with capacitive touch screens are able to sense micro current, allowing users to interact with the devices using their fingers, and using one's finger to write on a tablet computer is defined as finger writing for the purposes of this study. Based on previous studies, red, blue, yellow, green and white are adopted as experimental colors, while saturation change is beyond the scope of the present study.

1.2   Educational Application of Tablet Computer Technology

Hulls (2005) reviewed studies on the use of tablet computers in classroom instruction, and found that the ability to use of colored markers, draw shapes and make annotations directly in the interface served to attract students' attention and improve understanding. Thus students who used tablet computers in class experienced better learning results.

1.3   The Impact of Color on Behavioral Performance

Different colors can have an impact on human emotion and behavior. For example, Sinclair (1988) found that students taking an accounting examination performed better when the exam was printed on blue paper than when it was printed on red paper. The changes of the subject's cognition to extend the mode in which emotion plays a role of message transmission. Specifically, the test performance enhancement associated with the use of the color blue may be due to the color transmitting a signal that indicates "relative seriousness" of the task and the "need for careful and systematic handling". The relatively poor performance associated with the color red may be due to the color transmitting a signal that indicates that the task is "more neutral and does not require systematic treatment." The transmission role played by emotion in the model has been acknowledged and extended in many studies.

The use of color has been shown to have an impact on student achievement. Therefore, this study selects the use of color as an impact factor for writing, with use of the two aforementioned media (paper and tablet computers) as the key variable. Because other studies have held that different colors have varying effects on human emotional recognition this investigation focuses on the emotional recognition corresponding to different colors.

1.4   Color/emotion Associations among Children

An understanding of how children react emotionally to culture can be used in the design of products and services for children, along with the design of learning tasks and materials. However, semantic analysis may not be applicable to an investigation of children's emotional preferences for color because, unlike adults, children may be unable to make specific semantic distinctions (Tharangie et al. 2009).

Terwogt (1995) replaced the semantic scale by asking children how they felt about six colors (yellow, blue, red, green, white and black) and listed six types of emotional adjectives in response: happy, sad, angry, frightened, surprised and annoyed. Tharangie et al. (2009) applied this modified semantic analysis method to examined the emotional response of Sri Lankan children to color. Similar to Terwogt (1995) they replaced the semantic matching scale by asking children, "What kind of feeling does this color give you" and listed 11 types of emotional adjectives happy, sad, angry, annoyed, frightened, shy, proud, delighted, kind, excited and surprised.

In addition, Boyatzis et al. (1995) observed children's emotional response to different colors. In addition to the adjectives proposed by Terwogt and Tharangie, they included strong, boring, quiet and tense. Together these studies provide a perceptual vocabulary for examining the emotions children project onto different colors.

1.5   Measuring Handwriting Standards

Currently, teachers and parents evaluate the quality of student handwriting by subjective comparison to standard forms, but legibility is still evaluated subjectively (Lam et al., 2011), which seems inadequate for such a complex handwriting process. Lam et al. (2011) suggested that accuracy is an appropriate standard for handwriting. Their study primarily focused on students with dyslexia, thus their standard of accuracy must consider common handwriting errors which they defined as follows: (1) writing outside the grid, (2) size deviates from average, (3) size deviates from standard, (4) accuracy percentage, (5) total incorrect strokes, which was further broken down as including, (a) number of missing strokes, (b) number of extraneous strokes, (c) number of mirror side errors, (d) number of inverted strokes, (e) number of incomplete strokes, (f) number of connection errors, and (g) number of stroke crossing errors.

In addition, most handwriting evaluations emphasize writing speed and cannot provide data on the actual handwriting process, which is needed to indicate root problems (Rosenblum et al., 2006). Thus Luria et al. (2010) used the length and width of letters as a standard measure for handwriting, positing that increased cognitive loading would result in handwriting exceeding the length standard.

2   Research Methods

2.1   Research Subjects

To prevent results from being impacted by inconsistencies by skill development issues and to ensure that the test subjects could easily follow the experimental instructions, we selected 6th grade elementary school students with normal or corrected vision, and without color blindness. In total, 18 girls and 13 boys were included, and all test subjects were right handed. Two experienced elementary school teachers, aged 34, were enlisted to assist with the evaluation.

2.2   Experimental Use of Color

Based on the relevant literature, this study used white, yellow, red, blue and green backgrounds for writing tasks. Following the L*a*b range definitions devised by Lin et al. (2001) for color. To confirm that the colors used in the expeirment are consistent with human visual perception of those colors, and to ensure the consistency of color between the paper and tablet computer tasks, the researchers first tested the paper three times with a spectrophotometer, taking the average of three readings. This average value was then simulated in Adobe Photoshop on the tablet computer to render the same color as the background for the tablet.

2.3   Experimental Setup and Environment

The experimental setup primarily consisted of an iPad, paper in five different colors, black markers and video recording equipment.

To prevent distraction or unease among students, the experiments were conducted in their classrooms. To prevent environmental variation from creating color perception errors, experiments were conducted using natural light rather than fluorescent lighting, with the controlled environment color temperature between 5000K-6500K and illumination between 500LX-1000LX, while the experimental environment color temperature ranged from 5517K-6124K, and illumination ranged from 517LX-995LX. Expeirments were run at 10:00 in the morning to avoid errors caused by excessive sunlight. Measured color L*a*b* values, environmental color temperature and illumination were measured using an X-rite Eye-one Basic spectrophotometer, model i1-006. The tablet computer writing experiment was conducted using the LINE BRUSH (NAVER, Japan) program.

2.4   Writing Tasks

Table 1 shows the basic structure devised by Lam et al. (2011) for Chinese character writing tasks (independent, left-right, up-down, up-middle-down, left-middle-right, and inside-outside). This structure is used in the present study. To prevent the test subject performance from being impacted by any gap in prior learning, the writing task consisted of a single six-character phrase "提升國家藝術". Test subjects were provided with a pre-formatted grid of six boxes in which to write the phrase (see Fig. 1).

Table 1. Basic structure

Content	提	升	國	家	藝	術
Structure	Left-right	Independent	Inside-outside	Up-down	Up-middle-down	Left-middle-right

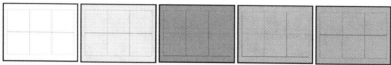

Fig. 1. Writing screen interface: Grid configuration for writing on the tablet computer screen with different color backgrounds (white yellow, red, green and blue)

2.5   Writing Evaluation Standards

In the subjective evaluation process, the researchers and elementary school teachers first discussed evaluation criteria. The teachers then evaluated the task performance in terms of correctness and neatness, and provided a subjective evaluation score.

Each subject was identified by a serial number. Adobe Photoshop was used to render all handwriting examples as black writing on a white background. The teachers were then asked to subjectively evaluate each writing output based on a five-point Likert scale with higher scores indicating better performance.

In addition to this subjective evaluation, we referenced the accuracy evaluation criteria used by Lam et al. (2011). However, these criteria were developed for errors commonly made by dyslexic students, thus following discussion with the teachers, our researchers eliminated mirror errors, inversion errors, and broken stroke errors, and combined the missing stroke errors and extra stroke errors into a single error type. Thus, as shown in Table 2, the scoring criteria used in this study included four error types: incorrect strokes, linking errors, crossing errors, and out-of-grid errors.

Table 2. Error criteria

Linking errors	Crossing errors	Out-of-grid	Incorrect stroke

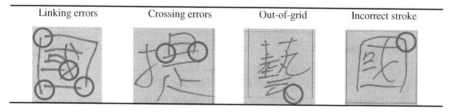

Also, as discussed in the literature review, handwriting performance considers handwritten information in addition to subjective evaluations. Thus, length and width are measured in cm according to the handwriting criteria devised by Luria et al. (2010).

2.6   Color Emotion Questionnaire

This study aims to determine the impact of color on the handwriting performance of children. Controlling for age and understanding of semantic analysis concepts to ensure the suitability of learner understanding and communication skills, previous relevant studies on children first selected adjectives to express common emotions, and then asked the students to match those adjectives to various colors.

Terwogt (1995), Tharangie et al. (2009) and Boyatzis et al. (1994) provided children with adjectives to describe emotions: Happy, sad, angry, annoyed, frightened, shy, proud, delighted kind, excited, surprised, strong, boring, calm and nervous. The questionnaire asked subjects to pair these adjectives to the colors white, yellow, red, blue and green.

2.7   Experimental Procedure

The researchers first explained the experimental process and asked the participants to write a single six-character phrase in a six-box grid on five types of colored paper and on a tablet computer, thus each subject wrote the same phrase ten times. Mistakes could not be corrected or erased.

Step 1: Participants were given five minutes to write the phrase "提升國家藝術" on five sheets of colored paper (white, red, yellow, green and blue) presented in a random order.

Step 2: The participants were given five minutes to write the same phrase on a tablet computer five times, each time with a different background color (white, red, yellow, green and blue). Due to the application restrictions, when the subject completed writing on one color background, the researcher assisted in changing the background to another color selected at random. While the total time for each step was five minutes, participants were free to use that time as they saw fit for each sub-task.

Step 3: Subjects answered the color emotion questionnaire, matching emotion adjectives to each of the test colors (white, yellow, red, green and blue).

3   Results

3.1   Impact of Media and Color on Handwriting Performance

Through the teachers' subjective evaluation, objective criteria, and length and width measurements, we conducted MANOVA analysis for media x color x writing performance. Descriptive statistics were also used to describe the characteristics of data, and impact trends for observable factors.

3.2   Impact of Media and Color on Subjective Ratings

In the teachers' subject evaluation of the students' handwriting, use of different media had a significant impact ($F>1$, $P<0.05$). However, the interactive relationship between color and color with media does not meet the conditions of F>1, P<0.05, and is thus not statistically significant.

Descriptive statistics show that paper tests had an average subjective score of 3.14, as opposed to 2.77 for tablet computers. In addition, the average scores for the five colors indicate that red had the best performance for both paper and tablet computers, while that for green was lowest.

3.3   Impact of Media and Color on Objective Evaluations

The total number of handwriting errors (including incorrect strokes, linking errors, crossing errors and out-of-grid errors) was statistically positive for both media and color (F>1, P<0.05).

From the descriptive statistics, the average total number of errors for the paper test was 3.92, as opposed to 11.77 for the tablet computer test. In addition, red backgrounds produced the lowest average total errors (i.e., best performance) for both the tablet computer and paper tests, while blue produced the highest.

Tukey's post hoc test was used to determine that red and blue have significant impact on the objective assessment for total errors (including incorrect strokes, linking errors, crossing errors and out-of-grid errors), with a P value of 0.021.

The objective evaluation of total errors applies MANOVA analysis to errors grouped under categories of incorrect strokes, linking errors, crossing errors and out-of-grid errors to find that media is significant for all error types, but that color is only significant for linking errors.

3.4   Impact of Media and Color on Length and Width

Luria et al. (2010) suggested that increased psychological loading would cause subjects to write characters with increased length (i.e., from top to bottom). Thus, standard criteria were set for the length and width of handwritten characters. We found media to have a statistically significant impact on length and width (F>1, P<0.05), while color did not (F>1, P<0.05).

3.5   Impact of Interactive Operation

Interactive operations were found to not be significant, indicating a lack of interactive operation between media and color. Thus, for the subjects, color did not arouse different emotional responses between the tablet computer and paper, suggesting that the experimental design for this research was successful in reproducing the exact same color for the task backgrounds in both media.

3.6   Color Emotions

The chi-square test was used to determine the independence of a child's emotional response to color (i.e., whether the child can distinguish emotional responses to colors), with a significance level of 0.000. Thus, descriptive statistics could be used to explore the children's emotional tendencies for the various colors. We found that children associated red with "exciting", white with "calm", blue with "delighted" "calm" and "friendly", and green with "delighted" and "friendly", while yellow had no significant emotional associations.

4   Discussion

This section uses the experimental analysis results and related literature to explore potential causes for the experimental results and provide recommendations.

4.1   Media Impact on Handwriting Performance

The analysis shows that different writing media has an impact on handwriting performance. Writing on paper earned higher subjective scores with fewer errors, and the characters tended to be shorter and narrower. A possible reason for the improved performance on paper is that test subjects were more familiar with writing on paper. This is supported by the better control over character length and width – the characters written on the paper test were significantly smaller than those on the tablet computer test because subjects were accustomed to writing characters of a certain size. Using pencil and paper, students were less susceptible to the influence of color, or perhaps due to increased writing automation, the task required less attention and control, and because their writing actions were more reliant on habit (Tucha et al., 2006) the impact of color was reduced.

4.2   Impact of Color on Writing Performance

The Tukey test showed red and blue had a significant impact on the objective evaluation of total error instances. Descriptive statistics indicate that red had the lowest average number of errors on the tablet computer (average: 9.35) and on paper (average: 2.48), indicating better performance, while blue had the highest average number of errors for both the tablet computer (average: 13.97) and paper (average: 4.74). Although color was not significant for the height and width of the characters, descriptive statistics indicate that, compared to other colors, red backgrounds produced larger characters (average height: 36.37; average width: 34.27), while blue produced smaller ones (average height: 35.84; average width: 33.36).

4.3   Impact of Specific Colors on Writing Performance

Although color did not have a significant impact on subjective scores, descriptive statistics indicate that, compared to other colors red resulted in higher subjective scores for both the tablet computer (average: 2.92) and paper (average: 3.18) and lower numbers of errors (including incorrect strokes, linking errors, crossing errors and out-of-grid errors), while green had lower scores for both the tablet computer (average: 2.58) and paper (average: 3.08). Red also produced larger character length and width values.

4.4   Impact of Color Emotion on Handwriting

Most test subjects were found to positively associate red with "excited", unlike Tharangie's (2009) Sri Lankan children who associated it with "frightened", and this may have contributed to their improved performance with red backgrounds. In addition, statistically the subjects were found to associate primary colors with positive emotions (happy, friendly, excited and calm), indicating that color projection was relatively positive. Blue and green had similar emotional responses (happy, pleasant). Subjective score results for green were relatively low, while blue had lower total errors, and smaller heights and widths.

4.5   Difference between Subjective Scores and Objective Evaluation

The different media produced different results for subjective and objective evaluations due to the use of scores in the subjective evaluation: good performance was scored 4 or 5, while flawed characters were scored 2 or 3, and poor performance was scored as 1.

While the subjective and objective evaluation results may vary, bivariate correlation analysis found the two evaluations to be significantly and negatively correlated (Pearson correlation coefficient 0.556, P=0.000) because better samples of handwriting performance, which scored higher in the subjective assessment typically, had fewer errors according to the objective criteria. From this, we can see that the subjective and objective evaluations are still consistent, but because the objective assessment calculates the number of errors, it is better able to analyze the types and trends of handwriting errors.

4.6   Conclusions

The key goals and results of this study are as follows:

1. Explore whether medium and color have an impact on children's writing performance.

   a. Media was found to have an impact on handwriting in terms of subjective scores, objective evaluations of total error instances, and character length and width. Paper-based tasks were found to produce smaller and more proportional characters than tablet-based tasks.
   b. Color was found to have an impact on the objective evaluation of total error instances.
   c. No interaction was found for color and media.

2. Analyze whether specific colors can lead to improved (or degraded) writing performance: using red as the background color produced higher subjective scores

and fewer total errors, along with larger, proportional characters. Results for the paper and tablet-based tests were similar.

3. Explore whether children's emotional response to or preference for different colors has an impact on student writing: color preference was found to be correlated with subjective scores and character length and width. Red was found to be associated with positive emotional adjectives and the use of red backgrounds produced improved performance.

4.7   Contributions and Suggestions

There is a trend towards increased use of tablet computers in schools. Unlike previous studies which conducted experiments using paper-based tasks alone, this study includes an investigation of writing tasks on new media forms and uses descriptive statistics to determine that red backgrounds have a positive impact on both tablet and paper-based writing tasks, both in terms of subjective scores and objective evaluation total error instances. The use of red also corresponds with greater length and width. Thus, the results of this study indicate that red consistently produces better results.

In addition, when students are less familiar with the writing media, their writing is less automatic and they are unable to rely on muscle memory. Thus the use of less familiar writing media can easily impact the writing process, and thus they can be used as tools to assess handwriting capability or fine motor skills.

Children were found to perform less well on writing tasks on tablet computers than on paper. Recording stroke order tablet computers provides useful information in understanding the writing errors, which is required for optimal performance. However, because color impacts handwriting performance, designers should consider incorporating red backgrounds into products, services, learning strategies and educational software for children. Designers also need to consider children's color preferences and emotional associations in that using a color with positive associations may help to improve learning outcomes.

References

1. Arnold, E.C.: Ink on paper 2: a handbook of the graphic arts. Harper and Row, New York (1972)
2. Boyatzis, C.J., Varghese, R.: Children's emotional associations with colors. The Journal of Genetic Psychology 155(1), 77–85 (1994)
3. Fordham, D.R., Hayes, D.C.: Worth repeating: Paper color have an effect on student performance. Issues in Accounting Education 24(2), 187–194 (2009)
4. Hulls, C.C.W.: Using a Tablet PC for classroom instruction. In: Paper Presented at the Proceedings of the 35th Annual Conference Frontiers in Education, FIE 2005 (2005)
5. Iovino, I., Fletcher, J.M., Breitmeyer, B.G., Foorman, B.R.: Colored overlays for visual perceptual deficits in children with reading disability and attention deficit/hyperactivity disorder: Are they differentially effective? Journal of Clinical and Experimental Neuropsychology 20(6), 791–806 (1998)

6. Lam, S.S., Au, R.K., Leung, H.W., Li-Tsang, C.W.: Chinese handwriting performance of primary school children with dyslexia. Research in Developmental Disabilities 32(5), 1745–1756 (2011)
7. Lin, H., Luo, M., MacDonald, L., Tarrant, A.: A cross-cultural colour-naming study. Part III—A colour-naming model. Color Research & Application 26(4), 270–277 (2001)
8. Luria, G., Rosenblum, S.: Comparing the handwriting behaviours of true and false writing with computerized handwriting measures. Applied Cognitive Psychology 24(8), 1115–1128 (2010)
9. McClanahan, B., Williams, K., Kennedy, E., Tate, S.: A Breakthrough for Josh: How Use of an iPad Facilitated Reading Improvement. TechTrends 56(3), 20–28 (2012)
10. Rosenblum, S., Chevion, D., Weiss, P.L.: Using data visualization and signal processing to characterize the handwriting process. Developmental Neurorehabilitation 9(4), 404–417 (2006)
11. Sinclair, R.C., Soldat, A.S., Mark, M.M.: Affective cues and processing strategy: Color-coded examination forms influence performance. Teaching of Psychology 25(2), 130–132 (1998)
12. Terwogt, M.M., Hoeksma, J.B.: Colors and emotions: Preferences and combinations. The Journal of General Psychology 122(1), 5–17 (1995)
13. Tharangie, K., Marasinghe, A., Yamada, K.: When Children Sense in Colours: Determinants of Colour-Emotion Associations. In: Paper Presented at the International Conference on Biometrics and Kansei Engineering, ICBAKE 2009 (2009)
14. Tucha, O., Mecklinger, L., Walitza, S., Lange, K.W.: Attention and movement execution during handwriting. Human Movement Science 25(4), 536–552 (2006)

The Relation between Online and Print Information Graphics for Newspapers

Ricardo Cunha Lima[1], Rafael de Castro Andrade[2], André S. Monat[3],
and Carla Galvão Spinillo[4]

[1] Esdi-UERJ, Rio de Janeiro
rclima@gmail.com
[2] UFPR, Paraná
ancara@gmail.com
[3] Esdi-UERJ, Rio de Janeiro
andresmonat@yahoo.com.br
[4] UFPR, Paraná
cgspin@gmail.com

Abstract. In this article we make a critical assessment of the relation between online and print design, focusing on the graphic language of newspaper infographics. A lot of the work done in this area consists in adapting print newspaper infographics to online versions. The problem with many of these adaptations is that there are losses in reading strategy and structure of their online versions, offering readers a mainly linear reading experience. To understand this fact, we compare print infographics and their digital versions through the analysis of layout and cognitive load. In a time when the knowledge of computer programming seems to be crucial to editorial design, we reflect on the importance of layout, which is the principle design structure to help readers access and understand information.

Keywords: Information graphics, information design.

1   Introduction

Newspaper design is a specialized field that, with the aid of technological advances, was included in the wider area of graphic design. Gradually, journalists became aware of the need to have a more effective typographic structure in newspaper layout. The traditional formula of newspaper layouts, with text and pictures (including photography) presented separately, was not enough to explain to the general public complex facts and processes, therefore graphical structures that could integrate both became necessary. In a parallel process, information graphics, or infographics, also developed from simple diagrams to complex non-linear graphic narratives. Technological innovation was an important factor in the inclusion of infographics in news design. When the North American newspaper USA Today came into existence in 1982, a four color printing process was chosen because popular journalism valued color pictures and infographics (Moraes, 2013). Although infographics is not a new

A. Marcus (Ed.): DUXU 2014, Part III, LNCS 8519, pp. 184–194, 2014.
© Springer International Publishing Switzerland 2014

way of communication, it has aroused great interest in recent years with the development of online information technology. With the current dissemination of information, infographics have helped readers to understand and process information quickly. This occurs, in part, by the varied means of symbolization available in an infographic, which makes it more adaptable to new contexts of information communication than other forms of traditional journalism (Lima, 2009).

Journalistic infographics is not a traditional form of iconography like illustration (including photography) it is in fact a kind of news story in which text and iconography are interdependent (Lima, 2009). Unlike traditional journalism, the written text is not necessarily the preferred source of information. Furthermore, the reading strategy may develop in a non-linear manner. That is, the reader can choose the order in which he reads, something that is somewhat problematic in a traditional linear text. Michael Twyman (1979, 1985) proposed that graphic language was composed of different modes of symbolization that are pictorial, verbal and schematic. Infographics integrates all of them through a non-linear layout structure, not only this but recently, online journalism made sound available to designers, bringing new possibilities for graphic language.

In this article, we show the problems faced in print infographics when they are adapted to online newspapers. In many cases, the principal strategy of the adapted infographics is the use of a sequential narrative. The infographic is divided into screens that can be accessed by the reader, one at a time. The problem with this strategy is that it conditions the reading process, creating a poor notion of the whole narrative, with limited choices of interaction. To understand this process we discuss the relevance of layout in the theory of graphic language proposed by Rob Waller (1985, 2012), problem of cognitive load in learning experience from the work of Mayer (2005) and Sweller et al. (1998).

2   Layout and Infographics

Rob Waller (2012) discusses the problems that graphic designers have been facing with the transition to online platforms and how layout has affected in this process. Waller was influenced by Michael Twyman (1979), who proposed that a page is diagrammatic, which means that readers understands text not only as words but as a structure of different forms of graphic language. Waller (1985) suggests that the linear structure of a traditional textbook tends to be that of prose, such as a transcript in graphic communication, verbal language. However, this can present miscommunication for certain types of information in certain contexts. Waller (1985) suggests that specialized scientific texts are not the norm when it comes to understanding documents. Newspapers and magazines are perhaps better examples, because they are developed taking into account the graphical structure of their content. Other good examples of texts that recognize the need to clarify its content graphically are reference Books and technical manuals (Waller, 1985:107).

To meet these varied reading strategies, Waller (1985) proposes the concept of text as diagram, i.e., a structure of non-linear text with a diagrammatic quality. When the text is placed in the form of a diagram, the structure becomes more accessible to a less linear reading, enabling readers to choose ways to understand the text and create their your own reading strategy. Therefore, these texts have multiple columns and complex typographic grids. Waller's focus is on the linearity of typographical texts (verbal graphic language) and its structure. However, the author does not neglect the role of pictorial images in the process. For Twyman (1985) the problem with pictorial language, is that it does not follow a well-defined grammar in the same way words do. Pictorial language is characteristically nonlinear. Twyman suggests (1985) that sequential images (graphic novels) or infographics can fuse the pictorial to the words graphically.

The structure of the diagram, the most typical form of an infographic, is perhaps the key to understanding how an infographic is configured. Infographics are essentially diagrams in the way that pictures, words and schematics are arranged in a layout. These multimodal structures are conceived with a nonlinear reading strategy in mind, providing more freedom to the reader (Lima, 2009). Each infographic is arranged according to certain rules of use compatible to its genre, as Waller (2012) points out:

The graphic layout of such genres effectively contains the rules or affordances for their use: Engaging layouts and large headings invite the magazine reader to browse; the orderly layout of a user guide invites systematic reading, referencing a task outside of the text through diagrams, and providing large numerals as a visual target to the returning reader (Waller, 2012:13).

Waller (2012) proposes that readers know (or find out) how to read a 'text' depending on access structures (the 'rules for use') of each document genre. A printed newspaper article is not read in the same way as its web counterpart. This is partially a technological matter, the Internet and print are simply not the same medium, they have different 'natures' and, therefore, should have different layouts configurations. What Waller points out is that, when print newspaper article is adapted to their online versions, there are many losses in reading strategy and structure. Online texts tend to be more constrained, in many cases, presented in single columns, offering little variety in its layout structure. If compared with their print counterparts, these online texts have fewer possibilities for interaction, offering readers a mainly linear reading experience, which is ironic because nonlinearity is considered one of the main characteristics of online texts.

This transition adaptation can be compared to problems with the transition between medieval manuscripts to the printed book. The illuminated manuscript, through the nature of its manufacturing methods, offered a close integration with the pictorial and verbal graphic content. The same could not be said of the printed book. Typography and iconography were separated with the invention of the movable type. Only later, through the development of new printing methods and mass media, could text and pictorial images be integrated once again.

What crucial is that the way a reader understands a online document genre is determined, in many ways, by paradigms shaped through older genres. For many online document their access structures are originally determined in print. And as Waller (2012) mentions, each new technology goes through a period of adaptation, but that the new medium does not render old ones completely extinct.

Fig. 1. A comparison between the online and print versions of a news story for the daily newspaper Folha de São Paulo. As we can see, the varied of layout structure of the print version (right) is reduced to a one column linear text without the aid of illustration (left).

3   Cognitive Theory of Multimedia Learning and Infographics

In most adaptations to online articles and infographics, much of the layout structure is lost, and with it most of the graphic content originally proposed. To better understand these 'losses' in many online layouts, we can look from the point of view of cognitive psychology. Some studies of cognitive psychology investigate how individuals learn through multimedia materials using different modes of presentation. One of the most cited is the cognitive theory of multimedia learning (CTML). Mayer (2002, 2005) formulates suggestions for the development of multimedia learning materials. The term multimedia is generally used to refer to varied uses of media (video, music, animation, etc.) but for Mayer the term has to do with multimodality, i.e., the set of different modes in which information is presented.

Mayer bases his theory on three assumptions:

1. The visual and verbal information are processed in different channels, derived from theories by Baddley (1974) and Paivio (1986);
2. Each channel has a limited capacity for information processing that originated from the cognitive load theory proposed by Sweller et al. (1998).
3. The processing of information in different channels actively promotes the construction of coherent mental representations, derived from the theory of active processing by Wittrock and SOI model, by Mayer (1996) himself.

These assumptions propose a better use of visual and verbal channels, adapting the cognitive load resources, resulting in a more meaningful learning process. The cognitive load is connected to the information processing capacity of current memory (or working memory), according to Sweller et. al (1998) there are three types of load (Sweller et al, 1998): intrinsic load, extraneous load and germane load. For a significant learning experience the intrinsic and extraneous loads should be minimal, because the focus of the cognitive resources should be on germane load, which is connected to the construction of learning.

From Sweller's perspective, the intrinsic load is related to the complexity of the information. The number of relationships between its components defines this complexity. Certain types of information are more complex. For example, learning a foreign grammar is inevitably more complex than learning a new vocabulary, i.e., the translation of individual words. The intrinsic cognitive load is produced by the complexity of the system. This load can not be fully minimized without compromising the complexity inherent to certain systems. The solution proposed by the authors is to divide the information into parts. Thus the reader only has to grasp part of the information each time, without covering the whole complexity at once. In this way the reader can experiences the intrinsic load gradually. When reading an infographic, complexity is an important factor because of its multimodal, non-linear layout.

Thus the suggestions of CTML focuses on strategies to minimize extraneous load and foster the relevant load. The extraneous load is coming from mental activity generated by the multimedia materials that is not related to learning. An example would be a picture that is complementary to a block of text in a layout, but they are presented in a way in which there is no clear correlation between them. This layout taxes the cognitive capacity of the reader because he has to pay more attention to the layout to understand the correlation. This kind of poor design configuration leads to a high amount of extraneous cognitive load. However, when the layout aids a better understanding of the content, this promotes a germane cognitive load.

From this perspective, at first glance, it is possible to consider an infographic as a complex material, which naturally leads to a substantial intrinsic load, because of a high number of relations between elements. However, some common features of infographics are compatible with the strategies recommended by the CTML. For example, the multimedia principle and the principle of contiguity. Mayer (2005) suggests, with the multimedia principle, that explanations that use image and text promote a deeper learning, this relation between image and text is a feature found in many definitions of infographics (Pablos,1999; Rajamanickam, 2005; Colle, 2004; Teixeira, 2010). In the contiguity principle, the author argues that multimedia elements must be spatially proximate so as to minimize an extraneous load.

Waller (2012) reminds us that, in design education, the "visual syntax of the page" is understood through perceptual principles established by the Gestalt psychologists. These principles are independent of specific content and are compatible with the principle of contiguity proposed by Mayer (2005). They are generally known as the proximity principle, "where that things that are physically close on the page are related in some way", and a similarity principle, "that things that look similar are members of the same category" (Waller, 2012:11). So it is widely accepted by designers that formal contiguity helps readers understand graphic relations and to distinguish categories. In infographics we can observe a close integration of elements in their layout, a practice that improves the reader's learning process without an unnecessary extraneous cognitive load.

When Mayer (2005) considers the advantages of contiguity, he only mentions the relation between text and image. He doesn't consider the variety of graphic elements available (such as sequential images, animation, etc.). But the author's scope is limited to learning materials, his theory does not examine the complexity of news and document design. In this sense, Waller (2012) seems to understand more fully the part played by layout in contiguity.

4   Analysis and Conclusion

Below is a brief analysis of the infographic "Tapuiassauro, the new dinosaur from Brazil", published in both online and printed versions of the Brazilian daily newspaper O Estado de São Paulo. Note that in 2011 the online version of this infographic received the gold medal in the online category of Malofiej, most important international award of infographics. The infographic provides information about the paleontological discovery of the dinosaur Tapuiassauro. A pictorial representation of the dinosaur and details of the fossils found.

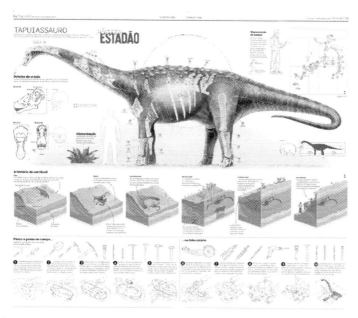

Fig. 2. Infographic "Tapuiassauro, the new dinosaur from Brazil" for the print version of daily newspaper O Estado de São Paulo. Design: Glauco Lara.

The print infographic was published in a double page (newspaper standard format). The content is structurally divided into three main parts:

4. A dominant descriptive picture of the dinosaur with sub-items that detail the main description.
5. "The history of the fossil", a sequential representation of the fossilization of the dinosaur.

6. "Step-by-step of the dig", an inventory of instruments and a sequence describing the procedures in a paleontological dig.

The print infographic allows the reader to get a sense of the whole, allowing him to decide his own reading strategies, creating relations between blocks of information. In "Step-by-step of the dig", different categories of information are presented together, in a structure similar to a table, allowing for comparisons between the bones of the skeleton, the tools and the stages of fossilization.

The online version was built using Flash and is divided in four screens that can be accessed through interactive tabs that form a sequence, like chapters: 1."Tapuiassauro", 2."dinosaurs in Brazil", 3. "a history of the fossil", 4. "step by step".

The first screen (Fig. 3) has the dominant image of the dinosaur with the sub-items present in print infographic. However, the online version offers interactive objects to reveal the skeleton. By passing the mouse over the dinosaur it is possible to do an x-ray, revealing the bones of the skeleton, with a "magnifying glass". While the reader scans the dinosaur, above the map, he can see where that bone was located in the plan of the dig. This interaction provides a direct observation of the elements, but in relation to the print version it remains compartmentalized, without offering an overall vision of the layout.

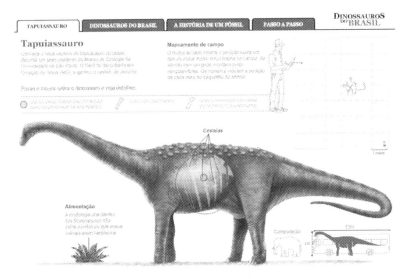

Fig. 3. "Tapuiassauro", first screen of the online version of the infographic

The second screen, "dinosaurs in Brazil" (Fig. 4), allows for a comparison of the scale and other dinosaurs found in Brazil. With mouse-over interaction the reader can select a dinosaur and locate where it was found, on a map of Brazil, and the period it existed. This section is not present in the print infographic because the online medium usually has more space available to offer content, it is not limited to a printed page format.

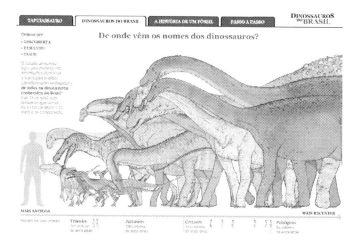

Fig. 4. "Dinosaurs in Brazil", second screen of the online version

The third screen (Fig. 5) provides a step by step representation of the fossilization of the dinosaur in segmented slides. A linear narrative control allows the reader to go forward and back between the slides.

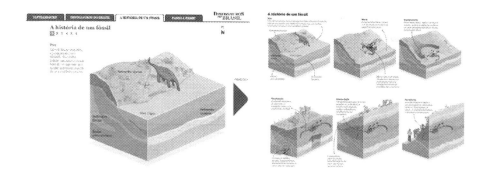

Fig. 5. "A history of the fossil", third screen of the online version

A fourth screen (Fig. 6) has the same inventory of instruments and procedures present in the print version. But the reader cannot see all of them at once, they are divided in two screens, one for fieldwork and another for laboratory work.

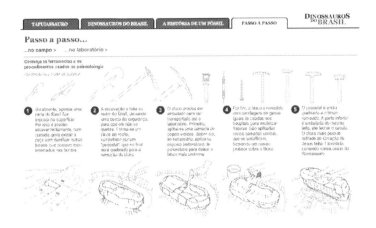

Fig. 6. "Step by step", fourth screen of the online version

Some types of simple controls, such as linear narrative and content selection. These controls seem to condition reading, restricting one of the main characteristics of the infographic, which is its non-linear reading structure, something that helps readers navigate blocks of information in the infographic, creating their own reading strategy.

In the sequence of slides, "a history of the fossil" (fig. 5), the reading process is fragmented into blocks of information, but maintaining a linear narrative. If the reader wishes to make a comparison between the stages of fossilization, he needs to read each one individually. This structure breaks the contiguity between the different stages taxing the reader's capacity to memorize the details of each one, creating a large amount of extraneous load. Something that does not occur in the print version, where a complete overview of the sequence of fossilization is offered.

Linear narrative controls and content controls do not seem to have been specially useful in promoting a better understanding of the content of the online infographic. In part because it is an adaptation of a print infographic. The elements do seem to have been chosen to meet the demands of the informational content, but to solve problems of adaptation between digital and print media.

Infographics published in Brazilian news websites tend to only have simple forms of interactions, such as content selection and linear narrative controls (Miranda, 2013). These interactive resources break the infographic into smaller pieces, as we have seen in the "Tapuiassauro" infographic. This could seem beneficial since it would reduce intrinsic load, as proposed by Sweller. However it seems that in the case of infographics, this high complexity has many benefits. The reader is invited to explore and make comparisons between the informational aspects of the infographic. In the online version of the "Tapuiassauro" infographic, the major loss occurred in the absence of contiguity between the different parts that structure the layout.

The richness in the complexity of the layout of an infographic is in the relations between the multimodal elements.

Although this tendency towards linear reading strategies is common in online publications some experiments using kinetic and interactive resources, with intention to break with this linearity, have been made. The content adaptation reflects an adjustment phase between print and online content. But the solutions will not necessarily come from advances in technology. Newspapers must invest in design teams that are willing, and have the resources, to experiment with the problems of online graphic language. In a time when the knowledge of computer programming seems to be crucial to editorial design, we must reflect on what must be expected from a designer. We believe that the focus should continue to be in layout, which is the principle design structure to help readers access and understand information.

References

1. Baddeley, A.D.: Working Memory. Oxford University Press, Oxford (1986)
2. Colle, R.: Infografía: tipologías. Revista Latina de Comunicación Social (58) (2004), http://www.ull.es/publicaciones/latina/latinaart660.pdf
3. Lima, R.C.: Análise da infografia jornalística. Dissertation (Master of Science) – Universidade do Estado do Rio de Janeiro, Escola Superior de Desenho Industrial, Rio de Janeiro (2009)
4. Mayer, R.E.: Learning strategies for making sense out of expository text: The SOI model for guiding three cognitive processes in knowledge construction. Educational Psychology Review 8, 357–371 (1996)
5. Mayer, R.E.: Cognitive Theory and the Design of Multimedia Instruction: An Example of the Two-Way Street Between Cognition and Instruction. New Directions for Teaching and Learning 2002, 89 (2002)
6. Mayer, R.E.: Cognitive Theory of Multimedia Learning. In: The Cambridge Handbook of Multimedia Learning, Cambridge University Press (2005)
7. Miranda, F.: Animação e interação na infografia jornalística: Uma abordagem do Design da Informação. Dissertation (Master of Science). Universidade Federal do Paraná, Curitiba (2013)
8. Moraes, A.: Infografia – História e Projeto. Blucher, p. 90 (2013)
9. Pablos, J.M.: Infoperiodismo: el Periodista como Creador de Infografia. Síntesis, Madri (1999)
10. Paivio, A.: Mental representations: A dual coding approach. Oxford University Press, Oxford (1986)
11. Rajamanickam, V.: Infographics seminar handout, Ahmedabad (2005), http://goo.gl/mlL5p
12. Swelller, J., Merrienboer, J.J.G., Pass, F.: Cognitive architecture and instructional design. Educational Psychology Review 10, 251–295 (1998)
13. Teixeira, T.: Infografia e Jornalismo – Conceitos, análises e perspectivas. EDUFBA (2010)
14. Twyman, M.: A schema for the study of graphic language. In: Kolers, P.A., Wrolstad, M.E., Bouma, H. (eds.) Processing of Visible Language, vol. 1. Plenum, New York (1979)
15. Twyman, M.: Using pictorial language: a discussion of the dimensions of the problem. In: Duffy, T.D., Waller, R. (eds.) Designing Usable Texts. Academic Press, New York (1985)

16. Waller, R.: Text as diagram: using typography to improve access and understanding. In: Jonassen, D. (ed.) The Technology of Text, vol. 2, pp. 137–166. Educational Technology Publications, New Jersey (1985)
17. Waller, R.: Graphic literacies for a digital age: the survival of layout. The Information Society: An International Journal 28(4), 236–252 (2012)
18. Wittrock, M.C.: Learning as a generative process. Educational Pyschologist 11, 87–95 (1974)

Prototyping in a Learning Environment - Digital Publishing Projects from the Escola Superior de Desenho Industrial

Marcos André Franco Martins

Esdi-UERJ, UX Design Professor, Rio de Janeiro, Brazil
marc.a.martins@gmail.com

Abstract. This paper focuses on the educational role prototyping plays on interaction design projects. Three case studies from ESDI (Escola Superior de Desenho Industrial, Rio de Janeiro, Brazil) will show different solutions for displaying visual information on tablets. Each case will show different approaches, namely: low and high fidelity and experience prototyping. It will be argued that the activity of prototyping stimulates student's critical thinking and encourages the search for innovation.

Keywords: Low and high fidelity prototyping, experience prototyping, visual information, digital publishing, pedagogy.

1   Introduction

With the introduction of tablets in the 2000's, visual information displayed on a screen has for the first time encountered ergonomic conditions similar to that of printed media. More portable and lighter than laptop computers, tablets have joined input and output on a single plane, approximating the screen's format to that of a page. The transposition of the page from print to digital touches a much broader historic and technological issue: new technologies tend to import features of previous ones before introducing their particular formal and experiential innovations. As Marshal McLuhan, has explained to support his well-known dictum *the medium is the message*, "...the content of any medium is always another medium. The content of writing is speech, just as the written word is the content of print..." [1]. Implied in this statement is the weakening of the rigid limits between form and content. Following McLuhan's reasoning, in the tablet's case the printed page, being considered the "content" of e-book readers, would have (as it did) formal implications on its designs. This influence is subtly noticeable in Amazon Kindle's preserving of typographic and layout conventions (page number and chapter name positioning, for example) [2].   Much less discreet is iPad's first e-book interface design, which visually mimics, with realistic detail, the tactile aspects of the book. While these imports might fairly indicate usability concerns (allusions to a traditional technology would facilitate intuitive navigation), they actually may reveal a resistance to engage in new mediums' design innovative opportunities [3]. Such conservative spirit is also

A. Marcus (Ed.): DUXU 2014, Part III, LNCS 8519, pp. 195–206, 2014.
© Springer International Publishing Switzerland 2014

noticeable in stereotyped and pre-formatted design decisions and assumptions that are embedded in software tools – the preservation the "form page" being an important example.

This paper presents three case studies of student's projects for digital publishing that challenge these aprioristic postulates with inventive solutions brought about through the practice of prototyping. At the Escola Superior de Desenho Industrial (ESDI) we stimulate students to prototype very early in the development of design projects and to keep doing it through all phases of the process. By constantly simulating, in rudimentary or sophisticated ways, how devices, actors, environments behave in a given proposal they learn to respond to the continuous formulation and reformulation of design problems. I intend to show that prototyping, when taken as a pedagogical tool, can establish a fertile and investigative learning environment that leads students to both achieve creative solutions and to gain an awareness of software tools biases and limitations. As I present the projects, I will emphasize, in each case, different approaches: low fidelity, experience and high fidelity prototyping.

Low-fidelity prototypes have been defined as exploratory tools that are quickly made, using materials not meant to be included in the final project. They are also identified by their low cost and communicative capabilities [4]. Bill Buxton prefers to name these early "instantiations of design concepts" as sketches. While prototypes are more refined and ready for usability tests, sketches – quicker and cheaper – are more connected to ideation phases within the design process [5]. The cases analyzed here are, I believe, more accurately qualified as prototypes and not sketches because some of the insights they have triggered reached an almost tangible presence in the later stages of the process. In the first example – Duotone magazine – playing with paper has inspired a form of navigation that became definitive in the final rendering of the interface.

In the second one, TxtoTracker, students used video recording to document the enacting of a proposed interaction in a real scenario. Not only the ideation phase, but also the final stages of this project were decisively influenced by experience prototyping. A concept that amplifies traditional definitions, it includes aspects like role-playing, time pressure, social interaction and environmental concerns. [6] There is, of course, a variety of specific techniques that can be combined, including paper prototyping, storyboarding, using index cards, live prototyping, animation, video recording and even faking. One should not forget, however, that prototyping techniques are constantly changing and multiplying, "fueled", as Bill Moggridge has put, "by the increasing complexity of design contexts" [7]. As Marion Buchenau and Jane Suri propose, experience prototyping is "less a set of techniques, than an attitude, allowing the designer to think of the design problem in terms of designing an integrated experience, rather than one or more specific artifacts ..." [6].

One might be led to think that such an attitude could only take place through the use of improvised, sketch, non-professional means. The third case study will demonstrate that it is not quite so. Wide World, a sci-fi story, employed high-fidelity prototyping, which is typically characterized by being fully interactive and having the exact look and feel of the final product [4]. The subtle experiences this project provides show how software tools, when used intelligently, can lead to creative findings. We will see that the project's author was able to employ pre-defined solutions in a remarkably idiosyncratic way.

These three approaches were not necessarily committed to commercial efficiency. In a professional design process, prototypes are valued as aids for ideation, communication, testing and innovation. While the case studies analyzed here may confirm this, I will focus in understanding the pedagogical value of prototyping. This value should not be confused with the teaching of prototyping techniques but understood in terms of how they can be used to develop in students the ability of specifying design problems. As Swiss designer Karl Gerstner has stated, back in 1964, "to describe a problem is part of the solution". Implied in this idea is the notion that "for no problem there is an absolute solution… there is always a group of solutions, one of which, is the best under certain conditions" [8] Prototyping, being essentially characterized by experimentation, is evidently an excellent tool for describing problems. In the course of perfecting such descriptions, we will see, students also improve their critical thinking.

2   Exploring Electronic Magazine Navigation

Considering today's technological acceleration, one would expect interaction design to follow the same pace. However, there are several design solutions that become essentially unchanged for certain periods of time. That's the case with tablet's digital publishing design. One of the dominant trends since the launching of the first iPad has been, as mentioned earlier, the insistence in references to traditional media. Apple's e-book reader's first interfaces emulate not only the unity of the page, but also its texture and physical turning effect, a trend that has been called "skeuomorphism" [9]. In one advertising, for instance, we notice a rhetoric approximation of the reading experience provided by the app to its printed counterpart: "reading in an iPad is exactly like reading a book… turn pages with a flick", says the apple's ad [10]. In other companies' marketing strategies we also see that even to show off technological advances, this is done through references to the well-known format of the traditional page. In an *Outside* magazine's ad film we hear: "we've all seen sci-fi movies where magazines and newspapers have their pictures moving right on the page… that's what we're doing here". [11]. These are just two examples of interface designs that, even with all innovation brought about by tablets, insist on the model of the "page".

This very model is challenged by project Duotone, developed by students Aline Alonso and Isabelle Lavigne ad ESDI in 2010. The idea was to create a magazine containing two issues in one. The students had developed, one year before, a printed version of the project. So, they already had text and photos as content to work with. Instead of merely transposing that content from one media to another, they forgot about the original design and engaged in experimenting with a bunch of fragments of photos and texts. They came up with a vague idea of arranging those items in a plane with irregular page boundaries. To experiment with this concept, they assembled a collage of what would later, in the final prototype, become the representation of one entire story. Navigation would, then, take place not by page turning but by plane panning in all directions "underneath" the tablet's screen (Fig. 1).

Fig. 1. First low fidelity prototype for *Duotone*

Fig. 2. (A) Out of focus area signals another plane and (B) the icon on the bottom left launches the 3D vision that can be rotated and used as a selector of sections

Playing with this physical prototype has also inspired the solution for the problem of how to navigate from one story to another. Because at this stage the bi-dimensional plane was *physically* available, students were able to perceive its potential three-dimensionality. They have decided that the magazine would contain several piled planes and that the user would be able to somehow switch planes. But what could be an interesting and effective interactive design solution for this concept? The releasing of planes in space called attention to a visual manageable feature: that of focusing. Displaying an out of focus plane, the interface managed to both signal the existence of more content *and* provide a "button area" that, when clicked, could bring the user to a different level/story (Fig. 2A). Here, the metaphor derives not from a magazine page but from cinematic and photographic features. Having solved this navigation problem, there was yet another challenge: how would the user change the view from one issue to the other, considering that the whole idea of *Duotone* was to present two issues in one. By clicking the magazine's icon on the lower right corner, one can access 3D navigation layers, where it is possible to choose not only the "reverse" issue but also one story within that issue (Fig. 2B).

Duotone, in short, presents three inventive ways of displaying visual information in a digital publishing environment: panning navigation on a plane that is not shaped as a rectangle; the attribution of semiotic and interactive qualities to depth of field; and a 3D representation that is also operative in navigation terms. All three aspects are the result of an exercise in describing a problem as part of a solution, as Gerstner has proposed [8]. While Apple's and Outside magazine were describing the problem how to transpose the printed page to digital form, Duotone has taken one step back and described another problem: how to present a certain content that include photos, text, audio and video, in a touch screen device. If we analyze the path that led to the final solutions, we conclude that (1) manipulating paper, glue and paper cutter and (2) being able to perceive a space between a paper mask and the content planes, played a fundamental role: that of providing a distance from pre-defined solutions and opening up a terrain suitable for innovation.

3   Vision Information in an Augmented Space

The combination of the Internet with mobile communications has, from the common user's standpoint, freed digital information from the ergonomics of desktop computers. The popularization of the word *cloud* as synonym for data storage is an indication of information's putative omnipresence. People are getting as used to expect instant access to personal or public data anywhere they go as they are to the idea of *ubiquitous computing*. Mark Wiser, PARC's scientist who coined the term, has stated: "The most profound technologies are those that disappear. They weave themselves into the fabric of everyday life until they are indistinguishable from it." [12]. But one would be mistaken to take the *cloud* for the same thing as *ubiquitous computing*. The two concepts have a strong difference: While the first one symbolizes information that can be accessed virtually anywhere, the latter points out to interactions that take place locally with devices (hidden as they may be) that *physically* sense the presence of an individual in specific places, promoting exchange of data between them. Concerned with the phenomenological aspects of such interactions, Lev Manovich has created the term "augmented space", derived from the older concept "augmented reality", coined around 1990. As Manovich puts it, this new space is distinguished by "*overlaying dynamic data over the physical space*". It is not to be thought, however, as one single space for everyone. Each "space is unique – since the information is personalized for every user, it can change dynamically over time" [13]. Given such dynamism, the stability of the tablet's "page" might give in to different design forms, which could represent and evoke the new phenomenological experience with augmented space. This is precisely what project *TxtoTracker*, developed by student Clarissa Baumann in 2010, was intended to.

Fig. 3. TxtoTracker's interaction's basic diagram

Fig. 4. TxtoTracker's activation icon "sticks" on any reading application

The project's proposal was to establish a connection between certain urban places and the uploading and downloading of text fragments being read by passerby users on a tablet. A typical interaction sequence would go like this: (1) a user is passing by a certain place and activates a mode that allows access to what s/he is reading; (2) another user, passing by the same place, turns the app on and have access to what the first reader was reading in situation 1; (3) users can select other users as favorites so that a web of "friends" is created, and each person can follow the chosen ones through other places and moments (Fig. 3).

The interface design seems at first very simple: just one icon – a blue circle – stands at the upper right corner of any reading application. When touched, the circle turns into the app's icon, an open eye, signaling that the mode "capture" is on. This means that whatever s/he is reading is being accessed and stored. The icon's drawing is purposely childish and unsophisticated so that it will look weird in the usual professional looking graphic interfaces of most reading apps (Fig. 4).

While in "capture" mode, two things would happen: the text being read by the user would be uploaded and all texts left at that location from other users would become available in a temporary memory in his/her tablet. The design problems, up to this point, were solved. The student then turned to the problem of selecting downloaded texts.

Her first idea was to display text fragments in different orientations and sizes on the reading plane. Such solution was, though, merely intuitive and not really connected to the project's general concept. She was encouraged to try experience prototyping in order to have an approximate idea of how would it feel to "collect" information from a spot in real space and see it on the tablet's screen. Having gathered some friends, she took a tablet to a square nearby the school and filmed enacted situations trying to rehearse all interaction steps (Fig. 5). Since no software was implemented in the tablet, each student's attention was driven to how it felt to be sitting or standing in the middle of a square concentrated on the tablet screen.

Fig. 5. Enacted experience prototyping with post-production

Fig. 6. On the left, an animation still showing the representation of augmented space. On the right the design solution for navigating and selecting text fragments on a tablet's screen.

The enacting confirmed initial assumptions that the sensation of finding information in specific places created an interesting awareness of today's augmented spaces. But it was in post-production that this experiment proved to be more effective. Text was added to the filmed sequence so as to represent the hybrid environment. When the student positioned the text boxes over the filmed image it became obvious that each of them had to follow perspective rules in order to appear either foreshortened or distant. This logic was a base for the design solution (Fig. 6). It is important to notice that, in spite of resembling Duotone magazine's 3d navigation, TxtoTracker's solution provides an all over effect that is remarkably different from the vertically ordered planes we saw earlier. The contact with real space tri-dimensionality inspired the student to create a 3d view of text fragments that would enrich the perception of overlaying real and virtual spaces.

4   Innovating with Available Tools

At the time Duotone and TxtoTracker were conceived, (2010) there was no affordable tool to create functional prototypes for tablet's e-publishing design. In 2011, Swedish media firm Bonnier Corp. released Mag+, an Adobe InDesign plug-in that could be downloaded and installed for free. In spite of some inconsistencies and incomplete documentation, Mag+ appeared to be a very interesting tool for exploring tablet interaction features. But we did not use it right away after its releasing. In 2012 I was more concerned with assignments involving Processing and Arduino open source platforms, and left e-publishing design aside for a while. In 2013 the theme was reintroduced in the course and students received Mag+ with enthusiasm. Especially attractive were the possibility of using a tool – InDesign – most were familiar with and also the easiness how Mag+ provided fast reviewing in the tablet itself. The tool, as expected, had its own preset of design solutions, the most striking one being a combination of horizontal navigation through "pages" with vertical scrolling in a layer-based design.

Project Wide World made no use of the vertical navigation option, and adopted the metaphor of sequential pages as in a printed publication. Renan Porto, who developed the project, took inspiration from tablet's typical orientation feature, associating vertical and horizontal positions with structural elements of his sci-fi story: in vertical position one sees an ordinary reality, and in horizontal position the same scenes are modified or amplified to show the Wide World, an augmented reality. The story is set in a psychiatric hospital where a physician gradually establishes connections across stories told by different patients. These ones, in the "normal world" (vertical) are depicted as mentally ill and in the "wide world", the doctor discovers, they live a perfectly sane, yet amplified, life.

Fig. 7. Wide *World*'s first sketches

The visual solutions for these narrative ideas started with sketches depicting the relationship between the two worlds (Fig. 7). At this stage there was still no clear definition of how exactly this "wide world" would be depicted. Figure on the right's scrambled lines point to a somewhat chaotic intertwining between the two worlds. Note that the figure on the left obeys comic books' framing graphic behavior. As the project evolved the "wide world" was conceived as being not so different from the "normal world". For example, as we see in Fig. 8, the vertical position displays a group of three young men chatting, while in the horizontal version of the same scene other characters are added, graphically differentiated by the use of color. In these second sketches, one notes the abandonment of the comics' framing visual language.

Fig. 8. Wide *World*'s second sketches

Fig. 9. Final illustrations show an economy of means: no comic book framing and very subtle use of color to identify elements of the "wide world"

In the final, fully functional high fidelity prototype (Fig. 9), color became restricted to a blue "aura" around the head of one character and to the text balloon. The prominence of black and white invests the story with austerity. In this and in all other scenes, the difference between "worlds" is very subtle. As a whole, from the first sketch to the final rendering there has been a movement towards economical solutions not only in graphic but also in interactive terms.

The opting for black and white language, for abandoning comic book's framing and for ignoring Mag+'s double navigation feature reveal an economy of means that is in itself a statement: choosing not to make use of available powerful tools, the author creates an experience that attain maximum effect with minimal interactive or graphic features. What was it to be gained? Answer: the narrative, that many times in interactive editorial pieces runs the risk of being relegated to second plane, is again the center of attention. The simple trick of turning tablet orientation has nothing attractive in itself: it is only an interactive tool at narrative's service. In the case of Wide World, innovation comes, paradoxically, from refusing to innovate: in a milieu – digital publishing – where the imperative is to create mesmerizing interactive experiences, Wide World presents us with black and white austerity and minimum interaction acrobatic novelties. It was not, however, a matter of a merely conceptual exercise. User experience is itself displaced from sensorial seductions into evocative thinking. It is an interesting case of high fidelity prototyping at the service of simplicity that shows the student's awareness of a set of predefined design solutions he has chosen not to use.

5   Conclusion

The importance of prototyping as a crucial activity in designing interactions is frequently explained in terms of time and money saving, creativity stimulation, team communication, usability validation, among other aspects. This paper was dedicated to see prototyping as a pedagogical tool. The three case studies have presented educational gains in different areas of interaction design problems.

With Duotone magazine, students learned how to reformulate the description of a problem. The kind of low fidelity prototype they executed provided a way of describing differently the problem of displaying publishing content in a digital environment. Instead of assuming the form "page" as a given, they devised a 3D layered-plane representation derived from the manipulation of paper cutouts.

Project TxtoTracker has lead students to employ enacting methods typical of experience prototyping. The interactive omnidirectional space created by type reinforced the project's concept of navigation on an augmented space. Again, such an abstract idea was represented by inspiration drawn directly from the prototyping experience.

Finally, Wide *World*'s visual and interactive solutions revealed a minimal style deliberately imposing a distance from today's inflated interactive possibilities and visual pollution. In this project a sophisticated tool (InDesign's plug-in Mag+) had its multiple possibilities restricted in favor of a much older technology: the narrative itself.

In the first two cases, students have experienced a way of projecting interaction that made them reformulate problems and find inventive solutions. One might argue that those solutions are not exactly unheard of. However, from the students' standpoint, it was a great novelty to find out that the page form was not a definitive solution for displaying publishing content. From a pedagogical point of view, it can be concluded that low fidelity and experience prototyping proved to be effective as tools for innovation.

One would be tempted to rapidly conclude that these low fidelity approaches would be superior to high fidelity functional prototypes, developed on the third example. While in terms of innovating in interaction and experience design this may be true, one cannot overlook the advantages of using a tool that makes it possible previewing designed pages right on the tablet's screen. This speed and the easiness of doing it have released time for the conceptual elaboration that gave birth to the also inventive visual and interactive statements implicit in an apparent simplicity. As a final conclusion, I would like to suggest that both pedagogical approaches are important and, obviously, non exclusionary.

But an aspect present in all three examples needs underlining: all three processes show that the students have been empowered with an awareness of design-presupposed solutions. Both the page and the software were understood as technologies to be used if / when necessary. The practice of both low and high fidelity prototyping has enabled autonomous decisions and provided a conscience of the transient and circumstantial status of any technology.

These cases are examples of how prototyping can work as a powerful tool for "unlearning" taken-for-granted solutions, being them embedded in software tools or established by cultural stereotypes. In a designer's formation, to be able to continuously move in and out presuppositions is the only way to innovation. To exercise this flexibility is, I believe, the greatest gain provided by prototypes in a learning environment.

References

1. McLuhan, M.: Understanding Media: the Extensions of Man. MIT Press, Cambridge (1994)
2. Hobbs, T.: Can We Please Move Past Apple's Silly, Faux-Real UIs? Fast Company, Mansueto Ventures (2012), http://www.fastcodesign.com
3. Martins, M.A.F.: Novas Formas para a Palavra Escrita, Resistências Históricas à Tecnologia. In: 10° P&D Design – Congresso Brasileiro de Pesquisa e Desenvolvimento em Design, São Luis, MA, Brasil (2012)
4. Preece, J., Rogers, Y., Sharp, H.: Interaction Design: Beyond Human-Computer Interaction. J. Wiley & Sons, New York (2002)
5. Buxton, W.: Sketching User Experiences: Getting the Design Right and the Right Design. Elsevier/Morgan Kaufmann, Amsterdam, Boston (2007)
6. Buchenau, M.S., Fulton, J.: Experience Prototyping. In: ACM (ed.) 3rd Conference on Designing Interactive Systems: Processes, Practices, Methods, and Techniques, pp. 424–433. ACM, Brooklyn (2000)
7. Moggridge, B.: Designing Interactions. MIT Press, Cambridge (2007)
8. Gerstner, K.: Designing Programmes. Lars Müller Publishers, Baden (1964, 2007)
9. Thomson, C.: Clive Thompson on Analog Designs in the Digital Age. Wired. Condé Nast (2012), http://www.wired.com/magazine/2012/01
10. http://www.apple.com/ibooks/
11. Henry, A.: Living Magazine Cover and Spread - Outside Magazine (2009), http://www.youtube.com/watch?v=3WeaC5QDUpg
12. Wiser, M.: The Computer for the 21st Century. Scientific American 265, 94–104 (1991)
13. Manovich, L.: The Poetics of Augmented Space (2005), http://manovich.net/

Logograms: Memory Aids for Learning, and an Example with Hearing-Impaired Students

Ligia Medeiros[1], Marcos Brod Júnior[2], and Luiz Vidal Gomes[1]

[1] Universidade do Estado do Rio de Janeiro, Rio de Janeiro, Brasil
ligia@esdi.uerj.br
[2] Universidade Federal de Santa Maria, Rio Grande do Sul, Brasil
brodjr74@gmail.com

Abstract. This paper describes a methodology for teaching design based on the use of a set of memory aids named *logograms*. Users' experiences involving the usability of logograms as a teaching support are being registered throughout empirical research during the last ten years by the authors. More recently, the technique was applied with success to hearing-impaired students. The material described here includes phonographic and iconographic elements aiming at the organization of a logographic system that, in addition to sign language, supported a more inclusive education. Some of the logograms presented refer to stages and procedures of the design process, and were converted into LIBRAS – the Brazilian Sign Language with the intensive participation of the users (interpreter, students and teacher). The process consisted in: establishment of keywords; denotative and connotative analysis of keywords; search of applicable signs within LIBRAS; creation of new signs when there were no codified signs for design technical terms in dactylology; validation by the interpreter and student; systematization of use through photographs; verbal description of the agreed gestures. The logograms are perceived as innovative ways to teach product and graphic design in undergraduate and graduate courses, and their use can be combined to software programs and Internet resources in new curricular approaches.

Keywords: perception of visual information, teaching of hearing-impaired and speech-impaired people, logograms.

1 Introduction

In 2003, in Brazil, the document "Program for Inclusive Education: the right to diversity" was launched by the Ministry of Education aiming at "guarantee that pupils with special educational needs have access to regular education in schools" [2]. That Program encouraged schools to provide proper facilities for disabled people, and faculty members to become aware of special education. In order to fulfill the objectives of the program, education managers should be able to enroll students with special needs in their under graduation courses, and teachers should be flexible in adopting new activities for educating, instructing and imparting knowledge.

A. Marcus (Ed.): DUXU 2014, Part III, LNCS 8519, pp. 207–216, 2014.

In 2007, a student with hearing difficulties was admitted in one the Design Courses established in Porto Alegre city, Brazil. Promptly, an interpreter of LIBRAS (Brazilian Sign Language) was hired to assist the communication between design teachers and the deaf student. However, despite the efforts of the interpreter and the attentiveness of the student, difficulties in communication were causing a significant loss of the teachers' explanations. The main problems were not related to the cognitive capabilities or psychomotor skills of the student, but with the lack of codified signs for design technical terms in dactylology (the use of the fingers and hands to communicate and convey ideas, as in the manual alphabet used by hearing-impaired and speech-impaired people). An agreement was made among a teacher of graphic design, the student and the interpreter to expand the use of an existing methodology for teaching design based on logograms. The teacher responsible for the discipline has had previous experiences with the use of logogram charts as a teaching resource and as memory aid [3, 10, 11, 12]. Moreover, he has done extensive research on the aspects of perception of visual communication addressing the needs of employees with hearing impairment in manufacturing workplaces [4] (Figure 1).

Fig. 1. Logograms, pictograms and sign language created during a PhD research on Production Engineering [4], aiming at inclusive manufacturing workplaces.

As a preliminary solution, a handout with logograms of relevant terms of the design process was prepared, and after, a broader instructional system was developed to promote a better understanding of the main notions employed during the course.

Most if not all engaged in making the teaching/learning process successful will agree with the idea that it is part of a teacher's job to improve instruction methods to suit their students' manual skills and mental capabilities. When facing the challenge of teaching hearing-impaired people, for example, it becomes more than natural for teachers to use visual aids. Motivated by the need to communicate with all design students, whether listeners or non-listeners, the authors developed a method integrating verbal, gestural and logographic language. The words and logograms presented here are related to the stages of the creative process and how those arbitrary signs were "translated" into the Brazilian Sign Language. To make such didactic effort useful and usable, the design teacher relied on the fundamental advice of the certified interpreter of LIBRAS, and also on the monitoring of the learning progress of the deaf student. Nowadays, the logograms charts and the related LIBRAS signs facilitate the learning of other design students with hearing difficulties.

2   Teaching Design with Memory Aids

In 2002 we started the experience of rendering design contents using metaphors from mathematical expressions to stimulate students to use abstract, modular and rhythmic reasoning. In order to find original images to represent design knowledge, some logograms were sketched to help technical product analysis. From the teacher's position, logograms became practical as "traffic signs", conventionalized graphic icons employed to guide procedures, to define techniques and to call students attention about the steps of the design process. It is relatively easier to remember or guess the meaning of logograms than to remember or guess the sound of alphabetic written words. In addition, a single logogram may be used by a variety of languages to represent words with similar meanings.

There are three referential words in our search to improve the use of logograms as memory aid in design teaching. The words are: (i) a noun, utility, that states the quality of being of use and service useful; (ii) an adjective, usable, meaning the extent to which a product can be used by specified users to achieve some goals with effectiveness, efficiency, and satisfaction in a specified context of use; and (iii) an adverb, utterly, connoting a way to maximize the experience of learning.

We have been observing from empirical research that logograms charts are valuable as teaching resource in that they respond promisingly to some basic usability issues: 1. Which difficulties students face in their first use of logograms to perform basic design tasks? 2. How is the rhythm and pace of performance of design tasks by students after having learned to use logograms? 3. How is their acquisition of such skill/knowledge? 4. Do logograms induce students to make mistakes? 5. Do students have an enjoyable learning process with the method with logograms? 6. Are the images of logograms self-explanatory, or are they arbitrary signs to be learnt with teachers support?

Logograms represent ideas by means of icono- and phonographic elements of visual language, and are being employed to describe tasks and procedures employed in the design process. In the first experiences as teaching tools, logograms were distributed to students during classes and seminars, for a simple recognition exercise. The participants of the experience told that the logograms facilitated the recall of the situation represented, even when they cannot say it from memory. It appears that the image activated the understanding of a whole chain of ideas, and when the logograms came to mind the creative and projectual processes was easily codified.

Pictorial images are central elements in the composition of visual languages to improve the recognition of situations, to ease the human capacity to retain information, to memorize facts and phenomena. Iconographic representations appear among the universal principles of design [13]. On that subject, the Symbol

Sourcebook, written by Henry Dreyfuss (1904-1972), and published in 1972 is still a reference. In the preface of Dreyfuss' classical work, the architect and philosopher Buckminster Fuller (1895-1983) stated an idea that motivated the development of the logograms: "the ideographic language, basically visual, developed for the primitive people, now tends to bring the basic tools of communication to the universal understanding and use" [8]. Two other texts, written by Charle K. Bliss (One Writing for One World) and by Marie Neurath (Education Through the Eye), complete the Symbol Sourcebook introduction. Henry Dreyfuss affirmed that no book related to symbols would be complete without mentioning the Semantography, by C. K. Bliss, a complete system which crosses the barriers of language. "The lines and curves of his symbols can be translated into any language and therefore his words and ideas are enclosed in my book". [8].

Dreyfuss also highlighted the work developed by Otto and Maria Neurath, at the Isotype Institute Ltda. Otto Neurath (1882-1945), a social scientist and Austrian professor, included the "isotype" (an acronym for International System of Typographic Picture Education) as part of his theory of education, and defended the idea that images are better than words, at least in the initial stages of knowledge acquisition. To translate complex images into forms that are both significant and accurate for the great public, Neurath suggested not only a series of fine pictograms, but also the techniques for their drawings and application. These principles, then, are the basis for the proposal of logograms as a tool to universal communication (based on Fuller); a system of lines and curves conventionalized as signs to effective communication (based on Bliss in "Semantography"); learning in the initial design training with something similar to the isotypes of Neurath.

Dreyfuss suggested that to deal with more complex instructions and meanings, it is necessary to combine basic and conventional signs together with other newly developed. The contribution of Rudolf Modley must be mentioned too. Neurath and Modley, in 1942, indicated three phases for the conception of iconographies:

1. Analysis of the fact or the situation that you want to conventionalize and to select the main illustrative elements;
2. Selection of the images that can be simplified and, therefore, are more adequate to represent the fact or the situation to be drawn;
3. Development of layouts that allow a simple and fast understanding of the information, essential to its history [14].

Aicher and Krampen [1] made reference to Neurath and Modley who also deal with the history of the modern pictograms.

During the conception and elaboration of logograms, we perceived that, according to the definition of the Dictionary of Symbols [6], we were dealing with "signs" and not with "symbols". When drawing logograms we traced "conventional signs", i.e. marks and ideograms, that have symbolic meaning in its origin and in the way they influence those who contemplate or use them". When calling them "conventional signs" we intended to nominate more or less arbitrarily established relations. Hydraulic codes, topography, meteorology, and the mathematics, all use systems of conventional signs that are also used in the traffic signs, in the industry, and even in music [6]. Our logographic system (Figure1) is based on stenography:

(a) The configuration of the logogram can be visually distinct from the original iconographic element;

(b) The seminal meaning can be extended to analogous situations [9];

(c) Its configurations offer more possibilities of structural combination than imitative sketches [5].

Logograms charts were systematized as a set of arbitrary signs relating to: creative movements, types of ideas association; symmetry laws; basic graphic elements of designing; intellectual capabilities; types of design meetings; main creative techniques; taxonomy of educational objectives and the stages, steps and phases of the creative process applied (Figure 2).

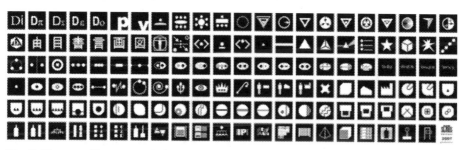

Fig. 2. First set of logograms designed as memory aid for learning. Illustrative elements for the situations were selected; images were simplified and the more adequate to represent design process were drawn. Seminal meanings were extended to analogous situations to apply to product design, graphic design, packaging design, etc.

One of the difficulties in conducting research on the usability of logograms is the lack of applicable assessment methods to measure and monitor students' learning. Current research has been done using observation and interviews with students as they interact with the logograms [10, 11].

In 2008/2009, a new set of logograms was designed to teach the urban signaling systems; and one of the findings was that the assessment of students' learning became easier: they could straightforwardly dissertate about each of methodological design moment from a single arbitrary sign sketched (Figure 3).

Fig. 3. Assessment of the learning process made easier through the recognition and application of logograms. When students know the learning objectives and how to achieve them, teachers and students together can monitor the learning progress.

3   Improving Teaching Methods to Suit Students' Needs

Logograms have been employed as memory aid to guide project works as varied as graphic analysis of the Brazilian vinyl record sleeves [15] and the design of urban signs system for Porto Alegre city [7]. From all teaching experiences, the more thought-provoking was the one that included a deaf student in the classroom. To cope with that challenging situation, teacher and interpreter expanded a methodology previously developed to help deaf people in manufacture industries from the South of

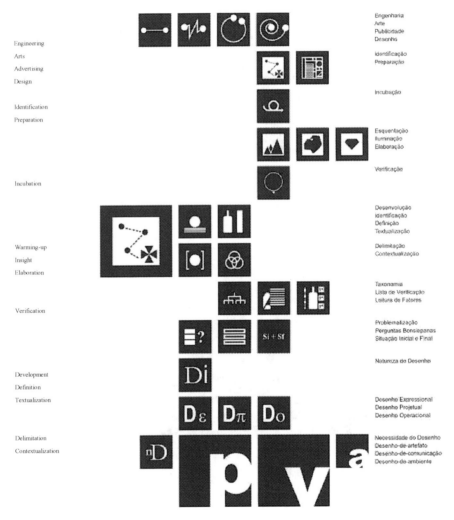

Fig. 4. Example of one of the large format posters displayed in the classroom for explanation of the design process, the meaning of logograms and their use as memory aid

Brazil. The theoretical basis was explained not only on the PhD thesis [4] but also on academic papers [3, 10, 11] and in a book [12]. The process of creation the visual aids for teaching design to deaf students was divided into steps. Initially, the theoretical basis of the design process was studied with the entire class, making sure that interpreter and students grasp the meaning of the keywords for procedures and techniques. Posters were displayed in the classroom for explanation of the logograms and their meaning (Figure 4).

Denotative and connotative analyses for keywords were made to find precise definitions and to corroborate their appropriateness, avoiding undesirable hidden meanings. Special attention was paid to prevent reappearance of words to designate different concepts. Signs within the Brazilian Sign Language were searched to match those keywords.

It became evident that new gestural signs were necessary, what is perfectly acceptable, since deaf people and interpreters regularly improve and supplement their vocabulary. The process of creating signs and testing their suitability and understanding was a meticulous job of the interpreter with the help of the student, in an iterative process. The new gestural signs were thoroughly recorded through photographs and the verbal description of the way in which the signs should be performed was reported so that other people could reproduce them as accurately as possible.

Figure 5 demonstrates four moments of the process. First column contains some of the concepts to be learned, represented by words. Second column contains logography, that is, visual symbols representing words rather than the sounds or phonemes that make up the word. The columns with photographic pictures contain the documentation of the gestures required to perform each key concept. The column on the right contains the verbal description of the gesture.

The deaf student, presently a graduated designer, stated: "When I started the Design course I was concerned if I could follow the lectures and other activities. When Rejane (the interpreter) arrived, my learning was very much facilitated, but sometimes we could not find the better words to represent the design techniques because there were no signs for them. Rejane and I created new signs relating words and meanings. It helped me to understand what the teacher was explaining. First was the contextualization of words and then the search for applicable signs, the combination and adaptation of them. The teacher had the wonderful idea to make a manual and posters with logograms, so it helped me and other students. After deciding the signs, I started drawing many own logograms for an easier learning of the signs. The objective is to engage the deaf person in the creation of new signs as well as logograms related to the meanings."

In 2013, in design classes at the Federal University of Santa Maria, students have demonstrated an amazing capacity to understand the logograms as a technique for learning industrial design. In some of their written exercises, taken as research protocols, students revealed an enjoyable self-oriented learning process and quickly begun to draw their own category of logograms (Figure 6).

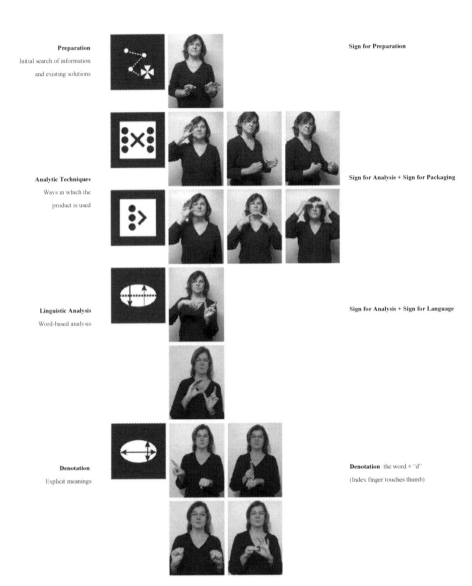

Fig. 5. First column contains words for some of the concepts to be learned. Second column shows the related logograms. Photographs demonstrate the gestures required to perform the key concepts. Verbal descriptions for the gestures are presented on the right column.

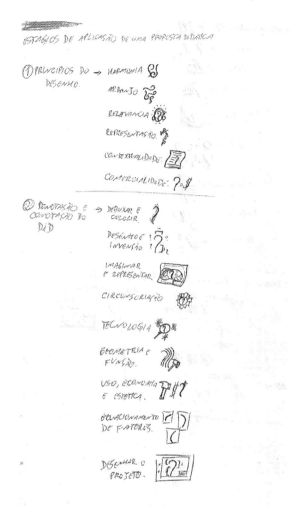

Fig. 6. Experience of students as users of logograms as a technique for teaching/learning product and graphic design

When used in association with theoretical basis and practical activities logograms assisted the students in their creative actions, increasing an awareness of their learning process. When creating their own logograms, students enrich their project with a powerful and yet synthetic piece of graphic-visual communication. Now, after the creation of 210 signs in LIBRAS, we are in the process of reviewing the manual that illustrate the correlation of word and logograms employed in the learning of the design process. Logograms are perceived as an innovative way to teach product and graphic design in undergraduate and graduate courses, and their use can be combined to software programs and Internet resources in new curricular approaches.

216   L. Medeiros, M. Brod Júnior, and L. Vidal Gomes

References

1. Aicher, O., Krampen, M.: Sistemas de Signos en la Comunicación Visual. Gustavo Gili, Barcelona (1979)
2. BRASIL, Educação inclusiva: direito à diversidade. Documento orientador. Ministério da Educação, Brasilia (2005), http://portal.mec.gov.br/seesp/arquivos/pdf/orientador1.pdf
3. Brod Jr., M., Gomes, L.V.N., Medeiros, L.M.S., Jucá, D.: Package Design: Graphic and Glyphic Modeling for Environmental Awareness. In: International Association of Societies of Design Research. IASDR, Seoul (2009)
4. Brod Jr., M.: Engenharia de Produção Inclusiva: a linguagem gráfico-verbal, gráfico-visual e gesto-visual para Atividades de Produção. DSc Thesis. UFRGS, Escola de Engenharia, Porto Alegre (2010)
5. de Campos, H. (org.): Ideograma: Lógica, Poesia e Linguagem. USP, Soa Paulo (1994)
6. Cirlot, J.-E.: Dicionário de Símbolos. Morales, São Paulo (1984)
7. D'agostine, D., Gomes, L.V.N.: Design de Sinalização: Planejamento, Projeto e Desenho, p. 95, 212. UniRitter, Porto Alegre (2010)
8. Dreyfuss, H.: Symbol Sourcebook. Paperback edition. John Wiley and Sons, New York (1984); (1st edn. McGraw–Hill (1972))
9. Gomes, L.V.N.: Desenhando: um Panorama dos Sistemas Gráficos. UFSM, Santa Maria (1998)
10. Gomes, L.V.N., Brod Jr., M., Medeiros, L.M.S.: Logogramas: desenhos para projeto. In: 8 Congresso Brasileiro de Pesquisa e Desenvolvimento em Design/P&D Design, SENAC, São Paulo (2008)
11. Gomes, L.V.N., Brod Jr., M., Medeiros, L.M.S.: Logogramas: desenhos para projeto. Estudos em Design (Online) 18(2), 2453–2464 (2010)
12. Gomes, L.V.N., Brod Jr., M.: Logogramas: Desenho para Projeto. sCHDs Editora, Porto Alegre (2007)
13. Lidwell, W., Holden, K., Butler, J.: Universal principles of design: a cross-disciplinary reference. Rockport Publishers, Massachusetts (2003)
14. Modley, R.: Handbook of Pictorial Symbols. Dover, New York (1976)
15. Santana, V.N.: O Desenho de Capas de Discos Bossa-Novistas e Tropicalistas. Master Dissertation, pp. 168–172. PPGDCI/UEFS, Feira de Santana (2013)

SMART Note: Student-Centered Multimedia Active Reading Tools for Tablet Textbooks

Jennifer George-Palilonis and Davide Bolchini

Indiana University Purdue University Indianapolis, School of Informatics and Computing,
535 W. Michigan Street, Indianapolis, IN 46202, USA
{jpalilon,dbolchin}@iupui.edu

Abstract. Active reading is a fundamental task for the study experience, yet existing tablet textbook platforms fail to provide the wide range of flexibility required for active reading, particularly when multimedia content is included. To address this, we propose SMART Note, a set of active reading tools that provides learners with novel annotation and reorganization methods intended to better support active reading in the tablet environment. In an evaluation study with SMART Note prototypes, users had high success rates with usability inspection tasks and rated novel annotation and reorganization tools more favorably than tools offered by most existing tablet textbook platforms. Our work builds a foundation for future research that explores how SMART Note affects active reading and learning with multimedia tablet textbooks.

Keywords: Active reading, tablet textbooks, educational multimedia, usability.

1   Introduction

With the advent of tablet devices, a new breed of textbook is emerging that combines the physical affordances of traditional textbooks with rich multimedia. Tablet textbooks are now designed to look like browse-able books and often seamlessly integrate interactive, multimedia content and tools to support user interaction and active reading. As tablet textbooks become more prevalent, so too will the inclusion of audio and video in educational textbooks. However, existing tablets and eReaders fail to provide learners with the wide range of flexibility that is required for active reading [4, 17]. Likewise, students may have difficulty migrating from the print textbooks with which they are familiar to interactive digital textbooks, particularly when multimedia is added. In the digital world, learners are accustomed to *reading* text, *watching* video, and *listening* to audio. Yet, they must *study* all three in a tablet-based multimedia textbook. Therefore, the strategies they have been accustomed to using for static, print textbooks may not be sufficient for tablet textbooks.

The physical nature of active reading involves several strategies that generally fall into one of four categories: annotation (highlighting, note taking), reorganization (outlining, summarizing), cross-referencing (working back and forth among documents, annotations, etc.), and browsing (studying artifacts developed during the

A. Marcus (Ed.): DUXU 2014, Part III, LNCS 8519, pp. 217–229, 2014.

other phases). These strategies are meant to assist an active reader in the necessary cognitive processes for learning, which include describing, critiquing, and building an analysis of a document in order to form an understanding of it. Generally accepted methods for active reading include highlighting, making notes in margins, organizing notes into outlines, making flash cards for future review, and other similar practices. These activities are help learners identify important parts of a text and organize notes in meaningful ways that are conducive for repeated review. However, recent studies suggest certain reading tasks, such as preparing for exams [19], reviewing texts for research or to prepare for class [18], and reading to learn specific information [13] are challenging with eReaders. Likewise, annotating can be cumbersome, as mechanical interaction with the device often interrupts the flow of learning. This raises several important questions about the learning process when it comes to tablet textbooks. For example, what does it mean to study integrated multimedia content–i.e., multiple videos/animations, audio clips, expository text, interactive graphics, and more–in the context of an interactive, digital document designed to look like a browse-able book? Additionally, what types of tools must be developed for users to achieve all of their active reading and learning goals in the multimedia textbook?

To address these concerns, we propose SMART Note, a set of tablet textbook tools that provides learners with novel annotation and reorganization methods intended to better support active reading in the tablet environment. The SMART Note design is based on findings from a prior study that suggests existing active reading tools do little to support learners when they struggle to make sense of and subsequently remember content delivered in multiple media formats, are distracted by the mechanics of interactive content, and grapple with the transient nature of audiovisual material. Specifically, this paper makes the following contributions:

- Introduces SMART Note, a novel active reading tool that is based on the learner behaviors specific to a multimedia tablet textbook;
- Assesses usability of SMART Note at two stages of fidelity with 20 users;
- Envisions possible improvements in the learning process when SMART Note is applied to an interactive, multimedia tablet textbook.

Following is a review of related literature and existing tools. We then report on results from an iterative design and usability study that assessed SMART Note at two stages of fidelity. Directions for future research and development are also addressed.

2   Related Work

This work draws on three interrelated fields: 1) active reading, 2) multimedia learning, and 3) current state-of-the-art in tablet textbooks and active reading technologies.

2.1   Active Reading and the Digital Space

Active reading involves reading and studying to understand a document's structure or purpose [1] and reorganizing (e.g., outlining or summarizing) and browsing (e.g., studying annotations and outlines for future recall) [2]. Most research on active reading has focused on the strategies enacted on paper and with narrative text. However, a few studies have indicated that students may have difficulty migrating from print textbooks to interactive digital textbooks, particularly when multimedia is added. Students also exhibit trouble building mental maps of content when it is presented in a nonlinear fashion [19]. Likewise, they have difficulties adjusting to new ways of annotating [14]. Because of this, prior research has indicated that in spite of some novel affordances offered by digital reading devices, learners still generally prefer paper because it easily supports a wide range of active reading requirements [17]. Although significant progress has been made for supporting active reading in the digital space, most systems fall short of providing an active reading experience that fully matches the flexibility learners' desire [16]. At present, college students are moderately traditional in their attitudes toward using tablets and eReaders for textbooks because they believe tools intended to aid in studying are in need of further improvement before they will be fully accepted and widely used [8].

2.2   Multimedia Learning Theory

The Cognitive Theory of Multimedia Learning [15] is a foundation for exploring active reading of interactive, multimedia textbooks. The theory asserts that the presentation of information in both words and pictures facilitates optimal learning conditions. Well-designed multimedia messages therefore foster deeper understanding when they rely on the brain's dual coding ability, processing words and visuals through two different channels of the brain and maximizing understanding. In this regard, multimedia messages are learner-centered rather than technology centered. There is consensus among scholars that technology-centered approaches to learning generally fail to lead to lasting improvements in education [7]. Deficiencies in active reading support among existing tablet textbook environments, therefore, necessitate further research to determine how multimedia textbook developers can implement established principles of multimedia learning to better facilitate active reading. Furthermore, research has shown that processing educational video increases cognitive load because it is difficult for students to synthesize visual and auditory streams of information and extract the semantics of the message [10]. Therefore, a key concern in using video as an instructional device is creating conditions for learners' cognitive systems that help address the processing demands needed to organize and integrate knowledge from dynamic media like video [11]. Ultimately, novel active reading tools must provide learners with better annotation and organizational support.

2.3   Tablet Textbooks and Active Reading Technologies

Tablets have gained traction in education as a number of publishers, namely Pearson and McGraw Hill, have taken the lead in the tablet textbook market. Both companies are partnered with digital publisher Inkling to test-drive new interactive textbooks at several universities [6] and re-imagine the traditional textbook to provide students with a tablet-based multimedia experience. Inkling books boast a number of active reading features, including the ability to highlight text, take notes and explore clickable keywords (annotation); add bookmarks and mark notes others have posted in a social learning network (reorganization); and browse collections of highlighted text, notes, and glossary terms (browsing). New systems that simulate paper and support novel ways of annotating text have also surfaced. Multi-Slate [4] is composed of several interconnected "slates" to provide learners with flexibility required for active reading. Similarly, PapierCraft [12] simulates paper with tablet PCs. Usability research suggests that these and similar systems that combine the affordances of paper and computers may be promising alternatives for overcoming some challenges students encounter with educational content on tablet devices.

3   SMART Note: Student-Centered Active Reading Tools

SMART Note is envisioned as a suite of multimedia annotation tools for tablet textbooks that integrate traditional narrative text with interactive, multimedia content. SMART Note includes features meant to improve two main aspects of the active reading experience. First, SMART Note allows learners to enact several different annotation strategies on multimedia content, while minimizing interaction with the device. Cumbersome interaction mechanics often distract users from content and take attention away from the flow of learning. Second, SMART Note offers more concrete reference points for mentally mapping a collection of annotations back to their original media sources. When content is presented in multiple media formats, it may become difficult to remember from where individual pieces of information originated.

3.1   SMART Note Rationale and Key Requirements

We conducted an exploratory field study to elucidate the nature of active reading in the tablet textbook [9]. Results suggest that this environment represents a heightened level of complexity for learners. Specifically, we identified key active reading behaviors learners enact in the multimedia tablet textbook environment, as well as breakdowns in their ability to access and study annotations effectively:

Sketching Video Frames. Participants often sketched on paper while watching videos to replicate the visual frames in their notes. Some combined several frames of an animation into a single sketch. Participants who did this said it helped them capture information delivered in transient and consequently elusive moving images and audio.

Annotating Connections among Notes and Media. Learners often created diagrams to indicate the media format in which individual pieces of information were originally delivered (i.e., *v*=video). They also drew additional marks to indicate when concepts in their notes were in some way connected. Many said they did this because important contextual connections are lost when annotations are viewed as a list. They also said that when annotations over audiovisuals are combined with annotations from text-based content, it is difficult to mentally map information to its original source.

Fixating on Animation Mechanics. Learners often tried to describe what they remembered seeing in the visual sequences of a video, but failed to render complete or accurate explanations. In these cases, learners seemed to remember the general mechanics of the videos but had less firm a grasp on the descriptive content.

Ultimately, the tensions between learning with and engaging with a multimedia tablet textbook must be minimized for learners to have efficient and satisfying active reading experiences. SMART Note is designed to help learners to achieve their goals while mitigating challenges faced when interactivity and multimedia are integral parts of studying. The following requirements have, thus, driven the SMART Note design:

R1. Develop new annotation tools that better support active reading strategies applied to audiovisuals.

R2. Provide more concrete ways to access important information presented in the often transient and elusive audiovisual format.

R3. Improve the organization of annotations so learners are more easily able to recall the original source format of an individual note, filter notes by type, and make conceptual connections among notes combined in a study guide.

R4. Allow learners to enact their active reading goals without taking them out of the flow of learning, which involves careful attention for effective comprehension.

3.2   Primary Features

SMART Note presents learners with four main ways to annotate video (Figure 1), three of which are new and allow learners to annotate audiovisuals in different ways with a simple button tap. Annotation features are designed to mitigate distractions often caused by the mechanics of interaction and keep learners in the flow of learning. A study guide tool is also included and serves as a visual outline of the most salient portions of a text and a logical organization of a learner's annotations.

Annotation. Included in the SMART Note interface are three new audiovisual annotation features: *Segment Capture*, the ability to capture and annotate short segments from a longer video; *Transcript Annotation,* the ability to highlight and annotate a transcript that corresponds with the audio track; and *Key Term Capture*, the ability to capture key term definitions as they are revealed in a longer video. Like other systems, SMART Note also allows learners to annotate points along a timeline that corresponds with a video. The new tools allow learners to be more granular with their annotations and more easily access portions of a longer video for future review.

Segment Capture directly ties to results from the preliminary study that indicate annotating a single point along a video timeline doesn't provide users with context for an individual note. By allowing users to capture and annotate shorter segments, they are able to easily and quickly access portions of a longer video and avoid grapping with interface mechanics. *Transcript Annotation* allows learners to see a dynamic text version of audio accompanying a video or animation. The transcript can be highlighted, saved for future review, and used to navigate to the corresponding point in the video. The transcript annotation feature directly ties to results from the preliminary study that suggest that audiovisual content is often transient and elusive. Transcript annotation provides learners with a concrete artifact that is easier to access and review later when preparing for exams or assignments. *Key Term Capture* allows learners to activate a *popup view* that alerts them when keywords and phrases are mentioned in a video. Learners may choose to capture a key term and definition, which are then saved separately with other annotations. The key term capture feature also provides learners with a concrete artifact for sometimes transient audiovisuals.

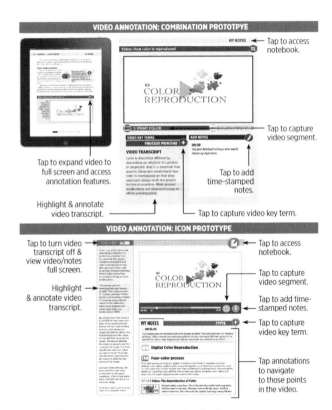

Fig. 1. SMART Note allows users to annotate video in four key ways: segment capture, key term capture, transcript annotation, and time-stamp annotation

Reorganization. SMART Note also includes a notebook and Concept Map Study Guide (Figure 2) where learners can access and review annotations in one place. Other systems often present annotations in a long list with little to no reference to their originating sources. SMART Note provides additional contextual cues and allows users to choose from two different presentation views. *List View* is organized by different kinds of annotations in the order they wee made, and learners can view all annotations at once or filter them by type. Labels or icons also indicate the type of media format in which the original content was delivered. *Map View* presents learners with an interactive concept map or flow chart that illustrate connections among main concepts in the chapter. The concept map is organized topically so learners can see a complete framework for the material they read and so their annotations can be mapped back to key topics covered in the chapter. The Concept Map Study Guide feature ties results from the prior study that indicated it is difficult to make connections among content in the tablet textbook.

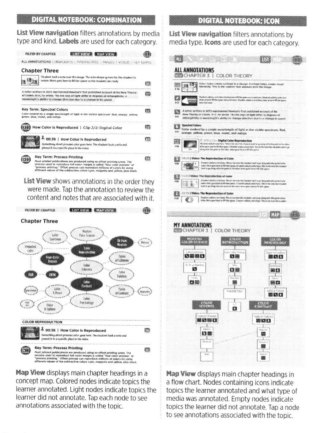

Fig. 2. The *Combination Prototype* (left) makes use of icons and text-based labels for annotation category filters and concept map labels. The *Icon Prototype* (right) makes use of icons for annotation category filters and flow chart labels.

4   Evaluation Study

A task-based study explored usability and user experience on SMART Note at two levels of fidelity. Following is a detailed explanation of the procedures and results.

4.1   Participants, Procedure and Stimuli

Participants. Twenty undergraduate or graduate students (aged 18-26; 10 male, 10 female) at a mid-sized Midwestern University were recruited to participate in the usability study via an all-campus email. The only inclusion criterion was that they own or have extensive experience with a tablet device, such as an iPad or Android tablet.

Procedure. Participants first completed informed consent and brief demographic and reading habits questionnaires. For both rounds of testing, each participant engaged in a 16-task session (complete task table: http://tinyurl.com/ko3t2n7) with each of two versions of SMART Note prototypes. Participants were not given any training about the interface prior to the usability inspection. The nature of tasks was twofold: 1) Seven articulation tasks required participants to explore parts of the prototype and explain how they believed it would function. 2) Nine interaction tasks required participants to complete a number of specific annotation strategies, exposing them to all of the key features in the SMART Note design.

The order in which alternative designs was presented was counterbalanced across participants to minimize learning effect. During task-based inspections, participants rated the perceived difficulty of each task and the researcher completed a success rating for each task. Participants also completed the Systems Usability Scale (SUS) [3] for each prototype. Follow-up questions about usability and preferences regarding the prototypes rounded out the research.

Stimuli. Each stage of testing exposed participants to two fully interactive SMART Note prototypes. Each was designed with content from a chapter on color theory currently used in 100-level graphic design courses. The prototype contained the body of the chapter, with three pages of narrative text and visuals, and the digital notebook, which included six pages of annotations in list view and a concept map study guide that organized notes by key headings and subheadings from the chapter.

There were two main differences between the prototypes, the first semiotic and the second structural. The *Combination Prototype* included both icons and word-based labels for buttons used to operate key annotation and study guide features, while the *Icon Prototype* included only icons for those controls. Additionally, the Concept Map structure in the *Combination Prototype* was a web-like diagram in which nodes represented main topics and key terms in the chapter with lines connecting related concepts. Nodes were also color coded to indicate which topics had been annotated by the learner and which had not. Alternatively, the Concept Map structure for the *Icon Prototype* displayed main chapter headings in the form of a linear, hierarchical flow chart. In each node, icons were used to indicate which sections had been annotated by the learner and which had not. Furthermore, icons were used to provide the learner with visual cues about what kinds of media had been annotated.

In the first round of testing, wireframes included narrative text on color theory with black boxes as placeholders for visual and/or multimedia content. After the first round of testing, prototypes were revised and the level of fidelity was also improved. In the second round of testing, actual images, graphics, and videos were included.

4.2   Results

Overall response to SMART Note prototypes across all participants was positive. All seven of the SMART Note annotation features explored in the usability inspections received favorable ratings from users (Figure 3). On average, participants found SMART Note annotation features easy to learn (average responses ranged from 4.0 to 4.9 out of 5 for all prototypes) and easy to use (average responses ranged from 3.8 to 4.2 out of 5 for all prototypes). Most participants also reported they would use SMART Note frequently if it were available (average responses ranged from 4.1 to 4.3 out of 5 for all prototypes). Figure 4 displays average responses to the Systems Usability Scale.

Evaluation Stage One. For both the *Combination Prototype* and the *Icon Prototype* wireframes, participants had no problems with interaction tasks. A few articulation tasks were more challenging.

Combination Prototype–Wireframe. Three articulation tasks proved problematic in this prototype, all of which related to users' inability to immediately understand the meaning of interaction icons. Users had the most trouble making sense of the video segment capture button (40% success rate). In most cases, users weren't even able to make a guess at what the button meant or would do. Participants also struggled to understand what would happen if they tapped the icon used to navigate to the Concept Map Study Guide (50% success rate). In this version, most

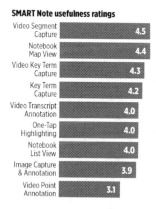

Fig. 4. Participants rated the usefulness of each SMART Note annotation feature. (5-Very Useful; 1-Very Unuseful).

mistook it for a menu button. Participants were equally confused by the icon used to represent key term capture (50% success rate), noting that the grabbing hand looked more like a punching fist. Figure 5 illustrates the problematic icons.

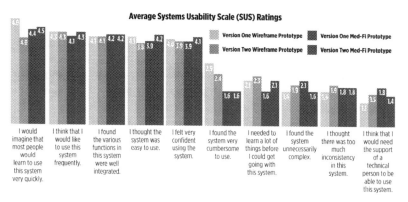

Fig. 4. Systems Usability Scale ratings

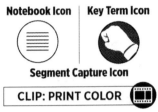

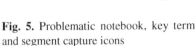

Fig. 5. Problematic notebook, key term and segment capture icons

Fig. 6. Problematic video annotation design

Icon Prototype–Wireframe. Three articulation tasks were challenging. Although users more easily understood the meaning of key term capture button in this version (60% success rate), when used with video, it was more difficult for users to correctly identify (30% success rate). If they noticed it at all, most users thought the "+" sign and key term placed on top of the video was a label for the video as opposed to a key term mentioned in the audio that accompanies the video. The video segment capture feature was also elusive in this prototype (30% success rate), with most users not realizing that it was a button and some indicating they thought it would pull up a new video if tapped. Finally, the Concept Map Study Guide navigation button (a pencil) was again confusing (30% failure rate), with most users reporting they thought it was for note taking. Figure 6 illustrates the problem issues with this prototype.

Evaluation Stage Two. Prototypes were revised to address problems, and the level of fidelity was improved. Success rates for interaction and articulation tasks improved.

Combination Prototype–High-Fidelity. In the redesigned prototype, the segment bar is labeled with the name of the corresponding video segment and the button associated with each segment highlights as the video plays. This redesign improved participants' understanding of this feature (90% success rate). Figure 7 illustrates the redesigned buttons and video annotation features. No other interaction or articulation tasks proved problematic, with success ratings for all other tasks at 60% or more.

Icon Prototype–High-Fidelity. Video key terms were changed to look less like labels and more like independent elements. The new design improved users' understanding (70% success rating). The video segment capture design was modified to provide users with more visual feedback related to its function, which improved participants' understanding (80% success rate). Finally, the Concept Map Study Guide button was changed to look like an actual notebook. This improved users' understanding (70% success rate), and most users preferred this approach. Figure 8 illustrates redesigned buttons and video annotation. No other interaction or articulation tasks were problematic, with success ratings for other tasks at 70% or more.

Fig. 7. Combination *Prototype–High-Fidelity*: Redesigned video annotation screen

Fig. 8. Icon *Prototype–High-Fidelity*: Redesigned video annotation screen

5   Discussion and Directions for Future Work

The generally high success ratings across all prototypes suggest that the SMART Note conceptual and interaction designs provide a sound user experience. However, it is important to highlight what we learned at each stage of evaluation that will inform our future work. For both wireframe prototypes tested in the first stage, users struggled most with articulation tasks that involved describing the meaning and function related to certain icons. Specifically, the most problematic icons–video segment capture, key term capture, and Concept Map Study Guide navigation–were very difficult for users to grasp. Although it is not surprising that users would struggle explaining features they are not familiar with, this did raise the question of just how much visual feedback and/or on-screen labeling users need to fully understand the meaning and function of such features. For example, users clearly needed more feedback to understand not only what the segment capture button does, but also how it works in concert with the video as it plays. Thus, redesigns of both prototypes for the second stage of testing allowed us to experiment with two different degrees of visual feedback. The *Combination Prototype–High-Fidelity* used highlighting labels and the *Icon Prototype–High-Fidelity* used a highlighting video timeline to provide visual feedback indicating which segment was currently playing. In both cases, learners were more immediately able to articulate what was happening and see the relationship between the highlighted segment and the video capture button. Similar visual and textual affordances were added to the key term capture button to give learners a few more clues as to their meaning and function, which also improved performance on related tasks.

In addition, participants' positive feedback regarding the perceived usefulness of each SMART Note annotation feature was also promising. Specifically, it is worth noting that participants rated SMART Note's three novel audiovisual annotation features–video segment capture, video key term capture, and video transcript annotation–to be more useful than video point annotation, a feature currently offered by most video annotation platforms. Likewise, the Concept Map Study Guide *map view* feature was rated higher in terms of perceived usefulness than *list view*, also currently offered by most tablet textbook platforms. Collectively, these results indicate that SMART Note shows promise as a means for improving active reading and learning with interactive, multimedia tablet textbooks. Future work will include an experimental study that compares SMART Note annotation and study guide features to annotation and notebook features commonly offered by existing tablet textbook platforms. Ultimately, the goal is to provide students with better study tools to help them more easily migrate from the printed textbooks they are familiar with to the emerging multimedia books increasingly available on their tablets.

References

1. Adler, M., van Doren, C.: How to Read a Book, The Classic Guide to Intelligent Reading. Simon & Schuster, NY (1972)
2. Aubert, O., Champin, P., Prié, Y., Richard, B.: Canonical processes in active reading and hypervideo production. Multimedia Systems Journal 14(6), 427–433 (2008)
3. Brooke, J.: SUS-A quick and dirty usability scale. Usability Evaluation in Industry 189, 194 (1996)
4. Chen, N., Guimbretiere, F., Sellen, A.: Designing a multi-slate reading environment to support active reading activities. ACM Trans. Comput.-Hum. Interact. 19(3), 1–35 (2012)
5. Clark, R.C., Mayer, R.E.: e-Learning and the Science of Instruction: Proven Guidelines for Consumers and Designers of Multimedia Learning. Pfeiffer (2011)
6. Coombs, B.: Tablets make digital textbooks cool on campus, USAToday.com (June 17, 2011), http://usatoday30.usatoday.com/tech/news/2011-06-17-digital-textbooks_n.htm
7. Cuban, L.: Teachers and machines: The classroom use of technology since 1920. Teachers College Press, NY (1986)
8. Doering, T., Pereira, L., Kuechler, L.: The use of e-textbooks in higher education: A case study. Presented at the E-Leader 2012 Conference, Berlin, Germany (2012)
9. George-Palilonis, J., Bolchini, D.: InterActive reading: Understanding strategies learners use to study interactive multimedia content. Presented at Int'l Conf. on Books & Publishing, Regensburg, Germany (September 2013)
10. Homer, B.D., Plass, J.L., Blake, L.: The effects of video on cognitive load and social presence in multimedia-learning. Computers in Human Behavior 24, 786–797 (2008)
11. Ibrahim, M.: Implications of designing instructional video using cognitive theory of multimedia learning. Critical Questions in Education Journal 3 (2012)
12. Liao, C., Guimbretiere, F., Hinckley, K., Hollan, J.: PapierCraft: A gesture-based command system for interactive paper. ACM Trans. on Computer-Human Interaction 14(4), 1–27 (2008)
13. Lorch, R.F., Lorch, E.P., Klusewitz, M.A.: College students' conditional knowledge about reading. Journal of Educational Psychology 85(2), 239–252 (1993)
14. Marshall, C.: From paper books to the digital library. In: Proc. DL 1997, pp. 131–140 (1997)
15. Mayer, R.E.: Multimedia Learning. Cambridge UP (2009)

16. Morris, M.E., Bernheim Brush, A.J., Meyers, B.R.: Reading revisited: evaluating the usability of digital display surfaces for active reading tasks. In: Proc. TABLETOP, pp. 79–86 (2007)

17. O'Hara, K., Taylor, A.S., Newman, W.M., Sellen, A.: Understanding the materiality of writing from multiple sources. Int'l Journal of Human-Computer Studies 56(3), 269–305 (2002)

18. Tashman, C., Edwards, W.K.: Active Reading and Its Discontents: The Situations, Problems and Ideas of Readers. In: Proc. 2011 Annual Conference on Human Factors in Computing Systems, pp. 2927–2936 (2011)

19. Thayer, A., Lee, C.P., Hwang, L.H., Sales, H., Sen, P., Dalal, N.: The imposition and superimposition of digital reading technology: The academic potential of e-readers. In: Proc. 2011 Annual Conference on Human Factors in Computing Systems, pp. 2917–2926 (2011)

Design, User-Experience and Teaching-Learning

Cristina Portugal

Pontifical Catholic University of Rio de Janeiro, Rio de Janeiro, Brazil
crisportugal@gmail.com

Abstract. This paper has a reflection about how to design digital environments that offer quality of experience to the user. It assumes that the user experience is the set of sensations, values and conclusions that the user gets from using equipment. The values coming from this interaction are not product of the functional experience, but also of the esthetical experience. The quality of this experience may be found in the result of the user goals, of the cultural variables and of the interface design. This article presents a brief discussion about the concept of user experience and after that presents the use of a hypermedia e-book as a pedagogical tool in a graduation course in Design and observations about this digital environment.

Keywords: Design, Hypermedia, User experience, Teaching-learning.

1   Introduction

This paper is part of a research project called "Contemporaneous Design: systems, objects and culture", that is being developed in the Post-Phd graduate program. – it is born from the experience gained in the research work developed during the Post-Phd internship supported by National Council of Scientific and Technological Development (CNPq), an agency of Brazil's Ministry of Science, Technology and Innovation (MCTI). (2010-2012), which resulted in a teaching material called "Design, Education and Technology", which received the "Aid for Publishing" (APQ 3) – 2012.2 - Faperj , constituted by two complementary parts which proposed the experiencing of languages as approached from the printed book, and from the digital book (e-book).(http://www.design-educacao-tecnologia.com/). For Gamba Jr.[1], the author, when devoted to the relations of Design with Learning, makes this study almost a meta language of contemporaneous knowledge, where new media, informational and cognitive models propose an innovative learning perspective.

The characteristics brought by contemporaneous digital technologies create a "new way to conceive and produce design". This study aims to create solutions to reduce this problem and to give interdisciplinary theoretical knowledge which supports discussions about the digital technologies applied to Design learning focused in the user experience aiming the educational, technological development and the innovation with the proposal of helping the propagation and the deepening of this knowledge area.

A. Marcus (Ed.): DUXU 2014, Part III, LNCS 8519, pp. 230–241, 2014.

This paper has a reflection about how to design digital environments that offer quality of experience to the user. It assumes that the user experience is the set of sensations, values and conclusions that the user gets from using an equipment. The values coming from this interaction are not products of the functional experience, but also of the esthetical experience. The quality of this experience may be found in the result of the user goals, of the cultural variables and of the interface design.

However, it becomes hard to have an understanding about concepts which fulfill the study about user experience. At first because user experience is associated to a wide range of diffuse and dynamical concepts, including emotional and affective variables, hedonic as esthetical experiences. Besides, the unity of analysis for the user experience is very malleable, ranging from a single aspect of the individual interaction of the final user with an independent application, up to all aspects of the multiple interactions of end users with the company, and its range of services from multiple disciplines. And, finally, the research panorama in user experience is fragmented and complicated by several theoretical models with different foci, such as: pragmatism, emotion, affection, experience, value, pleasure, beauty, hedonic quality, etc. [2].

The goal of this paper is to bring a reflection about the elements which characterize the user experience, what usability criteria could ease the obtention of positive experiences in users and what characteristics must have a good UX designer.

This discussion is justified, because today there is available a large amount and diversity of literature about usability for software, games, sites, etc. However there are insufficient data determining guidelines for a joint line of work between Design and the several areas which must collaborate in the construction of multimedia systems for Learning which consider the user experience in the teaching-learning process.

This shows the fragility of a conduct lacking criteria in development and utilization of contemporaneous digital technologies in education and the direct consequences of this shortage is an expressive distance between the regular teaching in schools and universities and the possibilities of teaching-learning made available by the new media. This fact becomes more serious in the teaching and formation in design, since a designer must be a translator of signs and languages and, therefore, must be ready to understand and act with the contemporaneous technologies, present and disseminated by the systems and digital languages related to information and communication. If the teaching and formation in design does not allow the access, involvement and knowledge of those technologies in its primary base, which professionals and researchers are we forming for the next future?

This article presents a brief discussion about the concept of user experience and after that presents the use of a hypermedia e-book as a pedagogical tool in a graduation course in Design and observations about this digital environment.

2   Concept of User Experience

The concept of user experience is associated to the before, during and after the interaction and may be understood as a subjective quality of users with regards to a product or service.

In this sense, user experience includes all emotions, beliefs, preferences, perceptions, physical and psychological responses, behaviors and realizations of the user that happen before, during and after the course.

The user experience is a consequence that happens through the brand image, presentation, functionality, system performance, interactive behavior and assistive capabilities of the interactive system, internal and physical state of user resulting from previous experiences, aptitudes, abilities and personality and use context.

Discussions about user satisfaction in face of his experiences have been studied and we may mention the author Mihaly Csikszentmihaly[3], which investigates, by psychology, how to have a happy life; for this, the author finds that the attention of the person must be focused in things that do good to him – things that make him feel the flow, in other words, the person feels immersed, focused in the momentary activity, ignoring external stimuli. Generally, people become apathetic when the perception and the cognitive system have no incentives. However, when overloaded, they become stressed and frustrated.

Some elements which characterize the flow theory are listed below, but it is still unknown which ones of those elements must be present for the flow to exist.

- Challenges that may be overcome;
- Attention focus without significant distraction;
- Clear and defined goals;
- Immediate answer with rewards for actions and overall performance;
- Loss of consciousness about daily worries and frustrations;
- Sense of control over actions, activities and environment;
- Loss of concern about itself, such as hunger and thirst;
- Different sense of time.

For the development of projects focused in the human being it is appropriate that all responsible by planning the project consider the importance about human/ergonomic factors considering [4]:

- how usability is related with the object and use of the product, system or service (for instance, size, number of users, relation with other systems, personal safety or health problems, accessibility, specific application, extreme environments;
- the levels of different kinds of risk that may result from bad usability (in other words, financial, low differentiation of products, personal safety, required level of usability, acceptation);
- the nature of the development environment (in other words, project dimension, marketing team, range of technologies, internal or external project, type of contract).

The International Organization for Standardization (ISO) is a world federation composed by national standardization organizations.

The User Experience Wheel by Magnus Revang [5], it is a model that tries to explain "what is user experience?"

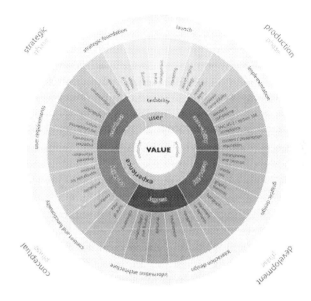

Fig. 1. The User Experience Wheel by Magnus Revang (2007)

According to ISO 9241-11, usability is about the capacity of a product to be used by specific users to reach specific goals with efficacy, efficiency and satisfaction in a specific user context. Efficacy refers to the precision and completeness for specific users to reach specific goals in particular environments. Efficiency is about resources spent with regards to accuracy and integrity of the goals reached. Finally, satisfaction is related to comfort and acceptance of the work system by its users and other people affected by its use. In face of that, the e-book Design, Education and Technology, object of this study, comes from the concern of the author, Cristina Portugal, with the development, understanding, use and efficacy of object systems in the different relations of Design in Situations of Teaching-Learning, having as the main focus the development of hypermedia systems that reinforce the interaction of its praxis with teaching and society where it is inserted.

Aiming to evaluate this e-book, a group of students from the third period of the course of graduation in Design was selected for, during one school year, testing the digital environment Design, Teaching and Technology. Those students were appointed to develop tasks in the system so that data can be collected in order to, latter, analyze and implement the due fixes or changes in the system so that it reaches a better usability and quality rate of user experience.

3   The Digital Environment and the Teaching-Learning Process

The use of the digital environment (e-book) Design, Education and Technology during the teaching and formation in design, gives for Design students an hypermedia tool aiming to collaborate in the teaching-learning process. The contents which compose this version of the e-book are presented in a non-linear way, bringing theoretical and esthetic reflections about the role of Design in the development of Hypermedia environments. The texts present in the book are supported by several pictures and bibliographic references. The item about information that complements the main texts must be highlighted. It offers a selection of books, sites, games, videos and apps which stimulate the book user to go deeper in each particular theme. The e-book content contemplates themes such as: color, typography, image, accessibility, usability, cognition, interaction, materiality, process, technology, reception. Those are some of the questions necessarily involved in the interface between human and physical reality. For Gamba Jr. [1], this is where is founded the challenge and value of Design. The author Cristina Portugal faces this complexity with the systematization needed for keeping the projectual method. Today it is possible to really elaborate a knowledge that allows to coincide, overlap, or to put in dialogue knowledge areas normally set apart by culture, but generously amalgamated by Design. Thus, in order to analyze the use of this e-book as a contemporaneous pedagogical tool in the area of Design, workshops about the theme were developed in seven classes of the third period of the graduation course in Design. Each class went through three stages during the e-book evaluation, which will be presented below. In the first stage the e-book was presented as a supporting tool to Design teaching with the updated content of the class using the e-book – Module Color – a video was played with basic concepts about color and theoretical concepts about hue, value, saturation using the digital environment Design, Education and Technology.

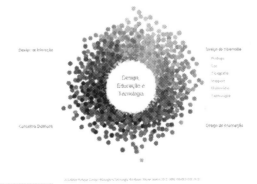

Fig. 2. Home page of the e0book Design, Education, and Technology by Portugal [6]

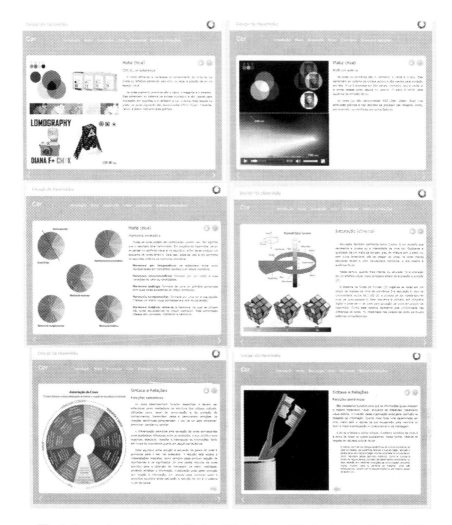

Fig. 3. Screns from hte e0book Design, Education, and Technology by Portugal [6]

The activity of this class was based in content learned by the students, they had to create a line of products (chocolate truffles). Each student in a group should develop a truffle respecting the Design style determined by the group, and the shape and colors should be in accordance with the goal and target group of the project.

For development of the line of truffles the students had to relate color with – flavor – aspect/shape – goal/target public – project resources. Each student should create a truffle using modeling clay according to criteria defined by the group. The access to contents in the e-book were open for research or for solving questions. At the end, the truffles developed by each student should be adequate in order to create a truffle line.

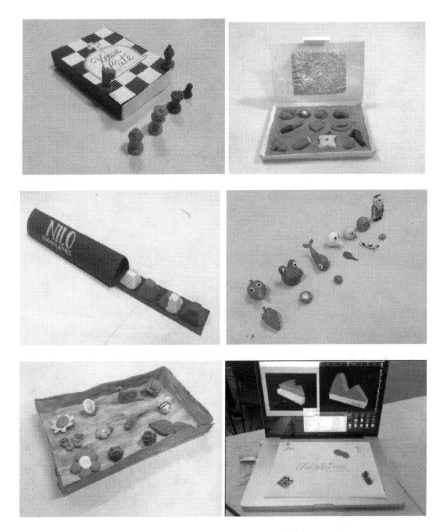

Fig. 4. Results of the students activities

In the second stage the e-book Design, Education and Technology of Cristina Portugal – Module Color – is presented, aiming to make available for the student a material for theoretical study and strategies to allow the access to several experiences in the use of color. For development of activities, the stages followed were:

1. Expository class with visual resources about color theory.
2. Experiences with chromatic harmonies from primary colors.
3. Formation of groups - Brainstorm with the goal of representing, by chromatic harmony criteria, the theme defined by the students.
4. Selection of one criteria of chromatic harmony and creation of a color palette communicating the project theme (objective and target public).

5. Development of layouts of a color composition representing the project theme of each group. The composition created should be brought in the next class, specifying contents learned during the class and which resources of the e-book were used for deepening the theme.

Fig. 5. Students doing the activities

In the third stage the e-book Design, Education and Technology of Cristina Portugal [6] – Module Color – is presented, aiming to work with the students the taxonomic and semantic relations. In this class were discussed the taxonomic relations about the use of color to organize, prioritize and highlight information, also enabling other applications, such as creating perception plans, directing and/or masking the reading, as well as treating the semantic relations of color which comprise its use for acclimatize, symbolize, denote or connote.

The digital resources available in the e-book during the class were video (Beau Lotto: Optical illusions show how we see), images and links for deepening the theme. As an activity for this class a brainstorm was performed aiming to represent, by taxonomic and/or semantic relationships of color with project theme. The proposed activity was to develop a poster about the project theme that the students should have been developing in the discipline "project 3", considering that the color may be considered an information every time that its application is responsible by organizing and prioritizing data or when it can attribute some meaning, in other words, acting individually or integrated and dependent of other elements. The result expected from this exercise is the possibility of communication by color and other graphical resources of each group's project theme.

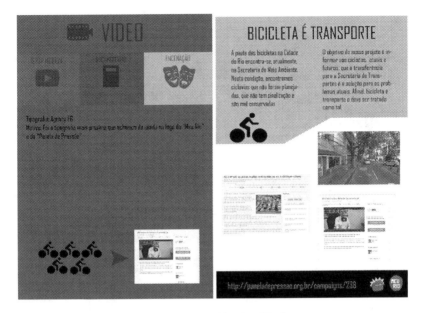

Fig. 6. Results of Student Work

Fig. 7. Results of Student Work

Fig. 8. Results of Student Work

4   Conclusions

Main questions observed in interviews with students during observations collected from students of the graduation course in Design about using the e-book Design, Education and Technology of Cristina Portugal as a teaching resource for the teaching-learning of Design.

4.1   Main Questions Observed

About Number of Accesses. Most of students accessed hypermedia from 0 until several times;

Generally, the accesses were related with three factors: performing active ties, individual learning process and ease of access during class.

Availability of Information. The Wi-Fi network available, in classrooms, collaborated both during presenting the content of e-book Design, Education and Technology as well as during the development of activities, because the students with their laptops, tablets and smartphones could use the available resources such as videos, links, e-book sites easing the search of contents needed for development of tasks.

Among the mostly mentioned contents were the ones related to the development of activities; such as developing the color palette for building the boards for presenting the works.

Some students identified that the videos played in classroom and then posted on Facebook contributed for the learning about color content. It was observed that videos posted in Facebook were viewed by a large majority of students in each class.

About Readability. Almost all students considered the e-book text as readable in their personal computers; however when exposed via data-show in classroom it was necessary to magnify them, so that the students could read.

Association between readability and amount of text was a favorable item, because the students considered the contents as knowledge pills that could be deepened in the e-book itself, as well as in references made available on the field "Learn more".

Content Organization. A large part of students understood the organization of color contents. They considered that the e-book content, as a whole, eased the development of tasks, since the e-book offered theoretical and aesthetic concepts about the Design field as a whole.

Text Language Used. Consistent information. The volume of text on screen was considered large for some students. Considered to be adequate to the use context;

Good receptivity from students to the use of images as examples of content and, specially, videos.

Features Found While Navigating. Students considered easy to navigate the system and find the links on the landing page; some have difficulty in finding the link for the landing page.

The menu and advance/return buttons were mentioned as easier to use navigation tools.

Association between Media Resources. Generally, perceived as adequate by students;

The most celebrated association by students was between text and video, image and text, perceived as fundamental for understanding the context.

Navigation Path and Completeness of Search Results. Some students have difficulty identifying the navigation tools; such as the icon for bibliography and the one for "Learn more".

Generally, opening modules in new tabs caused confusion in students;

The field "Learn more" was considered as important by students for deepening the content, however many did not use it by lack of time.

Generally the e-book content highlight was the clarity in organization and presentation of contents, simplicity and easiness of navigation, consistent presentation of information.

To finish, when analyzing a hypermedia pedagogical tool it was verified that regarding usability, the experience is normally defined considering the ease of use. However, the experience encompasses more than only function and flow, but the understanding compiled through all senses. For Shedroff [7],, the user experience is about the global, general or specific experience that a user, customer or member of the public has with a product, service or event.

According to Couto [8], in today's society, full of changes, the need of reevaluating teaching practices is pressing, leaving aside traditional methodologies. In order to that, the new trends and the use of innovative material must be considered. In this sense, the e-book of Cristina Portugal constitutes an invaluable source of research.

References

1. Gamba Jr.: 4° capa. In: Portugal, C. (ed.) Design, Educação e Tecnologia. Rio Books, Rio de Janeiro (2013)
2. Law, E., et al.: Understanding, Scoping and Defining User Experience: A Survey Approach. In: Proceedings of the Conference on Human Factors and Computing Systems Proceedings, Boston, pp. 719–728. ACM Digital Library, New York (2009)
3. Csikszentmihalyi, M.: Flow: The Psychology of Optimal Experience. Harper Perennial, New York (1991)
4. Associação Brasileira de Normas Técnicas. CEE 126: ergonomia da interação humano-sistema – Parte 210: Projeto centrado no ser humano para sistemas interativos. [S.l.] (2011), http://www.faberludens.com.br/files/ABNT_NBR_ISO_9241-210_2011.pdf (access July 13, 2013)
5. Revange, M.: The User Experience Wheel b (2007), http://userexperienceproject.blogspot.com.br/2007/04/user-experience-wheel.html (access January 30, 2014)
6. Portugal, C.: Design, Educação e Tecnologia (onlibe). Rio Books, Rio de Janeiro (2013), http://www.design-educacao-tecnologia.com/index.html (access July 30, 2013)
7. Shedroff, N.: An Evolving Glossary of Experience Design, http://www.nathan.com/ed/glossary/index.html (access January 20, 2014)
8. Couto, R.: Prefácio. In: Portugal, C. (ed.) Design, Educação e Tecnologia., Rio Books, Rio de Janeiro (2013)

Design for Mobility, Transport and Safety

Challenges in Implementation of TVM (Ticket Vending Machine) in Developing Countries for Mass Transport System: A Study of Human Behavior while Interacting with Ticket Vending Machine-TVM

Mazhar Abbas

Department of Product Design University of Gujrat, Gujrat Pakistan
mazhar.abbas@uog.edu.pk

Abstract. This article aims to identify the problems faced by passengers in developing countries of suburbs and city containing facility of mass transportation system. The research was focused on the difficulties of common passengers that rises up to 80,000 passengers each day in acquiring ticket/tokens for travelling on Metro Bus System (MBS). Particularly the article focuses on the Ticket Vending Machine (TVM) procedure for tokens acquiring and smart card facility procedure for regular MBS users. Beside the role of literacy and training this article also aims the user behavior in adaptation of newly introduce intelligent ticketing system for MBS facility in Lahore. Absence of user friendliness in TVM and few other key issues has been also investigated in this Article. A discussion on highlighted fact that the interface has been adopted from turkey where the scenario and user both have vast difference from the user and scenario here in Pakistan; therefore users found confused in adaptation of such smart facility for MBS in shape of TVM. A rigorous field work was conducted for collecting behavioral and other routine practicing data. It has been done by visual observation (incl. photography), the behavior of everyday commuters and interviewing them using a structured questionnaire. Identification of negligence factor was the part of study in the efforts made by the government; to provide ease for passengers, who interact with TVM, specifically by elderly, disabled and underage travellers at MBS.

Therefore beside the other prospects of this research the main focus of this study is to identify the TVM usage as ignored facility. Suggestions for the future prospects of TVM in Pakistan are also addressed.

Keywords: User experience, Ergonomics, Interface Design, Modern technologies.

1 Background

Due to rapid population growth in and around Lahore; transportation issues has been raised simultaneously. Punjab government has realized the importance of mass transportation system and promptly initiated MBS (Metro Bus Service) in Lahore and

A. Marcus (Ed.): DUXU 2014, Part III, LNCS 8519, pp. 245–254, 2014.

this is the first step to induce mass transportation system in Pakistan of its kind. Metro Bus Service is effectively fulfilling the needs as mass transit system for common masses around city. The success of this project can be evaluated by the frequency of use of this MBS. On an average 4000 -12000 tokens are being sold from each station. Approximately 80,000 travellers use this mass transport system on daily basis. There have been many challenges in handling of MBS. But the prominent challenge of MBS is the ticketing procedure. As per defined procedure there are two ways to get on board to utilize MBS facility for any passenger; popular way of using this facility is token and the other method is smart card facility. Token can be acquired from token booths and Ticket Vending Machine (TVM). There is no tariff and zonal categorization for MBS fare mechanism and upon payment of Rs. 20 travellers can be able travel from station 1 to station 27th.

Overall 36 TVMs are being installed on 27 MBS stations. Tokens are based on RFID (Radio Frequency Identification) technology. This technology earlier used for various transportation networks including the Transport for London which is the largest RFID based operational setup and over 5 million commuters uses this facility on daily basis. (Shin'ichi Konomi, 2006)

Smart card can also be acquired from token booth and it can be recharged from TVM. TVM is commonly called Projected Capacitive Touchscreen Ticket Vending Machine. The manufacturer of installed TVM is Kentkart.

A Tukish IT based transport management service providers. Kentkart introduced their distinguished products including; Automated fare collection, Vehicle management and Smart stop products to MBS.

1.1   Objectives

Following objectives has been determined as foremost goals of this research.

- The key challenge of this study is to investigate the reasons of low attention in using TVM as public facility in comparison of traditional method of acquiring tokens from ticket booth by MBS travellers.
- To investigate the user experience problems while using TVM. Potential of road network transportation ticket usage through TVM in developing countries especially in Pakistan.
- To investigate the differences between elderlies and young generation in relation to easiness in using modern technologies.
- Possibilities of redesigning the TVM for uneducated and untrained travellers

According to the current statistics given by Punjab Metro Bus Authority (PMA) only 5 percent of MBS users are using TVM for attaining the facility of smart card rest of the 95 percent of passenger depending on token booths. The research was conducted to know the reasons of low interest among common masses of MBS users.

The TVM has been introduced for the first time as public facility in Pakistan but most of the passengers do not prefer to use TVM instead standing in long queues.

Studies shown that even in modern day; commonly peoples are not proficient and comfortable in using modern technologies. Furthermore technologies are inducing complications day by day for those who have less technical aptitude thus they get gradually cut off from modern culture in society .(Günther Schreder, 2009).

1.2   Infrastructure for MBS

There is an important factor observed during the research that is pedestrian bridges. These pedestrian bridges are being used by all pedestrians whether they use MBS or not. This activity is in practice due to unavailability of specified facility or location for crossing the road for non MBS users. This cause heavily engaged pedestrian bridges other than the activity of token booth and TVM due to this rush and congested situation on pedestrian bridge is common situation over the pedestrian bridge. Thus MBS users experience difficulties in availing the facility of token booth and TVM.

Fig. 1. Queues for acquiring ticket from Ticket booth

The associated facility for the MBS and pedestrian bridge users is escalator which is especially installed for senior citizens and disables passengers but unfortunately there is no facility for wheel chair users neither the height of TVM allows any wheel chair user to operate it appropriately.

1.3   Operational Responsibility

Overall Punjab IT Board (PITB) is responsible for the operational responsibilities but PITB further assigned to Inbox to deal all IT related functions and procedures including viewing and monitoring of the ticketing system. Additionally on everyday basis these tokens required to get refresh this practice avoid any unfair use of these travelling tokens. Each token can be used within 72 hour otherwise it gets expired and required recharge to get operational again.

2   Methodology

Twofold methodology was adopted in the research. The procedure of investigating TVM usage is based on field survey; that holds mainly interviewing of MBS passengers, additionally observation was also played vital role in gathering important findings. In the observation part actual user experience has been recorded to identify the real time problems in TVM currently being used in Lahore MBS.

Research has been accomplished keeping in view the existence of communal gaps. As study verifies mid-90s research that an important indicator of communal gaps exists in shape of literacy social status, ethnicity income and gender (Günther Schreder, 2009).

Interviews have been taken of 180 passengers including both genders of men and women from 14-55 years of an age. Observation of 60 passengers has also been recorded with a team of 12 Surveyors. Two members of each team spent approximately 4 hours independently on specified locations. The survey was conducted two days twice a day on the basis of routine and peak hours. Further survey was conducted on Sunday and Monday to distinguish the situations in holiday and working day.

Additionally interviews of key operators of MBS have been conducted to acquire the statistics of MBS and TVM.

2.1   Observations

In the first phase there was field observation accompanied on 6 busiest stations of MBS these stations are located in the suburbs of Lahore (Pakistan) that contained the blend of educated and uneducated passengers, keeping in view of covering the suburban area where education and living standard are on an average line.

In the observation phase passengers were observed while they were acquiring or using smart cards or tokens either from token booths or from TVM. Observers were instructed to notice the fault closely as the correct procedure of Interactive systems is based on true input by the user and flawless process by the Interactive system.(Paul Curzon, 2007) . Additionally latest trends of automatic fare collection systems (TVM in our case) required precise performance and faultless reliability. (Akio Shiibashi, 2007). There is need to acknowledge that the very design of technological products can be effected in the growth of digital divide and as well minimize the difference by using "universal design" methodology. (Michael Sengpiel, 2011).

Following are the key segments of field survey in observation phase

- Procedure of acquiring tokens from ticket booth
- Procedure of acquiring smartcard
- Procedure of recharging smartcard from TVM
- Procedure of acquiring tokens from TVM

To acquire the travelling token for MBS; users are require to either reach token counter booth or TVM, that is on the similar location over pedestrian bridge and in most of the stations it is adjunct to token booth.

Ticket Booth: A prepaid token can be acquired by paying 20 Pak rupees only for any destination from any of the 27 stations. The token booth representatives are consisting of at-least 2 and maximum up to 4 members and duties of these workers are on shift basis.

TVM: In mostly MBS stations TVM is hide behind the queue of passengers who are waiting for their turn to acquire the token from token booth. TVM is basically installed to accomplish following functions.

Acquiring travelling tokens by paying currency notes
Acquiring travelling tokens by paying coins
Smart card recharging up to rupees 1000 maximum

2.2   Interviews

The important most phase of the field survey was interviewing with travellers. Travellers of MBS are most likely shown their keen interest in giving interviews. The interviews were consisting 10 short questions. Including their personal information, MBS performance, acquiring RFID based tickets and problems in using TVM

3   Results

Study has shown that passengers feel missing user-friendliness approach in TVM beside high ratio of currency note rejection. Following opinions were studied in the portion of questionnaire to know the main factor of TVM negligence.

1. Lack of appropriate training among TVM users
2. Hesitation while using TVM due to illiteracy
3. Unfriendly TVM interface and design
4. High rejection currency ratio
5. Insufficient classification for returning money in shape of coins

Results have shown that users of MBS do not choose TVM to acquire travelling tokens due to the fact that most of the passengers hesitate to use TVM and the reason of hesitation is that the large numbers of travellers doesn't even experience computer or smart phones and ATM machines in past.

Travellers of MBS can be distinguished into regular and non-regular (occasional) users. The huge number of occasional users has been identified in the field survey but overall regular users dominate as shown in the figure 2.

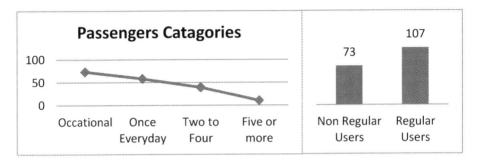

Fig. 2. MBS frequency of use by various traveller groups

Both categories of users are satisfied with the efficiency of MBS but demanded more token booths to avoid time and energy loss in acquiring tickets. In the category of occasional users most of the users are independent travelers who mentioned that MBS facility should be extended to their area as they have no such facility at their routine route. Occasional travellers use MBS for roaming around for meeting or approaching certain markets and places covered MBS route.

Only 1/4th of the travellers belongs to female category as majority of the MBS travellers are male. Survey shown that in Pakistan male passengers are culturally permissible to travel independently even if they are under age instead female travellers even though 50% of the seats in Buses are reserved for female travellers

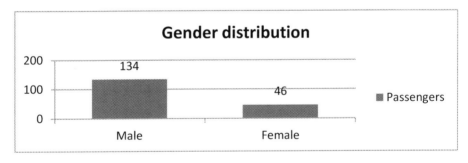

Fig. 3. The MBS is being used by male travellers dominantly

Trend of smart card found encouraging in regular users of MBS but the pace of adaptation of novel technology is very slow. Initially it has been understood that currency note rejection and difficult interface are the key indicators in avoidance of TVM by the travellers but most of the passengers have no experience of using modern technologies including computers, smart phones and TVM machines.

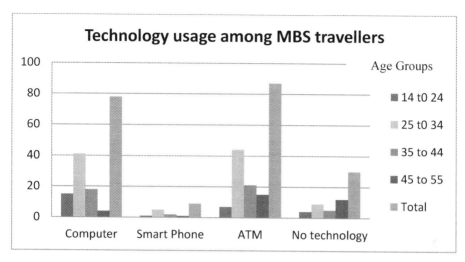

Fig. 4. Modern technologies trend of use among MBS travellers

Results prove less practice of novel technologies among MBS travelers including touchscreen interface and other related technologies. This impacts the user behavior in motivation of using TVM interface and other computer based technologies.

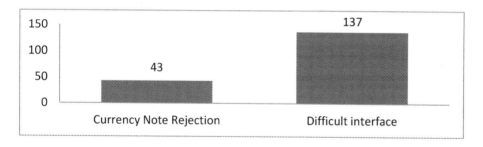

Fig. 5. Identified problems in TVM usage- TVM hardware and software behavior

The issues in hardware and interface difficulties also investigated from user experience point of view and it was only questioned to those who got tokens from Token booth. The answer of 137 travellers claimed that they either avoid or not willing to experience the TVM due to the reason that TVM interface is not user friendly. 43 passengers claimed that they have experienced more than once but currency note rejection frustrates to avoid the facility. The sophisticated TVM sensors doesn't accept flimsy, old and folded corner currency notes thus currency note rejection causes delay and incomplete operation.

In answer of high currency note rejection the PMA conclude that due to bad condition of currency note possession by travellers is the key reason of currency rejection otherwise RFID travelling tokens can be acquired easily against inserting coins instead currency.

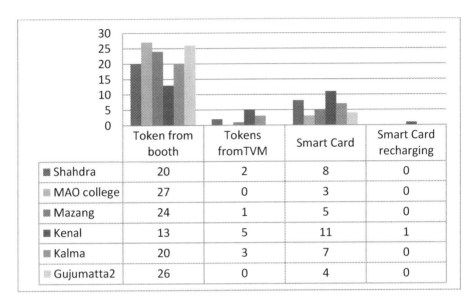

Fig. 6. Tokens and smart card usage at various MBS stations

Trend of acquiring tokens from token booths is common practice apparently the usage of TVM that is very low on every station. Adaptation of smart card is growing in regular travellers but overall awareness of this facility is missing among common MBS passengers.

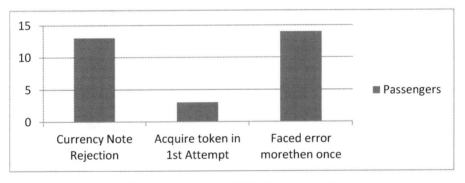

Fig. 7. User experience of TVM- Observation Phase

In the observation phase it has been observed that to acquire a token from TVM in first attempt is a big challenge as shown in figure 7. Very few numbers of travellers successfully obtained tokens in their first attempts. Results indicate that it is a huge challenge for travellers with no experience to attempt for hit and trial and consume their time in acquiring token from TVM.

the installed facility of TVM for acquiring token. and go

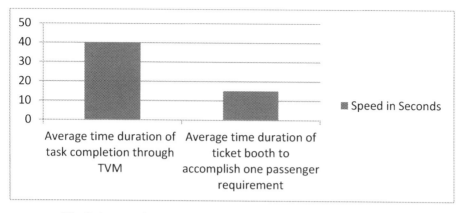

Fig. 8. Average duration of acquiring token from ticket booth and TVM

An average speed for facilitating one passenger is approximately 15 seconds from token booth. Therefore approximately 12 passengers are being facilitated in 3 minutes as buses are scheduled to arrive at any MBS station after every 3 minute.

Conventional ticket acquiring procedure through token booth is comparatively fast in terms of window operation but if it includes the time of standing in queues so that would be bit higher and it takes 4-6 minutes on an average in routine time and peak time it rises to 15 minutes or higher.

4   Discussion and Conclusion

Blend of multiple problems are recognized as cause of low interest of using TVM among MBS travellers.

Technological Trends: The important identification of undeveloped trend of TVM use is inappropriate background of novel technology usage by the MBS travellers. Passengers of above 45 years age hardly tried to acquire token from TVM as they rarely experience such devices thus they hesitate using TVM to avoid any inconvenience. Female travellers are also required to encourage utilizing the TVM. The ratio of user experience of smart technologies is increasing day by day as smart technologies are becoming part of routine practice among common masses especially by youngsters.

Literacy: In our case literacy can be acknowledged as another significant barrier in understanding vocal and written instruction to perform the task. Literacy is the barrier in understanding and follow-up of instructions. Beside the literacy factor the training factor is dominantly missing as an illiterate balloon seller proved his proficiency in using TVM as he operated TVM upon the guidance of our surveyors only once.

Interface Design: Study identified multidimensional problems that may be resolved by improving the design of TVM interface. The Interface can be redesign by using training videos including more graphical icons for illiterate and untrained travellers.

Another possibility of training travellers is to educate users in onsite training session. Usage of smart card among MBS frequent users to avoid hassle and other failure is appreciable. Additionally e-ticketing for more convenience of MBS travellers can be introduced. A bright future of e-ticketing can be seen in various international projects furthermore these technologies embrace the time management and most progressive solutions in terms of cost effectiveness.

TVM Efficiency: On an average currently installed TVM takes about 20-40 seconds on each transition and if PMA increases the number of TVMs up to 4 on each station and improve the efficiency by reducing the processing time then the productivity of TVMs can be raised and enough to facilitate 30 travellers in 8-10 minutes. additionally running cost of TVM is more viable in comparison of human based token booth existing solution.

Acknowledgements. I would like to thank all team members of Product Design Department University of Gujrat for their active participation in Field survey specially Tahir Shafiq who facilitate surveyors to conducted field survey.

References

1. Zolfaghari, S.: A model for holding strategy in public transit systems with real-time information. International Journal of Transport Management 2, 99–110 (2004)
2. Schreder, G., Siebenhandl, K., Mayr, E.: E-Inclusion in Public Transport: The Role of Self-efficacy. In: Holzinger, A., Miesenberger, K. (eds.) USAB 2009. LNCS, vol. 5889, pp. 301–311. Springer, Heidelberg (2009)
3. Konomi, S.: Ubiquitous computing in the real world: lessons learnt from large scale RFID deployments. Pers. Ubiquit. Comput. 11, 507–521 (November 2007)
4. Curzon, P.: An approach to formal verification of human–computer interaction. Formal Aspects of Computing 19, 513–550 (2007)
5. Shiibashi, A.: High-speed processing in wired-and-wireless integrated autonomous decentralized system and its application to IC card ticket system. Innovations Syst. Softw. Eng. 3, 53–60 (2007)
6. Sengpiel, M.: Young by Design: Supporting Older Adults' Mobility and Home Technology Use through Universal Design and Instruction. In: Stephanidis, C. (ed.) Universal Access in HCI, Part III, HCII 2011. LNCS, vol. 6767, pp. 230–239. Springer, Heidelberg (2011)

Simulation of Wireless Sensor Network for Flood Monitoring System

Manal Abdullah

Faculty of Computing and Information Technology FCIT,
King Abdulaziz University KAU, Saudi Arabia
maaabdullah@kau.edu.sa

Abstract. Monitoring environmental disaster such as flooding is highly improved using ICT. Deployment of sensor networks to monitor physical environment is one of the most important applications for Wireless Sensor Networks (WSNs). In this paper, we model and simulate flood monitor case in Jeddah, Saudi Arabia. Using OMNET++ simulator , we employ Direct Diffusion DD routing protocol to operate flood case.. We first have developed one of the well-known sensor network protocols which is DD. Then, we evaluate the performance of our simulated case by computing several statistics including power consumption, end-to-end delay, throughput to measure the availability and scalability of the network and decide the best possible configuration that well monitor our case. Our results determined that the best sensor network configuration for flood monitor system in the area of interest is 135 sensors with memory capacity of 80 to 120 message entries.

Keywords: WSN, Flood control, Direct Diffusion, Discrete Event Simulation, OMNET++.

1   Introduction

Flooding is a growing problem in the world. In Jeddah, Kingdome of Saudi Arabia (KSA), we have a special interest with the flooding problem because this disaster happened twice in the few recent years. It has a significant effect on residents, businesses and commuters in flood areas. The cost of damage caused by flooding correlates closely with the warning time given before a flood event, and this makes flood monitoring and prediction critical to minimizing the cost of flood damage. Wireless Sensor Networks (WSN) has proven its worth in monitoring physical quantities and environmental disasters. That is because this technology has the capability of quick capturing, processing, and transmission of critical data in real-time with high resolution. Environmental disasters are one of the major applications of wireless sensor networks. Jeddah in KSA has faced flood disasters that could have less harm on citizens with an advanced networking monitoring and alarming system.

WSNs consist of individual nodes that are able to interact with their environment by sensing or controlling physical parameters; these nodes have to collaborate to fulfill their tasks as, usually, a single node is incapable of doing so; and they use wireless

A. Marcus (Ed.): DUXU 2014, Part III, LNCS 8519, pp. 255–264, 2014.
© Springer International Publishing Switzerland 2014

communication to enable this collaboration. Sensor is the object used to gather information about a physical object or process, including the occurrence of events (i.e., changes in state such as a drop in temperature or pressure). These are called remote sensors. From a technical perspective, a sensor is a device that translates parameters or events in the physical world into signals that can be measured and analyzed [1]. In most cases, it is very difficult and even impossible to change or recharge batteries for these sensor nodes. For this reason, energy efficiency is of primary importance for the operational lifetime of a sensor network. [2],[3]

The focus of this work is to simulate a wireless sensor network flooding monitoring system. The system will be responsible for water level monitoring during the flooding periods.

OMNeT++ [4] is a discrete-event simulation platform that is trusted to model and simulate variety of networking systems. As a first step, we have developed one of the well-known sensor network routing protocols which is Directed Diffusion. We evaluate the performance of our simulator by computing several statistics including many performance parameters to measure the availability and scalability of the network and decide the best possible configuration. Some previous work has proven its worth using same type of monitoring. It shows how to benefit from WSN and solve this problem.

Hughes, et. al.[5] introduced two main classes of flood prediction models. The first is referred to as spatial models, and the second class is referred to as point prediction models. Traditional flood monitoring approaches impose a rigid separation between the on-site WSNs that are used to collect data, and the off-site computational grid which is used to analyze this data.

Castillo, et. al. [6] presented the ongoing effort in providing the population of the Andean region of Venezuela with a flashflood alerting system by making use of wireless communications and information technologies. A key component is a WSN that is used for monitoring the environment and tracking the disaster. The main objective of the system is to gather environmental information and, based on the collected data, to alert the authorities and the population at risk autonomously.

Price, et.al.[7] developed an environmental sensor network deployed in the Great Crowden Brook catchment area of the Peak District, United Kingdom. The main aim was to assess the deployment methodology for "multi hop" networks and assess the sensor node technology choices from an operational perspective. The area of interest is deep within a steep sided valley where there is no GSM coverage, and thus the only cost effective way to transmit real-time sensor readings to a remote lab is via multi-hop networking. The design strategy has been to minimize the duration and frequency of communications, and limit such communications to the transmission of summary data (from node to node) and alarms from base-station to end user.

2   Sensor Network Architecture

Wireless Sensor Network (WSN) is a type of networks that consists of individual nodes and are able to interact with their environment by sensing physical parameters.

There are two types of node: Source which is the sensor that provide sensed information, Sink which is the base station that acts as the destination where the information should be delivered.

Sensor networks are usually related to real-time computing. Despite the differences in purposes of sensor networks they all share the need for distributed form of organization[8]. The following subsections detail the WSN components.

- **Sources:** they are the entities which provide information that is the actual nodes which sense data. [8]
- **Sinks:** They can be called the destination where the information should be delivered to. They could be in 3 types: just sensor/actuator node – entity outside the network e.g. *Personal Digital Assistants* (PDA) or handheld – gateway to another larger network such as Internet [8].
- **Base Station (BS):** It is a single powerful node, usually a sink node, which is used to connect a WSN to a wired network. BS is supported with powerful resources and extra capabilities in communication and processing compared to a normal wireless sensor node [9].

2.1   Sensor Node Hardware Overview

A basic sensor node comprises five main components [8] as shown in Figure 1

- **Controller**: The controller is the core of a wireless sensor node. It collects data from the sensors and processes this data. It is the *Central Processing Unit* (CPU) of the node.
- **Memory** Some memory to store programs and intermediate data is required.
- **Sensors and actuators:** The actual interface to the physical world; devices that can observe or control physical parameters of the environment.
- **Communication devices:** It is used to exchange data between individual nodes.
- **Power Supply:** As usually no tied power supply is available, some forms of batteries are necessary to provide energy.

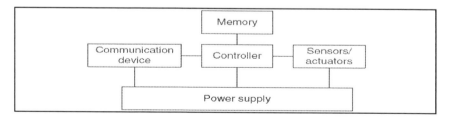

Fig. 1. Overview of main sensor node hardware components [8]

2.2   Water Level Sensors

Liquid level sensors as its name indicates are used to detect the level of the liquid and the interfaces on the liquids, where the liquid in the intended network is water. Three level sensors types, that are Ultrasonic, submersible and bubbler. These sensors are considered to be used for water level monitoring in the case of floods. Comparing between them, submersible sensor seems to be the most suitable. Ultrasonic sensor has the disadvantage of being damaged by floods. This is critical since our network will deal with floods caused by rains so the reliability of the sensor is not guaranteed. Bubbler sensor has the disadvantage in terms of maintainability which will require continuous visits to refill the tanks. In addition, the power consumption is large in this type of sensor that besides the cost [10][11]. In contrast, submersible sensor is waterproof, using power moderately, requires little maintenance and easy to install. For those reasons it will be the choice for the network. [10]

2.3   Routing Protocols

Recent advances in wireless sensor networks have led to many new protocols specifically designed for sensor networks where energy awareness is an essential consideration. The four main categories explored for WSN are data-centric, hierarchical, location-based and Network Flow and QoS-aware protocols [12].

Direct Diffusion is a data dissemination and aggregation protocol, which is data centric and application aware. It has several key elements as follows:[13][14]

- *Data naming:* sensing tasks are sent by the sink in attribute-value pairs.
- *Interests and gradients:* Each named task description constitutes an *interest* that has a timestamp field and several *gradients* fields. As *interest* propagate through the network it, and the *gradient* from source back to sink is setting up.
- *Reinforcement:* at the beginning the sink sets low data rate for all the incoming events. Then it can reinforce one particular sensor to send the events with a higher data rate by resending the original interest message into a smaller interval.

This protocol meets the main requirements of WSNs such as energy efficiency, scalability, and robustness. However, it has some limitations such as; the implementation of data aggregation requires some synchronization techniques that are not realizable yet in WSNs. Also, DD can't be applied in applications that require continuous data delivery to the BS [13],[14],[15]. For these limitations, we developed DD protocol for our flood monitoring system by modifying the original DD in application and network layers.

3   Problem Formulation

Many agencies over the world are taking care of the weather and environmental phenomena. In Kingdom of Saudi Arabia (KSA), we have the Center of Excellence in Environmental Studies (CEES), as one of the excellence centers affiliated to King Abdulaziz University (KAU). Also, the General Directorate of Civil Defense (GDCD) and Presidency of Meteorology and Environment (PME) in KSA who warn people by sending warning reports to media and GDCD. The scenario of operation is illustrated in figure 2 .

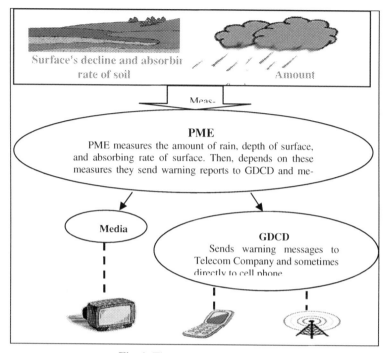

Fig. 2. The scenario of flood alert

3.1   Simulation Setup

The following information is used for model setup

- **The Monitored Area:** Bani Malek St. 4896.27m [from Google Earth]. This street was the most street that have been affected by floods in 2011.
- **Number of Base Stations (sinks):** one placed in the middle of the street.
- **Number of Sensors (sources):** Obstructions assumed to be presented, so the radio frequency for the sensor is almost 305m. This leads to 16 sensors to cover one side of the street. For self-healing purposes we will add another sensor in the opposite side of the street which form zigzag shape, as shown in figure 3 .The total number of sensors are 32.

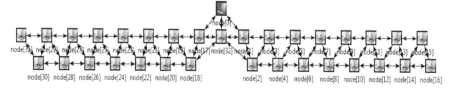

Fig. 3. WSN Configuration in OMNet++

- **Sensor Installation:** 1 meter altitude from the surface of the street. Thus the ground height is the zero level of the sensor.
- **Interest:** According to *Federal Emergency Management Agency* (FEMA), six inches of moving water could breakdown most of cars and make the walker fall [16].

For energy saving, all sensors are off and wake up when tasked by the sink. The sink sends a task or interest at specific periods. The sensor which measures an event will send back the response to the same gradients. Once the sink received event, it resends an interest with higher data to Reinforce specific path. The flood monitoring system work flow is illustrated in figure 4.

The above information has been used to setup the simulation model using OMNET++ [4]. The parameters adopted during simulation test along with their respective values are summarized in Table 1.

Table 1. Simulation Parameters Configuration

Values	Simulation Parameter
17400	Network size (m2)
135	Number of sensors
100	Broadcasted message entries
62	Packet size (byte)
6	Threshold (inch)
1.9	Interval (s)

4   Results and Discussion

4.1   Performance Metrics

The high growth of WSN research has opened challenging issues about their performance evaluation. Performance is affected by several issues. In this section we review performance based on the scalability and availability which we have used in our research.

In scalability, WSN consists of hundreds of sensor nodes, densely deployed in a regional area[17]. Protocols must thus scale well with the number of nodes. This is often achieved by using distributed and localized algorithms, where sensor nodes only communicate with nodes in their neighborhood [18]. In availability, as most sensor nodes will be restricted concerning their energy capacity, all protocols and algorithms must be energy-efficient and save as much energy as possible. Since the most energy is consumed during the wireless communication, the radio must be turned off most of the time. But also the transmission of data should be energy-efficient in order to minimize the number of sent and received packets [18].

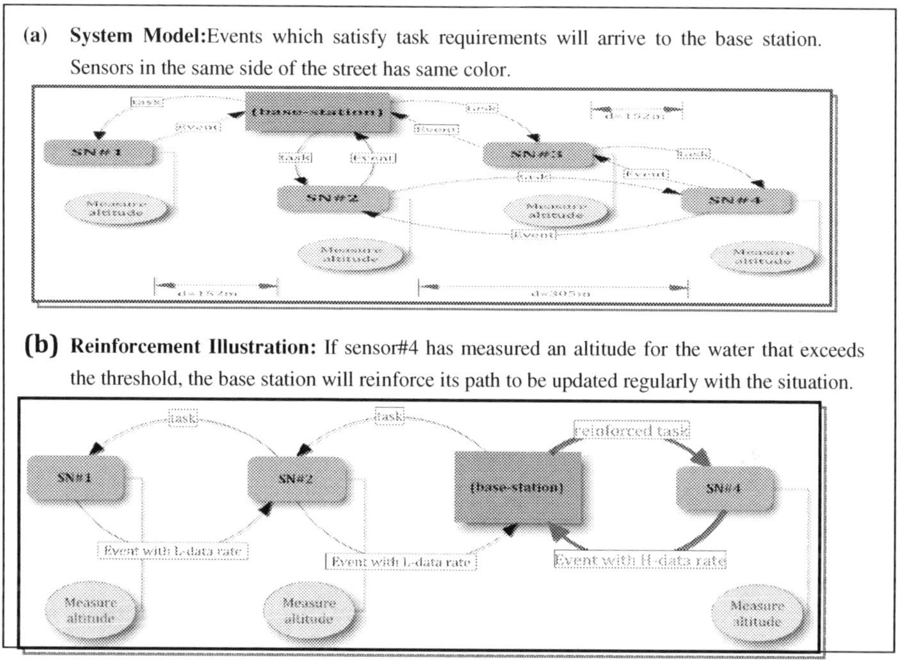

(a) System Model:Events which satisfy task requirements will arrive to the base station. Sensors in the same side of the street has same color.
(base-station)
SN#1
SN#2
SN#3
SN#4
task
Event
Measure altitude
(b) Reinforcement Illustration: If sensor#4 has measured an altitude for the water that exceeds the threshold, the base station will reinforce its path to be updated regularly with the situation.
task
reinforced task
(base-station)
SN#1
SN#2
SN#4
Event with L-data rate
Event with H-data rate
Measure altitude

Fig. 4. Flood Monitoring System workflow

Our research is evaluated against availability and scalability. Availability is determined by two metrics: average energy cost and storage capacity. While scalability is measured by throughput and delay.

4.2 Availability

Availability is the property of the system being in function. In our research , we have measured the availability using two metrics: average power consumption and throughput. Figure 5 shows the average energy consumption of the network while the number of nodes varies from 18 to 264. Energy consumption is increased with increasing the number of nodes in the network due to routing process.

Power Consumption (mW)
Number of Nodes

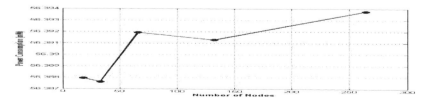

Fig. 5. Average energy cost per node versus number of sources

Storage affects on routing process since it is based on how many packets will be sent/forwarded via the network. The factors used in this metric are the number of data packet forwarded versus the max number of entries in the network. Figure 6 shows relationship between number of entries in the network and number of packets forwarded. The importance of increasing storage has benefit in conserve the network traffic by decreasing the number of packets forwarded through nodes.

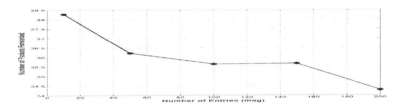

Fig. 6. Cost of storage (Packet forwarded versus network entries)

4.3   Scalability

The number of nodes in WSN has an impact on network scalability. Scalability could be measured with the following metrics: End-to-end delay and throughput. A higher latency when network workload is high due to increasing sources and the network contention caused by path sharing between different sources. From figure 7, the max end to end delay exists at 132 network nodes after which we have very small decrease of latency.

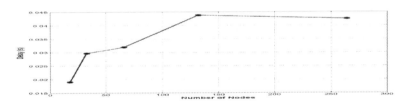

Fig. 7. End-to-End transmission delay versus number of sources

Throughput is a measure of network performance that is the average rate of bit per second (bps) that has successfully deliver over a communication channel. Figure 8 shows that throughput decreases with the increase of number of nodes. This is because the network is not sufficiently loaded and the required transmission messages are less than the network capability. At nearly 70 nodes, the throughput starts increasing.

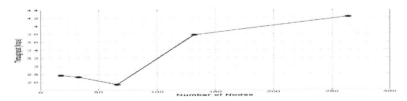

Fig. 8. Throughput versus number of nodes

5   Conclusions

The wireless sensor network used in our simulation scenario consists of 32 stationary sensors and a base station. The nodes are supposed to be aligned in the monitored area of 17400 m2. At each simulation test, the nodes transmit sensed data during their corresponding time slots, only when an incident is detected. This happens whenever the current value of the sensed attribute is greater than the threshold value which is set to 6 inches according to FEMA [16].

In order to experiment the performance for our simulated network, we review the performance based on the scalability and availability . In addition, the results of analysis to check that the results conform to the rules defined by the requirements. We have reached the optimum configuration of WSN Flooding System in the assigned area as:

The number of sources must be more than 132 node to operate with minimum delay. Using 132 nodes, the longest delay between two nodes is less than 0.04 s. The number of nodes between 70 to 150 nodes would also optimizes the network power consumption.

The importance of increasing the storage has benefit in conserve the network traffic. However, because memory capacity is limited, between 80 and 120 message entries are quite enough and result in a reasonable number of forwarded packets.

Acknowledgement. I would appreciate the support and help of the computer science department at Faculty of Computing and Information Technology FCIT, King Abdulaziz University KAU.

References

1. Ahmed, A., et al.: Wired Vs Wireless Deployment Support for Wireless Sensor
2. Oh, E.: Study of Network Design Factors That Influence Industrial Fieldbus Network-Based System Integration. In: Industrial and Systems Engineering. The Ohio State University (2009)
3. Dargie, W., Poellabauer, C.: Sensor Classifications. In: Fundamentals of Wireless Sensor Networks: Theory and Practice, p. 336. John Wiley & Sons, United Kingdom (2010)
4. OMNet++, User Manual Version 4.3, http://www.omnetpp.org/doc/omnetpp/manual/usman.html (last retrieved at December 2012)
5. Hughes, D., Greenwood, P., et al.: An intelligent and adaptable grid-based flood monitoring and warning system. Citeseer (2006)
6. Castillo-Effer, M., Quintela, D.H., et al.: Wireless sensor networks for flash-flood alerting. In: Proceedings of the Fifth IEEE International Caracas Conference on Devices, Circuits and Systems (2004)
7. Price, M.C., et al.: Development & Demonstration of the Utility of Wireless Environmental Sensors Incorporating a Multi-hop Protocol. IEEE (2008)
8. Karl, H., Willig, A.: Protocols and Architectures for Wireless Sensor Networks, p. 526. John Wiley & Sons, England (2005)

9. Irrigation Training and Research Center. Water Level Sensor Testing Summary. ITRC, California Polytechnic State University, San Luis Obispo, California, USA (2004)
10. Andreas, T.G., et al.: Comparative Simulations of WSN (2008)
11. Jevti, M., Zogovi, N., Dimi, G.: Evaluation of Wireless Sensor Network Simulators (2009)
12. Noury, N., Herve, T., Rialle, V., Virone, G., Mercier, E., Morey, G., Moro, A., Porcheron, T.: Monitoring behavior in home using a smart fall sensor. In: IEEE-EMBS Special Topic Conference on Microtechnologies in Medicine and Biology, pp. 607–610 (October 2000)
13. Rabaey, J.M., Ammer, M.J., da Silva Jr., J.L., Patel, D., Roundy, S.: Picoradio supports ad hoc ultra-low power Wireless Networking 38, 333 (2002), IEEE Computer Magazine
14. Petriu, E.M., Georganas, N.D., Petriu, D.C., Makrakis, D., Groza, V.Z.: Sensor-based information appliances. IEEE Instrumentation and Measurement Magazine, 31–35 (December 2000)
15. Montresor, A., Caro, G.D., Heegaard, P.E.: Architecture of the Simulation Environment (2003)
16. FEMA. During a Flood (August 11, 2010), http://www.fema.gov/hazard/flood/fl_during.shtm (retrieved June 7, 2012)
17. Busse, M.: Wireless Sensor Networks, http://pi4.informatik.uni-mannheim.de/pi4.data/content/projects/wsn/
18. Chipara, O., et al.: Real-time power-aware routing in sensor networks. IEEE (2006)
19. Lee, J., et al.: RFMS: Real-time Flood Monitoring System with wireless sensor networks. IEEE (2008)
20. Standard Emergency Warning Signal (SEWS), http://www.emergency.nsw.gov.au/content.php/491.html (retrieved June 6, 2011)
21. Khadari, F.: Weather Index, http://www.pme.gov.sa/WeaIndex.asp (retrieved June 9, 2011)

Enhance User Experience Moving in Campus through Understanding Human Spatial Cognition

Szu-Miao Chen[1], Yi-Shin Deng[2], Sheng-Fen Chien[3], and Hsiao-Chen You[4]

[1] Institue of Creative Industries Design, National Cheng Kung University
[2] iNSIGHT Center, National Taiwan University
[3] Department of Architecture, National Cheng Kung University
[4] Department of Multimedia Design, National Taichung University of Science and Technology
{mszu.2003,yishin.deng,hcyous}@mail.com, schien@mail.ncku.edu.tw

Abstract. There are always interactions between people and environment involved in our daily activities. People gather different kinds of information from their surroundings; after interpreting by mental models, they give responses to environment. Among all the information, spatial information is the one which played an important role in supporting our living activities such as traveling or commuting. Besides, people in the same environment will form cognitive map differently owing to their mental model, which process perceived information, and purpose of activities. Therefore, to construct better information architecture for providing needed information, the understanding of differences of spatial cognitions between individuals is essential. This paper explored different kinds of users' spatial representations about a specified semipublic space, university campus; and through applying user interview as well as living lab concept, the findings can be referred for future study to build an customized, comprehensive spatial information providing system.

Keywords: User Experience, Spatial Cognition, and Information Architecture.

1 Introduction

As one of the most significant parts in living activities, the interaction between people and environment has great influences on our daily experience. Through the continuous interactions with surrounding environments, people learn and build their own knowledge about the space. Furthermore, they can form cognitive map of that place [1].

However, people learn spatial knowledge differently according to their mental models, purposes of activities, and cultural backgrounds, which leads to the differences of spatial representations between individuals. Besides, context changes while people are moving within places. Which means that even with the same goal, the information needed will be different based on their location.

Therefore, spatial information should be customized provided in order to support activities and enhance user experience in an environment. To reach this target, the understanding of how different people learn a certain environment based on their purposes and backgrounds is essential. What's more, the findings of those spatial

A. Marcus (Ed.): DUXU 2014, Part III, LNCS 8519, pp. 265–272, 2014.
© Springer International Publishing Switzerland 2014

representational differences between individuals could be further analyzed to build comprehensive information architecture.

This paper, as part of a large holistic study on spatial cognition and information, explored different kinds of users' spatial representations about a specified semipublic space, university campus, which is seldom being discussed before. As a semipublic space, campus is generally open to public; however, unlike parks, campus was built for certain purposes such as lecturing, administrations with specific target audiences, students and faculties, within a time period. In other words, it includes both public and private functions. For this purpose, taking advantages of its convenience as well as flexibility, an online web application was built after conducting some user studies as a method to collect various perspectives of how people understand the place.

2   Theoretical Background

In our everyday life, we use mental models to process surrounding information and figure out ways to solve problems. Accordingly, mental model basically governs our behaviors; it influences how we respond to external world. In other words, when we see and perceive descriptions from a world, we can construct a similar, yet less rich, representation—a mental model of the world based on the meaning of the description and on our knowledge [2].

Mental model creates the lens through which we see the world, however in most situations we merely notice its existence. Besides, because mental model is formed by learning and experiences, it may differ from person to person. Yet the diversity of ways how people see descriptions from the same world is valuable. Multiple mental models bring multiple perspectives to bear. Through the understanding of how different people see a same world, and how they interpret perceived spatial information based on their mental model, the differences as well as the patterns can be found to help construct more comprehensive information architecture for environmental learning.

Spatial representation is a process through which people gather spatial information from surrounding environment and form an internal mental understanding of that spaces which can be expressed by symbols or texts. In other words, the representations of space show how people interpret spatial information, and in which way they express the information (Fig. 1).

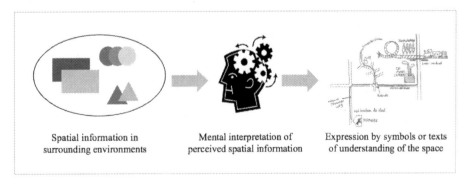

| Spatial information in surrounding environments | Mental interpretation of perceived spatial information | Expression by symbols or texts of understanding of the space |

Fig. 1. The process of spatial representation

What's more, spatial information exists in many forms in our living environments. For example, in the famous book, The Image of the City (1960)[3], Lynch has contributed five identified features of environment that are assumed mostly likely to be perceived— edges, paths, nodes, districts and landmarks— by asking people to describe cities they lived in.

A well-formed spatial representation contains enough and clear information which is all what users need. As many psychologists claimed, too much information may cause cognitive overload and may therefore make situation even worse.

In addition, while conducting activities especially navigation activities within an environment, there are three forms of knowledge being involved in the perception of spatial information: Landmark knowledge, route knowledge, and survey (i.e., map) knowledge [4]. Both of the landmark and route knowledge are egocentric, which means we measure the information such as distance and height of a landmark or a route according to where we are. Yet the survey knowledge is allocentric. It is objective and irrelevant to our position. That is, we can acquire survey knowledge of a place even we are not in there.

3   Methodology

In the past, spatial cognition research in spatial activities such as navigation mainly focuses on the discussion of linguistic representations. Whereas, the purpose of this study is to explore different kinds of users' spatial representations about a semipublic university campus, National Cheng Kung University, through applying Living Lab concept.

As mentioned before, after a certain time of learning, the environmental familiarity increased. The familiarity to an environment is formed by two components: specific experience of given locality and global experience of city structure, hierarchy of roads, traffics and directing signs. Both of these two components are forming directly yet only representing part of individual's total spatial knowledge. There is other part

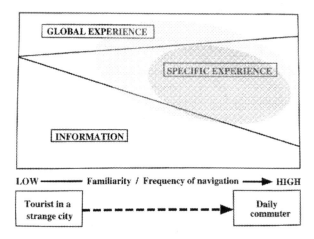

Fig. 2. Components of spatial knowledge and its change according to familiarity

of information acquired from external sources, such as maps, navigation media, street signs, people, and so on. The illustration (Fig. 2, without colored highlight) below made by Eliahu Stern & Juval Portugali (1999) [5] well expresses the three main components of forming spatial information and the change according the familiarity.

The red-colored, highlighted part in the illustration above shows the focus this study is going to explore. The global experience will be less considered than specific experience, because we assumed that all subjects participated in the experiments are sharing certain degree of the same cultural background and knowledge living in this country.

3.1   Living Lab Approach

Living lab concept originates from MIT, Boston, professor William Mithchell, MediaLab and School of Architecture and city planning. According to Schumacher (2007) [6], this new research method has many characteristics. With its "users as innovators" approach, Living Lab needs users' involvement in the all R&D and evaluation cycle, instead of joining at the end phase of development as trail testers. In addition, in order to get access to the users' ideas and their knowledge, the researchers need to build multi-contextual sphere in which an interactive and co-creative approach can be applied between developers and users over the whole process. Besides, with the use of ICT (Information and communication technology), the interactivity of Living lab can therefore reach a bigger community than traditional method. The comparison between Living Lab and traditional research method is illustrated by Schumacher A.J. and Feurstein B.K. (2007) as below. (Fig. 3)

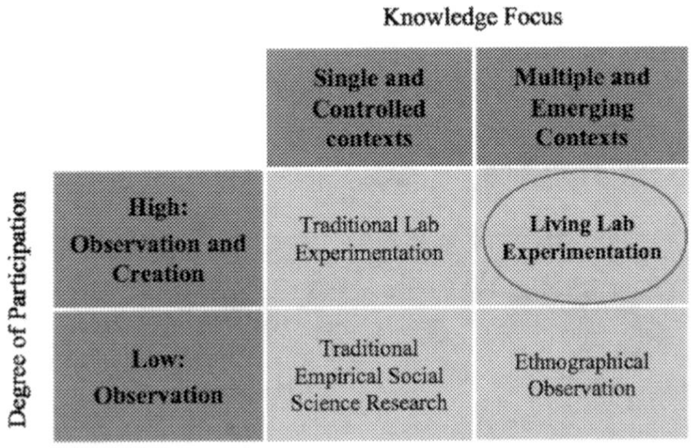

Fig. 3. Participation and Context of innovations according to Schumacher (2007)

This paper mainly focuses on the research question: What kinds of spatial cognitions will be formed by people with various purposes of activities in the campus?

3.2   Designing Experiments

The exploration was divided into two parts: user interview and online data collecting. In the user interview session, five subjects who have experiences either studying or visiting NCKU were interviewed for their image about the environment of the campus. Any way to describe the image such as by talking, by drawing, or by sharing photos is allowed for the purpose of maximizing the diversity of possible spatial cognition.

According to the findings from user interviews, we built an online application which combines both the questionnaire and a map-based painting board. The questionnaire is designed to collect basic user information which may be considered relevant to the differences of their spatial cognition, for example, their background knowledge about selected place, their reasons and experiences of being in the campus; whereas the online painting board (Fig. 4) is designed to widely collect spatial understandings about the place from as many people as possible. Compared to traditional ways of user data collection such as Probe [7], the reasons to use web-based application to collect data is because it can gather much information in a short time, without considering time and weather constraints. And when the amount of collected data becomes larger, the analysis after data collecting is more likely to be holistic. These advantages are corresponding to the characteristics of Big Data: volume, variety, and velocity. Besides, through online application, updates and adjustments can easily be made, which ensure the flexibility of data collecting.

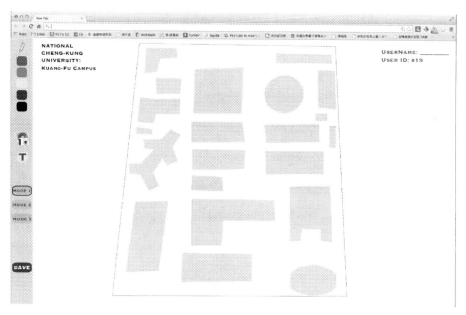

Fig. 4. Template of web-based painting board

4   Discussion

The findings from the user interviews with five subjects who have been staying in the campus, either for long-term studying or for short-term visiting, confirmed that individuals learned and formed their own spatial cognitive maps according to both experience gained in the place and internal mental models. Besides, the context in which people acquire spatial knowledge is quite influential on their forming of spatial cognitive maps.

In other words, they are two factors we found based on the interviews that can be seen as variables during the forming process of spatial cognitive map: time and purpose of activities. As Tolman(1948) [1] mentioned, cognitive map of a space can be formed after a period time of learning about that environment; however we found that people start build and organize acquired spatial knowledge as soon as they get into the place. Some people may present poor spatial understanding due to less information noticed and perceived, or it is just because ignored information is relatively not important while considering their purpose of activities.

4.1   Results and Findings

As you can see in the figures below (Fig. 5), both of the two figure (a) and (b) are drawn by 20s-year-old male master students respectively. The only difference between them is how much time they have spent in this environment. The subject who drew figure (a) visit campus only for meeting friends, he stayed for only three hours in the campus; whereas the subject who drew (b) has lived and studied in NCKU for over five years.

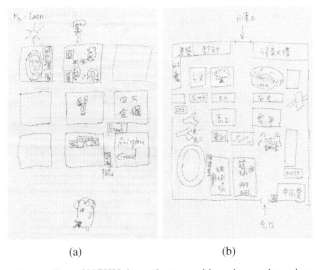

(a)   (b)

Fig. 5. Spatial understanding of NCKU drawn by two subjects in user interviews. (a) Drawn by a NCKU visitor after his second-time visiting the university and stay for approximately three hours in the campuses. (b) Drawn by a second-year master student studying at NCKU. The drawn part is the one of nine campuses of NCKU where his department is located.

Hence, as what we can expect, there are some obvious differences between the two drawn illustrations (a) and (b):

Firstly, the scale is different. This shows that subject who is familiar with certain area will tend to describe it in details compared to subject who is a foreigner in the environment. Those details come from the accumulation of spatial knowledge by actively living and learning about a place.

Secondly, in addition to more details can be described by subject who is familiar with the place, the location accuracy of those provided spatial information is also higher than subject who is unfamiliar with the campus.

Thirdly, though people with higher familiarity with the environment can provide more detailed description with more accurate location, the two subjects are just holding different perspectives toward the same place. Not only the ways they described a place are different, but what they've noticed, and what kind of information they've perceived are also varied. In summary, a tourist may see something a resident has never noticed; and vice versa.

Based on those findings, a web-based quantitative user study was therefore conducted. In order to collect as diverse as possible more spatial cognitions from people with different mental models in different context, we allowed users to paint, to add notes, and to attach images, as long as it can well represent their understanding about the place. Additionally, after carefully considerations, two scales (which are mode1, mode 2) with relative locations of buildings are provided as references to assist users' to draw their spatial descriptions. (Refer to Fig. 4)

4.2   Future Work

In future work, we plan to bring the implementation of the web-based survey application to more quantitative study with at least 50 data collected for further analysis. Besides, the concept of GIS (Geographic Information System), which is highly involved in our daily life, and its operational and transactional characteristics are all considerable extension.

Due to time constraints, only some areas of the campuses can be covered in the research; yet the findings as well as the designed method of how to efficiently collect individual's spatial understanding can be referred in the future study. In addition, the user experience in city mobility, which has larger area and more complex contexts, may also be discussed in the future.

5   Conclusion

In order to explore different kinds of users' spatial representations about a specified semipublic space, university campus, which is seldom being discussed before, we taking advantages of the convenience as well as flexibility of technology: an online web application was built after conducting user interviews as a method to collect various perspectives of how people understand the certain place.

Considering there are little studies discussing about the diversities of human spatial cognition according to the two factor: time and context, in campus environment, this study contributed to the relevant literature by providing findings to improve user experience moving in university campus.

References

1. Tolman, E.C.: Cognitive maps in rats and men. The Psychological Review 55(4), 189–208 (1948)
2. Johnson-Laird, P.N.: Mental models and human reasoning. Proceedings of the National Academy of Sciences 107(43) (2010)
3. Lynch, K.: The image of the city. MIT, Cambridge (1960)
4. McCall, R., Benyon, D.: ENISpace: Evaluating navigation in information space. In: de Bra, P., Leggett, J. (eds.) Proceedings of WEBNET 1999, pp. 1344–1345. AACE, VA (1999)
5. Stern, E., Portugali, J.: Environmental cognition and decision making in urban navigation. In: Wayfinding Behavior: Cognitive Mapping and Other Spatial Processes, pp. 99–118 (1999)
6. Schumacher, A.J., Feurstein, B.K.: Living Labs - a new multi-stakeholder approach to user integration. In: Gonçalves, R.J., Müller, J.P., Mertins, K., Zelm, M. (eds.) Enterprise Interoperability II, R, vol. 2007, pp. 281–285. Springer, London (2007)
7. Information & Design, http://infodesign.com.au/usabilityresources/culturalprobes/

Pilgrim Smart Identification
Using RFID Technology (PSI)

Abeer Geabel, Khlood Jastaniah, Roaa Abu Hassan,
Roaa Aljehani, Mona Babadr, and Maysoon Abulkhair

King Abdulaziz University, Jeddah, KSA
{aboor_19,k.jastaniah,r0ro4ever,lolo_1409,muna_bader}@yahoo.com,
{Mabualkhair,kjastaniah}@kau.edu.sa

Abstract. Yearly, from all around the world, different nations millions of pilgrims gather for Hajj season in holy Makkah to perform Hajj rituals, so Saudi government and Hajj institutions facing a big challenge and a lot of problems summarized in losing the official identification documents, language barrier in communicating with the authority especially in emergency cases (need guidance when missing directions, and medical problems) and determining the identity of dead pilgrims.

The aim of Pilgrim's Smart Identification (PSI) system is to improve the current identification method by using RFID (Radio Frequency Identification) technology.

Keywords: RFID Technology, Hajj, Hajj Campaign, Smart Identification.

1   Introduction

Yearly, from all around the world, different nations and cultures millions of pilgrims are gathered for Hajj season in one spot in holy Makkah to perform Hajj rituals, doing the same things at the same time. The Hajj is held in the second week of the last month of the year in Hejri calendar (Thul' Hijjah).

Hajj is the fifth pillars of Islam. Every Muslim has a good health and enough money must perform Hajj once at his life time. The Hajj season is the most crowded event that is repeated every year and the number of pilgrims is rapidly increasing year after year. That means the Saudi government in collaboration with Hajj institutions must do their best to make it the most beautiful and comfortable journey for every pilgrim. However, Saudi government and Hajj institutions facing a big challenge and a lot of problems due to the huge number of pilgrims summarized in language barrier, pilgrim identification in case of losing etc. So, they try to solve these problems especially lost problem by nominating a worker for every group of pilgrims to look for and guide the pilgrims by checking their names' lists and passports many times to make sure that none of them are lost. This process is a waste of time and effort.

A. Marcus (Ed.): DUXU 2014, Part III, LNCS 8519, pp. 273–280, 2014.
© Springer International Publishing Switzerland 2014

2   Problem Definition

During Hajj season many of the Saudi ministries, government's sectors and other committees who are responsible for managing and coordinating the pilgrims' services face hard time in organizing the Hajj process. The difficulties in organizing the Hajj process come from many issues dealing with the rite of the pilgrimage, because it is a unique gathering of an extensive number of Muslims who came from various countries to join processions of hundreds of thousands of people, who simultaneously converge restricted area on Mecca for the second week of the Hajj, and perform a series of rituals.

The large gathering of people raised many critical issues for the organizations and committees who have a full responsibility to take care of them. Some of these issues are summaries in:

— Losing the pilgrims' identification documents.
— Lacking of knowing the direction to re-join their campaign.
— Communicating with the guidance and authorities in case of missing or losing properties.
— Knowing the health medical record of the pilgrims.

For instance, if a pilgrim does speak neither Arabic nor English language, his\her doctor will not be able to get any information about his\her medical history. In emergency situations, the patients might come to the hospital in a coma, stroke or any critical state when the doctors have to find out the reason as soon as possible so the proper action can be taken immediately to save their lives. In presence of language barrier the situation will be more difficult to manage. The technology has made things easier for doctors in term of patient's life saving. Validity of patient's data in a special (card or tag) including chronic illnesses, current medications, previous surgeries and allergy to some food, material or drugs can help the emergency team to act rapidly and therefore saving the patient's life. For example, the patient who comes with coma due to overdose or side effect   of his/her own medicines can be treated and improve dramatically if the specific Antidote given after identifying the drug that caused this coma, in this case the patient is unconscious and presence of his/her current drugs list will be enough to save life. This is a simple data that has significant benefit so how if a proper health record is available.

Last ten years ago, the Ministry of Hajj has provided nine computerized centers which operated by a total of 350 manpower. The ministry has also established 21 guidance centers to assist and help pilgrims in the holy places under their supervision [1].

According to the data that the Saudi government has shown that "18 percent of the second proportion of pilgrims suffered from being lost; that percentage represent 200 thousand pilgrims a year, and 84 percent of the lost pilgrims agree that this problem discomfort and confuse their Hajj journey" [1].   Arafa, Mena, Mozdalefa and also the holly Mosque are a very wide area that pilgrims go to and gather in during the Hajj season.

It is obvious that the language barrier is considered one of the main difficulties in communication. According to the reported interview done with one of the hiring guidance, worked as a guide man on one of the past Hajj seasons, who pointed to the difficulties that happened due to the lack of having a way to find the location of each pilgrim professionally. This guidance mentioned that he had communicated with pilgrims who spoke different languages daily using an information card carried by each pilgrim. However, he emphasized that the process in this case required walking with each pilgrim to his camp for a simple reason because of the language barrier and the lack of understanding. He said: "I am having a big difficulty with pilgrims who missed their cards that indicate the position of their camps, which means that I have to contact with all the Hajj campaigns, one after the other and tell them the description of the lost pilgrim until I find the right campaign"[2]. Furthermore, the Ministry of Hajj recruited many multilingual translators to facilitate the communication with the pilgrims from non-Arab nationalities; additionally it requested all owners and investors of residential units and hotels to provide identification cards and distributed them to all pilgrims [1].

The other problem is raised during the pilgrims' transportation, when the responsible workers for the Hajj campaign check out each pilgrim's passport, in order to ensure that they are carrying the same group of pilgrims. The process of checking the pilgrim's identity during the transportation consumes a lot of time and it is obvious to lose some of them.

To avoid all the mentioned problems, we decided to implement "Pilgrims Smart Identification" (PSI) system using RFID technology. PSI is aimed to identify the lost, die, sick pilgrims and guide the lost pilgrims to their camps and overcome the language barrier.

Radio-frequency identification (RFID) is a technology that uses the radio waves to exchange the data between the RFID reader and the electronic tag attached to an object, for identification purposes. RFID makes it possible to give each pilgrim its own unique identity number [3]. In other words, it does not require line of sight to "see" an RFID tag, the tag can be read even if it is a few meters away, and unlike barcodes RFID tags can be read hundreds of tags at time.

3   Objectives

The main objectives of PSI are including the following:

1. Make Hajj journey easier for pilgrims and reduce the problems that possible occurs.
2. Save Hajj authorities time and efforts in identifying pilgrims.
3. Overcome the language barrier obstacle between the pilgrims and Hajj authorities in case of losing or missing.
4. Identify the lost, died, and sick pilgrims.
5. Know the health medical record of the pilgrims.

4   Automatic Identification Related Work

RFID-Based Pilgrim Identification System proposed by Mohandas which a prototype for identifying pilgrims to facilitate the declaration of the pilgrims in case of dying or missing. He used RFID passive technology for the performance of the prototype, and he concentrate on storing pilgrims' information such as personal information, medical information and contact information of the pilgrim's Hajj campaign. [4].

Additionally, [5] proposed RFID Based Library Management System (LMS). The library management system is used to save the time to the members who work on the library, fast access to the book in searching, and decrease errors that for example happen in put book in shelf etc. RFID used here rather than barcode because it can be re-used tags many times, to speed up self-check in/out processes, to make the library secure from the theft, tags cannot be visible like put it in cardboard cover of book, and can store data such as stack number, book number, author information but barcode just store identification number. It used RFID technology with two readers: Work-about Pro Ultra High Frequency (UHF) RFID handheld reader that has Windows Embedded CE 5.0 and full Video Graphics Array (VGA) that use for searching, and Mercury4 RFID reader used to transfer data to a remote computer over a network, EPC global Generation2 UHF passive RFID tags. In LMS the RFID has three integration modules: Searching module for fast searching of books, transaction module provided transaction forms, and monitoring module to monitor the incoming and outgoing things [5].

Furthermore, RFID has been used to manage the patient in the hospital [6]. Hospitals always used paper to save information of the patient during registration and updated by nurse. This is inaccurate because it written by hand. Nurse takes care for inpatient and outpatient. The Hospital Patient Management System (HPMS) provides low cost of health care, easy automate and simple patient identification processes in hospitals and use mobile device for design a health care management system. The system used RFID technology, to update information Wi-Fi connection using mobile devices such as PDA. RFID tag is put on wristband and has an identification number with password to protect it, and can store patient data such as name, patient ID, drug allergies, drugs that the patient is on today, blood group. Each patient wear wristband and contains an antenna and a tiny microchip. The data can read from the tag even the patient was sleep without disturbing them. The data can enter/update by HPMS application developed by Agile System Development Methodology (ASDM) using C# in Microsoft Visual Studio.net 2003 environment [6].

5   PSI Methodology

The first step the developers need to decide in order to produce the desired system is the instruments and tools used for the data collection. Thus, PSI developers decided to use interviews and questionnaire instruments to help them understand the Hajj campaign mechanisms in dealing with their pilgrims' identification in case of getting lost and treating them when they have health problems. Also, through the interviews with the Hajj campaigns, the PSI developers investigated about the different ways to organize work for the Hajj campaigns' workers. The other instrument in the data collection is the distribution of the questionnaire to recognize the users' characteristics and the most important tasks that need to be included in the PSI project.

The PSI developers realize that, in order to facilitate storing and retrieving the information, they need to build a database.

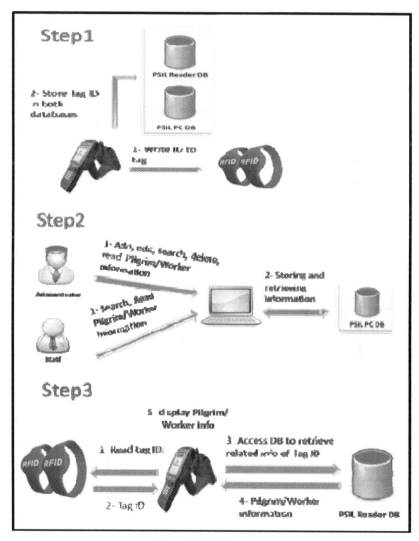

Fig. 1. PSI Architecture

6   PSI Architecture

PSI system is based on utilizing the RFID technology, and it consists of four components, which are RFID wristbands, end terminal PC, the database, RFID reader. Figure -3 shows the PSI components and architecture.

The RFID wristband is a basic component in PSI system which plays a major role in saving the pilgrim's or worker's information. The wristband is distributed to each pilgrim and worker. It's used as an identifier; it has a unique tag id stored in it.

The stored information will include the following:

- Personal information like the name, telephone number and address in Saudi Arabia and in Home country, nationality, etc.
- Medical condition information
- Contact information of his Hajj campaign.
- Picture of the pilgrim or worker.

PSI system consists of two applications; the first one is on the PC and the other is on the RFID handheld reader. Both have a graphical user interface which is developed by Visual Studio 2008 and C# to facilitate the data entry as shown in figure -2 and figure -3 respectively. Every application has its own independent database. So, PSI system has two databases which are used to store pilgrims, workers and login data, one of them stored in the PC which is developed by SQL server 2005 and the other one is in the RFID reader (CSL CS101-2 EPC Class 1 Gen 2) which is developed by SQL compact edition 3.5. The replication is used between the two databases.

RFID reader sends periodic signals to inquire about any tag in the surrounded area. The tag is represented in PSI system as a wristband.

The passive tag draws the power from RF field of the reader to operate its microprocessor that strengths the data, then the RFID tag reflects the signals which contains the tag ID that's stored in the manufacture. These tags will be reassigning them with a new tag id by the hajj campaign based on their rules by using the function (Write Tag ID) at the reader application.

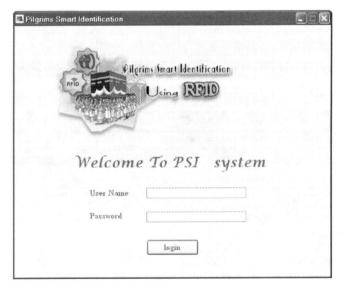

Fig. 2. PSI PC's Application

Through PSI PC's system the administrator assigns pilgrim/worker information to these tag ids. PSI PC's application has two types of accounts; one for administrator with the ability to add new pilgrim or worker, edit pilgrim or worker information, read pilgrim's or worker's information, delete pilgrim or worker, search for pilgrim or worker information, add new administrator, add new staff, delete staff and change password. Staff account also interacts with PSI system by read pilgrims or workers information, search for pilgrim or worker information and change his password. The adding and deleting on the PC's application will be stopped at a specific time after insuring that every pilgrim and worker in the campaign has been registered to the system. The PSI reader's application is also standalone, its main functionality is to read the stored Tag Id on the wristband's tag, retrieve the related information of the pilgrim or worker and display it in the RFID reader screen, only if the tag is assigned to a pilgrim or worker in the database. Also this application has the ability to add and delete pilgrim's or worker's information in case of emergency.

The entire previous scenario is done to achieve PSI system's objectives and goals.

Fig. 3. PSI Reader's Application

7   Conclusion

PSI system is developed to facilitate most important Hajj obstacles from different aspects. Mainly, from Hajj authority perspective, it saves Hajj authority's time and efforts by facilitating pilgrims' and workers' information registry. Additionally, PSI system helps guiding lost pilgrims to their campaigns by using RFID reader to read campaign information (campaign name, address and phone). Also the stored information helps to contact with pilgrims' family in their countries in emergency cases.

In addition to making Hajj journey comfortable for every pilgrim by avoiding big troubles due to lack of communication and understanding because of the language barrier that appears in different areas. From the medical side, PSI helps doctors to know the health medical records of pilgrims by correctly diagnosing the emergency cases. Also it helps in identifying lost, sick and deceased pilgrims.

PSI system is composed of PC application and RFID reader application both are developed using C# and .Net farmworker. In PC application, PSIL is used to register pilgrims' and workers' information and modify operations to the SQL server database which makes them easier and faster than manual registration. Also it enables the person responsible to view the list of all pilgrims and workers and to search about a specific pilgrim and worker.

While the reader application provides different functionalities. for example, programming the wristband with a given tag id, which reads multiple tags at one time then displays pilgrim or worker information in the reader screen related to the selected tag from SQL compact Edition database. In unusual cases, there is an ability to perform add and delete operations from the reader application.

Finally, both applications are user-friendly and have simple interfaces, the developers hope PSI system will have a good impact on social services and help Hajj authorities to manage Hajj problems in an efficient way.

8   Future Work

PSI system is developed to help Hajj authorities in identifying pilgrims and workers. It consists of two parts: the first part is a PC application which is used to facilitate entering pilgrims' and workers' information (add, edit and delete) operations and the second part is Reader Application which is considered as the core of the system. In addition to pilgrims' and workers' information entry process, it is used to write id tags, read tag id and retrieve the related information from the database.

1. Implementing GPS to determining the pilgrim's position
2. Help request feature: possibility of guiding the pilgrims to their camps in case of losing direction.
3. Encryption the stored information in the database.
4. Generalize the RFID technology to all the Hajj sectors to minimize the common problems that occur during Hajj season.

References

1. Mufdila, M.: Loss of pilgrims to the absence of a uniform system of addresses for cities and neigbohoods. Okaz 3351 (2010), http://www.okaz.com.sa/new/Issues /20100820/Con20100820368420.htm
2. Fakihi, H.: Scouts go beyond the language barrier and guide the pilgrims with different languages. AlSharq Al-Awsat 11325 (2009), http://www.aawsat.com/details. asp?section=4&article=546499&issueno=11325
3. RFID: An Introduction (2006), http://www.msdn.microsoft.com/en-us/ library/aa479355.aspx
4. Mohandes, M., Turcu, C.: A Case Study of an RFID-based System for Pilgrims Identification and Tracking in Sustainable Radio Frequency Identification Solutions, pp. 87–104. InTech, Dahran (2010)
5. Dhanalakshmi, M., Uppala, M.: RFID Based Library Management System

Timeaxis Design of a Service System Growing Values of Mobility Using the M-V Model

Kei Kamiya[1], Akira Kito[1], Jaime Alvarez[2], Koichiro Sato[3], Hidekazu Nishimura[4], Yoshiyuki Matsuoka[3], and Satoru Furugori[5]

[1] Graduate School of Science and Technology, Keio University, Yokohama, Japan
`k.kamiya.0123@gmail.com`, `fa0kitou@hotmail.co.jp`
[2] Monterrey Institute of Technology and Higher Education, Monterrey, Mexico
[3] Department of Mechanical Engineering, Keio University, Yokohama, Japan
`{k.sato,matsuoka}@mech.keio.ac.jp`
[4] Graduate School of System Design and Management, Keio University, Yokohama, Japan
`h.nishimura@sdm.keio.ac.jp`
[5] Mazda R&D Center Yokohama, Yokohama, Japan
`furugori.s@mazda.co.jp`

Abstract. This paper describes the design of a service system which belongs to a basic system realizing a Value Growth Mobility: a concept of next generation mobility intended to increase the different values that the user feels towards the mobility. The concept is proposed based on Timeaxis Design incorporating the viewpoint of time into the theory and methodology of design. To design this service system, the M-V model is used. This model is an integrated model of the M model, which focuses on design activity, and the V model, which visualizes a system development process. As the result of design, it is proposed a system consisting of subsystems including an emotion recognition system, a camera system, and a social networking service. These subsystems provide services encouraging the growth of values through interactions between the user and the mobility system.

Keywords: Timeaxis Design, M Model, V Model, Service Design.

1 Introduction

Recently, design of robust and attractive products is highly demanded due to environmental degradation, aging of the population, and advancement of information society [1]-[2]. To deal with these issues, Timeaxis Design (TAD), which incorporates the viewpoint of time into the theory and methodology of design, has been proposed [3]. On the other hand, Value Growth Design (VGD) [4] is concept of design growing values of a product through usage embodying TAD. As examples of VGD, leather gloves and fountain pens create growth of perceived values by fitting to the user through usage, keeping qualities by maintenance, and developing a sense of attachment caused by long-term usage. By realizing VGD based on Value Growth Model, it is considered possible to design products adaptable to various circumstances and values that are variable over time.

A. Marcus (Ed.): DUXU 2014, Part III, LNCS 8519, pp. 281–292, 2014.

In the previous study, a Value Growth Mobility was proposed by applying VGD to mobility [5]. The Value Growth Mobility is a concept of next generation mobility, and increases different values that user feels towards the mobility, by means of a mobility system. This concept contributes to address problems surrounding mobility, such as environmental degradation, passenger accidents, and a decrease of interest in vehicle purchasing. In this research, the mobility system not only refers to the vehicle, but includes services and infrastructures surrounding the vehicle. In previous studies, the Core Module system and the service system have been obtained as basic systems, as the result of conceptual design of the Value Growth Mobility [3]. The Core Module system is installed in the vehicle, and enables to adapt the vehicle to driving circumstances and user's conditions. This system uses the algorithm of the Emergent Control System [6] that allows adjustment to various driving circumstances. By using this system, it is confirmed a 36% improvement in fuel efficiency and battery life in the simulation of assumed hybrid cars. By contrast, the service system is assumed to encourage the growth of values that user feels towards the mobility through the interaction between the user and the mobility system. However, this system has not been designed towards the development.

Against this background, this research is aiming to develop the service system encouraging the growth of values that a user feels towards the mobility. To realize the growth of values, it is necessary to consider psychological elements that user feels towards the mobility. Additionally, it is assumed that the service system will become complex and large against a backdrop of the progression of ICT or infrastructures [7]. Hence, the M-V model is used to develop the service system. The M-V model is an integrated model of the M model (Multispace design model) [8], which models design acts and knowledge for these acts by using multiple spaces, and the V model [9], which supports to develop the complex and large systems. In this paper, a basic design of the service system based on the M-V model towards the development including verification and validation is described.

2   The M-V Model and a System Design Method Based on the M-V Model

2.1   The M-V Model Integrated the M Model and the V Model

The service system is designed based on the M-V model integrating the M model, which models acts and knowledge of design by multiple spaces, and the V model, which visualizes a process of a system development.

Fig. 1 shows the M model [8]. This model is composed of thinking space describing designing, and knowledge space describing knowledge used in designing. In this model, designing is defined by induction, abduction, and deduction in thinking space based on factors in knowledge space. Thinking space is comprised of psychological space including psychological elements that a user feels towards the design objective, and physical space including physical elements that realize psychological elements.

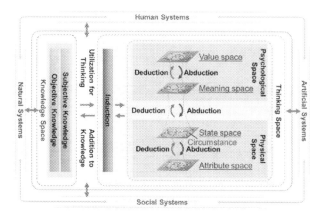

Fig. 1. M model

Psychological space consists of value space and meaning space. By contrast, physical space consists of state space and attribute space. Value space consists of numerous values such as social, cultural, and individual values. Meaning space is built of functions and images. State space includes characteristics of the system, dependent on its circumstances. Attribute space is constructed of characteristics independent of circumstances. In this model, circumstances refer to the usage environment, including the user and the ways in which artifacts are used. Knowledge space is comprised of objective knowledge and subjective knowledge. Objective knowledge holds generalities such as theories and methodologies, including physical laws in natural sciences, social sciences, and humanities. Subjective knowledge contains specialties that depend on individual contexts. When designing based on viewpoint of the M model, bottom-up generation of ideas caused by the extraction of elements and detection of relationships is supported. Thereby, it encourages emergent design which includes the bottom-up process. In addition, it promotes development that does not depend on apparent requirements. However, it cannot manage a whole process of development involving realization, integration, and validation.

On the other hand, the V model [9] is a valuable tool for visualizing and managing the systems engineering process. Fig. 2 shows the architecture V model. The left leg of the V represents system decomposition and definition of system architecture based on requirements of systems derived by analysis of stakeholder's requirements. The right leg represents realization of the lowest configuration items, architecture integration with verification of satisfaction to requirements, and validation of the system. At each decomposition level, there is a direct correlation between activities on the left and right sides of the V. For example, a test case confirming a completion of a system must be determined by an operation scenario clarified on the left. The V model can clarify each activity in a systems engineering process to multidisciplinary team. In addition, by using this model, it is possible to support the systems engineering developing solutions in response to expanded requirements by the growing scale and complexity of large systems. However, the systems engineering along the V model tends to develop requirements analysis and system definition based on apparent requirements in the early stage

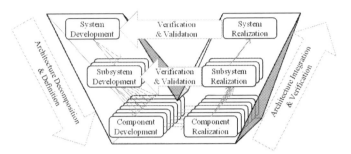

Fig. 2. Architecture V Model

of development. Thereby, there is a possibility that it is difficult to derive latent requirements. Additionally, it may be difficult to perform emergent derivation for new values in the systems engineering process due to the tendency to be top-down development in the range of determined requirements and specification. Hence, it is expected to propose the system with new values differ from existing systems by encouraging bottom-up idea generation that does not depend on apparent requirements in the stage of determining requirements or specification of systems.

There are complementary relationships between the designing based on viewpoint of the M model and the systems engineering along the V model. In the designing based on viewpoint of the M model, psychological elements and physical elements are organized from the viewpoint. Thereby, there are expected to realize the bottom-up generation of ideas caused by the extraction of elements and the detection of relationships which do not depend on apparent requirements. This idea generation may cover the top-down design based on requirements in the early process of the systems engineering. On the other hand, in the systems engineering along the V model, it is possible to support the whole systems engineering process from the system requirements analysis to the latest validation. Furthermore, the systems engineering along the V model enables to support the verification in each stage due to ensuring traceability through the whole systems engineering process.

Based on the complementary relationships, in this research, an M-V model integrating the M model and the V model is used to design the service system. Fig.3 shows the M-V model. This model indicates the systems engineering process along the V model adopting the viewpoint of the M model. A system design method based on the M-V model, ensures traceability between psychological elements including value and meaning and physical elements realizing psychological elements. By using this method, the method enables to organize elements extracted in process of realization, verification, or after provision in the systems engineering process. Therefore, it is expected to perform emergent derivation of value and meaning that was not assumed in decomposition and definition process. These effects are obtained by the M-V model integrating concepts of the M model and the V model. However, they are difficult to obtain just combining the design method based on the M model, which does not manage the process of verification and validation, and the systems engineering, which develops the system based on apparent requirements.

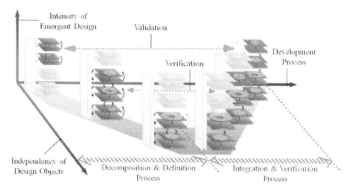

Fig. 3. M-V model

2.2   A System Design Method Using the M Method and SysML

To design a system based on the M-V model, the system design method combining the M method with an elements relationship diagram [10] and SysML (Systems Modeling Language) [11] is employed. The M method with the elements relationship diagram is a design method based on the viewpoint of the M model. On the other hand, SysML is a modeling language realizing the systems engineering along the V model.

The M method is the design method that adopts viewpoints of the M model. In this method, the system is developed by organizing elements and relationships between elements in circumstances and four types of space: value, meaning, state and attribute. In this research, the M method with the elements relationship diagram is used. The elements relationship diagram describes each element and their relationships included in each space of the system. This method enables to develop the design considering both psychological elements and physical elements at the same time.

On the other hand, SysML is a graphic modeling language that supports specification, design, verification, and validation of complex systems. The language describes systems, their components and environment, and supports modeling the whole system by using nine diagrams classified into four groups: requirements, behavior, parametrics and structure diagram. SysML enables the development of solutions which address expanded requirements of large and complexity systems.

By using the M method with the elements relationship diagram and SysML, it is expected to structure systems that enable to adapt changing conditions of users and circumstances over time. Fig. 4 shows the combined system design method. Here, the four steps listed below are repeated optionally.

1. Modelling elements relationship diagram by the M method

> Extract elements and organize relationships between elements. In this step, design considering elements of psychology, physics, and circumstances are developed to extract and organize elements by viewpoints of multispace.

2. Translating to SysML

> Translate elements and relationships to SysML. Viewpoints of the M model are included to systems engineering through SysML. For example,

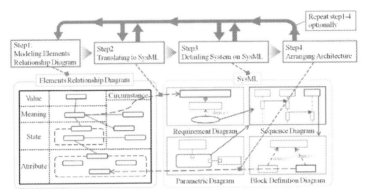

Fig. 4. Flow of Proposed System Design Method

value and meaning elements are described in SysML as the basic elements of requirements.

3. Detailing System in SysML

Detail system in SysML, along with systems engineering process. For instance, behaviours and structures of the system are newly derived from requirements based on value elements.

4. Arranging Architecture

Translate extracted elements from SysML to their elements relationship diagram, and arrange system architecture. To ensure traceability, describe in each element about relationships of it and SysML diagrams which detail it. For example, subsystems derived in SysML are arranged as attribute elements in the elements relationship diagram, and IDs of SysML diagrams that describe behavior or structure of those subsystems are put down in each attribute element.

By repeating these steps, the system architecture is modelled. In the process of realization, verification, and validation, the system is developed based on models obtained in the process of design.

3   Proposal of the Service System Realizing the Value Growth Mobility

3.1   The Service System Including Viewpoint of Timeaxis Design

The Value Growing Mobility is proposed based on Value Growth Design (VGD), which is a design concept realizing Timeaxis Design (TAD). TAD incorporates the viewpoint of time into the theory and methodology of design, enabling to adapt various circumstances and user's conditions as well as changing the two over time to be considered. VGD is proposed based on this concept of TAD. By applying the VGD to products, values, which the user feels towards the products, increase proportionally to the amount of usage. In previous studies of VGD, a Value Growth Model is proposed as a model describing changes of values over time in the process of product's value growth [4]. In this model, from the time before the user purchases the product to the time the user disposes it is divided by 5 phases describing different features: value discovery phase, value realization phase, value growth phase, value establishment phase, and value tradition phase. The value discovery phase occurs when the user discovers values of an object or product before purchase. The value realization phase is when, after purchase, the user uses the product or system or learns about its different functions and reconciles expectations and the actual use of a product. The value growth phase is when the user employs an object over time and develops a sense of attachment to it. The value establishment phase is when the value as a whole eventually stabilizes. The value tradition phase occurs when the value begins to decrease due to physical decay, and is transferred to the next generation of that product or system. By using viewpoints of each phase, it is considered possible to design the service system encouraging the growth of values that the user feels towards the mobility.

Based on viewpoints of the Value Growth Model, the service system realizing the Value Growth Mobility is designed by the system design method as it was explained in the previous section. The system is designed based on a concept of encouraging the growth of values that the user feels towards the mobility by making delight through travel with the vehicle. Fig. 5 shows the element relationship diagram describing key elements of the system derived from the concept. In the following sections, the service system consisted of these elements and services that they provide are explained.

3.2   Structure of the Proposed System

Fig. 6 shows an internal block diagram describing the structure of the proposed service system. The internal block diagram represents interconnection and interfaces between blocks. For example, Fig. 6 describes interactions between the block on the left side, "user" and blocks representing structural elements of the service system. Nested blocks within "vehicle" or "Service Department" represent subsystems of each

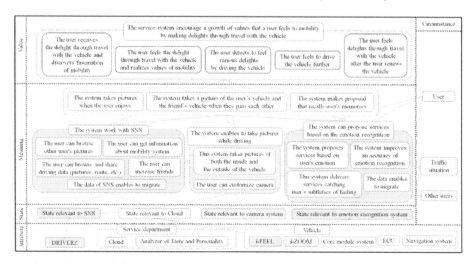

Fig. 5. Elements Relationship Diagram Describing Key Elements of the Service System

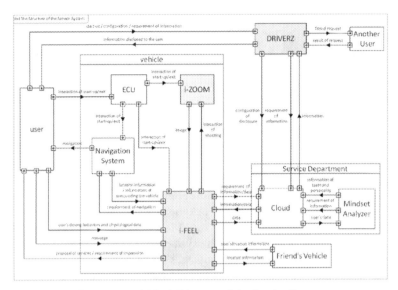

Fig. 6. Internal Block Diagram of the Service System

system. As to main subsystems which encourage the growth of values that user feels towards the mobility, "i-FEEL", "i-ZOOM", and "DRIVERZ" are proposed. First, "i-FEEL" is an emotion recognition system carried inside the vehicle. This system recognizes emotions of the user analyzing his behaviors and physiological data, and provides services based on emotions. Secondly, "i-ZOOM" is a camera system carried inside the vehicle. This system safely takes pictures of both the inside and the outside of the vehicle based on directions of the user or cooperation with "i-FEEL" while the user is driving. At last, "DRIVERZ" is a social networking service (SNS) and this system facilitates communication between users through the vehicle by sharing information such as pictures and driving routes. By combining these subsystems, the service system encourages the growth of values that user feels towards the mobility.

3.3   A Process of Service Delivery to User

To encourage the growth of values that a user feels towards the mobility, the service system provides services appropriate to relationship between the user and the vehicle with the use of the vehicle. Fig. 7 shows the Value Growth Model and major services in each phase. Along this model, a process of value growth is explained.

In the value discovery phase, the user can get information about mobility system including the vehicle and the service system. Additionally, the user can interact with other users owning vehicle by making friends in DRIVERZ. By these features, the user receives the delight through travel with the vehicle and discovers fascination.

In the value realization phase, the user then begin realizing values of mobility through usage of the mobility system. For example, by combining i-FEEL and i-ZOOM, i-ZOOM can take pictures of both the inside and the outside of the vehicle when the user enjoys. The service system provides interactive services between the

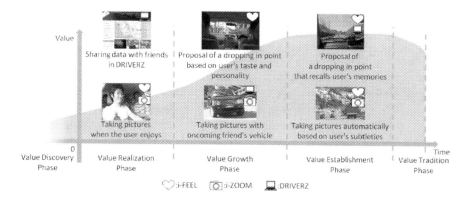

Fig. 7. Images of Services

user and the vehicle by the application of emotion recognition technology. Pictures taken while driving and information of driving routes are stored in cloud computing. The user can manage these data in DRIVERZ, such as browsing and editing data, or sharing data with friends. By combining the vehicle and DRIVERZ, the service system enhances interaction with other users more than before the user purchases the vehicle. Through these function, the user feels the delight through travel with the vehicle and realizes values of mobility.

In the value growth phase, values that the user feels towards the mobility grow the most. Based on the user's data stored in the cloud computing including user's feeling recognized by i-FEEL and sites that user browsed in DRIVERZ, the service system analyzes user's mindset, and delivers services according to them. For example, in the case there is a site around a drive route where the user would be interested, i-FEEL proposes the site as a point of dropping in. If the user decides to drop in the point and conveys the decision to i-FEEL, i-FEEL navigates the user to the point. This information of interaction between the user and i-FEEL through services are stored in the cloud computing, and used to improve analysis of user's mindset. In addition, by using information of user's friends, the service system takes a picture of the user's vehicle and the friend's vehicle when they pass each other. This function promotes interaction of users while driving. In this phase, the user detects to feel various delights by driving the vehicle. Thus, values grow in this phase.

In the value establishment phase, values that the user feels towards the mobility become stable. In this phase, because accuracy of analysis about user's mindset is high, i-FEEL delivers services catching user's subtleties of feeling. For example, when the vehicle finds a view matching user's mindset, the vehicle automatically takes a picture of it without user's directions. Furthermore, the service system becomes capable of delivering proposals that make the user recall memories stored through interactions with the mobility system. For instance, when the vehicle approaches a point visited in past, i-FEEL proposes to drop in the point with pictures at the present time. In this phase, because the mobility system gives these delights through travel with the vehicle, the service system contributes to developing a sense of attachment in the user. Thereby, the user gets motivated drive the vehicle further.

In the value traditional phase, the user renews the vehicle. The data stored in the cloud computing and data of user's mindset analyzed by the service department are continuously used to deliver services after the user renews the vehicle. Therefore, the user can interact with a new vehicle in a similar way as the vehicle that the user used. Hence, values that the user feels towards the mobility are inherited after the user renews the vehicle.

These services are described in detail by diagrams representing behavior in SysML, and essential systems to realize services are derived. Fig. 8 shows one of sequence diagrams. Sequence diagram represents behavior in terms of a sequence of messages exchanged between parts. This diagram enables to specify the interaction between the user and the mobility system. Time proceeds vertically down the diagram. Fig. 8 is an example of the sequence diagram specifying a behavior "the vehicle recognizes user's emotion". First, i-FEEL obtains user's driving behaviors and physiological data, and analyzes this data and recognizes user's emotion. Then, i-FEEL stores user's emotion and elements causing it in the system and the cloud computing. By doing this, the service system enables to recognize user's emotion and to deliver services based on the particular emotion. In addition, data stored in i-FEEL and the cloud computing are used to improve accuracy of the emotion recognition, as well as to analyze user's mindset. For these reason, it is found that i-FEEL requires a database to store user's data. Thereby, systems that construct the service system are derived by the analysis of behaviors.

3.4   Provision of Services to Realize Delights through Travel with the Vehicle

As described in earlier sections, items that construct the service system and services that are provided by these items are assumed to support growth of values that the user

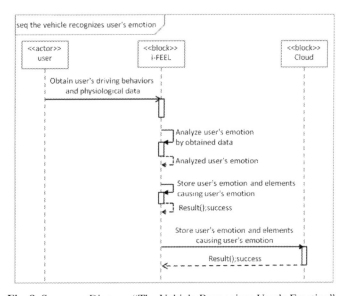

Fig. 8. Sequence Diagram "The Vehicle Recognizes User's Emotion"

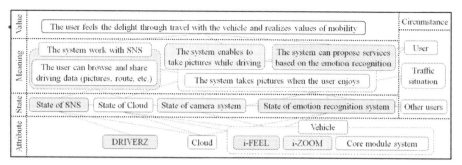

Fig. 9. A Part of Elements Relationship Diagram

feels towards the mobility. Fig. 9 shows a part of an elements relationship diagram arranged architecture of the service system. This diagram describes psychological elements that the user feels towards the mobility and physical elements that realize psychological elements in the value realization phase. Subsystems of the service system including "i-FEEL", "i-ZOOM", and "DRIVERZ" are described as attribute elements. These attribute elements realize state elements, and state elements realize meaning elements such as "the vehicle automatically takes pictures which the user wants" and "the user shares pictures with other users in SNS". These elements satisfy a value element "the user feels the delight through travel with the vehicle". Thus, the service system promotes interaction between the user and the mobility system through SNS not only when the user drives the vehicle, but also when the user is not driving the vehicle. As the result of the interaction, the user feels the delight through travel with the vehicle by using the service system, and this system encourages the growth of values that the user feels towards the mobility.

3.5   Future Tasks towards Embodiment the Service System

Towards the realization of the proposed service system, a design of the lowest configuration items is currently developed. Drive recording technology, which is already been commercialized, enable to realize i-ZOOM. Additionally, DRIVERZ can be realized by technologies used in existing SNS to architect software and usage of internet. Similarly, systems generated based on technology seeds are realized by using attribute elements, which are bases of the idea generation, as the lowest configuration items or directly. By contrast, the emotion recognition system that is the core of i-FEEL is difficult to realize by using seeds of technology, because technologies of emotion recognition are in the process of development. Thus, it is necessary to consider in detail about index parameters and methods for emotion recognition based on existing technology. As these index parameters, user's behaviors and physiological data are proposed. However, this system has not been developed in detail for embodiment. As a future task, it is necessary to verify feasibility of emotion recognition based on proposed index parameters. As the result of system verification, the lowest configuration items of the emotion recognition system can be decided. Additionally, it is necessary to define items of other systems and develop the design of the service system towards validation, whether it encourages the value growth of mobility or not.

4   Conclusion   •

In this research, the design of the service system realizing the Value Growth Mobility is developed by the system design method based on the M-V model. As the result of the design, the service system consisting of subsystems including i-FEEL as an emotion recognition system, i-ZOOM as a camera system, and DRIVERZ as a social networking service is proposed. This service system enables to provide interactive services between the user and the mobility system or other users, such as taking pictures automatically based on the user's emotion and sharing information with friends through SNS. By these interactions, it is expected to encourage the growth of values that the user feels towards the mobility.

In further research, toward a validation whether the proposed service system encourages the growth of values of mobility, it is necessary to continue the design of the service system.

References

1. Mitsubishi Research Institute, Inc., The Grand Design for The New Century, Nikkei Inc. (2000) (in Japanese)
2. Tanaka, S.: Mirai yosoku report 2009-2015, Nikkei Business Publications, Inc. (2008) (in Japanese)
3. Matsuoka, Y.: Dawn of Timeaxis Design, pp. 46–72, 95–104. Maruzen Publishing Co., Ltd. (2012) (in Japanese)
4. Kanazawa, S., Sato, K., Matsuoka, Y.: Value Growth Design Model Based on Design Science. In: The 15th International Conference on Machine Design and Production, UMTIK, Turkey (2012) [CD-ROM]
5. Kamiya, K., Kito, A., Alvarez, J., Sato, K., Nishimura, H., Matsuoka, Y., Furugori, S.: Design of a Service System for Vehicle Users by Applying Multispace Design Method and SysML. In: Proceedings of the Asia-Pacific Council on Systems Engineering Conference 2013, APCOSEC, Japan (2013) [CD-ROM]
6. Furugori, S., Yamazaki, T., Kuroda, Y., Suetomi, T., Nouzawa, T., Ujiie, Y., Nakazawa, K., Matsuoka, Y.: Value Growth Design in a Next Generation Mobility. Oukan, The Journal of Transdisciplinary Federation of Science and Technology 6(1) (2012) (in Japanese)
7. Kawamoto, T.: Vision of Future Automobile. In: JIDOSHA-GIJUTSU. Journal of Society of Automotive Engineers of Japan 67(1) (2013) (in Japanese)
8. Matsuoka, Y.: Multispace Design Model Towards Integration between Industrial Design and Engineering Design. In: Proceedings of Design Research Society 2012. Design Research Society, Thailand (2012)
9. Forsberg, K., Mooz, H., Cotterman, H.: Visualizing Project Management: Models and Frameworks for Mastering, 3rd edn. John Wiley & Sons, Inc., New Jersey (2005)
10. Matsuoka, Y., Ujiie, Y., Asanuma, T., Takano, S., Izu, Y., Sato, K., Kato, T.: M method - Design Thinking on Multispace. Kindai-Kagaku-Sha, Tokyo (2013)
11. Friedenthal, S., Moore, A., Steiner, R.: A Practical Guide to SysML. The Morgan Kauffman OMG Press (2008)

Developing the HMI of Electric Vehicles

On the Necessity of a Broader Understanding of Automotive User Interface Engineering

Christian Knoll[1], Roman Vilimek[2], and Inken Schulze[2]

[1] BMW Group, User Interface Concept BMW i
[2] BMW Group, Concept Quality, Munich, Germany
{christian.m.knoll,roman.vilimek,inken.schulze}@bmw.de

Abstract. BMW i, as a sub-brand of the BMW Group, targets on delivering sustainable solutions for individual mobility. One of the most important steps on this path was the introduction of the all-electric BMW i3 in 2013. In order to design not only the vehicle in itself, but also especially the newly developed electric vehicle related functions for optimal customer experience, the HMI design process substantially relied on repeated usability testing and large international field trials. With more than 34 million test kilometers absolved during the MINI E and the BMW ActiveE field trials an extraordinary knowledge base about customer needs related to e-mobility contributed valuable input to the development of the user interface of the BMW i3 and HMI challenges beyond the vehicle like charging wallbox, smartphone app and web portal related to driving electric. The paper reports on the unique process of defining the user interface of the BMW Group's first purpose-designed electric vehicle including the non-vehicle-based e-mobility infrastructure components. Based on selected use cases, the interplay between evolutionary steps in the HMI and continued usability testing shows how user-centered design is applied for a completely new kind of vehicle, thus providing insights on the necessities of iterative testing for disruptive innovations.

Keywords: MINI E, BMW ActiveE, BMW i3, BMW i, user interface, HMI, ConnectedDrive, 360° Electric, BMW iRemote App, web portal, wallbox Pure & Pro, charge, AC, DC, car sharing, DriveNow, ChargeNow, eDRIVE.

1 BMW i3: Design Background

The BMW i3 is not just another car in the portfolio of the BMW Group. It is the pioneer to a new era of electric mobility and represents the BMW Group's first purpose-built and volume-produced model driven purely by electric power. Some important characteristics which strongly influence the development of the user interface are:

- A new LifeDrive vehicle architecture with the battery pack housed in the aluminium drive module and a lightweight carbon fibre life cell on top. This design provides a spacious passenger cabin with an even floor free of obstacles and *no constructive separations* between the passengers.

A. Marcus (Ed.): DUXU 2014, Part III, LNCS 8519, pp. 293–304, 2014.
© Springer International Publishing Switzerland 2014

- BMW eDrive hybrid synchronous powertrain developed specifically for the BMW i3, maximum output: 125 kW/170 hp, peak torque: 250 Nm (184 lb-ft) which results in an unusually *silent* yet powerful propulsion.
- Extremely ambitious sustainability targets (concerning production: 70% less water consumption, 50% less energy consumption covered by 100% renewable energy) which lead to an exceptionally high proportion of naturally treated, recycled, and renewable raw materials. This creates a *puristic* interior which resembles more a lounge than a cockpit.
- A built-in SIM card as standard equipment which allows *permanent connectivity* with the BMW backend server. Thus, highly demanding user requests can be processed outside the car (like e.g. real time intermodal routing) and the result of the calculation is then sent back into the car. On the other hand, the user can always stay in contact with the car from anywhere in the world.
- A minimalistic project approach: The BMW i3 is designed for a range of 130-160 km because after years of field tests we know that this provides a fully adequate autonomy for more than 90% of all mobility demands involving a car of that-size[1]. In order to fulfill the sustainability and efficiency targets this means that *efficiency information* concerning range, how to optimize it and how to avoid waste of energy becomes crucial. It also means that *minimalism* or as we call it "clever simplicity" must be the guideline for the overall user interface. It also means *weight* plays a crucial role and every LED, every button and every cable would have to be justified.
- Yet a holistic project approach which offers not just the car, but anything else a user, leaser, or owner of the car might need: From a green electricity contract to a solar car port, from a ChargeNow RFID card which allows charging at most European public charging stations towallboxes for faster home charging, from a smartphone app for Apple and Android devices (BMW iRemote App) to a relaunchedConnectedDrive web portal which allows to change car settings, share information with other users and stay informed if anything happens which can potentially influence the disposability of the car. To sum it up, when we speak about the user interface, we do not only mean the car but *all* these*touchpoints*.
- And last but not least the pursuit of globally addressing *new user groups* who either do not own a car at all or just use one occasionally, who are not technically minded and do not have experience with BMW interaction principles.

2   Development Process

The aspects mentioned above only form a subset of constraints and objectives. They were enriched by a large set of product requirements defining the story of the car and its functionality. But it is important to mention that the development process was not linear. As e-mobility is a comparatively young field of intense research and development, the initial set of requirements kept changing, too. As for example drive train and battery proceeded, new constraints and requirements came up, leading to a constant discussion on where the boundaries of customer relevance lie. At the same time not only the BMW engineers kept learning, but also the global legislation and homo-logation landscape was and still is subject to drastic changes.

Thereby, an important reference point for development was the idea of a minima-listic car which is part of a larger, sustainable, and premium quality mobility system and which emphasizes the aspect of sharing the drive with others. Another was the target to form a user interface which is clever (meaning: offering adequate solutions for the user) yet as simple as possible (meaning: less features and buttons and knobs, low number of alternatives provided, few interaction steps, clear priority of informa-tion). These references helped to define two initial UI foundations:

1. The so-called **basic layout** which determines position and distribution of all con-trols and displays in the cabin
2. The **size of the displays** which clarifies the informatory focal points

Working on these two lead to a set of more specific requirements:

- In contrast to other BMW motorcars, the cockpit should not provide driver-orientation – neither physically nor in terms of informatory exclusiveness. Only those controls and displays *essentially* needed for driving should be grouped around the steering wheel and designed in a highly minimalistic manner. Instead, emphasis should be put on information which is relevant and accessible for all pas-sengers in the car. The result is a cluster instrument which is formed by a 5,8" LCD screen with additional tell tales, accompanied by a 10,2" center display for all na-vigation, ConnectedDrive, infotainment, communication, and setup functions ("iDrive") as standard equipment.
- To fulfill the functional grouping of drive functions and to allow a much more flexible usage of the interior space the gear selector needs to be moved from its typical position between the front seats to the steering wheel area.
- As the whole startup and driving is silent, appropriate feedback must be provided to ensure mode awareness.
- The so-called one-pedal-feeling which is applied in MINI E and BMW ActiveE must be preserved and improved. This means that lifting the foot from the drive pedal activates a regenerative braking which decelerates the car to a full standstill. At the same time solutions for easy maneuvering in tight spaces and on slopes – fulfilled by idle creep on conventional combustion cars with automatic gearboxes – must be found.
- The fact that the car needs to be charged brings a totally new activity to the majori-ty of users. So the overall procedure in terms of ease of use, cable stowing and handling, feedback, controllability etc must be highly user friendly and inviting.
- As we could also learn from an extensive social media analysis and from years of MINI E and BMW ActiveE field tests, detailed information must be provided on how to drive efficiently and thus maximize range. Hereby maximum advantage should be drawn from the built-in connectivity.
- Car, smartphone app, and web portal must work togetherseamlessly and speak the same "language". Also its aesthetic structure should form a clear link to the BMW i brand.

The iterative development process included the following phases, including a constant monitoring of social media postings and testing of competitor's cars.

1. Initial ideation, utilizing key findings of MINI E field studies.
2. Construction of a functional mock-up with simulated displays.
3. Mock-up usability testing (in a static driving simulator). Focus: Cluster instrument layout, air conditioning controls, and gear selector.
4. Development and testing of the BMW ActiveE UI especially focusing on newly developed EV specific functions as pre-production versions of the BMW i3.
5. Construction of a fully roadworthy prototype (called "I/One") on technical basis MINI E with fully integrated simulation of system behavior, demonstrating the full interior, exterior, and smart phone app UI.
6. I/One usability testing (on test track).
7. I/One usability testing (on test track) of the redesigned overall UI.
8. Usability tests of smartphone app and wallbox professionalUI.
9. Cross cultural usability testing with BMW dealers from US and China and J.D. Power representatives from ECE, US, and China.

The following chapters point out some highlights which might serve as good examples to illustrate how the above mentioned requirements and objectives were finally united into one concept. All examples show the ECE / German UI. US and China UI can differ.

3   Highlights of the BMW i3 UI

3.1   Cluster Instrument

The cluster instrument is the driver's primary source of information and as such plays an important role in reflecting the whole story of the car. In case of the BMW i3 that was an extremely challenging task because from a company's perspective it is not easy to quit with the design paradigm of driver orientation and to abandon its iconic, brand shaping center instrument (Fig. 1).

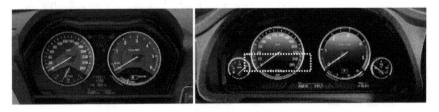

Fig. 1. BMW heritage (Fotocredit: BMW Group): The current "two eyes" (F20 1 series, left / A0161657) and "four eyes" (F10 5 series, right / A0173684) cluster instruments. Dotted line (right) indicates the display size of the BMW i3 cluster instrument display in comparison.

The display of the BMW i3 cluster instrument (Fig. 2) bears all basic driving information – such as speed, range, drive train info etc. Because of the minimalism design requirements this display measures half of the display area in the 5 series cluster instrument depicted in Fig. 1 – and the 5 series instrument is additionally equipped with four analogue pointer instruments [2]. It is obvious that this ambitious target size required a radical reduction of information both in terms of quantity and complexity.

Fig. 2. Cluster Instrument BMW i3 (Fotocredit: BMW Group): Display area with current speed, drive train gauge, fill levels andranges for petrol (range extender version) and battery. Top left on board computer (toggle). Top right Trip. Green speed indication: Current speed = ACC or DCC resume speed. ECO PRO: Current mode).

First thing to be eliminated was the analogue speedometer. It has doubtlessly clear advantages when it comes to quantitative judgment and the perception of disproportionally varying values [3]. But in the context of a car for metropolitan areas, with a limited top speed of 150 km/h (93 mph) and without manual gearbox it is more important to respect the inner city speed limit rather than to compare at a glance speed and revs to choose the right gear. To partly compensate the higher mental workload of reading digital numbers instead of interpreting a pointer angle, the speedometer numbers are more than double the size recommended in EN ISO 15008:2009 and form the center of the instrument.

Below, a drive train gauge is the only remaining indicator resembling an analogue instrument. It shows current deployment or regeneration of electric power and provides subtle efficiency information: The blue brooch marks the limits of efficient acceleration and deceleration (without using the foot break the white pointer would not exceed the left efficiency limit). The thickened zone around the coasting point in 6 o'clock position recommends a smooth driving style which results in moderate needle movements (white marker). Few information on this instrument have its exclusive display areas, like current speed and range. Large parts of the display area are used in multiple ways: A Check Control Message or person warning overrule fill levels and trip, but never current speed and electric range (Fig. 3).

Fig. 3. Cluster Instrument BMW i3 (Fotocredit: BMW Group): Check Control Message (left) and person warning (right) overrule information of lower priority

Total mileage, clock, and current consumption is default content on most BMW cluster instruments. Here, a rigid selection had to be made: The clock is anyhow shown on most iDrive menus (in the status bar) so it was integrated into the on board computer list. There one can also toggle to total mileage and current consumption. This reduction of information density and unnecessary redundancy is what is meant by "clever simplicity". More than ten layout versions were designed and evaluated in expert assessments, in the end three were extensively tested in the mentioned usability tests on the driving simulator and on board the I/One test platform, leading to significant changes from each iteration step to another.

3.2   Gear Selector

As the drive train of the car is operating with a fixed gear, the user can only choose between P, R, N, and D. No manual gears have to be selected. This also means that the interaction frequency is lower in comparison to a car with manual and automatic gearbox. However, it quickly became clear that this component demanded for a specific set of requirements, including ergonomic, technical, and aesthetic aspects. Amongst these are

- Distinctive representation of the electric drive train
- Defensive interaction gesture in contrast to "sporty" gear shift sticks
- Clear semantic concerning mechanical degrees of freedom
- Optimized interaction without visual control
- Still full visibility and reachability for all percentiles

Moving the gear selector functions to the steering wheel area can be made in multiple ways. Push buttons for P, R, N, and D are one option, as realized in other EVs/cars on the market, but this form of interaction requires additional hand-eye-control and may increase driver distraction. Literally hundreds of sketches and long discussions later the following design took form: A rotary, monostable control, mounted on the steering wheel with the scheme aside (Fig. 4).

Fig. 4. Gear shifter BMW i3 (Fotocredit: BMW Group)

This design allows achieving another advantage: Compatibility between operation direction of the control and the activated direction of drive. So, moving the rotary lever forwards activates "D", pulling it backwards "R". With respect to the target group of novice users who typically perceive the classic automatic gearbox scheme P-R-N-D with "P" in front and "D" in reverse position as a hassle, this is a clear progress towards intuitiveness. Tests also confirmed that users who are accustomed to the classic scheme very quickly adopt to the inverted i3-logic – thanks to the combination of new position, new touch, and new interaction gesture.

At the same time the position behind the steering wheel and the kinematics that require the deployment of a momentum, make unwanted operations (by falling objects, playing children,…) practically impossible. As a consequence we also omitted the shift lock button which is integral part of all BMW gear shifters. The START STOP-button (SSB) is integrated as well, with slight restrictions in terms of reachability but optimal visibility. The close grouping of SSB and rotary control also makes it comfortable to drive off with one hand gesture – like the one-pedal-feeling does by reducing the number of shifts from one pedal to the other. The design also allows to integrate a READY indication which is important when it comes to mode awareness.

3.3   Indicating READY State

The silent start of an electric car is fascination and system ergonomic challenge at the same time – this is a clear feedback from the usability tests: Unambiguous feedback on whether the car is in ready state or not is crucial to avoid user irritations because of the missing engine sound. Note that the BMW i3 is equipped with keyless go and does not have a key insert. Finally, a combination of visual feedback in the cluster instrument, visual feedback on the gear shifter, and acoustic feedback is indicating READY. After unlocking the car and opening the door, a short welcome animation is shown. It remains in the state depicted in Fig. 5.

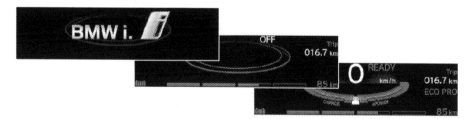

Fig. 5. Cluster Instrument BMW i3 (Fotocredit: BMW Group): Welcome (top), STAND BY (middle), READY (bottom)

In this state practically no primary, secondary of tertiary functions are available which is symbolized by an empty screen. Pushing SSB without footbrake leads to STAND BY state. Now all iDrive-functions are active, range and fill level are alive, on board computer can be toggled. But it takes pushing the footbreak to activate READY state. Now current speed is displayed, the drive train gauge is shown, and

READY is depicted explicitly. This differentiation helps to distinguish the states and still highlights the only state with full functionality.

Simultaneously, an orange light band embracing the SSB keeps flashing in all non-READY states to catch the user's attention and help him find the first step to get the car started (Fig. 6). As soon as the footbrake is pressed, the flashing becomes brighter. In the transition phase towards READY state, the light band first expands towards the rotary lever and then changes color to electric blue. This color coding was chosen to indicate electricity as well as efficiency messages. The expansion of the light band unites SSB, scheme, and rotary lever and so conveys the message: "time to turn the lever".

Fig. 6. Gear Shifter BMW i3 (Fotocredit: BMW Group): non-READY state (left), transition to READY state (middle), READY state (right). Night design, "P" active.

Additionally, an acoustic sound indicates activation (increasing frequency) and deactivation (decreasing frequency) of READY state. In contrast to the indications in cluster instrument and gear shifter, this indication is temporary during the transition phases to preserve the quietness of the car but feedback when necessary. Of course it is fundamental that all three feedback mechanisms work together synchronously.

3.4   Selected e-Mobility Functions of iDrive

To enhance comfort or to convey efficiency information as requested during the field tests, several e-mobility specific functions were added, and some were removed: As range plays an important role the user wants to be in control how to use onboard electricity. Dominant factor is the driving style and a large set of functions help to drive efficiently (drive train gauge, ECO PRO modi), to motivate the user (ECO Tips, efficiency challenge via smart phone app,...), and to offer solutions before situations become critical (see section 3.6).

But an influencing factor is the usage of auxiliary consumers, too - especially A/C. The car heating in the winter can reduce the net range drastically. 2°C more or less cabin temperature can make the difference if the destination can be reached or not. In order to provide maximum transparency, a highly reliable range prediction is calculating in real time. Additionally, the new menu "Auxiliary consumers" clearly depicts how much range is currently consumed by the A/C system. This menu also indicates the effect of the seat heating which issurprisingly low: Setting both seat heatings on MAX would always result in a range reduction below 1km. With this information the user can easily decide how to compromise best between climate comfort and range (Fig. 7).

Fig. 7. NewiDriveMenue "eDRIVE" BMW i3 (Fotocredit: BMW Group): Auxiliary Consumers. Seat heatings are turnedoff, so no range potential is displayed.

On the other hand,functions from the BMW i3 predecessor BMW ActiveE were abandoned to reduce complexity, to avoid irritations amongst our non-early adopters clientele, and simply because improved technical solutions have been found which made monitoring of certain parameters unnecessary. The BMW ActiveE "eDRIVE" menue "Battery Info" is a good example for that (Fig 8). It gave technical insight into the state of health of the high voltage battery, including the parameters battery temperature and state of charge (SoC) in [%]. It has been removed from the BMW i3 menus, raising questions among the early adopters community. The reason is: In contrast to the MINI E and BMW ActiveE cars which the early adopters have been using for a long time, the BMW i3 is equipped with a highly effective thermal HV-battery management and, as already stated, a very reliable range prediction.

Fig. 8. Removed iDriveMenue "eDRIVE" BMW ActiveE (Fotocredit: BMW Group / A0145735.): Battery Info including Battery Temperature, SoC, and Range.

As both was not the case in MINI E and BMW ActiveE, users were accustomed to make their own range calculations and therefore needed SoC in [%]. Also, monitoring battery temperature used to be necessary to predict degradation effects – in the rare case of a degradation this information is now integrated in the BMW i3 drive train gauge.

3.5   Charging the Car

To increase intuitiveness, charging functions were redesigned from the socket to the app: The cable is stowed in its own compartment to keep the interior clean and tidy. The plug socket is brightly illuminated to facilitate connecting at night and also incorporates a clear color and frequency coded indication of all relevant states, e.g. "charging" with blue flashing and "fully charged" with constant green (Fig. 9).

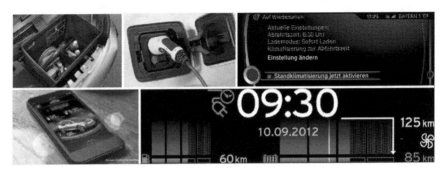

Fig. 9. Charging features of BMW i3 (Fotocredit: BMW Group / A0145735.). Top: Cable box under the bonnet, illuminated socket, Goodbye Screen. Bottom: BMW iRemote App, charging screen (range extender version).

After plugging in, the instrument cluster converts into a charging screen, informing about all relevant details such as time until full charge or chosen timer settings and range after a full charge. To keep operation easy, by default the user does not have to make any difficult decisions or settings: Just plug in and charge. Those who use the car regularly will find the week calendar helpful. It allows to set departure times and precondition battery and cabin – a feature that enhances comfort and range. All these settings are kept very clean, and when the drive is ended with a push on the SSB, a "Goodbye Screen" is shown, summing up the most important parameters. Also, setting changes can be made right from that screen. Charging progress, timer settings etc. can always be monitored via BMW iRemote App to ensure flexibility and to keep the user informed about the vehicle status – push and pull wise.

3.6   Selected Satnav Functions

A powerful set of satnav functions will help to cure "range anxiety": By default the map provides two outlines indicating the range in all directions in current drive mode and in the most efficient one named ECO PRO + (Fig. 10).

Hereby, traffic conditions, topography, week day, temperature, and road net are incorporated, calculated on the backend server. Also charging stations can be displayed, including detailed information on socket types and (depending on data provider) availability and ChargeNow readiness. In Fig. 10, close to the current car position a green symbol is half hidden. It represents a user chosen "preferred charging station".

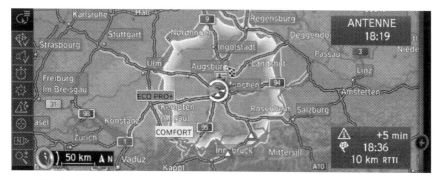

Fig.10. iDrive menu "NAV" BMW i3 (Fotocredit: BMW Group): Range map

Fig.11. iDrive Range Assistant BMW i3 (Fotocredit: BMW Group): Pop up

A so-called Range Assistant permanently monitors it and as long as the symbol is green it is possible to reach it. If returning there becomes tight, a pop up window warns in time, providing alternatives how to get back safely (Fig. 11). This happens independently of the navigation system guiding status. But the range assistant also takes action if range and distance to destination do not match, shown in Fig 11, too: The flag symbol represents the current navigation destination, the plug the favorite charging station. In the header in blue "Electric range not sufficient" is inscripted, providing the alternatives to change route criteria to ECO PRO Route, to select ECO PRO + mode or to search for charging stations along the route. In this example, only switching to ECO PRO + mode would allow to reach the destination *and* get back "home". Again, the layout of the pop up window was iteratively modified until it got its dominantly graphical expression: It allows a quick comparison between the criteria "arrival time", "buffer", and "comfort" (note that ECO PRO + switches A/C off – the user is informed about that when ECO PRO + is activated) – which the user prioritizes situatively.

4 Conclusions

Selected aspects of the BMW i3 UI show how MINI E and BMW ActiveE field tests laid the road to its development. The user's voice has been constantly heard over a period of 6 years, additionally including numerous iteratively applied testing methods corresponding with the increasing level of BMW i3 UI maturity (cf. also [4]). A particular challenge was the application of a highly minimalistic yet clever approach which underlines the whole "project i"story. We are convinced to deliver not only ease of use but also: Sheerpleasure.

Acknowledgments. The authors would like to acknowledge the project i team at BMW Group and our academic research partners. Most of allwe would like to thank our customers and usability test participants for their support and inspiring feedback.

References

1. Vilimek, R., Keinath, A., Schwalm, M.: The MINI E Field Study - Similarities and Differences in International Everyday EV Driving. In: Stanton, N.A. (ed.) Advances in Human Aspects of Road and Rail Transport, pp. 363–372. CRC Press, Boca Raton (2012)
2. Eckstein, L., Knoll, C., et al.: Interaktion mit Fahrerassistenz- und Fahrerinformationssystemen im neuen 7er BMW. 24. VDI/VW-Gemeinschaftstagung Integrierte Sicherheit und Fahrerassistenzsysteme. VDI (2008)
3. Bernotat, R.: Anzeigengestaltung. In: Schmidtke, H. (ed.) Ergonomie, p. 563. Hanser, München (1993)
4. Vilimek, R., Keinath, A.: User-Centred Design and Evaluation as a Prerequisite for the Success of Disruptive Innovations: An Electric Vehicle Case Study. In: Regan, M., Horberry, T., Stevens, A. (eds.) Driver Acceptance of New Technology: Theory, Measurement and Optimisation, pp. 169–186. Ashgate, Farnham (2014)

Examining the Functionality and Usability of Interactive Wayfinding Design within Cities in China

Fung Ha Sandy Lai

Department of Information Art and Design
Academy of Arts & Design, Tsinghua University, China
jjsandylai@gmail.com

Abstract. In recent years, wayfinding is one of the aspects in urban city design that emerge with digital technologies in the *smart city* [1] development in China. However, before building a smart city, some issues need to be solved in the wayfinding system within cities in China such as misleading signs, irrational roadway design in transportation. This field study report is part of my research project, in which examples of three prime cities (Beijing, Shanghai, Hong Kong) and two 2nd tier cities (Suzhou, Nanjing) are discussed to examine the functionality and usability of interactive wayfinding design. The findings of this report showed that emerging new technologies with wayfinding concept and theory that is based on user experience makes wayfinding more effective and functional. Some alternative guidelines and solutions of usable wayfinding design are provided to help people live in a safe environment rather than live in just a fully digitalized city.

Keywords: interactive wayfinding, wayfinding design, user experience, urban infrastructure, mobile internet.

1 Introduction

In China, over a hundred cities have planned to transform themselves into smart cities.[2] Wayfinding design in transportation is one of the important aspects in urban city infrastructure [1]. The question now is what role could "wayfinding" play in the planning and development of smart cities in China? Wayfinding is a kind of systematic *communication* [3] which helps people find their way. Basically, the purpose of wayfinding is to help people obtain quick and accurate communication and information in terms of legibility, readability and convenience. It can be applied broadly in urban informatics, infrastructure service, transportation, city planning, travel spots, and more. Traditionally, graphical elements and tools like graphs, diagrams, data, charts, colors, typography, images, sound tracks, via maps, symbols, signs or billboards, information kiosks are used for wayfinding.

With the rapid development of new technologies in recent decades, the definition of wayfinding became broader. An experienced architect, Kelly C. Brandon, explained how wayfinding could contribute to the urban design process: "*Wayfinding design is the*

A. Marcus (Ed.): DUXU 2014, Part III, LNCS 8519, pp. 305–316, 2014.

process of organizing spatial and environmental information to help users find their way. It should not be considered different activity from traditional signage design, but rather a broader, more inclusive way of accessing all the environmental issues." [4] He also quoted Kevin Lynch's city elements (ie. Paths, Edges, Nodes, Landmarks and Districts) in urban design [5], the idea of which is used for mapping information easily.

Nowadays, ubiquitous digital technologies are integrating with wayfinding design, and are making both more interactive and dynamic. Technology is changing the traditional form of wayfinding design via different digital means, such as touch screen, sensor system, smart card, media facades, digital signage, internet system, GPS, automation and so on. In addition to the convergence of pervasive, interactive and digitalized tools for wayfinding, the functionality has become more globalized, locative and informative in real time mode to let people find their way much easier.

According to China Daily (13-8-2013), *"The smart city program aims to create an innovation network, optimizing the use of technology in the design and operation of infrastructure and buildings in a way that meets the city's current and future demands."* [6] However, smart city development cannot just rely on digital hardware and should avoid excessive emphasis on emerging IT technologies while neglecting the basics of urban design. To this end, the method that can deliver a clear guideline and alternative solutions on wayfinding design which integrates with cultural elements, user experience design and emerging IT technologies, such as GPS mapping, touch screen and voice control technology, internet or mobile user platforms, etc., in urbanization should be applied.

This paper is part of the research report of *"Examining the functionality and usability of interactive wayfinding design within cities in China"* which will take about two more years to complete. The field study, which forms the backbone of the research report, had taken six months and involved three prime cities (Beijing, Shanghai, Hong Kong) and two 2nd tier cities (Suzhou and Nanjing) in China. Those cities were used as examples to examine the functionality and usability of interactive wayfinding design. The report will consist of case studies and analysis and is divided into five major parts: 1. Introduction; 2. Overview of Interactive Wayfinding; 3. Digital Platform Wayfinding Solutions; 4. Wayfinding Concept and Theory Application; and 5. Human Factors in Wayfinding Design. During the research process, it is found that mobile internet and voice control technology would become a very important tool to emerge in interactive wayfinding in the future.

In the coming 18 months, ongoing research including survey will be continued. Municipal authorities, design participants and general public in China are the targets. The objective is to give an overview with comparison of the merits and drawbacks in the existing wayfinding design in aforesaid cities, and highlighting the potential obstacles / problems envisaged in order to providing solutions with practical alternatives and strategies for future development.

Furthermore, the report will also discuss how to motivate people in China to use the wayfinding design and enforce the execution of the design, especially in the view point of municipal governments. Because different provinces are using different standard for implementation of the system in urbanization, some fundamental issues and problems in the current wayfinding design therefore need to be addressed and discussed before building a smart city.

The concept and theory of "wayfinding" was quite new to people in the past decades in China. Most of the books were targeted only at educators, students and used for curriculum. Theories, case studies, photos were often taken from foreign countries. Only a few of the foreign books on "wayfinding" had been translated into Chinese for local people's reference [7-9]. To make it more useful for China, it is worth to examine the principles of wayfinding design and to integrate them properly with interactive design, emerging IT technologies and urban infrastructure service in the context of China.

Hopefully, the research at its completion will be beneficial to local governments as well as the general public in China by providing them with a wider perspective of wayfinding design and enhancing their awareness of the possible barriers in effective communications in urban infrastructure service.

2   Overview of Interactive Wayfinding

Hong Kong's infrastructure design, including interactive wayfinding design, is often used as example and reference for China's cities. Under the principle of one country, two systems, Hong Kong has become one of the prime cities in China since 1997 [10]. Hong Kong has been awarded numerous international rankings in different aspects [11-13]. Overall its infrastructure is highly ranked among other countries in the world. [14] Its wayfinding design is better than many other cities in mainland China. Because of these merits, its interactive wayfinding designs for its infrastructure, such as airport, subway and roadway, etc. are often taken as example and reference for China's cities. Similar contemporary design can be found in Beijing and Shanghai. Advanced technologies and applications are also integrated with interactive tools to help people get information easier and faster. For example: information kiosk (with sensor, touch screen, smart card, QR code, internet, GPS, mobile internet for checking real time traffic situation, destination and transport schedules), digital signage and media façade with motion graphics to deliver messages, etc.

Along with the increasing demand for transport service created by both international and local people in China [15-16], the wayfinding systems in transportation are also digitalized, modernized and commercialized, but neglecting the need of considering user experience in applying wayfinding concept and theory. As millions of rural people and foreigners are moving to prime and 2nd tier cities for jobs and business opportunities, it is necessary to foster the public to use new wayfinding systems with interactive tools and enforcing execution of applying a correct wayfinding concept and theory. This has become a real challenge to local governments.

3   Digital Platform Wayfinding Solutions

3.1   Digital Information Kiosk

Digital information application is popular in wayfinding in transportation, such as free stand information kiosks which are frequently used for people finding information and destinations at new airports, railway and subway stations. Some kiosks are there for checking real time highway traffic conditions to and from airport; others are for checking travel spots, desired destinations nearby, local weather and advertising.

Fig. 1. Different forms of interactive information kiosks are emerging in wayfinding Photo by Author - Location: Beijing, Shanghai

Most interactive information kiosks provide high resolution graphics, text, sounds, maps, GPS system, touch screen buttons and navigation bar. However, the design of most information kiosks still has a lot of room for improvements. For instance, most of the local brands of information kiosks provide information in the Chinese language only. This is a common problem – it is not user friendly for foreign commuters. (See Fig.2) For them, a few foreign brands provide multi-language but are found only at major transport hubs in Beijing and Shanghai, while none can be found in 2nd tier cities. From the field observation, each person spent around 3 to 5 minutes in average to complete the searching through clicking different interfaces in applications. That means in average a kiosk is able to serve only 12-15 users hourly. Therefore, information kiosks may not be an efficient means for mass transit wayfinding. It simply cannot cope with the increasing demand of passengers at the transport hubs at peak seasons, such as Lunar New Year and other long public holidays (according to China Daily, there will be more than 3.62 billion trips on roads, via trains, planes and ships during 2014 Lunar New Year) [17]. More alternatives need to be considered.

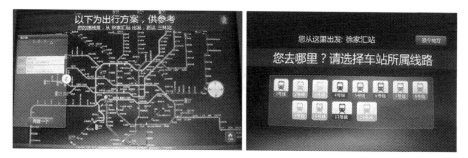

Fig. 2. Touch screen type of interactive wayfinding – only available in the Chinese language
Photo by Author - Location: Shanghai

3.2   Emerging Mobile Technology

Mobile phone platform as the tool in wayfinding would become more and more important in future. People can get information quickly and conveniently through the mobile internet. According to the report by (CNNIC) China Internet Network Information Center: *"the number of mobile internet users in China had reached 464 million by the end of June 2013, up by 43.79 million over the end of 2012. Amongst all the Internet users, those using mobile phones to access the Internet rose from 74.5% to 78.5%, a higher growth rate than that of the second half of 2012. According to the data released by the Ministry of Industry and Information Technology, the number of users who use mobile phone to access the Internet in China had reached 783 million by May 2013. Despite the difference, the data above indicated that the size of Chinese mobile Internet users is huge, and maintains a momentum of rapid development."* [18]

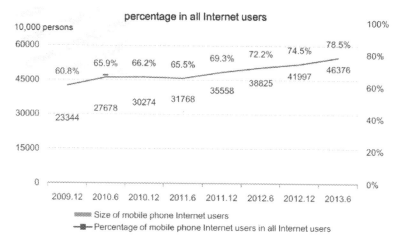

Fig. 3. Size of Mobile Phone Internet Users Source: CNNIC - Statistical Survey on Internet Development in China 2013

This data shows that the mobile internet would be the key tool for searching information in the future, provided that the right application interface is available, and utilization of mobile technology would be one of the effective alternatives for dealing with mass transit wayfinding. According to Phoenix New Media of the 2014-01-31 instant, over 60% passengers have purchased their railway tickets through the mobile internet during the 2014 Luna New Year [19-20]. Mobile phone users can use free Wifi to surf the internet for finding instant traffic schedules, ways of buying tickets, and their destinations in a quick and convenient manner instead of lining up to wait for their turn searching for information in front of the kiosk. It is unlike information kiosks which provide only limited real time mode in wayfinding within the related district. In a way, the information kiosk is only good for those who are not conversant with mobile internet applications, eg. some elderly or illiterate people. For mass transportation, the mobile platform is seemingly the most efficient tool for interactive wayfinding as of today.

3.3   Integrated Voice User Interface (VUI) Technology

Integrated with an advanced *voice user interface* [21] would also be a feasible wayfinding solution. According to the book *"Voice User Interface Design"* by Cohen Michael H. James Giangola. Jennifer Balogh: *"VUI would free the user to be far more mobile, as speech input eliminates the need to look at a keyboard...Hand-held devices would be designed with larger, easier-to-view screens, as no keyboard would be required. Touch-screen devices would no longer need to split the display between content and an on-screen keyboard, thus providing full-screen viewing of the content."* [22], it inspired that when VUI further develops, its voice control elements could be applied and integrated with the interactive wayfinding system. The developed VUI eliminates the cumbersome steps and layers of guiding or directing interfaces, enabling people to communicate directly with the voice responder to retrieve target wayfinding information more efficiently, and could therefore get information more conveniently.

3.4   Collaboration between Government and IT Industries

In mainland China, the only internet service provider (the China Internet Network Information Center) and the mobile telecommunication providers (like China Mobile, China Unicom, China Netcom and China Telecom) are all state-owned enterprises under the control of Chinese Government. Therefore, it is crucial to obtain enough support from the Chinese Government for any wayfinding system to be integrated with digital applications for the purposes of large scale usage, eg. the use of mobile technology in transport services, where massive data and high performance speed access at busy locations are carried out through the mobile network to deliver real time information, identify the current location, checking traffic, tickets, or weather. In order to develop the right strategies and solutions for dealing with such, one may need to go even further to collaborate with IT industries and research organizations for leveraging with say, *cloud service, graphical processing unit (GPU), QR codes apps and mobile location apps,* [23-26], *etc.* An example of such successful cooperation is 'Di Di Taxi Calling' application. This App was developed by private enterprises in China. Basically, it integrates the taxi calling system with a GPS, so that a customer through the mobile network can notify the nearby taxi drivers of his/her request for a taxi service whilst the driver can see the calling customer's location through the GPS. If a driver decides to take the job, he can reply to the customer and that call order will be deleted on the mobile screen. With this App, the driver can capture much more business opportunities and it offers the customer much more effective way of finding a taxi.

Fig. 4. "Di Di Taxi Calling" App in transport wayfinding in China. Screen Source: HKTVB News

In fact, some overseas industries have used mobile voice technology in wayfinding such as the "Apple iOS ICar" in automobiles [27]. (See Fig.5) Mobile voice technology eliminates the cumbersome procedures of going through numerous layers or interfaces using tiny buttons on the touch screen to operate the system [28]. For the mobile voice technology to be successfully adopted in China, it needs the support and collaboration between the Chinese government and private enterprise, particularly, in establishing a common standard or interface that can be shared by all or at least most of the mobile network service providers in order to enhance the usability of the wayfinding system in China.

Fig. 5. "Apple iOS ICar": iPhone mobile voice control system integrated in wayfinding in automobile industry Screen Source: youtube.com

4   Applying Wayfinding Design Concept and Theory

During the field study research, there has been found to be misuse of wayfinding design in transportation as illustrated below. This finding reflected that the fundamentals of wayfinding concept and theory such as sign placement, position, typography, colors, size as well as spatial and environmental organization have been neglected. This kind of misuse of design would surely affect the quality and image of a smart city.

4.1   Placement, Typography, Colors, Position, Scale

When cities in China took reference of Hong Kong's wayfinding design, some improper designs were also borrowed. (See Fig.6)

Fig. 6. (Left) Confusing and chaotic queue lines in Hong Kong's Mass Transportation Railway System (Right) The confusing sign was adjusted by tapping yellow sign in Suzhou Subway line Photos by Author - Location: Hong Kong and Suzhou

(Fig.6) The design of the queue lines was intended to guide commuters to line up in proper order at the train doors (Left photo). The package consists of 6 lines and 5 arrows. The column in the middle is for commuters leaving the train, while the others are for commuters boarding the train. The problem here is that the total width of the columns is much greater than the width of the train door. It creates chaos, especially during busy hours. The same wayfinding design can also be found in many subway and railway stations in China. In Suzhou, (right photo) the original sign was found to cause confusion and chaos, the design was manually adjusted by using a yellow tap sign on the floor. If the wayfinding design has taken into account the spatial organization effects in terms of user needs and experience, this problem would not have happened.

Inconsistent street names and road signs can often be found in cities in China. They are unclear, hard to read or understand, thus creating potential risks for both the drivers and pedestrians. In addition, incorrect signs with misspelled words cause confusion. Some signs show only Simplified Chinese words, while others are using *Pinyin* [29] (using Latin letters to help pronounce the Chinese words), which is the only recognized translation system being enforced in mainland China [30]. If foreigners do not recognize Chinese, what is the use for them to spell the Pinyin, even with correct intonation? They do not know the meaning. It is difficult for them to memorize the strange combination of Pinyin Latin letters of street names and places. Foreign visitors simply cannot find their ways using these types of road signs for wayfinding.

Fig. 7. Misused typography and color in one of the signs of a busy subway station Photo by Author - Location: Beijing

(Fig.7) Line No. 13 is one of the busy subway lines in Beijing. The word "Driction" on the top sign plate is a typo and the correct word should be 'Direction'. The even more correct translation is 'To DONGZHIMEN'. Station names are only available in Chinese, without any Pinyin. The yellow and white colors are in weak contrast, thus reducing legibility and readability in wayfinding.

Fig. 8. Misplacement of sign plates at escalators in the newly built Nanjing railway station Photo by Author - Location: Nanjing

(Fig.8) The sign label on the escalator floor is wrongly placed. Both the sign label with the text 'Please hold the handrail' (left photo) and the sign label with the text 'Please keep clear' (right photo) are placed upside down. Although it may not be the designer's mistake, it has defeated the purpose of the wayfinding design and reflects that there is a lack of wayfinding knowledge or poor management in implementing the wayfinding design.

Fig. 8. Large Scale Traffic Signs Photo by Author - Location: Nanjing

(Fig.9) This is a good example of applying a wayfinding concept and theory. The size of the digital traffic timer and arrow signs is much larger than those found in many other cities in China. It is highly visible for both drivers and pedestrians at the road intersection whether at day or nighttime. It helps provide a safe and convenient environment for users in the city. It also reflects that different provinces are using different standards for building their wayfinding system in urban development.

4.2   Urban Planning Design

Urban planning design can also affect the functionality and usability of wayfinding. Some irrational infrastructure design appearing in the new city planning and development in China reveal that there is insufficient application of a wayfinding concept and theory based on a user's need and experience. In Fig.10 below, the bus station (left photo) and the bush fencing (right photo) is constructed in the middle of the zebra crossing. The road crossing function and the bus waiting / loading & unloading function are crashing. This is a representative example of irrational urban planning in wayfinding.

Fig. 10. Irrational road design in wayfinding Photo by Author - Location: Shanghai

5   Human Factors in Wayfinding Design

No matter how a city is integrated with advanced technologies to improve a citizen's quality life, it would be worthless if people are to abuse the wayfinding system and do not follow the rules in a city. For example, see Fig.11. Zebra crossing is one of the wayfinding features commonly found in roadway systems. Around the world, pedestrians always have the right of way crossing the road. In China, it is seldom the case. Many drivers violate this code of traffic and challenge pedestrians walking on the zebra crossing, causing chaotic and dangerous situations on the roads. To improve the situation, tighter enforcement of the traffic laws and regulations as well as more advertising and education are advised to foster people, including drivers and pedestrians, to better make use of wayfinding tools.

Fig. 11. Chaotic and dangerous scenes at zebra crossing happen frequently in China Photo by Author - Location: Beijing

6   Conclusion

In this field study report, it is revealed that though the proposed smart city may emerge with new high-tech applications, a poor wayfinding design in urban infrastructure system would decrease its efficiency and weaken the city image. It needs a proper balance between emerging technologies and wayfinding concept and theory application which is based on user experience. Three prime cities (Beijing, Shanghai, Hong Kong) and two 2nd tier cities (Suzhou, Nanjing) were examined to explore the positive and negative scenarios of interactive wayfinding in transportation in China. The report showed that mobile voice control technology is effective digital platform solutions that would be the future wayfinding tools and would be widely applied in smart cities in China. However, it is necessary to obtain enough support and collaboration between the Chinese Government and private enterprises to enhance the effectiveness of the interactive wayfinding platform. As a guide for design practitioners and local government officials who are responsible for the implementation of the wayfinding design, the basic concept and theory of wayfinding must be considered and incorporated with the urban design of the city in order to make it a smart city.

In my ongoing research project, a smart city will be chosen for further in-depth surveying and experiment for wayfinding design. Hopefully, the final paper would be beneficial to local governments and general public in China by providing them with a wider perspective of wayfinding design and enhancing their awareness of the possible barriers in effective communications in urban infrastructure service.

References

1. Smart City, http://www.ibm.com/smarterplanet/us/en/smarter_
   cities/overview/?lnk=fkt-scit-usen
2. Smart City: Opportunity and Challenge for Enterprises, http://www.chinadaily.
   com.cn/bizchina/2012-11/15/content_15935688.htm
3. Shannon, C.E., Weaver, W.: The Mathematical Theory of Communication, 1st Printing
   edn. University of Illinois Press, USA (1971)
4. Brando, K.C.: Wayfinding definition, http://www.kellybrandondesign.com/
   IGDWayfinding.html (retrieved)
5. Lynch, K.: The Image of the City. The MIT Press, USA (1960)
6. http://china.org.cn/china/2013-08/13/content_29707492.htm
7. Gibson, D.: The Wayfinding Handbook: Information Design for Public Places. Liaoning
   Science and technology Publishing House, China (2010) (Chinese Edition)
8. Berger, C.M.: Oriented Logo: Graphical Navigation System Design and Implementation.
   Electronic Industry Press, China (2013)
9. Calori, C.: Signage and Wayfinding Design. Publishing House Electronics Industry, China
   (2013) (Chinese Edition)
10. http://www.basiclaw.gov.hk/en/index.html
11. http://www.worldairportawards.com/
12. http://www3.weforum.org/docs/CSI/2012-13/GCR_Rankings_2012-13.
    pdf
13. http://www.discoverhongkong.com/eng/about-hktb/awards-and-
    achievements.jsp
14. http://www.photius.com/rankings/infrastructure_quality_count
    ry_rankings_2011.html
15. http://www.aci.aero/Data-Centre/Monthly-Traffic-
    Data/Passenger-Summary/Monthly
16. http://news.cnr.cn/native/gd/201401/t20140102_514555471.shtml
17. http://www.chinadaily.com.cn/china/2014-01/17/content_
    17240283.htm
18. CNNIC - Statistical Survey on Internet Development in China (June 2013), http://
    www1.cnnic.cn/IDR/ReportDownloads/201310/P020131029430558704
    972.pdf (retrieved)
19. http://finance.ifeng.com/a/20140129/11582020_0.shtml
20. http://news.ifeng.com/gundong/detail_2014_01/17/
    33097983_0.shtml
21. http://www.dictionaryofengineering.com/definition/voice-
    user-interface.html
22. Cohen, M.H., Giangola, J., Balogh, J.: Voice User Interface Design. Addison-Wesley
    Proessional, USA (2004)
23. Cloud, http://www.pcmag.com/encyclopedia/term/39847/cloud
24. GUI, http://global.britannica.com/EBchecked/topic/242033/
    graphical-user-interface-GUI
25. QR code, http://www.pcmag.com/encyclopedia/term/61424/qr-code
26. Mobile location apps, http://www.webmapsolutions.com/mobile-location-
    apps
27. http://www.autoexpress.co.uk/car-news/85505/apple-icar-ios-
    coming-your-vehicle
28. Apple iOS ICar, http://www.youtube.com/watch?v=M5OZMu5u0y
29. http://en.wikipedia.org/wiki/Chinese_Phonetic_Alphabet
30. http://qhs.mca.gov.cn/article/zcwj/dmgl/200711/2007110000444
    1.shtml (Chinese)

The Encourage Operators to Promote Manual Flight Operations- a Pandemic in Modern Aviation

Edgard Thomas Martins[1], Isnard Thomas Martins[2], and Marcelo Márcio Soares[3]

[1] Universidade Federal de Pernambuco Recife- Pernambuco, Brasil
edgardpiloto@gmail.com
[2] Universidade Estácio de Sá- Rio de Janeiro, Brasil
isnardthomasmartins@gmail.com
[3] Universidade Federal de Pernambuco Recife- Pernambuco, Brasil
soaresmm@gmail.com

Abstract. Advances in technology have enabled increasingly sophisticated automation to be introduced into the flight decks of modern airplanes. Generally, this automation was added to accomplish worthy objectives such as reducing flightcrew workload, adding additional capability, or increasing fuel economy. To a large extent, these objectives have been achieved. Safety also stood to benefit from the increasing amounts of highly reliable automation. Indeed, the current generation of highly automated transport category airplanes has generally demonstrated an improved safety record relative to the previous generation of airplanes. Vulnerabilities do exist, though, and further safety improvements should be made. To provide a safety target to guide the aviation industry, the Secretary of Transportation and others have expressed the view that the aviation industry should strive for the objective of none accidents. Training standards and currency in manual flying skills may well have deteriorated, but are these changes in proportion to the tasks and situations typical of modern operations, or really at the root of handling related safety concerns [9].

Keywords: Automation, Manual procedures, Pandemia.

1   Introduction

This appears to be what the FAA have done (*a pandemic in modern aviation*); but it's easy to find error as it is a normal aspect of human behavior. However, without evidence that these 'errors' directly contribute to reduced safety (and what are these errors), more of 'this or that' simple solution will not guarantee any improvement. You may only improve the skill in *'flying one-engine ILS (Instrument Landing System)*. The FAA's investigation has used pilot error as a stopping point; the human is at fault, thus train the human – more currency. This simplistic approach may miss underlying problems, and until these and the contributing factors are understood then any meaningful intervention cannot be formulated. What about the organization, economic, and social changes; has the baseline human behavior been affected by these [1]. Modern views of human factors by-pass human error with the concept of variability;

A. Marcus (Ed.): DUXU 2014, Part III, LNCS 8519, pp. 317–325, 2014.
© Springer International Publishing Switzerland 2014

this is a performance characteristic necessary to manage daily activities. No situation is perfect / clear cut, work activity is a compromise. So one aspect to consider is if pilots are sufficiently trained / skilled in the process of compromise – the judgment that originates from situation assessment and choice of action (aspects of airmanship), and which also involves risk management, and the skills of thought when stressed. This thread talks about manual handling errors. But it's not about "faults". It's more about lack of being able to fulfill the role the human still has his place in the cockpit: To take over when the electrons go the wrong way. See figure 1.

Fig. 1. The ILS-(Instrument Landing System)

Training standards and currency in manual flying skills may well have deteriorated, but are these changes in proportion to the tasks and situations typical of modern operations, or really at the root of handling related safety concerns [2].

Again, you sound great intellectually and such questions might be worth investigating. They expect us to be able to take over, fly the airplane out of any danger irrespective to any of the above (and even you are a customer every now and then). Even on newer cars equipped with cruise-controls and distance monitoring/intervening you still need to be able to brake yourself. We know what you mean, but still insist that the underlying problem here, is that the basics are not taught well enough and the acquired is not maintained enough. This might be simple, but then it's just as simple to remedy it [3].

2   Contextualization

On April 26, 1994, an Airbus A300-600 operated by China Airlines crashed at Nagoya, Japan, killing 264 passengers and flightcrew members. Contributing to the accident were conflicting actions taken by the flightcrew and the airplane's autopilot. The crash provided a stark example of how a breakdown in the flightcrew/automation interface can affect flight safety. Although this particular accident involved an A300-600, other accidents, incidents, and safety indicators demonstrate that this problem is not confined to any one airplane type, airplane manufacturer, operator, or geographical region. This point was tragically demonstrated by the crash of a Boeing 757 operated by American Airlines near Cali, Columbia on December 20, 1995, and a November 12, 1995 incident (very nearly a fatal accident) in which a American Airlines Douglas MD-80 descended below the minimum descent altitude on approach to Bradley International Airport, CT, clipped the tops of trees, and landed short of the runway[4].

As a result of the Nagoya accident as well as other incidents and accidents that appear to highlight difficulties in flightcrews interacting with the increasing flight deck automation, the Federal Aviation Administration's (FAA) Transport Airplane Directorate, under the approval of the Director, Aircraft Certification Service, launched a study to evaluate the flightcrew/flight deck automation interfaces of current generation transport category airplanes. The following airplane types were included in the evaluation: Boeing: Models 737/757/767/747-400/777, Airbus: Models A300-600/A310/A320/A330/A340, McDonnell Douglas: Models MD-80/MD-90/MD-11, Fokker: Model F28-0100/-0070 [5].

The Federal Aviation A chartered a human factors (HUMAN FACTOR) team to address these human factors issues, with representatives from the FAA Aircraft Certification and Flight Standards Services, the National Aeronautics and Space Administration, and the Joint Aviation Authorities (JAA), assisted by technical advisors from the Ohio State University, the University of Illinois, and the University of Texas. The HUMAN FACTOR [6]. Team was asked to identify specific or generic problems in design, training, flightcrew qualifications, and operations, and to recommend appropriate means to address these problems. In addition, the HUMAN FACTOR Team was specifically directed to identify those concerns that should be the subject of new or revised Federal Aviation Regulations (FAR), Advisory Circulars (AC), or policies. The HUMAN FACTOR Team relied on readily available information sources, including accident/incident reports, Aviation Safety Reporting System reports, research reports, and trade and scientific journals. In addition, meetings were held with operators, manufacturers, pilots' associations, researchers, and industry organizations to solicit their input. Additional inputs to the HUMAN FACTOR Team were received from various individuals and organizations interested in the HUMAN FACTOR Team's efforts [7].

When examining the evidence, the HUMAN FACTOR Team found that traditional methods of assessing safety are often insufficient to pinpoint vulnerabilities that may lead to an accident. Consequently, the HUMAN FACTOR Team examined accident precursors, such as incidents, errors, and difficulties encountered in operations and training. The HUMAN FACTOR Team also examined research studies that were intended to identify issues and improve understanding of difficulties with flightcrew/automation interaction. In examining flightcrew error, the HUMAN FACTOR Team recognized that it was necessary to look beyond the label of flightcrew error to understand why the errors occurred [8].

We looked for contributing factors from design, training and flightcrew qualification, operations, and regulatory processes. While the HUMAN FACTOR Team was chartered primarily to examine the flightcrew interface to the flight deck systems, we quickly recognized that considering only the interface would be insufficient to address all of the relevant safety concerns. Therefore, we considered issues more broadly, including issues concerning the functionality of the uderlying systems. From the evidence, the HUMAN FACTOR Team identified issues that show vulnerabilities in flightcrew management of automation and situation awareness and include concerns about:

- Pilot understanding of the automation's capabilities, limitations, modes, and operating principles and techniques. The HUMAN FACTOR Team frequently heard about automation "surprises," where the automation behaved in ways the flightcrew did not expect. "Why did it do that?" "What is it doing now?" and "What will it do next?" were common questions expressed by flightcrews from operational experience.

- Differing pilot decisions about the appropriate automation level to use or whether to turn the automation *on* or *off* when they get into unusual or non-normal situations (e.g., attempted engagement of the autopilot during the moments preceding the A310 crash at Bucharest). This may also lead to potential mismatches with the manufacturers' assumptions about how the flightcrew will use the automation.

Flightcrew situation awareness issues included vulnerabilities in, for example:

- Automation/mode awareness. This was an area where we heard a universal message of concern about each of the aircraft in our charter.

- Flight path awareness, including insufficient terrain awareness (sometimes involving loss of control or controlled flight into terrain) and energy awareness (especially low energy state).

These vulnerabilities appear to exist to varying degrees across the current fleet of transport category airplanes in our study, regardless of the manufacturer, the operator, or whether accidents have occurred in a particular airplane type. Although the Team found specific issues associated with particular design, operating, and training philosophies, we consider the generic issues and vulnerabilities to be a larger threat to safety, and the most important and most difficult to address. It is this larger pattern that serves as a barrier to needed improvements to the current level of safety, or could threaten the current safety record in the future aviation environment. It is this larger pattern that needs to be characterized, understood, and addressed. In trying to understand this larger pattern, the Team considered it important to examine why these vulnerabilities exist [9]. The Team concluded that the vulnerabilities are there because of a number of interrelated deficiencies in the current aviation system:

- Insufficient communication and coordination. Examples include lack of communication about in-service experience within and between organizations;

incompatibilities between the air traffic system and airplane capabilities; poor interfaces between organizations; and lack of coordination of research needs and results between the research community, designers, regulators, and operators.

- Processes used for design, training, and regulatory functions inadequately address_human performance issues. As a result, users can be surprised by subtle behavior or overwhelmed by the complexity embedded in current systems operated within the current operating environment. Process improvements are needed to provide the framework for consistent application of principles and methods for eliminating vulnerabilities in design, training, and operations.

- Insufficient criteria, methods, and tools for design, training, and evaluation. Existing methods, data, and tools are inadequate to evaluate and resolve many of the important human performance issues. It is relatively easy to get agreement that automation should be human-centered, or that potentially hazardous situations should be avoided; it is much more difficult to get agreement on how to achieve these objectives.

- Insufficient knowledge and skills. Designers, pilots, operators, regulators, and researchers do not always possess adequate knowledge and skills in certain areas related to human performance. It is of great concern to this team that investments in necessary levels of human expertise are being reduced in response to economic pressures when two-thirds to three-quarters of all accidents have flightcrew error cited as a major factor.

- Insufficient understanding and consideration of cultural differences in design, training,_operations, and evaluation. The aviation community has an inadequate understanding of the influence of culture and language on flightcrew/automation interaction. Cultural differences may reflect differences in the country of origin, philosophy of regulators, organizational philosophy, or other factors. There is a need to improve the aviation community's understanding and consideration of the implications of cultural influences on human performance.

3   Method

Based on our investigations and examination of the evidence, these concerns represent more than a series of individual problems with individual, independent solutions. These concerns are highly interrelated, and are evidence of aviation *system* problems, not just isolated human or machine errors. Therefore, we need *system* solutions, not just point solutions to individual problems. To treat one issue (or underlying cause) in isolation will ultimately fail to fundamentally increase the safety of airplane operations, and may even decrease safety[10].

The flaws in the commitment of decision-making in emergency situations and the lack of perception related to all elements associated with a given situation in a short space of time indicate, often, lack of situational awareness. Automation always surprises the crews and often prevents them from understanding the extent of this technology that is very common in aircraft units with a high degree of automation. These facts are discussed in a subtle way by aircraft drivers who can not do it openly, as it might create an impression of professional self-worthlessness (self-deprecation). This leads to common questions like: What is happening now? What will be the next step of automated systems? This type of doubt would be inadmissible in older aircraft because the pilot of those machines works as an extension of the plane. This scenario contributes to emotional disorders and a growing hidden problem in the aeronautical field [11]. These unexpected automation surprises reflect a complete misunderstanding or even the misinformation of the users. It also reveals their inability and limitations to overcome these new situations that were not foreseen by the aircraft designers. Our studies showed a different scenario when the accident is correlated with systemic variables. It has identified the problems or errors that contribute to the fact that drivers are unable to act properly. These vectors, when they come together, may generate eventually a temporary incompetence of the pilot due to limited capacity or lack of training in the appropriateness of automation in aircraft or even, the worst alternative, due to a personal not visible and not detectable non-adaptation to automation. We must also consider in the analysis the inadequate training and many other reasons, so that we can put in right proportion the effective participation or culpability of the pilot in accidents. Our doctoral thesis presents statistical studies that allow us to assert that the emotional and cognitive overload are being increased with automation widely applied in the cockpits of modern aircraft, and also that these new projects do not go hand in hand with the desired cognitive and ergonomic principles.

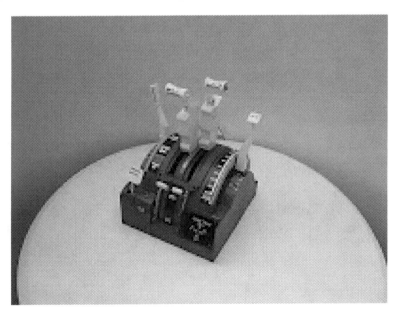

Fig. 2. Throttle Quadrant (http://aeroprado737-800ng.blogspot.com.br/2013/07/tq-conjunto-de-manetes.html)

4   Conclusions

As with many airlines it is self-funded by the student and thus is kept to a minimum number of sessions. As with other airlines the type rating is combined with an OPC. A few decades ago, in my early life entering the airlines, we were taught to fly the Authomatic Control in the Throttle Quadrant (TQ) course, with SOP's (Standard Operating Procedure) attached. The line operations were refined during line training. The initial emphasis was knowing how the automated new system worked and how to fly it. The line training refined these skills and expanded how to operate it within the airways system and a multitude of busy airports and small visual airfields. Understanding the complexities of the systems came with our 'apprenticeship', which had started.   When automation became readily available we used it to reduce workload when we felt like it. We didn't really trust it but we used it knowing we could easily disconnect it when it didn't do what we wanted. Now some airliners want everything done on autopilot because it can fly better than any pilot. Airlines hire young pilots with little experience and they are shown how you don't need to hand fly any more because of automation. Labor is cheap. Then Air France Flight 447 accident shows the world how wrong that was. All that flight needed was one pilot in the cockpit who knew how to hand fly but they didn't so everybody died for no reason. Nowadays the TQ (Throttle Quadrant - see figure 2)

The course seems to shift the emphasis more towards SOP's (*Standard Operating Procedures*) during the maneuvers, some of which are with normal & non-normal scenarios. Some of the non-normals scenarios are non reported. It was not the complexity of their feelings which did put them into trouble, it was the lack of training, Understanding of those systems. This ignorance created a complex system when in fact with proper training it would have been quite simple. One wonders if the policy of many airlines to use relatively (2 years experience). They have followed the self same course of knowing what to do, but not the how and the why. They then pass on this diluted knowledge to the next generation of cadets who will become the next generation of equipments and so the downward spiral of knowledge continues. SOP's are so intense that the first thought of a pilot in a less than ideal situation is to ask, "what does the book say?" Second, if at all, comes "what is the most sensible airmanship thing to do?" By the time you arrive at the 2nd option it might be too ate as the a/c was still traveling very fast during the first phase of questioning confusion. The oldies do what is best instinctively, and within the book boundaries, but are not afraid to bend the SOP's; the newbie are terrified to even blow at the boundaries and thus delay making some decisions and then have to race to catch up. All old farts were newbies once, but mostly with a longer and deeper apprenticeship than today.

If the industry is gong to continue making captains with relatively low hours then the training of manual skills, and especially systems knowledge and understanding of all their possibilities, needs to be more in depth to compensate for the shorter apprenticeship. Too many commands can be given to those whose professional checks are above average and the knowledge is perfect. So we can not cover all eventualities. Most incidents and accidents started quite subtly and the human intervention, or lack of it, caused a can of worms to develop, when it was preventable. And that's a whole other discussion about a good crew being preventative rather than reactive. Slavishly following this scenery is not always preventative, but that was touched upon in an earlier thread. I guess lack of training never applied to us old guys. We kind of trained ourselves. We couldn't afford a lot of formal training. Our first few thousand hours had no automation so we just took our hands and did what was needed to fly. The HUMAN FACTOR Team developed recommendations to address the vulnerabilities and deficiencies from a system viewpoint. Our consideration of human performance issues, however, was focused primarily on the flightcrew [13]. We did not attempt to address human performance issues associated with other personnel involved in the aviation system, such as flight attendants, ground personnel, air traffic services personnel, or maintenance personnel. Because the system is already very safe, any changes should be made carefully to avoid detracting from existing safety practices. The Team believes we must improve and institutionalize:

- Investments in people (designers, users, evaluators, and researchers). For example, flightcrew training investments should be re-balanced to ensure appropriate coverage of automation issues.

- Processes. It is important to improve how design, training, operations, and certification are accomplished. For example, regulatory authorities should evaluate flight deck designs for human performance problems.

- Tools and methods. New tools and methods need to be developed and existing ones improved to accompany the process improvements.

- Regulatory standards. Current standards for type certification and operations have not kept pace with changes in technology and increased knowledge about human performance. For example, flightcrew workload is the major human performance consideration in existing regulations; other factors should be evaluated as well, including the potential for designs to induce human error and reduce flightcrew situation awareness.

References

1. Eugenio, C.: Automação no cockpit das aeronaves: um preciosoauxílio à operação aérea ou um fator de aumento de complexidade no ambiente profissional dos pilotos, 1st edn., vol. 1, pp. 34–35, São Paulo, Brasil (2011)
2. Henriqson, E.: A coordenação como um fenômeno cognitivo distribuído e situado em *cockpits* de aeronaves- Coordination as a distributed cognitive phenomena situated in aircraft cockpits Aviation in Focus (PortoAlegre), Porto Alegre, vol. 1(1), pp. 58–76 (Ago/Dez. 2010)
3. Reason, J.: Human Error. Cambridge University Press, Cambridge (1990, 2012)
4. Rasmussen, J.: Human errors: a taxonomy for describing human malfunction in industrial installations. Journal of Occupational Accidents 4, 311–333 (1982)
5. Sternberg, R.J.: Cognitive psychology. Ed Artmed, Porto Alegre (2000)
6. Green, R.G., Frenbard, M.: Human Factors for Pilots. Avebury Technical. Aldershot, England (1993)

7. FAA-Federal Aviation Administration, DOT/FAA/AM-10/13, Office of Aerospace Medicine, Causes of General Aviation
8. Accidents and Incidents: Analysis Using NASA Aviation, Safety Reporting System Data. Press, Washington, DC (September 2010, 2011, 2012)
9. Dekker, S.: Illusions of explanation-A critical essay on error classification. The International Journal of Aviation Psychology 13, 95–106 (2003)
10. Martins, E.: Study of the implications for health and work in the operationalization and the aeronaut embedded in modern aircraft in the man-machines interactive process complex, Estudo das implicações na saúde e na operacionalização e no trabalho do aeronauta embarcado em modernas aeronaves no processo interativo homemmáquinas complexas, thesis, Centro de Pesquisas Aggeu Magalhães, Fundação Osw Cruz, pp. 567–612, Perna, Brasil (August 2010)
11. Martins, E.: Ergonomics in Aviation: A critical study of the causal responsibility of pilots in accidents. Ergonomia na Aviação: Um estudo crítico da responsabilidade dos pilotos na causalidade dos acidentes, Msc. Monography, Universidade Federal Pernambuco, Brasil, Pernambuco
12. Federal Aviation Administration Human Factors Team Report on: The Interfaces Between Flightcrewsand- Modern Flight Deck Systems (June 18, 1996)

Hardwired Critical Action Panels
for Emergency Preparedness:
Design Principles and CAP Design
for Offshore Petroleum Platforms

Bojana Petkov and Alf Ove Braseth

Institute for Energy Technology - IFE, Halden, Norway
{bojana.petkov,alf.ove.braseth}@hrp.no

Abstract. Critical action panels (CAPs) are hardwired safety panels installed in control rooms of oil and gas platforms. They are used as redundant backup for safe shutdown in cases where software systems fail. The panels of many installations in the North Sea today do not follow modern standards and regulatory requirements, while other installations have not yet implemented CAP panels. These use instead large safety matrices, which can cause information overload as they are also used for process operation. This paper presents design principles for modern CAP design followed by a conceptual CAP design layout. The design rationale is primarily based on a study for an operational installation on the Norwegian continental shelf. Regulatory demands as well as user requirements and needs were followed to create a functional display. The objective of the design was maintaining the user's situation awareness while harmonizing with the software-based interfaces in the control room. The CAP design was reviewed against requirements and proved acceptable.

Keywords: Critical action panel, control room, petroleum platform, interaction design.

1   Introduction

The first Norwegian oil platform began production mid June 1971. Today, this number has expanded to 76 fields, making it by far Norway's largest industry. In 2012 it represented more than 23 per cent of the country's total value creation [1]. To maintain the safety of a steadily growing number of platforms, operators and workers, new standards and regulation are being put in place, requiring improvements of the oldest installations.

Modern oil and gas production process use software-based semi-automated systems for process monitoring and interaction from the platform's central control room (CCR). The Norwegian Institute for Energy Technology (IFE) in Halden has a long history of performing safety oriented research for both the petroleum and nuclear industry. Focus areas have been on supporting process overview, production optimization, plant safety and designing software-based interaction solutions. But what hap-

A. Marcus (Ed.): DUXU 2014, Part III, LNCS 8519, pp. 326–337, 2014.

pens when software systems fail? How do operators maintain safety, and in a controlled way stop and shut down the plants production systems?

The main system used for this is the critical action panel, CAP, a simplified safety panel primarily used as the last resort to shut the platform down safely [2]. The CAP can also be used to restart the main electrical functions on platforms that have been completely shut down and possibly even abandoned.

The panels are hardwired to installation safety functions as a redundant backup system, typically wall mounted and ranging in size from A3 to A0. The panel is typically positioned near the operator's normal seated position, but not necessary placed in normal field of view. Typical CAP designs are shown in figure 1.

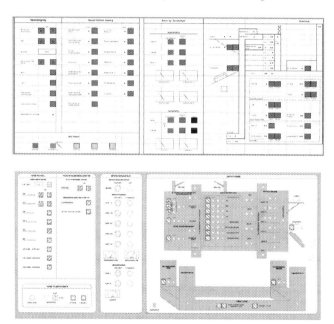

Fig. 1. Example of CAP designs from other platforms (Source: IFE design)

Upon failure of electricity or of the normal control and display systems (often software based), the operators require access to key functions such as fire and gas (F&G), emergency shutdown (ESD), and communication to be accessible on the panel. One of the key challenges is observing and differentiating relevant findings and problems in time constrained situations. According to Meshkati [3], the use of decision and memory aids can minimize failures and human errors during abnormal situations. These challenges are not domain specific, and can also be experienced for other complex fields such as nuclear power plants [4].

The daily operation of a platform is typically done on operator station (OS) computer screens and large screens displays (LSDs). The LSD is used for a 'big picture' overview, whereas the OS is used for detailed in depth process interaction. As the

CAP is rarely used, the panel design should be harmonized with the daily used OS and LSD interfaces, matching their mental models of the problem [3] and aid in making correct decisions. One challenge of the CAP design described in this paper was visual harmonization to inform operators of structural and functional interrelations as suggested by Javaux et. al [5], making the unfamiliar, familiar.

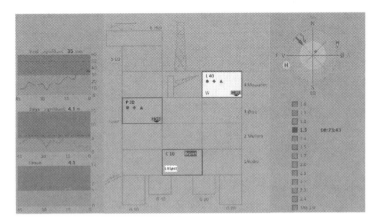

Fig. 2. Example of graphical elements from LSD with which the CAP should harmonize (Source: IFE design)

The rationale of the design presented in this paper is primarily based on a collaboration of CAP development with a Norwegian platform (not named here for commercial reasons). The platform was in use of extended safety matrices for fire and gas, and emergency shutdown. The matrices contained most safety depending functions in addition to many operational functions, cluttering the panel with too much information. Per definition, the contents of operational functions impeded the matrices of being labeled a CAP panel. The matrices did not follow all requirements and regulations of modern platforms nor were they consistent with the newer software based solutions, e.g. colour coding for different alarms and statuses. The background for the project was that no single standard covering human factors of CAP design is currently available for the industry.

This paper is organized in the following way; relevant background material for CAP design is identified with a description of the design process. Based on this, design principles and CAP design is explained by figures and text. Lastly we outline a conclusion and suggest topics for further work.

2   Design Approach: CAP Design Basis

The following chapter outlines relevant background material for CAP design and work method. The project followed a work process as described in ISO 9241-210 [6], providing requirements and recommendations for design principles throughout the life cycle of computer based interactive systems. Systems designed by use of human computer design (HCD) methods are described as easier to understand and use, more productive, and efficient while reducing discomfort and stress [6].

The method has emphasis on the users, their needs, skills and judgment. According to Nielsen [7] however, this does not mean that the users should be entitled to design the panel freely, as users can be coloured by learned habits and behavior and don't like to deviate from current incorporated practice [8]. The project also identified human cognitive capacity limitations as important for CAP design. Humans have limited cognitive abilities and are prone to make errors; especially when put in situations they are not used to or feel comfortable in [8]. These limitations emphasize the importance of designing for human support and aspects such as situational attention drawing, limited memory requirements and intuitive mental perception.

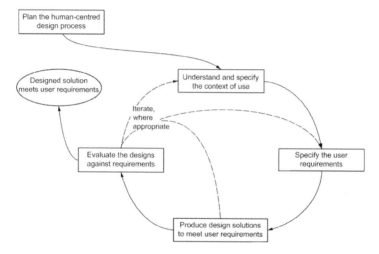

Fig. 3. Interdependence of human centered design activities (Source: ISO 9241-210, p. 11)

The first step of designing a usable, intuitive panel was however to scope the context of use and identify user needs under relevant situations. Who will be using the panel, apart from the operators and in which situations? What safety functions are required for a safe shutdown? How can the physical design layout help to prevent accidents related to human error?

2.1 Scoping: Context of Use

The primary use of the panel is when all software systems fail and the control operators have to safely and securely shut down the platform, in many cases before abandoning the offshore platform. In some cases this can be under heavy seas or loss of electricity and work light. The buttons and alarm lights must therefore be constructed in a clear and visible manner with safety locks or hatches to prevent accidental activation. A set of overall functional and ergonomic requirements was set at the start of the project to define a common goal for development. This guide for scoping CAP use, was used during all project meetings and workshops:

1. The CAPs intended use is when the software system fails to safely shut down the platform. It's not designed to maintain production.
2. The CAP shall be clearly marked in the CCR.
3. The CAP interface shall be suitable for awareness and actions during emergency situations with a simple and clear command structure.
4. The CAP shall be independent of other control and display systems.
5. The text should be readable at arm's length in Norwegian, (here translated to English).
6. All functions and alarms must have a clear meaning and be consistent with other equipment in the CCR such as the large screen display and the operator stations software displays.

As the CAP will not be in daily use, the information on the panel has to be self-explanatory and logical for the user. They have to perceive the status and dynamics happening around them, understand what that information means and its projection in the future [9], described as maintaining situation awareness. The operators need to concentrate solely on what is going on in those situations, preventing the mind from wandering to render vivid and detailed observations, often referred to as mindfulness [10].

2.2   User Requirements and Work Process

The control room operators are the primary users of the panel, however, there are certain electrical aspects such as isolation of various areas and rooms of the platform that trained electricians are responsible for and are considered the secondary users of the CAP. Another group is the emergency preparedness team, usually situated somewhere near the control room, that require platform situation information without disrupting the operators in their work. This group is in need of read only availabilities. Finally, cleaning and technical groups require accessibility for maintenance.

The project identified user requirements from relevant standards and guidelines. They were composed as a combination of acquiring rules and regulations form standards such as ISO and NORSOK (Norwegian continental shelf competitive position), technical requirement reports from the petroleum authority of Norway and interviews with the end users. Table 1 shows a short summary of the required safety functions extracted from standards and regulations.

A draft list of all obligatory, recommended and nice to have requirements was listed before user involvement. The interviews and conversations with the users were performed in groups with all participants present to stimulate ideas and transfer knowledge and experience. Each of the listed requirements were discussed with the operators and approved or rejected for use on the CAP (where regulations allowed) during an extensive workshop. The conclusions resulted in a list of design principles followed by multiple design iterations that were repeatedly evaluated against requirements and user satisfaction.

Gestalt principles such as proximity, closure, colour coding, consistency and similarity [13], were used in the design process aiming to formulate the layout and use based on input from regulatory specifications and users needs, skills and knowledge.

Table 1. Requirements with corresponding proposed design principles for CAP design

Standard requirements basis	Design principles
Firewater and foam pump systems • Fire fighting release activation status • Start of fire water (FW) or foam pumps called for • Selection of FW/foam pumps for standby/duty • Manual start/stop of FW/foam pumps	Firewater pressure in the fire fighting water and foam pumps should be displayed with a gauge. Relevant limits should be presented. A geographical layout of the F&G areas should be used to help the operator faster comprehend where the alarm was initiated.
Emergency Shutdown (ESD) • Activation of all safe shut-down levels • Activation of blow down (BD)	There shall be a clear grouping offering control and display functions for isolation and shutdown.

Ergonomic Considerations. The size of the panel is set to 1200x700 mm with all functionality included in the current layout. A specific detailed design solution will be necessary for each platform as the details of production and safety differs. The project identified relevant ergonomic data from guidelines for the related nuclear domain, NUREG 0700 [11]. The size fits well in to the typical ergonomic placement guidelines of the standard, stating that working panels should be placed no lower than 760 mm above the floor and no higher than 1930 mm [11].

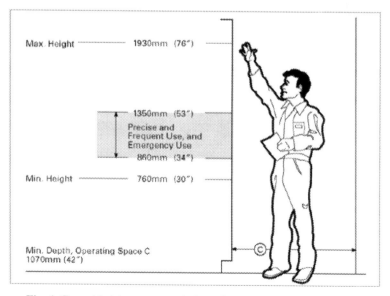

Fig. 4. Control height recommendations (Source: NUREG 0700, p 424)

The buttons of the panel should be big enough to be activated even if the operators are wearing gloves approximately 20x20 mm based on NUREG 0700 guideline stating that legend pushbuttons (illuminated with internal light) should be 19-38 mm wide and high [11]. All buttons should be slip resistant and equipped with a safety lid to prevent accidental activation. The lid will also allow for safe maintenance and cleaning of the panel without shutting down the entire system [12].

The alarm lamps are only meant to give information and have been made circular and smaller than the push buttons, 8 mm in diameter, not to distract the user with too much information at once and to properly differentiate between information given (circles) and actions to be performed (square buttons).

2.3   Harmonizing CAP Design with Software-Based Interfaces

The software based information systems give detailed picture of the overall process state and afford in-depth details. The CAP however, only presents main critical functions, primarily fire and gas, and emergency shutdown. The CAP panel has partly automated functions, and will shut down certain high danger systems, even if operators have given no input action. The operators have to be able to distinguish what functions (1) are activated because they have to or have been automatically activated by the system, (2) require a release or activation, (3) contain errors or (4) have been blocked. The project identified for this reason the following as important characteristics supported by the CAP panel: mental models, consistency principles, colour coding and recognition of software functions will help the operators determine what information is important to attend to in what order.

3   Results: Design Principles and CAP Design

This chapter presents the paper's contribution of proposed design principles for CAP design followed by the actual design layout with corresponding design rationale.

3.1   Design Principles for CAP Design

The following are the proposed design principles for CAP design for Norwegian petroleum platforms:

- All text on the CAP shall be in Norwegian and terms should be written as used in daily life. It should be readable at arm's length and be in a sans serif font.
- Groupings of control and display function shall be used, based on relatedness and arranged in order of performance and use.
- A geographical layout of the F&G areas shall be used to help the operator faster comprehend where the alarm has been set.
- The contents of CAP groupings shall be organized from left to right and top to bottom, e.g., first the alarm lamp, followed by function, execution, confirmation and potential blockings, also with corresponding confirmation of blocking action, based on sequences of use.

- Alarm lamps for display functions shall differ in shape and size from the action implementing buttons. The action button shall be placed before any confirmation lamps.
- The alarm lamps' colours shall be consistent with the software-based systems.
- Similar alarms placed together shall be distinguishable in appearance.
- All buttons and rotary knobs should have prevention against accidental activation. The more important button functions should have additional colour coding for easier recognition.
- All buttons should be made as a latch on/off in order for the operator to both activate and cancel actions. The light in the button shall be turned on and off.
- Less important buttons such as "Lamp test" and "Acknowledge alarm" should be placed outside the main area of sight.
- The CAP and control functions on it shall be positioned in accordance with NORSOK S-002 [2] (standard for technical safety) and a commonly used human factors standard such as NUREG 0700 [11] or the applicable standard at the time of detailed design, to allow reach by all expected operators.

3.2   CAP Design

One of the main issues of the design was to give the operators a good visual interpretation of the overall safety related functions on the platform, as well as details over certain critical areas. On the operator stations this is possible by browsing through multiple pictures. This was on the CAP solved by grouping together all similar functions and buttons, and arranging them in close proximity to each other by level of use and physical placement on the platform following Gestalt principles [13]. The operators can take a step back to see the overall situation of the platform or immerse themselves in a certain aspect of the process, a group of functions. The illuminated alarm lamps will be seen in the peripheral vision and the alarm colour will determine whether the operator needs to change task focus or continue what he's working on.

Different functionalities based on actions and alarms are grouped together and separated by distance and the use of a dull grey colour background. The layout and outline closure of the platform itself with deck-based functions is perceived faster in a more logical manner. The layout is also recognizable from the software based visual interfaces of the large screen and operator stations, see figure 2, and helps the operators maintain a mental picture of situation placement [10].

The groups are placed top to bottom, left to right based on frequency of use. The functions most often used are in the users primary eye level, with less critical functions placed to the left and most critical to the right.

The principle of mental modeling [8, 13] has also been used regarding visual interpretation of pressure measurements. In the pictures on operator stations, pressure is primarily displayed as a number. When the number reaches a high or low, an alarm will initiate, drawing the operator's attention. On the CAP however, it is of less importance to know the exact number, as when running the process, but rather is there enough pressure for firewater to reach all areas of the platform? A gauge going from a normal state, in the middle, to a low red area on the left will quickly indicate potential danger if a fire would occur. If the pressure goes beyond warning, a red level-1 alarm will initiate.

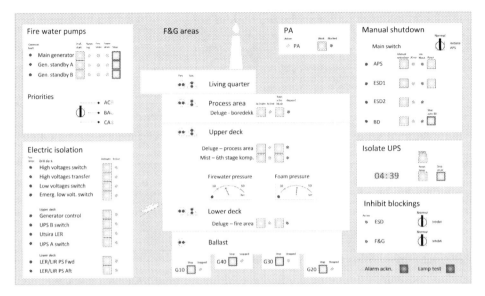

Fig. 5. The CAP design as specified by requirements and design principles (Source: IFE design)

Fig. 6. Pressure gauges are a good mental model for detecting early signs of failure

Consistency and design affordances with the software systems have been maintained also by the use of colour coding of alarms and general information given by the software. The use of colour has been used conservatively to avoid bringing the users attention to things that are of less importance. The human eye can only process and distinguish a limited number of colours at a glance, depending on the design [13]. The design presented in this paper only uses 4; (1) red for alarm level 1, (2) yellow for alarm level 2, (3) blue for blockings, and (4) white for initiated sequences and functions that have to or should be activated. The figures show how the panel will look when the alarms are active and illuminated, the worst-case scenario. During normal state operation the colours will be less bright and attention demanding.

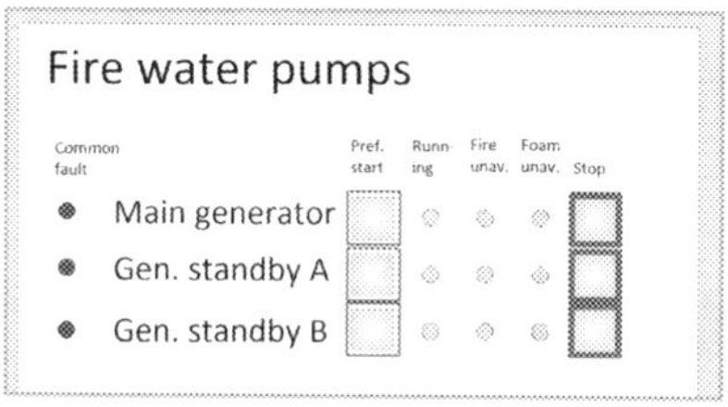

Fire water pumps
Common fault
Pref. start
Running
Fire unav.
Foam unav.
Stop
Main generator
Gen. standby A
Gen. standby B

Fig. 7. Example of Gestalt principles where similar functions are grouped vertically while item-related functions are displayed in one horizontal line

In some cases it is not enough to differentiate between functions solely with the use of colour if many alarms are located in too close proximity. Fire and gas alarms on the different decks are placed close together and are even displayed with two level-1 alarm lights, one for detected fire or gas alarm and the other for confirmed. The difference of which is important because it allows the operators to decide the next step in fire fighting more directly. Figure 8 shows a geometric symbol around the alarm lights. The circle indicates a fire while the triangle indicates gas making them easily distinguishable. These symbols are also used on the large screen display and therefore easily recognizable by the users, see figure 2. In addition, the positioning of detection and confirmation alarms, on top of or next to each other, will help minimize human errors and wrong functionality activation.

Fire
Gas
Living quarter
Process area
Activate
Active
Auto activ. block
Blocked
Deluge - boredekk
Upper deck

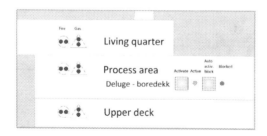

Fig. 8. Colour coding alone isn't enough to differentiate all alarms

The design presented in this paper differs strongly from safety matrices used to maintain normal operation and many other CAPs in the concise way information is observed by the user and given to the system. All information displaying alarms and notifications are shaped like circular lamps and all tangible interactive measures are shaped like square buttons. The buttons are also equipped with a light to confirm that a function has been activated. When the action is deactivated, the light will illuminate. This consistency does not apply for all panels in use today, see figure 2.

All the information is consistently presented when reading from left to right. Faults and alarms are placed to the far left, followed by the name or placement of the alarm. Next comes actions, confirmation of activation, and finally any blockings or stops of functions.

Fig. 9. Examples of special buttons, such as stop functions

Certain functions and buttons are more important to recognize, particularly when it comes to actions that should be stopped or terminated. The buttons are displayed with a coloured frame. Stop of ballast pumps and valves that are used to regulate the ballast and horizontal orientation of the platform in the water is marked with a red frame (see figure 9 left). If the platform starts to tilt above a certain angle, the big movements may hurt people and equipment onboard. Similarly, stop of pumps and valves in the process can have severe after effects and cause injuries. These stops and shutdowns will have a different effect on the platform that is easier to stabilize; they are marked with a black frame (see figure 9 right, stop of automatic blow down - BD).

4   Conclusion and Further Work

This paper presents CAP design principles with a corresponding conceptual CAP design. The contribution is an interface design focusing on maintaining users situation awareness and mindfulness during highly stressful situations of emergency preparedness. This was accomplished partly through harmonization with the known software-based interfaces of the control room.

The results presented in this paper were developed based on a design development performed for a Norwegian oil and gas platform in the North Sea. The functions were determined based on standard requirements and regulatory demands as well as the feedback from a user group of operators from the platform in question. The safety functions have been reviewed against the requirements and design guidelines proposed in the project, and proved acceptable.

We suggest performing studies comparing the operator performance of the newly developed CAP versus the old safety matrices. This would be beneficial before installing the CAP design, to verify the added value of the panel. This study can be performed using a large interactive touch screen for verification of functionality and usability.

Following the prototype production there is also a need for further user testing in a real setting, located in a control room, preferably under simulated stressful situations. Measured quantitative performance data would be beneficial for such studies.

Finally, before CAP detailed design, operators should go through simulator training not only to learn how the panel works, but also to be reassured that all safety related functionality has been included in the new panel and is in fact responding to actions in the desired manner.

Even though the CAP design presented here is developed for Norwegian platforms, some of the proposed applied principles and conceptual design is of generic value also for other domains. However, detailed clinical CAP design should be taken in consideration for each individual installation's functionality and requirements. In this project, we found it valuable following an iterative user centered design method, to aid in mitigating installation's specific needs. We therefore suggest this as an appropriate method for other installations along with performing user studies and design verification before the panel is installed in the control room. These actions could help prevent and minimize problems in the CAP detailing phase.

Acknowledgements. We thank the platform operators for their contribution on specifying requirements and valuable feedback during design development. We also thank the contributors of the internal report and study this work is based on, Stephen Collier and Per Kristiansen.

References

1. Alveberg, L.-J., Melberg, E.V.: Facts 2013: The Norwegian Petroleum Sector. 07 Media, Oslo (2013) ISSN 1502-546
2. Standards Norway, NORSOK S-001: Technical Safety. Standards Norway, 4th edn. Lysaker (2008)
3. Meshkati, N.: Safety and Human Factors Considerations in Control Rooms of Oil and Gas Pipeline Systems: Conceptual Issues and Practical Observations. International Journal of Occupational Safety and Ergonomics 12(1), 79–93 (2006)
4. Mumaw, R.J., Roth, E.M., Vicente, K.J., Burns, C.M.: There is More to Monitoring a Nuclear Power Plant than Meets the Eye. Human Factors: The Journal of the Human Factors and Ergonomics Society 42(1), 36–55 (2000)
5. Javaux, D., Colard, M.-I., Vanderdonckt, J.: Visual Display Design: A comparison of two methodologies. In: Proc. of 1st Int. Conf. on Applied Ergonomics, ICAE 1996, Istanbul, pp. 662–667 (1996)
6. International Standards Organization: ISO 9241 Ergonomic Design of Control Center – Part210: Human Centered Design for Interactive Systems. ISO 9241-210, 1st edn., Geneva (2010)
7. Nielsen, J.: Usability Engineering. AP Professional, Cambridge (1993)
8. Sharp, H., Rogers, Y., Preece, J.: Interaction Design: Beyond Human-Computer Interaction, 2nd edn. John Wiley & Sons, Ltd., England (2007)
9. Endsley, M.R.: In: Lee, J.D.: Kirlik (eds.): Situation Awareness in The Oxford Handbook of Cognitive Engineering, pp. 88–108. Oxford University Press, New York (2013)
10. Weick, K.E., Sutcliffe, K.M.: Managing the Unexpected: Resilient Performance in an Age of Uncertainty, 2nd edn. John Wiley & Sons, Inc., San Francisco (2007)
11. NUREG 0700, Human System Interface Design Review Guidelines, US Nuclear Regulatory Commission, rev 2, Washington (2002)
12. Mohla, D., McCLung, B.L., Rafferty, N.R.: Electrical Safety By Design. In: Industry Applications Society 46th Annual Petroleum and Chemical Industry Conference, San Diego, pp. 363–369 (1999)
13. Lidwell, W., Holden, K., Butler, J.: Universal Principles of Design: 125 Ways to Enhance Usability, Influence Perception, Increase Appeal, Make Better Design Decisions, and Teach Through Design. Rockport Publishers Inc., Massachusetts (2010)

Designing the User Experience for C4ISR Systems in the U.S. Army[*]

Pamela Savage-Knepshield, Jeffrey Thomas, Christopher Paulillo,
James Davis, Diane Quarles, and Diane Mitchell

U.S. Army Research Laboratory, Human Research and Engineering
Directorate, Aberdeen Proving Ground, MD, USA
{pamela.a.savage-knepshield,jeffrey.a.thomas132,
christopher.r.paulillo,james.a.davis531,diane.l.quarles,
diane.k.mitchell}.civ@mail.mil

Abstract. A unique set of challenges exist for implementing user-centered design principles in the context of military acquisition over and above those typically encountered by user experience designers. This paper focuses on the tools and techniques that we have utilized to help ensure that a positive user experience (UX) will result when Soldiers and systems interact under harsh conditions on the battlefield. Insights gained from applying these techniques to system design and evaluation early in the acquisition process and the impact that their use has had on training and system design are discussed.

Keywords: Agile development incorporating DUXU, design philosophy and DUXU, usability methods and tools.

1 The U.S. Army MANPRINT Program's Focus on UX

MANPRINT or Manpower and Personnel Integration was incorporated in the U.S. Army during the mid-1980's and is the U.S. Army's implementation of human systems integration. It forced a radical change in the way that defense contractors did business with the U.S. Army, requiring them to focus on the human and on the design of systems that would better fit Soldiers' needs and capabilities [1]. This is significant because in the military stakes are high; failures in human system interaction at the user interface (UI) not only result in loss of productivity, but also contribute to catastrophic incidents with loss of life and limb. Military system acquisition design successes as well as failures across the joint services have been documented in the public press and scientific and technical publications. And, in concert with efforts by organizations such as the National Research Council, whose mission is to improve government decision making and public policy, have raised awareness of the importance of considering human factors and human systems integration earlier in the acquisition process and have positively impacted acquisition policy and procedures [2].

The U.S. Army's MANPRINT program places the user – the American Soldier – squarely in the center of the design process to ensure that their needs are the foremost

---

[*] The rights of this work are transferred to the extent transferable according to title 17 U.S.C. 105.

A. Marcus (Ed.): DUXU 2014, Part III, LNCS 8519, pp. 338–346, 2014.
© Springer International Publishing Switzerland 2014

consideration when making design trade-offs and decisions [3]. The processes and procedures used to procure equipment have evolved to meet the urgent demands of our forces in the field. Most notably is the U.S. Army's Agile Process, which has sought to keep pace with technological advances and accelerate the pace of network modernization [4]. The Agile process seeks to meet capability gaps by rapidly integrating emerging Command, Control Communications, Computers, Intelligence, Surveillance and Reconnaissance (C4ISR) systems and iteratively testing their effectiveness during Network Integration Evaluation (NIE) test events. This process has raised further challenges for UX designers as we seek to understand our users' goals, intentions, and behaviors and use this information to shape the behavior of the technology so Soldier-system interaction appears natural to the user. Lessons learned including what has worked well and what has not as we move to become more fully engaged earlier in the Agile and "traditional" acquisition processes are presented.

2   Cognitive Workload Modeling and Simulation of the UX

Modeling & Simulation (M&S) tools developed by the U.S. Army to support MANPRINT practitioners help ensure that the UX is optimized throughout the acquisition cycle. One of the key principles of UX is to incorporate user feedback as a design evolves. MANPRINT practitioners do this by incorporating user feedback as inputs to the models they develop during each phase of the acquisition cycle. They develop their models early in the cycle during the Analysis of Alternatives phase [5], the technology demonstration phase [6, 7], and continue throughout the acquisition cycle [8].

Using the U.S. Army-developed tool, the Improved Performance Research Integration Tool (IMPRINT), to design the UX for a C4ISR system, analysts adhere to the experimental design process replacing experiments with models in the process. They conduct cognitive task interviews with Soldier subject matter experts (SSMEs) and include the data obtained as a key step in their model development process. This step is critical because each IMPRINT model is a hierarchical network of the mission, functions, and tasks Soldiers perform with the interface associated with the C4ISR system. Tasks within the models are verified by the SSMEs and modified as necessary to ensure user feedback is a part of the M&S process. Each model run is a dynamic, stochastic simulation of Soldiers performing their tasks with the C4ISR system. Once verified, the models are run multiple times.

Multiple IMPRINT models can represent C4ISR systems with alternative designs. By comparing mission performance across the models, analysts can predict the impact of the alternative C4ISR UI designs on mission performance. The output IMPRINT provides to analysts for comparisons can include mission success or failure, mission performance time, function times, task times, cognitive workload, and task failures. In addition IMPRINT output can include the effects of environmental variables such as heat, cold, and clothing. The predicted mission performance highlights issues that should be the focus of research studies, usability testing, and field tests as the system design matures. In turn, the completed models and predicted results are verified by

SSME performance and feedback during usability studies and field tests during later stages of the acquisition cycle. Any required model modifications are made by the analysts and the revised models become the baseline for analyses of modifications to the system design for the next iteration of the acquisition cycle.

2.1   Applying IMPRINT to Measure the UX

Currently, MANPRINT practitioners are using IMPRINT to compare the human machine interface (HMI) of the manpack radio (AN/PRC-155), to a notional HMI for the radio. In this example, an analyst used the task-by-task instructions provided in the radio's operator manual to an operational vignette provide by SMEs to build an IMPRINT model that reflects how Soldiers are using the fielded radio during missions. Next, the analysts walked-through the model with SMEs and incorporated the operators' feedback within a revised IMPRINT model. To compare an alternative design, the analyst is building an IMPRINT model representing a notional radio concept in which the radio operator is guided through the radio operation by an operational aid or "wizard". Once again, SSMEs will provide feedback on the model and it will be revised if necessary. One performance measure that will be included within each model as output is the number of times that a radio operator requires the assistance of a maintainer to obtain help. Another is operator response time to critical messages transmitted or received. Mission performance measures will include quantitative measures such as wait time for the radio maintainer to respond, costs for radio maintainers, additional costs for training to task proficiency, mission failures due to lack of required message response time, and percentage of time in cognitive overload. Results are being provided to acquisition leadership to demonstrate the trade-offs between design for usability and its impact on training and performance. Because Soldiers were part of the model development process the results reflect user feedback and support UX design concepts. Because the results are quantified, leadership is likely to accept the trade-off data and this, in turn, should support selection of the optimum design.

2.2   Applying Human Figure Modeling to Predict the UX

One of the U.S. Army's programs which is primed to seek out more efficient ways of executing program acquisition while also integrating the UX is the Enhanced Medium Altitude Reconnaissance and Surveillance System (EMARSS). The EMARSS consists of a commercial derivation aircraft equipped with a variety of intelligence collection systems. It has leveraged 3-Dimensional (3D) human modeling to refine system design and examine design tradeoffs to increase the functionality of the workstation and the usability of its UIs. In doing so, the program was able to identify a serious safety concern prior to system design – the likelihood for a torso strike should the aircraft decelerate quickly – see Figure 1(a). These 3D models also facilitated the identification of physical dimension concerns that could potentially result in serious ailments after prolonged use due to the wrist angle for the operators (i.e., carpel tunnel syndrome) – see Figure 1(b). As a result of the 3D modeling efforts, the program was able to investigate and integrate an alternative seat into the aircraft which significantly mitigated these safety and physical dimension concerns.

Safety   **Physical Dimension**

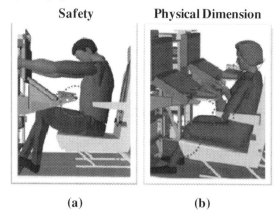

(a)   (b)

Fig. 1. EMARSS 3D modeling to identify UX issues early in the design process

3   The U.S. Army Agile Process

3.1   Early UX Assessment during the NIE

The NIE is a major test and evaluation event in which C4ISR equipment is assembled and configured to form the U.S. Army's tactical internet. There are many components that are in varying states of maturity with varying acquisition strategies. Some components are in the traditional acquisition process, others are a combination of commercial or modified commercial equipment, and many components are born from the Agile acquisition process. During NIE, a brigade combat team uses the equipment to conduct war games as part of their training while testing new capabilities. The team exercises its mission planning functions, intelligence gathering, and movement and maneuvers over a vast area in the desert with an opposing force that does the same.

In May and June 2011, the U.S. Army executed the first of six NIEs designed to test the effectiveness of networked technologies in an operational environment. The focus was on technical integration, and the intent was to determine how well these systems met the networking requirements of our Soldiers executing tactical missions. However, by the second test, NIE 12.2, system design attributes such as ease-of-use, accessibility, and trainability were recognized among core integration evaluation criteria. These criteria also became integral in the candidate assessment and source selection processes for future NIEs as part of the U.S. Army Agile Process (A2P).

The U.S. Army recognized that complex system designs increase training time for Soldiers to become proficient operators and maintainers; increase reliance on engineers/field service representatives (FSRs) to troubleshoot, fix, and repair systems in field; and degrade the collective unit's overall ability to complete tactical missions in a timely, safe, and efficient manner. According to the Government Accountability

Office, after reviewing five NIEs the U.S. Army found it needed the ability to "...automatically reconfigure radios and other systems remotely ... these systems require intense pre-configuration and manual interface." [9, p. 16]. Additionally, the Director, Operational Test and Evaluation concluded in their review of NIEs in FY12 that the:

> "Network component, both mission command systems and elements of the transport layer, are excessively complex to use. The current capability...is diminished due to pervasive task complexity. For example, what should be relatively simple tasks of starting up and shutting down systems requires complex series of actions by the operator" [10, p. 8].

Additional findings from the review noted that planning and loading tactical radios was cumbersome and time consuming processes; and that there is a distinct correlation between the dependency on FSRs and excessive complexity of using network systems.

In late FY13, in response to NIE findings and equipped with specific MANPRINT lessons learned from MANPRINT risk mitigation efforts on select U.S. Army programs, our organization partnered with the System of Systems Integration and Evaluation Directorate, of the Assistant Secretary of the Army for Acquisitions, Logistics, and Technology to ask the "right" questions of system developers, in the A2P. It was evident that U.S. Army officials and our Soldiers needed trained advocates, involved in initial system assessment, selection and evaluation to identify, discuss, and eliminate, where necessary, proposed system designs that did not fully consider how Soldiers would operate or even integrate the system into a network mission. We ensured that system providers supplied evidence that their systems were designed with the Soldier and their missions in mind. Thus, a complete answer was based on the presence of data or reports as evidence that the system: (1) underwent a Soldier-centric system design process, and (2) engineers were able to identify and describe Soldier critical tasks. Critical tasks were those that would result in unintended operational downtime or mission failure.

The A2P – MANPRINT Risk Readiness methodology and report engages the A2P through the Product Supportability Integrated Product/Process Team (PS IPT). The PS IPT, also referred to as Factor IV (Burdens), assesses systems under evaluation along lines of sustainment supportability, associated costs, and training requirements when compared to similar existing U.S. Army systems. These assessments are based on hardware and software support logistics, safety, survivability, reliability, maintainability, and MANPRINT aspects. In this forum, MANPRINT practitioners collaborate with logisticians, systems engineers, and reliability engineers to generate the initial white paper requirements by which industry candidates are evaluated; in generating specific requests for information for the technical interchange meeting and NIE Bull Pen (described in more detail below); and in coordinating and collaborating on systems under evaluation assessments generated during and post NIE execution.

One of the more significant achievements of the PS IPT has been the updated Product Support Questionnaire. This tool was fully updated and incorporated in the request for candidates to participate in NIE 14.2. More than 25% of the Product Support Questionnaire (or 13 of 50 questions) was either updated or new questions added to emphasize MANPRINT and system design characteristics. These questions include but are not limited to: "Does the system require 'round-the-clock' or sustained attention?" and "What types of evaluations of the system's Soldier-machine interfaces (physical and software) or usability have been performed?" The intent was to leverage the sources sought process as a forcing function for industry to more fully consider users' goals, intentions, and behaviors to improve Soldier-system interactions.

Another accomplishment for MANPRINT has been to have representation during the NIE Bull Pen. The NIE Bull Pen provides another touch-point in the A2P in which systems selected to participate in the NIE receive additional screening to understand their sustainment impact to the U.S. Army. This includes an assessment to understand burdens Soldiers may experience in system set-up, operations, transport, maintenance, and tear-down. Soldier burdens include identifying special tools and training necessary for troubleshooting and maintenance; understanding the time and the number of steps required to start-up or shut-down systems; and a discussion about the manpower and personnel skills required to successfully operate the system with minimal disruption to operational availability. This also includes determining the extent to which a system supports the information needs of its users to minimize operational downtime due to a loss of network, power, or incorrect system setup resulting in degraded or lost communication capabilities. This is discussed in greater detail pertaining to the evolution and operational testing of tactical radios in the next section. Findings from the Bull Pen inform evaluation and data collection priorities to ensure the UX is explicitly assessed as part of the A2P.

Fully integrating MANPRINT within the A2P through the PS IPT and NIE Bull Pen have increased the opportunities available to MANPRINT practitioners to emphasize the UX and to apply lessons learned from the field to influence the initial assessment, selection, and ongoing evaluation of future C4I systems.

3.2   Assessing the UX During NIE Testing

Over the last 25+ years, C4ISR technology has advanced exponentially. Tactical radios, once used primarily for voice communication and limited data transmission such as position reports, have been replaced by smaller and more capable devices that transmit and receive voice and enormous amounts of data traffic across the tactical internet which did not exist 20 years ago. Before 2000, tactical radios were typically large, heavy and had limited modes of operation. Radio control consisted of various knobs, switches, buttons (i.e., hard controls) with a small display used for system feedback. This old technology has been replaced by high powered computers that have operating systems, universal transceivers and store the software logic, algorithms, and operational data to emulate the capabilities of all the old radios that it replaces as well as new communication capabilities that tie into the tactical internet.

New C4ISR technology has allowed information to reach the battlefield's leading edge – the dismounted Soldier. The new generation radios serves as the conduit to the tactical internet, the US military's information highway. This presents a big UI design challenge. End user equipment operation for communicating voice and data across the battlefield must be simple, intuitive, require minimal attention demands, and training time. The equipment must not require any specialized skill more than that required to fight the fight, whether the Soldier is executing a mission on foot, riding in ground vehicle, or supporting ground troops while flying a helicopter.

To further add to the UI design challenges, C4ISR equipments must meet hundreds of performance requirements. Each performance requirement translates to one or more system design requirements, each which can potentially be decomposed into several derived design requirements. Considering system performance requirements, size, weight, power, environmental requirements, information assurance compliance requirements, and the general purpose user requirement, compromises must be made because many of the requirements do not co-exist very well. It is imperative that a qualified MANPRINT professional with UI design experience participates early in the system engineering process, understands the design challenges that the other engineering disciplines face, and is capable of identifying and communicating MANPRINT issues. Otherwise, there is a high degree of likelihood that the initial system design will have usability problems.

New generation multi-mode radios have been the centerpiece during NIE test events. While the radios are capable of interoperating with legacy radios, the new "digital radio" voice and data communication capability uses an internet protocol address to maintain connectivity with all the radios in a group. Large groups of users can split into smaller groups and merge back into a large group and maintain communications to support missions of the dismounted Soldier below the platoon level. Range extension radios strategically positioned on ground and aerial platforms can connect groups that may have split or connect two independent groups. Also, it is possible to monitor five groups of radio traffic at once whereby the groups monitored may only receive traffic from their own group. The concept of operation is quite different than what Soldiers have experienced using legacy equipment.

During system development, we support UI-centered design events, heuristic evaluations, and iterative usability testing as the design matures. Approximately half the systems participating at NIE have had some level of our support during development. Unlike UI test and evaluation activities that occur during system development, NIE evaluation can yield findings that could never have been made in a controlled test environment. This is because the equipment is being used in a manner and context truly representative of war fighting and the evaluator is exposed to the Soldier's experience to some degree (www.youtube. com/watch?v =Ovj4hFxko7c). Our evaluators observe system training and communication exercises that test the system.

When the games begin, we travel to the test units during breaks in the mission during resupply and other logistics-related activities and interview users. These times are typically very early in the morning and very late in the evening. Soldiers are asked questions such as whether or not the equipment was used, was it needed, how well did it work, was it easy to use, and what improvements are recommended. When possible, Soldiers demonstrate problems that they experienced with the equipment. As the mission continues and the troops drive further into the desert, the evaluators coordinate with the test officer and visit the units while they are receiving logistics support. Missions occur over the course of three weeks and over time, users and evaluators get to know each other. Soldiers tend to become more comfortable with the evaluator and speak more freely with them allowing the evaluator more access to the user's world.

Not only does the evaluator collect data on the equipment under evaluation, but they learn how the mission went the night before, the problems that were encountered when a vehicle made the wrong turn, an injury sustained during an accident, dynamics within the fighting unit, and the extreme cognitive and physical workload that users endure. If new to the U.S. Army culture, participating in the NIE is a great opportunity to learn how the U.S. Army does business. If one has served in the past, it is good opportunity to learn how it does business *today*. This insight into the user's experience is a great reminder that the equipment is merely a tool to assist Soldiers in executing their mission, in the case of tactical radios; their mission is not focused on operating radios.

Insight to the UX via NIE participation has allowed us to identify usability problems that are difficult to detect during heuristic reviews and usability evaluations. It is especially advantageous when we have had the opportunity to participate in UI development activities because this information enables us to give special attention to known UI weaknesses as NIE evaluators. Generally speaking, one of the most common usability problems that Soldiers experienced with the new generation of tactical radios was their inability to determine the radio's state of readiness following prolonged periods of non use. Soldiers needed to quickly assess whether the radio was set to communicate and make any changes if it was not. Soldiers had difficulty remembering how to accomplish this during times of stress and high workload. To add to the challenge, there are many processes that occur with networking radios that are transparent to the user. We documented the findings along with recommended solutions and passed them on to project management.

To mitigate communications issues that we observed at NIE, we entered into a partnership with the U.S. Army Training and Doctrine Command to study the relationship between usability and trainability. Refer to Section 2.1 for a discussion of this effort.

3.3   Refining Training Based on UX Feedback

During NIE, MANPRINT practitioners observe training and collect data via surveys and interviews from participating Soldiers. The data enables to understand the Training UX and revise programs of instruction to better meet the needs of Soldiers.

Initially, the Maintainer course was conducted over two days. Maintainers are the Soldiers who install, maintain, and troubleshoot signal support equipment and terminal devices. The first course was conducted with seven Soldiers and operator tasks were covered on the first day and troubleshooting the radio was covered on the second day. Troubleshooting encompassed using both the radio and a subset of the vehicle mounts to which it could be mounted to (e.g., tanks and other tactical ground vehicles) on tabletop trainers. All components associated with a radio's vehicle installation were provided with the exception of the actual vehicle. At the conclusion of the training, a group interview was conducted to obtain feedback. All Soldiers wanted the training to be increased to three days and suggested changes to the course structure.

346 P. Savage-Knepshield et al.

The Maintainers commented that the tabletop trainers worked well, but not every Maintainer was able to have hands on time with all three systems provided during the course. The Maintainers wanted everyone to have the opportunity to put each tabletop system together and break it down. This would allow them to ask questions and receive assistance from the training instructors if needed.

NIE provides the opportunity to follow up with the Soldiers during the test event. Three maintainers were interviewed during NIE to assess training coverage sufficiency for the problems that they encountered in the field and several additional coverage gaps were identified.

The Maintainer course was increased to three days and the tabletop trainers continue to be used. The focus has shifted to providing sufficient hands on time for the various vehicle installations and verifying that the training is providing the necessary information for maintainers to troubleshoot the radios and get them operational again.

References

1. Skelton, I.: MANPRINT for the US Army. Congressional Record—House, H8269-71 (1997)
2. Pew, R.W., Mavor, A.S. (eds.): Human-System Integration in the System Development Process: A New Look. National Academy Press, Washington, DC (2007)
3. Savage-Knepshield, P.A.: Soldier-Centered Design and Evaluation Techniques. In: Savage-Knepshield, P., Martin, J., Lockett III, J., Allender, L. (eds.) Designing Soldier Systems: Current Issues in Human Factors, pp. 275–307. Ashgate, Farnham (2012)
4. Army News Service: Army Demonstrates New Agile Acquisition Process to Industry Partners. DefenceTalk (2011), http://www.defencetalk.com/army-demonstrates-new-agile-acquisition-process-to-industry-partners-37071
5. Mitchell, D.K., Samms, C.L., Henthorn, T.J., Wojciechowski, J.Q.: Trade Study: A Two-Versus Three-Soldier Crew for the Mounted Combat System (MCS) and Other Future Combat System Platforms (ARL-TR-3026). Army Research Laboratory, Aberdeen Proving Ground (2003)
6. Mitchell, D.K., Brennan, G.: Soldier Workload Analysis of Infantry Vehicles With Alternative System Designs (ARL-TR-6375). Army Research Laboratory, Aberdeen Proving Ground (2013)
7. Mitchell, D.K., Brennan, G., Lobo, B.: Workload Analyses of Reconnaissance Vehicle Commander: With and Without Robotic Asset Responsibilities (ARL-TR-6607). U.S. Army Research Laboratory, Aberdeen Proving Ground (2013)
8. Mitchell, D.K.: Workload Analysis of the Crew of the Bradley Infantry Fighting Vehicle: Baseline IMPRINT Model (ARL-TR-6083), U.S. Army Research Laboratory, Aberdeen Proving Ground (2012)
9. U.S. Government Accountability Office: Army Networks: Opportunities Exist to Better Utilize Results from Network Integration Evaluations: Report to the SubCommittee on Tactical Air and Land Forces, Committee on Armed Services, House of Representatives (GAO Publication No. GAO-13-711) (2013), http://www.gao.gov/products/GAO-13-711
10. The Office of the Director, Operational Test and Evaluation: DOT&E FY2013 Annual Report (2013), http://www.dote.osd.mil/pub/reports/FY2013

A Mobile Application for Controlling
Domestic Gas Cylinders Remotely

Wafaa M. Shalash, Salha Al-Behairi, Nada Al-Qahtani,
Mashael Al-Muzaini, Bayan Sharahili, and Aisha Alawi

Information Technology Department, King Abdul Aziz University
P.O. Box 42808, Jeddah 21551, Saudi Arabia
Wafaa1@yahoo.com

Abstract. The domestic gas cylinders or cooking gas are considered as the source of energy commonly used at homes but, the potential for a serious accident such as gas leak from organizations or flow valves if the gas cylinder or its attachments are not treated properly or simply if the user forgot to close the gas before leaving home. The current project aims to develop a mobile application in order to control the gas cylinder remotely by mobile application in an effective way. The system consists of two parts. A specially designed controller connected to the gas cylinder organizer and an android mobile application to control the cylinder remotely through it. The main functions of this application are, controlling one or more domestic gas cylinder remotely, sending an audio alarm to the user if he leave while the gas cylinder opened and close it, providing an alarm if there is a gas leakage and close it and finally if the system fail to close it due to any reason it call the civil defense.

Keywords: Intelligent home, gas remote control, GSM, PIC controller, Android application.

1 Introduction and Related Works

The world has seen a great development and interest in intelligent home application and products. As the standard of living improves, people focus more on the home safety and the warehouse safety, and the demand of the protection on the gas leakage and the fire in the room higher and higher [1].

Smart homes contain multiple, connected devices such as home entertainment consoles, security systems, lighting, access control systems and surveillance. Intelligent home automation system is incorporated into smart homes to provide comfort, convenience, and security to home owners [2-4]. Home automation system represents and reports the status of the connected devices in an intuitive, user-friendly interface allowing the user to interact and control various devices with the touch of a few buttons. Some of the major communication technologies used by today's home automation system include Bluetooth, WiMAX and Wireless LAN (Wi-Fi), Zigbee, and Global System for Mobile Communication (GSM)[5]. All GSM is one of the most widely used cellular technologies in the world [6,7]. With the increase in the number

A. Marcus (Ed.): DUXU 2014, Part III, LNCS 8519, pp. 347–356, 2014.

of GSM subscribers, research and development is heavily supported in further investigating the GSM implementation [5].

Among the cellular technologies, GSM network is preferred for the communication between the home appliances and the user due to its wide spread coverage [6,7] which makes the whole system online for almost all the time. Another advantage of using the GSM network in home automation is its high security infrastructure, which provides maximum reliability whereby other people cannot monitor the information sent or received. Hence, this research work implements DTMF based control for home appliances using the GSM architecture in order to provide remote control to home gas cylinder safely.

2   System Architecture

The proposed system consists mainly of two parts hardware and software. The block diagram of the proposed GSM base system is shown in figure1.

2.1   Hardware

The hardware first part contains mainly of PIC16F886 microcontroller circuit which control the gas valve. The microcontroller is managed using DTMF and GSM base technology as it contains mobile modem and SIM card. The second part is the flammable gas sensor (MQ- 2) which is attached to the circuit and finally the gas control valve attached to a special controller to open and close it. The DTMF IC works as an interface between the GSM modem and the PIC microcontroller. Figure 1 shows a general layout of the system. Figure 2 shows the circuit diagram and figure 3 shows the prototype of the proposed system hardware. Figure 4 shows the used gas sensor.

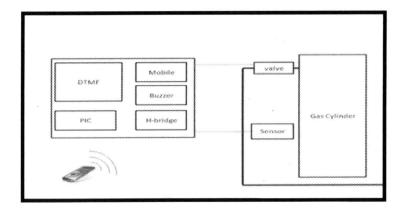

Fig. 1. Shows a general layout of the system

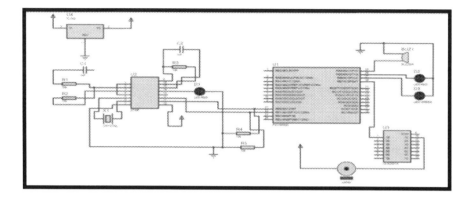

Fig. 2. Main controller circuit diagram

Regarding to figure 1 the main components are:

1. PIC (Peripheral Interface Controller), is the system's processor which has been programmed to read the sensor and issuing Software commands.
2. DTMF (Dual Tone Multi-frequency), which is dedicated to the reception of sound waves from mobile and convert it   to digital
3. Buzzer which is responsible for determining resonance
4. The sensor which is testing if there is a leakage
5. The valve which is responsible for closing and opening the gas cylinder.
6. Data SIM-Card using the Global System for Mobile (GSM) to make a cell phone call with the application installed on an android system.
7. H-bridge (electronic circuit) which is used for the electrical voltage to prevent reflection of electric current.

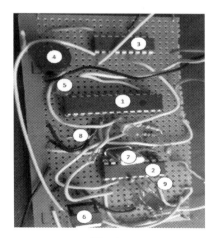

	Elements
1	Microcontroller
2	DTMF
3	ULN
4	Buzzer
5	LED
6	Voltage Regulator
7	CRYSTAL
8	Resistor
9	Capacitor
1	MQ-2 gas sensor

Fig. 3. The prototype of the proposed system hardware

Fig. 4. MQ-2 gas sensor for flammable gas

2.2   Software

The android based software package is designed to enable user to control one or more domestic gas cylinder remotely by, sending an audio alarm to the user if he leaves while the gas cylinder is opened and close it, providing an alarm if there is a gas leakage and close it and finally if the system fail to close it due to any reason it call the civil defense.

The diagram level zero (figure 5)shows that the system takes his input from: users and make some processing then you can see the output on the gas that could be turn on or off according the command and the user can see the output of the processing as graphs.

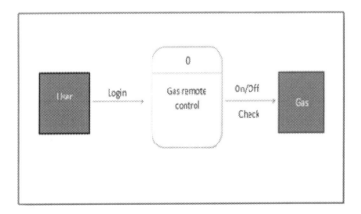

Fig. 5. Data flow diagram (level 0)

Figure 6 shows the data flow diagram (level 1) of the mobile application. It shows the interaction between entities, data base and processes. It shows the source of each command and data and its direction. The user can access user_ personal_ info, and the gas_ info to sore and remove data. The user can access the gas_ info to store his gas information where the user accesses them to retrieve it and then control gas.

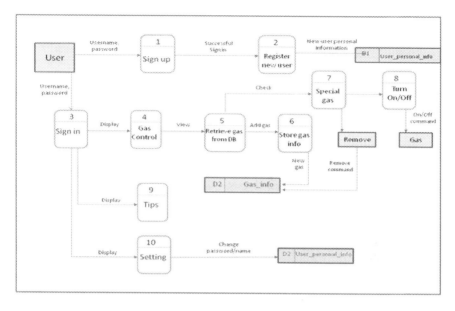

Fig. 6. Data flow diagram level1

The following figures (7 – 12)show the designed GUI of the system which is designed as simple as possible in order to make its critical function easy for the user. A well designed usability test has been performed in order to test the efficiency of the designed GUI.

Fig. 7. Login/ sign up interface

Fig. 8. Set location

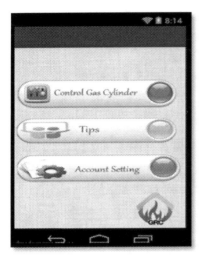

Fig. 9. Main Menu interface

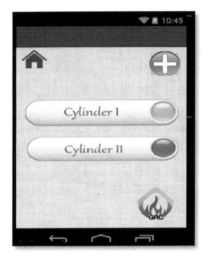

Fig. 10. Control cylinder interface

Fig. 11. Turn the gas cylinder   on or off
screen

Fig. 12. Notification the popup window

3   Usability Test and Results

Before performing the test, the test   general goals that will be tested have been decided and the chosen   tasks depending on those goals. Each task will be given to the
user and the user action and comments will be observed as they can gain results that
help in better design choices.

3.1   Participant

They conducted the test on ten user all of them are educated and their age between 20 and 35 year old. Users have experience in using mobile application.

3.2   Task Scenarios

1. User has six tasks to do:
2. Add new gas cylinder
3. Change id and name gas Cylinder
4. Remove gas cylinder
5. Turn On/Off gas cylinder
6. Tips
7. Change account information

Table 1. Tasks correct path

Task No.	Correct Path
Task#1	log in => Control gas cylinder => Add new gas cylinder
Task#2	log in => Control gas cylinder => Chose gas cylinder => Change id and name of gas cylinder
Task#3	log in => Control gas cylinder => Chose gas cylinder => Remove gas cylinder
Task#4	log in => Control gas cylinder => Chose gas cylinder => Turn On/Off gas cylinder
Task#5	log in => Tips
Task#6	log in => Setting account => Change user name and password

3.3   Preparing Tasks Resources

Time: 25 minutes
   Place: They decided to conduct the test at the university, some others was at home.

3.4   Performance Measures

1. Time to finish each task
2. Number of clicks
3. Number of wrong clicks
4. Subjective measures:

These measures are participants' perceptions, opinions and judgments. So the developers need to take their rating.

1. Ease of use
2. Clarity of labels and button names

Table 2. The three level of criteria

Criteria	Excellent	Acceptable	Unacceptable
Task#1 : Add new gas cylinder			
Time to finish the task (in seconds)	00:20:07	00:24:00	00:29:00
Number of clicks	3	4	5
Number or wrong clicks	0	1	2
Task#2 : Change id and name gas Cylinder			
Time to finish the task (in seconds)	00:21:00	00:25:00	00:30:00
Number of clicks	4	5	7
Number or wrong clicks	0	1	2
Task#3 : Remove gas cylinder			
Time to finish the task (in seconds)	00:18:03	00:22:00	00:24:03
Number of clicks	4	5	7
Number or wrong clicks	0	1	2
Task#4 : Turn On/Off gas cylinder			
Time to finish the task (in seconds)	00:18:03	00:22:00	00:24:03
Number of clicks	4	5	6
Number or wrong clicks	0	1	2
Task#5 : Tips			
Time to finish the task (in seconds)	00:09:00	00:13:00	00:16:00
Number of clicks	2	3	4
Number or wrong clicks	0	1	2
Task#6 : Change account information			
Time to finish the task (in seconds)	00:26:00	00:30:00	00:30:00
Number of clicks	3	4	5
Number or wrong clicks	0	1	2

The Levels of Criteria Are Established

1. Excellent; This means the program is easy to use according to the performance in this task.
2. Acceptable: This means the user is satisfied with this level performance on this task.
3. Unacceptable : If user encounters problems when performing the task.

Table 3. Usability test sammary

Task	User1	User2	User3	User4	User5	User6	User7	User8	User9	User10	Total	Average	Task performance
Task1	4	3	3	3	3	3	4	3	5	3	34	3.4	Excellent
Task2	5	5	5	6	6	5	4	4	6	5	51	5.1	Acceptable
Task3	5	4	6	4	5	6	5	6	5	5	51	5.1	Acceptable
Task4	5	4	4	4	4	4	6	5	5	4	45	4.5	Excellent
Task5	2	2	2	2	2	2	2	2	2	2	20	2	Excellent
Task6	3	3	3	3	3	4	3	3	3	3	31	3.1	Excellent

4   Conclusion

Recently intelligent home applications and products including remote controlling devices such as air-conditions heating and lighting are considered as a promising field needs more researches and products. We present an ongoing project to produce a home gas cylinder remote controlled system base on using GSM technology which provides high security and reliability to the system as it will make the system online almost all the time[]. The system also is dedicated to provide remote control for only flammable gas cylinder instead of controlling other home devices like many other applications which make it low cost companied with other solutions. The proposed system was implemented using PIC16F886 microcontroller and DTMF with the co-operation of GSM and an Android application which provides the gas cylinder re-mote. The system prototype was tested and the results shows a promising results.

5   Future Work

In future we are going to add many other features to the system such as:

- Schedule timers
- Cloud service allowing access via multiple devices
- Supports multiple IP cameras

References

1. Tang, Z., Shuai, W., Luojun: Remote Alarm Monitor System Based on GSM and ARM. Procedia Engineering 15, 65–69 (2011)
2. Ahmad, A.W., Jan, N., Iqbal, S., Lee, C.: Implementation of ZigBee-GSM based Home Security Monitoring and Remote. In: Proc. 2011 IEEE 54th International Midwest Symposium on Circuits and Systems (MWSCAS), Seoul, pp. 1–4 (2011)
3. Begum, T., Hossain, M.S., Uddin, M.B., Chowdhury, M.S.H.: Design and development of activation and monitoring of home automation system via SMS through microcontroller. In: Proc. 2009 4th International Conference on Computers and Devices for Communication (CODEC 2009), Kolkata, pp. 1–3 (2009)
4. [4] Zhai, Y., Cheng, X.: Design of smart home remote monitoring system based on embedded system. In: Proc. 2011 2nd International Conference on Computing, Control and Industrial Engineering (CCIE), Wuhan, pp. 41–44 (2011)
5. Teymourzadeh, R., Ahmed, S.A., Chan, K.W., Hoong, M.V.: Smart GSM Based Home Automation System. In: 2013 IEEE Conference on Systems, Process & Control (ICSPC 2013), Kuala Lumpur, Malaysia, December 13-15 (2013)
6. Gu, G., Peng, G.: The survey of GSM wireless communication system. In: Proc. 2010 International Conference on Computer and Information Application (ICCIA), Tianjin, pp. 121–124 (2010)
7. Mingming, G., Shaoliangshan, Huixiaowei, Sunqingwei: The System of Wireless Smart House Based on GSM and ZigBee. In: Proc. 2010 International Conference on Intelligent Computation Technology and Automation (ICICTA), Changsha, pp. 1017–1020 (2010)

Virtual Personas: A Case Study on Truck Cabin Design

Jos Thalen and Mascha van der Voort

University of Twente, Enschede 7500AE, The Netherlands
{j.p.thalen,m.c.vandervoort}@utwente.nl
http://www.ctw.utwente.nl/opm/en

Abstract. User involvement can help designers reach beyond functionality and usability, and identify the user's deeper needs for a pleasurable product experience. In practice, direct user involvement can be limited by a lack of knowledge of appropriate techniques, confidentiality constraints or limited access to end-users. Alternatively, *personas* can be used as a substitute for direct user involvement. Personas, however, often end up as posters in the hallway of a design department without being used, for instance because personas are not sufficiently realistic, or because the personas are insufficiently communicated within the design department. This paper presents a case study featuring Virtual Personas. This application allows designers to create and review use scenarios in a virtual world, featuring digital avatars. Although the application has been successfully deployed, it was found that additional effort is required for designers to really reach beyond the level of functionality and usability.

Keywords: personas, scenarios, roleplaying, virtual reality, case study.

1 Introduction

Product design is no longer driven by functionality alone. In addition to usefulness and ease of use, *experiential qualities* such as pleasure of use are now also playing an important role [1]. Consequently, the need to inform the design process about the expectations of the users, as early as possible, is vital. A study of the current state of user involvement in design practice, in which the authors were also involved, revealed however that design practice has not yet caught up with design literature [2]. The study captured the current state of user involvement in design practice, and identified common pitfalls and challenges faced in design practice, such as a lack of concrete user involvement techniques, a non-user centred company culture and several practical constraints such as limited access to end-users and confidentiality issues.

This paper presents a case study carried out for one of the companies that was also involved in the aforementioned study, as part of a larger research project [3]. The company, situated in the Netherlands, is involved in the development, production, marketing and sale of medium and heavy-duty commercial vehicles. The company's design department faces several challenges with respect to user

A. Marcus (Ed.): DUXU 2014, Part III, LNCS 8519, pp. 357–368, 2014.

involvement. Firstly, direct user involvement is not possible because of confidentiality constraints. The designers therefore have to rely on input from the marketing department (which conducts interviews and surveys) and on the input from end-user representatives; company employees who have a truck drivers licence. Furthermore, the attempts to increase indirect user involvement through personas have failed because of a lack of concrete guidance on how to adopt them in the design process. The case study introduces *Virtual Personas*. With Virtual Personas, personas are represented by interactive digital avatars rather than text based descriptions or photos. The virtual personas 'live' in an interactive virtual environment, in which designers can act out future use scenarios, reflect on product proposals or generate and discuss new ideas.

The paper is structured as follows. In section 2 we describe the background of the techniques that form the basis of the Virtual Persona technique. Section 2.1 introduces personas and several related techniques, including scenario based design and roleplaying. Section 2.2 briefly outlines the current state of VR *(Virtual Reality)* techniques in the field of product design, particularly looking at VR applications in the early stages of the product design process. Section 3 presents the approach and proceedings of the case study, and presents an evaluation of the results. In section 4 the paper reflects on the case study and discusses the contributions to design practice.

2   Background

The following subsections introduce the traditional persona technique and further explain related design techniques, including scenario based design and role playing. Subsequently, a brief introduction to VR is presented along with a motivation for using this technique as a new medium for personas.

2.1   Personas, Scenarios and Roleplay

A definition of personas is given in [4]: *User models, or personas, are fictional, detailed archetypical characters that represent distinct groupings of behaviours, goals and motivations observed and identified during the research phase.* These user models should become a 'real' person in the mind of the designers, and help them to make appropriate design decisions 'on behalf' of that user. Since its introduction by [5] in the '90s, personas have been widely discussed in literature. In this overview however, we focus on the practical aspects of using personas.

In design practice, a common challenge of working with personas is the lack of concrete guidelines on how to actually apply them in a design process, as for instance discussed in [6]. The authors describe additional challenges, such as a lack of believable personas, a lack of communication of the personas, and a lack of high-level support or encouragement. These issues are addressed by presenting an approach for creating believable personas, and by proposing concrete design techniques that use and communicate personas, such as priority matrices, posters and foundation documents.

Another development that intends to make personas a more engaging design technique is the combination of personas with scenarios. Scenarios, as introduced in [7], are stories that describe the use of a product by a user, in a certain setting. In [8] it is proposed to use personas to make the 'user' (or actors) in scenarios more engaging. Seeing personas in a specific context makes it easier to understand their actions and consequently help move designers in 'the right direction'. In [9] it is argued that scenarios should be formed around personas to "[...] obtain a far more powerful level of identification and engagement [...]", similar to how people identify with characters from a soap opera series on TV. Similarly, in [10], theatre techniques were used to effectively communicate personas and scenarios within a group of software designers. While human role playing transfers personas from paper to more 'engaging' stories, there are some drawbacks. Firstly, it takes quite some time to get used to acting out scenarios in front of colleagues. Alternatively, professional actors could be used, but this may lead to an increase in time and costs. Secondly, role playing still takes quite some imagination to 'see' the correct context in which a story is taking place. Thirdly, analysing the data from such sessions is time consuming; raw video has to be analysed in order to extract information relevant for the project.

Combining personas, scenarios and role play is expected to contribute to the adoption of personas by the designers of the company involved in the case study. However, given the aforementioned drawbacks of traditional role playing, we propose to use VR technologies to create virtual environments in which designers can use virtual personas to create, act out and evaluate scenarios. The following section further discusses the opportunities of VR.

2.2   Virtual Reality

VR technologies create an alternative reality in which worlds, objects and characters can be experienced that may not yet be available in reality. VR was initially considered a high-end design technique for large industries such as aerospace and automotive design. Over the years however, advancements in hardware and software reduced costs and extended the application scope of VR to simulation, training, prototyping and evaluation purposes (see [11] for an extensive overview).

Given the increasing availability of off-the-shelf VR hardware and software, it is becoming an interesting technique to facilitate user involvement in the early stages of the design process. In [12] it is argued that successfully user involvement requires explicit representations of design information, realistic interaction between the user and design information, and users should become conscious of the consequences of design decisions. These requirements are in line with the characteristics of VR: it can provide realistic and interactive representations of (future) products, allowing end-users to create, experience and assess future use situations. [13] provides a more extensive overview of example applications.

In the current case study VR is employed to create engaging, realistic and interactive representations of use scenarios, featuring virtual personas. It is expected that, through this new medium, designers are encouraged to step in to the shoes of specific personas, and reach a deeper level of understanding of their needs, wishes and desires.

3   Case Study

The case study focuses on the design of the truck cabin, from which truck drivers not only drive the truck, but, especially in case of long distance trips, in which they live as well. The design of the cabin therefore has a significant effect on how the truck is experienced by the driver. This goes beyond the driving characteristics of the truck itself. It concerns the layout of the interior, the lighting design, in-vehicle media system user interfaces and the design of the sleeping area.

The *vehicle definition* department is in charge of cabin design. A separate *product planning* department provides this department with insights in current market needs, not only from vehicle drivers but also from vehicle buyers. The insights are gathered through interviews and field studies carried out by the product planning department. Apart from this indirect user involvement, user involvement is limited by confidentiality constraints. Consequently, in order for the vehicle definition department to conduct tests and evaluations they have to rely on end-user *representatives* rather than actual end-users. End-user representatives are co-workers who either have experience as a truck driver themselves, or are in direct contact with real end-users.

As explained in the introduction, the designers attempted to address the lack of direct end-user involvement by creating personas. Rather than working with statistical data from the product planning department, designers could use personas to think from the perspective specific individuals. However, a lack of concrete guidance on how to apply the personas in practice has caused the personas to fail in reaching designers and engineers.

Therefore, the problem definition of the case study is twofold. Firstly, the lack of direct end-user involvement in the design process makes it difficult for designers take future use scenarios and experiences into account. Secondly, a feasible solution to the first issue failed to be adopted in practice. The *Virtual Persona* application aims to provide a more vivid representation of the established personas. The application combines the advantages of role playing (resulting in engaging stories) with advantages of VR, namely the explicit and interactive visualisation of future use situations.

3.1   Approach

The case study addresses three research questions. Firstly, does the Virtual Persona session stimulate designers to put themselves in the shoes of end-users? If so, what kind of product insights (in terms of functionality, usability and experiential) can be obtained? Lastly, are there specific benefits of using VR techniques in this application? To investigate these questions, the Virtual Persona application will be deployed and evaluated using the following steps.

1. **Prototype development** A functional prototype of the Virtual Persona
   application will be developed to allow the designers to experience what it
   is like to use the application in practice, and to provide the researcher with
   feedback on how to improve the application.
2. **Test case** A test case is carried out in which the application prototype is
   deployed. This phase also involves the definition of a design session structure
   of which the Virtual Persona application is part.
3. **Evaluation** The test case will be evaluated by transcribing and analysing
   video recordings of the session, and by gathering insights through post-
   session evaluation forms.

The following subsections further elaborate on the individual steps.

3.2   Prototype Development

A functional prototype of the envisioned Virtual Persona application was developed in collaboration with the participating designers from the company.
The basis of the application resembles a theatre layout; a large screen is used
to present a group of designers with a live view of the virtual world in which
the scenarios are acted out. The virtual world includes an urban environment
as well as a highway, a truck parking lot and a petrol station. The environment
also includes interactive objects, such as autonomous traffic and driveable trucks.
Within the virtual world, virtual personas are represented by digital avatars. The
different types of personas are represented by their clothes, physical appearance
and facial features (see figure 1). An on-screen user interface allows designers to
control the avatars (e.g. their behaviour and movements in the virtual world),
but also provides access to virtual world settings, such as lighting and camera
viewpoints.

To facilitate rapid and flexible development of the prototype, the Blender
Game Engine[1] was used as a development platform. This suite supports 3D
modelling as well as behaviour modelling through scripts, real-time rendering
and interfaces well with external devices such as the Microsoft Kinect. The latter allowed the researcher to experiment with using gestures to control the virtual personas. During an early review session however, designers did not see any
added value in being able to control the avatars through gestures and motion
tracking. The use of a mouse and keyboard controls was considered more effective; this would allow the designers to position the avatar anywhere in the
virtual world by simply clicking on the desired position. Additionally, designers
indicated that the virtual personas should be properly introduced before using
them in a scenario. This could be achieved by creating a short introduction
video of each persona. Furthermore, the visual appearance of the avatars should
be improved by using more distinct clothing and facial textures, and by using
different body models.

---

[1] See http://www.blender.org

Fig. 1. Digital avatars represent specific personas. Mouse controls allow designers to control individual limbs using 'handles' and to automatically position personas, for instance on a seat in the cabin.

3.3   Test Case

In this step the prototype application is deployed in a realistic test case. The test case concerns the idea of developing a new device to control various truck functions, such as the lights and the central locking system. The feasibility of this idea is to be assessed by the participants in this session, who are experts in specific areas such as mechanical engineering or HMI design. In particular, the designers and engineers are to evaluate the concept from the perspective of two personas embodied in virtual avatars.

The test case comprises two identical one hour sessions, each involving four different participants from the company. Session participants include designers and engineers who will work on a fictional design case defined for this session. The two sessions were facilitated by the researcher, who made sure that the following steps were carried out.

1. **Case Description (3 min.)** - The participants are asked to assess a proposed product concept. This step introduces the product and explains the aim of the session.
2. **Scenario Setting (2 min.)** - A scenario is provided as a starting point for the brainstorm: *You are near the end of a long driving day. Because of driving time regulations you are forced to spend the night at a trucker's parking space near the highway. It's around 17:00 when you arrive at the parking space. There is a gas station and small snack/restaurant nearby. After parking your truck, the evening starts...*
3. **Brainstorm (10 min.)** - The participants are asked to brainstorm about what tasks a driver would have in this period of time and what events could take place. Participants write down the tasks and events on cards and put them on a whiteboard.
4. **Persona Introduction (5 min.)** - A short 1-minute video of each persona (Jim and Stanley) is shown. 'Jim' is a young and technology oriented driver,

Fig. 2. An overview of the Virtual Persona session, involving the virtual environment (1), the operator (2), the tasks and events (3) and the design team (4)

who loves his job. 'Stanley' is an older driver, who drives his truck just to make money.

5. **Scenario Generation (40 min.)** - The task and event cards are used to create a scenario that can then be acted out in the virtual environment. The virtual environment is operated by one of the participants, supported where needed by the facilitator.

The proceedings of the test session are captured on video and the participants are asked to fill out an evaluation form after the session.

3.4   Results

This section briefly describes the proceedings of the test session, and summarises the insights gathered through the post-session evaluation forms. Section 4 further elaborates on the results.

Proceedings. Both groups successfully managed to complete the design session. During the sessions the virtual environment played a balanced role as one of four elements that interacted during the session (see figure 2). Throughout the session, there were interactions between the group of designers, the tool operator, the virtual environment and the list of tasks and events. In the first few minutes of each session designers systematically picked an item from the list of tasks and acted this out in the virtual environment. As the session advanced, most of the time was spent on group brainstorms and discussions, fed by information from the virtual environments or events from the list.

Post-session Evaluation The post-session evaluation form consists of three parts, asking the participants to reflect on the persona engagement, the product insights and the added value of VR.

1. **Persona Engagement.** The majority of the participants (6 out of 8) indeed felt like they have been evaluating the product concept from two different user perspectives, and all participants consider this activity to be useful especially in the early stages of the PDP. Tables 1 and 2 list the expected benefits and drawbacks of using Virtual Personas. Furthermore, participants also mentioned some of the risks related to the use of (virtual) personas. For instance, it was noted that 'we [designers] should not presume to know everything about a user', and that the focus on personas sometimes distracted from the actual use case.

2. **Product Insights.** The insights gained during the session primarily include refined or new product ideas for the use case of the session[2]. The results of the evaluation indicate that participants expect 'Jim' to accept, like and use the application, while 'Stanley' will probably not use it. Furthermore, the *consequences* of not using the new product concept were discussed explicitly in Stanley's scenario, as illustrated by the following fragment:

   > *"Stanley has to do the truck administration manually, from his driver seat. This takes a bit more time than doing it digitally, and it's not automatically updated with the home office. [...] He will give his wife a call to say he won't be eating at home. He uses his own phone for this."*

   This is also reflected by some of the answers to a question in which the designers are asked about the expected use of the product concept. In their answer, designers reason from the perspective of the persona: *"Eventually yes, because it will make his job easier. The threshold is high, and he will only use a small part of all functions/features"*, and *"Yes, he grew up with technology like this en is very capable of using them."*.

3. **Added Value of VR.** The participants indicated that the virtual environment helps with imagining use situations and with explaining and understanding user-product relations. The environment sometimes reminds them of small details or very 'standard' tasks or actions that would otherwise have been overlooked. On the other hand, the use of the virtual environment sometimes distracted designers from a discussion. Furthermore, it lacks a good simulation of 'time pressure' (e.g. in real-life truck drivers are always trying to reach a destination in time, while the application did not include such aspects), and similar aspects may be forgotten if there are no 'triggers' present in the virtual environment. For instance, in this session objects like a coffee mug and a sandwich triggered designers to think about lunch, which may have been overlooked if the virtual sandwich and mug were not included in the environment. Lastly, the development and extension of the virtual environment is time consuming.

---

[2] The exact results of the session (i.e. the resulting scenarios, functions and requirements) are not included because of confidentiality reasons.

Table 1. Potential benefits identified by designers after the test session

Potential benefits of using Virtual Personas
"Exchange experiences between participants"
"Seeing line of sight, imagining things, immersing in a situation"
"Interactions, and to remind you of simple things (such as opening doors)"
"Understanding/immersing in the user"
"Imagination/immersion in character"
"Especially in early stage it will help with setting boundary conditions and a scenario"
"You are encouraged to think about details"
"The tool keeps you focused, constantly reminding you of the persona"

Table 2. Potential drawbacks identified by designers after the test session

Potential drawbacks of using Virtual Personas
"Takes time to extend"
"Takes time and it may distract"
"Could be negative; you might forget things if the environment doesn't show them"
"Maybe we focused to much on the 'perfect user'"
"Real circumstances are missing, such as time pressure. These make the experience slightly less realistic"
"It's time taking/cumbersome to work with the scenario, difficult to get the right level of detail"
"You can't do everything in the environment, it still takes some imagination"

4   Discussion

The Virtual Persona application succeeded in getting the designers to step into the shoes of two specific end-users. They acted out use situations, came up with new product functions, identified several problem scenarios and refined some of the preliminary product requirements. While this positively answers the first research question (see section 3.1) the remaining two questions should be further discussed.

4.1   Product Insights

As shown in section 3.4, the insights gained during the session primarily concern the functionality and usability of the product concept. Especially in the case of the tech-oriented 'Jim' persona, designers were constantly coming up with new functions for the product to provide. While idea generation is acceptable in the early stages of a design process, it can be questioned whether it is also desired in a review or evaluation session: the generation of new ideas distracts designers from looking into the deeper issues related to new product concepts or interaction styles.

Although the designers primarily came up with functional ideas, issues and requirements, there are indications that a deeper understanding of and engagement with the personas was achieved. While designers came up with new functions for 'Jim', they were also triggered to think about the consequences of these functions for 'Stanley'. Questions like 'will Stanley feel left out when we make a product like this?' were raised and discussed. For example, using a smartphone as a platform for various cabin functions would allow 'Jim' to easily fine tune his environment. 'Stanley', who does not use a smartphone, might feel like he is missing out on something. Participants started a discussion about what kind of cabin fine tuning would a person like Stanley need, or what kind of interactions should we design to accommodate Stanley's needs? These discussions illustrate that although starting on a superficial 'functional' level, the designers eventually touch the persona's deeper needs and requirements.

It is expected that, apart from the goal of the session, the persona descriptions and their level of detail have caused a focus on functionality and usability. The test case featured two relatively flat and extreme characters that easily evoke caricature behaviour: Jim prefers to have as much features in one product as possible, while Stanley is old fashioned and hates electronic devices. Similar to [5], it is expected that more detailed virtual personas will evoke more user specific product functions.

4.2   Added Value of VR

The results of the post-session evaluation forms indicate that participants find it difficult to pinpoint the added value of using a virtual environment and virtual personas. Although it is generally acknowledged that the explicit and interactive representation of personas in a future use situation is useful, it can be argued that this could also be achieved with live role playing, animated scenarios or storytelling. A formal comparison of virtual personas with such alternative techniques could provide more insight into the benefits or drawbacks. Based on the observations made during the test session however, there are several aspects considered to be unique to using virtual personas, and several areas of potential added value.

The primary benefit of using an interactive virtual environment is that even with a limited level of realism and only few means of real-time modification, it provides designers with a lot of freedom to explore foreseen as well as unforeseen use scenarios (created ad-hoc). In the test session we observed how small objects and actions can evoke new use scenarios. Even when a use scenario required the avatar to do something that was not pre-defined (e.g. checking tire pressure outside the cabin), an approximation of the actions and events was enough to initiate relevant discussions concerning this particular scenario. This level of flexibility is quite difficult to reach with pre-recorded animated scenarios or storyboards.

Another relevant benefit is that, compared to role playing or acting out scenarios, the Virtual Persona application is quite a safe way of stepping into the shoes of a persona. The designers, as a group, instruct the application operator how to act out the scenario. Especially in the field of engineering (e.g. truck manufacturing and machine design) this reduces the threshold for designers to express their ideas. Apart from the application operator, the participants do not need specific skills or preparation to contribute to the session.

Lastly, there are various potentially beneficial features that have not yet been implemented in the application prototype. For example, designers indicated that it would be useful to record the use scenarios generated during the sessions. The recordings can be used for future reference within the design team, but also to communicate the results to other departments. Furthermore, by recording the actual events in the 3D environment, it would be feasible to 'revisit' scenarios later on in the design process, and validate new product concepts in a specific use scenario. Another opportunity identified by the designers was for the environment to contain detailed 3D and 2D models. This would for instance allow designers to evaluate the user interface of a new dashboard or car radio from the perspective of personas, in specific use situations.

5   Conclusion

The Virtual Persona application helps designers to start thinking from the perspective of specific end-users. As such, it is a feasible alternative when direct end-user involvement is impossible. The results of the test session presented in section 3 show that designers mainly discussed product functionality, and to some extend usability and experience. As explained in section 4, it is expected that a deeper level of engagement with the virtual personas can be reached when more detailed persona descriptions are used. Additional factors include the time available for conducting a virtual persona session, and the number and diversity of virtual personas used.

The case study did not involve an explicit comparison of Virtual Personas to alternative techniques, such as animated scenarios or role playing. Nevertheless, we identified several unique aspects of this application, namely the level of flexibility designers have in creating and reviewing use scenarios and the low threshold for designers to contribute to the session. Additional opportunities, such as recording and re-visiting scenarios, have been proposed by the participating designers.

5.1   Future Work

We propose two directions of future work. Firstly, the application prototype and session structure developed in this case study can be used as a starting point for a more elaborate test case to further validate the effectiveness of the Virtual Persona application. In particular, a deeper level of insights (i.e. beyond functionality and usability) could be obtained when the shortcomings of the current test case, such as the limited time available for creating scenarios and the lack of sufficiently detailed and distinct personas, are addressed. Secondly, to gain insight in the added value of VR in the Virtual Persona application, the technical setup could be extended in two directions, namely a more high-end (e.g. using more detailed avatars, fully immersive VR and natural interfaces for controlling the avatars) and a low-end (e.g. using physical drawings or sketches).

A comparison of these three versions will provide insight into whether VR actually adds something to traditional personas, and, if so, whether or not the current implementation is sufficient.

References

1. Jordan, P.W.: Designing Pleasurable Products: An Introduction to the New Human Factors. CRC Press (August 2002)
2. Ozcelik, D., Quevedo-Fernandez, J., Thalen, J., Terken, J.: Engaging users in the early phases of the design process: Attitudes, concerns and challenges from industrial practice. In: Proceedings of the 2011 Conference on Designing Pleasurable Products and Interfaces, DPPI 2011, pp. 13:1–13:8. ACM, New York (2011)
3. Thalen, J.: Facilitating user centred design through virtual reality. PhD thesis, University of Twente, Enschede. The Netherlands (2013)
4. Calde, S., Goodwin, K., Reimann, R.: SHS orcas: the first integrated information system for long-term healthcare facility management. In: Case Studies of the CHI 2002: AIGA Experience Design FORUM, CHI 2002, pp. 2–16. ACM, New York (2002)
5. Cooper, A.: The Inmates Are Running the Asylum. Macmillan Publishing Co., Inc., Indianapolis (1999)
6. Pruitt, J., Grudin, J.: Personas: practice and theory. In: Proceedings of the 2003 Conference on Designing for User Experiences, DUX 2003, pp. 1–15. ACM, New York (2003)
7. Carroll, J.M.: Scenario-based design: envisioning work and technology in system development. Wiley & Sons, New York (1995)
8. Blomkvist, S.: The user as a personality. In: Position Paper for the Course Workshop on Theoretical Perspectives in Human-Computer Interaction at IPLab, KTH (2002)
9. Grudin, J., Pruitt, J.: Personas, participatory design and product development: An infrastructure for engagement. In: Proc. PDC, vol. 2002, p. 7 (2002)
10. Carmichael, A., Newell, A.F., Dickinson, A., Morgan, M.: Using theatre and film to represent user requirements. In: Proceeding of Include Conference Royal College of Art, London, vol. 5 (2005)
11. Jimeno, A., Puerta, A.: State of the art of the virtual reality applied to design and manufacturing processes. The International Journal of Advanced Manufacturing Technology 33(9-10), 866–874 (2006)
12. Tideman, M., van der Voort, M., van Houten, F.: A new product design method based on virtual reality, gaming and scenarios. International Journal on Interactive Design and Manufacturing 2(4), 195–205 (2008)
13. Thalen, J., van der Voort, M.: Facilitating user involvement in product design through virtual reality. In: Xinxing, T. (ed.) Virtual Reality - Human Computer Interaction, pp. 105–124. InTech (September 2012)

A Pilot Study Using Virtual Reality to Investigate the Effects of Emergency Egress Signs Competing with Environmental Variables on Route Choices

Elisângela Vilar[1], Emília Duarte[2], Francisco Rebelo[1,3],
Paulo Noriega[1,3], and Ernesto Filgueiras Vilar[4]

[1] Centre for Architecture, Urban Planning and Design (CIAUD), Rua Sá Nogueira,
Pólo Universitário, Alto da Ajuda, 1349-055 Lisboa
elipessoa@gmail.com, {frebelo,pnoriega}@fmh.ulisboa.pt
[2] Unidcom, IADE – Creative University. Av. D. Carlos I, 4, 1200-649 Lisbon, Portugal
emilia.duarte@iade.pt
[3] Ergonomics Laboratory, Universidade de Lisboa, Alameda da Universidade,
1649-004 Lisboa
{frebelo,pnoriega}@fmh.ulisboa.pt
[4] Beira Interior University – Communication and Arts Department, Rua Marquês d'Ávila e
Bolama 6200-001 Covilhã, Portugal
ernestovf@gmail.com

Abstract. Emergencies (e.g., fire egress) into complex buildings are stressful situations which can provoke unexpected, undesired and sometimes unsafety behaviors in the users. Thus, the main objective of this pilot study was to investigate the relative influence of new technology-based exit signs, when compared to the conventional static ISO-type counterparts, in the users' wayfinding behavior during an emergency egress. A critical situation was designed in which the environmental variables and exit signs, at the 12 decision points, were giving conflicting directional information. Thirty participants were randomly assigned to the two groups (i.e., Static signs and dynamic signs), and their route-choices in the 12 decision points displaced along a route into a virtual hotel were collected using a Virtual Reality-based methodology. Findings suggest that for the group exposed to static ISO-type exit signs, the reliance on environmental variables decreased along the egress route, and for the first intersection about 73% of participants preferred to follow by the direction which was the opposite of that posted on the egress sign. However, when technology-based signs were used, the influence of the environmental variables was weak from the first decision point to the end, as suggested by a compliance rate with the exit signs reaching almost 98% along the entire route.

Keywords: Emergency egress, wayfinding, virtual reality, technology-based signs, exit signs.

1 Introduction

Emergencies (e.g., fire egress) into complex buildings are stressful situations which can provoke unexpected, undesired and sometimes unsafety behaviors in the users.

A. Marcus (Ed.): DUXU 2014, Part III, LNCS 8519, pp. 369–377, 2014.

Examples are the wrong decisions in following the marked emergency routes, increasing the egress time over the limit or even trapping the users inside the building. Such problem can be aggravated when the environmental variables (e.g., light, corridors' width), acting as "attractors", are communicating contradictory information to the users. In such cases, the conflicting cues can increase the users' uncertainty regarding the route decision and lead to an escalation in the number of victims.

Previous studies [e.g., 1, 2] verified that some environmental variables can be considered affordances that, somehow, attract the users toward them in a route-choice decision. In a previous study [i.e., 3] was also found that when such environmental variables are competing with ISO-type conventional static emergency exit signs, the users' wayfinding behavior at the beginning of the egress route was not the intended (i.e., at the first route-decision, most of the participant did not comply with the exit sign, and took the opposite corridor). The results reveal worrying low rates of compliance (about 70%) for the first three decision points, with an increment of the compliance along the route.

Considering this, the main objective of this pilot study was to investigate the relative influence of new technology-based exit signs, when compared to the conventional static ISO-type counterparts, in the users' wayfinding behavior during an emergency egress. A critical situation was designed in which the environmental variables and exit signs, at decision points, were giving conflicting directional information (i.e., in a two ways intersection, one of the available paths was brighter and wider than the other, attracting participants' to it. However, an exit sign was placed pointing to the opposite direction, a darker and narrower corridor).

To conduct the study, a virtual building was designed and a Virtual Reality (VR)-based methodology was used to facilitate the manipulation and control of the variables, as well as to allow the exposition of participants to a stressful emergency situation without submitting them to a real hazard. The use of VR to study behavior during emergency situations has been studied by Gamberini and colleagues [4]. These authors used VR to examine how people respond during a fire in a public library by manipulating variables such fire intensity and the initial distance to the emergency egress. Their results suggest that users seemed to recognize a dangerous situation within the context of a simulation and readily produced adaptive responses, thereby indicating that VR is a suitable venue for emergency simulations.

2   Experiment

2.1   Design of the Experiment

The study used a between-subjects design. The dependent variable was the participant route-choice at pre-defined decision points (i.e., 12 corridor intersections). Two experimental conditions were considered:

- Static – With an emergency directional system composed by conventional static ISO-type emergency exit signs;

- Dynamic – With an emergency directional system composed by new technology-based emergency exit signs.

2.2   Participants

Thirty university students, 15 females and 15 males, aged between 18 and 35 years (M = 21.67, SD = 3.809) participated in the study. They were randomly distributed across three experimental conditions:

- Static: Fifteen participants, 8 females and 7 males, aged between 19 and 35 years (M = 22.20, SD = 4.828);
- Dynamic: Fifteen participants, 7 females and 8 males, aged between 18 and 28 years (M = 21.13, SD = 2.475).

All participants had normal sight or had corrective lenses, as well as normal color vision, screened with Ishihara, 1988 [5]. They also reported no physical or mental conditions that would prevent them from participating in a VR simulation. All participants were asked to sign an informed consent form.

2.3   Experimental Task

Critical situation. The critical situation was created taking into account the existence of contradictory information that was manipulated by inserting posted static emergency signs or technology-based emergency signs pointing to the opposite direction of the corridors that were the most chosen by participants. The most chosen corridors were selected from a previous study carried out by Vilar and colleagues [2] about navigational choice preferences associated with environmental variables (i.e., corridor width and brightness). For the current study, only twelve corridors intersections (Fig. 1) of fifty-seven different situations studied earlier [2] were selected. Corridor selection followed the criteria: i) the most chosen corridors considering the available alternative corridors (i.e., left vs. right, front vs. left, and front vs. right) for each situation (i.e., only corridor width, brightness enhanced in the wider corridor and brightness enhanced in the narrower corridor), ii) the intersection type (i.e., "T-type" and "F-type"), and iii) the narrower corridor when the difference across the percentage of choices was less or equal to 1%.

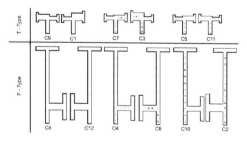

Fig. 1. The twelve "T-type" and "F-type" corridor intersections selected from the study of Vilar and colleagues [6]

The factors of attraction (i.e., corridor width, brightness enhanced in wider corridor, and brightness), attractors direction (i.e., left, right and front) and percentages of choices toward the attractor attained by Vilar and colleagues [2] for the twelve selected corridor intersections can be seen on Table 1.

Table 1. Percentages of choice for the twelve most chosen corridor intersections from Vilar and colleagues [6] used as the basis for the design of the virtual building and signs placement

Corridor intersection	Variable (attractor)	Direction	% of choices towards the attractor
C1	Width	Right	72.05
C2	Brightness	Front	75.83
C3	Brightness and width	Left	87.87
C4	Brightness and width	Right	89.58
C5	Brightness	Left	81.67
C6	Brightness and width	Left	91.25
C7	Brightness and width	Right	89.58
C8	Width	Right	63.75
C9	Width	Left	72.92
C10	Brightness	Front	78.33
C11	Brightness	Right	83.68
C12	Width	Left	57.50

Virtual Environment (VE) - The Hotel. For the design of the hotel building used in the present study, twelve corridor intersections previously selected (Table 1) from Vilar and colleagues [2] were used. These twelve corridor intersections were mixed and then randomly divided into three groups of four corridors each that comprise three sections of the building floor plan. Each section was designed to have the same travel distance, regardless of participants' directional choice at each choice point (Fig. 2).

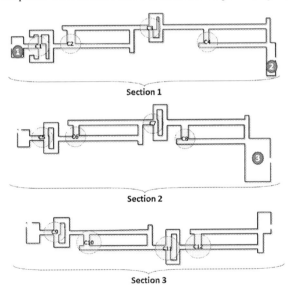

Section 1

Section 2

Section 3

Fig. 2. Top view of the floor plan with the three sections and with the location of the 12 selected corridor intersections. Numbers 1, 2 and 3 show where the wayfinding instructions were delivered to the participants

The virtual hotel was generated based on requirements operationalized during systematic meetings involving experts in Ergonomics, Architecture, Psychology, Design and Computer Engineering. Requirements were mainly related to the context, the building's design aspects, the wayfinding tasks that participants have to perform, the navigational aspects and the strategies to enhance the sense of presence and involvement.

The experimental conditions were created considering two emergency directional system composed by conventional static ISO-type exit signs (Static condition) and by new technology-based exit signs (Dynamic condition).

Static ISO-type exit signs are symbol-based and consistent with the International Organization for Standardization (ISO) standard [7]. ISO standard exit signs are required by law to illustrate an arrow and running figure in a doorway (Fig. 3).

Fig. 3. Static ISO-type emergency exit signs used for the Static condition

Technology-based emergency exit signs used for the Dynamic condition were developed by a design team considering the User-Centered Design methodology. A behavioral intention test was also performed with thirty university students. For this, an animation with the designed technology-based emergency exit sign was presented to the participants and they had to ask two questions: i) what is this sign? ii) What would you do if you see this sign? Most of the participants (67.2%) considered the sign an emergency exit sign. Most of them (76.6%) also reported that if they saw the sign they would follow its direction through an emergency egress.

Screenshots of the static ISO-type and the technology-based exit signs used for Static and Dynamic experimental conditions can be seen on Fig. 4.

To create the critical situations, the signs were always positioned to point to the directions opposite to those that were considered the most probable choice (see Table 1) according to the results of the study conducted by Vilar and colleagues [2].

Fig. 4. Screenshots from the Dynamic and Static conditions

Scenario and Wayfinding Task. To increase participant involvement, a scenario was created. At the beginning of the experimental session a cover story was given to the participants. The cover story created was that the participant had to give a lecture in an important conference at a hotel and conference center, however he/she was late and still had to talk to the receptionist to complete his/her conference registration and to know the location where the presentation would be made. When the participant reached the second floor, where the presentation would occur, he/she was informed that a fire has been detected on the premises. Participants were also told that they should behave as they would in a real-life situation. Fig. 5 shows screenshots of some fire locations within the building.

Fig. 5. Examples of fire with smoke in the second floor of the VE during the emergency

It was considered a controlled navigation approach because the corridors already passed by the participant were closed by doors during everyday wayfinding and by fire and smoke in the emergency situation. Thus, for each choice point, when participants chose one of the two alternative corridors, the corridor of the path that was not chosen was closed by a door (or fire), forcing them to continue along their initial selected path. At the beginning of each section, there was a room which was used to deliver the wayfinding task via virtual characters and to calculate the participants' partial performance.

2.4   Experimental Settings

The VE was projected onto a screen using a stereoscopic projector (i.e., Lightspeed DepthQ 3D) and visualized by the participants through active shutter glasses (i.e., MacNaughton Inc.'s APG6000). The projected image size was 1.72 m (59.7° of horizontal field-of-view - FOV) by 0.95 m (35.2° of vertical FOV) with an aspect ratio of 16:9. The observation distance (i.e., the distance between the observers' eyes and the screen) was 1.50 m.

A Logitech®Attack™ 3 joystick was used as an input device to collect the participants' answers. The movement's speed gradually increased from stop (0 m/s) to a maximum speed (3 m/s). Wireless headphones (i.e., Sony® MDR-RF800RK), allowed the participants to listen to instrumental ambient music, the wayfinding task instructions given orally by the virtual characters, and the sounds of a fire siren and fire.

2.5   Procedure

Before starting the experimental session, all participants were asked to sign a consent form and advised that they could stop participation at any time. The average duration of the entire experimental session was approximately 30 minutes, divided into a training session and a VR-based component. Participants were told that they ought to fulfil the given tasks as accurately and as quickly as possible.

The training session had the following main objectives: i) to familiarize participants with the simulation setup; ii) to allow them to practice the use of navigation and visualization devices, to bring their virtual movements closer to their realistic/natural actions; iii) to homogenize differences in the participant's performance using joystick; and iv) to make a preliminary check for symptoms of simulator sickness (participants were asked to report whether they felt any discomfort). For this, participants were encouraged to explore freely and navigate into a training VE, as quickly and efficiently as they could, without time restrictions. The researcher monitored participants' control of the navigation device by verifying their accuracy in executing some tasks, such as circumnavigating a pillar placed in the middle of a room without bumping into this element and walking through a zigzag corridor without touching the walls. Participants were also instructed to inform the experimenter when they felt relaxed and comfortable with the equipment. Only after verifying some of these equipment-related skills did the researcher permit the participant to start the VR-based component. No dialogue between the participant and the researcher was allowed after the simulation started.

The interaction started in the ground floor of a hotel and convention centre where participants received three wayfinding tasks (i.e., find three different locations in the building) from virtual characters present in the VE. The last task sent the participants to the second floor of the building via an elevator. Once they exited the elevator, an auditory alarm sounded and they were prevented from further elevator use. Thus, participants were faced with finding an emergency egress point by navigating through the second floor to escape from the fire.

If the participants reached a time limit of 20 minutes inside the simulation, the experiment was stopped to prevent eye fatigue, or simulation sickness, or both. Simulator sickness was mainly evaluated through participants' verbalizations. However, the researcher also monitored them during the interaction for symptoms such as redness of face, nausea, dizziness, and sweating [8, 9].

At the end of the VR-based component, a post task questionnaire was used to collect demographic information such as age, gender, occupation and dominant hand.

3   Results

Criteria for presenting results are related to the choices favoring the direction pointed by the signs considering the experimental conditions (i.e., Static and Dynamic). Participants' route performance considers the directional choices recorded for the entire route (12 corridor intersections). Table 2 summarizes the results obtained for all conditions. The corridors are presented according to their disposition on the building's plan. All statistical analyses were conducted using IBM SPSS v.20. The statistical significance level was set at 5%.

Table 2. Results considering the predicted directions from previous study [2], participants' route performance, percentages of choices contrary to and favouring the posted emmergency signs in static and dynamic conditions. Corridors were arranged according to their disposition on the building's plan.

Corridor (intersection type)	Variable (predicted attractor)*	Variable Direction*	% of choices contrary to the environmental variable*	Experimental conditions			
				Static		Dynamic	
				% choice contrary to sign direction (N)	% choice favouring sign direction (N)	% choice contrary to sign direction	% choice favouring sign direction
C1 (T)	Width	Right	72.0	73.3 (11)	26.7 (4)	6.7 (1)	93.3 (14)
C2 (F)	Brightness	Front	75.8	26.7 (4)	73.3 (11)	6.7 (1)	93.3 (14)
C3 (T)	Brightness and width	Left	87.9	26.7 (4)	73.3 (11)	- (0)	100 (15)
C4 (F)	Brightness and width	Right	89.6	- (0)	100 (15)	- (0)	100 (15)
C5 (T)	Brightness	Left	81.7	13.3 (2)	86.7 (13)	- (0)	100 (15)
C6 (F)	Brightness and width	Left	91.2	6.7 (1)	93.3 (14)	6.7 (1)	93.3 (14)
C7 (T)	Brightness and width	Right	89.6	13.3 (2)	86.7 (13)	6.7 (1)	93.3 (14)
C8 (F)	Width	Right	63.7	6.7 (1)	93.3 (14)	- (0)	100 (15)
C9 (T)	Width	Left	72.9	6.7 (1)	93.3 (14)	- (0)	100 (15)
C10 (F)	Brightness	Front	78.3	- (0)	100 (15)	- (0)	100 (15)
C11 (T)	Brightness	Right	83.7	6.7 (1)	93.3 (14)	- (0)	100 (15)
C12 (F)	Width	Left	57.5	6.7 (1)	93.3 (14)	- (0)	100 (15)
Participants Route Performance (%)				15.6	84.4	2.2	97.8
SD				20.2	20.2	3.3	3.3

*Predicted results were attained from Vilar and colleagues (2013) study.

A chi-square test of independence was performed to examine the relation between participants' route-choices favoring the direction posted by the sign and the emergency sign type for the 12 corridor intersections. The relation between these variables was significant only for the corridor intersection C1 ($X^2(1) = 13.889$, $p < .01$) and C3 ($X^2(1) = 4.615$, $p < .01$). However, differences were not statistically verified for the others analyzed corridor intersections ($p > .05$). Thus, technology-based emergency exit signs were more likely to be followed by the participants when seen for the first and third times than static ISO-type emergency exit signs.

4　Discussion and Conclusion

Preliminary data attained in this pilot study provide insights about the importance of verifying effectiveness of emergency exit signs considering users' wayfinding behavioral while interacting with a simulated emergency situation. The main objective of this pilot study was to investigate the relative influence of new technology-based exit signs, when compared to the conventional static ISO-type counterparts, in the users' wayfinding behavior during an emergency egress. A critical situation was considered (i.e., environmental variables and direction posted in the signs present conflicting information, for instance, in a two ways intersection, one of the available paths was brighter and wider than the other, attracting participants' to it and an exit sign was placed pointing to the opposite direction, a darker and narrower corridor).

Main results shown that high percentages of participants in an emergency and stressful condition chose not to follow the direction posted in static ISO-type emergency exit signs when the sign was available for the first time (C1). Considering that missing the right direction in the first available exit sign could foreseeably make people walk greater distances and spend more time than necessary to escape from a hazardous situation and could potentially increase the likelihood of injury or death, this result is disturbing. When technology-based emergency exit signs were considered, higher percentages of participants preferred to follow the direction indicated in the sign since its first appearance.

Main limitation of this study was the reduced number of participants. A large sample could represent different results, mainly related with the differences in the percentages of choices for the following corridor intersections. Considering other dependent variables than participants' directional choices, such as partial and total egress times and travelled distance, could also reinforce the need of new alternatives for the emergency exit signs generally used for emergency indoor signage.

References

1. Taylor, L.H., Socov, E.W.: The movement of people toward lights. Journal of Illuminating Engineering Society 3, 237–241 (1974)
2. Vilar, E., et al.: The Influence of Environmental Features on Route Selection in an Emergency Situation. Applied Ergonomics 44(4), 618–627 (2013)
3. Vilar, E.: Using Virtual Reality to Study the Influence of Environmental Variables to Enhance Wayfinding within Complex Buildings. In: Ergonomics 2012. University of Lisbon, Lisbon (2012)
4. Gamberini, L., et al.: Responding to a fire emergency in a virtual environment: different patterns of action for different situations. Ergonomics 46(8), 842–858 (2003)
5. Ishihara, S.: Test for Colour-Blindness, 38th edn. Kanehara & Co., Ltd., Tokyo (1988)
6. Vilar, E., et al.: The influence of environmental features on route selection in an emergency situation. Applied Ergonomics
7. International Organization for Standardization (ISO), Graphical Symbols - Safety Colors and Safety Signs. Part 1: Design Principles for safety Signs in Workplaces and Public Areas. ISO 3864-1. International Organization for Standardization, Geneva, Switzerland (2002)
8. Kennedy, R.S., Hettinger, L.J., Lilienthal, M.G.: Simulator sickness. In: Crampton, G.H. (ed.) Motion and Space Sickness, pp. 317–342. CRC Press, Boca Raton (1990)
9. Keshavarz, B., Hecht, H.: Validating an Efficient Method to Quantify Motion Sickness. Human Factors: The Journal of the Human Factors and Ergonomics Society 53(4), 415–426 (2011)

Impact of Multi-sensory On-Bicycle Rider Assistance Devices on Rider Concentration and Safety

Chao-Yang Yang[1], Yu-Ting Wu[2], and Cheng-Tse Wu[3]

[1] Department of Industrial Design, Tatung University, No.40, Sec. 3,
Zhongshan N. Rd., Taipei City 104, Taiwan
dillon.yang@gmail.com
[2] Department of Industrial Design, Chang Gung University, 259,
Wen Hua 1st Rd, Kuei Shan, Tao-Yuan, Taiwan
hope790406@gmail.com
[3] Department of Industrial Design, Chang Gung University, 259,
Wen Hua 1st Rd, Kuei Shan, Tao-Yuan, Taiwan
woolmonster@gmail.com

Abstract. This study evaluated the impact of multi-sensory information cues from on-bicycle rider information assistance devices (OBRAD) on hazard perception performance. Experiments tested the impact of distraction from different combinations of visual, auditory and tactile sensory aids on the subject's ability to maintain peddling frequency while conducting eight different tasks. The results indicate that the integrated use of different sensory cues (e.g., text, audible alerts and vibration) can decrease cognitive loading, with each sensory combination, particularly those involving tactile stimulation, having different levels of effect. Tactile sensory aids helped reduce the degree of rider distraction, thus helping maintain a high sensitivity to danger (hit rate mean: 0.34). Cycling performance was further improved through combining tactile stimuli with auditory cues for assistance in the secondary task. The implications of these findings and the need to integrate and manage complex OBRAD information systems are discussed.

Keywords: cycling performance, multi-sensory, hazard perception, cognitive loading.

1 Introduction

Increased popularity of recreational bicycling has driven sales of On-Bicycle Rider Assistance Devices (OBRADs), which offer an increasingly broad range of information, including location and route information (including altitude and slope gradient), and physiological monitoring data including heart rate and cadence.Use of OBRADs can impact the rider's speed control, reaction time, ease of learning and level of psychological stress in emergency situations. Rockwell (1988) recommended a "two-second rule" for OBRAD use, suggesting that any device which requires drivers to look away from the road for more than two seconds has a significantly negative impact on safety. In consideration of the rider's posture and the design of bicycle

A. Marcus (Ed.): DUXU 2014, Part III, LNCS 8519, pp. 378–388, 2014.

frames, OBRADs are usually placed on the handlebars to optimize access and visibility to the rider. However, the rider's pedalling action has a constantly shifting impact on his/her line of sight, level, and observational capacity.

The impact of multitasking on driver performance and safety has been widely studied (Salvucci, 2002), but little attention has been focused on the use of OBRADs by cyclists, thus this study begins by reviewing the relevant literature for automotive OBRAD use. Cycling and driving are similar in that they are both multitasking activities primarily concerned with the safe transport of the rider/driver, and both require training to successfully accomplish subtasks including observing road conditions and maintaining constant speed. Lansdown et al. (2004) suggested that driving task demands are variable, and at times the driver may be left with considerable spare capacity which can be used to undertake secondary or dual tasks. Use of OBRADs and similar devices significantly increases the amount of visual information riders must process, thus increasing the potential for distraction and accidents. For example, reading route guidance systems is likely to considerably increase rider's cognitive loading and cause distraction. Given that cyclists today can reach speeds of 40-60 kph, potential harm due to distraction is no less serious for cyclists than for car drivers and entails a risk of serious injury or death. Previous research has shown that cyclists are highly prone to single-driver accidents, often resulting from behavior including excessive speed, lack of attention, breach of traffic regulations or poor co-ordination (Eilert-Petersson & Schelp, 1997). In addition, "looked, but didn't see" is a puzzling but common type of error, potentially caused by negligence and poor judgment (Stanton & Salmon, 2009).

Receiving and processing riding information occupies physiological resources, including visual, operational, cognitive and auditory. Previous studies have shown that engagement in non-essential activities degrades driver performance, with contributing factors including attentional allocation (Matanzo & Rockwell, 1967), driving experience (Summala et al., 1998), age (Brouwer et al., 1991; Korteling, 1994) and mental workload (Hancock & Verwey, 1997). Dingus (2006) suggested that drivers cannot drive safely while dividing their attention between multiple visual stimuli, and Droll (2011) found that alternating one's gaze between the road and the radio leaves drives vulnerable to collisions. Gopher (1990) suggested that increasing the difficulty of the primary task increases the impact of multi-tasking on overall performance, potentially resulting in fatally delayed response times. However cognitive loading is difficult to measure directly, and is thus typically assessed through the use of subjective ratings or measurements of physiological responses. Studies of drivers' visual attention indicate that night time and rainy driving conditions increase cognitive demand, which thus may reduce the useful field of view (Konstantopoulos et al., 2010). Others have shown that mental workload affects driving performance (Lee et al., 2007; Recarte & Nunes, 2003) resulting in increased response times (Plainis & Murray, 2002).

Human reactions to their surroundings can be broken down into three stages: stimuli recognition, reaction choice and reaction step. The process of reaction, from stimulus input through message processing and control operation to reaction output, is a holistic operation and the time required to execute this process is referred to as total reaction time (TRT). From an operational perspective, TRT can be split into reaction time (RT) and movement time (MT), such that TRT = RT+MT (Sagberg &

Bjørnskau, 2006). Gopher (1990) suggested that adding a secondary task to a difficult primary task can exceed the operator's central processing capacity, thus significantly decreasing primary task performance. Empirical support was provided by Salvucci (2002) who demonstrated that driving involves continual multitasking of a number of sub-processes which show a clear (and significant) task effect, with reaction times increasing from 1.6 seconds to 2.2 seconds when a second task is added.

One's ability to foresee potential traffic accidents is referred to as "hazard perception", and explains the difference between novice and experienced drivers in dealing with distractions without causing collisions (Sagberg & Bjørnskau, 2006). Some investigations of hazard perception have assessed traffic conditions prior to accidents. These studies used a variety of images (Tränkle et al., 1990), vocal descriptions (Guerin, 1994), video (Renge, 1998) or actual traffic flows (Bragg & Finn, 1985) to assess hazard perception. Other studies have investigated driver reaction time as a way to assess the likelihood of collision. Some of these studies were based on physical models of traffic situations (CURRIB, 1969) while others used video (Congdon, 1999; McKenna & Crick, 1997).

Hazard perception studies can be broadly divided into two types: the first primarily focuses on investigating the scene of the potential hazard, while the second is primarily concerned with investigating driver reaction times. The present study is concerned with whether cyclists' hazard perception and reactions undergo significant changes when using OBRADs; thus this study is primarily concerned with the second approach to hazard perception. The present study uses a virtual cycling environment combined with real bicycles to identify the key risk factors for concentration impairment to provide a reference for the formulation of traffic safety standards. In addition to assessing the degree of distraction caused by the use of OBRADs, we also investigate the use of different information reception modes to determine which mode best reduces riders' psychological loading, thus reducing distraction and the risk of collision. This research also measures riders' visual concentration during instances of head movement. Doshi and Trivedi (2008) showed that head movement enables drivers to receive correct information and thus improve the accuracy of their judgments vis-à-vis potential hazards.

Warning signals and stimulus signals can be conveyed as visual, auditory or tactile cues through lights, buzzers, vibration or text (Magill & Anderson, 2007). Auditory stimuli are characterized by short reaction time, judgment direction, distance perception and high conspicuousness. Jones and Furner (1989) noted that, "audition is intimately connected with the arousal and activation systems of the nervous system," indicating that sound can produce faster reaction times than visual stimuli (Welford, 1980). Equally important is that auditory cues can be perceived without the use of either eyes or hands, making them an important means of communication in everyday life and a potentially superior form of alert for OBRADs. Using a driving simulator, Van Erp and Van Veen (2004) found that assistive information (such as alerts) communicated through vibration reduces visual loading. Qian et al. (2011) used the vibrating alert from cell phones to test the degree of information reception among test subjects without increasing visual loading. Burnett and Porter (2001) showed that tactile cues can be substituted for visual cues, and can supplement auditory cues as a channel for information transmission.

The present study uses auditory and tactile cues to replace visual cues for assistive information transmission in OBRADs to assess the impact on cyclist cognitive loading and reaction times. This study uses SDT and Likert response instrument to measure cognitive loading in detecting hazards to explore risks to cyclists as follows:

1. Assess the cognitive loading of cyclists using OBRADs;
2. Explore the potential for reducing cycling risks through the use of single-sensory /multisensory information cues.

2   Methods Used

This study uses signal detection theory to investigate the effects of various OBRAD information transmission modes on bicyclist behavior through lab-based simulations of authentic riding conditions.

2.1   Experimental Setup

To ensure consistent environmental conditions (e.g., weather or traffic), and to prevent differences in individual riding skill from affecting the results, experiments were conducted in a lab environment (see Fig. 1). The bicycle used in the experiment was a 48" steel frame road bike, which had been previously identified by Rodgers (1998) as being a type of bicycle highly prone to collisions. The bicycle was fitted to a Tacx™ Fortius-Multiplayer T1930 virtual reality trainer using the Tacx 2.0 (T1990.02) software. An Epson EB410 short focus projector was positioned 230cm from a 4:3 aspect ratio screen, which was 170cm in front of the test subject's eyes. A Garmin® Edge705 trip computer was fitted to the bicycle with text size set to 36pt, 40cm from the test subject's eyes. The entire process was recorded on video to collect the following data:

1. Conditions presented on the screen
2. Average rotations per minute (RPM)
3. Head movement
4. Reaction to perceived hazard

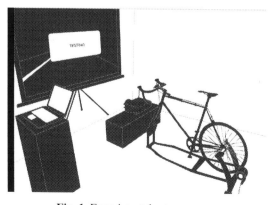

Fig. 1. Experimental setup

2.2   Test Subject Selection

The experiment was conducted using 30 test subjects, including 16 male and 14 female undergraduate and graduate students from Chang Gung University, aged between 18 and 26 (mean 21.13, SD = 3.54). Test subjects ranged from 165 to 180 cm
in height (mean 172.82, SD = 4.95). All test subjects had an average of 10 years or
more of cycling experience, none suffered from color blindness or any other eye disease. Degrees of corrected vision ranged from 0.8 to 1.2, and all were right handed.
The test procedure lasted 90 minutes. To reduce fatigue and the memory effect, test
subjects were separately tested twice. Each test subject was paid the equivalent of
US$10 after completion of the second test. Prior to testing, the bicycle seat was ad-
justed to suit the rider's height. To reduce psychological loading, the bicycle's gearset
was fixed at 50*14.

2.3   Experimental Design

Reaction time is the time from when the person perceives the stimulus signal to when
he or she makes his or her first reaction. To calculate reaction time, we select a more
clearly defined stimulus (see Table 1) (e.g., an oncoming car or a car overtaking from
behind) and avoid other unnecessary stimuli. A large button is positioned on the bicycle's handlebars and test subjects can easily press the button without changing position, thus significantly reducing the physical difference in reaction behavior. Test
subjects press the button in response to perceived hazard. When the button is pressed,
a visible red laser dot to appear on the projection screen, and reaction time is calculated as the interval between the initial appearance of the hazard and the red dot appearing on the screen.

Table 1. Hazard stimulus definitions

Oncoming car from left	Overtaking car	Oncoming car	Oncoming motorcycle	Bicycle

The experiment was divided into nine tasks. In each task, the test subject was asked
to respond to a perceived hazard (e.g., oncoming or overtaking vehicle) by pressing
the button once. Task 1 was a warm-up in which participants were asked to ride the
bicycle through a rural area for three minutes. In tasks 2 through 9, riders were asked
to maintain a cadence of between 55 to 65 RPM while receiving visual, auditory and
tactile cues from the multimedia trip computer. Each ride simulated resistance road
training with the road gradient set to within 3%, and included a selection of over ten
hazard stimuli distributed through each task. In the interval between tasks, test subjects were asked to provide feedback about the information they'd received from the
OBRAD and road conditions in the previous task through answering short and simple

interview questions which were recorded, and through filling out a Likert response table. These responses provided an understanding of the riders' degree of distraction while receiving information from different message modes.

3   Experimental Results

The operating variables used in this study include visual message reception, auditory message reception and tactile message reception.

3.1   Cognitive Loading

After each task the participants asked to complete a Likert response instrument to measure cognitive loading. Responses ranged from 1 (strongly disagree) to 7 (strongly agree).

Table 2. Task content of T value test

One-Sample Test

					95% Confidence Interval of the Difference	
	t	df	Sig. (2-tailed)	Mean Difference	Lower	Upper
ND	20.696	29	.000	4.80000	4.3256	5.2744
V	41.713	29	.000	6.00000	5.7058	6.2942
A	11.239	29	.000	4.43333	3.6266	5.2401
T	13.681	29	.000	3.90000	3.3170	4.4830
VA	15.183	29	.000	4.83333	4.1823	5.4844
VT	14.516	29	.000	3.96667	3.4078	4.5256
TA	12.349	29	.000	4.13333	3.4488	4.8179
VAT	15.751	29	.000	4.80000	4.1767	5.4233

Test Value = 0

Table 2 shows that the various tasks have significantly different impacts ($P<0.05$, V has the greatest impact on riding task performance (M=6.00 ,$P<0.05$), followed by VA (M=4.83,$P<0.05$). T has the smallest impact (M=3.90,$P<0.05$), followed by VT (M=3.96,$P<0.05$).This finding indicated that subjects felt the use of visual aids was more likely to affect their cycling performance and hazard perception, but that adding other information transmission forms would reduce workload. In terms of secondary aids, tactile cues produced better results than auditory inputs. Participants indicated that tactile inputs were less distracting than auditory inputs which tended to startle the rider, thus increasing mental workload and degrading primary performance.

3.2   Hit Rate

Fig. 2 shows that ND indicates that the test subjects maintained their RPM within the target range without using the OBRAD, while maintaining a mean hazard detection hit rate of 0.36. Observations indicated that tactile cues had the least impact on riding safety, followed by visual cues. The results can be divided into two main groups: the first group has a higher Hit Rate, and includes Tasks ND, T, TA and VAT, while the second group has a lower Hit Rate and includes Tasks V, A, VA and VT. These results show that tactile cues can be used to effectively transmit information while causing a level of distraction comparable to that when no assistive devices are used (i.e., Task ND), and this lack of interference in hazard detection is worthy of further investigation. Task T is the only task which does not use visual cues to score a low hit rate through the use of tactile cues alone. Task VAT is the only member of the high hit rate group to use visual cues which did not provide optimal performance, which indicates that simultaneous use of all three sensory cues does not optimally affect the detection of traffic conditions, and the use of visual devices greatly reduces the rider's ability to detect hazards.Of the tests using visual cues, Task V produces a relatively high hit rate, indicating that using other sensory cues in addition to visual cues exacerbates rider distraction.

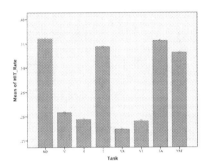

Fig. 2. Hit rate mean linear change

3.3   Reaction Time

Fig.3 shows that reaction time varies among the groups, with reaction times mostly averaging between 3s~4s. Hazard detection results are similar, and we find that Tasks V, A, VA, and VT have higher reaction times (3.47s~3.59s), indicating that test subjects react more slowly after becoming aware of the stimulus, while Tasks ND, T, TA and VAT have lower reaction times. Observations indicated that tactile cues had the least impact on riding safety. Using visual plus auditory cues (VA) or visual cues alone (V), test subjects maintained a high degree of hazard perception.

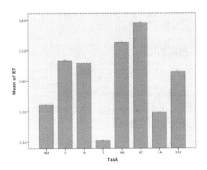

Fig. 3. Reaction time mean linear change

3.4   Sensitivity of d'

Figure 4 shows the mean change of d', where Task TA has the highest sensitivity (d' mean=1.06), followed by Task T (d' mean=0.95), while the sensitivities of Tasks ND, A, VT and VAT are largely similar, and Tasks V and VA have relatively lower sensitivity.The d' value of Task ND is significantly lower than that of Tasks V, VA and VT. Using multiple tactile cues can lighten the rider's visual loading, thus increasing hazard detection capability. The difference between the prior hit rate and RT for Tasks V and VT is due to the addition of the FA variable to the value of d', which results in a reduction of the rider's mean hazard detection capability reflected in the hit rate and RT for these two tasks. However, the d' value indicates fewer misjudgments in Task VT, and more misjudgments in Task V. Task T only uses vibration cues, while Task TA uses both auditory and tactile cues, and results for both tasks indicate that the use of tactile cues effectively increases rider sensitivity to incoming information. Next, we look at Tasks V and VA, which exhibited a relatively low value for d'. These two tasks show that the use of visual cues corresponds to reduced rider sensitivity. Finally, Tasks ND, A, VT and VAT exhibit mid-range values for d'. Task ND uses no sensory cues, while Task A uses only auditory cues. This, plus the relatively high mean values of d' for Tasks T and TA, indicate that excluding visual cues results in heightened sensitivity. Results for Tasks T, VT, TA and VAT show that the use of tactile cues, regardless of whether used alone or combined with visual cues, results in a higher d' value, indicating that test subjects are more sensitive to potential risks. However, using both auditory and tactile cues for Task VA results in the lowest recorded d' values, indicating that the tactile cues are clearly more effective at conveying information than visual or auditory cues, and the inclusion of tactile cues seems to compensate for the poor performance of other types of cues.

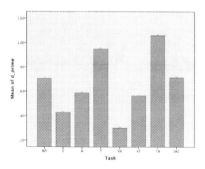

Fig. 4. d' mean linear change

3.5   Head Movement

Figure 5 shows that head movement in Tasks V, VA, VT and VAT can be divided into two groups, with Tasks V and VA having a higher incidence of head movement than Tasks VT and VAT. Task VA has the highest mean incidence of head movement (mean=3.05). Given that this task involved visual and auditory cues, we can speculate that the use of auditory cues had a significant impact on the test subjects' reception of information and increased the number of head movements.Task VA includes auditory cues, but does not result in a higher degree of distraction than pure visual cues. However, distraction levels for Task VAT are considerably lower than for Task VT, suggesting that matching multiple sensory cues in a single application requires careful adjustment.

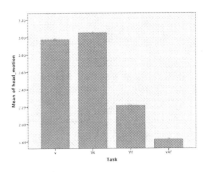

Fig. 5. Head movement mean linear change

4   Discussion

Cycling entails continuous posture and position adjustments which place additional stress on rider concentration capacity. Experimental results indicate that the use of visual and auditory prompts in OBRADs can lead to rider distraction and reduce rider sensitivity to potential hazards, while tactile cues are found to reduce the likelihood of distraction. The results emphasize the importance of coordinating various sensory inputs to optimize reaction time. Properly coordinating sensory cues can effectively reduce visual loading and contribute to the improved design of cycling information interfaces, thus reducing the potential for cycling accidents.

5   Conclusion

Safety is an important consideration for the design and use of cycling information systems. Given the high degree of environmental interference inherent in cycling, the use of existing cycling trip computers seriously exacerbates the risk of accidents. The results presented here not only contribute to the improved design of trip computer interfaces, but also provide deeper insight into rider performance, mental workload and safety.

References

1. Bragg, B.W., Finn, P.: Influence of safety belt usage on perception of the risk of an accident. Accident Analysis & Prevention 17(1), 15–23 (1985)
2. Brouwer, W.H., Waterink, W., Van Wolffelaar, P.C., Rothengatter, T.: Divided attention in experienced young and older drivers: lane tracking and visual analysis in a dynamic driving simulator. Human Factors: The Journal of the Human Factors and Ergonomics Society 33(5), 573–582 (1991)
3. Burnett, G.E., Mark Porter, J.: Ubiquitous computing within cars: designing controls for non-visual use. International Journal of Human-Computer Studies 55(4), 521–531 (2001)
4. Congdon, P.: VicRoads Hazard Perception Test, Can it Predict Accidents? (1999)
5. Currib, L.: The perception of danger in a simulated driving task. Ergonomics 12(6), 841–849 (1969)
6. Dingus, T.A., Klauer, S.G., Neale, V.L., Petersen, A., Lee, S.E., Sudweeks, J.D., Perez, M.A., Hankey, J., Ramsey, D.J., Gupta, S., Bucher, C., Doerzaph, Z.R., Jermeland, J., Knipling, R.R.: The 100-Car Naturalistic Driving Study, Phase II - Results of the 100-Car Field Experiment (2006)
7. Doshi, A., Trivedi, M.: A comparative exploration of eye gaze and head motion cues for lane change intent prediction. 2008 IEEE Paper Presented at the Intelligent Vehicles Symposium (2008)
8. Droll, J.A.: The Velocity of Visual Attention in Vehicle Accidents. American Association for Justice (2011)
9. Eilert-Petersson, E., Schelp, L.: An epidemiological study of bicycle-related injuries. Accident Analysis & Prevention 29(3), 363–372 (1997)
10. Gopher, G.: Attentional allocation in dual task environments. Attention and Performance III (1990)
11. Guerin, B.: What Do People Think About the Risks of Driving? Implications for Traffic Safety Interventions1. Journal of Applied Social Psychology 24(11), 994–1021 (1994)
12. Hancock, P., Verwey, W.B.: Fatigue, workload and adaptive driver systems. Accident Analysis & Prevention 29(4), 495–506 (1997)
13. Jones, S., Furner, S.: The construction of audio icons and information cues for human-computer dialogues. Paper Presented at the Contemporary Ergonomics: Proceedings of the Ergonomics Society's 1989 Annual Conference (1989)
14. Konstantopoulos, P., Chapman, P., Crundall, D.: Driver's visual attention as a function of driving experience and visibility. Using a driving simulator to explore drivers' eye movements in day, night and rain driving. Accident Analysis & Prevention 42(3), 827–834 (2010)
15. Korteling, J.H.: Effects of aging, skill modification, and demand alternation on multiple-task performance. Human Factors: The Journal of the Human Factors and Ergonomics Society 36(1), 27–43 (1994)
16. Lansdown, T.C., Brook-Carter, N., Kersloot, T.: Distraction from multiple in-vehicle secondary tasks: vehicle performance and mental workload implications. Ergonomics 47(1), 91–104 (2004)
17. Lee, Y.-C., Lee, J.D., Boyle, L.N.: Visual attention in driving: the effects of cognitive load and visual disruption. Human Factors: The Journal of the Human Factors and Ergonomics Society 49(4), 721–733 (2007)
18. Magill, R.A., Anderson, D.: Motor learning and control: Concepts and applications, vol. II. McGraw-Hill, New York (2007)

19. Matanzo, F., Rockwell, T.H.: Driving performance under nighttime conditions of visual degradation. Human Factors: The Journal of the Human Factors and Ergonomics Society 9(5), 427–432 (1967)
20. Plainis, S., Murray, I.: Reaction times as an index of visual conspicuity when driving at night. Ophthalmic and Physiological Optics 22(5), 409–415 (2002)
21. Qian, H., Kuber, R., Sears, A.: Towards developing perceivable tactile feedback for mobile devices. International Journal of Human-Computer Studies 69(11), 705–719 (2011)
22. Recarte, M.A., Nunes, L.M.: Mental workload while driving: effects on visual search, discrimination, and decision making. Journal of Experimental Psychology: Applied 9(2), 119 (2003)
23. Renge, K.: Drivers' Hazard and Risk Perception, Confidence in Safe Driving, and Choice of Speed. IATSS Research 22(2), 103–110 (1998)
24. Rockwell, T.: Spare visual capacity in driving-revisited: New empirical results for an old idea. Paper Presented at the Vision in Vehicles II. Second International Conference on Vision in Vehicles (1988)
25. Rodgers, G.B.: Factors associated with the crash risk of adult bicyclists. Journal of Safety Research 28(4), 233–241 (1998)
26. Sagberg, F., Bjørnskau, T.: Hazard perception and driving experience among novice drivers. Accident Analysis & Prevention 38(2), 407–414 (2006)
27. Salvucci, D.D.: Modeling driver distraction from cognitive tasks. Paper Presented at the Proceedings of the 24th Annual Conference of the Cognitive Science Society (2002)
28. Stanton, N.A., Salmon, P.M.: Human error taxonomies applied to driving: A generic driver error taxonomy and its implications for intelligent transport systems. Safety Science 47(2), 227–237 (2009)
29. Summala, H., Lamble, D., Laakso, M.: Driving experience and perception of the lead car's braking when looking at in-car targets. Accident Analysis & Prevention 30(4), 401–407 (1998)
30. Tränkle, U., Gelau, C., Metker, T.: Risk perception and age-specific accidents of young drivers. Accident Analysis & Prevention 22(2), 119–125 (1990)
31. Van Erp, J.B., Van Veen, H.A.: Vibrotactile in-vehicle navigation system. Transportation Research Part F: Traffic Psychology and Behaviour 7(4), 247–256 (2004)
32. Welford, A.T., Brebner, J.M.T.: Introduction: an historical background sketch, New York (1980)

Design for Rural, Low Literacy and Developing Communities

Barriers and Reforms for Promoting ICTs
in Rural Areas of Pakistan

Aneela Abbas[1], Mubbashar Hussain[1], Muddesar Iqbal[1], Sidra Arshad[1],
Saqib Rasool[1], Muhammad Shafiq[2], Wasif Ali[1], and NadeemYaqub[1]

[1] Faculty of Computing and Information Technology
University of Gujrat, Pakistan
{aneela.abbas,mubbashar.hussain,m.iqbal,
saqib.pk,wasif.ali}@uog.edu.pk, comcidra_111@yahoo.com
[2] Department of Information and Communication Engineering
Yeungnam University, South Korea
{shafiq.pu,nadeem.yb}@gmail.com

Abstract. Pakistan is a developing country and peoples of more than 50,000
areas, cover 64% of the whole population, belong to rural. ICTs are the essence
of this modern age but unfortunately, the services of ICTs have failed to trickle
down the rural masses of Pakistan. We believe that the inadequacy of infrastructure, i.e., behavioral, cultural and social barriers, is debarring ICTs to
strengthen its roots in the rural areas. The most vital task is to wipe out this digital division to change the patterns of thoughts and behaviors of the masses of
rural areas. In Pakistan many efforts are in the pipeline to reveal the concrete
paybacks of ICTs for rural population. The need of the hour is to do so in a way
that makes economic reimbursements. This paper deals with the potential barriers barring ICTs in far wide areas of the Pakistan, various fruitful steps taken
by the Government of Pakistan to introduce ICT reforms, various policies
framed for boosting ICTs and computer literacy in rural areas.

Keywords: Digital divide, IT infrastructure, ICT reforms, Computer literacy.

1 Introduction

A report by the World Economic Forum, illustrates a miserable condition of ICTs in
Pakistan by assigning it at 105 among 144 countries. (The Global Information Technology Report, 2013) In comparison with urban areas, rural areas are far behind in
adopting ICTs due to certain reasons. The importance of rural development is not
always understood, as the urban people are more visible and more vocal than their
rural counterparts [12]. Information and Communication Technologies (ICTs) denotes
to the electronic centered technologies like computers, mobile phones and tablets to
collect information, and to connect with others [2]. ICTs offer major opportunities to
the developing areas in boosting the economic growth, local development and reduction in poverty [3]. Although, it seems absurd that modern information technology
facilities, associated in our minds, have any relevance for remote areas of the country

A. Marcus (Ed.): DUXU 2014, Part III, LNCS 8519, pp. 391–399, 2014.

where many millions still lack basic necessities of life. But nevertheless, this IT revolution may become a major source of social and economic development of the rural areas of the country. Rendering to Universal Service Fund, 480 cities and towns of Pakistan are deprived of broadband services with the chief percentage encompassing the rural areas [16]. Furthermore, extensive load shedding in the rural areas has aggravated the condition. Nevertheless, spreading of ICTs in rural areas of Pakistan will be a problematic task [15].The goal can be endorsed to the point that with the fruition of technology, outspreading ICTs set-ups to rural zones has been a consistent challenge [1] [4].

Modern Facilities are concentrated in urban areas. Provision of health facilities, construction of universities, libraries and hospitals, all confined to the big cities, whilst, Rural areas are deprived of all these. If provided in villages, they are not sufficient or in poor condition. Online education and online libraries are alternative solution to the imperfect facilities of education. BHU (Basic Health Unit) commonly known as dispensaries and lady health workers are the only health facility provided to the villagers. Telemedicine is a feasible proposed solution to provide basic health facilities to the remotes areas of the country. This study is aimed at promoting ICTs for the development of rural zones. Part one of the paper deals with the barriers and hurdles, which ceased the multitudes of countryside to embrace technology. Second part of the papers is about the ICTs reforms introduced in the country. In third part some practicable solutions and recommendations are given to promote ICTs in rural areas of Pakistan. At the end conclusion and future work is stated.

2   Objectives

The core objectives of this study were:

- To explore the barriers refraining these underprivileged folks to reap the benefits of ICTs which have revolutionized the whole world.
- To see if the execution of ICTs in Rural areas of Pakistan would have any influence on the life of the masses living in the remote areas of the country.
- To give an insight to the Government of Pakistan about the depressed ICTs condition in rural areas of Pakistan, anticipating some necessary and corrective measures by the concerned authorities.
- To give some suggestions for stimulating and enriching information and communication technologies in rural areas of the country.

3   Barriers in Adopting ICTs in Rural Areas of Pakistan

3.1   Language Barrier

A key handicap in implementation of ICTs in rustic areas is that the information content is not pertinent to the masses for which it is deployed. As these systems are developed by the people living for away from the rural areas, consequently they have a dense urban-bias. Low literacy rate is a big factor, which debars people to clinch technology, as mostly kiosks and software's are in English language and the people only know their national or regional languages in most of the areas of the country. So the ICTs and kiosks, therefore have limited efficacy for the masses of rural areas. This problem can be overcome by developing relevant content in native lingoes and propagating it to more and more rural zones.

3.2   Cultural Barriers

There are some demographic and cultural barriers in promoting ICTs in remote areas of the country. Due to gender divide and stereotypical attitude of the people towards the females, particularly in the far wide areas of the country, acceptance ratio of ICTs in rural areas is far more less than the urban areas. It would be perceived very bizarre in underdeveloped and backward areas, if females use technology and latest communication conveniences like cell phones, Face book and Skype.

3.3   Lack of Awareness

Another key aspect is the unwillingness of the people to adopt change. Low literacy rate is a major cause of this conventional approach of people towards technology. People with backward mindset repel latest technology. They will prefer to do their work manually rather than invoking ICT's. Lack of awareness is a major reason of low penetration and acceptance of ICTs by villagers as they are unaware of the benefits they could reap by opting ICTs.

3.4   Computer Literacy

An acute impediment in promoting ICTs in rural areas is computer illiteracy and ignorance. With poor literacy rate of 53%, the ICT literacy rate particularly in the rural areas of Pakistan is insignificant [3]. The ICT curriculum presently introduced in schools all over the country, does not cater to localization. Even though some schools have facility of computer labs, yet student lack sufficient knowledge to operate computers. Some prominent grounds of low computer illiteracy in these areas are lack of adequate facilities such as adverse IT infrastructure and scarcity of computers, labs and skilled IT staffs in schools of rural areas.

3.5   Affordability of ICTs

Poverty and insufficiency of resources are predominantly a rural problem in Pakistan. It is widely concentrated in rural areas where most of the people are living their life below the poverty line. Rural folks comprising of 2/3 of the country's population, encompass 80 per cent of the country's deprived people [5]. Poor economic condition of the rural masses is a major barrier for less adaptation of technology. In rural areas most of the people have low purchasing power. It's not easy for the people depriving of basic necessities of life to afford these expensive technologies. Subsequently, there are a very limited number of expected users of technology. However, extension and adaptation of ICTs in rural areas can help to accelerate economic growth. These can play crucial role in eradicating poverty in vulnerable remote areas of the country.

3.6　Electricity Shortfall

Pakistan's desperate energy crisis is proving a serious mess for its economy. The energy crisis has shattered Pakistan. Pakistan's development has come to a standstill due to the energy crunch. The country's energy problems are deeper and complex in rural areas. This prevailing power crisis throughout the country, in the rural areas particularly, is another significant factor affecting the smooth operations of the operators and service providers. Thousands of cell sites have to remain functional (24×7 basis) in order to keep the network alive and maintain the quality of service as well. Resolving Pakistan's energy catastrophe will no doubt, help to promote ICTs in rural areas and urban areas as well, but it depends, after how long Pakistan rides out this storm. Extension and promotion of ICTs in rural as well as urban areas owes greatly to viable sources of power [13]. Fig.1 illustrates the barriers debarring ICT's in rural areas of Pakistan.

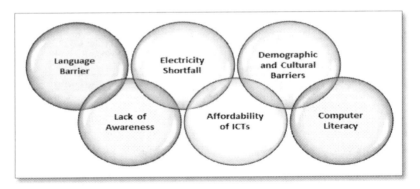

Fig. 1. Barriers of adopting ICTs in Rural areas of Pakistan

4　ICTs Reforms: Steps towards Improvement

Being abreast of the problem and admitting the need of ICTs public and private sector has taken some initiatives to promote ICTs in rural areas of the country. Many NGOs are also playing their role in this context. Below are discussed some reforms introduced in the country.

4.1　Laptop Scheme

Pursuing ICT reforms in country, Laptops distribution scheme was introduced by Chief Minister of Punjab Mian Shahbaz Sharif in January 2012 for the students of the Punjab. Now government of Pakistan has made a decision to begin Laptop scheme for students throughout the country. Nevertheless, it's a major milestone in promoting ICTs in far and wide areas of the country. This scheme, no doubt; would leave an extensive impact on the education sector by delivering a prospect to the students of both urban and rural areas to benefit from the latest technology in their academic hunts [20].

4.2   IT Labs Project

Introducing IT labs in far wide areas of the country is a big milestone and achievement as well. Targeting to boost computer literacy in the state, the Government of Punjab laid down the foundation of an ambitious initiative of Punjab IT Labs Project [7] [8]. The Punjab Government envisioned this project to provide computer access to 3.4 million students all over the province. Chasing this goal, the government set up well-resourced computer labs in the 4,286 schools across the far wide areas of the province. If same schemes would be introduced in remote areas of other provinces, it will surely promise ICT revolution throughout country.

4.3   Computer Education and Training

To make the students of the country computer literate, computer education is declared mandatory right from school to university level. Government and policy makers should concentrate on updating the syllabus regularly to keep the students abreast of latest computer knowledge and expertise [6]. Many technical and vocational training institutes like TEVTA are playing their part in this context by offering computer short courses and certifications.

4.4   Contribution of Private Organizations

Many private organizations like 4CCI, ADP and SACHET are also contributing for promoting computer literacy in rural areas of the country.

4.4.1   Children Community Initiative (4CCI)

Rendering to 4CCI (4 Children Community Initiative) computer technology is a solo factor that would take schools and educational institutes from good to best. With this perception, they offer technology incorporated syllabuses augmented by technology setup. These organizations are trying to boost computer literacy all over the country by introducing computer labs crossways the rural areas of Pakistan. This access to computers is intensely complemented by trainings of teachers and students [17].

4.4.2   Association for the Development of Pakistan (ADP)

ADP (association for the development of Pakistan) is backing for launching computer lab and computer learning program in a government school in Noor Lakhan (NLS), Ghotki, Sindh. It targets to extend computer literacy in rustic zones to develop necessary competencies for both education and job effectiveness [4].

4.4.3   SACHET

SACHET established its first computer training center in Village Shahdara in January 2000, for promoting computer awareness and skills in computer illiterate masses of this area. Now it has stretched it branches in other remote areas of the country as well [19]. Fig.2 demonstrates various steps and reforms introduced to promote ICTs in rural areas.

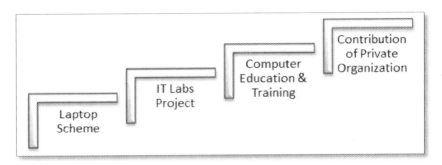

Fig. 2. ICT Reforms- Steps towards improvement

5   Solutions and Suggestions

Beneath are revealed some viable solutions and suggestions to resolve this desperate condition of ICTs, envisioning a revolution in the destitute rural areas.

5.1   Encouraging Telecom Operators

Government and concerned authorities should encourage telecom operators to invest in rural and far wide areas of the country. By facilitating and giving incentives to operators and ISPs government could "play its role" in encouraging ICTs all over the country. It would be productive if private sector lends a helping hand to the government. Government should encourage competitive entrants of technology to reduce the cost of ICTs. New connection fee should be reduced for rural area.

5.2   Vernacular Language Software

The problem of language barrier could be overcome with vernacular language software. Softwares are mostly developed in English language. The need of the hour is to realize that most of the people in rural areas are familiar with their native languages only. So it would be a big deal for them to understand and operate softwares in extrinsic language. In this scenario, it would be desirable to develop computer softwares in vernacular languages, just like China, France, Saudi Arabia and others, to cater non-English speaking people, to ease our illiterate people and to draw them towards latest technologies.

5.3   Community Information Centers

Let's go for notion of "Community information centers", community library Centers and Panchayat Centers throughout the country, making sure the availability of IT infrastructure and services. This worthy concept of a community information center has been proposed by IT Task Force. These community centers could turn into pivots of information and education and it would be a source of ICTs awareness to the people on a mass scale. The community computer can be positioned in internet booths at public places, where people can get information for a small price. Practice has revealed that any kind of workout for the training of the rural people inevitably requires interactivity. By invoking ICTs tools, collaborative learning along with dissemination media such as television and radio would be imaginable [10], [11].

5.4   Teleconferencing and Distance Learning

If, after incurring huge expenditure on various educational schemes, rural areas have not become fully literate, the need of the hour is to transform the education system. There is unanimity among experts and scholars that assimilation of ICTs in education will have a progressive influence on the learning atmosphere and consequently boosting education in these areas. It is evident that ICTs could be implemented fruitfully to stretch out a larger number of students, to whom education was hitherto not easily manageable. In presence of ICTs geographical distance will no more an unbeatable impediment to promote education in far wide areas of the country. Verily, teleconferencing and distance learning would be a viable solution for promoting education in these areas [5].

5.5   Introducing ICTs for Farmers

To improve socio-economic status of folks in villages is to make certain that their yields and merchandises trace right kind of markets within no time and without involving various middle men. Introducing ICTs in rural areas will definitely provide promising opportunities to the producers of rural harvests. By providing direct access to rural markets, internets will permit to promote merchandises of rural and remote areas of country to global markets. The farmers can access latest information on farm technology and produces. The government and development agencies have acknowledged the potential of ICTs and online technologies as an essential tool in promoting agriculture, hence various radical communication and technology schemes have been launched [2]. Fig. 3 gives some guidelines and recommendations to promote ICTs in depriving areas of the country.

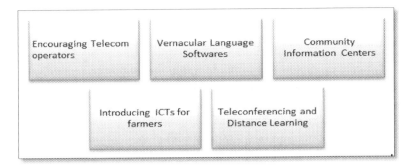

Fig. 3. Solutions and suggestions

6   Conclusion

In nutshell, Improvement in adverse conditions of rural areas owes greatly to ICTs. Information technology could play a crucial role in improving socio-economic conditions of the far wide areas of the country. The upswing of various ICTs and their growing reception and implementation by rural zones will no doubt, provide distinctive openings which could possibly stimulate education, accelerate health facilities and uphold agriculture sector of the country. It's vital need to gauge the adverse situation of ICTs and to take corrective measures to promote them in remote areas of the country. This is the only way to eradicate this digital divide between urban and rural areas.

7   Future Work

Future research is needed to augment this research study by conducting a survey in the rural areas to figure out which barriers are more hampering and to identify the views and anticipations of rural masses regarding ICTs.

References

1. Alleman, J., Rappoport, P., Banerjee, A.: Information Universal service: a new definition 34(1-2), 86–91 (2010)
2. Angello, C., Wema: Availability and usage of ICTs and e-resources by livestock researchers in Tanzania: Challenges and ways forward. International Journal of Education and Development the Developers (IJEDICT) 6(1), 53–65 (2010)
3. Mamaghani, F.: The social and economic impact of information and communication technology on developing countries: An analysis. International Journal of Management 27(3), 607–615, 777 (2010)
4. Qureshi, A., Yasmin, R., Ilyas, Whitty, M., Khan, J.: Information Communication Technologies (ICT) and its Impact on the Livelihood of Communities Involved in the Agriculture: A Case Study of Pakistan (2013)

5. Information and Communication Technology for Education in India and South Asia, Infodev (2010)
6. http://15cci.org.pk/FocusAreaComputerLiteracy.php
7. An evaluation report of IT/Computer Science Teachers, Lab In-charge & Computer Labs Project-Matching Program with Government of Punjab (September 2008)
8. A New Dawn for Millions of Students in Pakistan. Ncomputing (2012)
9. A Review of the Research Literature on Barriers to the Uptake of ICT By Teachers By British Educational Communications and Technology Agency (2004)
10. Sharma, D.C.: http://pib.nic.in/feature/feyr2000/faug2000/f030820002.html
11. Ansari, S.: Telecenters and Community Resource and Information Centers in Pakistan (October 2006)
12. http://www.economic-review.com.pk/may-2013/pakistan-in-the-global-ict-rankings
13. Saleem, H.: (2013), http://insider.pk/national/load-shedding-has-devastated-pakistan/
14. Zaidi, A., http://www.ifad.org/operations/projects/regions/pi/factsheets/pk.pdf
15. Industry Overview. The new economy, economies, http://www.pseb.org.pk/, Information Economics and Policy (retrieved on 24, March 2013)
16. Iftikhar, P.: Universal service fund telecom for all (2012), http://usf.org.pk/FCKeditor/editor/filemanager/connectors/aspx/UserFiles/resources/newsletters/USF%20Presentation%20at%20Secretaries%20IT-Edu%20Conference%20.pdf (retrieved on 28, March 2013)
17. http://4cci.org.pk/ComputerLiteracy.php
18. http://developpakistan.org/
19. http://www.sachet.org.pk/web/
20. http://www.currentaffairspk.com/tag/laptop-scheme-in-punjab/

Positive Technology and User Experience for Human Needs in Developing Countries: Some Considerations

Nils Backhaus, Stefan Brandenburg, and Anna Trapp

Technische Universität Berlin, Chair of Cognitive Psychology and Cognitive Ergonomics
nils.backhaus@tu-berlin.de

Abstract. The present paper highlights the importance of positive technology, user experience, and needs fulfillment in developing countries. It proposes a theoretical framework that enables engineers and interaction designers to develop products that help users to fulfill their interaction needs in this special environment. Put in other words: the proposed environment-sensitive user-centered design framework elicits positive technology for users in developing countries. Adequate methods corresponding to this framework are summarized and effects of positive technology in developing countries are discussed.

Keywords: Rural areas, developing countries, user experience, human needs, socio-technical system approach, user-centered design.

1 Introduction

In western, developed societies technological progress has often been discussed as a trigger to overcome poverty, starving, illiteracy, and social inequality. Comparably to western societies emerging nations like China, India, or Brazil reveal the empowering forces of technological change. Technological development boosted China's economy for example. Economically, China will gain influence in the next years and is likely to become the most powerful economy worldwide before 2030 [1]. However, developing countries seem to miss the boat of technological progress. Their technological level is assumed to be low and technologies are largely non-digitized. From the western perspective the constriction of starvation and poverty as well as of political and social instability can be supported by financial aids and development assistance. Technological progress comes second and is often ignored although it could become a growing resource for developing countries. Information and telecommunication technologies offer benefits for the developing world [2], especially in rural areas. They enable people to easily access knowledge and information via fast communication channels. Hence, information and communication technologies can improve peoples' education [3]. Moreover they give people in geographically outlying regions a voice to make their presence felt in other parts of the earth. Therefore technology can bridge infrastructural shortcomings and empower the lives of humans and help gratifying human needs.

Of course, special challenges on several layers must be kept in mind when developing technology for rural areas in developing countries. In this paper we focus on

A. Marcus (Ed.): DUXU 2014, Part III, LNCS 8519, pp. 400–410, 2014.

user experience (UX) and its requirements as one of the key phenomena of information and communication technology. In literature UX is a buzzword for the holistic quality of interaction between a user and a technology or service [4]. It has been argued that UX is essentially related to perceived usability and aesthetical aspects of an artifact [5] and that it impacts the usage of technical artifacts [6]. Moreover, UX influences user's preferences for a certain product [7]. In addition, both perceived usability and aesthetics affect the user satisfaction [8]. Thus, designing any piece of technology or service should involve the development and evaluation of UX.

Amongst many others, two things are of importance when considering UX in the product development process, the target group and their contextual setting [9]. There are main UX research strands in the western, developed areas that incorporate these issues when developing human machine interfaces. However, when designing for emerging nations the target group and their contextual setting change dramatically. This paper addresses these changes. It argues that elements of the socio-technical system approach should be integrated in the user-centered design process in order to build up UX-sensitive technology and services for rural areas in developing countries. The aim is to show how the western user-centered design process needs to be extended by a human-centered view to make it work for developing countries as well. Therefore this paper presents a new environment-sensitive design model. Subsequently the model will be discussed regarding its implications for the design of human-machine interaction (HMI) and evaluation methods in rural areas in developing countries.

2   User Needs

Technology is delivered in order to please the user and to improve his or her well being [10]. In terms of Maslow's hierarchy of needs [11], positive technology addresses the top of the needs pyramid; the top includes self-actualization and personal growth. Hence, all basic needs like physiological (e. g. food, water) or safety needs (security of the body, health) should be satisfied before people have the need to use pleasing technological artifacts. However, this position of positive technology in Maslow's needs pyramid must be treated with caution since it is culturally coined against a western, individualistic, and capitalistic background [12]. Nowadays it is assumed that needs of different hierarchy levels can co-exist. Therefore needs regarding technological progress may exist even if basic needs are not fully met. Hancock et al. [13] even put up a needs hierarchy for technical artifacts (Fig. 1). In this hierarchy Ergonomics form basic needs. As in Maslow's hierarchy, safety aspects are most important. Besides safety aspects, functionality, and usability aspects belong to ergonomic needs. Usability is to some extent part of the hedonic needs. Here personal preferences and pleasurable experiences play an important role for the user. Comparably to Maslow's hierarchy it can be assumed that the steps of the technological needs are not fully distinct as well. Hence, users might have strong needs regarding a pleasurable (user experience) and satisfactory interface (usability) even if the functionality of the device can be improved.

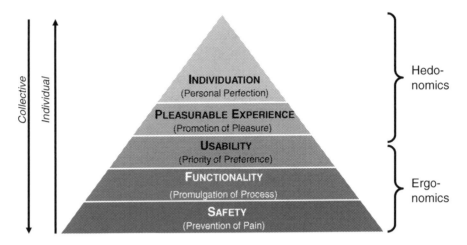

Fig. 1. The technology hierarchy of needs (from [13])

3   User-Centered Design

User-centered design starts with the needs of users [14]. Since users interact with the system via its interface, user needs should be reflected in the interface as well. Users should know where to look for important information. Moreover, they should understand how to access this information. Positive technology and positive UX resolve from interfaces that fulfill user needs. These interfaces can be realized by engineers and interaction designers through user-centered frameworks [e.g. 15–17]. User-centered frameworks define an iterative process and stress that user needs are centered in the middle of the design challenge. Therefore the focus on user needs has to be set very early in the product development process. Users have to participate in each step of the process [18]. Decisions whether the design of an artifact is completed or not, are made based on the degree of the fulfillment of user needs. Usually user centered design frameworks emphasize an iterative design cycle that comprises of four steps: (1) context and demand analysis, (2) requirements definition, (3) drafts, prototyping, and (4) prototype evaluation (see Fig. 2). In addition the user-centered design process proposes a whole lot of methods that can be applied to gather information in each step of the process. Step one of the user-centered design considers the context of use and users demands. However this step loosely subsumes context factors of the environment like lighting conditions [17]. Broader issues like the users' cultural settings are not taken in account. Most methods of demand analysis propose to simply ask users. Hence they assume reflective users and a good understanding between users and the usability engineer. Demand requirements and prototyping may work without too much user involvement. In contrast the prototype evaluation does hardly work without users. For a prototype evaluation it is typically assumed that users are able to read and write. Users should be able to verbalize their thoughts in terms of usability or user experience issues. It is evident that especially the first and last steps of the user-centered process heavily rely on cultural and user characteristics. Hence the theoretical framework has to be adapted in order to account for differences in context and target user groups of developed and developing countries.

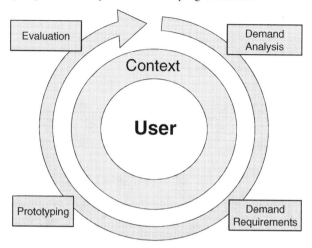

Fig. 2. An exemplary user-centered design process

4   The Socio-Technical System Approach

In HMI research, the perspective of the socio-technical system approach evolved years ago in the wake of the famous Tavistock Studies [19]. It focuses on a holistic perspective on human-machine interaction incorporating man and machine in their respective contexts. In contrast engineers and system designers often emphasize just one single part, either the human or the machine of the HMI system [20]. Tavistock Studies showed that changing either technology or human effects the other part, too. This leads to the credo of the socio-technical HMI definition: Human and machine work together (they interact) to solve a task in a goal-oriented way [21]. This cooperative system generates outputs like services or products. This view of an HMI emphasizes its local environment at a certain time and place (narrow definition in Fig. 3).

However, the global environment affects socio-technical systems as well. There are contextual factors that might be invisible at first sight but have large effects on the over-all system. Integrating the tangible and intangible environment of the HMI leads to a broader view on socio-technical systems (broad definition in Fig. 3). Several factors of the tangible and intangible environment influence both, human and machine. In this paper we emphasize intangible factors like cultural or societal issues and tangible factors, i.e. directly observable factors like weather conditions or the infrastructure of an area where an artifact is implemented. Both shape a HMI implicitly but in a clearly recognizable way and therefore have to be considered in the product development process. Product engineers and product users mostly share large parts of their tangible and intangible world. Therefore considerations of the global environmental (broad definition in Fig. 3) of the socio-technical system are negligible. But as soon as engineers adopt their products and product development processes in culturally different backgrounds, the global environment turns out to be vital and must be taken into account.

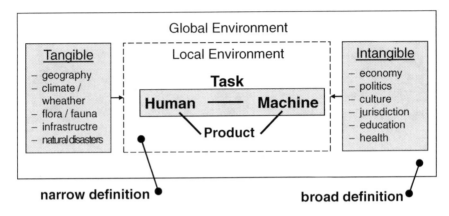

Fig. 3. Framework of socio-technical systems

The adaptation of the socio-technical system approach to developing countries calls for a certain understanding of key factors of this special environment of HMI implementation. Following [22], many developing countries share a number of common characteristics that affect the tangible and intangible properties of the global environment (see also [23], [24]):

- *Economic characteristics:* Due to low aggregate value added, no accretion is attained. Developing countries tend to rely on the primary economic sector (retrieval and production of agricultural and mineral raw materials).
- *Ecological characteristics:* Developmental countries are often faced with ecological problems (species extinction, soil degradation, wood clearing, and high exposure to natural disasters).
- *Demographical characteristics:* The dynamics of the population is coined by a high birthrate, a high (but declining) death rate and infant mortality rate, as well as a low life expectancy, leading to uncontrolled population growth and migration.
- *Public health characteristics:* Unhygienic conditions, shortcomings in medical care and education, and malnutrition often lead to different diseases and pandemics (HIV/Aids).
- *Socio-cultural characteristics:* The coincidence of cultural, societal, and religious behavioral patterns lead to several aspects like sex discrimination or social inequality. Furthermore things like illiteracy, hoarding of the upper classes, child labor can be subsumed under this topic.
- *Political characteristics:* A low efficiency and stability of political institutions and a lack of presence in decentralized regions are often prominent in developing countries. Other aspects cover illiberal regimes, violent conflicts, or civil wars.

Of course not all of these characteristics apply for all developing countries anytime. Oil-exporting countries often have a flourishing economy with a huge social inequality. Newly industrialized economies are defined to be developing countries but miss typical characteristics being at the threshold to an industrialized country. The characteristics of developing countries should be kept in mind when designers and engineers work at new products for developing countries because these characteristics frame the user-centered product development process.

5   The User-Centered Design Process in Developing Countries

As pointed out earlier, designers of technology mostly derive from a developed, western-oriented culture. If they build technical artifacts for developing countries they need to become culturally reflective and sensitive for the factors of the global environment of the socio-technical system. Because the user-centered design process is geared to the local environment of the socio-technical system (see Fig. 3), it is desirable to integrate the factors of the global environment to the user-centered design process. Figure 4 shows the environment-sensitive user-centered design framework. The user and his interaction with the technical artifact are located in the center of the concept. This user-machine dyad, with the task being immanently present, is also called the local environment in the narrow definition of the socio-technical environment. In contrast to the standard user-centered design process the present model proposes that the user and his local environment are itself located in the global environment. As in a multi-shell model, the interaction between user and artifact is not just influenced by his or her immediate surroundings, but also by the large-scale factors of the global environment. These large-scale factors constrain the user's local environment and set the boundaries for the user and his or her possibilities to accomplish his or her needs in an interaction with a technical artifact. Hence, the user-centered design process needs to be sensitive to both, the local and the global environment. This assumption has implications for the user-centered design methods also.

6   Methods

Methods for user-centered design in developing countries should take the HMI local and global requirements in account. Several methods of analyzing the different needs fall short in meeting these requirements. However, some of them may be adapted to these requirements of developing countries.

6.1   Methods and Tangible Requirements

Tangible requirements constrain the type of methods applicable to developing countries. Especially in rural areas there is only little equipment or infrastructure for the methodological approach to HMI. Depending on the degree of urbanization vs. ruralization, there may be no facilities like buildings for testing or interviewing potential users. Methods should be feasible at many different places without a complex setup. Extreme weather conditions call for robust and made-to-last, weatherproof equipment. If electronic technology is used, durable batteries or solar-powered devices should be used to avoid blackouts. Wireless data processing should be kept to a minimal level since the network coverage is often not very high. For example methods like event-related diary studies might work for the documentation of needs (Fig. 4, step 1: demand analysis) and usability problems (Fig. 4, step 4: evaluation)

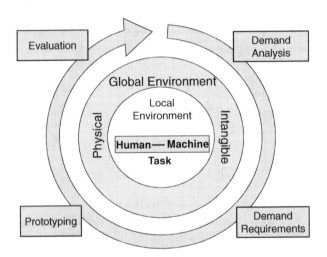

Fig. 4. The environment-sensitive user-centered design framework

6.2   Methods and Intangible Requirements

Intangible characteristics like the ones presented in Fig. 3 form the second set of constraining factors for selecting applicable methods in the environment-sensitive user-centered design process. Especially cultural influences need to be considered. As to that gender roles can play an important role during recruitment of participants and implementation of methods. Women might interact more openly with other women and men feel more respected by male interviewers; in extreme cases woman might even be prohibited to talk to foreigners at all [25]. Another challenge in cross-cultural interaction deals with criticism and feedback. In some cultures it is not appropriate to criticize others, especially people from other cultures. Hence, needs elicitation methods or evaluation methods need to embrace more than just verbal statements like think aloud protocols. Moreover, participants' educational background should be regarded since illiteracy prevents using standard questionnaires. Language barriers can be compensated via translators but the quality of translation and motivational issues of the translator need to be thought of. Minor prior experience with technical devices constrains subjects in their ability to use prior knowledge for interacting with the technical artifact. This might lead to ceiling or floor effects when judging the usability of a technical system. Politics, jurisdiction and peer pressure can influence participants' behavior due to prohibitions and the fear of punishment and embarrassment. Thus methods should always be applied in confidential settings that represent a safe place for communication. Since all intangible factors have a rather soft character, it is advisable to take time to deal with them. For example methods could be integrated into the community before using them.

6.3   Methods Applicable to Developing Countries Settings

Given the tangible and intangible constraints of the global environment, qualitative methods should be favored for gathering information in the environment-sensitive user-centered design process. Qualitative methods have a lot of advantages [26]:

- Due to less standardization and equipment needs, these methods are very flexible and can be easily adjusted to the subjects and the situation.
- Qualitative methods are very open and exploratory to unravel new and unknown issues. Without constraints of the method, subjects often react more freely and openly giving more subjectively information to the interlocutor. Especially for demand analysis, the content focus of the method is chosen by the respondent [27].
- That enables him or her to talk freely about his or her needs and wishes. The respondent can highlight what he thinks is important.
- Qualitative data requires fewer respondents but produces a lot of detailed data.

The disadvantages of qualitative methods should be addressed, too [26]:

- Qualitative methods require much time to approach the respondent.
- The requirements for the interviewer in qualitative settings are very high. He has to be very empathetic, sensitive, and eloquent towards the respondent.
- This requirements increase in developing countries since the interviewer involved in qualitative methods should be familiar with the intangible, cultural background of his or her respondents.

A number of qualitative methods might be appropriate for the situational background of developing countries with none or little adaptation. Qualitative interviews (non-structured) may be used to analyze the wishes, needs, or opinions towards a certain topic in an open way. These interviews may vary in their form. Episodic interviews may deal with a specific situation. For example in HMI this may be the situation of a problem or critical incident that the product is going to address [28]. Narrative interviews inquire a topic very intensively and request the respondents to tell stories [29]. A similar method, using larger samples, is the focus group or group discussion. A moderator leads a discussion concerning a certain topic or issue. Here social interdependencies may drive the discussion [28]. Applying this method one has to be careful because different cultural backgrounds may influence the quality of the method. Many ethnographical methods deal with the topic of observation of respondents. Here respondents are observed in order to gather insights as to the behavior, actions, and the effect on other respondents or persons. The collected data may be used to analyze situations in which a product is used (demand analysis, demand requirements in

Fig. 4) or to analyze the interaction of respondents with an artifact or prototype (prototyping, evaluation in Fig. 4). The interaction can be observed participatory or non-participatory (i.e. the engagement of the observer in the observation), direct and indirect (i.e. recorded/reported or live), and may be open or covert (i.e. the respondents know about being observed). Observational methods often require a large amount of involvement with the people in an environment to analyze their motives and needs deeply.

Whereas qualitative methods bear many advantages for testing and evaluating, some research objectives require a quantitative approach. Quantitative methods aim at generalizability and have their main advantage in the possibility of hypothesis testing [29]. Quantitative data is often based on standardized testing materials. To adjust these methods to developing countries, one needs to anticipate possible obstacles in the subject's interaction with the material. Coping with illiteracy could be implemented via reading questions and items aloud and replacing verbally or numerical anchored scales using a visual analogue scale. Depending on the content visual analogue scales can vary from continuous lines with two end-points to simple pictures or sound files [30]. Emotional content that has a vital relevance in UX testing, can be sampled with a set of different smileys since emotional expressions are assumed to be cross-cultural [31]. However, an unavoidable consequence of adjusting standardized methods is pretesting them.

7   Discussion and Outlook

This paper argued that it is important to develop positive technology for developing countries. Positive technology leads to positive user experience that in turn is related to feelings of competence and the motivation to learn [10]. Hence positive technology might help to motivate people to use technical artifacts and therefore to overcome gaps between developing and developed countries. However, most of the paper focused on a theoretical approach that enables engineers and interaction designers to cope with the special characteristics of developing countries. The environment-sensitive user-centered design framework places the user and his needs accomplishment in the middle of the product development process. In addition the model highlights the role of the global environment. In contrast to other researchers [32] we believe that the environment-sensitive user-centered design framework demonstrates the feasibility of the user-centered design approach in developing countries. However, empirical evidence is still needed to validate the model. This is subject to further investigation.

References

1. Lin, J.Y.: Demystifying the Chinese economy. Cambridge University Press (2011)
2. Munyua, H.: Information and communication technologies for rural development and food security: Lessons from field experiences in developing countries. Sustainable Development Department, Food and Agriculture Organisation of the United Nations (2005)

3. Traxler, J., Kukulka-Hulme, A.: Mobile learning in developing countries. Technical report. Commonwealth of learning: Vancouver (2005)
4. Hassenzahl, M., Tractinsky, N.: User experience - a research agenda. Behav. Inform. Technol. 25, 91–97 (2006)
5. Lee, S., Koubek, R.J.: Users' perceptions of usability and aesthetics as criteria of pre and post-use preferences. Eur. J. Ind. Eng. 6, 87–117 (2012)
6. Zhang, P., Li, N.: Love at first sight or sustained effect? The role of perceived affective quality on user's cognitive reactions to information technology. In: Proceedings of the Twenty-Fifth International Conference on Information Systems (ICIS), pp. 283–296 (2004)
7. Hartmann, J., Sutcliffe, A., de Angeli, A.: Towards a theory of user judgment of aesthetics and user interface quality. ACM T. Comput. -Hum. Int. 15, 15:1–15:30 (2008)
8. Lee, S.: Understanding user experience with computer-based applications with different use purposes. Int. J. Hum. -Com. Int. 29, 689–701 (2013)
9. Law, E.L.C., Roto, V., Hassenzahl, M., Vermeeren, A., Kort, J.: Understanding, scoping and defining user experience: a survey approach. In: Proceedings of 27th International Conference on Human Factors in Computing Systems, pp. 719–728 (2009)
10. Riva, G., Baños, R.M., Botella, C., Wiederhold, B.K., Gaggioli, A.: Positive Technology: Using Interactive Technologies to Promote Positive Functioning. Cyberpsychol. Behav. 15, 69–77 (2012)
11. Maslow, A.H.: A theory of human motivation. Psychol. Rev. 50, 370–396 (1943)
12. Hofstede, G.: The cultural relativity of the quality of life concept. Acad. Manage. Rev. 9, 389–398 (1984)
13. Hancock, P.A., Pepe, A.A., Murphy, L.L.: Hedonomics: The Power of Positive and Pleasurable Ergonomics. Ergonomics Des. 13, 8–14 (2005)
14. Norman, D.A.: Cognitive Engineering. In: Norman, D.A., Draper, S.W. (eds.) User Centered System Design: New Perspectives on Human Computer Interaction. Erlbaum, Hillsdale (1986)
15. ISO 9241-210:210: Ergonomics of human-system interaction – Part 210: Human-centred design for interactive systems. ISO Geneva (2010)
16. Mayhew, D.J.: The Usability Engineering Lifecycle – a practitioners handbook for user interface design. Academic Press, San Diego (1999)
17. Wickens, C.D., Lee, J.D., Liu, Y., Becker, S.E.G.: An Introduction to Human Factors Engineering. Pearson Education, Upper Saddle River (2004)
18. Schuler, D., Namioka, A.: Participatory Design: Principles and Practices. Lawrence Erlbaum Associates, Hillsdale (1993)
19. Trist, E.: The evolution of socio-technical systems: a conceptual framework and an action research program. Occasional paper (No. 2). Ontario Quality of Working Life Centre, Toronto (1981)
20. Ropohl, G.: Philosophy of Socio-Technical Systems (1999), http://scholar.lib.vt.edu/ejournals/SPT/v4_n3html/ROPOHL.html#emery
21. Timpe, K.-P., Jürgensohn, T., Kolrep, H.: Mensch-Maschine-Systemtechnik: Konzepte, Modellierung, Gestaltung, Evaluation. Symposion, Düsseldorf (2002)
22. Wikipedia (2014), http://de.wikipedia.org/wiki/Entwicklungsland#Gemeinsame_Merkmale_der_Entwicklungsl.C3.A4nder
23. United Nations Development Programme: Human Development Report 2013. Technical Notes. United Nations Organization, New York City, NY (2013)
24. Campbell, D.F.J.: The Basic Concept for the Democracy Ranking of the Quality of Democracy. Democracy Ranking, Vienna (2008)

25. IDEO: Human-Centered Design Toolkit (2011), http://www.ideo.com/work/human-centered-design-toolkit
26. Flick, U., von Kardorff, E., Steinke, I.: Qualitative Forschung: Ein Handbuch. Rowohlt, Reinbek (2000)
27. Millen, D.R.: Rapid ethnography: time deepening strategies for HCI field research. In: Proceedings of the 3rd Conference on Designing Interactive Systems: Processes, Practices, Methods, and Techniques, pp. 280–286 (2000)
28. Lazar, J., Feng, J.H., Hochheiser, H.: Research methods in human-computer interaction. John Wiley & Sons, Hoboken (2010)
29. Häder, M.: Empirische Sozialforschung, 2nd edn. VS Verlag für Sozialwissenschaften, Wiesbaden (2010)
30. Schrammel, J., Geven, A., Tscheligi, M.: Using Narration to Recall and Analyse User Experiences and Emotions Evoked by Today's Technology. In: Karlsson, M.A., Desmet, P.M.A., van Erp, J. (eds.) Proceedings from the 5th Conference on Design and Emotion (2006)
31. Ekman, P., Friesen, W.V.: Constants across cultures in the face and emotion. J. Pers. Soc. Psychol. 17, 124–129 (1971)
32. Shen, S.-T., Woolley, M., Prior, S.: Towards culture-centred design. Interact. Comput. 18, 820–852 (2006)

Transforming Data into Information Experiences

María González de Cossío

Universidad Autónoma Metropolitana Cuajimalpa,
Av. Vasco de Quiroga 4871, Delegación Cuajimalpa de Morelos, D.F. 05300, México
mgonzalezc@correo.cua.uam.mx

Abstract. The focus/perspective described in this paper relies on the different experiences visitors have through the interaction with an information space, in this case an exhibition on social mobility. Two levels of knowledge appropriation are described. First, the exhibition takes visitors from a general / local environment; to an individual space; to an intimate introspection life and planning; and finally, to the integration with others. Second, the exhibition provides valuable information to understand social and economic issues; invites visitors to identify and see themselves reflected on the information; creates the environment to share ideas with others and learn from success stories; and lastly, the exhibition presents examples that show that social mobility is easier when one works within a group. Information design is at the core of the exhibition and brings together verbal graphic language using a variety of means to convey the message of social mobility through education.

Keywords: Information, interaction, knowledge appropriation, graphs, rhetoric.

1 Introduction

Mexico is a country with poverty and inequality. By 2006 it did not have, as many countries in the world, studies that show if there was any socio economic evolution between generations. The NGO Espinosa Rugarcía Foundation (ESRU) carried in 2006 and then in 2011, the only intergenerational social mobility surveys in the country. The studies offer data that show to what extent Mexican society has been moving in the socioeconomic ladder[1] in the last forty years. Data also depict the interaction among variables such as age, education, migration, intergenerational social movement, women status, and income level from different generations. The 2011[2] survey is the only study that provides data that differentiates roles between male and female as household heads, and in topics such as education, salaries, occupation, living conditions, etc. In this text, the main topic regarded is social mobility through education.

Results show that there are two factors that condition social mobility in Mexico [3]; on the one hand, public policies are essential, such as social infrastructure, teachers'

---

[1] ESRU's Foundation definition of social Mobility is: 'the easiness with which a person can climb to a higher level in the socioeconomic ladder' [1]. (Serrano and Torche, 2007).
[2] The survey is referred to as EMOVI 2011 [2].

A. Marcus (Ed.): DUXU 2014, Part III, LNCS 8519, pp. 411–422, 2014.

study levels, quality education and laws, etc depend on the government. On the second hand, the results show that personal and family context and decisions are crucial for a better outcome. Decisions such as whether to study or not, finish a whole educational cycle, hard work, discipline, and others, are in parents and children's hands. Sometimes, parents and even teachers do not grasp the importance of those decisions.

Looking at this panorama, and after several studies directed to public policies, ESRU decided to approach the second factor, namely the personal and family decisions and contexts, to enhance social mobility. Ordinary people, young people, parents and teachers were approached to convey the importance of education to enhance social mobility. The proposal was to develop an exhibition on the topic and to present it in various places in Mexico.

2 The Design Problem

The design problem consisted of developing an information system on how to communicate the main ideas behind social mobility and education. The results of the survey done by ESRU in 2011, suggest that people's attitudes are fundamental to promote social mobility. This was the basis for the exhibition, to address people's awareness and acknowledge the importance of education in order to achieve a better socioeconomic level. The solution should be easily understandable, effective, and should shake people's minds and attitudes. The design solution should empower users into new ways of viewing their future and foresee the possibilities they could have if they make a proper decision.

The solution should offer a new way to convey the importance of education to move in the socioeconomic ladder, and reach as many people as possible, especially those who have fewer opportunities. The goal was to have visitors appropriate the experiences and information presented at the exhibition and transform them into knowledge.[3]

Interactive graphs[4] previously designed [6] on this topic were the cornerstone for the itinerant exhibition that would travel throughout the country. The exhibition is the result of an interdisciplinary team who applied a thorough design process, from the conception of the project to the evaluation of its impact on visitors. It is relevant to say that there are no recollections of previous exhibitions on the topic.

---

[3] Shedroff [4] explains this chain in his diagram 'The scheme of understanding' where data is transformed into information; information into knowledge; and knowledge into wisdom.

[4] A group of 7 graphs on topics such as perception of Mexicans on their socioeconomic level; indigenous jobs; children's education in relation to their parents' education, etc can be consulted at the Centro de Estudios Espinosa Yglesias' site [5].

3   Main Questions to Be Answered

There were main questions that had to be answered in order to design the exhibition such as, What for and for whom? Which data? How it should be transformed into information? What kind of media should be presented? Should interactions with the information be included? How visitors appropriate information?

3.1   What for and for Whom?

The objective of the exhibition was to promote young people's awareness of the importance of education to improve their socioeconomic level. The exhibition should empower users into visualising new ways of imagining their future, as well as foreseeing the possibilities they could have, if they made a proper decision related to education. The exhibition was addressed to young people from 14 to 24 years old from low and medium income levels that might be at risk of abandoning their studies or who do not appreciate the advantage of studying. Teachers and parents should also be considered as important users (indirect users) involved in this project because they are direct influences, –and even decision makers–, on young people's development. Therefore, relevant materials should also be included in the exhibition for parents and teachers.

For the development of the exhibition, two focus groups were observed when general concepts for the exhibit were presented. It was important to see their reactions and listen to their opinions to enrich the initial proposal. The first focus group consisted of young university students and the second group consisted of young people who dropped out of school, mainly because of economic reasons. A strong comparison between groups was observed, from open beliefs and optimism to depression and failure. Both types of participants came from medium low socioeconomic levels, without training or the habit to read graphs or economic data. Their reading and language skills were in development, attracted to visuals, eager to interact with technology and sensitive to music.

The specific objectives of the project were:

- Visitors should develop awareness on the data presented.
- Visitors should understand the basic concepts on social mobility through clear and simple information.
- Visitors should be stimulated to change attitudes.
- Visitors should appropriate information for their lives.
- Policy makers should also become aware of the socioeconomic situation.

3.2   Which Data? How should it be Transformed into Information?

The surveys on Social Mobility [7] were the main data source. The selection of topics, under the guidance of development economists, was carefully put together. The main topics selected for the exhibition were: data on poverty and inequality, social mobility and its relation to education, the importance of individual social mobility, and social mobility within the community.

The transformation of these data into information required careful consideration of users/visitors[5] as the centre of the exhibition. Visitors characteristics guided into design decisions, such as:

- The language should be simple, clear and concise, either in verbal or written texts.
- Narratives should be meaningful; some narratives should be addressed to young people, and others to teachers and parents.
- The images should help visitors identify[6] with the contents; images should complement and visualise the text.
- Use of innovative technology to surprise visitors.
- Interactions should be simple so as to let visitors share their opinions; interactions should enable them to achieve good results and feel successful.
- Storytelling as a means to connect with visitors.
- Music should appeal emotions.

There were other constraints related to the design of the structure and the space modelling. The exhibition should be inexpensive, but attractive; easy to pack and unpack, but strong, and light weighted for easy transportation. It should also be possible that the exhibition could be hosted in spaces with different shapes. Therefore, it was designed in modules that could be organised in different ways without loosing its concept: as a square, as an L shape or in a linear way. The panels should carry their own lightning and electric power. The exhibition space should be covered to keep off from sunlight and give proper conditions for electronic equipment and video projections.

The exhibition space should invite people to go inside, provide environment for interaction, hold the groups of visitors together and should be meaningful to those who visit it.

3.3   Rhetorical Approach to the Exhibition

Visitors at the exhibition should react and respond to the different messages. The exhibition was planned to promote questioning, thought and change of attitudes. Aristotle defines three main ways of rhetorical communication: the appeal to reason and logic (logos); the appeal to emotions and feelings (pathos); and the appeal to moral and ethical values (ethos) [9]. Designed objects should have the three components to provoke a response.

The objects at the exhibition were carefully selected and designed to have a balanced combination of the three appeals, and for the different types of visitors (young people, parents and teachers).

---

[5] In this information design project, 'visitors' will substitute the term 'users'.

[6] Shah and Hoeffner [8] distinguished three major processes of graph comprehension; first, users must identify visual presentation of the graph, second, viewers must relate the visual features to the concepts represented, and third, users should be able to identify the referent of the concepts in the graph.

4   How Visitors Appropriate Information?

Why appropriation? Appropriation entails taking something for oneself by own right, and it is considered a distinctive relationship than that of learning or assimilating [10]. The appropriation of main concepts is achieved through various ways and it can happen when people interact with objects of their interest. 'Knowledge evolves through the interaction –reciprocal action- of an individual with other entities; information is conceptualised and used in an efficient way every time the person is confronted with new situations that require such knowledge' [11]. Therefore, knowledge appropriation involves a person, a knowledge object, and a context of interaction.

   In a similar way, Kosslyn [12] explained that for effective communication, designers should use familiar concepts and display formats to the user. He also refers to this as the Principle of Appropriate Knowledge: 'Readers can know how to interpret a display only if they have already stored the necessary background in memory. […] Know your audience, and present your information accordingly'.

   These premises were applied to the exhibition. Besides, a trained guide accompanied each group of visitors through the exhibition to assure understanding and appropriation. In each room knowledge objects were placed with significant information, such as visual graphs, videos, texts to appeal in various ways to visitors. The exhibition guide facilitated with explanations, discussions and interactions. As a result, in each room there was a different and unexpected way to approach visitors. The initial pieces presented theoretical and objective information about the topic. Whence this information was presented, visitors were expected to think about the information, question it, relate to it, and wrap up the experience with interaction. Through this process of appropriation, the person built, constructed new representations or interpretations, and new perspectives emerged. While visiting the exhibition, 'it is important to facilitate emotional experiences and conversations, fun, interaction, make feasible that visitors interpret meanings, analyze them, make inferences and give explanations' [13].

   Information and interactions were structured in two different levels, related to the type of contents presented at the exhibition and the type of experiences visitors could have.

4.1   First Level

What the contents of information should be? What cognitive processes should visitors experience in each of the four rooms of the exhibition? In the first room, the information space should take visitors through a narrative that makes them face and understand the information provided. In the second room, visitors should identify their family situation with the graphs and images shown, and develop relationships to their family social mobility. In the third room visitors should question themselves and answer specific issues. Lastly, in the fourth room, visitors should confirm what others have achieved working together.

4.2   Second Level

What visitors should experience at the exhibition? What other cognitive and emotional processes should visitors go through at the exhibition? This could be explained as a trip from general information to its appropriation, and then to personal insights. In the first room, the information space should make visitors glance through the national socioeconomic situation to become aware and sensitive to the problems depicted. In the second room they should arrive at their immediate living conditions of their own family and project themselves in the graphs and images shown. In the third room visitors should think about their intimate life; they should go through introspection and imagination of their own future. Finally, in the last room visitors should foresee their connection to others.

Information design underlies the four exhibition rooms, but the degree of logical and objective explanations varies from room to room. There are some pieces that are more directed to the emotional or pathos appeal, and others to the ethical one. Here is a description of the two levels in which visitors engage in the information space:

When visitors arrive at the exhibition, they have to separate themselves from the outside world and immerse in a new space and into the same reality, here and now. Visitors start their engagement in the first space by viewing Mexico's contrasts, poverty and inequality. For example, they are faced with the crude reality that is ignored from everyday life's sight, they see graphics that show the slow evolution of Mexico in comparison to a rich country such as Sweden[7], inequality between boys and girls' education, men and women salary differences, and income inequality between rich and poor Mexicans. During the explanation, the guide asks questions to assure that visitors understand the concepts and are engaging in the topic. Awareness of the country's situation is the main objective of the information presented.

While looking at the different pieces, visitors perform various mental operations such as: making comparisons, questioning issues, contrasting information, making relations to personal situations, and making logical operations such as understanding definitions. The first space is key in preparing visitors' consciousness for the next exhibition room.

In the second space, visitors are taken from the general depiction of the country, to their local family situation throughout time. They are presented with few basic definitions of social mobility, absolute and relative mobility; graphic descriptions that relate income level to education level; quotes addressed to teachers; graphs that show students performance in relation to the teacher's involvement. Visitors have to identify publicly or privately what kind of living conditions had their grandparents and which is their present living environment. Through these selections they figure out if their family has moved in the socioeconomic ladder, either upwards or downwards. In this space they focalised from general situation to their close and immediate environment. The information objects make them understand social mobility, identify their home situation, know how education influences income level and project themselves in the different cases depicted.

In the third space, after being in touch with their immediate reality, and having familiarized with topics on poverty and inequality, and education and social mobility, visitors are asked to go through an introspective phase. They are asked to share with

---

[7] Sweden was in a similar situation as Mexico 75 years ago, but with the government's action to educate people, they became in one of the most equal societies [14] [15].

the group their thoughts and insights to plan their future through an interactive experience[8]. The guide poses four questions to the group, such as: who they are, what they want to achieve, what are the obstacles and opportunities they face in order to achieve their goals. Visitors are invited to answer one question at a time. They write the answer in tablets and when they are satisfied with the text, they publish their thoughts and feelings. Their answers appear on an interactive touch table, which is at the centre of the room. The answers are then shown on a screen as a word cloud that expands as words are repeated. The guide's role is very important because he/she gives visitors the confidence to share their thoughts and discuss them openly with the group.

After sharing their views and discussing how they would like to see themselves in the near future, visitors listen to recorded testimonies of people who have moved into a better life.

In the fourth and last space, visitors realise the importance to be in contact with others. They go from their intimate reflection and examples of people who achieve a higher socioeconomic level in the previous space, to the importance of considering and connecting to 'the others'. Participation of the transformation of public space is the first example they see. People from a small community changed their street by painting their houses and dignifying their immediate environment. Visitors also witness disciplined and committed teamwork shown in a video of a children's orchestra. Afterwards, they experience working together through the interaction with a video game trying to imitate the children's orchestra performance. This game requires working as a team to achieve a number of points. Different quotes and graphics are placed at the room to remind visitors that education is the key component for social mobility. Final pieces at the exhibition leave visitors a positive feeling and wish for a better future.

As one can see, the two levels described before mingle together in four spaces, that make visitors go sequentially from immersion in the country's reality –and possibly their own situation– to their close environment, to intimacy and the importance of others. Visitors also engage in understanding information, identifying in the situations depicted, and sharing their own ideas and projects with others.

4.3   What Were Visitors Responses to the Exhibition?

In four months time, the exhibition has been hosted by two different venues[9] in Puebla, Mexico, and has already received 6,300 visitors from different areas and back-

---

[8] Simon [16] says that the best participatory experiences are in small groups. They should support people to feel comfortable engaging in the activity. 'It requires a careful balancing act between structure and flexibility'.

[9] The first institution that hosted the exhibition was Universidad Iberoamericana Puebla (UIA-P); it is a private university whose doors are not opened to everyone. People have to show an identification card to enter at the university. The second venue is a public university, Benemérita Universidad Autónoma de Puebla (BUAP) and the exhibition could be accessed through a direct door to the streets of the city centre. This venue received many more groups coming from public high schools and people walking on the street.

grounds. Knowing people's reactions to the exhibition was indispensable to find out whether the objectives were fulfilled.

Two types of testing were designed for this purpose: a quantitative test of 4,089 visitors and applied by an external consultant, and a qualitative test of 10 visitors performed by the author.

1. Quantitative test. Visitors answered either in printed or electronic media a questionnaire regarding taste, definition of social mobility, main obstacles for moving, main opportunities identified for success, a one-word definition of the exhibition, and additional comments. The results show that the exhibition's message is very clear and conclusive. Education and will are the major incentives; oneself and apathy are the main slow downs to education. However there are situational aspects or group dynamics that influence these last results [17].

However there are some differences in the results depending of which of the two venues visitors attended to.

Table 1. Quantitative results: opportunities and obstacles

Visitors answers	First venue (UIA-P)	Second venue (BUAP)
Visitors mentioned that they have opportunities such as study and learning	39.7%	32.8%
Visitors mentioned that they have opportunities related to attitudes, self-effort and will	19.3%	27.8%
Visitors mentioned having obstacles such as: oneself, will, conformism, fear	24.4%	38%
Visitors mentioned obstacles such as: laziness, apathy and comfort	16%	7.7%

Table 2. Quantitative results: One-word description of the exhibition

Description of the exhibition	First venue	Second venue
Excellent, extraordinary, awesome	26.7%	20.2%
Educational, informative	21.1%	10.9%
Good, intelligent	14.9%	21.6%
Thoughtful, conscientious, provoking	10.1%	8.7%
Stimulating, inspiring	9.2%	14.2%
Dynamic, creative, interactive	4.8%	3.6%
Fun, entertaining	3.2%	4.5%
Innovative, creative	2.7%	8.7%
Negative comments	0.8%	0.8%

2. Qualitative test. Visitors were asked to select the three pieces per room that were more meaningful to them, in terms of the information presented, of their emotional responses and their credibility to the pieces presented. In other words, the three

rhetorical ways of convincing established by Aristotle were questioned. Visitors explained their reasons for each piece selected.

Visitors' selection was varied; they chose almost every exhibition panel. However, there were pieces that were frequently selected. Here is the distribution of their choices by room.

Visitors also answered how they would describe and recommend the exhibition to other people.

Some significant phrases they mentioned were:

'We were confronted with reality. It is true'

'It made us think, question and share'

The interactive table was also mentioned several times. Visitors mentioned that they were given the opportunity to think about their future and share their feelings. They seemed not having these kind of questioning.

Some visitors appreciated the opportunity they had to think freely and to imagine how they would like to be in the future, share their views and discuss them with the group. They suggested visiting the exhibition without parents or grandparents because they felt controlled.

Some visitors asked the organizers if the exhibition could travel to their hometown because they wanted their own people to see it and experience it.

As one can see from both, quantitative and qualitative tests, the exhibition had a strong impression on visitors.

Fig. 1. The first graph shows the differences of goods and services of two parents and children. The pictures show the comparison between Mexico and Sweden households lowest socioeconomic levels. The text says: "if you were in the lowest socioeconomic level, this would be your house".

Table 3. Answers to qualitative questions

Exhibition rooms	Pieces frequently selected	Visitors' comments
Room 1. This is Mexico	Comparison between Mexico and Sweden	'If Sweden could achieve a higher level, why Mexico cannot?' 'Sweden is clean, ordered.'
Room 2. Social mobility and education	Graphs on education and income	'If we had more opportunities we would have a better national level.'
	Intergenerational mobility	'I only studied highschool. Here, I commit to study a Bachelor's.'
Room 3: Imagine your future	Interactive table	'It gave us the opportunity to think about our lives, question it and share it with others.'
	Testimonies	'One can confirm ideas. These examples show you that it is not too late to study, because some voices are not that young.'
Room 4: social mobility and the community	Children's orchestra	'Inspiring' 'These children learn to value.'
logical appeal (logos)	Graph on goods and services	'It provokes a private commitment with oneself.'
Emotional appeal (pathos)	Video on poverty [18]	'Indifference to poverty. We do not see it anymore.'
Ethical appeal (ethos)	Various answers, but inequality was the most repeated	

5   Conclusions

The information design system proved to be very effective. Quantitative tests results show that a large percentage of visitors left the exhibition with understanding social mobility concepts and clear ideas on the importance of education to achieve a higher socioeconomic level. Qualitative tests results show that the exhibition was meaningful to most visitors. Young people realised that they have not had the chance to think about their future, question it and plan their future.

It was relevant to test from an external consultancy because they could give objective data on the impact of the exhibition, which was later confirmed by the 'in-house' qualitative test, which shed additional and detailed information.

Interdisciplinary teamwork was crucial in the concept development, graphic and information design, industrial design, interactive design, film, and the general organization of the exhibition. Information design considered the whole range of issues, contents, language use, adequacy of images, narrative, organization of the venues, development of manuals, engagement of institutions that support education, testing, legal permissions, etc.

This project showed that it is possible for information designers to intervene in social issues of this importance.

Acknowledgements. The interdiscipline team that worked together for the exhibition were: Centro de Estudios Espinosa Yglesias (Study on Social Mobility, socioeconomic data: Roberto Vélez), Abracadabra (Graphic design: Benito Cabañas), Core design (Industrial design: Rigoberto Cordero), Rayya (videos: Gerardo and David Sánchez Yanes), Efectos Digitales Interactivos (Interactive design: Ariel Molina), Centro de Estudios Avanzados de Diseño (general coordination: Cecilia Orvañanos and María González de Cossío), Factum (marketing studies: Alberto Martínez de Velasco).

References

1. Serrano, J., Torche, F.: Nos movemos? In: La movilidad social en México, Fundación ESRU, México (2008)
2. Centro de Estudios Espinosa Yglesias, http://www.ceey.org.mx
3. Centro de Estudios Espinosa Yglesias: Informe. Movilidad social en México 2013. Imagina tu futuro. Editorial CEEY, Mexico (2013)
4. Shedroff, N.: Information Interaction Design: a Unified field Theory of Design. In: Jacobson, R. (ed.) Information Design, pp. 267–292. MIT Press, Massachussets (1999)
5. Centro de Estudios Espinosa Yglesias, http://www.ceey.org.mx/site/movilidad-social/graficas-interactivas-sobre-movilidad-social-mexico
6. González de Cossío, M.: Social Mobility in Mexico. Information Design Journal Graphs that help in Understanding the Relation Between Education and Socioeconomic Level 17(3), 246–260 (2009)
7. Centro de Estudios Espinosa Yglesias: Informe. Movilidad Social en México 2013. Imagina tu futuro. Editorial CEEY, Mexico (2013)
8. Shah, P., Hoeffner, J.: Review of Graph Comprehension. Research: Implications for Instruction. Educational Psychology Review 14(1), 47–69 (2002)
9. Ehses, H.: Design on a Rhetorical Footing. CEAD, Puebla (2009)

10. Peñalosa Castro, E., Méndez Granados, D., García Hernández, C., Espinosa Meneses, M.: La apropiación del conocimiento en comunicación y educación para la ciencia: una propuesta de conceptualización. Universidad Autónoma Metropolitana Cuajimalpa (manuscript)

11. García Hernández, C., Espinosa Meneses, M.: Espacio, cuerpo y apropiación de conocimiento en los museos. Universidad Autónoma Metropolitana Cuajimalpa (manuscript)

12. Kosslyn, S.M.: Graph Design for the Eye and Mind, p. 34. Oxford University Press, New York (2006)

13. García Hernández, C., Espinosa Meneses, M.: Espacio, cuerpo y apropiación de conocimiento en los museos, Universidad Autónoma Metropolitana Cuajimalpa (manuscript)

14. Maddison, A.: Historical Statistics (2012), http://www.ggdc.net/maddison/Maddison.htm

15. World Bank: Indicadores (2012), http://datos.bancomundial.org

16. Simon, N.: The Participatory Museum, Museum, California, vol. 20, p. 269 (2010)

17. Factum: Movilidad social. Estudio cuantitativo. Reporte total de resultados Iberoy BUAP. Puebla (2014)

18. Museo de Memoria y Tolerancia: http://www.youtube.com/watch?v=rq5QzqmgNzI

Design for Rural Community Regarding Health

Shahzaib Iftikhar, Umar Muzaffer, Abbas Illyas,
Tayyab Asif Butt, Hassan Ejaz, and Muhammad Faraz Khokhar

University of Gujrat, Gujrat, Pakistan
(10050656-068,10050656-087,10050656-096,10050656-115,
10050656-091,10050656-021)@uog.edu.pk

Abstract. Pakistan is a developing country and it has lot of issues but health is its one of the leading issue because up to 67% of its population is currently in rural areas. Rural community of Pakistan is badly affected by this issue. Allocation and distribution of resources in the Pakistan is un equal because of this inequality, rural community suffers a lot regarding serious health issues and facing many dangerous diseases. Both developed and developing countries report geographically skewed distribution of healthcare professionals, favoring urban and wealthy areas, despite the fact that people in rural communities are experiencing many health related problems. To prevent from this big problem govt. should distribute the resources equally and provide the necessary staff and skilled professionals to rural community and introduce such a system which helps them to decrease the healthcare issues. We are going to propose a design for the rural community which helps them to facilitate with first aid in emergency problems and give them relief. It can help them in a cases like maternity etc.

Keywords: Facilities, Maternity, Resources, Health, Govt. Expenditures, Rural Areas, Pakistan, Problems.

1   Introduction

Health plays the productive role in determining the human capital. A better health improves the productivity of labor force. In all over the world Pakistan considered as developing country and the population of Pakistan is almost according to the research of 2008 is 130 million. Pakistan facing many critical problems in which two problems are inversely proportional to each other one is illiteracy and other is high fertility rate and according to economic scenario Pakistan's economic graph go down and down with the passage of time. The ratio of maternity mortality is 340/100,000 live births as well as infant maternity rate is 86/1000 live birth. In the case of health women and children are the most UN protected segment against maternity attack. The statistics about mortality which is given above is the worst statistics in the world. The cause of mortality in the present age of medical is much avoided.

Deaths because of pregnancy of women who lived in Pakistan are 1 in 80 compared to 1 in 61 in developing countries statistics as a whole in 40.85 in industrial countries. A high maternal issue in Pakistan is due to absence of maternal health data. The accurate measurement regarding maternal mortality is quiet difficult in rural

A. Marcus (Ed.): DUXU 2014, Part III, LNCS 8519, pp. 423–431, 2014.
© Springer International Publishing Switzerland 2014

community. Sindh is most populous province of Pakistan after Punjab. "Majority of population of Sindh lived in rural areas". [1]in this province high fertility rate with addition to high mortality rate show the bad governance and dismal picture of health in the province. "The women in this area which are pregnant 40 percent of them suffer from anemia" [2] and also facing hemorrhagic complications in pregnant women in rural areas of Sindh. There is need of most effective and efficient strategies regarding health care in rural area of Pakistan in case of maternity.

"Women were asked whether there were any deaths due to obstetric complications in the household in the last three years.61% women received their antenatal care in their last pregnancy"[3]

According to the Economic survey of Pakistan in (2005/06), on health sector Government of Pakistan spent their 0.75% of GDP to make their population more healthy and sturdy. In this way numerous numbers of programs are run regarding health facilities in Pakistani rural areas. Many agencies and NGOs spent their time to help needy people and try to reduce poverty but they also don't have many facilities to entertained people. [4]

First aid precautions about this disease also play a vital role to save the lives of rural community. Government spends its expenditures in health sector just 0.7% per year but it's not enough for massive populated areas in developed country like Pakistan. The education sector also infected from this budget. [5]

2   Literature Review

Although about 68 percent of Pakistan's population lives in rural areas. While some small groups and UN bodies observe health problems in Pakistan, most national NGOs, the government and the media do not give special attention to the rural area's health problems. The health care system in Pakistan [11] is beset with numerous problems like structural fragmentation, gender insensitivity, resource scarcity, inefficiency and lack of accessibility and utilization.

2.1   Problem Identification

The issue which is faced by rural community is lack of emergency maternity health care centers. The survey was conducted from May 2010 to December 2011. Survey based on 314,623 women at 16 facilities in Punjab, Sindh and Islamabad, who were studied to determine the occurrence and management of maternal and neonatal problems.. There were 94 near-miss maternal mortality cases and 38 maternal deaths, giving a maternal mortality ratio of 299 per 100,000 births.

Much of this stems from the low incidence of skilled birth attendance and high fertility rates. What is more alarming is that the rate of skilled birth attendance a proxy for maternal mortality has actually declined from 48 percent in 2004–06 to 41 percent in 2008/09 (Pakistan, Planning Commission, 2010). The situation is even worse in rural areas where the maternal mortality rate is almost double that of urban areas: 319 per 100,000 in rural areas and 175 per 100,000 in urban areas (Pakistan, Planning Commission, 2010). [6]

The report suggested four main reasons of this in which two of them related to accessibility i.e.

- Delay in transporting patient to primary or secondary health care centers.
- The delay occurs at health care centers due to unavailability of professional medical staff.
- Another important aspect related to this is the absence of decision maker.
- Due to strong cultural and religious norms; traveling of rural women is very limited and often household head is responsible for distant travel decisions.

2.2 Policies Emphasizing Health Care Services in Pakistan

Pakistan is in the middle of epidemiological transition where almost 40 percent of total burden of disease (BOD) is accounted for by infectious/communicable diseases. These include diarrheal diseases, acute respiratory infections, malaria, tuberculosis, hepatitis B&C, and immunisable childhood diseases. Another 12 percent is due to reproductive health problems. Nutritional deficiencies particularly iron deficiency anemia, Vitamin-A deficiency, iodine deficiency disorders account for further 6 percent of the total BOD.In Pakistan, the Statistics of dying under the age of five child mortality is at 101 per 1,000 live births with a life expectancy of 62 years. Table below indicates some comparative health indicators. The major problem in Pakistan seemed by some specialist in reference of child mortality. In 2004 on immunization of children under 12 month age shows that 33% didn't get immunization against measles and 20% didn't get immunization against tuberculosis, diphtheria, pertussis and tetanus.[6] According to age wise the expectation of life in Pakistan are given in the table below:

There are numerous number of policies held for providing better health care service in Pakistan. Including Millennium Development Goals (MDG), Poverty Reduction Strategy Papers and National Health Policy.

Table 1. Source: WHO (2006)*Calculated by NIPS (2006)

	Total Popula-tion(000)	Life Expec-tancy at Birth(Years) Both Sexes	Probability of Dying (per1000) underage 5 years Both Sexes	1 Year Old Fully Immunized (%) Against Measles	TB	Population Growth Rate(%) 1994-2004	Physicians (per100 ,000 People) 1990-2004
Bangladesh	139,215	62	77	95	77	2.0	26
Bhutan	2,116	63	80	92	87	2.2	5
China	1,315,409	72	31	94	84	0.8	106
India	1,087,124	62	85	73	56	1.7	60
Nepal	26,591	61	76	85	73	2.3	21
Pakis-tan	154,794	62	101	80	67	1.9*	74
Sri-Lanka	20,570	71	14	99	96	1.0	55

2.3   Health Millennium Development Goals(2015)

Pakistan has adopted 16 targets and 37 indicators from 18 targets and 48 indictors fixed by the UN Millennium Declaration for achieving eight millennium goals. Pakistan is the only country which was signed to UN Millennium Development Goals (MDG), 2000-2015. Three of the eight MDGs emphasize directly to health sector with four targets and sixteen indicators. The MDGs include: Reducing Child Mortality (1 target, 6 indicators); Improving Maternal Health (1 target, 5 indicators) and Combating HIV/AIDS, Malaria and Other Diseases (2 targets, 5 indicators). [6]

Table 2. Reduce by Three-quarters, between 1990 and 2015, the Maternal *Mortality Rate*

Indicators	Definitions
Maternal mortality ratio	No. of mothers dying due to complications ofpregnancy and delivery per 100,000 live births
Proportion of births attended by skilled birthattendants	Proportion of deliveries attended by skilledhealth personnel (MOs, midwives, LHVs)
Contraceptive prevalence rate	Proportion of eligible couples for family planning programs using one of the contraceptive methods
Total fertility rate	Average number of children a woman delivered during her reproductive age
Proportion of women 15-49 years who had given birth during last 3 years and made at least one antenatal care consultation	Proportion of women (15-49) who deliveredduring the last 3 years and received at least one antenatal care during their pregnancy period from either public/private care providers

2.4   Access to Health Care Centers in Rural Areas

The major challenges in Pakistan rural areas facing by Pakistan underlining are maternal mortality and morbidity. Progress underlining proportion of women (15-49) who gave birth in last 3 years and are attended by the skilled birth attendants is somewhat satisfactory; however the maternal mortality is unsatisfactory.

There has been negative improvement in the mortality ratio for example Out of 100,000 live births 350 mothers died due to complications of pregnancy in 2000-2001 and it reaches 400 deaths in 2004-2005 whereas MDG targets is 140 in decade time. On the other hand, targets for skilled birth attendants and antenatal care are on track but still need efforts to achieve the MDG targets in Pakistan. This major factor of increasing in deaths is due to unavailability of gynecologist doctors whether its male/female, in rural areas and also there is no first aid maternal health care centers. The proper treatment of pregnant women during the period of pregnancy would reduce the complications facing by them.

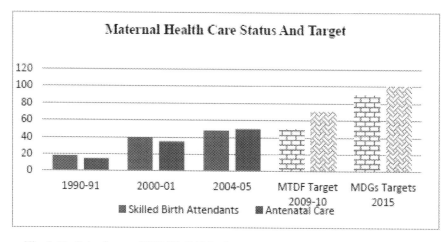

Fig. 1. Fig **2.4.** : Source: PMDGR (2005). Chart shows that a year wise birth attendants.

3   Research Focus

The research will conduct from different divisions of Pakistan like Gujrat, Gujranwala, Lahore and Rawalpindi etc. The reason to choose these areas is that the villages are more effective by the deaths of maternal cases. The overall data will be collected from taking interviews. The interviews will be taken from households and in some areas where women don't allow to come outside for interviews, their we will take interviews from men.

3.1   Survey

We will choose our suspects randomly from different interviewers from above mentioned districts. There will be 15 villages which are estimated by us to collect data. We will take interview from 10 villagers from total population of per village. The Table below shows the criteria for collecting data about specific maternal issues.

Table 3. Total population and collected data

Survey	Population Size	Total number of Villages
Interview (villagers)	10* 15 = 150	15

According to above table it is assume that from 15 villages there are 150 interviews will be taken from different people related from different fields of life. In interviews we will discuss face to face every small a minor issues which are facing by rural community.

4   Purposed Solution

The main part of our study is to purpose the best solution for the villagers to reduce the rate of deaths due to maternity cases. From different researches about health and education in held in Pakistani rural areas it is assume that maximum part of the rural community is un-educated. So by take into account the rate of illiteracy amongst the rural community in Pakistan we want to purpose the icon base design. In this form of design there will following important things present.

- Mobile Application (ICON based application).
- Information System (For technical Person).
- Ambulance Availability for emergency situations

4.1   Propose Framework

The following Design for an application and IS will be made.

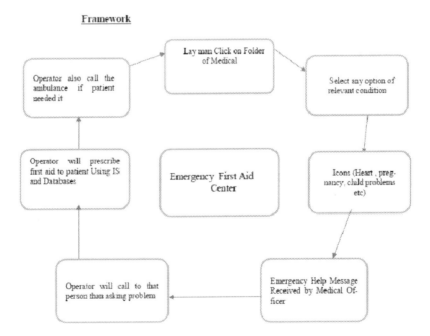

Framework

We want to introduce new design for rural community[13][14] to facilitate them. This design will help them in emergency situations when they need first aid to survive. Our design will facilitate them by providing emergency medical offices located in every Union Council. As the design [12][15][16] discuss above in a figure that describes each and every point very clear. First we want to make an application for Symbian cells because according to the reference of research in Pakistani rural areas there are 75% people using Nokia Symbian cell phones to communicate with each other.

5   Expected Results

The results according to our point of view will be 100% chances of decrease of death rate and educate rural community in the form of first Aid precautions in a related emergency situation.

The following points will give benefits to people, that are as follow.

- Fast communication between a layman and a technical person.
- Time saving
- Give help to fast decision making
- Helpful for first aid precautions
- Will receive a best service on early basis.
- No delay of transport
- Free of cost transport availability.
- Free of cost First Aid Precautionary measures.

6   Discussion

During study we realized the main reason that why most of the women in rural areas of Pakistan died when they were in the stage of giving birth to baby. The big reason was their husbands didn't allow them to operate from male gynecologist doctors that is caused by the strong cultural [17] or religious norms present in that particular area. So that's why most of the women died during the last moment of giving birth due to unavailability of lady doctors in the rural areas of Pakistan.

Another reason of sudden deaths of pregnant women is their men take a long time to make decision to go to hospitals for treatment. Decision making was not taken on the early basis, the decision making delayed due to much illiteracy amongst the people. That reason also makes big hurdles to save the lives of women. During interviews some respondents also reveals the major issues like delay of transport, men don't allow their women to go to hospitals, also they didn't trust on doctors for treatment, that issues were caused due to lack of facilities like transport, ignorance percentage in rural areas etc.

Following chart reveals, the permission is necessary for women for going to hospitals from different family members.

Table 4. Person's Permission for going to hospitals in case of Emergency situations. (n=1176)

Persons	%
Husbands	55
Mother-In-Laws	25
If husbands are not presents then Father-In-Laws/Brother-In-Laws	10
Permission is not necessary for going to health care centers	10

With the reference of above discussion it is concluded that Pakistan has a high rate of deaths in maternal cases. There is no attention of Government and other public or private NGO's which working for health care centers in Pakistan's rural areas.

References

1. Government of Pakistan, Economic survey of Pakistan, Islamabad, Ministry of Finance (2000)
2. Pakistan Medical and Research Council. National Health Survey 1990-94: health profile of the people of Pakistan. PMRC, Islamabad (1994)
3. United Nations Children Fund, State of the World's Children. UNICEF, New York (2001)
4. Alam, A., Khan, M.: Problems and Facilities In Prenatal And Postnatal Conditions to Rural Women At Palosi. Peshawar, Pakistan.Sarhad J. Agric. 24(3) (2008)
5. Akram, M., Khan, F.J.: Health Care Services and Government Spending in Pakistan. In: PIDE Working Paper 2007, p. 32 (2005)
6. Chaudhry, R.: Health matters: Maternal mortality high despite solutions availability, Islamabad, Pakistan
7. Afzal, U., Yousuf, A.: The State of Health in Pakistan. Center for Research in Economics and Business(CREB), Lahore School of Economics, Pakistan
8. Shah, N., Hussain, N., Shoaib, R., Hussain, A., Gillani, R., Khan, N.H.: Socio-demographic Characteristics and the Three Delays of Maternal Mortality, Pakistan (April 2005 to May 2008)
9. Waite, M.D., Ward, P.: Increasing contraceptive use in rural Pakistan: an evaluation of the Lady Health Worker Programe, Center for Population Studeis, London School of Hygiene and Tropical Medicine, London, UK and Oxford Policy Management, Oxford, U.K.
10. Safdar, S., Inam, S.N.B., Omair, A.: (Department of Community, Health Sciences, Ziauddin Medical Unversity,42-a,Sindhi Muslim Housing Society, Karachi.) S.T. Ahmad (Health and Nutrition Development Society (HANDS), 42-a, Sindhi Muslim Housing Society, Karachi), Maternal Health Care in a Rural Area of Pakistan
11. Anwar, N., Sheikh, J.A.: Healthcare Practitioers and the role of Ergonomics in Information Technology. In: Proceedings of 1st International Conference on Informationand CommunicationTechnology Trends (ICICTT 2013), Pakistan (2013)
12. Duncker, E., Sheikh, J.A., Fields, B.: From Global Terminology to Local Terminology: A Review on Cross-Cultural Interface Design Solutions. In: Rau, P.L.P. (ed.) HCII 2013 and CCD 2013, Part I. LNCS, vol. 8023, pp. 197–207. Springer, Heidelberg (2013)

13. Sheikh, J.A., Fields, B., Duncker, E.: The Cultural Integration of Knowledge Management into Interactive Design. In: Smith, M.J., Salvendy, G. (eds.) HCII 2011, Part I. LNCS, vol. 6771, pp. 48–57. Springer, Heidelberg (2011)
14. Sheikh, J.A., Fields, B., Duncker, E.: Cultural representation by Card Sorting. Ergonomics for All: Celebrating PPCOE's 20 years of Excellence. Selected Papers of the Pan-Pacific Conference on Ergonomics, November 7-10, pp. 215–220. Taiwan CRC Press, Kaohsiung (2011a)
15. Sheikh, J.A., Fields, B., Duncker, E.: Multi-Culture Interaction Design. In: Advances in Cross-Cultural Decision Making, pp. 406–415. CRC Press (2010b)
16. Sheikh, J.A., Fields, B., Duncker, E.: Cultural based e-Health information system. In: Presentation at the Health Libraries Group Conference 2010, July 19-20, CILIP, Salford Quays (2010a)
17. Sheikh, J.A., Fields, B., Duncker, E.: Cultural Representation for Interactive Information system. In: Proceedings of the 2009 International Conference on the Current Trends in Information Technology, Dubai (2009c)
18. Sheikh, J.A., Fields, B., Duncker, E.: Cultural representation for multi-culture interaction design. In: Aykin, N. (ed.) IDGD 2009. LNCS, vol. 5623, pp. 99–107. Springer, Heidelberg (2009)

Content Management and User Interface
for Uneducated People

Zainab Mahmood, Syeda Sana Shahzadi, and Sahar Tariq

Department of Computer Sciences
University of Gujrat Hafiz Hayat, Gujrat ,Pakistan
{10070619-023,10070619-075,10070619-100}@uog.edu.pk

Abstract. This study will be conducted to propose such system that contains contents that meet capability and preference of Un-Educated user of rural community of Pakistan by making the websites more interactive and understandable for them. Visually with pictures, video or text, acoustically with sound or spoken Language considering regional languages (*Voice* Directions gives you turn by turn *navigation* instructions in *voice), icons and menus.*Our Proposed interface will robust the needs of Un-Educated people including information retrieval and learning. It will meet needs of illiterates and deal with the barriers they face in communicating to web. This work will help them to reduce their anxiety and fear of technology. The proposed prototype will support Un-Educated users through an interface that does not require reading skills to understand or use.

Keywords: Web Contents, Uneducated people, Text-Free Interface, Auditory Interface, Sensor Based Interface.

1 Introduction

Most computer applications pose an accessibility barrier to those who are unable to read fluently. Excessive use of readable content hinders the illiterate or semi-literate users to have fruitful results from such computer applications [1]. It was realized that in order to achieve the significant economic contribution in development from rural community, we have to provide an effective and viable solution so that Un-Educated people can take advantage of the technology and compete with literate community. As cited in [4] the restrictions for the development of information technology are financial limitations. The countries that suffer the most financial hardships are third World countries. The ability to access technological and scientific information does not just give a nation power, but it enables that nation to lead a better life in all aspects .Effective information delivery system should be provided to ensure that service reach to target group according to their needs. Pakistan is sixth most populous country on globe and second largest country in South Asia, reported to have79% illiteracy [2][3].

A. Marcus (Ed.): DUXU 2014, Part III, LNCS 8519, pp. 432–441, 2014.
© Springer International Publishing Switzerland 2014

2   Literature Review

From literature review we found that many research have been conducted to provide interactive interfaces for Un-Educated users. Research work that investigates user interfaces [43][44][49] for Un-Educated users work is recent and few research groups have looked at designing for this population. As Cooper says, Different kinds of techniques are used to aid Un-Educated people in interacting with web content, as Un-Educated users are very different from the target user imagined by most user interface designers. Striving for digital society ensures an ICT driven knowledge-based society and in order to build a digital society it needs to reduce the gap between information rich and poor in the community[47]. It needs to build a system where information will be readily available online and people from different parts of the country will avail themselves of the information through different channels [4][45][46][48].The areas of study contributing to our research dimension are Text free interface with visual and graphic aids ,Auditory interfaces with voice navigations and Sensor based human-machine interfaces.

2.1   Text Free Interface with Visual Aids for Un-Educated

Less text- More graphics technique is commonly used for this type of interface. For information communication symbol systems have been introduced such as universal language to enable interpersonal communication between people speaking different languages. Charles Bliss developed his semantography in 1949, a communication system based on a set of symbols which can be used to break down language barriers. Every symbol is abstract meaningful; they can be placed together to form sentences [5][6]. Indrani, Toyama [7] Proposed the design for text free interface. They proposed ethnographic design in collaboration with a community of Un-Educated domestic laborers in three Bangalore slums. They designs text-free employment search engine matches domestic laborers with jobs in Bangalore, India.

Christer [8] proposed text free interface to make a prototype of an icon based menu for mobile phones that can support Un-Educated users through an interface that does not require reading skills to understand or use. He also discussed the design issue and revealed what factors are necessary in order for an iconic interface to have best possible chance of being correctly understood. Concreteness, proper amount of detail, intuitive placement of icons and icons with actions are factors that affect any user of the interface.

Medhi et al. [7] compared text-free interface designs for an employment search application and a map application to corresponding text-based versions. An evaluation with low literacy users (0 to 6 years of education) showed that the text-free versions were preferred and increased task accuracy.

Kentoy, Medhi, ravin [9] proposed the benefits of an asynchronous communication tool like email might be made accessible to populations with little to no literacy. Their goal was to create a communication experience built on standard email protocols. They presented the design and evaluation of a prototype video-mail application that uses a combination of graphics, animation and voice assistance to empower illiterate users to be completely self-reliant right from setting up accounts through communicating using it.

Matthew [10] traces the initial stages of URSULA (User-Interface Recommendations supporting Universal Literacy Accessibility) work, and it demonstrates how a conceptual interface design approach, Hypothetical User Design Scenarios (HUDS), can be used to drive the design process. User-Interface Recommendations Supporting Universal Literacy Accessibility (URSULA) is a project to create user-interface guidelines for developers who are writing applications and websites that may be used by illiterate users. Simputer was a small information access device to be distributed in India. Because of low literacy levels among the target population for this device and the diversity of languages used throughout India, special considerations were exercised when designing applications such that they are understandable by users who lack written language literacy. Joy, Dipin [11] proposed an integrated solution using a mobile computing device suitable for use by illiterate people in mainly rural areas. Modifications in supported applications including telephony, messaging and browser to enable them to be used text free were described. The design combined the speech recognition and Image based approaches. It incorporated AI and speech recognition to translate speech into text, Siri like interfaces to invoke specific apps, interfaces for browsers and to invoke search engines, using Bluetooth or other technologies to send VCF cards to store in memory, way to make a call to an existing contact without pressing any numbers, apps to learn reading and writing, using images instead of text to convey information. Their approach was to use technology to empower illiterate people at a level which they can presently relate to, rather than focus on technology to promote literacy .The patent by Rama[12] speaks of various mobile phone based apps customized for the use of an agriculture worker, facilitating access to various agricultural services, with apps for labor markets for farmers, markets to sell their produce and social groups on the internet.

There have been a number of articles related to technology access, using mobile phones, for illiterate people. Most of them speak of initiatives launched by various organizations such as TCS to identify the unique needs of such users and improving literacy with the help of technology [13].

2.2   Auditory Interface for Un-Educated

Speech assistance is also provided like voice auditory interfaces. There are research papers which have demonstrated the utility of auditory icons in addition to standard graphical feedback in communicating information to Un-Educated users. Alvin, Richard [14] developed the "Lingraphica" system. It was designed based on a database of"word-concepts" connected with an icon to enable communication for people with aphasia. Patients can point on these icons and drag them together on storyboards. Lingraphica automatically translates these sentence-like constructions into text and spoken words.

In Project Health Line [15] the target audience was low-literate community health workers. In rural Sindh province Pakistan research was conducted .The goal was to provide telephone-based access to reliable spoken health information and the speech interface. This project also highlighted the challenges in eliciting informative feedback from low-literate users. A joint project between researchers at Carnegie Mellon University (CMU) in Pittsburgh, Pennsylvania, USA and at Lahore University of Management Services (LUMS) in Lahore. They deployed a speech application, called "Polly", to Pakistan that allows users to access entertainment and information just by using voice over a simple (not smart) phone. Their work recently published at the ACM SIGCHI Conference on Human Factors in Computing Systems (CHI) [16]. More recently, in a study comparing participants' understanding of health information represented as text, drawings, photographs, videos or animation, all with and without audio, the conditions with audio resulted in higher understanding and task accuracy than conditions without audio [17].

Plauche [18] discussed a voice user interface designed to enable low-literacy farmers in the Tamil region in India to have access to market information on agricultural produce. In this design, the prompts were restricted to simple yes or no answers so that the interactions were simple enough for higher accuracy. The application was a Tamil spoken language system designed by Berkeley's TIER group to test speech interface in low-literacy environment .

. In the design of a financial management system for rural micro-credit groups in India, Parikh [19] conducted iterative design sessions with 32 women. The final design included numbers to leverage numeracy skills, icons, audio, and text in the local language. Audio augmentation was found to be useful for disambiguating items. Although the impact of different levels of literacy was not the focus of their research. Parikh [20] have also confirmed the importance of audio in the context of a cell phone application for capturing paper-based information. Rural literate users who tested a text-only version of the interface after using it with both audio and text preferred the version with audio.

Ravin [9] conducted research in Semiliterate and illiterate ability for audio text and text free interaction in Karnataka, India. They conducted two studies that explore how semiliterate users with very little education might benefit from a combination of text and audio as compared to illiterate and literate users. Results show that semiliterate users reduced their use of audio support, illiterate users showed no similar improvement. Semiliterate users should thus be treated differently from illiterate users in interface design.

Deepak [21] conducted a research in which he presented a framework that can be used to check the most important aspects required in designing an appropriate VUI (voice user interface) for low literate users. The research ends with successful paper prototype VUI for m-Event Organizer. This research helped other designers during the process of designing a VUI prototype for low literate users. Istanbul researchers [22] proposed a novel design for a basic mobile phone, which is focused on the essence of mobile communication and connectivity, based on a silent speech interface and auditory feedback. This assistive interface takes the advantages of voice control systems while discarding its disadvantages such as the background noise, privacy and social acceptance. The proposed device utilizes low-cost and commercially available hardware components. Thus, it would be affordable and accessible by majority of users including disabled, elderly and illiterate people.

Researchers of Finland [23] studied the deployment of voice-based mobile educational services for developing countries, especially in India. Their research was mainly based on a Spoken Web technology developed by IBM Research Labs. In a program level they studied how in agriculture, primary healthcare, education, banking and microfinance and entertainment these services can be deployed. In this paper they focused on educational services. The results of the project can be applied for similar market areas, such as Africa and Latin America. It also provides a platform for the reverse innovation system building, especially in speech and symbol inter-face based applications for focused areas in developed countries.

Indian Researchers used a Featherweight multimedia device that combined audio with non-electronic visual displays (e.g., paper). Because of their low cost, customizability, durability, storage capacity, and energy efficiency, they are well-suited for education and information dissemination among illiterate and semi-literate people. They presented taxonomy of featherweight multimedia devices and also derive design recommendations from their experiences deploying featherweight multimedia in the agriculture and health domains in India. They found that with some initial guidance, illiterate users can quickly learn to use and enjoy the device, especially if they are taught by peers [24].

Paul, Jason [25] presented two experimental prototypes that explore technical solutions and identify an application architecture suitable for literacy e-Learning. E-Learning has been defined as the use of Internet technologies to deliver a broad array of solutions that enhance knowledge and performance and can provide benefits such as reducing travel, infrastructure and training expenses, while allowing wide access and scalability.

It was estimated in OECD International Adult Literacy Survey that up to 500,000 Irish adults were functionally illiterate, that is many people had difficulty in reading and understanding everyday documents. They addressed this problem by allowing users to interact with speech enabled e-Learning literacy content using multimodal interfaces. The implementation of an evolutionary prototype that uses client side technology was described and feedback from that phase of the project was reported [26]. Tucker [27] developed a framework for localization of text to speech(TTS) for voice access to information, describing various components of a TTS solution. Plauche, Nallasamy [28] designed a text free system for farmers in Madurai using speech recognition technologies, and also studied barriers for designing such a system. Among the barriers they identified were dialectical variation, multilingualism, cultural barriers, choice of appropriate content, and the expense of creating the necessary linguistic resources for effective speech recognition.

2.3   Sensor Based Human-Machine Interfaces

LeBlanc, Ahmed, Selouani, Bouslimani and Hamam [29] proposed an infrared sensor based cost effective human-machine interface interpreting the user's hand or head gestures. This system targets people suffering from reduced mobility as well as specific professionals operating in constraining situations. This design allows using simple head movements to perform basic computer mouse operations, such as moving the mouse cursor on a computer screen. The proposed design was based on infrared distance measuring sensors which detect the head movements and convey that information to the PC by means of a microcontroller and a USB connection.

Deo [30], Lalji [31]and Parikh [32] also studied issues related to technology usage and needs of illiterate and semi-literate users. Katre [33]focused on the usability of thumb as the means of interaction for illiterate mobile users and made some design recommendations .Yulia, Oleg and Veikko [34] presented a novel vision-based perceptual user interface for hands-free text entry that utilizes face detection and visual gesture detection to manipulate a scrollable virtual keyboard. The system gave a reasonable performance in terms of high gesture detection rate and small false alarm rate. A majority of the proposed vision-based interfaces provide point-only functionality by tracking face/head or facial features and using the location of the tracked object as a camera mouse [3][36][37][38].

Betke [39] tested normalized correlation template feature tracking in a typing board application. The reported text entry speed was 31 cpm (chars per minute) when a dwell time of 0.5s was used. Hansen [40] used a marker-based head tracking for typing with a dwell-based dynamic typing application. The reported speed of communication on the first day was ~25 cpm for Danish keyboard and ~44 cpm for Japanese keyboard. Several authors developed point-and-click visual-based interfaces which combine both camera mouse and visual gesture detection to eliminate the use of dwell time and to emulate a computer mouse's "single click"functionality. Grauman et al. (2003) utilized voluntary blinks and brow raises detected by motion analysis and normalized correlation template matching as selection gestures. The interface was tested in a letter-scanning application that required two selections to enter a single character. The typing speed (selection-only) was 5.7 cpm [41]. Varona [42] designed a system that used nose tracker to move a computer pointer and eye wink detection to execute mouse click events. The interface was applied in menu selection tasks; its text entry performance was not tested.

2.4   Problem Statement

Content and interface of web is not easy to understand and appropriate for Un-Educated people. Un-educated people are certainly part of the group which has been referred to as the "Information Poor". With weak reading skills they cannot navigate, explore, and use the web effectively and understand information presented there.

2.5   Research Question

A detailed review of the accessible literature leads us to the question "How to enhance the information gathering (from web) method for un-educated user?"

This study will be conducted to propose such system that contains contents that meet capability and preference of Un-Educated user of rural community by making the websites more interactive and understandable for them. Visually with pictures, video or text, acoustically with sound or spoken Language considering regional languages (Voice Directions gives you turn by turn navigation instructions in voice), icons and menus.

- To examine the rural community's need of information gathering
- Provide interaction styles for information presentation

The one objective of this research is to find out how to manage the content on web that are useful and understandable for Un-Educated people. That is why we need to use such content management system that manages the content in a way which effectively and efficiently deal Un-Educated people. This method will provide highest level of satisfaction and minimal frustration. Another objective is to define interactive user-friendly interface that can be used for Un-Educated people, as poor interface cause catastrophic errors and may people leave using any web because of poor user interface design.

3   Research Methodology

This study will be conducted in rural community. Questionnaires will be designed to get information from target community, to find out the level of web services usage in that community. We will also conduct sessions for presenting voice recordings, videos, animations, and pictorial representation to identify the reaction of target community to what extent they understand the delivered information. Regional languages will also be considered.

4   Expected Results

Our Proposed interface will robust the needs of Un-Educated people including information retrieval and learning. This work will help them to reduce their anxiety and fear of technology. The proposed prototype will support Un-Educated users through an interface that does not require reading skills to understand or use.

References

1. Aman Sagar, Kentaro Toyama, and Indrani Medhi, "Text-Free User Inter faces for Un-Educatedand Semiliterate Users", Microsoft Research India, 2007
2. UNESCO, Pakistan stands at 180th number in literacy at world level (2013), http://brecorder.com/top-news/1-front-top-news/147197-pakistan-stands-at-180th-number-in-literacy-rate-at-world-level-unesco.html (January, 02, 2014)
3. Khan, G.M.: Literacy and Pakistan, 2013, http://x.dawn.com/2013/05/22/literacy-and-pakistan/ (January 02, 2014)

4. Anwarul Islam, M., Tsuji, K.: Bridging digital divide in Bangladesh: study on community information centers. Department of Information Science & Library Management and Information and Media Studies. The Electronic Library 29(4) (2011)
5. Adam, H.: Mit Gebarden und Bildsystemen kommunizieren. Edition bentheim, Wurzburg (1996)
6. Nsung-nsa, M.H., Emmanuel, E.A., Sibanda, K.: A voice user interface for low-literacy users in a rural community. International Journal of Computing and ICT Research 7(1) (June 2013)
7. Medhi, I., Sagar, A., Toyama, K.: Text-free user interfaces for illiterate and semiliterate users. In: Proc. ICTD 2006, pp. 72–82 (2006)
8. Nordberg, C.: Exploring the text free interface for Un-Educatedusers Designing an icon-based prototype for mobile phones, Department of Information Science and Media Studies,University of Bergen (Spring 2001)
9. Medhi, I., Prasad, A., Toyama, K., Ravin: Exploring the Feasibility of Video Mail for Illiterate Users. In: Computer Science, Microsoft Research India, University of Toronto, MicroSoft Research India Bangalore (2008)
10. Rao, R.: Mobile device for access to agricultural services by non-literate and semi literate users, US Patent No. US 2010/0035597 A1
11. Bose, J.: Dipin K. P, A solution for a mobile computing device along with supporting infrastructure for the needs of illiterate users in rural areas, Samsung India Software Operations (SISO) Bangalore, India (2012)
12. Rao, R.: Mobile device for access to agricultural services by non-literate and semi literate users, US Patent No. US 2010/0035597 A1
13. Sterling, B.: Connectivity for the illiterate, Wired (March 11, 2010)
14. Sacks, A.H., Steele, R.: A journey from concept to commercialization-Lingraphica (May 1993), http://171.64.252.73/Publications/issue5.html (Cited August 17, 2000)
15. Sherwani, J., Ali, N., Mirza, S., Fatma, A., Memon, Y., Karim, M., Tongia, R., Rosenfeld, R.: Healthline: Speech-based access to health information by lowliterate users. In: International Conference on Information and Communication Technologies and Development, ICTD 2007, pp. 1–9. IEEE (2007)
16. Ali Raza, A., Ul Haq, F., Tariq, Z., Pervaiz, M., Razaq, S., Saif, U., Rosenfeld, R.: Job Opportunities through Entertainment: Virally Spread Speech-Based Services for Low-Literate Users. In: Proceedings of the 2013 ACM SIGCHI Conference on Human Factors in Computing Systems (2013)
17. Medhi, I., Prasad, A., Toyama, K.: Optimal audio-visual representations for illiterate users of computers. In: Proc. WWW 2007, pp. 873–882 (2007)
18. Plauche, N., et al.: Speech Recognition for Illiterate Access to Information and Technology. In: ICTD (2006)
19. Parikh, T., Ghosh, K., Chavan, A.: Design studies for a financial management system for-micro-credit groups in rural India. In: Proc. CUU 2003, pp. 15–22 (2003)
20. Parikh, T., Javid, P., Kumar, S., Ghosh, K., Toyama, K.: Mobile phones and paper documents: Evaluating a new approach for capturing microfinance data in rural India. In: Proc. CHI 2006, pp. 551–560 (2006)
21. Chhetri, D.: Voice User Interface Design for m-Event Organizer, Master Thesis, Vrije Universirty, Amsterdam (2012)
22. Ali Yuksel, K., Buyukbas, S., Hasan Adali, S.: Designing Mobile Phones using Silent Speech Input and Auditory Feedback, Sabanci University, Istanbul (2011)

23. Ruohonen, M., Turunen, M., Linna, J., Hakulinen, J.: Amit A. Nanavati and Nitendra Raj-put, E-Inclusion Innovation for Rural India: Mobile Voiceand Tablet Based Educational Services, University of Tampere, Finland (2013)

24. Chu, G., Satpathy, S., Toyama, K., Gandhi, R., Balakrishnan, R., Menon, S.R.: Feather-weight Multimedia for Information Dissemination. Microsoft Research India (2008)

25. Walsh, P., Meade, J.: Speech Enabled E-Learning for Adult Literacy Tutoring. In: Pro-ceedings of the 3rd IEEE International Conference on Advanced Learning Technologies, ICALT 2003, Cork Institute of Technology, Ireland (2003); Abbott, K.: Voice Enabling Web Applications: VoiceXML and Beyond. APress,

26. Abbott, K.: Voice Enabling Web Applications: VoiceXML and Beyond. APress (2002)

27. Tucker, R., Shalonova, K.: The Local Language Speech Technology Initiative– localiza-tion of TTS for voice access to information. In: SCALLA Conference, Nepal (2004)

28. Plauche, N., et al.: Speech Recognition for Illiterate Access to Information and Technolo-gy. In: ICTD (2006)

29. LeBlanc, Ahmed, Selouani, Bouslimani, Hamam, Computer Interface by Gesture and Voice for Users with Special Needs, Université de Moncton, Moncton Campus, Shippagan Campus, NB, Canada

30. Deo, N., et al.: Digital Library Access for Illiterate Users, Intl. Res. Conf. on Innovations in Info. Tech. (2004)

31. Lalji, Z., Good, J.: Designing new technologies for illiterate populations: A study in mo-bile phone interface design. Interacting with Computers 20 (2008)

32. Parikh, T., Ghosh, K.: Understanding and designing for intermediated information tasks in India. Pervasive Computing 5(2) (April 2006)

33. Katre, D.: One-handed thumb use on smart phones by semi-literate and illiterate users in India. In: Workshop on Cultural Usability and Human Work Interaction Design, NordiCHI Conference, Lund, Sweden (2008)

34. Gizatdinova, Y., Špakov, O., Surakka, V.: Face Typing: Vision-Based Perceptual Interface for Hands-Free Text Entry with a Scrollable Virtual Keyboard, University of Tampere, Tampere, Finland

35. Palleja, T., Rubion, W., Teixido, M., Tresanchez, M., del Viso, A.F., Rebate, C., Palacin, J.: Using the optical flow to implement a relative virtual mouse controlled by head move-ments. J. Universal Comp. Science 14(19), 3127–3141 (2009)

36. Findlater, L., Ravin, Toyama, k.: Comparing Semiliterate and Illiterate Users' Ability to Transition from Audio+Text to Text-Only Interaction Computer Science, University of British Columbia, University of Toronto Microsoft Research India (2009)

37. Laursen, L.: Designing a Smart-Phone Alphabet for the Illiterate, MIT Technology (March 30, 2012), http://www.technologyreview.com/news/427376/designing -a-smartphone-alphabet-for-the-illiterate/

38. Rebeiro, J.: IBM will Research Mobile Access for Aged and Illiterate, (March 09, 2010), TechHive   http://www.techhive.com/article/191063/article.html (accessed: January 29, 2014)

39. Betke, M., Gips, J., Fleming, P.: The Camera Mouse: Visual tracking of body features to provide computer access for people with severe disabilities. IEEE Trans. Neural Systems and Rehabilitation Engineering 10(1), 1–10 (2002)

40. Hansen, J.P., Tørning, K., Johansen, A.S., Itoh, K., Gaze, H.A.: Typing compared with in-put by head and hand. In: Symposium on Eye Tracking Research & Applications, pp. 131–138 (2004)

41. Grauman, K., Betke, M., Lombardi, J., Gips, J., Bradski, G.R.: Communication via eye blinks and eyebrow raises: Video-based human-computer interfaces. Universal Access in the Information Society, 2-4 (2003)

42. Varona, J., Manresa-Yee, C., Perales López, F.J.: Handsfree vision-based interface for computer accessibility. J. Network and Comp. Applications 31(4), 357–374 (2008)

43. Duncker, E., Sheikh, J.A., Fields, B.: From Global Terminology to Local Terminology: A Review on Cross-Cultural Interface Design Solutions. In: Rau, P.L.P. (ed.) HCII 2013 and CCD 2013, Part I. LNCS, vol. 8023, pp. 197–207. Springer, Heidelberg (2013)

44. Sheikh, J.A., Fields, B., Duncker, E.: From Global Terminology to Local Terminology: A Review on Cross-Cultural Interface Design Solutions. In: Smith, M.J., Salvendy, G. (eds.) HCII 2011, Part I. LNCS, vol. 6771, pp. 48–57. Springer, Heidelberg (2011)

45. Sheikh, J.A., Fields, B., Duncker, E.: Cultural representation by Card Sorting. Ergonomics for All: Celebrating PPCOE's 20 years of Excellence. Selected Papers of the Pan-Pacific Conference on Ergonomics, pp. 215–220. Taiwan CRC Press, Kaohsiung (2011a)

46. Sheikh, J.A., Fields, B., Duncker, E.: Multi-Culture Interaction Design. In: Advances in Cross-Cultural Decision Making, pp. 406–415. CRC Press (2010b)

47. Sheikh, J.A., Fields, B., Duncker, E.: Cultural based e-Health information system. In: Presentation at the Health Libraries Group Conference 2010, CILIP, Salford Quays, UK, July 19-20 (2010a)

48. Sheikh, J.A., Fields, B., Duncker, E.: Cultural Representation for Interactive Information system. In: Proceedings of the 2009 International Conference on the Current Trends in Information Technology, Dubai (2009c)

49. Sheikh, J.A., Fields, B., Duncker, E.: Cultural Representation for Multi-culture Interaction Design. In: Aykin, N. (ed.) IDGD 2009. LNCS, vol. 5623, pp. 99–107. Springer, Heidelberg (2009)

Rural Area Development through Multi-interface Technology and Virtual Learning System

Faizan ul Mustafa, Adeel Mushtaq, Shakra Mehak, Salman Akbar, Usman Ahmad, Sara Mobeen, Hassan Ejaz, Tayyab Asif Butt, and Muhammad Faraz Khokhar

University of Gujrat, Pakistan
faizan_ab@gmx.com,
{ch.adeelmushtaq,shakramehak,finalyear0,itprof.usman}@gmail.com,
sarah_mobeen@yahoo.com,
{10050656-091,10050656-115,10050656-021}@uog.edu.pk

Abstract. This paper presents the concept of multi interface technology based on psycho-logical factors of an individual that determine likes and dislikes of a person. According to this concept modern devices will be able to read an individual's likes dislikes and then automatically change their interface including color combination, language, design etc. based on a person's desire. In this paper e-learning concept is also introduced through which we can educate enough to understand a particular technology. After implementing this approach, we will be able to bring people close to the modern technology and can minimize the gap between technology and understanding of a common person living in a backward area.

Keywords: Multi interface, smart interface, interface that can automatically change, rural area development, human likes and dislikes and technology.

1 Introduction

Technology has changed the World. The progress and improvement of technology has improved people's lives. It has led to a far better, easier and very comfortable life for the people. But in rural area of progressing countries especially Pakistan and In-dia, people are still facing many problems in technology adoption. A big part of these countries consists of rural areas especially in Pakistan where 113,678,524 peoples of total population are living in rural areas. Most of them are illiterate people; they don't have knowledge to use a particular technology. That's why people living in rural areas are facing technology emergence.

This paper focuses on the psychological factors that plays major role in a person's liking. For example, according to modern researches, group of people belonging to same blood group, age and birth order, have many common personality traits. They have common likes and dislikes towards a particular design and combination. While color psychology helps us to find personality traits of those people who have same favorite colors. This research paper discusses that how we can make such user interfaces that can automatically change their behavior by fetching the certain personality

A. Marcus (Ed.): DUXU 2014, Part III, LNCS 8519, pp. 442–451, 2014.

traits of the user. In villages most of people follow old trends, they don't believe on modern healthcare facilities and technology. If we change their thinking level we can bring a massive change in villages in all dimensions. For this, virtual education system can play a vital role. According to this approach, interface should be able to teach user how to interact with technology, how to deal with health related problems, traffic rules etc. in his own native language. This is the virtual learning concept that is discussed in this paper. A villager who works in fields' the whole day and cannot go to school, he can get basic knowledge from the device that is being used by him. Government can run these projects parallel to those that are being executed by them.

In section 2 problem background scenario is discussed, here in this section it is briefly stated that why people feel it difficult to adopt technology instead of old local methods. In section 3 related work is discussed which is based on current research on both psychological factors that affects human like's dislikes and interfaces. In section 4 solution of problem is explained in details. This section includes three parts, in 4.1 overview of solution is given, while in 4.2, Technical details of solution are explained. Section 5, 6, 7 and 8 have expected results and, conclusion respectively.

2   Problem Background

With the growing progress in Information technology is offering the potential for improving the life style of the people. Rapid growth in Technology has brought people closer and minimized the class difference among them. After the invention of graphical user interfaces GUI, people's views and perception about the technology has drastically changed. This tremendous change in the technology has deep effects on life style of the people living in the backward areas. Nonetheless, in many progressing countries like India and Pakistan people especially in rural areas are part of worst digital divide. According to the World Bank report of 2012 almost 1.5 billion of the world's poorest people live in rural areas. They have poor infrastructure, a huge gap in communication means, old tradition and living style, lake of living facili-ties like electricity, water and health centers. These rural people supply food to other-world but majority don't use modern equipment and technology. Another thing that is very important 37.6% land of rural areas of World and 34.4% of Pakistan's land is agricultural land [1]. Unfortunately this ratio is becoming less and less day by day because population of these areas is increasing rapidly. This is really dangerous and can affect food availability in World. Governments of all countries are developing roads infrastructure, providing subsidies to farmers but rural areas are still different and backward than other areas.

Technology adoption is a critical problem in these rural areas. Because of the literacy rate that is very low, people don't know how to use the modern technology in their daily life. They are not able even to operate a smart phone that connects them with other World. User interface plays a critical role during the interaction with technology. A user interface provides optimum communication between the user and the device. Although user interfaces are designed to facilitate user to interact with the technology but they are many factors that varies person to person[14]. If an interface is good according a person living in USA, at the same time it may be bad for another person living in a village of Subcontinent. So it was needed badly such an interface that should be smart enough to change itself automatically according to an individual's liking. Our cities are advanced because people are educated they can understand their responsibilities well; they can get good facilities than others. But in villages most of people follow old trends, they don't believe on modern healthcare facilities and technology. If we change their thinking level we will bring a massive change in villages in all dimensions. For this virtual education system can play a vital role. So it is need of time to develop such a interfaces which not only automatically change but educate their users too. That's why we have proposed multi-interface technology and virtual learning concept in order to overcome technology adoption problems in rural areas.

3   Related Work

Basically Pakistan is an agriculture country. More than two-thirds of Pakistanis live in rural areas, of which about 68 percent are employed in agriculture, agriculture is backbone of Pakistan's .these people provide us food but they didn't have good meal of one time, the rural people are mostly facing poverty.   More than 60 percent of poor rural do not have basic facilities that we can imagine our lives without these facilities like water for drink, food, electricity, health center etc. Mostly these poor people do not have educational background that is the main reason that they are facing crisis. .

3.1   Digital Divide

Due to the gap between digital and non-digital world, a bridge is created between rural and urban areas, called Digital Divide. There are several major causes to the digital divide including technology emergence for illiterate people. As expected, the people in rural areas have less know how about digital devices. Studies of digital divide often focus on lack of technology. Moves to expand computer availability with simple interfaces will help to increase usability of machines[10]. In order to bridge this Digital Divide, global Organization is making long-term investments to collect and distribute technological devices and teach people how to use technology. Organiza-tion such as the United Nations, World Bank and other not-for – Profit Organization are working toward closing the gap between the digital and non-digital Divide.

3.2   Psychology Related Review

There are some biological attribute that influence human behavior. The attribute we have used is blood group. A natural experiment was conducted in japan in 19878-1988 to examine the relationship between blood groups and human behavior. Japanese people propose a prophecy that blood groups have great influence on human personalities. This phenomena constructed Japanese beliefs that they started to use this study in social psychology, educational psychology, clinical psychology Organizational and industrial psychology. They conducted an open personality test where people can participate. There they practice many activities to judge personality. Before this test, they classified them according to their blood groups.

After accomplishment of this study, they analyze the results. At very extent, the persons having same blood groups have same results in activities that had performed during test. Experts note down their personalities qualities then they concluded about blood-typical personality's stereotypes [2]. This topic of blood groups and humans personality is very popular domain. Research is going on upon this topic from a long time ago. In 1964 a research was conducted to study the relationship among human personality and blood groups. A group of people was studied according to their blood groups. Results of the comparison over all 14 HSPQ factors indicated that only factor I reaches a substantial level of significance. Consideration of the adjusted means for the blood group on this factor indicates that highest scores on I are associated with type A, somewhat lower scores with types and B (in that order), and the lowest scores with type AB. Just short of significance at the 5% level is Factor J, asthenia (the common feature of neurasthenia and psych asthenia), the AB type being low on this factor. As human's age grows, his likes, dislikes and perception toward things changed [3].

Study was conducted to know the impact of human age on his behavior. They had divided this study into two portions, the first portion is about the typical middle-age adult and the other is about typical young-age adult. The sample of this study was 1,267,218 people from population between ages of 10-65 years. After testing on sample they had developed a personality mode that was called Big Five traits domains. According to this study, people are:

Extraversion (Quick in decisions, hard work), agreeableness (pleasant personality), Conscientiousness (shy, take time to make decisions), Neuroticism (moody, calm in tension), and openness to experience (defender, use their experience in decision making). This Big-five model planned a test to judge people about their personalities. The available results indicate that from emerging adulthood through middle age, conscientiousness and agreeableness show positive age trends, Neuroticism shows a negative age trend, and Extraversion and openness to experience show flat trend.

These studies provide an informative sketch of age differences in personality traits but there is need to complete this picture so further work is required.[4]

Color has increased the learning efficiency. Color is a kind of factor which has a great impact on human emotions, mind and decisions. This paper has analyzed impact of color factor on human learning. Color is due to a wavelength spectrum of exposure to the human eye, and causes the retina to produce visual excitement by color vision cell [5]. Hue, saturation and lightness are three basic characteristics of color. Color psychology is the subjective psychological reaction caused by objective color world. Learning efficiency is the ratio of quantity and quality for the time, energy consumption and outcomes though studying. It has a good effect for learner, for example light blue color helps to take concentration, and similar color has great impact on human mood and behavior. Pleasant color brought good change in human. In this paper, a color testing was performed on thirty students having same characteristics, to check their learning efficiency in different color's environment. It was concluded that the formation of a specific color of color vision psychology, given the character and association of different color. So when people see the different colors will produce the appropriate physiological and psychological changes. This change will turn affect the learner's learning efficiency [6].

According to social and clinical psychology there are many factors that decide human likes and dislikes and general behavior towards a certain event. A study was conducted in 2001 that covers the review of twenty five years of research on human evaluation conditioning [7].

3.3   HCI Related Review

Although the details of how people use command-line interfaces are fairly well known that how complex to remind commands to operate machine. Few decades ago, computer experts an introduced graphical user interface (GUI). GUI has brought a tremendous change to adopt technology, but still the problem exist that for a lay person , it is difficult to operate to understand interface of machine, so the sub-field Computer Sciences, Human Computer Interaction (HCI) has been working to overcome this problem. The GUI is based on a hybrid mechanism that combines ranking and rating. It has been used based image for rating. It presents a base image for rating its similarity to seven peripheral images that are simultaneously displayed in a circular layout. The user is asked to report the base image's pair wise similarity to each peripheral image on a fixed scale while preserving the relative ranking among all peripheral images. The collected data are then used to predict the user's subjective opinions regarding the perceptual similarity of images. We tested this new approach against two methods commonly used in perceptual similarity studies: (1) a ranking method that presents triplets of images for selecting the image pair with the highest internal similarity and (2) a rating method that presents pairs of images for rating their relative similarity on a fixed scale. We aimed to determine which data collection method was the most time efficient and effective for predicting a user's perceptual opinions regarding the similarity of mammographic masses. Our study was conducted with eight individuals. By using the proposed GUI, we were able to derive individual perceptual similarity profiles with a prediction accuracy ranging from 76.83% to 92.06% which was 41.4% to 46.9% more accurate than those derived with the other two data collection GUIs. The accuracy improvement was statistically significant [8].

To overcome a gap between current representational capabilities[11][12][13][14][15][16] of cognitive models and the requirements for cognitive modeling in human-computer interaction a research was conducted that proposed that introduced the understanding of human-computer interfaces as devices and a form of representation where information is exchanged between an artificial and natural representation system, in order to accomplish tasks cooperatively. The representations of the computer system and the cognitive system are mutually modulating and influencing each other. The goal is to establish a process of cooperative human-machine cognition [9].

Similarly in 2009 a research was conducted in which various interaction models are explored and investigated when used in designing interactions. Object Action Interface model is studied in detail and its shortcomings are identified [10].

4   Proposed Solution

Majority of people who belong to rural areas are illiterate. Main problem that an user interfaces while interacting with software embedded devices is to understand the interface. Although software developers try their level best to minimize this gap but 100% perfection is not possible. A common lay man who uses the technology faces many problems during his interaction with device.

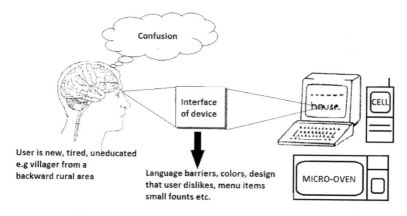

(Major problem in rural areas while using software embedded devices)

Fig. 1. Device usage issues

4.1   Overview of Solution

We have proposed multi interfaces technology concept to overcome technology adoption gap. Parallel to this, for enhancing user's literacy level virtual learning concept has been introduced. According to this concept, the device that is being used by a non-technical person will get some information about user. This data will be collected by user with the help of a simple questionnaire before using a device. This information will include following points

- Age of user
- Blood group of user
- Favorite color
- Birth order of the user
- User's Education
- Area

According to psychology above mentioned information has deep concern with an individual's likes and dislikes. By analyzing above mentioned information with the help of psychological theories we can predict following points about user

- Education level
- User's language
- Color combination that user likes
- Design pattern that user likes

After analyzing this information device will search most suitable interface pattern from its built-in memory and will generate a view in user's native language according to user's preferences. This will help user to use a particular device more easily.

4.2   Technical Approach

In technically language this research has been divided into three steps which are listed bellow as:

- User Authentication
- Machine Response
- System Updating

The whole process is described through following figure.

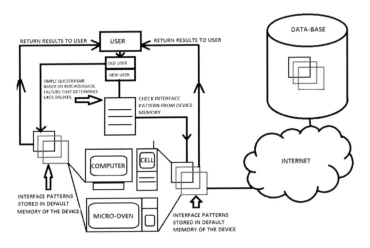

(HOW A MULTI-INTERFACE APPROCH WORK)

Fig. 2. Technical model for the process

User Authentication. Whenever a user will interact with the device, device will ask him to confirm whether user is old or new. If the user is new it means that he is using the device first time then the device will ask user to provide some information about him through a simple questionnaire. Questionnaire will have following questions

- Age of user
- Blood group of user
- Favorite color
- Birth order of the user
- User's Education
- Area

After getting this information device will allocate user, user ID number and will allow user to use the device. In case of old user machine will require only user's ID and precede the next process.

Machine Response. We are assuming that our devices are smart enough and have built in memory with it. All possible interface patterns are stored in device's memory based on the questionnaire. After data collection from the new user, device will analyze data and match this information with the interface patterns stored in default memory of device. If the pattern is found, device will change its interface according to that pattern.

If the pattern is not found, device will return interface pattern close to user's information and call the database to send interface patterns of based on user's information so that when user comes second time device will allocate new interface.

System Updating. Although devices will have the entire possible interface patterns stored in their default memory but exceptions are still possible. If a device does not find a pattern related to users information, it will store user's info in its memory and will make a connection with main database to update its record with new patterns. User can also update his device with new interface pattern whenever he wants.

Virtual Learning. Virtual education system can play a vital role. According to this approach, interface should be able to teach user how to interact with technology, how to deal with health related problems, traffic rules etc. in his own native language. This is the virtual learning concept that is discussed in this paper. A villager who works in fields' the whole day and cannot go to school, he can get basic knowledge from the device in his native language that is being used by him. Government can run these projects parallel to those that are being executed by them.

Technical this idea runs similar as mentioned above in figure number 2.

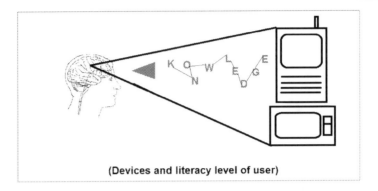

Fig. 3. Virtual learning model

5   Expected Results

In future, we will implement this idea and the expected result according to our re-search will increase use of technology in rural areas. People belonging to backward areas will have confidence in technology devices. There will be a chance to control digital dived that has divided a world into different parts. There are following benefits of overcoming digital divide that will be seen when this idea will be implemented, these are:

1. Those without enhanced data capability will be able to access the benefits ex-pected particularly in relation to education, health and government services.
2. Concern that people in the developing countries will enjoy the benefits of the new knowledge-based economy using technology.
3. It will remove disempowers, discriminates and dependency, and reshape the map of the world.
4. If people adopt technology easily, it is solution for traffic and fuel pollution
5. Key to establishing availability, accessibility and affordability for people.

6   Conclusion

In this study, various human attributes are explored and investigated to understand human personality and machine interface Designing. These attributes are age of user; blood groups, color, user education etc. proposed model is represented in the form of set of finite interfaces that are designed according to mentioned attributes. As user fulfill the form requirement, the system will response and machine interface will be changed according to person's psychological attributes.

The implementation of a set of infinite interfaces based on this proposed paradigm is the future work. We will also evaluate developed interfaces using qualitative usabil-ity evolution measurement methodologies.

References

1. World Bank, http://data.worldbank.org/indicator/SP.RUR.TOTL
2. Sakamoto, A., Yamazaki, K.: Blood-typical Personality Stereotypes and Self-fulfilling Prophecy (April 2002)
3. Cattell, R.B., Boutourline Young, H.: Blood groups and personality traits. Supported by public health grant MH 01733-17 by Grant Foundation of New York (received February 17, 1964)
4. Soto, C.J., John, O.P., Gosling, S.D., Potter, J.: Age Differences in Personality Traits From 10 to 65:Big Five Domains and Facets in a Large Cross-Sectional Sample. Journal of Personality and Social Psychology 100(2), 330–348 (2011)
5. Cigić, D., Bugarski, V.: Personality traits and color preferences, Research Article UDC 159.937.51
6. Hartman, T.: The Power of Color: What Does Your Color Say About You. Colorcode.com
7. Houwer, J.D., Thomas, S., Baeyens, F.: Associate learning of likes and dislikes. Psychological Bulletin 127(6), 853-869 (2011), copyright 2001 by American psychological association, Inc., 0033-2909/01/$5.00, doi:1037///0033-2909.127.6.853
8. Seneler, C.O., Tugrul, N.B.: A Taxonomy for Technology Adoption: A Human Computer Interaction Perspective. In: PICMET 2008 Proceedings, Cape Town, South Africa, PICMET (July 27-31, 2008)
9. Markus, F., Peschl, Stary, C.: The Role of Cognitive Modeling for User Interface Design Representations: An Epistemological Analysis of Knowledge Engineering in the Context of Human-Computer Interaction, ICPC: PIPS No.: 160298 (mind:mindkap.cls) v.1.15 mind287.tex;11:57 (October 21, 1998)
10. Rashid, U., Niaz, I.A., Amin, M.W., Bhatti, M.A.: Designing Interactions using OAI Model: A New Interface Modeling Paradigm. In: International Conference on Emerging Technologies (2009)
11. Sheikh, J.A., Fields, B., Duncker, E.: Cultural representation by Card Sorting. Ergonomics for All: Celebrating PPCOE's 20 years of Excellence. Selected Papers of the Pan-Pacific Conference on Ergonomics, November 7-10, pp. 215–220. Taiwan CRC Press, Kaohsiung (2011a)
12. Sheikh, J.A., Fields, B., Duncker, E.: Multi-Culture Interaction Design. In: Advances in Cross-Cultural Decision Making, pp. 406–415. CRC Press (2010b)
13. Sheikh, J.A., Fields, B., Duncker, E.: Cultural based e-Health information system. Presentation at the Health Libraries Group Conference 2010: CILIP, Salford Quays, UK, July 19-20 (2010a)
14. Sheikh, J.A., Fields, B., Duncker, E.: Cultural Representation for Interactive Information system. In: Proceedings of the 2009 International Conference on the Current Trends in Information Technology, Dubai (2009c)
15. Sheikh, J.A., Fields, B., Duncker, E.: Cultural Representation for Multi-culture Interaction Design. In: Aykin, N. (ed.) IDGD 2009. LNCS, vol. 5623, pp. 99–107. Springer, Heidelberg (2009b)

Traffic Management in Rural Networks

Rodrigo Emiliano[1], Fernando Silva[1], Luís Frazão[1], João Barroso[2],
and António Pereira[1,3]

[1] School of Technology and Management, Computer Science
and Communication Research Centre, Polytechnic Institute of Leiria, Leiria, Portugal
rodrigoemiliano@hotmail.com,
{fernando.silva,luis.frazao,antonio.pereira}@ipleiria.pt
[2] INESC TEC (formerly INESC Porto) and Universidade de Trás-os-Montes e Alto Douro,
Quinta de Prados, 5000-801 Vila Real, Portugal
jbarroso@utad.pt
[3] Information and Communications Technologies Unit, INOV INESC Innovation-Delegation
Office at Leiria, Leiria, Portugal

Abstract. The internet is increasingly present in people's lives, being used in diverse tasks, such as checking e-mail up to online gaming and streaming. The so-called "killer applications" are applications that, when not properly identified and prevented, have more impact on the network, making it slow. When these applications are used on networks with limited resources, as happens in rural networks, they cause a large load on the network, making it difficult its use for work purposes. It is important then to recognize and characterize this traffic to take action so that it does not cause network problems. With that in mind, the work presented in this paper describes the research and identification of cost free traffic analysis solutions that can help to overcome such problems. For that, we perform preliminary testing and a performance comparison of those tools, focusing on testing particular types of network traffic. After that, we describe the analysis and subsequent modification of the source code for storing important traffic data for the tests, as well as the test scenarios in laboratory and real-life environments. These tasks are aimed on collecting information that assists in taking action to improve the allocation of network resources to priority traffic.

Keywords: Internet, Network Traffic, Rural Networks, Traffic Analysis, Deep Packet Inspection.

1 Introduction

The number of people with access to the Internet has been growing very quickly over the years. It is estimated that 1 in 3.5 people in the world have internet access [1]. These figures suggest the global character of this service, resulting from its increasing availability and from its decreasing access prices.

Nevertheless the Internet is still not available equally to all people. Unfortunately, the more remote and distant areas of the cities are the most affected, due to the cost and non-profitability of implementing an Internet service with good quality in those areas [2].

A. Marcus (Ed.): DUXU 2014, Part III, LNCS 8519, pp. 452–461, 2014.
© Springer International Publishing Switzerland 2014

Most of those zones are rural areas that by not having a large population density are set aside for not presenting a benefit for the implementation of such service.

Generally, if an access service to the Internet exists in rural areas, it is fairly limited, slow and with a low bandwidth. Therefore, when a large number of people accesses this service at the same time, a huge load is caused on the network. This load can be caused by the use of "killer applications" such as BitTorrent clients, peer-to-peer (P2P) programs, or even services that require lots of bandwidth, such as video and movies streaming. This compromises the proper functioning of the network and the quality of the service for other users that needs the internet for work purposes [3].

This is a difficult problem to tackle due to the weak network resources and the lack of control regarding the use of these "killer applications". One possible solution to this problem is the use of network traffic analysis tools to identify and control the traffic generated by these applications. Deep Packet Inspection (DPI) is a form of network packet filtering that allows identifying this type of traffic by checking the data packet origin application, as well as allows identifying the users that are responsible for its generation. The identification of this traffic and the implementation of measures that modify the allocation of resources to these applications, assist to a better management of the network resources, allowing a fair differentiation of applications and thus, preventing overloading the network with "unwanted" traffic and, consequently, its malfunction.

The research, testing and implementation of cost-free applications that perform this type of analysis, is the way forward to prevent the application of large load in rural networks.

This paper is organized as follows. In the next Section we introduce concepts underlying our research on traffic analysis technologies. Sections 3 and 4 describe our proposed solution and its application to a rural network, respectively. In Section 5 we describe our test scenarios on the selected application and in Section 6 we describe the adaptations made to its source code and the tests performed. Section 7 presents the results that we were able to observe, both in a laboratory and in a rural network. Finally, the ending Section presents final considerations on our work and topics for future work.

2   Traffic Analysis and Deep Packet Inspection

The traffic analysis on a network is increasingly important, contributing not only to understand the type of traffic flowing in the network, but also to prevent its congestion and ensure information security. This section presents DPI as a valuable traffic analysis approach.

2.1   Traffic Analysis

The traffic analysis on a network is widely used in the detection and resolution of network problems, thus improving the network in order to improve its operation in the future [3]. The traffic analysis makes the examination of packets passing a network card interface into promiscuous mode, or through Port Mirroring or Network Taps, and it generally allows deducing information from patterns in this communication.

2.2   Deep Packet Inspection

The Deep Packet Inspection (DPI) is a form of filtering/analysis of data packets, which examines more than the destination and source addresses. This parses the packet from layer 2 to 7 of the OSI model. This type of packet analysis allows a more complete monitoring and management of the network, by collecting information from headers, data, and protocol structures, in order to identify and classify the type of package or communication [4]. However, although this type of analysis is already being used for some time now in advertising or even in preventing spam emails, it creates many conflicts among the defenders of neutrality on the Internet due to its intrusive nature. Nevertheless, despite this ethical issue, DPI helps on several network tasks [4].

3   Proposed Solution

To collect and store the information in the network, we propose the model for the collection and processing of information illustrated in Fig. 1. This model consists of the following modules: gathering, filtering, storage, parsing and action.

Fig. 1. Proposed model for traffic analysis

Collection: The first step in processing information flowing in the network is the collection of such information. This collection must gather all of the data circulating on the network, such as the actors involved in the communication, the application that is transmitting the information, among others.

Filtering: The data collection should be filtered to display only the information relevant for the traffic analysis to subsequently proceed to its storage.

Storage: The filtered information should be stored in a media where it can be accessed. This storage will allow building the network traffic history.

Parsing: When necessary, the filtered information should be processed in order to easily understand what it concerns. This step also allows the reorganization of information in order to be saved in a format that can be imported by different programs.

Action: In the future, this information will provide the basis for the imposition of rules of distribution of resources and improvement of the network.

4   Solution Applied to a Rural Network

In order to improve resource allocation in networks with limited resources, a rural network was chosen to test the architecture proposed in Section 4.

Due to not having a large population density, many rural areas have very limited access to internet services, since they do not present a clear benefit to the operators of this service. Even when an internet service exists, it is rather poor in its quality. It is important then, to improve the allocation of resources in these networks, as the management of broadband networks in rural areas is of great importance. Fig. 2 shows how our solution can be applied to a rural network for management and traffic analysis purposes.

The proposed architecture has the following main objectives:

- Gathering all the information that enters/exits the network: This objective is illustrated through the use of a Central Server, where all traffic entering or leaving the network flows. Since the majority of the network traffic flows through this point it is ideal for collecting all of the necessary information. Therefore, this server will run the tool that collects information about network traffic. Using a Central Server simplifies the data collection and analysis processes, since it is not necessary to place the traffic analysis tool in many different parts of the network.
- Remote Administration: This allows non-presence maintenance of the solution, which represents a clear advantage. Thus, software maintenance and configuration is easily achieved, as well as the collection and observation of the data.
- Modelling of the network: After collecting and storing information, the network must be modelled so that all available resources are allocated according to the current needs. This modelling will avoid an excessive load on the network and, consequently, will result in its proper functioning.

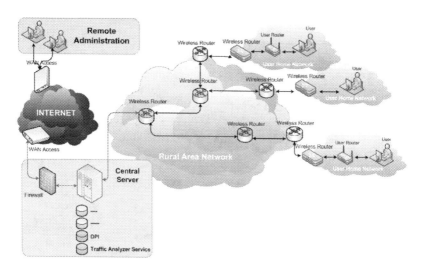

Fig. 2. Proposed solution architecture

5   Testing Settings

As one of the major objectives of this work is the detection of harmful traffic to the network, it is necessary to identify its different intervenient in order to perform the management that allows the proper functioning of the network.

One possible way to discover the application that is responsible for sending traffic is through the identification of its operating port [5]. However, due to technology advancements, there is increasing difficulty in identifying an application through the packet headers. Hence the use of DPI, which identifies those applications and all of the traffic present on the network [4].

During the initial stage of this study we have investigated several network traffic analysis programs, in order to find the tool that best fits our goals. After this extensive research, and taking into account different criteria, ntop [6] was chosen as the most appropriate tool. Ntop is very easy to install and to setup. Also, it has an advanced DPI library and it allows gathering relevant information that will help on managing the network load [7]. Being an open source tool, it is possible to edit its source code in order to perform additional functions as required, such as automation of traffic analysis and data storage. It is also possible to perform its configuration remotely, which represents an advantage since it is not necessary to travel to the site to perform tasks.

Using ntop, several test sessions were held, each with the duration of one hour, for the identification of applications and application protocols. These tests consisted in using controlled traffic with the aim of identifying it through the DPI. The traffic generated by applications such as Twitter, YouTube, Skype, among others, was tested. The results were then registered for each one of the tests performed.

After knowing the features of ntop and finishing the preliminary testing, the tests with "killer applications" were performed. Several P2P programs were tested and compared.

5.1   Peer to Peer (P2P)

P2P networks are applications with distributed architecture that distribute tasks among peers. All of the peers have the same permissions, capabilities and responsibilities to each other, in which they differ from the client/server architecture, where some of the actors are dedicated to serving others. This type of architecture is quite simple and it does not require coordination by a central authority.

P2P is often incorrectly used for setting up file sharing, such as music, video or game files via the Internet. However, its usefulness is much wider.

5.2   Unknown Traffic

Although DPI allows a very rich data analysis, there are still many applications and types of traffic to be identified. The traffic that ntop is unable to identify is classified as "unknown". During some sessions, the initial traffic was detected as "unknown". This happened when the web interface was started, suggesting that some kind of connection exists.

However, it was observed that there are more cases in which traffic is marked as "unknown". These cases are mostly related to P2P traffic. By enabling protocol encryption, the BitTorrent clients prevent their traffic identification, which is then identified as "unknown". The traffic generated by these clients is quite bulky and causes a large load on the network, therefore, although not identified, it does not go unnoticed. Even when identified as "unknown" there is some traffic that is correctly identified as "bittorrent". Knowing that there is BitTorrent traffic flowing in the network and that there is also a large volume of unknown traffic, it is safe to infer that these two types are related. Then, it is important to identify, not only those involved in BitTorrent traffic, but also the ones involved in the unknown traffic.

5.3   Protocol Encryption and DPI

Protocol encryption is widely used by BitTorrent clients. This happens because many Internet Server Providers (ISPs), block P2P traffic in order to prevent the network bandwidth overload [3]. Due to protocol encryption, BitTorrent traffic remains undetected by ISPs. The DPI analysis also fails on its identification, marking it as "unknown" traffic. Therefore, we infer that the majority of the unknown traffic is possibly caused by BitTorrent clients' protocol encryption. In order to detect and register the perceivable changes that this traffic causes on the network, we have tested different BitTorrent clients.

KTorrent. It is fairly easy to install on UNIX operating systems. When performing the tests, it was found that all of the captured traffic was recognized by P2P filtering. However, this BitTorrent client supports encryption protocol, making it unrecognizable to the DPI.

OpenBitTorrent. This is a tool that usually comes included with Ubuntu 12.04 operating system. It is quite simple; however, in the tests performed, the DPI did not identify its traffic as "bittorrent". Instead, this traffic was identified as "unknown", which suggests that this client uses protocol encryption.

UTorrent. It is one of the most widely used BitTorrent clients. It can be identified by ntop's DPI. Due to its importance, our tests are mostly focused in this tool.

In order to know how traffic changes with the different possible configurations, we started by using Utorrent default settings. We observed that near 90% of the traffic was correctly identified as "bittorrent". However, UTorrent supports protocol encryption, which makes its traffic unrecognizable to ntop's DPI.

Relationship between P2P, Hosts, and Active Sessions. When a new actor is detected in the network traffic, it is added to a ntop list of hosts, storing several information about its data, such as name, IP address and amount of sent and received traffic, among others. As the P2P connection uses multiple peers, it detects much traffic with different origins [8]. Thus, during the tests with BitTorrent clients, multiple hosts from different countries, with high amounts of traffic sent/received, were detected.

6   Source Code Analysis, Implementation and Testing

Because many BitTorrent clients are configured for protocol encryption and much of the information that is detected cannot be extracted through the available mechanisms, we have proceeded with the study of ntop's source code. Thus, we sought to understand the packet capture functioning and its respective analysis and processing, for subsequent amendments in the code for collecting the required information.

After confirming the architecture of ntop, we have identified the code snippets responsible for capturing and processing packages: *startSniffer()*, *processPacket()*, *isP2P()*. However, these snippets do not distinguish relevant traffic for the data collection. For this, we have deepened our study to the DPI code.

Within the protocols folder of the DPI code, we find different files for identifying the different protocols, as illustrated in Fig. 3. For example, for the discovery of BitTorrent traffic, there is a file named "bittorrent.c". However, for HTTP traffic, such as YouTube and Twitter, there is only one file: "http.c".

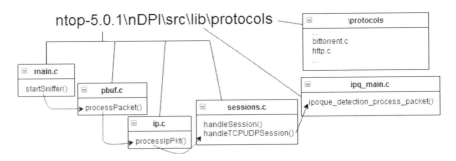

Fig. 3. Ntop's architecture

The study of the DPI code and the tests performed on BitTorrent clients, allowed us finding areas in the code where it is possible to collect information concerning hosts that carry harmful network traffic. For this purpose, it is necessary to perform the information collection within each file responsible for the different protocols.

6.1   Bitorrent.c

This file's functions allow determining if a data packet is originated by BitTorrent traffic. Thus, it is possible to find those responsible for this traffic by simply performing a *printf* of the data packet. In the code, the packet is located within an *ipoque_packet_struct* structure, which in turn is within the *ipoque_struct* structure.

The collected information was not in a suitable format, so a parser was made to treat this information. The data taken from the "bittorrent.c" file were the destination IP address, the source IP address, the Terms of Service (TOS) and the source and destination ports.

6.2   Extension of Data Collection to the "unknown" Data Type

Capturing traffic identified as "unknown" is of major importance, because a great majority of P2P traffic is marked as such. However, there is no source file to treat unknown traffic, therefore we have climbed in the file hierarchy and we have analysed the "ipq_main.c" code file. This file has the *ipoque_detection_process_packet()* function, which is responsible for discovering the application that is sending a given data packet. This function discovers the application protocol of the data packet. We assume that whenever it is not possible identifying the application, it should be identified as "unknown". Therefore, in these cases, we collect this type of information by making the function return the value "unknown".

6.3   Collecting Information on the Size and Timestamp of the Packet

After collecting the information on the different intervenient and on the applications of a given data package, we have captured more information which help us on building statistics about the data. This information is the size and the timestamp of the package. This information also helps on identifying network traffic delays.

6.4   Using Wireshark to Compare Data

Throughout the testing of our solution, all collected data were compared with data from the Wireshark tool [9], which also allows the collection and analysis of traffic. These comparisons were made using samples of traffic used in the tests performed with ntop. As these samples can also be read by Wireshark, it was possible to check the accuracy of the proposed solution.

6.5   The Parser

A parser, written in PERL, was created to handle data. This parser is designed to perform its conversion to a suitable and perceivable format that the *printf* function does not always allows achieving.

The parser converts the IP and port address from the decimal format, to dotted decimal and port, respectively. Then, it converts the protocol number into a string, which can present the values "UDP" or "TCP". After that, it performs the conversion of application number into the corresponding application, through an additional file containing the correspondence "application → value". Finally, it stores the converted information into a file, using the Comma Separated Value format (.csv), as illustrated in Fig. 4.

	A	B	C	D	E	F	G	H
1	Application	Protocol	Source IP	Port	Destination IP	Port	TOS	Size
2	[UNKNOWN]	[TCP]	77.243.180.38	80	10.0.1.2	49596	0	1480
3	[UNKNOWN]	[TCP]	77.243.180.38	80	10.0.1.2	49596	0	1480
4	[UNKNOWN]	[TCP]	10.0.1.2	49596	77.243.180.38	80	0	52
5	[UNKNOWN]	[TCP]	77.243.180.38	80	10.0.1.2	49596	0	1480

Fig. 4. Sample of parser's processed file

6.6   Automation

In order to reduce the human interaction to a minimum, we opted for using automation for the data collection and its processing procedures. The main objective of this automation is to perform an action that depends on the current results. For that purpose we use the cron program, which allows the automatic execution of a given program [10]. Thus, a simple change via cron enables the automatic collection and processing of data, continuously or through sample packets.

7   Results

The laboratory results show that it is possible to discover the interveners in heavy traffic in the network and collect proper information on that same traffic. However, in order to ensure that these results are also observed in a real environment, we have implemented our model to Memória Network.

The Memória Network was the result of a project entitled Memoria Online [11], which consisted on the implementation of a network in this rural location, granting to its inhabitants access to the internet. However, due to the number of clients using this network, its resources must be well distributed, in order to maintain its quality and speed. So, our proposed solution was implemented in this network in order to collect and analyze traffic, for helping to perform a better modeling of the network.

After applying our model in Memória Network, data collection was performed over a period of 3 hours. This collection has captured about 10 million packages. After analyzing the collected data, we conclude that it is possible to identify camouflaged P2P traffic in the network. This traffic is then queued in the low priority Quality if Service (QOS) list in order to not disturb the other traffic on the network. We also observe that the traffic is being well identified, allowing to detect if that same traffic is being correctly classified and marked by the QOS mechanisms.

In sum, the proposed model allows unmasking the camouflaged traffic and that affects network performance, as well as provides efficient mechanisms that help optimizing the network.

8   Conclusion

The aim of this project was to create a model that would allow improving resource allocation in networks with scarce resources, such as rural networks. This would require using cost-free solutions of network traffic analysis and the ability to perform data filtering through DPI.

Ntop is a network traffic analysis tool that complies with the requirements of the project. It was preliminarily tested in controlled environments for identifying applications generating traffic considered harmful and not harmful. Then, its source code has been modified to allow storing the information relating to the most harmful network traffic. Solutions that enable automation of the model and evaluating the classification accuracy of the collected data were also implemented.

The results show that our model allows unmasking the camouflaged traffic that negatively affects scarce resource networks, simultaneously providing relevant information for improving network management.

We conclude that ntop is a very good tool for the identification of network traffic, especially for identifying harmful network applications. Being an open-source tool and having a good capacity for analysis and identification of traffic through the DPI, it is a viable option for implementing in resource-limited networks, or even in networks that seek an intelligent management of their traffic.

For future work, it is important to perform additional tests on other real scenarios, as well as to collect additional information that enables a richer statistical analysis. It is also important to investigate other tools for analysing traffic on large networks such as ntop next-generation [12], which allows network analysis with great resources and with high speed traffic exchange.

References

1. Internet World stats, "Usage and population statistics", http://www.internet worldstats.com/stats.htm (date accessed, January 2014)
2. Liew, J.H., Yeo, A.W., Hamid, K.A., Othman, A.K.: Implementation of wireless networks in rural areas. Computer Science and Information Tech., Malaysia Univ., Sarawak (2004)
3. Feitosa, E., Souto, E., Sadok, D.H.: An orchestration approach for unwanted Internet traffic identification. Computer Networks 56(12), 2805–2831 (2012)
4. Mueller, M.L.: Convergence of control? Deep packet inspection and the future of the internet. Communications & Convergence Review 2(2), 92–103 (2010)
5. IANA, Protocol Numbers, http://www.iana.org/assignments/protocol-numbers/protocol-numbers.xml (date accessed, January 2014)
6. ntop, "ntop", http://www.ntop.org/ (date accessed, January 2014)
7. Bujlow, T., Carela-Español, V., Barlet-Ros, P.: Comparison of Deep Packet Inspection (DPI) Tools for Traffic Classification. Technical Report, Universitat Politècnica de Catalunya (2013)
8. Gomes, J.V., Inácio, P.R.M., Pereira, M., Freire, M.M., Monteiro, P.P.: Detection and Classification of Peer-to-Peer Traffic: A Survey. ACM Computing Surveys 45(3), 1–40 (2013)
9. Wireshark, "Wireshark", http://www.wireshark.org/ (date accessed, January 2014)
10. LinuxQuestions, "Tcpdump with cron", http://www.linuxquestions.org/questions/linux-software-2/tcpdump-with-cron-121727/ (date accessed, January 2014)
11. Salvador, N., Filipe, V., Rabadão, C., Pereira, A.: Management Model for Wireless Broadband Networks. In: 3rd International Conference on Systems and Networks Communications, pp. 38–43. ICSNC (2008)
12. ntop, "ntopng", http://www.ntop.org/ (date accessed, January 2014)

Usability Guidelines for Designing Knowledge Base in Rural Areas

Towards Women Empowerment

Javed Anjum Sheikh, Hafsa Shareef Dar, and Farzan Javed Sheikh

Faculty of Computing & IT, University of Gujrat, Gujrat, Pakistan
{javedanjum,hafsa.dar,13041719-019}@uog.edu.pk

Abstract. The paper discusses issues related to Design, User experience Usability involved in designing the interface to be used in rural areas. This study analyses the problems based on tests done on the interface in the villages of Punjab, Pakistan. Rural development is based on economic, social and human development. Whereas, Software Requirement Engineering focuses on how requirements can be gathered to achieve better end product. We aim to discuss software requirement gathering process in rural areas and attempting to elicit requirements from Pakistani rural woman. This could help us in bridging the technological gaps exist between rural and remote areas. Our aim is to find a solution for this barrier by designing software for rural woman of Pakistan. Further break down of our study is health issues with rural woman by adopting software requirement gathering on various e-health issues.

Keywords: software Requirement Gathering, Requirement Elicitation, Software Development Life Cycle, SDLC, Rural Development.

1 Introduction

The purpose of this study is to investigate how Pakistan farmer can be benefitted by modern technologies. This study also assumes that famers are already engaged in tacit knowledge directly or indirectly therefore how tacit knowledge can meet explicit knowledge to foster effective knowledge sharing. It is also to be noted that traditional forms of communication such as radio and televisions overlook the rural community. On the other side, mobile phones and computers both are out of their reach. Pakistan is one of the six most populous countries on globe and second largest country in South Asia. People living in rural areas according to the World Bank report 2012, have a literacy rate of 44 percent overall (58 percent for men and 29 percent for women). According to a survey in 2006-07, roughly agriculture is accounted for between 38-45 % of world's labor force whereas in the developing countries it is about 55% of the labor force in agriculture. Agriculture is the largest income and the employment-generating sector of Pakistan's economy. Services are provided via Mobile phones and other means like websites to the laymen. But still such services are not that much famous due to different reasons.

A. Marcus (Ed.): DUXU 2014, Part III, LNCS 8519, pp. 462–469, 2014.

According to the survey presented by Pakistan Survey Organization, women hold 52% of total population of Pakistan whereas 68% of them are living in rural areas. There are various factors like economic, social and human development on the basis of which rural community develops. Due to cultural issues [14][15][16][17][18][19], men's control and religious boundaries rural women do not have less access to information. Due to the technological barrier, rural areas of Pakistan are still far behind in helping Pakistan in socio-economic development. Various aspects of women's status in Pakistan are treated as independent variables, but she herself could decide whether she remains independent or not. Some of the aspects are: mobility, economic autonomy, access, fear of husbands, communication with spouse and decision making.

Women living in rural areas has to face challenges like literacy, socio-economics, religion and technology. Current research focusing on information technology diffusion in rural markets highlights a variety of challenges like socio-cultural and technological infrastructure of rural communities. Rural development is based on economic, social and human development. Rural areas in general are mostly illiterate. Consequently, these areas are far behind the urban areas.

Neils (13) proposed 7 C s, i.e., Connectivity, Content (Static and Dynamic), Context, Cash, Culture, Community and Communication for rural areas. He did not consider rural culture in general specially developing countries. He also ignored the role of tacit and explicit knowledge. We need to understand rural areas' norms, their values and diverse dynamics. Nonaka and Takeuchi's (11) model can be helpful to achieve successful result. The tacit knowledge of a rural community needs to transform into explicit knowledge. Rural community based on their local knowledge instead of global knowledge. Rural area needs bridge between local knowledge and global knowledge. This bridge can be built by providing information according to their preferred mode. Davenport and Prusak (10, cited by Hess, 11) proposed principles for knowledge sharing. His principles emphasis on good relationship shared knowledge by training, meeting places and times to exchange the ideas and incentive for those who share knowledge etc. According to Hess (11) rural knowledge can perform better if all are agree on same objectives, interest, contribute their experience and a place to share all these.

A requirement is a necessary attribute in a system, a statement that identifies a capability, characteristic, or quality factor of a system in order for it to have value and utility to a user.   This paper further stated that 85 percent of the defects in developed software originate in the requirements. It is widely recognized that requirements gathering is vital to the SDLC process. This is because the quality of any software product depends on the quality of the raw materials that are fed into it. Thus, poor requirements lead to poor software. A special document that lists all requirements is software requirement specification, which is again helpful for documenting user requirements. The great challenge of the requirements process is finding a way to uncover and capture the needs of the business and communicate those needs to a software development team in a language and style that facilitates the software design process, producing a result that precisely solves the business problem.

2   Literature Review

More than of half of Pakistan's population lives in rural areas. They can have a lot of benefit of using technologies but it's worthless if it is not used for the benefits made for. Rural areas can get the more benefits from them in various fields such as in Education. ICT has become the most important tool for the increasing adoption and access of education. The adoption of education is near to the ground in Pakistan due to inadequate situations. Lack of motivation at Primary Level, lack of education at undergraduate level, lack of infrastructure, poverty and Gender Biasness are common factors which are major barriers in implementation of ICT in rural areas of Pakistan. People don't have education but they have experience. They can do well in most of fields. ICT can help them to work in a formal and best way in their working. People of rural areas have not as much of education status. All people use ICT openly or in some other way but they don't be familiar with the convention of it. They assume that usage of these technologies have terrible impact on their lives and don't know about the helpful impact of ICT in their lives. Higher the number of uneducated people lowers the quality of governance. Young people of rural areas are excluded from ICT. Rural areas users are illiterate they don't be familiar with the significance of education. We have divided our literature review into three parts:

1. Software Requirement gathering Process
2. Requirement Elicitation Technique
3. Requirement Elicitation in Rural Areas

2.1   Software Requirement Gathering Process

Software requirement gathering is sub domain of software requirement engineering of software engineering. It is first step of traditional SDLC.

According to [7], Gathering, understanding and managing requirements is a key factor to the success of a software development effort. There are several techniques available for requirement gathering and most of them involves customer interaction with the development team.

As discussed in [12], the most difficult part in gathering requirements is not documenting the user requirements it is the effort of helping users figure out what they 'need' that can be successfully provided within the cost and schedule parameters available to the development team. The paper further discussed Industry experience has shown that customers and system developers should jointly evaluate stated requirements to ensure that each is a verified need. It is estimated that 85 percent of the defects in developed software originate in the requirements. Once defects are embedded in the requirements, they tend to resist removal. They are especially difficult to find via testing.

Another paper [9] discusses requirements must be determined and agreed to by the customers, users, and suppliers of a software product before the software can be built. The requirements define the "what" of a software product. Business requirements define the business problems to be solved or the business opportunities to be addressed by the software product. In general, the business requirements define why the software product is being developed. The authors mentioned various levels and types of requirement in figure 1:

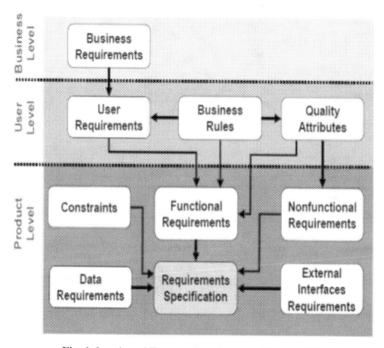

Fig. 1. Levels and Types of Requirements (Source: [9])

The authors further mentioned that if software requirements are not right, companies will not end up with the software they need.

2.2   Requirement Elicitation Techniques

Within the requirement engineering process is to use requirement elicitation and then requirement prioritization. Our aim is to discuss requirement elicitation in this section.

The main challenge of the software engineering community is to satisfy the customer needs and possibly exceed his expectations in an economic, rapid and profitable manner. Requirements engineering can help organizations develop quality software systems within time and budget constraints which are true reflection of customer needs [10]. The paper further stated that the primary success factor of requirements elicitation is that requirements meet end user needs. This outcome is difficult to achieve because users often have trouble identifying and articulating their needs and because those needs often change as a result of system implementation. Mistakes made in elicitation have been shown many times to be major causes of systems failure or abandonment and this has a very large cost either in the complete loss or the expense of fixing mistakes.

Some of the challenges discussed are: The majority of requirements elicitation techniques fail to address the less conspicuous and often more tacit requirements, priorities, and issues that analysts do not know to ask about and those users do not or cannot readily identify and articulate. Traditional techniques are unable to fully diagnose how such contextual issues will affect system requirements, system development, and system evolution. The methods to develop requirements are under the engineer's control [20]. An overall knowledge about the requirements development methods is important for engineers to predict the requirements development process and select a proper method. There are number of requirement elicitation techniques [4][10][20] available in literature. Some of the techniques discussed by various authors are presented in table 1

Table 1. Requirement Elicitation Techniques

Techniques	Details
Interviews	Conducted from groups of people with pre-defined agenda
Workshop, focus groups	To create/review high level features of desired products
Questionnaires	During early stages of requirement elicitation
Brainstorming	Rapidly generates broad and large list of ideas
Prototyping	A version of software which is incomplete
Win-win approach	Stakeholders negotiate to resolve disagreements about user requirements
Repertory Grids	To identify the similarities/differences between different domain entities
Card Sorting	To sort a series of cards into groups according to their own understanding
Joint Application Development	Stakeholders discusses the problems and all possible solutions

2.3   Requirement Elicitation in Rural Areas

It is necessary to understand the current scenario of requirement elicitation in rural settings in order to know the evolving technology. The hesitation is more pronounced with the rural users because they are not exposed to new technologies. For requirement elicitation, the author has discussed in [1], there are influential people in the villages like doctors, teachers, rich farmers and the elderly who are trusted sources of information for the village. These are the people accessible to almost all the villagers and can influence individual and collective decisions.

Much of the communication in rural areas is restricted to physically close locations, the nearby towns and villages. For this intra and inter village communication, word of mouth information exchange is most widely used. People gather at public places like local market, bus stop etc. and discuss various issues concerning them. This is also the place where social consensus is made and decisions taken. However inaccuracy is a major problem with this communication system. Most of the written communication done by the illiterate population like filling up government forms, Insurance formalities, and even writing letters is through agents/middlemen. This can be attributed to low literacy levels, unfamiliarity with the "official" language used and lack of information resources.

In practice it is much more difficult as finding useful information implies that the actual end-users understand what the problem is and ask the 'right questions' which get the 'right answers' so that the resulting information is pertinent and applicable. Expressing oneself with the 'right questions', understanding the 'questions right', and giving the 'right answers' are all learnt skills which, because of their socio-economic situation, people in rural communities may not have had the opportunity to develop [8]. As discussed in [3], author said that the first obstacle to overcome would be the general level of computer literacy of the people in the area. Merely providing the technology will not lead to a large number of people using it, similarly training would be sufficient. Studies in rural areas in Asia showed that in the battle against poverty, micro-finance has emerged as one of the most potent weapons.

3   Problem Analysis

There is Lack of awareness about ICTs in villagers as they are unaware of the fact that what benefits they may reap with Technology. There are a very limited number of expected users of technology in rural areas due to many demographic, cultural and economic barriers, as many people cannot afford these expensive technologies. Also it is perceived very weird in underdeveloped and backward areas, if females use technology and latest communication conveniences like cell phones, Face book and Skype. Low literacy rate is a major cause for this conventional approach of people towards technology. Affordability of ICTs is also a major factor for less adaptation of technology, because masses living in remote areas of Pakistan mostly have poor economic conditions. Lack of technical human resource in village areas to sort out technical problems is also a major reason. Low literacy rate is a big factor, which debars people to embrace technology, as mostly kiosks and Softwares are in English language and the people only know their national or regional languages in most of the areas of the country. By reviewing literature, we observe that technology adoption is a barrier between rural and remote communities of Pakistan specifically women. It is difficult to understand the perception of messages of illiterate women. Women living in rural areas are more subject to these aspects because of more challenges like literacy, socio-economics, religion and technology. Rural woman hardly have any interaction with technology.

4   Methodology

The method to conduct our research will be survey based and evaluation of system for rural communities. This survey and participatory audience research will be conducted from some selected rural areas of Punjab. The expecting finding in the study will have a guideline to design an interface to meet the need of rural community. Fig 2

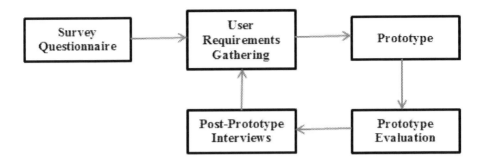

Fig. 2. Framework

5   Expected Results

Information technology may play a crucial role in improving socio-economic conditions of the far wide areas of the country; it may allow better access to the health and educational facilities in the rural areas of the country. Modern and updated Facilities are concentrated in urban areas, provision of health facilities, construction of universities and Libraries, all confined to the big cities and towns, whilst, Rural areas are deprived of all these, if provided in village, they are not sufficient or in poor condition Government and Local government started rural development program and uploaded their information about development program on websites for rural people.

References

1. Aditya, C.: Designing for the Indian rural population: interaction design Challenegs, Development by Design, Bangalore (2002)
2. Davenport, T.H., Prusak, L.: Wenn Ihr Unternehmen wüsste, was esalles weiß. Das Praxishandbuch zum Wissensmanagement. Landsberg/Lech (1998)
3. Delene, H.: Can a centered approach to designing a user interface for rural communities be successful? Durban Institute of Technolog. (2005)
4. Didar, Z., Chad, C.: Requirements Elicitation: A Survey of Techniques, Approaches and Tools. Engineering and Managing Software Requirements 19-46 (2005)
5. Duncker, E., Sheikh, J.A., Fields, B.: From Global Terminology to Local Terminology: A Review on Cross-Cultural Interface Design Solutions. In: Rau, P.L.P. (ed.) HCII 2013 and CCD 2013, Part I. LNCS, vol. 8023, pp. 197–207. Springer, Heidelberg (2013)
6. Hess, C.G.: Knowledge Management and Knowledge Systems for Rural Development. In: READER: GTZ Knowledge Management. GTZ Sector Project Knowledge Systems in Rural Development (2006), http://www.gtz.de/agriservice
7. Kavitha, C.R., Sunitha, M.T.: Requirement Gathering for small Projects using Agile Methods, IJCA Special Issue on Computational Science - New Dimensions & Perspectives, NCCSE (2011)
8. Kristina, P., Radhakrishnan, T.: A multimedia tool to elicit information needs in rural communities. In: CHI 2008, Florence, Italy, April 5-6. ACM (2008) 1-58113-000-0/00/0004

 9. Linda, W.: Software Requirements Engineering: What, Why, Who, When, and How. The Westfall Team (2006)
10. Nilofer, M., Sheetal, G.: Comparison of Various Elicitation Techniques and Requirement Prioritization Techniques. International Journal of Engineering Research & Technology (May 2012)
11. Nonaka, I., Takeuchi, H.: The Knowledge-Creating Company. Oxford University Press, New York (1995)
12. Ralph, R.Y.: Recommended Requirements Gathering Practices, Northrop Grumman Information Technology (April 2002)
13. Roling, N.: Extension Science, Information System in Agricultural Development. Cambridge University Press, Cambridge (1988)
14. Sheikh, J.A., Fields, B., Duncker, E.: The Cultural Integration of Knowledge Management into Interactive Design. In: Smith, M.J., Salvendy, G. (eds.) HCII 2011, Part I. LNCS, vol. 6771, pp. 48–57. Springer, Heidelberg (2011)
15. Sheikh, J.A., Fields, B., Duncker, E.: Cultural representation by Card Sorting. Ergonomics for All: Celebrating PPCOE's 20 years of Excellence. Selected Papers of the Pan-Pacific Conference on Ergonomics, November 7-10, pp. 215–220. Taiwan CRC Press, Kaohsiung (2011a)
16. Sheikh, J.A., Fields, B., Duncker, E.: Multi-Culture Interaction Design. In: Advances in Cross-Cultural Decision Making, pp. 406–415. CRC Press (2010b)
17. Sheikh, J.A., Fields, B., Duncker, E.: Cultural based e-Health information system. In: Presentation at the Health Libraries Group Conference 2010, CILIP, Salford Quays, UK, July 19-20 (2010a)
18. Sheikh, J.A., Fields, B., Duncker, E.: Cultural Representation for Interactive Information system. In: Proceedings of the 2009 International Conference on the Current Trends in Information Technology, Dubai (2009c)
19. Sheikh, J.A., Fields, B., Duncker, E.: Cultural Representation for Multi-culture Interaction Design. In: Aykin, N. (ed.) IDGD 2009. LNCS, vol. 5623, pp. 99–107. Springer, Heidelberg (2009)
20. Zheying, Z.: Effective Requirements Development – A comparison of Requirements Elicitation Techniques, Department of Computer Science (2005)

The Contemporary Rural Landscape
in the South-Western Region of Poland (Sudeten Region)
– A Search for Spatial Order

Elzbieta Trocka-Leszczynska

Faculty of Architecture of Wroclaw University of Technology
elzbieta.trocka-leszczynska@pwr.wroc.pl

Abstract. Architecture of rural settlements situated in the south-western region of Poland is distinguished by its vernacular character – the so-called "Sudeten architecture". Characteristic features of this architecture are visible in pre-war buildings of Sudeten villages both in two-story and single-story structures and include pitched gable roofs, a wooden residential section and a brick maintenance section. Another characteristic feature of Sudeten villages, also called "chain villages", is their homogenous layout, i.e. a detached but uniform arrangement of buildings. On the other hand, buildings which were erected in the southern part of the Lower Silesian province after 1945, which was a new economic and political situation, evolved away from the pre-war Sudeten vernacular architecture. With their randomly chosen architectural forms, flat roofs, concrete constructions, inappropriate colors and excessively dense arrangement, these new buildings introduced spatial chaos into the homogeneous structures of villages. Due to the landscape qualities of this region, it is important to establish precise rules for erecting new buildings in the existing context, and to popularize traditional architecture of the region (e.g. by organizing architectural contests for contemporary Sudeten buildings). Such projects could help residents to better understand the qualities of existing settlements and justify the requirement to follow rules when renovating and modernizing buildings. The purpose of these actions is to create new vernacular architecture for villages, which will both fulfill the requirements and needs of contemporary work and life, and also harmoniously complement the existing cultural and rural landscape.

Keywords: Corporate culture and/or country culture, rural landscape of Sudeten region.

1   Definitions

In his book,, From a Traveller's Perspective" Stanisław Vincenz remarks that landscape functions both as a historical background and as the result of history. He adds that landscape is not merely an artistic or visual effect, but also the soil on which we tread and toil, the hills and plains, the waters, rivers and moors, the air we breathe: all these things shape the activity of human beings and their footsteps, work, arms and

A. Marcus (Ed.): DUXU 2014, Part III, LNCS 8519, pp. 470–481, 2014.

legs, and their foundation [1]. On the other hand, Christian Norberg Schulz answers the question of what landscape is by stating that it is the space in which life of man takes place, the inhabited space between the earth and the sky. He notices that the act of inhabiting requires a place which has a distinct character and which enables living life to its fullest [2]. A description of an inhabited place underlines its features, which are a material expression of the culture of a given community, and, in effect, emphasizes such places as so-called architectural regions that share similar characteristics of development. A set of such characteristics (urbanistic, architectural, structural, or functional) assigned to particular areas is called vernacular architecture. Using this approach, the Sudeten were identified as a region in Poland with distinct characteristics of rural development [3].

The landscape is a dynamic system. Its functioning is determined by its components, the relations between them and the dominant processes [4]. In the case of areas with valuable characteristics of material culture, the notion of cultural landscape applies. The changing circumstances within this landscape determine its change and transformation, which in most cases consists not only in creating esthetic values, but also, or rather most importantly, in doing good and evil [5, p. 37]. Therefore, the most popular value these days, especially in rural landscapes, is spatial order, which is understood as doing good as opposed to the concept of spatial chaos, i.e. doing evil (Fig. 1, 2).

Fig. 1. A harmonious panorama of the village of Trzebieszowice with its vernacular architecture and dominating church tower (photo by E. Trocka-Leszczynska, 2011)

Fig. 2. A chaotic panorama of the village of Oldrzychowice Klodzkie ruined by high-rise prefab buildings located amongst single-story houses with steep roofs (photo by E. Trocka-Leszczynska, 2012)

In areas with homogenous architecture erected before 1945, spatial order may manifest itself as the continuation of traditional characteristics, forms or spatial arrangements, which have been classified as valuable and worth preserving. Spatial chaos is the uncontrolled process of erecting buildings and other elements in their surroundings. The study of spatial order in areas where characteristics of traditional development have been preserved is carried out by researchers of material culture and architecture of such areas. The activities of architectural scholars have produced another notion of regionalism, which was coined by Władysław Orkan at the turn of the 19th and 20th centuries. Initially this term referred to the cultural social movement aiming to stimulate the province, make it independent and to underline and respect its local tradition [6, p. 157]. In the 1970s regionalism was associated with the attitudes of opposition to uniformization and was considered a response to stereotypes and oversimplifications in spatial development [7, pp. 3-16]. However, regionalism vernacular architecture in this sense was often criticized because it frequently led to many forms which did not match particular areas and eliminated the traditional, often very valuable, characteristics of sub regions. Sometimes these solutions were also impractical and represented "imaginary" architecture, which disregarded the context of the place where these solutions were located [8, pp. 58-61].

The interpretation of the concept of regionalism should not result in a faithful reconstruction of old solutions or in the creation of open-air museum (Skansens). Only those actions should be considered that can produce architecture which is consistent with the surroundings and which continues the tradition of the area where the structure is to be built, but which also takes into consideration technological progress and meets contemporary needs. These issues are particularly problematic in areas where, after the Second World War, the political, administrative and economic system changed dramatically and where whole local communities were replaced and the cultural continuity was severed [3].

2   The Sudeten Region: Tradition and Modernity

The character of rural development resulted from the wisdom of local builders, who, for centuries, had been adapting the architectural solutions to the local environmental conditions, i.e. the climate, terrain, soil type and available building materials. This rural development was transformed in the spirit of that time, with the goal to meet the work and life needs of that day. The historical analysis of this development shows that subsequent stages of transformation were closely connected with traditional solutions and aimed at improvement without breaking the ties with the past. What resulted was the "continuity of rural architecture", which is manifested in the progressive transformation of urbanistic, architectural, functional and cultural characteristics. This was also the foundation for the traditionalism of vernacular architecture, which resisted the impact of the rapidly changing new architectural trends [9, p. 170].

2.1   Sudeten Before 1945 – Characteristic Features of the Landscape and Regional Architecture

The Sudeten mountain range was constantly affected by environmental circumstances typical for that area (i.e. the mountain climate and terrain, type of soils and available building materials: stone, slate, timber, clay) as well as changing anthropogenic circumstances (political, administrative, economic, etc.). As a result, the rural (vernacular) architecture of Sudeten, which had been shaped since early Middle Ages, was fairly homogenous and uniquely combined a variety of influences, including material culture of Germany, Czech Republic, Lusatia and Poland. This architecture was ultimately shaped in the 18th and 19th centuries, and has many common features, such as: the type of settlement arrangement ("chain villages") and characteristic types of homesteads – on farm land the so-called enclosed farmsteads with multiple buildings (Fig. 3), including a residential house, barn, and livestock pens. On the other hand, in mountain areas, where the terrain is diversified, single-story residential and livestock buildings emerged, which had all the homestead functions under one roof [3].

Fig. 3. Multi-house enclosed homesteads with an internal farmyard and a shrine at the entrance (Oldrzychowice), (photo by E. Trocka-Leszczynska, 2009)

The forms of these building are characteristic: elongated shape, tall, pitched symmetrical roof with a pitch of 45°-55°, identical spatial and functional systems based on the so-called Franconian house, in which the residential, utility and livestock sections were connected under one roof. Their floor plans are also similar with a centrally-located hall with residential rooms on one side and utility and livestock rooms on the other. Walls in the buildings in this area are also specific and the structures of external walls match the functions of the rooms: timber walls are used in the residential section, brick walls in the hall and livestock rooms, and trabeated or boarded walls in the utility and storage section.

The structure of the residential section (made of timber in older buildings) is a combination of different structures that exist in the Silesian region. The trabeated, stone and log houses are combined into one original construction, the so-called Lusatian half-timbered framing (German: Umgebinde), in which the posts surrounding the log wall of the ground floor support the trabeated upper floor and steep timber roof, or only the wooden rafter frame [10, pp.148-156].

These houses also have a similar architectural detail: a triangular, symmetrical gable with vertical boarding, characteristic wooden window bands and stone portals. This type of construction was built by the locals until the end of World War II (Fig. 4).

Fig. 4. Lusatian half-timbered houses, which combine all types of structures that exist in the Sudeten region: on the left – Sokolowsko, on the right – Olszyna Lubanska (photos by E. Trocka-Leszczynska, 2007)

2.2   Sudeten – Rural Architecture After 1945

After the Second World War, Polish borders were redrawn and incorporated the so-called Western Lands where most of the development had not been destroyed by military operations. The fundamental social and economic problem in these lands is that the population was replaced, i.e. the local communities were deported west to Germany and people from the Eastern regions of Poland were repatriated to the abandoned towns. The misunderstanding and ignorance of history and material culture of these areas, and especially the different reality of post-war socialist economy, were the main causes of the gradual ruin of the local development, destruction of spatial order and, ultimately, the degradation of the cultural landscape of the Sudeten. In the post-war period there are four phases that depict the attitude of both users and authorities to the existing development, as well as the impact of political, legal and economic circumstances on the protection and conservation of the existing and emerging development [3], [11].

The people deported to the Sudeten region found themselves amidst a high economic and technological standard and a different type of development, which was adapted for: different methods of farming connected with cultivating large areas, well-developed tourism, craft (weaving), local services (taverns, inns, hotels) and light industry (logging, mining, small hydroelectric power stations, etc.).

The unfamiliarity of the existing urban, architectural and technological solutions, was detrimental to their usage [12]. The migrants adapted the existing spatial arrangements of Sudeten houses to their current needs. Most frequently, this was synonymous to the destruction of former functional systems of buildings, either by using only one section of the huge homestead, and thus letting the remaining area deteriorate due to lack of conservation, or by populating them with many families, whereas when former homesteads were divided into smaller apartments, large rooms were partitioned, and multifunctional cookstoves, characteristic of this region, used for heating, cooking and baking bread, and connected with the so-called black kitchen, were demolished because they were difficult to fuel. After a period of uncontrolled management and use of the existing development, the construction industry in this area fell into stagnation, which was caused, on the one hand, by insufficient funds for renovations and modernizations, and, on the other hand, by the obstacles in erecting new structures. The former development was considered in this period as "culturally foreign", and its original characteristics were eliminated and obscured by amateur renovations [3], [11].

In the 1950s it became impossible to continue the traditional features in new development due to new legislation, which rationed building materials, introduced building typification, and forbade the use of timber, steep roofs or individual designs in rural architecture. Typification of construction in combination with industrialized building technologies, based on prefabricated reinforced concrete, introduced into Sudeten villages cuboidal single-family houses, in the shape of reinforced-concrete cubes, with flat roofs covered with tar paper. Such architectural solutions brought chaos into the landscape of Sudeten villages. Additionally, they were not properly designed to be inhabited by the village people because their functional system was typical for an urban single-family house with a limit of 110 m² on usable floor area (Fig. 5).

Fig. 5. Typical single-family and multi-family development (Oldrzychowice Klodzkie 2012) (photo by E. Trocka-Leszczynska)

Due to the lack of proper construction supervision, many unplanned changes to typical and obligatory architectural designs were introduced nationwide, with disregard to regional diversity. Most often, the floor area was increased by adapting basements and garages for residential use. This caused an increase in the number of stories and, in effect, in the height of buildings, which stood out in the local landscape. Moreover, new architectural details were introduced in the form of "Italian" arches, baroque terraces with balusters and prefabricated fences or fences made of scrap steel from production of e.g. ice skates. This typification also pertained to high-rise multi-family buildings, which were built near State Agricultural Farms and had cuboidal shapes and flat roofs. The inappropriate scale and form of this type of development ruined the spatial order of small Sudeten towns [3], [11].

The need to build new houses was also common, as the people deported from destitute rural areas did not want to continue their own or local rural architectural traditions. A new villa-type stone house, characterized by vertical proportions, became the desired symbol of social advancement and of breaking ties with the traditional, poor, timber single-story "cottage".

It was only in the 1980s, when postmodernism was developing in Europe, that "regionalism" was born, which piqued the interest of decentralized architectural departments in local architecture. This resulted in, among others, documents which systematized the solutions of Sudeten regional architecture.

Initially, during this phase, people built duplicable buildings, printed in catalogues, with features based on the so-called "mountain architecture". In result, the following characteristics were introduced, which were foreign to Sudeten: very steep roofs, wooden rafters, and boarding of external walls and balustrades. Although these buildings were designed for the Sudeten region, they did not have any local vernacular features. They were rather features of "universal mountain architecture" due to their steep roofs and wooden details, which were introduced after the period of modernist cubes (Fig. 6).

Fig. 6. Homes from that period: on the left – a much taller house with an asymmetrical roof (Oldrzychowice), in the center – a house with a steep asymmetrical roof and arches (near Ladek), on the right – a house with a „mountain" roof and boarding on balustrades (photos by E. Trocka-Leszczynska)

Only after the political and economic changes in Poland in the 1990s came a significant breakthrough in rural architecture of that region. There was a boom in investments and in renovations and modernizations of the existing development, all of which resulted from the following: clearly defined ownership of buildings, access to construction loans, possibility to renovate and build houses based on individual designs, accessibility of building materials, and appearance of private construction companies. However, most of the renovations done "independently" by owners, without proper construction supervision and knowledge of local architectural features or local construction methods, in most cases led to the demise and disappearance of original local features (Fig 7). Very often, owners replaced traditional small-paned windows with "large" plastic windows, roof coverings with "modern and more colorful" ones, wooden walls with stone or insulated and plastered walls, and since recently, with walls with siding.

The 1990s brought a generation change – most of the buildings are inhabited by people born in the region – and a change in the awareness of the young people living in this area.

People started showing interest in the history of these areas and old development is no longer treated and "foreign", but as "own". Old buildings are also eagerly bought, e.g. as second homes, renovated and inhabited, and the renovations serve as examples of good practices and as encouragement for neighbors and designers.

Fig. 7. Amateur renovations: on the left and in the center – the wooden walls of the ground floor and gable have been walled up (Wlosien 2006), on the right– the wooden structure of the round floor has been walled up (Bratkow) (photos by E. Trocka-Leszczyńska)

Slightly different problems emerge in terms of designing and erecting completely new structures. The basic difficulty in the Sudeten region is that no one has developed any models for shaping contemporary regional architecture. The previous attempts to preserve old traditions in newly designed buildings have been mostly unsuccessful, unskilled and with their foreign form, proportions and detail (Fig. 8) and ostentatious colors, stand in contrast with the existing development [11].

Fig. 8. Newly built homes in the Sudeten region: on the left – a home near Swieradow (2009), on the right – in Jerzykow (2012) (photos by E. Trocka-Leszczynska)

2.3   Continuation of Architecture in the Sudeten Region

The results of analyses show that the new buildings built in the region after the end of the Second World War, and in new political and economic circumstances, did not continue any of the features of pre-war architecture, but instead introduced spatial chaos into the homogenous Sudeten development. The first individual architectural designs in the 1980s were unsuccessful as they were not based on theoretical foundations and mostly had universal features of the so-called "mountain architecture", which were borrowed from other areas. The architectural features of Sudeten were ruined by people who disregarded local architecture and irresponsibly implemented architectural features that are foreign to the Sudeten region, such as e.g. steep asymmetrical roofs, foreign architectural details. This whole process was additionally aided by amateur renovations and modernizations of old developments, which were carried out without proper construction supervision (Fig.9).

Fig. 9. An unsupervised extension of a 19th century cottage eliminated the original features of the house: on the left – the original form as of 1996, on the right – the same building as of 2012 with a new reinforced-concrete porch (Wilkanów) (photos by E. Trocka-Leszczynska)

The Sudeten landscape is also being invaded by architectural designs from various "catalogs", which are erected in an unsupervised manner. This phenomenon popularizes structures, such as timber frame houses and log cabins, which are foreign to this area. Such buildings ruin the order and harmony of the Sudeten landscape by introducing, e.g. relatively flat hip roofs, thatched roof coverings, manor development (very popular in other Polish regions), or the very popular and structurally simple log cabins, which originate from eastern regions of Europe (Fig.10).

Fig. 10. Homes built from catalog designs: on the left – a „Polish manor" house, on the right – a timber frame house (photos by E. Trocka-Leszczynska)

At the turn of the 20th and 21st centuries one can notice a gradual rebirth of Sudeten architectural traditions. This is visible in the growing interest in both professional renovations and in the search for contemporary form of regional homes. For this purpose special architectural contests are announced, which are focused on the Sudeten region. For example in 2009, there was an architectural contest for "a Sudeten House with features of vernacular architecture of the Klodzko Land", and in 2012, a "Contest for a conceptual design of a contemporary half-timbered house" (Fig. 11).

Fig. 11. Contest for a conceptual design of a contemporary half-timbered house – winners of the second prize (first prize was not awarded): on the left – team: Aleksandra Doniec, Agata Kaczmarek, Katarzyna Sobuś, Marcin Wajda, in the center – PAG Głowacki Architectural Studio, Wroclaw; Tomasz Głowacki, Katarzyna Filipiak, Magdalena Ciszak, Magdalena Kornacka, on the right – Paweł Czeszejko, Katarzyna Antosik, Warsaw (photos by E. Trocka-Leszczynska)

The submitted projects are published in special catalogs and will help future investors to choose a design of a regional home which is appropriate for this area.

3   Conclusions

Theoretical design objectives can result from different approaches to the challenge of introducing new architecture into the existing cultural context. When searching for activities which could do good to the cultural landscape, what comes into focus is the concept of continuation of traditional architectural characteristics. Such activities, however, require that the elements which should be preserved and which will receive a new purpose in the landscape, be chosen objectively, without relying on personal preferences. What is also important here is the purpose for the survival of elements of the landscape (i.e. economical, historical, social, aesthetic values, etc.) [5, p 39].

A diversified approach to the existing cultural context, as well as the diverse cultural and historical values of existing housing complexes, determine how new development is built in their vicinity. New structures can either be copies of original solutions, such as open-air museums (Skansens), or can be inspired by local characteristics by creatively alluding to regional features, or can be negations by creating contemporary architectural forms, which are not related to traditional architecture.

Speaking of the continuation of regional architecture in areas, where ties with the past have been severed, one can recall the statement of Paul Ricoeur – It is a fact: every culture cannot sustain and absorb the shock of modern civilization. There is the paradox: how to become modern and to return to sources; how to revive an old, dormant civilization and take part in universal civilization [13]. Others insist on being critical in drawing from architectural history and taking into consideration the value of the context [14]. Others require that we do not directly draw from the context, but that a need of identity of place emerge, which seems a difficult and long-lasting process in the studied area [15, pp. 96-109].

By eliminating inappropriate trends, tightening the construction law, and raising the awareness of investors and designers it is possible to create contemporary regional rural development, which, on the one hand, could cater for the requirements and expectations of contemporary life and work, and on the other, could harmoniously complement and extend the existing rural and cultural landscape of the Sudeten region. Continuation of regional architecture requires special aid of regional architectural departments, i.e. their help in finding the right solutions, encouragement in pursuing them and special preparation and crediting for such projects.

It is also important to support the slow process of developing interest in old architecture and rebirth of Sudeten architectural traditions. Such initiatives are taken during, e.g. Open Days of Half-Timbered Homes, which are organized in Sudeten towns near the Czech and German border. At these events one can see properly made renovations or displays of architectural skills needed to perform renovations (Fig. 12).

Fig. 12. Open Day of Half-Timbered Homes, Bogatynia – popularization of the craft of joinery and a presentation of log carving for log walls (photos by E. Trocka-Leszczynska, 2010)

The following are also helpful in this process: training of craftsman, especially in the difficult and somewhat forgotten craft of wood carving, special training for architectural departments and popularization of knowledge of local architectural features, as well as activities aimed at increasing the awareness of cultural values of the development in this region.

References

1. Vincenz, S.: Perspektywy z Podróży, Kraków, pp. 362–363 (1980)
2. Norberg-Schulz C., Genius l.: Towards fenomenology of Architecture, Londyn (1980); Królikowski J.T.: Wieś i miasteczko – próba analizy znaczeń; Wieś i miasteczko u progu zagłady, PWN, Warszawa, p. 34 (1991)
3. Trocka-Leszczyńska, E.: Wiejska zabudowa mieszkaniowa w regionie sudeckim, Wrocław, Oficyna Wydawnicza PWr., Wrocław (1995)
4. Armand, D., Nauka o krajobrazie. Podstawy teorii i metody logiczno-matematyczne, PWN, Warszawa, p. 335 (1980)
5. Królikowski, J.T.: Wieś i miasteczko – próba analizy znaczeń, In: Wieś i miasteczko u progu zagłady, PWN, Warszawa, p. 37 (1991)
6. Tondos, B.: Regionalizm w aspekcie historycznym, In: Wieś i miasteczko u progu zagłady, PWN, Warszawa, p. 157 (1991)
7. Kurzątkowski, M.: Architecture vernaculaire = architektura rodzima? Ochrona Zabytków 1(148), 3–16 (1985)
8. Radziewanowski, Z.: Logika architektury regionalnej. Architektura (3), 58–61 (1985)
9. Tłoczek, I.: Dom mieszkalny na polskiej wsi, PWN, Warszawa, p.170 (1985)
10. Trocka-Leszczyńska, E.: Umgebindehauser in Niederschlesien. In: Umgebinde. Eine einzigartige Bauweise im Dreilandereck Deutschland – Polen – Tschechien, Die Blauen Bucher, Konigstein im Taurus: Langewiesche, pp. 148-156 (2007)
11. Trocka-Leszczyńska, E.: Tożsamość architektoniczna wiejskiej zabudowy mieszkaniowej", Kwartalnik Architektury i Urbanistyki 46(3), 299-308 (2001)
12. Nasz, A.: Przemiany kulturowo-społeczne na wsi dolnośląskiej po II wojnie światowej. In: Wieś Dolnośląska, PTL, Wrocław, pp.9-53 (1970)
13. Ricoeur, P.: History and Truth. In: Kolbley, C.A., (trans.): Northwestern University Press, Evanston (1965); Frampton, K.: Towards a Critical Regionalism: Six points of an architecture of resistance. The Anti-Aesthetic (red.) Hal Foster, Bay Press, Port Townsend, p. 16 (1983)

Mobile Money System Design for Illiterate Users in Rural Ethiopia

Mesfin F. Woldmariam[1], Gheorghita Ghinea[2], Solomon Atnafu[1], and Tor-Morten Grønli[3]

[1] Addis Ababa University
{mesfin.fikre,solomon.atnafu}@aau.edu.et
[2] Brunel University
george.ghinea@brunel.ac.uk
[3] Norwegian School of IT
tmg@nith.no

Abstract. Current mobile money systems provide users with hierarchical user interface and represent money as a positive rational numbers of the form 1, 3, 4.87...N. However, research indicates that rural communities that cannot read and write have a challenge entering such numbers in to mobile money system. Navigating through hierarchical text menu is also difficult to illiterate individuals. The present study uses concepts like memory placeholders, dragging & dropping; swiping, temporary holding space, and frequency counter and proposed a system that consists of three layers. The first layer denotes user interface and uses photos of currency notes, second layer is a placeholder memory that keep record of the frequency of currency bill, and the last layer keeps record of the total digital money in the system. We believe that the proposed system enables illiterate to identify currency notes while making payments and receiving payments, count digital money while making payments and or receiving payments during transaction.

Keywords: Color of money, mobile money systems, interface for Illiterate users, counting money.

1 Introduction

Mobile money can be classified as mobile transfer, mobile payments, and mobile financial services (UNCTAD 2012). M-transfer refers to when money is transferred from one user to another, mainly with the absence of exchanging goods and services. For example when one send or transfer money to his wife. In this case, mobile money replaces methods of sending money through friends or banks. On the other hand m-payments refer to when money is exchanged between two users that involves exchange of goods and services. Example, when customers pay bills to utility companies. Finally, m-financial services refer to when mobile money is linked to a bank account to provide the user with a whole range of transactions (savings, credits etc.) that they normally access at banks. This requires banks to integrate mobile

A. Marcus (Ed.): DUXU 2014, Part III, LNCS 8519, pp. 482–491, 2014.

money service with the normal banking system, so that mobile money users can withdraw and or deposit money without visiting agents. This makes possible to deposit cash directly into bank account, transfer money directly to another account. It also makes electronic based loan collection and disbursement possible. According to the GSM Association some 130 mobile money systems have been implemented since March 2012 and this number is increasing continuously1. Deploying and using each of the above types of mobile money requires different level of sophistication and complication.

Ethiopia is one of the fastest growing and second most populated African Counties. There is a huge gap between financial service provision and service demand from citizens. Financial institutions serve mainly the upper and middle class people residing in urban areas (Collins et al.; 2009), (Duncome and Boateng 2009), (Kristof 2010), (Rutherford 1999). Rural communities (whether they are poor or rich) and poor people in urban areas were marginalized by existing financial institutions' service delivery model. However, mobile technology has already proved mobile phones are the best solution to provide financial services to such marginalized poor and remotely living people. For example, in Kenya M-PESA, mobile phone based financial service enabled marginalized people get access to formal financial institutions. The success history of mobile money services in Kenya, Tanzania, South Africa, Brazil, India etc., attracted the attention of many telecommunication companies, development and aid NGOs like (DFID), World Bank's International Finance Corporation (IFC), Consultative Group to Assist the Poor (CGAP), Bill & Melinda Gates Foundation, Innovation for Poverty Action (IPA), research centre like the Institute for Money, Technology, & Financial Inclusion (IMTFI), Innovations for Poverty Action (IPA), and governments in hope of providing an alternative means to enable the rural community access financial services, irrespective of their being located remotely. But there are many challenges when we think of providing financial services to people who cannot read and write. Issues like interfaces are among the major challenges.

The state of mobile phone usage is relatively on a good status among rural Ethiopians. Even in villages without electricity, mobile phone ownership was surprisingly widespread. The primary use of mobile phones was to reduce money spent on transportation costs, to meet families in urban and other rural areas, and to get updated about market prices. They are quite aware of the utility of mobile phones and even non owners easily describe how they would make use of it if they had one. However, there is a problem of how to operate and use. Most of the old people generally need the assistance of others to make a phone call and even to answer an incoming call. Literacy wise, over 70% of the adult populations are functionally illiterate and uneducated. One in every two adults cannot read or write and the situation is worse for adult women. Many of them have low or no level of textual literacy, and they have no prior exposure to computing technology.

---

[1] http://unctad.org/en/Pages/newsdetails.aspx?OriginalVersionID= 134&Sitemap_x0020_Taxonomy=Technology%20and%20Logistics, retrieved on 15, June 2012.

In addition to the problem of illiteracy, there are many languages in the country, predominantly, Amharic, Oromigna, Tigrina, Somali, and Guaragigna that challenges digital communication. For example an Amharic speaker can communicate with Oromigna speaker through symbols like (color of money, showing fingers etc) or through some intermediaries that speak both languages. Color of money notes has dual purpose; as a means to identify among currency notes- by the illiterate individuals and as a means of communication language-when people speaking different language meet for transaction.

In addition to these, the physicality of money itself also enabled illiterate individuals to move money around and make simple mathematical computations (for example dividing 87 birr to 5 people), to sort money according to economic value. Thus it is interesting to examine how existence of many languages affects communication and transactions as we go from paper based money into digital money. Thus, it seems important to think the possibility of using photos of existing money color and denominations for interface design.

This paper is organized as follows: section two reviews the literature regarding interface design for mobile money systems, section three deals with problems of existing interfaces and mobile money representations, whilst section four presents money practices of illiterate users. Section five focuses on proposed mobile money system, while section six summarizes our work and highlights future work.

2   Interface Design for Mobile Money Systems

Literature like (Lehrer and West 2013) indicates literacy is the main challenge to bringing financial services to marginalized and poor people. Many of the information systems we talk about require some level of literacy and we have overlooked the experience and know-how of the poor with regards to how to use ICT systems. If one cannot read his/her name, cannot spell his identification number, cannot spell his phone number, cannot understand his/her receipt, it is simple to imagine the frustration he/she develop if transactions made digitally or if money goes digital. For example, a study in Bangladesh by (Ahmed, Zaber, and Guha 2013) found that the illiterate do not even remember their mobile phone number and have their number written on piece of paper for them. This makes the case to be even more challenging when it comes to the issue of mobile money.

Reviewing the literature for possible solutions to the illiteracy problem reveals the use of icons, verbal instructions, and photographs (Lehrer and West 2013). It is found that illiterate users that have no experience of using icons do not use them easily. The use of verbal instructions in interface design also revealed that users have some difficulties with making the translation from verbal instruction to manual action. Terms like "top, right" or "the square", "bottom" etc was confusing. This is the result of lack of previous exercise and practice with the use of such abstractions. They also experiment photograph for interface design and the result was quite impressive. Illiterate easily understand photos and there is no abstractions.

The study by Medhi et al. (2009) also revealed that illiterate users are comfortable with non-text designs over text-based designs. The use of images and or graph for user interface is also considered by researchers like Grisedale et al. (1997), Medhi et al. (2006) and Parikh et al. (2003). Research, such as that described in (Medhi et al 2006) and (Ruth 2013) also considered voice instructions and audio annotations as a powerful way to design user interface for the illiterates. Even though there are some authors (Parikh et al 2003) states the possibility of using numbers is acceptable, it appears this is not the case from the observation we made in the field.

Thus, it can be understood from the review of the literature, designing for illiterate people needs to consider principles like: (1) visual-illiterate people often do not learn to think in terms of abstractions, so signs, icons, and diagrams may not make sense to them, (2) illiterate people can be confused if what they see is different from what they know, (3) the use of audio based interfaces if recommended-as it avoids literacy related issues (Medhi et al., 2006) and (Ruth 2013, and (4) menu based interfaces are questionable for novice users (Jones et al 2000). Therefore, it appears important to explore the use of currency photos for interface design.

3   Existing Mobile Money Interfaces and Money Representation

Currently existing mobile money services use hierarchical menus, as indicated below and represent and store digital money as a positive rational numbers of the form 1, 2, 3, 4.25, 0.43, …, N and enable users get access to their accounts through some security codes based on either SMS or USSD. From the illiterate users' perspective both menu based interface design and money representations have challenges. A simple observation (Fig. 1 below) of M-birr in Ethiopia and M-PESA in Kenya reveals the interface is menu-based where transactions are conducted by selecting options that appear on the mobile phone's display, organized as hierarchical menu options. Users use up-down keys to select between options on the menu. As stated by previous research detailed in the previous section, such a textual menu-based interface is not easy for illiterate individuals. One can imagine how difficult the following interface will be to illiterate people that cannot read and write even their name.

Unlike previous solutions that represent digital money in a positive rational number avoiding the issue of color and denomination, this paper assumes that mobile money services will take money notes as they appear in their paper format, digitizing money notes while maintaining color and denomination. This means for example, we will have digital money of 5 cents, 10 cents, 25 cents, 50 cents, 1 birr note, 5 birr note, 10 birr note, 50 birr note, and 100 birr notes. Each of this will form a stack and will appear on top of the mobile phone screen when users swipe on the different colored money interface. As stated by the research described in the previous section, such use of photos of money and their denomination can enable illiterate individuals to understand and use such a system easily.

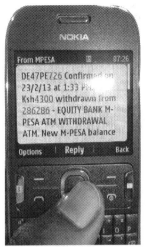

M-BIRR of Ethiopia   M-PESA of Kenya

Fig. 1. Interface of M-BIRR and M-PESA

4   Money Practices of Rural Illiterate Individuals

Field work undertaken in 2012 revealed that many old-aged women and men could not read in their own spoken language, and many of them could not read anything at all. Many of them do not understand symbols, icons, illustrations, and instructions. On the other hand, we contend that any system designed to serve them should work for them. Thus this brings a challenge to designers of the system to make sure such users can able to use their system. According to the field work, the majority of the study population identifies currency notes based on color, images, and sizes, and not based on values inscribed. This raises the question, how could illiterate individuals transact in an electronic payment ecosystem?

The physicality of money itself also enabled illiterate users to move money around and make simple mathematical computations (for example to divide 87 birr to 5 people), they lay say an amount of 10 birr into 5 places and keep on adding on to it until they exhaust the money to be shared. Individuals also arrange money from the smallest denominator to the largest (1, 5, 10, 50, and 100) birr money notes. Such sorting makes money counting easy and fast. Calculating the total is also easy when it is sorted than not sorted, said a respondent. Figure 2 shows how farmers sort money according to economic value from highest to the smallest denomination and identify based on color.

Fig. 2. Color based identification and sorting of money

In order to propose our mobile money system design for rural illiterate Ethiopians, it is important to look into the everyday practices of such communities. From the field work data of 2012, we found interesting practices that inform new system design and worth explanation: (1) practice of money counting while making payments and or receiving payments, to know balances at hand, (2) making money changes during transactions, (3) sorting and arranging money notes based on denomination, (4) making simple mathematical computation (addition, subtraction, division, and multiplication. Any new system to be designed for illiterates need to facilitate the execution of these practices in digital money form too. It is our belief that this paper has contributed towards many of these issues.

4.1   Money Counting Practice

Counting money bills is an important task during transaction even in normal circumstances. Be it during transactions or at other social and religious events, people do count money: while accepting payments, making payments, and making and accepting changes etc. As a matter of culture and practice, individuals count each time they receive cash payments and when they make payments, mainly during transactions. To do so, individuals sort every bill and arrange them from the biggest bill to the smallest one and count the bills. To count the money, they hold the stack of money in one hand and count with the other hand. Sometimes they count from both edges so that they can get around the situation when some bills are folded and counted as two bills. Figure 3 below shows this practice.

Fig. 3. Money counting practice

The issue is, given that digital money is represented by a positive rational number, how do illiterate users count money? This is one of the questions this paper addresses.

4.2   Changes During Transaction

If we assume digital money representation in the form of digitizing existing money bills by maintaining the color and denomination, the issue of changes during transaction and money transfer is important. For example, assume one has a digital money bill of 5 birr and wanted to pay 3 birr to a shoe polisher. In this case, similar to the paper money, one would give the shoe polisher 5 birr bill and expect him to give change to the value of 2 birr. Now the issue is how do we do this in digital money (mobile money)? One of the options is to design a mobile money system that can change a 5 birr bill into five (1 birr bills) so that a user can pay the three of them to the shoe polisher. In this case, the system will automatically update the frequency of 5 birr bill and 1 birr bills as well as the total value in the system. That is, it contains the idea of a system which splits bills automatically when needed!

4.3   Sorting and Arranging Money Based on Denomination

To count and keep money, individuals also arrange money bills according to their category. Again our proposed system introduces the memory placeholders' concept which enables to keep different money bills into different categories.

4.4   Undertaking Simple Mathematics Operations

The physicality of the bills also has another advantage to illiterate users, namely that they can do simple maths by moving money around. For example, if they want to divide 65 birr among 6 individuals, they do it step by step. Firstly, they approximately allocate 9 birr to each of them and when they remain with some extra, they keep on giving one additional birr to each individuals and keep doing so until they share it equally. Thus, again the current proposed system will have a feature that enables individuals to do such maths.

5   Proposed Rural Mobile Money System Design

Based on the above everyday money practices of illiterate individuals, we propose to use photographs of each bill and coin in use in Ethiopia for the interface design of mobile money system. The bills and coins are similar (same color, images, and denominations) to paper money, except they appear digitally in the apparatus. Accordingly, keeping these metadata of the bills serve the illiterate users as a means of: (1) communication among people of different language, (2) counting and making mathematical computations and (3) identifying and differentiating among currency notes. To address the issue of counting money, making money changes by the system, performing simple maths, we introduced concepts like: dragging and dropping, memory placeholder, swiping, frequency counter, total controller, audio assist, and temporary holding place. The design of the system has three layers as indicated in figure 4 below.

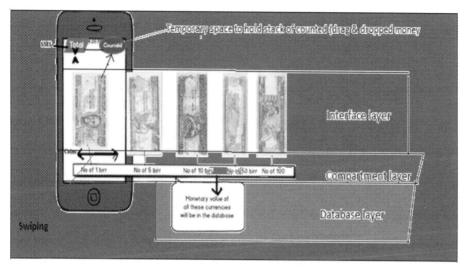

Fig. 4. Design of mobile money information system

We now describe the components that constitute the system.

5.1   Interface Layer

This layer displays the different money bills and cents one after the other. When the user swipes to the left side, cents of 5, 10, 25, and 50 will appear visible on the screen. Swiping to the right side will make bills (1, 5, 10, 50, and 100) to be visible on the screen one after the other. So, through swiping left and right, a user can get access to the cents or bills he/she would like to make use of.

5.2   Compartment Layer

This layer consists of compartments (memory place holders) for every money bill/notes and cents. This means that, when say a bill of 10 birr is visible and is on screen, it means that the user is reading this memory space. The memory spaces count and keep record of the frequency or number of the bills. For example if a user has 3 bills of 50 birr notes and expends 2 of them, the system will update data in this compartment to 1. The same logic is applicable for the other bills too.

5.3   Database Layer

This layer shows the total of monetary value (sum of all currencies and cents in their respective compartments/ memory place holder) that the user has. It displays the total amount of money in the phone at particular time. When money is expended or received, both the compartment and database layer will be updated automatically, to reflect current balance.

5.4   Top Two Icons (Red and Green)

As indicated in figure 4 above, our design also consists of other elements indicated by green and red colors. The placeholder marked by the red color is a space we place money to be paid. The user will count money by dragging and dropping through the interface layer from the compartment and places the counted money in this red color temporary holding place. The green one is an audio assisted icon that "speaks" the amount of money counted and placed to be paid or transferred.

6   Conclusion and Future Work

Designing mobile money systems to match the capabilities of the people they are meant to serve is essential to growing financial inclusion. Such systems enable illiterate users to develop confidence in the system and scale up financial inclusions. Based on the challenges of illiterate users and their transaction practices, we have proposed a mobile money system that enable them distinguish electronic money notes, and suit their transaction practice like the counting they know. We believe, this work will provoke researchers for more work in this area (either to advance the proposed idea or searching for another one). In our upcoming work, we are planning to consider some ways that enable individuals to be able to make changes, implement and evaluate our design.

References

1. Ahmed, I.S., Zaber, M., Guha, S.: Usage of the Memory of Mobile Phones by Illiterate People. In: Proceedings of the Third ACM Symposium on Computing for Development, New York, USA (2013)
2. Collins, D., Morduch, J., Rutherford, S., Rutheven, O.: Portfolios of the poor. Princeton University Press, Princeton (2009)
3. Duncome, R., Boateng, R.: Mobile phones and financial services in developing countries. Reviews of concepts, methods, issues, and evidence and future research directions. Working paper No. 37. Centre for development informatics, institute for development policy and management (2009)
4. Grisedale, S., Graves, M., Grünsteidl, A.: Designing a graphical user interface for healthcare workers in rural India. In: Proc. SIGCHI Conference on Human Factors in Computing Systems, Atlanta, USA, pp. 471–478 (1997)
5. Jones, M., Buchanan, G., Thimbleby, H., Marsden, G.: User interfaces for mobile web devices mobile workshop position paper. In: Proc. 9th International World Wide Web Conference (2000)

6. Kristof, D.N.: Cash is so 20th century. I have seen the future in Haiti (2010), http://www.nytimes.com/2010/12/05/opinion/05kristof.html?_r=1 (retrieved by March 31, 2011)
7. Rachel, L., Harry, W.: Literacy a Hidden Hurdle to Financial Inclusion (2014), http://www.cgap.org/blog/literacy-hidden-hurdle-financial-inclusion (retrieved on January 23, 2014)
8. Medhi, I., Gautama, N.S.N., Toyama, K.: A Comparison of Mobile Money-Transfer UIs for Non-Literate and Semi-Literate Users. In: CHI 2009, Boston, Massachusetts, USA, April 4-9, pp. 1741–1750 (2009)
9. Medhi, I., Sagar, A., Toyama, K.: Text-Free User Interfaces for Illiterate and Semi-Literate Users. In: International Conference on Information and Communication Technologies and Development, Berkeley, USA, pp. 37–50 (2006)
10. Parikh, T., Ghosh, K., Chavan, A.: Design Studies for a Financial Management System for Micro-credit Groups in Rural India. In: ACM Conference on Universal Usability, Vancouver, Canada, pp. 15–22 (2003)
11. Branvall, R.: Designing products and services for the illiterates. Inclusive business insights (2013)
12. http://community.businessfightspoverty.org/profiles/blogs/ruth-branvall-designing-products-and-services-fory-illiterate (retrieved on January 23, 2014)
13. Rutherford, S.: The Poor and their Money. An essay about financial services for the poor, Institute for development Policy and Management University of Manchester, UK (1999)
14. UNCTAD 2012, http://unctad.org/en/Pages/newsdetails.aspx?OriginalVersionID=134&Sitemap_x0020_Taxonomy=Technology%20and%20Logistics (retrieved on December 13, 2013)

Design for Environment
and Sustainability

Using Soft Systems Methodology (SSM) in Understanding Current User-Support Scenario in the Climate Science Domain of Cyber-Infrastructures

Hashim Iqbal Chunpir[1,2], Thomas Ludwig[1,2], and Amgad Ali Badewi[3]

[1] German Climate Computing Center (DKRZ), Bundesstr. 45a, Hamburg, Germany
{chunpir,ludwig}@dkrz.de
[2] University of Hamburg, Department of Informatics, Hamburg, Germany
[3] Cranfield University, Manufacturing Department, Bedforshire, United Kingdom
a.badewi@cranfield.ac.uk

Abstract. Cyber-infrastructures have transformed the practice of research. Researchers can now access distributed data worldwide with the help of cyber-infrastructures. User support services play an important role to facilitate researchers to accomplish their research goals with the help of cyber-infrastructures. However, the current user-support practices in cyber-infrastructures are not properly organized (at least in climate cyber-infrastructures) thus over-burdening human support agents. The paper describes the study conducted to evaluate the geographically distributed user-support system currently in practice in the leading cyber-infrastructure namely Earth System Grid Federation (ESGF). The members of the investigation team found out that the user-support in ESGF, a global climate cyber-infrastructure need more attention to make it resourceful as well as standardized. The findings about end-user support system were modelled using soft systems methodology (SSM). This approach helped to present the findings of this study to stakeholders in order to capture their feedback about the current system to further improve the system.

Keywords: Information visualization, e-Science, systems, research, user support, help desk, soft systems methodology, rich picture building.

1 Introduction

Cyber-Infrastructures (CI) has widely been deployed to access and share the knowledge, data, computing and even human resources to facilitate intra-disciplinary and inter-disciplinary research, also known as e-Research. Cyber-infrastructure is the coordinated aggregate of software, hardware and other technologies, as well as human expertise, required to support current and future discoveries in science and engineering. Networks that constitute cyber-infrastructure(s) are complex networks; users need an interface to access its resources usually data [1]. The interface includes command line tools, web portals, different application interfaces or Graphical User Interface (GUI) to access data holdings which are the main resources. However,

A. Marcus (Ed.): DUXU 2014, Part III, LNCS 8519, pp. 495–506, 2014.

during an interaction of a user with a cyber-infrastructure, a user may require help due to outages of some resources or any other anomaly in cyber infrastructure or a user requires particular scientific or technical information. In order to meet user support challenges, cyber infrastructures offer support, which even being a core activity has not received adequate attention since inception of cyber-infrastructures [2].

This paper describes the results of an investigation of the current user support system in climate cyber-infrastructure ESGF. The results are depicted using soft systems methodology (SSM). To improve a system or to develop an effective system to support users of a cyber-infrastructure, it is essential for all stakeholders to understand how support employees perform the tasks of helping users along with performing other core operational tasks of cyber-infrastructure development. For this purpose, SSM is used to portray the current user support practices that constitute user support system in ESGF (Earth System Grid Federation). Though various approaches have been used to model user support systems in industry [3–6] and education sector [7], hardly any study has been done using SSM approach. Secondly, few studies have been conducted that have investigated user support practices in cyber-infrastructures so far [2].

The rest of the paper is organized as follows: Section 2 describes the background of cyber-infrastructures, user support and the significance of user support in cyber-infrastructures. Section 3 describes the contemporary user support practices in ESGF as captured from diverse data and sources of information. Finally, section 4 describes the critique of the existing user support, followed by conclusion and discussion in section 5 and 6.

2   Background

The background related to this paper is divided into three main headings given in the sub-sections:

2.1   Cyber-Infrastructures

Cyber-infrastructures, also called e-Science, e-Science infrastructures, e-research, collaboratories, virtual science and Big Data Science [8], are based on technically connected networks through grid-computing technology [9], [10]. Furthermore, they are formed through collaboration of many organisations across national boundaries where hardware, software, human resources, and other instruments are under the jurisdiction of one or more institutes having their particular norms, standards and policies [8], [11]. The active domains supported by cyber-infrastructures include Earth Sciences, Climate Sciences, Bio-Informatics, and other fields. In cyber-infrastructures, much of funding and effort has been dedicated to develop and improve technologies such as anatomy of data-grid [5], middleware, storage of data in grid environment [8] as well as socio-structural aspects of e-Science for instance "Virtual Organisations" (VOs), CWE (Collaborative Work Environments), VRE

(Virtual Research Environments) [12]. Yet, the organization of user support has not been the subject of study in cyber-infrastructures [4].

Much has been changing over-time about cyber-infrastructures, as they are evolving with changing technologies and other socio-structural factors. Therefore this change has a direct effect on the user support. Investigating user support in cyber-infrastructures will reveal the common problems and their categorization scheme. Other contributions of this study include: organizing and managing user support in a better manner in CI by introducing a recommendation framework that will lead to user and employee satisfaction over the services of cyber-infrastructure. Furthermore, this study will contribute to cyber-infrastructure in letting it adapt to changes, scientific changes in the domain that a cyber-infrastructure serves.

2.2   Servicing Users

User support has been always seen as a subsidiary or additional function to the core services of corporations until start of 2000s, when it was realized that customer support should be made better with the application of business process frameworks to improve service quality and provide customer satisfaction [13]. Since then different support models and structures have been tried to suit the corporation business model of servicing customer and end-user concerns. User-support technologies and processes have evolved with the passage of time. The first help desk (HD) in the 80's had only a desk, pen and a telephone used by human support agent [13], [14].

Since then, the traditional HD afterwards had gone through different levels of evolution with the change in the commercial organizational set-up and needs of customers to employ techniques like Automatic Call Distributions systems (ACD) [15], Interactive Voice Response (IVR) systems [16], help desk management system (HDMS) along with associated reporting tools [17], help desk expert systems, knowledge-management centric help desks [18], embedding case-based reasoning (CBR) engine in help desk [19], [20], help desks based on corpus-based analysis (CBA) mechanisms [21], [22], use of remote control technologies to support end-users and web based e-support techniques with and without human support agents [23]. Studying ESGF user support as a use case will contribute to the "service desk" or "customer services" concept in distributed, research oriented, non-commercial environments.

2.3   Significance of User Support in Cyber-Infrastructures

In the last decade, the user-support in ESGF has been evolving mainly due to the change in ESGF cyber-infrastructure. For instance; looking at the history of ESGF development, the technological changes, organizational changes, introduction of new data projects served by the ESGF data archive system and the number of users and their needs have been on constant rise [24–27]. It is the right time to perceive and understand the dynamics of user support situation, its role and its interconnection with cyber-infrastructure operations because ESGF has reached a state of modular services-oriented architecture (SOA) forming a federated and distributed network.

The architecture of ESGF has been developed in such a way that new partners can easily join the federation with few changes in configuration through a central configuration scheme known as XML registry. The dynamics and complexity of ESGF operations influences the user support process thus making it also a dynamic process where a user request from any part of the world can come and is handled by any person in the participating institute of the federation. In order to save time and supporting efforts of human resources (cyber-infrastructure staffs) viz-á-viz user satisfaction, it is vital to investigate user support process using SSM so that the process may be made efficient in the near future.

3   Contemporary User Support Practices in Cyber-Infrastructures

3.1   Case Selection

An important practical use-case in the field of climate science cyber-infrastructures) is ESGF (Earth System Grid Federation) project. ESGF is the first inter-agency and international effort in the domain of Climate Science used for Earth Science Modeling (ESM) [8], [25], [27]. At the moment, more than two thousand researchers accessing huge amount of climate data for climate-model inter-comparison purposes from ESGF distributed data-archive worldwide that makes ESGF a effervescent infrastructure that supports ESM [2,7], which is a main reason to take ESGF as a use-case for this research.

Moreover, ESGF facilitates to study climate change and impact of climate change on human society and Earth's eco system [27]. Since physical phenomenon that govern Earth's climate are so complex and diverse, it is the most important scientific challenges of our time to undergo sophisticated model simulations that generate huge amount of data, collect observational data from various sources and share that data at a global scale. This is made possible by ESGF to discover, analyze and access the Climate data sets which are stored at multiple geographic locations across the globe [27–30].

3.2   Research Method and Its Justification

In this study single case study method is chosen as a research method. The information about current user support practices in ESGF, and similar cyber-infrastructures, was captured via; survey-questionnaire, participatory observation of the first author, ten interviews with stakeholders (of ESGF and C3Grid e-Science infrastructures having different backgrounds and roles), observing relevant documents such as reports, publications and archival analysis of user and staff communication within the user's mailing list of ESGF. The triangulation of sources of information was chosen to capture different perspective to validate and to contrast the findings [31–33].

3.3   Findings

This empirical qualitative cum quantitative investigation revealed number of issues where attention of ESGF executive team is needed in order to improve the existing user-support process in climate cyber-infrastructure projects. The issues about the existing user-support process in climate cyber-infrastructure projects include allocation of time, human resource, time to solve the user-problems, characteristics of user requests, support tools, support structure and many others. Following Checkland's seven stage overview "mode 1" of SSM, the current user-support situation in climate cyber-infrastructure projects (especially ESGF and its associated projects) is expressed in figure 1 in the form of *rich picture mind map*.

Fig. 1. The figure shows the user support process in climate-Science infrastructures in the form of rich picture mind map

The authors being the analyst found the current situation of user support problematic and expressed the situation in the form of what they call a *rich picture mind map*. Pictures can provide an excellent way of sorting out and prioritizing complex problem areas and therefore are used in SSM. In traditional SSM approach rich pictures are normally hand drawn and they describe elements of structure, process, issues, concerns or developments. There are no rules used in SSM rich pictures approach though matchstick people and bubbles coming out of people are common.

In figure 1, the current user support system scenario is described using thick lines that describe a particular concept associated to the user support system with in ESGF. The lined arrows originating from the main oval shaped system describes that the system contains or is dependent on these various concepts depicted via a thick line and a textual description on top of them. The dashed-lines arrows depict that a particular concept might have different attributes depicted by these lines. For example, if we look at the figure 1, user support system in ESGF cyber-infrastructure has communication channels via which users and staffs communicate in case of a problem. These communication channels are divided into asynchronous and synchronous type of communication channels, currently present in user support in cyber-infrastructures (in fig. 1 top left). The asynchronous communication channels in user support of ESGF are mailings lists (ML) and request tracking software (RT) (in fig. 1 top left). Most of the communication between users and climate cyber-infrastructure employees is via e-mail (through ML and RT). This result is in accordance to the distributed model and global nature of cyber-infrastructure.

Time is an important issue in user support in cyber-infrastructures. Staff's response time and solution time to a user request are important elements of an effective user support. Response time is further categorized into support staff's reply time, reply time between support staffs, i.e. response time of a support staff if a user request is escalated from another support staff who is the receiver of the user request at first. Finally, user response time to the support staffs response. For the time being response time and solution time though not systemized with the help of a service level agreement (SLA) works well for user support in ESGF cyber-infrastructure.

The user requests also known as incoming incidents can either be due to a problem in the cyber-infrastructure; e.g. outages of notes, or a user requires an information about a particular phenomenon; e.g. how a user shall register etc. All of these incidents or user requests can be categorized into respective categories. After analyzing the results of the survey questionnaire, these categories can be cited as: Data access and data download problems, user authorization; authentication and registration problems. These are the most common problems encountered in a current user support. Unfortunately, there is no central repository maintained by the current user support system in ESGF where the information about user requests can be stored and redundant user support enquires can be triggered. Moreover, currently there is no information retrieval system where users or support staff can search the relevant problem cases. However, partly some user support staffs do update the information useful for staff and users of ESGF system. The usability of the online help resources is not determined yet. Update of the online help websites is done if there is a new version or release of a software component of an ESGF cyber-infrastructure.

User support in ESGF cyber-infrastructure is present to facilitate ESGF users and is operated by its employees (see figure 1 top right). The operation of user support is based on employees' attitude, knowledge, analytical skills and satisfaction level with the support process that provide support to users. Similarly, users in their interaction with the cyber-infrastructure depend on their behavior of interaction (attitude) towards systems as well as their knowledge, analytical skills and level of satisfaction. According to survey results the employees who support users are skillful and qualified. Moreover, both users and employees are satisfied to some extent with the current user support facilities in ESGF and ESGF-like cyber-infrastructures but not completely satisfied.

The users of ESGF and ESGF-like cyber-infrastructures are divided into four main categories, working group 1: Advanced core climate scientists, working group 2: Impact scientists, working group 3: Integrated Assessment Modelling (IAM) scientists and finally non-climate scientists such as; policy makers, journalists and anyone who is interested in climate science. The employees of ESGF and ESGF-like climate science cyber-infrastructures are technical experts such as computer scientists, network administrators, data curators and climate scientists. The roles amongst the staffs of climate science cyber-infrastructures (ESGF and ESGF-like) are not completely specified. Therefore, there is no formal assigned role of *user support manager* in cyber-infrastructure organization. Any climate science cyber-infrastructure employee from any part of the world can jump in and answer a user request and provide solution to user's problem. Answering a user request or providing a solution to user's problem is a initiative of an employee (at least in ESGF). There are no explicit long-term support positions financed by the ESGF sponsors.

The ESGF data archive system and its sub-components such as authorization and registration sub-system, UI of gateways (portals) available to users to browse and access climate data-sets and others depends on user support. For instance if there is any disturbance in any function in any geographically distributed component of archive system, then the users experience it: Hence sending user requests which are entertained by cyber-infrastructure employees. There is no split of user support into user support levels such as first level support (FLS) or second level support (SLS).

3.4   Root Definitions and CATWOE

According to SSM; there is a *transformation process* in each conceptual system having a purpose, where an input is transformed into an output. The transformation depicted as "T" is a *Weltanschauung,* a German word equivalent to *worldview* in English. *Weltanschauung* "W" is a very dominant concept in SSM that determines the belief or point of view that makes transformation "T" rational. W and T form the core of a mnemonic CATWOE[1]. CATWOE analysis in SSM is used to create a root definition which is the third stage in Checkland's seven stage of SSM investigative process which has come to be known as "mode 1" SSM. ESGF user support system is a system that has a purpose (or purposes), it exists for a reason and achieves some change, or 'transformation'. ESGF promotes user problem solving; in the long run it educates users and promotes learning about its sub-systems. It 'transforms' unresolved user problems into solutions.

---

[1] In CATWOE, C stands for *customers,* A for *actors,* T for *transformation process,* W for *worldview,* O for *owners* and E for *environmental constraints.*

User Support requested   Transformation   User Support Delivered

Fig. 2. The transformation process in ESGF user support

Using SSM mode 1, CATWOE analysis in the context of ESGF user support system can be stated as in the following table 2:

Table 1. CATWOE analysis of user support system in ESGF cyber-infrastructure

Mnemonic	Description
C= Customers	users of ESGF system (victims or beneficiaries)
A= Actors	ESGF staff (Support staff and developers)
T=Transformation process	Transformation of user incidents into solutions monitored by E1[2] E2[3] E3[4]
W="Weltanschauung" or Worlds perspective	the belief that providing user support will benefit users in their research activities and interaction with the ESGF system monitored by E1 E2 E3
O=Owners	All stakeholders of ESGF
E = Environmental Constraints	Geographically distributed environment with components under control of different authorizes operated by different human resources

E1, E2, E3 can be defined in terms of ESGF user support system as:
E1: Are user support requests answered properly? E2: How many user support requests are answered keeping what standard and how many resources consumed? E3: Do users find user requests solved by employees and UI for self-help a useful way of reaching the research goals of users and interacting with cyber-infrastructures?

An ESGF user support system which is part of the ESGF system in the wider context can be defined in the form of SSM root definition as: *An ESGF user support system owned by ESGF-stakeholders (investors), operated by ESGF staffs (partly staff from node administrative bodies), to support users of ESGF by fulfilling their information needs in order to get information to achieve their research-oriented goals while constrained by ESGF financial, technology, human resources, cultural norms, geographic administrative and general policies.*

---

[2] Efficacy- does the system work?, is transformation achieved?
[3] Efficiency- a comparison of value of output versus value of input- is the system worthwhile?
[4] Effectiveness- does the system achive its longer term goals?

4   Critique

From the findings of survey questionnaire, one can observe that there is multiple communication channels offered in a user support system which is not bad. Nonetheless, different administrative nodes that form a user support unit have their own local usage of communication channels. For instance request tracking software (RT) are used by some locally and at the same time there does a mailing-list exist. Nevertheless, there is no storage of all the cases of user problem or information needs that have been already treated by user support employees. Since there is no incident repository or knowledge-base (KB), there is no central information retrieval system present in user support process that would help users (for self-help) and the staff. Though efforts made in the last several months, the online help websites are not updated regularly. Usability as well as accessibility of the websites can be further improved.

There is no formal designation of user support managers or employees, hence, no one is responsible for this activity rather user support activity is carried out by the employees on their own. This is the reason that user support requests are sometimes completely ignored, though this takes place not too often. Neither there is a user support task force nor committee, which collects the funding from the ESGF cyber-infrastructure sponsors, to standardize, measure, and control user support practices of ESGF. Partly this is because the research focus till now has been on stabilizing and developing the ESGF cyber-infrastructure itself. But since now the minimum level of maturity in ESGF cyber-infrastructure has been achieved it now time to streamline its user-support. At the moment, no formal concrete policy has been included in the manifesto of ESGF. Though the user support system works for now but as the number of users are on increase the user support needs monitoring, control of user support activities in order to streamline it.

5   Discussion

At first glance, information systems or cyber-infrastructures seem to be 'hard' designed physical systems, but experience shows that they seldom add value unless they are closely married to their organizational context and the people who use them [34]. Softer issues are important in information system planning, design, and implementation. 'Soft' has another, more specialist meaning. It includes people's perspectives; depending on the type of person you are, and your training and experience, you may understand 'systems' as tangible things which are really present in the world. In this paper user support process is shown in the form of a system where organizational and human context plays an important role as their influence cannot be ignored.

The aim of ESGF user support is to 'transform' unresolved user problems into solutions. Its performance though not formally measured at this point in time, however can be measured. With a measurement scheme the user support activities can be shown to be more, or less efficient, rate of service (transformation) can be judged with the help of resolution of queries and problems. It is important to introduce a mechanism for control of the whole user support process and a decision making process within a user support should be laid down i.e. a management structure of user support activities. The current user support is based on geographically distributed components (physical and human), which can themselves be taken to be systems administrative units as well as climate modelling units. All components are related, and sub-systems with a user support system interact with each other. The topic of user support in cyber-infrastructures is needed to be included in board meetings and face to face meetings of ESGF.

6   Conclusion

Since a human behavior is unpredictable, organizational and management problems are seldom clear-cut and well-defined; normally they are complex, with many indeterminable variables 'soft' systems. User support system in climate cyber-infrastructure can be represented with the help of SSM to represent its root definition, rich picture mind map and the conceptual model understandable to all stakeholders of cyber-infrastructures, which forms basis of enhancement needed to a system. Another governing principle of SSM is representation of user support as the idea of 'emergence' most simply expressed as 'the whole is greater than the sum of the parts.' When the constituent parts of a system act together they have properties which the individual parts do not have. Thus, staff and researchers are needed (as well as many other things) to make a cyber-infrastructure; not just a piece of hardware. The user support system is a major platform for collaborative development of cyber-infrastructure itself as well as its services.

Acknowledgement. We appreciate the sincere support of DKRZ and ESGF colleagues Dean Williams, Stephan Kindermann and others, including users.

References

1. Freeman, P.A.: Is It Possible to Define Cyberinfrastructure? First Monday 6(12) (2007)
2. Soehner, C., Steeves, C., Ward, J.: E-Science and Data Support Services (August 2010)
3. Jäntti, M.: Lessons Learnt from the Improvement of Customer Support Processes: A Case Study on Incident Management. In: Bomarius, F., Oivo, M., Jaring, P., Abrahamsson, P. (eds.) PROFES 2009. LNBIP, vol. 32, pp. 317–331. Springer, Heidelberg (2009)
4. Hess, J., Reuter, C., Pipek, V., Wulf, V.: Supporting End-User Articulations in Evolving Business Processes: a Case Study to Explore Intuitive Notations and Interaction Designs. Int. J. Coop. Inf. Syst. 21(04), 263–296 (2012)
5. Jäntti, M.: Improving IT Service Desk and Service Management Processes in Finnish Tax Administration: A Case Study on Service Engineering, pp. 218–232 (2012)
6. Jäntti, M.: Examining Challenges in IT Service Desk System and Processes: A Case Study, no. c, pp. 105–108 (2012)
7. Arora, A.: IT Service Desk Process Improvement – A Narrative Style Case Study s e i t i v i t c a r i e h t d n a s m a e t S S T - 1 e l b a T, no. Pacis (2006)

8. Hey, T., Trefethen, A.E.: Cyberinfrastructure for e-Science. Science 308(5723), 817–821 (2005)
9. Buyya, R., Venugopal, S.: A Gentle Introduction to Grid Computing and Technologies (July 2005)
10. Krauter, K., Buyya, R., Maheswaran, M.: A taxonomy and survey of grid resource management systems for distributed computing. Softw. Pract. Exp. 32(2), 135–164 (2002)
11. Hey, A., Trefethen, A.: The data deluge: An e-science perspective, pp. 1–17 (January 2003)
12. Jirotka, M., Lee, C.P., Olson, G.M.: Supporting Scientific Collaboration: Methods, Tools and Concepts. Comput. Support. Coop. Work, no. Ci (January 2013)
13. Kendall, H.: 'Prehistoric Help Desk!!'. Support World. Help Desk Institute, pp. 6–8 (October-November 2002)
14. Leung, N., Lau, S.: Information technology help desk survey: To identify the classification of simple and routine enquiries. J. Comput. Inf. Syst. (2007)
15. Underwood, J.A., Hegdahl, D., Gimbel, J.: A proper set of tools are needed to corral support. In: Proceedings of the 31st Annual ACM SIGUCCS Conference on User Services - SIGUCCS 2003, pp. 23–26 (2003)
16. Czegel, B.: Help Desk Practitioner's Handbook. John Wiley (1998)
17. Marcella, R., Middleton, I.: The role of the help desk in the strategic management of information systems. OCLC Syst. Serv. 12(4), 4–19 (1996)
18. González, L.M., Giachetti, R.E., Ramirez, G.: Knowledge management-centric help desk: specification and performance evaluation. Decis. Support Syst. 40(2), 389–405 (2005)
19. Aamodt, A.: Case-Based Reasoning: Foundational Issues, Methodological Variations, and System Approaches 7(1), 39–59 (1994)
20. Roth-Berghofer, T.: Learning from HOMER, a case-based help desk support system. Adv. Learn. Softw. Organ., 88–97 (2004)
21. Marom, Y., Zukerman, I.: Analysis and Synthesis of Help-Desk Responses, pp. 890–897 (2005)
22. Zukerman, I., Marom, Y.: A Comparative Study of Information-Gathering Approaches for Answering Help-Desk Email Inquiries, pp. 546–556 (2006)
23. Dworman, G., Rosenbaum, S.: Helping Users to Use Help: Improving Interaction with Help Systems, pp. 1717–1718 (2004)
24. Williams, D.N.: Earth System Grid Federation (ESGF): Future and Governance World Climate Research Programme (WCRP), Working Group on Coupled Modelling (WGCM)— Stakeholders and ESGF, pp. 1–17 (2012)
25. Williams, D.N., Bell, G., Cinquini, L., Fox, P., Harney, J., Goldstone, R.: Earth System Grid Federation: Federated and Integrated Climate Data from Multiple Sources 6, 61–77 (2013)
26. Bernholdt, D., Bharathi, S., Brown, D., Chanchio, K., Chen, M., Chervenak, A., Cinquini, L., Drach, B., Foster, I., Fox, P., Garcia, J., Kesselman, C., Markel, R., Middleton, D., Nefedova, V., Pouchard, L., Shoshani, A., Sim, A., Strand, G., Williams, D.: The Earth System Grid: Supporting the Next Generation of Climate Modeling Research. Proc. IEEE 93(3), 485–495 (2005)
27. Cinquini, L., Crichton, D., Mattmann, C., Harney, J., Shipman, G., Wang, F., Ananthakrishnan, R., Miller, N., Denvil, S., Morgan, M., Pobre, Z., Bell, G.M., Drach, B., Williams, D., Kershaw, P., Pascoe, S., Gonzalez, E., Fiore, S., Schweitzer, R.: The Earth System Grid Federation: An open infrastructure for access to distributed geospatial data. In: 2012 IEEE 8th International Conference on E-Science, pp. 1–10 (2012)

28. Earth System Grid Federation, "ESGF" (2013), `http://esgf.org/` (accessed: June 10, 2013)
29. "IS-ENES portal" (2013), `https://verc.enes.org/` (accessed: August 22, 2013)
30. Vu, L.: Earth System Grid Federation: A Modern Day 'Silk Road' for Climate Data. Energy Science Network (2013), `https://es.net/news-and-publications/esnet-news/2012/ESGF/` (accessed: August 23, 2013)
31. Yin, R.: Case Study Research: Design and Methods. Sage Publishing (1994)
32. Rocco, T.S., Bliss, L.A., Pérez-Prado, A., Gallagher, S.: Taking the Next Step: Mixed Methods Research in Organizational Systems 21(1), 19–29 (2003)
33. Buchanan, D.A.: Case studies in oranisational research. Qualitative Organisational Research: Core methods and current challenges. Sage Publishing (2012)
34. Checkland, P., Poulter, J.: Systems Approaches to Managing Change: A Practical Guide, pp. 191–242. Springer, London (2010)

Improving Sustainability through Usability

School of Industrial Engineering, School of Agriculture and Biological Engineering
Center for Environment, Purdue University
47907 West Lafayette, IN, USA
duffy@purdue.edu

Abstract. This article proposes methodologies and applications for sustainability solutions through usability. Usability and sustainability are defined in the context of human factors and ergonomics. Economic, social and ecological considerations form the basis for the three leg platform for sustainable development. A return to fundamentals in human factors, ergonomics and industrial and operations engineering can provide insight into effective implementation of sustainability solutions. Principles such as learning curves and economies of scale are highlighted in the context of sustainable energy. It is also suggested that exposure-response curves can be derived using Bayesian networks, giving insight into potential causal effects in existing ecotoxicology data. Ergonomists have used these tools in the past to evaluate performance of other engineering implementations while toxicology can initially provide some common basis for the historical and modern view of ergonomics in the context of sustainability. Sustainability can benefit from such tools that can evaluate potential interventions under uncertainty. From other engineering literature it appears that technical solutions are already available to support sustainability, while the lag may be occurring in coordinating the social, organizational and cultural response. Lessons learned in human factors and ergonomics can support sustainability related interventions building on experience in human-system interface design and visualizations that have been an integral part of the digital human modeling community especially over the last two decades.

Keywords: Usability, Sustainability, Design, Visualizations, Digital Human Modeling, Green Chemistry, Risk Management, Health and Safety.

1 Introduction

Administrative solutions and policy changes can be effective but typically take longer to implement than engineering solutions. They also face a constantly changing technology landscape. One can refer to some National Academies reports when determining next goals in sustainability, but not yet the next steps for achieving those. Insight into green product and process substitutes can bring opportunities for improved market share through early entry, as well as reduced potential for losses and adverse outcomes. Awareness of intangibles and monitoring of available quantifiable

A. Marcus (Ed.): DUXU 2014, Part III, LNCS 8519, pp. 507–519, 2014.
© Springer International Publishing Switzerland 2014

measures can influence individual and organizational decisions over the life-cycle of products and processes. In addition to learning and scalability, one may apply Bayesian networks as a special case of meta-analysis to give some insight under uncertainty. Perception of performance can be considered in usability evaluations while visualizations can support decisions in multi-disciplinary sustainability initiatives.

One may consider that the same treatments were used for childhood leukemia, but that those were modified in approach to implementation through coordinated care and communication among those with experience. It is reported that it took nearly 50 years for modifications to the implementation, while the underlying fundamentals of the regimen were unchanged over that time [1]. In the meantime, before process refinements many young children died without effective treatment or consistent implementation among various caregivers. It would be unfortunate if sustainability-related outcomes continue on a trajectory that appear unstable and out of control. Deviations from a balanced equilibrium in ecosystems have been shown to be the result of human activity [2].

1.1   Potential Value in Cross-Disciplinary Cooperation

There is support among our research colleagues in chemistry for cooperation on Green Chemistry and Health related initiatives [3]. These cooperative efforts could include (i) entrepreneurial efforts in development of clean pharmaceutical processes for new products, (ii) strategic reuse and reduction or capture of CO_2 emissions, (iii) safe nanotechnology development and implementation based on especially organometallic compounds [4]. Many nanotechnologies are based on metals in catalyst systems including small particle and powdered iron, aluminum, nickel, silver and gold as well as various oxide compounds utilizing iron, aluminum, zirconium, titanium and zinc [5]. Cooperation between our colleagues and students in industrial engineering and chemistry could contribute to a sustainable future, building especially on past experience some industrial engineering faculty have with industrial hygiene related professional affiliations and publications. The reduction of exposures to harmful chemicals is clearly within the scope of traditional work design and occupational ergonomics. Theodore [6, p.245-252] shows how various commonly known metals are forming the basis for new materials and the emerging science of nano-technologies.

[6]. However, lessons learned within the industrial workplace have applications in product design and community relations. Exposures previously considered as maximum permissible limits at work need to be considered in the context of the materials going out of our industrial facilities as waste, emissions and end-of-life products into the air, water, soil and ultimately our food chain. With the high and increasing incidence of various forms of cancer, it is imperative that the engineers provide a form of prevention at the product and process source while various medical communities continue to seek the cure. National Academies reports recognize that "meeting the goal of sustainable development requires an integration of social, environmental and economic policies, necessitating interdisciplinary coordination among federal agencies with varying missions…" [7].

With that, the engineering community has opportunity to support various industrial organizations via methods by which they can show their initiative and compliance with environment, health and safety regulations that are moving to the fore with reporting requirements increasing through, for instance, REACH in Europe. REACH regulations require various forms of Registration, Evaluation, Authorization and Restriction of Chemicals throughout their life cycle [8]. While all who do business in Europe will have increasing requirement for reporting the use, transport and manufacture of harmful chemicals it will be important that fundamentals be better integrated into existing engineering curriculum and not simply rely on applying the experience in entry level chemistry courses to provide sustainability outcomes that are needed.

1.2   Potential Consequences of Business-As-Usual

One may also consider the costs of adverse events that have escalated with a similar pattern to CO_2 emissions, as measured in the atmosphere, which have increased to near 400 parts per million (ppm). The costs of doing business as insurer now require new methods and models for setting policy premiums-revenues in addition to concerted efforts to drive costs down through design-related decisions. As noted in the book *Changing Planet, Changing Health*, a modest rise in average temperature by end of 21st century would trigger additional extreme economic and social consequences including the potential displacement of up to 200 million people for rising sea levels, floods and droughts in addition to likely crop failures and water shortages for one in six people worldwide [9, p.208]. Translated into dollar figures, business-as-usual greenhouse gas emissions could lead to economic losses of 5-20% of global GDP per year which could translate to between $1.7 trillion and $7 trillion per year suggesting a significant reduction of well-being and quality of life. This could potentially effect the poor in a disproportionate way, while current projections for increasing demand in developing countries assumes stability in short term 3-5 year timelines. Relatively modest expenditures on the order of 1% of global GDP could help avert such consequences [9, p.209]. Additional information about the Greenhouse effect and evidence for its enhanced effect as seen in the measure of increased CO_2 concentration (ppm) from 185 in the mid-1800s until today can be found in intrductory chemistry texts in the section on thermochemistry [10, p.250-251].

2   Usability and Sustainability

Usability is an emergent property that depends on the interactions among users, products, tasks and environments [11, p.1267]. The measurement or the accomplishment of global task goals could be considered as a primary focus of usability [11, p.1271]. Problem discovery could be a goal of usability testing [11, p.1268] and quality in use could form a measure giving insight into usability-related parameters such as functionality, reliability, efficiency and maintainability. Think aloud methods, where participants are encouraged to talk about their experience and give verbal reports, could give additional insights into potential measures and sustainability-related parameters that have traditionally not been considered in relation to usability. Intel is contributing to the development of such products that can include a smart thermostat, remote management and home screen [12]. These would have sustainability and energy management at the core among product functionality and performance objectives.

It is suggested that long term problems will require long-term solutions with deliberate, integrated and consistent and sustained actions to move us in a more secure and sustainable energy system that meets especially the nation's economic and environmental needs [7]. A new energy system may include a "smart grid" and related appliances that may not be initially of interest or easily usable without close cooperation among those with domain knowledge and expertise in usability. Prototypes, such as those at Intel, are available early in this transition which provides design opportunities for usability. The chemical related effects of various emissions provide additional opportunities for the use of visualizations in decision making and computer-aided engineering of new products and processes. Current digital human modeling tools may be limited in supporting these initiatives until sustainability objectives are more explicitly considered and included in computer-aided engineering and Product Lifecycle Management (PLM) systems.

Human performance and related simulations in the recent versions included anthropometric, comfort based on joint angles, motion timing, fatigue, strength, low-back risk assessments and human motion tracking [13]. A three leg model for sustainability shows social, ecological and economic objectives. Social refers to the consequences of a process including culture, justice, decision-making and equity. Ecological sustainability refers to the health of the ecosystems that support both human and non-human life. Economic sustainability focuses on the economic viability of process, project, enterprise or community [14].

Energy management has typically seen significant industrial emphasis when energy costs are high. However, sustainability has only recently become a catalyst for some energy management initiatives [15]. Industrial boilers account for 30% of energy used in manufacturing industries and manufacturing industries are responsible for 1/3 of all world energy consumption while contributing 36% of the CO_2 emissions [16].

Sustainability challenges have arisen in the past. An energy crisis developed toward the end of the 17th century when demand for wood for fuel exceeded supply [17]. For a time, wood buildings were banned in London. A new technology, coal-based power, provided a solution while coal was still hard to mine and led to visually noticeable pollution and health problems, especially when fog carried contaminants to low altitudes in towns and cities [17]. Some common experience has been seen in China in recent years and the need for engineering as well as administrative solutions has become evident to the Government of China. Achieving sustainability will require the participation of citizens to utilize and support solutions to these and other potential sustainability-related problems that are not always as visible.

Reliability and maintainability were at the core of system effectiveness criteria even before the quality movement. Reliability is generally defined as the probability that a given system will perform its intended function satisfactorily under the projected environmental conditions of use [18]. Maintainability is defined as the probability that a failed system can be made operable in a specified interval of downtime including failure detection, active repair time, logistics time for repair and administrative time giving indications for how long a system may remain in the failed state [18]. It is commonly expected that reliability and maintainability activities should span the entire life cycle of the system [18].

3   Quantifying Improvement

Scientists have reported that climate change is also largely caused by human activities, with CO_2 as one of the main greenhouse gases and direct atmospheric measurements increasing significantly in modern times [19, p.5]. Coal burning, as a means to meet growing electricity demand, is a significant contributor to CO_2 emissions that contribute trapped heat that can be measured in oceans and at the earth's surface [19].

Eccleston notes that the United Nations Agenda 21 declares environmental protection as an integral part of the development process and suggests that it should not be considered in isolation in order to achieve sustainability, while Sustainable Development is one of the U.N.'s stated Millenium Goals [18, p.60]. Specific to that, one objective or "target" is to integrate principles of sustainable development into country policies and programs. Another is to reduce the proportion of the population without sustainable access to safe drinking water and basic sanitation by half [18].

Though administrative objectives are proposed and supported through U.N. initiatives, it is expected that engineering solutions will ultimately need to also be implemented. It has been noted that engineering solutions are typically more effective than administrative solutions in the long term [20]. Past legislative solutions for pollution include the Clean Air Act which contains a combination of mandated administrative as well as engineering controls. While toxic chemical release reporting is already a part of Community Right to Know legislation [21, p.185], more recent court deliberations were about whether the U.S. EPA could consider regulating greenhouse gas emissions within the Clean Air Act [22, p.99].

A "safety first" corporate culture provides opportunity for improved sustainability related outcomes and relies on continuous improvement and quality related teachings of Deming [21]. An outline supporting companies interested in pursuing this in more detail is available as a part of Occupational Safety and Health principles as shown in Goetsch [21].

Haslam and Waterson consider definitions for sustainability including "development that meets the need of the present without compromising the ability of future generations to meet their own needs." A different definition these authors also offered for sustainability is "Improving the quality of human life while living within the carrying capacity of supporting ecosystems" [23]. Within the second definition there appear to be opportunities for further development of ergonomics science in the context of usability. Haslam and Waterson refer to estimates by Drury [24] that suggest "In the future, all of our actions as ergonomists will have to take into account their impact on sustainability"[23, 24].

Baird defines anthropogenic as a man-made influence [25, p.60] and shows how emissions of carbon-based compounds, as part of photochemical reactions [25, p.31], contribute to the increasing environmental effect experienced as weather extremes within climate change [25, p.62-63]. With emissions as catalysts [25, p.37] for these larger scale effects referred to in National Academies reports, a cradle-to-grave analysis is outlined and encouraged for pollution prevention [25, p.9].

Rouse and Boff propose a framework originally used in military for estimates related to toxic chemicals and suggest that it may have applications more broadly for cost-benefit analyses within human factors and ergonomics assessments [26]. In outlining strategies for sustainable energy, Tester, Drake and co-authors emphasize the need for life cycle assessment and show sample analyses related to learning curves and economies of scale [27]. They describe how economies of scale can be estimated mathematically using a scale exponent to illustrate how "bigger is cheaper" per unit output using renewable energy replacement options [27, p.225].

In Hancock and Bayha [28], it is shown that the number of cycles increases the time per cycle or cost per cycle decreases either as "human learning" or as "production progress functions". These can be considered in cost projections when assessing potential alternative materials, energies, process substitutes or modifications intended to reduce risk. Estimates of time standards and maintenance times should consider experience and be careful not to allow data for "inexperienced" operators or processes to improperly influence decisions [28].

4   Improving Health and Safety Outcomes

"Industrial Processes…are rarely benign. These processes often require strong acids, strong bases or other aggressive chemicals." Further "…the potential for problems is always present: technological processes have the 'potential to pollute (PTP)." As well, T.E. Graedel suggests that "…engineers and other technologists should take account of the potential environmental consequences of their engineering decisions, whether those consequences are immediate or may occur far into the future [29]. According to Graedel and Howard-Grenville, green engineering is a necessary (though not sufficient) condition for the sustainable development …" [29, p.19]

Green chemistry is founded on principles that reduce or eliminate the use or generation of hazardous substances in the design, manufacture and use of chemicals. By definition this design, manufacture and use is a 'usability' matter. "Green engineering seeks to provide a framework for the design of new materials, products, processes and systems that are benign to human health and the environment" [29].

Based on Karwowski [30], it is evident that a Committee on Human-Systems Integration from the National Academies is expected to provide new perspectives on theoretical and methodological issues concerning the relationship of individuals and organizations to technology and the environment [30, p.31]. Japan's Ministry of

Education, Culture, Sports, Science and Technology (MEXT) published issues and problem statements of interest in 21st century including nanotechnologies and changes in human habitat future directions and support the development of human factors and ergonomics a discipline focusing on the science, engineering, design, technology and management of human-compatible systems [30].

Cranor asks us to imagine a world in which companies' new and existing products would be tested to determine hazardous properties so that any risks would be reduced or the products would be removed or prevented from entering the market before contamination occurs [31]. Then there should have been no thalidomide babies or women with cervical cancer [31, p.208]. Persistent organic pollutants such as polychlorinated biphenyls (PCB), banned fire retardants such as polybrominated biphenyls (PBBs) and existing fire retardants (eg. PBDEs) may have affected few or no children. Men might be at lesser risk from prostate cancer and reproductive disfunction because of bisphenol A (BPA). Fewer children's cognitive function and behaiour might have been adversely affected by exposure to lead, mercury and other neurotoxicants [31].

Legislative and regulatory assumptions made years ago are being challenged as technological advances allow more sensitive measurement of toxic substances, present new risks or reverse beliefs about the relationship between certain hazards and health effects [32, p.vii]. Policy makers and judges are forced to deliberate about complex issues beyond the understanding of most jurists or elected officials while epidemiologists, geneticists, toxicologists and other scientists are regularly called upon in court proceedings [32]. A 2011 report concluded that green chemicals will save industry $65.5 Billion dollars by 2020 [33]. Engineering graduates and ergonomists need to know more about how substituting renewable energies and green chemicals contributes toward usability and improved sustainability.

For instance, coal can have significant environmental impacts at every stage of its production and utilization. Hence, in the context of life-cycle assessments, decisions to utilize coal-based electricity production need to be considered carefully for their potential health effects to the community in which the workforce resides [34]. Link and Albers considered uncertainty and a Bayesian Multimodel Inference in predicting the non-human reproductive pattern of certain birds under various non-lethal concentrations of methylmercury [35]. Spadaro and Rabl consider a dose-response function to provide an estimate of economic and social decrement by analyzing the cost of damage and loss of IQ (Intelligence Quotient score) from atmospheric emissions of methyl mercury [36]. There were documented diseases induced by metals that increased with increasing production of various metals such as copper, lead and zinc. [37, p.34]. As well, an increasing number of endocrine disrupters were shown in the environment and especially in water. These are chemicals that stimulate or retard the production of hormones [37].

In reviewing research incorporating no-observed-effect levels (NOELs) and lowest-observed-effect levels (LOELs), the authors conclude that there are flaws in practice of implementing environmental toxicology, risk assessment and management decisions [38]. Instead, although new to most environmental toxicologists, the editorial by Landis and co-author favors the derivation of exposure-response curves using a Bayesian approach [38]. Initial findings are described after using a software that performs Bayesian Inference Using Gibbs Sampling (BUGS). It is described as an expert system software used to determine a Markov chain-based Monte Carlo simulation scheme based on a Gibbs sampler and is shown at http://www.openbugs.info/w/. Additional information and sample analyses related to Bayes' Rule and Decision Trees can be found in Winston [39, p.767].

Much is known about toxicology in the workplace. Mercury and other Inorganic compounds are shown for their neurotoxic agents [40, p.6.13.2]. Many Threshold Limit Values (TLVs) were developed by the American Conference of Governmental Industrial Hygienists (ACGIH) [40, 6.13 p.1-12]. Information about the effects of various solvents is also shown. These are typically made of some type of hydrocarbon with fundamentals in organic chemistry. Additional information about the properties of solvent related organic molecules and the study of chemical reactions can be seen in Wade's book covering fundamentals of Organic Chemistry [41, p.38, 124].

Green substitutes and less hazardous solvents can be found in the literature and purchased from various sources. These need to be included in commercially available design software as material options during process and work design. Individuals typically try to minimize their expenses, but they do not always buy or do what is cheapest per unit of performance or cheapest over the long term [42, p.541]. In regard to environmental economics, some have proposed a Human Development Index as a supplement or substitute for the Gross Domestic Product (GDP) [42, p.543]. In the U.S. it was found that States with stronger environmental programs outperformed states with weaker programs in employment growth and wages [42, p.545].

"Decisions about ecological effects are often perceived as arising from selfless protection of the Earth." Instead they could be considered in the context of value placed on free services provided by our ecological systems. "These services include the generation of clean water, air and production of food..." [43, p.xv]. A framework for evaluating environmental costs is provided here. Environmental cost is not typically well captured in engineering economic evaluations [44].

Table 1. A Summary of Methods and Measures for Usability and Sustainability

Methods contributing to usability	Measures to assess improved sustainability
Thinking aloud	Reduced Greenhouse gas emissions including CO_2
Learning curves	Reduced exposures to harmful chemicals
Economies of scale	New pharmaceuticals developed in clean processes
Reliability	"Safety first" corporate culture
Maintainability	Reduction of Persistent Organic Pollutants such as PCBs, PBBs, PBDEs and BPAs
Digital Human Modeling	Monitor processes for their 'Potential to Pollute'.
Bayesian approach and networks	Green chemistry and Green manufacturing

These principles here include costs not normally assigned to individual projects such as administrative and regulatory environmental costs as well as liability or compliance costs typically assigned to overhead or indirect costs. And reducing the expected value of liability costs through improved usability can provide further opportunity to contribute improved profitability. Personnel costs associated with reporting as well as staff productivity, morale, and turnover can be influenced by poor environmental performance that may be reflected in workplace conditions increased rates of illness [44]. Personal protective equipment is a last line of defense [45, p.1072]. Engineering controls such as "substitute a less harmful material" are preferred over administrative controls including reducing exposure.

5   Systems Approaches in Usability, Water and Food Safety

The ergonomics community could justify participation in this area by considering prior definitions as inspired by Chapanis (1995) and shown by Helander [46, p.4-5]. "Ergonomics and human factors use knowledge of human abilities and limitations to the design of systems, organizations, jobs, machines, tools and consumer products for safe, efficient and comfortable human use." A new image of ergonomics emerged beginning in the early 1990s as the discipline of human-computer interaction developed further. Certainly usability and human reliability have been at the core of ergonomics in recent years [46, p.13]. A focus on continuous improvement in organizations provides additional opportunity to re-emphasize the safety aspects of human use [46].

For instance, number 48 rank on the top 100 ways to live to be 100 years of age is to *Test Your Tap Water for Toxins*. The EPA has found that 20 percent of public ground-water systems are contaminated with manmade pollutants and 1/3 of those serving larger communities are contaminated with chemicals [47, p.108] Life-threatening danger includes cancer, birth defects, miscarriages, heart abnormalities, hyperactivity and reduced mental functioning [47].

Fresh water has already been shown to be of limited availability in various countries in recent years while populations continue to move into areas with already limited water supplies and changing climate could reduce available fresh water supplies even further.   Some chemicals are not easily removed through water filtration systems [48]. Where risk typically has been considered in terms of human error probabilities multiplied by the severity of the hazard, in regard to sustainability one must consider the exposures. Manahan [49, p.456] shows that the risk is proportional to the severity of the hazard presented by a product or process multiplied by the exposure of humans or other potential targets or recipients. He points out that much of the design and practice of Green Chemistry is about risk reduction [49]. An appropriate implementation supported and influenced by ergonomists, engineers and correct visualizations can support usability and hence sustainability.

Additionally, foodborne illnesses can be linked to improper maintenance and reliability of process equipment [50]. Repair is essentially a human activity. Hence, designing for maintainability must include consideration for human capabilities and limitations in the maintenance environment. Human factors and ergonomics aspects include anthropometry, human perception and design of the controls, displays and tools and equipment and the workplace [51, p.270-273]. Effective strategies for supporting performance include fault isolation, part standardization and interchangeability, modularization and accessibility and proactive maintenance. Predictive maintenance methodologies are shown in more detail in Ebeling [51]. Such estimates can support further investment in usability and maintainability to support sustainability.

Usability specialists may borrow from lessons learned in standards previously implemented more broadly related to quality when considering energy management and environmental related objectives. An ISO 50001 flowchart shown by Eccleston and co-authors [52] includes establishing (i) general requirements, program and scope, (ii) roles, responsibilities and authorities of management, (iii) energy policy, (iv) plans, (v) operating, implementing and maintaining essential performance records, (vi) observe operations, examine records and report on performance, (vii) review and direct corrective and preventive actions to improve performance [52]. This framework is designed around the continuous improvement plan-do-check-act approach utilized in ISO 9001 for Quality and similar for ISO 14001 for Environmental Management [52].

6   Conclusions

In conclusion, a multi-disciplinary approach and contributions from various disciplines will be needed to ultimately achieve sustainability. Usability experts, ergonomists and industrial engineers have experience in providing safe human-systems interactions. Reducing exposures to hazardous conditions, some chemically-based, has some common elements in environmental chemistry. Environmental chemistry can provide a platform for decisions considering that materials coming into industrial facilities will go out as products or as waste. There are common necessary for consideration in minimizing exposure to chemically-based hazards inside and outside the factory that ultimately can effect water, soil, air and food. An understanding in these areas can provide a foundation for supporting and contributing to new ventures that can enable green substitutes in product and process design. These are core elements of sustainability that are highlighted within this paper, and they can be supported through traditional methodologies that facilitate good usability in operations and systems.

Acknowledgements. The author would like to thank the Fulbright Program in Washington, D.C. and Moscow, Russia. In addition to IIE (www.iienet2.org) and HFES (www.hfes.org), interested readers may find additional information on usability or sustainability at Institute for Ergonomics and Human Factors–formerly the Ergonomics Society (ergonomics.org.uk), American Society for Quality (www.asq.org), American Chemical Society (www.acs.org) and National Academies Press (www.nap.org).

References

1. Hannemann, R.E.: Professor of Biomedical Engineering and M.D. Personal Communication (February 25, 2014)
2. Melnyk, L., Hens, L.: Introduction. In: Hens, L., Melnyk, L. (eds.) Social and Economic Potential of Sustainable Development, p. 10. Sumy University Book Publishing Sumy, Ukraine (2008)
3. Zwier, T.S.: The M.G. Mellon Distinguished Professor and Head of Chemistry. Personal Communication (November 18, 2013)
4. Negishi, E.: The H.C. Brown Distinguished Professor of Chemistry. Personal Communication (December 13, 2013)
5. Theodore, L.: Nanotechnology. Wiley-Interscience, Hoboken (2006)
6. Konz, S., Johnson, S.: Work Design: Occupational Ergonomics, 7th edn. Arizona Chemical Environment, p. 455. Holcomb Hathaway Publishers, Scottsdale (2008)
7. Shapiro, H.: America's Energy Future. National Academies Press, Washington, D.C. (2009)
8. Plog, B.A., Quinlan, P.J.: Fundamentals of Industrial Hygiene. National Safety Council, pp. 840–841 (2012)
9. Epstein, P.R., Ferber, D.: Changing Planet, Changing Health, p. 3, 205–206. University of California Press, Berkeley (2011)
10. Silberberg, M.S.: Chemistry, 6th edn. McGraw-Hill, New York (2012)
11. Lewis, J.R.: Usability Testing. In: Salvendy, G. (ed.) Handbook of Human Factors and Ergonomics, 4th edn., pp. 1267–1312. Wiley & Sons, Hoboken (2012)
12. Intel. Intel Smart Home Dashboard. Embedded Computing. Intelligent Home Energy Management Proof of Concept (2009), http://intel.com/embedded/homeenergy (retrieved March 2, 2014)
13. Raschke, U., Schutte, L.M., Chaffin, D.B.: Ergonomics in Digital Environments. In: Salvendy, G. (ed.) Handbook of Industrial Engineering, 3rd edn., pp. 1111–1130. Wiley & Sons, New York (2001)
14. Kibert, C.J., Monroe, M.C., Peterson, A.L., Plate, R.R.: Working Toward Sustainability. Wiley & Sons, Hoboken (2012)
15. Turner, W.C., Kennedy, W.J.: Energy Management. In: Salvendy, G. (ed.) Handbook of Industrial Engineering, vol. 10(5), pp. 1–24. Wiley & Sons, New York (1982)
16. Yang, M., Dixon, R.K.: Investing in efficient industrial boiler systems in China and Vietnam. Energy Policy 40(1), 432–437 (2012)
17. Kapur, K.C.: Reliability and Maintainability. In: Salvendy, G. (ed.) Handbook of Industrial Engineering, vol. 8(5), pp. 1–34. Wiley & Sons, New York (1982)
18. Eccleston, C.H., March, F.: Global Environmental Policy: Concepts, Principles and Practice. CRC Press, Boca Raton (2011)
19. Cicerone, R.J., Nurse, P.: Climate Change Evidence and Causes. National Academy of Sciences with The Royal Society, Washington, D.C. (2014)
20. Wickens, C.D., Lee, J.D., Liu, Y., Gordon Becker, S.E.: An Introduction to Human Factors Engineering, 2nd edn., p. 374. Pearson, Prentice-Hall, Upper Saddle River, New Jersey (2004)
21. Goetsch, D.L.: Occupational Safety and Health, 7th edn. Pearson, Prentice-Hall, Upper Saddle River, New Jersey (2011)
22. Theodore, L., Dupont, R.R.: Environmental Health and Hazard Risk Assessment. CRC Press, Boca Raton (2012)

23. Haslam, R., Waterson, P.: Ergonomics and Sustainability (editorial). Ergonomics 56(3), 343–347 (2013)
24. Drury, C.: The Future of Ergonomics/the Future of Work: 45 years After Bartlett (1962). Ergonomics 51, 14–21 (2008)
25. Baird, C.: Environmental Chemistry, 2nd edn. (1999)
26. Rouse, W.B., Boff, K.R.: Cost-Benefit Analysis of Human-Systems Investments. In: Salvendy, G. (ed.) Handbook of Human Factors and Ergonomics, 3rd edn., pp. 1133–1149. Wiley & Sons, Hoboken (2006)
27. Tester, J.W., Drake, E.M., Driscoll, M.J., Golay, M.W., Peters, W.A.: Sustainable Energy. MIT Press, Cambridge (2005)
28. Hancock, W.M., Bayha, F.: The Learning Curve. In: Salvendy, G. (ed.) Handbook of Industrial Engineering, pp. 1585–1598. Wiley & Sons, New York (1992)
29. Graedel, T.E., Howard-Grenville, J.A.: Greening the Industrial Facility, p. 5. Springer, New York (2005)
30. Karwowski, W.: The Discipline of Human Factors and Ergonomics. In: Salvendy, G. (ed.) Handbook of Human Factors and Ergonomics, pp. 3–37. Wiley & Sons, Hoboken (2012)
31. Cranor, C.F.: Legally Poisoned: How the Law Puts Us at Risk from Toxicants. Harvard University Press, Cambridge (2011)
32. Brown, G.E., Cranor, C.F.: Regulating Toxic Substances. pp. vii–ix. Oxford University Press, New York (1993)
33. Environmental Protection Agency, Green Chemistry, http://www2.epa.gov/green-chemistry (retrieved March 2, 2014)
34. Tatiya, R.R.: Elements of Industrial Hazards, p. 45. CRC Press, Boca Raton (2011)
35. Link, W.A., Albers, P.H.: Bayesian Multimodel Inference for Dose-Response Studies. Environmental Toxicology and Chemistry 26(9), 1867–1872 (2007)
36. Spadaro, J.V., Rabl, A.: Global health impacts and costs due to mercury emissions. Risk Analysis 28(3), 603–613 (2008)
37. Yu, M.-H., Tsunoda, H., Tsunoda, M.: Environmental Toxicology: Biological and Health Effects of Pollutants, 3rd edn. CRC Press, Boca Raton (2012)
38. Landis, W.G., Chapman, P.M.: Well Past Time to Stop Using NOELs and LOELs (editorial). Integrated Environmental Assessment and Management 7(4), vi–viii (2011)
39. Winston, W.L.: Operations Research, 4th edn. Thomson Learning, Belmont (2004)
40. Lindstrom, K.: Toxicology. In: Salvendy, G. (ed.) Handbook of Industrial Engineering, vol. 6(13), pp. 1–7. Wiley & Sons, New York (1982)
41. Wade, L.G.: Organic Chemistry, 5th edn. (2003)
42. Matlack, A.: Green Chemistry, 2nd edn., pp. 216–217. CRC Press, Boca Raton (2010)
43. Newman, M.C.: Fundamentals of Ecotoxicology, 3rd edn. CRC Press, Boca Raton (2010)
44. Allen, D.T., Shonnard, D.R.: Green Engineering, pp. 402–412. Prentice-Hall, Upper Saddle River (2002)
45. Konz, S.: Environmental Design. In: Salvendy, G. (ed.) Handbook of Industrial Engineering, pp. 1047–1077. Wiley & Sons, New York (1992)
46. Chapanis, A.: Product Development: A Personal View. Ergonomics 38, 1625–1638 (1995); as cited in Helander, M.: The Human Factors Profession. In: Salvendy, G., (Ed.) Handbook of Human Factors and Ergonomics, 2nd Edn., pp.1–16. Wiley & Sons, New York (1997)
47. Inlander, C.B., Hodge, M.: 100 Ways to Live to be 100, Wings Books: Random House The People's Medical Society, Avenel, New Jersey (1992)

48. Kreith, F., Kreider, J.F.: Principles of Sustainable Energy. CRC Press, Boca Raton (2011)
49. Riccetti, S.: Designing Food Safety and Equipment Reliability Through Maintenance Engineering. CRC Press, Boca Raton (2013)
50. Manahan, S.: Environmental Chemistry, 9th edn. CRC Press, Boca Raton
51. Ebeling, C.E.: An Introduction to Reliability and Maintainability Engineering, 2nd edn. Waveland Press, Long Grove (2010)
52. Eccleston, C.H., March, F., Cohen, T.: Inside Energy. CRC Press, Boca Raton (2012)

Energy Graph Feedback: Attention, Cognition and Behavior Intentions

June A. Flora[1] and Banny Banerjee[2]

[1] Human Sciences & Technologies Advanced Research Institute and Solutions Science Lab
in Department of Pediatrics, Stanford University
MSOB 1265 Welch Road, Stanford California 94305, USA
jflora@stanford.edu
[2] Mechanical Engineering and Changelabs
Stanford University 210 Panama 104 Cordura Hall Stanford, CA 94305, USA
banny@stanford.edu

Abstract. Behavioral science has long acknowledged that informational and performance feedback is a key to behavior change. The *graph* features prominently as a feedback modality. Driven by the large scale deployment of energy sensing devices, graphs have become a ubiquitous visualization of household energy consumption. We investigate the influence of three energy graph formats (bar, line and radial) and two cue conditions (color or numeric cues) within four group conditions (cost or kilowatt hour subject matter with single graph or comparison graph feedback) on five outcomes. Ease of understanding, positive attitudes and involvement were higher for bar and line graphs. Novel graph formats – the radial graph, were attended to longer and associated with more learning. There were no overall behavioral change intention effects by condition, although a few individual energy behavior intentions did differ by condition. The importance of multiple outcomes of graph feedback and the relationships among outcomes are discussed.

Keywords: Energy feedback, graph perception, graph comprehension, graph formats, graph content.

1 Introduction

The increasing worldwide deployment of Advanced Metering Infrastructure (AMI) or smart meters in homes has transformed the amount, granularity, and type of informational and performance feedback that energy consumers have access to from their utility companies or other energy service providers. More than 65 million smart meters are expected to be installed in the U.S. by 2015 [1]. These meters bombard utilities with data, often passing along meter readings every 15 minutes or about 35,000 times a year offering individual energy consumers opportunities to view and understand their energy consumption in ways never before available. Graphic displays of household energy use have become ubiquitous in paper bills, websites, in home display devices and mobile applications [2-3].

A. Marcus (Ed.): DUXU 2014, Part III, LNCS 8519, pp. 520–529, 2014.
© Springer International Publishing Switzerland 2014

The need to create graphs whose informational feedback is intuitive, easily and quickly understood [2] [4] is increasing in importance with the growth of mobile, wearable, appliance use, and thermostat "smart" sensing devices. Advances in sensor technology have spawned more energy efficient instruments that collect more types of data with ever increasing granularity. These technological advances have so far outpaced the scientific community's ability to display the data visually so that consumers can quickly and easily comprehend content and be consistently engaged and motivated to use the information to meet their health, energy consumption, and economic goals [4].

There is a large research and design literature on graphic displays of information. The fields of psychology, education, risk and science communication, computer science, and statistics all invest in the study of graphs. Yet, there is no clear consensus on guidelines for the presentation and communication of graph feedback. Instead research results vary by discipline, methodology and studied outcome [5].

2   Literature Review of Graphical Displays

The study of graphic interpretation has long been of interest in social science and education fields and continues to advance along with the rapidly growing fields of human computer interaction, data visualization and data science [5-7].

A selected review of this sizeable literature on graph perception reveals differences in focus and methodology [5]. A widely cited article in statistical science presents a framework of aspects of graphical methods. Included in the framework are positions along a common scale, positions on identical and non-aligned scales, length (distance), angle, slope, area, volume, density (amount of black) color saturation, and color hue [6]. These aspects are ranked according to their accuracy judgments from graphical –perception tasks. Position along a common scale and position on identical but non-aligned scales were ranked one and two respectively in accuracy judgement.

Scholarship in neuroscience and cognitive psychology [8-9] has focused on the communication of information portrayed in graphs such that the reader/viewer can see the information the graph designer intends to convey. Eight psychological and communication principles are derived from this research [8-9], we focus on the following five:

1. Principle of Salience; attention is drawn to large perceptible differences;
2. Principle of Discriminability; properties must differ by a large enough proportions or they will not be distinguished from one another.
3. Principle of Perceptual Organization; people automatically group elements into units which they then attend to and remember, this principle holds true for graphs.
4. Principle of Informative Change; graph viewers will interpret change in the appearance of a display as conveying information.
5. Principle of Capacity Limitation; people have a limited capacity to retain and to process information.

Most of these psychological principles also are generally incorporated in graph research in education and guide the study of visual characteristics of a graph (e.g. format, color, use of legend, size etc.). In addition, education research focuses on characteristics of the graph viewing audience. Viewer knowledge about graphs and expectations about the content of the data in a graph feature significantly in education research on learning outcomes [5] [10-13].

To understand the role of graphical displays on *behavior and behavioral intentions*, the field of health risk communication yields other important cues to designing effective graphs [7]. A primary conclusion of an extensive review of graphical features in health risk communication is that features that improve the accuracy of quantitative reasoning differ from features most likely to induce change in behavior or behavioral intentions. Further, [7] concludes that features that viewers like may not be related to accuracy judgment or behavior change goals. Graphs that show part-to-whole relationships help people improve their judgments about risk, whereas graphical displays that show only the numerator are more likely to induce behavior change [14]. Viewers most often preferred graphs that had visual simplicity and familiarity, but these preferences were not associated with accuracy judgments.

3   Energy Reduction Feedback

Feedback as technology driven interactive communication process is currently considered as key to CO_2 emission and energy reduction [4] [16]. Feedback can potentially turn the invisible and unknown energy use into knowable, concrete, and changeable behaviors. Further, feedback can document and reward behavior changes that lead to reductions in environmental impact [15]. The graph features prominently in feedback. While the practice of using energy consumption graphs as a data visualization element is common, the empirical study of graph characteristics that continuously engage consumers, offer a user experience that is appealing, increases appropriate knowledge, and activates behavior change is relatively rare [16]. This study is an early attempt to empirically examine the effects of selected graphic elements on a hierarchy of attentional, affective, cognitive and behavioral outcomes.

4   Hypotheses (HYP) and Research Questions (RQ)

- **HYP 1:** Novel graphs, such radial dial graph will induce longer attention.
- **RQ1:** What graph features contribute to more learning about energy consumption?
- **HYP 2:** Graphs developed with high discriminability of features such as color cues will be perceived as easier to understand.
- **HYP3:** Graphs that are simple such as bar and line graphs will be perceived as easier to understand.
- **HYP4**: Familiar graphic formats (such as bar and line graphs) will be more likely to influence positive graph attitude and involvement.
- **HPY5:** Cost of energy consumption as graph subject matter, because of its relevance and tangibility, will be associated with greater intentions to change behaviors.
- **HYP6:** Graphs that portray subject matter comparisons on two different time periods (use of two graphs) will be associated with greater behavioral intentions.

5   Methods

A total of 211 community college students enrolled in the study, consented to participate based on a study description approved by the university institutional review board, and completed the online study. Overall the sample was: 79% female; 38% white, 12%Hispanic, and 34% Asian; 34% college sophomores. Income was measured on an 11-point scale, where 1 = "$9,999 or less" and 11 = "$100,000 or more". The overall mean of 7.2 corresponds to "$60,000 to $69,999".

5.1   Study Design

A factorial mixed design was used; a 2 (cost vs kWh graph content) X 2 (a single graph vs two comparison graphs) between factor and a within group factors with six graph formats. Participants were randomly assigned to one of four between factors conditions and graph formats were randomly ordered in the within group factor. Between group conditions were labeled accordingly, Condition 1: Cost with no comparison graph (C1); Condition 2; Cost with a comparison graph (C2), Condition 3; kWh graph with no comparison (C3); and Condition 4; kWh graph with a comparison graph (C4). Within each condition, participants viewed six graph formats that corresponded to the features of the condition (cost versus kWh subject matter and single versus comparison graph). The graph formats were line, bar and radial graphs with and without color cues for the highest and lowest energy consumption or cost.

5.2   Graph Stimulus Materials

All graphs were conceptualized to have a framework within which the following elements resided; an X-axis label, a Y-axis label (which was always hour of a 24 hour day), a title, a background, and the content graphed. Aspects of the framework that were standardized across all graphs: (a) the X-axis displayed time, 24 hours of a day, (b) all graphs had a yellow and blue background with low saturation grid lines on the Y-axis, and (c) all graphs showed a dual peak energy consumption shape over the 24 hour day, with peak electricity use/or cost at around noon and a second peak around 6 PM.

Aspects of the graph framework manipulated were: (a) content, the lines, bars, numeric symbols and other marks that specify relationships , (b) shape of the framework, the line and bar graphs were conveyed in a rectangular shape and the radial dial was a round shape, (c) subject matter was either the kWh consumed or the cost of the electricity consumed, and (d) use of color in all graph formats to highlight high, medium and low use or the use of numbers to specify highest and lowest use (or cost). Figures 1 and 2 show a sample of the graph images used within the subject matter and comparison conditions.

Cost: Radial Graph numeric cues

Electricity use: Radial graph with color cues

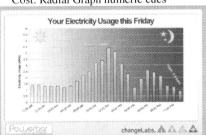
Electricity: Bar graph with numeric cues

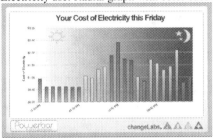
Cost: Bar graph with color cues

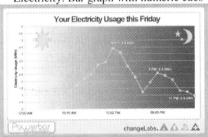
Electricity: Line graph with numeric cues

Cost: Line graph with color cues

Fig. 1. A sample of the three graph formats with color and numeric cues covering cost of electricity or kWh of electricity use

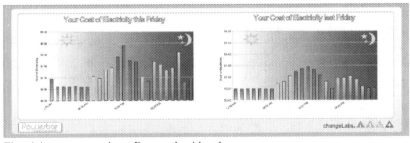
Electricity use comparison: Bar graph with color cues

Fig. 2. Sample comparison bar graph of electricity cost

5.3   Dependent Measures

There were five within subject dependent measures and two between subject dependent measures. Within subject measures were *attention*, operationalized as time in seconds spent on the graph page. Once participants viewed a graph they could not return to that graph.

Ease of understanding was a single question asking participants to rate their ease of understanding a graph on a one to five scale with one being not at all easy and five being very easy.

Knowledge was measured as the correctness of response to a single question. The knowledge question stem was tailored to the subject matter condition (cost versus kWh). The knowledge question also randomly asked in which time block (four time blocks were displayed) did you use the *most* (or *least*) amount energy (spend the most/least amount money).   The variation in the wording was used to inhibit participant's focusing only on the single graph feature (least or most).

Attitude toward the graph was assessed by an eleven question index using a 9-point semantic-differential scale adapted from [17- 18]. The scale instructions were modified to use the term graph instead of advertisement. The specific items were Like/Dislike,   Dynamic/Dull,   Interesting/Boring,   Favorable/Unfavorable, Unappealing/Appealing, Persuasive/Not Persuasive, Eye-catching/Not Eye-catching, Uninformative/Informative, Pleasing/Irritating. All 9 items were averaged to form the graph attitude index (Cronbach's alpha =.97).

Graph involvement was adapted from a six item scale of ad product involvement by [18-19]. Perceived graph involvement was measured on the following six 9-point semantic differential items: Matters to me/Doesn't matter, Relevant/Irrelevant, Unimportant/Important, Essential/Non-Essential, Wanted/Unwanted, Useless/Useful. Responses to these six items were averaged (Cronbach's alpha = .95).

There were two dependent measures for the four between conditions; short and long term *behavioral intention* to perform 48 energy reduction behaviors; 22 curtailment (routine or habitual) behaviors and 26 efficiency (product/device purchase) behaviors. The short term question was phrased as: How much do you intend to perform XXX behavior over the next week. The long term intention questions was: Over the next six months, how much to you intend to perform this action as often as necessary. Both questions use 10 point response scales ranging from do not intend to do to highly intend to do.

6   Procedure

The experiment was administered online to northern California community college students who signed up to participate in a one – two hour research project. Once participants went to the online study they saw a two minute video that reviewed the importance of energy reduction and showed images of the ways that individuals could reduce energy. Next participants saw a randomly ordered set of six graphs; after each graph participants answered the sixteen knowledge, ease of understanding, attitude toward the graph, and involvement with graph questions.

7   Results

Data analysis proceeded first with the use of repeated measures ANOVAs by condition to examine the five within subject dependent measures. Next, 2 (cue type) X 2 (subject matter) ANOVAs were used to test effects of condition on short and long term behavioral intentions.

HYP 1: Novel graphs would stimulate more attention to graphs was partially confirmed. There were only significant differences in graph cues and format within C1 [1]. Within the cost – no comparison (C1) condition, there was a significant interaction between graph format and graphs with color cues, F (2,328) = 9.18, P<.0001. Participants spent more time on the radial dial graph with color demarcations (Fig. 3a).

RQ1: What graph features (color cue or format) led to greater learning? In C1 and C3 graphs using color cues produced significantly more correct responses to the knowledge question (F(1,329) = 7.00, p<.001; F(1,311) = 6.13, p <.01   respectively). There was a significant interaction between graph format and color cues for C1, C3 and C4 (F (2,329) = 4.90, p<.001; F (2,311) = 13.35, p<.001; F (2,311) = 4.90, p<.0001) respectively. The interaction effects however were not parallel. In C1 and C3, the radial dial graph with colors produced more learning (73% and 73% correct). In C4 there was a significant interaction between graph format and color cues, F(2,317) = 16.59, p<.0001), the line graph with no color cues produced the greatest learning (70% correct) and the bar graph with no colors showed the least knowledge (32% correct)   For the C1, there were significant differences between graph formats (C1 F (2,305)=7.69, p<.0001), with bar graphs producing more learning (67% and 65%) and radial graphs producing the least amount of learning (41% and 45%) (Fig. 4).   We interpret these results as indicating that graphical knowledge if differentiated in simple graph conditions (C1 and C3) – that is, in a condition with no comparison graph, there was greater knowledge regarding the novel radial graph type.   In the more complex conditions, the influence of graph format and cues were less systematic. In the cost comparison condition, the two radial graphs produced less knowledge. In the kWh comparison condition (C4) the line graph produced the highest knowledge (70% correct).

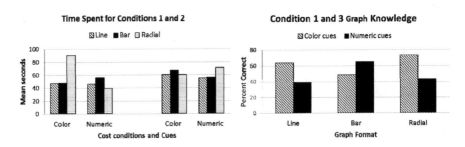

Fig. 3. Time spent on graphs in C1 and C2   **Fig. 4.** Knowledge of graphs in C1 and C3

---

[1]   Time spent on graphs in the two electricity conditions was not analyzed because of errors in collecting viewing time data.

HYP2: High discriminate cues will be associated with greater perceived ease of understanding. This hypothesis was not confirmed, there were no significant differences between graphs with color cues and those with numerical cues on ease of understanding.

HYP3 was confirmed, graph format was significantly related to ease of understanding, across all four conditions (p<.0001): C1: F (2,320) = 51.7, p<.0001; C2: F (2,280) = 78.45, p<.0001; C3: F (2,301) = 83.88, p<.0001; and C4: F (2,305) = 68.05, p<.0001. In all conditions, the radial formats were rated as much less easy to understand, bar graphs were rated easiest to understand (Fig. 5).

HYP4: Graph attitude and involvement will be influenced by graph format and graph cue was partially confirmed. Graph attitude was significantly related to graph format; C1: F (2,317) = 31.207, P<.0001; C2: F (2, 286) = 38.67, p<.0001; C3: F (2,304) 28.18, p<.0001; C4: F (2, 306) = 14.78, p<.0001 (Figure 6). In each condition, the bar graph was rated with the most positive attitude, the line graph as next and the radial graph was rated least positively. There were no significant differences by graph cue type; color or numeric cue.

Graph involvement was significantly different by graph format: C1: F (2,323) =28.67, p<.0001; C2: F (2,284) =74.37, p<.0001; C3: F (2,302) =65.70, p<.0001; C4: F (2,307) =42.29, p<.0001. There were no significant differences for cue type within any condition.

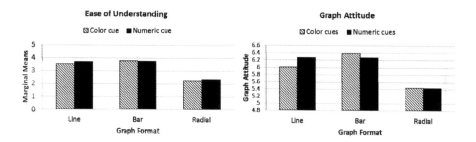

Fig. 5. Format, cues and ease of understanding   **Fig. 6.** Format, cues and positive attitude

HPY5& 6: Cost (C1 & C2) and comparisons conditions (C2 &C4) will be associated with greater short and long term behavioral intentions to change easy and difficult behaviors. This hypothesis was disconfirmed. There were no significant differences between conditions on short or long term curtailment or efficiency behavioral intentions. We also examined differences in short term intention behavior by behavior. There were significant differences in the comparison and non-comparison conditions for four behaviors, and subject matter and comparison interactions on two behaviors. In the no-comparison conditions (C1 & C3), turning the faucet to full cold position, and using the spin dry feature on the washing machine had higher behavioral F should be intentions, (F (1,201)=4.70, p<.05 and F(1,2000=11.59, p<.001, respectively. In the comparison conditions (C2 &C4) boil water with a kettle and seal around exterior doors had greater behavior intentions F (1,202) =9.76, <.01 and F (1,200) =4.76, p<.05 respectively. Intentions to use compact fluorescent bulbs showed the highest intentions in the cost comparison (C2) condition, an interaction effect F (1,202) =4.18, p<.05. Dressing warmly to avoid turning up the thermostat had the highest behavior intentions in the kWh comparison condition, F (1,201) =4.28 p<.05. Interesting, all of these behaviors are curtailment behaviors with the exception of using CFL bulbs.

8   Discussion

With the increasing availability of high resolution energy sensor data in energy, we aimed to examine graph features that are germane to energy feedback that has the potential to influence consumers' attention, knowledge and perceptions of ease, attitudes, involvement and behavioral intentions. Our results are intriguing; there are consistent patterns of preferences and affective engagement with specific graph features (e.g. the bar and line graph). However, a different pattern of results is revealed for attention and knowledge outcomes, the novel radial graph, while the least preferred, garners greater attention and increases in knowledge.

We were unable to significantly and consistently influence behavioral intentions. This may reflect the lack of personal relevance of our graphs or the inability of the viewer to interact with the graphs over time.   Graphs alone even with cues for interpretation may be insufficient to change behavior. Tips for behavior change, reminders   and embedding the energy lifestyle graph in family and community norms may be required to stimulate and maintain behavior change.

We offer several caveats to the interpretation of our data. Our audience was a young adult student audience, many of whom still live with their parents and likely have not yet paid their first electricity bill, making energy graphs to save money and energy irrelevant. A more age diverse audience engaged in bill paying may react differently to the subject matter of the graph and the implications of reducing consumption via behavior change. Attention results as measured by time spent on the graph page were intriguing, but only available in two of the four conditions. Future work should attempt to more rigorously assess attention via eye tracking or other means to insure that time on a page reflects graph attention.   We replicate others findings that preferences and attitudes towards graphs are not related to learning and attention [7].

More research is needed on the array of potential affective, cognitive and behavioral outcomes from graph-based feedback. Particularly needed is a systematic examination of the interplay of graphic display features and user experience outcomes and behavior change.

Acknowledgements. Study data analysis funded by Stanford University Precourt Energy Efficiency Center, Changelabs project funded in part by the Department of Energy ARPA-E award number DE-AR0000018, the California Energy Efficiency Commission award number PIR-10-054 and Precourt Energy Efficiency Center. We acknowledge the data analysis assistance of Melissa Saphir and Dave Voelker and the programming and implementation assistance of Anshuman Sahoo, Annie Scalmanini, Brian Wong, Alexandra Liptsey-Rahe, and Shaun Stehly.

References

1. IEE Report, Utility Scale Smart Meter Deployments, Plans and Proposals. Institute for Electric Efficiency, The Edison Foundation (2012)
2. Froehlich, J., Findlater, L., Landay, J.: The design of Eco-Feedback Technology. In: CHI 2010, Atlanta, Georgia, April 10-15 (2010)
3. Chiang, T., Natarajan, S., Walker, I.: A Laboratory Test of the Efficacy of Energy Display Interface Design. Energ. Buildings 55, 471–480 (2012)
4. Fischer, C.: Feedback on Household electricity consumption: A tool for saving energy? Energy Eff. 1 (2008)
5. Shah, P., Hoeffner, J.: Review of Graph Comprehension Research: Implications for Instruction. Ed. Psy. Review 14, 47–69 (2002)
6. Cleveland, W.S., McGill, R.: Graphical Perception and Graphical Methods for Analyzing Scientific Data. Science 229(4716), 828–833 (1985)
7. Ancker, J.S., Senathirajah, Y., Kukafka, R., Starren, J.B.: Design Features of Graphs in Health Risk Communication: A Systematic Review. J. AM. Med. Inform. Assoc. 13, 608–618 (2006)
8. Kosslyn, S.M.: Graph Design for the Eye and Mind. Oxford University Press, New York (2006)
9. Kosslyn, S.: Understanding charts and graphs. Appl. Cogn. Psychology 3, 185–225 (1985)
10. Shah, P., Carpenter, P.A.: Conceptual Limitations in Comprehending Line Graphs. J. Exp. Psychol. Gen. 124, 43–61 (1995)
11. Carpenter, P.A., Shah, P.: A model of the perceptual and conceptual processes in graph comprehension. J. Exp. Psychol.- Appl. 4(2), 75–100 (1998)
12. Friel, S.N., Curcio, F.R., Bright, G.W.: Making sense of graphs: Critical factors influencing comprehension and instructional implications. J. Res. Math. Educ. 32(2), 124–158 (2001)
13. Zachs, J., Levy, E., Tversky, B., Schiano, D.J.: Bars and Lines: A Study of Graphic Communication. Mem. Cogn. 27, 1073–1079 (1999)
14. Stone, E.R., Sieck, W.R., Bull, B.E., Yates, J.F., Parks, S.C., Rush, C.J.: Foreground: Background salience: Explaining the Effects of Graphical Displays on Risk Avoidance. Organ. Behav. Hum. Decis. Process 90(1), 19–36 (2003)
15. Dietz, T., Gardner, G.T., Gilligan, J., Stern, P.C., Vanderbergh, M.P.: Household Behaviors can Provide a Behavioral Wedge to Rapidly Reduce US Carbon Emissions. P. Natl. Acad. Sci. 106(44), 18452–18456 (2009)
16. Ford, R., Karlin, B.: Graphical Displays in Eco-Feedback: A Cognitive Approach. In: Marcus, A. (ed.) DUXU/HCII 2013, Part IV. LNCS, vol. 8015, pp. 486–495. Springer, Heidelberg (2013)
17. Burner, G.C.: Standardization and Justification: Do Ad Scales Measure Up? J. Cur. Issues & Res. Advert. 20(1), 1–18 (1998)
18. Sundar, S.S., Kim, J.: Interactivity and Persuasion: Influencing Attitudes with Information and Involvement. J. of Interactive Advertising 5(2), 5–18 (2005)
19. Zaichkowsky, J.L.: Measuring the involvement construct. J. Consum. Res. 12(3), 341–352 (1985)

User-Centred Design of an Audio Feedback System for Power Demand Management

Rebecca Ford[1], Joe Penn[2], Yu-Chieh Liu[2], Ken Nixon[2], Willie Cronje[2], and Malcolm McCulloch[3]

[1] School of Engineering and Computer Science Victoria University of Wellington PO Box 600, Wellington, 6140, New Zealand
rebecca.ford@ecs.vuw.ac.nz
[2] School of Electrical and Information Engineering, University of the Witwatersrand, Johannesburg, Private Bag 3, WITS, 2050, South Africa
joseph.penn@students.wits.ac.za,
{yu-chieh.liu,ken.nixon,willie.cronje}@wits.ac.za
[3] Department of Engineering Science, University of Oxford Parks Road, Oxford, OX1 3PJ, United Kingdom
malcolm.mcculloch@eng.ox.ac.uk

Abstract. Low-income houses in South Africa are supplied with a pre-payment meter and a circuit breaker that trips at a low power level (about 20A, 4.5kW), resulting in many nuisance trips. Four categories of audio cues, each being able to represent five levels of power consumption, are assessed. A survey of 62 people was conducted. The numerical analysis of the results and the perceptions of the respondents both indicate that the use of changing tempo and texture is the most effective at conveying feedback information on the power consumption in the home.

Keywords: audio cues, demand management, low cost, energy feedback.

1   Introduction

This paper addresses the issue of developing a design methodology for providing immediate and intuitive audio feedback about high power consumption to low-income residential users, particularly for periods when their demand is approaching the maximum capacity of the main circuit breaker in their home.

On any electrical power system (national grid, microgrid or nanogrid) it is extremely important that the flow of power between generators and loads is balanced at any instant in time. This ensures stable operation of the system and avoids the disruption that will ensue if the grid is blacked out due to instability. Stability can be addressed from the generation side as well as the consumption side. An adequate reserve margin on the generation side (embodied in the kinetic energy of the spinning turbo-generators, or stored battery charge on microgrids) gives the grid operators the freedom to dispatch more energy from the generators to the load side at short notice. South Africa in particular is facing severe generation constraints at the present

A. Marcus (Ed.): DUXU 2014, Part III, LNCS 8519, pp. 530–541, 2014.
© Springer International Publishing Switzerland 2014

moment in time; the generation reserve margin of the national utility company, ESKOM, was as low as 0.17% on 13 May 2013 [1].

Load side response (better known as demand side management) is now coming to the fore, as it has been demonstrated that it can be more economical than expanding the generation side [2]. However, demand side response is challenging because it requires that a large number of consumers actively participate. In South Africa, national campaigns are in place to encourage households to swap incandescent lights for more efficient lighting solutions and consumers are being offered rebates on solar water heaters [3]. Furthermore, real time alerts are displayed on state-owned television channels to reduce peak demand; this visual information system takes the form of a special graphical display at the bottom of the television screen that indicates the current demand status to households via the use of colours and bar charts. The scheme provides information to consumers about the state of the grid, and has been shown to have an impact at a national level [4], but it does not tell consumers much about their own contribution to the total demand. This is a problem because many residents in rural areas often have their power consumption limited by pre-paid electricity meters equipped with feed-in breakers, as shown in Fig. 1. These breakers trip at a modest level of 20A [5], frequently cutting off the power supply with no warning.

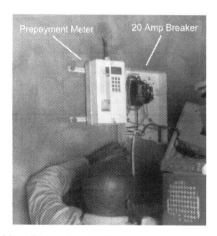

Fig. 1. A typical installation showing the pre-payment meter and 20A breaker

Although there is the occasional use of automation to disconnect hot water systems during periods of high power demand [6], this intervention is often not sufficient to prevent the breaker from tripping. Further intervention is frequently necessary, but the automation of additional household appliances becomes complex and is too expensive, especially given that most residences equipped with prepayment meters and feed-in breakers are low-income households.

However, site visits revealed that the combination of their low income and use of prepayment meters has made these residents both aware of their household energy usage and motivated to take action to reduce consumption and prevent tripping of the breaker. As there is a strong motivation amongst the community [7] this context presents an ideal case for integrating users into the demand management process. Feedback about household electricity demand is thus explored as a mechanism for encouraging and enabling users to better manage their energy consumption and prevent power outages.

This paper focuses on assessing the efficacy of cues to the user that enable them to manage their demand and limit high levels of energy consumption by prompting immediate action when the load approaches the trip level. Specifically, it addresses the question of which parameters within the cues produce consistent, accurate and meaningful responses from users. The work presented here does not include the deployment of any technologies into the field.

First, the relevant literature is explored to determine key aspects in the design of effective feedback mechanisms for demand management, and Section 2 concludes that, in general, user-centric design needs to fulfil four criteria. In Section 3 the specific context of this work is examined, particularly the need for users to respond immediately to the feedback to prevent power outages, and thus audio cues are suggested as an appropriate mechanism. Users also need to be made aware of situations when their use is approaching high power consumption (i.e. before it reaches maximum capacity), therefore we propose that a suite of cues is required. Section 4 discussed the design of these cues, and Sections 5 and 6 present findings from preliminary testing. Conclusions and recommendations for further research are discussed in Section 7.

2   Feedback as a Mechanism for Demand Management

Feedback about energy consumption has been used over the past 40 years as an effective mechanism for encouraging energy demand management. Feedback interventions are on the whole effective at encouraging users to reduce consumption, and they are cost effective when compared to other interventions [8]. However, the way that users respond to feedback varies significantly, and whilst feedback is effective on average, it is not so in all cases [9]. A more recent body of work in this space points to the importance of considering users when designing feedback interventions, particularly with regard to their interaction with the feedback technology [10,11].

Although the provision of energy consumption information is of considerable value, for the feedback system to be effective at bringing about the desired shift in energy behaviour it is important that the design process accounts for the way in which users interpret and respond to the feedback, as well as their behavioural and motivational psychological aspects in relation to energy use [12]. In addition, contextual constraints can limit a person's ability to respond to feedback regardless of their motivation to act [13], and therefore careful consideration of the specific purpose of the feedback, the context in which energy is being consumed, and the Living Standards Measure grouping and cultural background of the target demographic is important.

A key challenge is to develop a user-centric design of a system capable of providing households with real-time feedback about their consumption that meets the following four design criteria: (1) it is appropriate to the specific context in which it is intended to be used, (2) it is interpreted consistently and accurately, (3) it provokes a response at the appropriate point in time, and (4) it is positively perceived by the user. The context for this study is different from most feedback studies and therefore needs closer examination and is addressed in the next section.

3   The Case for an Audio Cue

Most feedback interventions aim to encourage consumers to reduce their overall energy consumption, and are designed and evaluated accordingly. However, these systems are not appropriate when trying to encourage reductions in peak usage, where the main concern lies around the simultaneous use of a number of high power appliances, leading to a power trip. This raises four issues.

Firstly the user response has to be immediate. Energy consumption is a measure of power demand aggregated over time and hence the timing of the feedback to the user is not critical. For this case the user can 'pull' the feedback from the device. However for peak power response the feedback must reach the user immediately, hence the device must 'push' the information to the user. Secondly *all* users in the home must be aware of the feedback, no matter where they are located within the home, as they may each cause the breaker to trip by increasing the load. Hence the feedback must not be a point source of information but rather have a ubiquitous reach. Thirdly, the feedback needs to indicate the current level of power demand, ranging from moderate to extreme. The reason for this is that, even at the moderate level (e.g. just the oven on), the addition of just a single further high power device (e.g. iron) and one medium power device (e.g. fridge) can lead to a trip. Finally, it is important to consider the context in which the feedback will be provided; the target community is low paid, and therefore cost is a constraint on the implementation.

Typically feedback is provided to users visually. A user information [13] unit has been trialled in South Africa where the user interface is a three colour (green, amber red) visual display. The feedback is triggered both by local measurements and by information communicated from a central control room. The drawback of the visual display is that the user is not always facing the information unit, or is perhaps not even in the same room.

Whilst visual displays have the potential to provide detailed information about electricity demand, they are not always located such that they are visible to the consumer at the necessary point in time. As users are often physically occupied with tasks that might increase their energy consumption, such as housework, they are unlikely to pay constant attention to the display. Instead, we propose that an audio cue may offer a superior interface [14] that reaches a greater area of coverage in the house, and provides immediate notification of usage status to the consumer, thus addressing issues one and two. Issue three can be achieved through the use of a range of cues provided via interactive technologies, though care must be taken to ensure that they do not become a nuisance to users [15]. As audio devices are low cost, the final is also solved.

Therefore the authors propose that the most appropriate form of feedback applicable to the specific context of power management (design criterion 1) is that of a suite of audio cues. The next section explores the idea that appropriately designed audio feedback can improve the level of positive responses from the end users. In addition this paper investigates whether different sound symbols can be used to effectively warn end-users about power as well as energy constraint. It also tries to determine if the audio symbols can be used to communicate a sense of the urgency of the problem.

4   Design Parameters for the Use of Audio Cues

For the audio cues to evoke an appropriate response from users they must be readily distinguishable from one another across the various levels of energy usage to which the signals have been allocated.   The implemented audio cue set must also be relatively intuitive to respond to, requiring a minimal learning period for users to become accustomed to the scale of intensity contained within the batch of samples. To achieve this, the musical parameters are progressively increased corresponding to an increase in power usage. However, the individual parameters for variation must be carefully identified in order to accommodate both the distinguishability and intuition requirements of the design so as to meet design criterion 2.

When choosing audio parameters to investigate, it is crucial to consider the impact that they might have upon the user once introduced into their domestic environment. The audio samples utilised must induce a sufficient trigger at the critical end of the scale to bring about alterations to user behaviour, yet must also be benign enough to avoid excessive irritation for lower energy usage levels [16]. If the audio cues are too demanding at all energy usage levels, users may be inclined to eliminate the audio functionality of the energy monitors entirely. In order to achieve this aim, the sound samples must increase in urgency, which can be achieved by changing certain properties as the level of energy usage increases.

Although certain elements (such as melody, harmony and rhythm) may be used to impart levels of urgency, they offer consistent irritation levels to users and thus are not appropriate for this application.   For example if a major-harmony themed melody is repeated over a sustained period it may impart less urgency than a minor-harmony themed alternative [16]. However, the constantly looping phrase is likely to be equally irritating to the user regardless of the variant, quite possibly resulting in deactivation of the monitoring device entirely. Accordingly, foundational musical elements that can be utilised with simple tones in order to create audio cues that feature high degrees of fundamental variation offer the best building blocks for the sonic elements required for this application.

The pitch (or frequency) of a note is a fundamental musical property that can be varied with profound effect. Whilst some people struggle to recognise subtle fluctuations in tones, most are capable of recognising substantial changes in pitch. As lower pitched tones sit quite subtly amongst background noise and higher pitched tones tend to cut through more noticeably, variations in pitch are an ideal parameter to explore in this domestic context.

Tempo (or speed) is one of the most basic musical devices, variations of which are instantly recognisable. As tempo is entirely independent of pitch, it may be recognised and experienced by even the most 'tone-deaf' and musically-uneducated amongst us. Furthermore, different tempos are easily distinguishable from one another, making tempo a natural element to be exploited in this application. Extremely slow tempos can result in long intervals between sonic elements, reducing the irritation and urgency factor associated with an audio cue. Fast tempos have the opposite effect, and hence tempo is deemed appropriate for further exploration in this work.

Texture is the tactile quality that may be ascribed to a sonic element; an abstract concept that often leads to the use of adjectives such as 'rough', 'smooth', 'round' or 'thin' in order to describe sounds. It is a fundamental building block of music, and is easily distinguishable to the human ear being entirely separate from harmony. Given that the textures of sounds can have effects on listeners that range from 'soothing' to 'jarring', this element is a natural candidate for inclusion here. However as the variations are subtler, it is used in conjunction with changing tempo.

In addition to such musically oriented parameters, we are subjected to a diverse range of audio stimulus that affects our behaviour, such as the hooting of car horns, barking of dogs and so forth. Accordingly, the use of such audio can be implemented in order to generate responses in people that are directly related to generic experiences of the world around us and do not require any level of musical abilities in order to distinguish. This makes the use of non-musical sonic samples, recorded from the surrounding environment worthy of investigation.

Thus the properties of pitch, tempo, texture and real-world association were chosen for evaluation in this application. The sonic samples utilised for the real-world association category of audio cues were selected from within an animal theme, using fairly generic animal sources. The noises selected for use were deemed to be both fairly universal (mainly domestic animals) and to provide a subset of sounds to which the vast majority of users would have been exposed with relatively high frequency during their lifetimes. To see how users would react to the sounds a survey was conducted.

5   Survey Methodology

The purpose of the survey was to determine how the effectiveness of each of the four categories (pitch, tempo, texture and real-world association) in distinguishing between the following five levels of power consumption:

1. Moderate power usage: above average rate of consumption.
2. Moderate-high power usage: significantly above average.
3. High usage: energy consumption should not be increased further
4. Very high power usage: approaching trip level of main breaker, reduce usage as soon as possible.
5. Extreme power usage: about to trip main breaker, immediate action required.

A ten second sound sample was generated for each level. The musical properties of interest were incrementally increased for each sound representing the correspondingly increasing power level.

A set of 15 randomly selected sound samples per category was placed in a video. The first five samples randomly covered all 5 levels. We call this the 'learning stage' as it is the first time the person is exposed to the sounds. The next 10 samples randomly covered each of the 5 levels twice. This latter data is evaluated for consistency and accuracy. As each sample was played, the person was asked to identify which level they thought the sound represented. To avoid bias users were not told how the sounds vary, and the categories were randomly presented to the users.

At the end of the survey, users were then asked two open questions: (1) which category they thought the most effective and (2) at which point they would take action. Anonymous demographic information was also collected.

6   Findings

There were 61 respondents (8 New Zealand, 21 South Africa, 32 UK; 19 female; 34 under the age of 20 and 10 over the age of 50). The mean time to complete the survey was 17 minutes. Three respondents that did not complete the survey were discarded.

6.1   Consistent and Accurate Interpretability

The second criterion is that the feedback cue is interpreted consistently and accurately. Consistency is evaluated using the metric of the percentage of users whose second and third responses to the same sound level were identical, as shown in Fig. 2. Accuracy is represented by the offset between the actual and the perceived level. The metrics used for evaluation are the mean and standard deviations of this offset, Fig. 3.

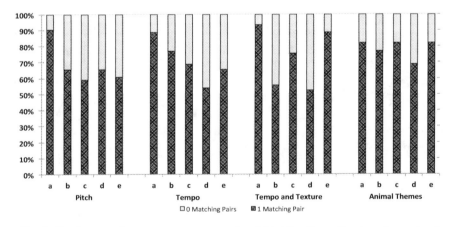

Fig. 2. Consistency of user responses to second and third iterations of each audio cue level

Pitch. Less than 66% of the respondents are consistent in 4 of the 5 levels. The exception is level (a), which has 90% consistency rate. However, it should be noted that the low frequency sample used for this set of audio cues could not be heard clearly on many laptop and cellphone audio-speakers, thus appearing as a change in both volume and pitch, which may explain the high level of consistency. This category had the worst overall results for consistency. The standard deviation and offset plots in Fig. 3 show a distinct worsening of performance as the pitch is increased. At level (e) the offset is greater than -1.5, indicating that on average all the respondents severely underestimated the urgency. This category had the worst overall results for accuracy.

Tempo. This category featured high consistency (> 70%) for the lower levels. However, the performance drops off for the higher energy consumption levels' of (c) – (e). This provides an indication of the existence of a tempo-urgency threshold, beyond which users find all cues to indicate extreme energy usage and thus struggle to make consistent associations. Accordingly some further method of differentiation may be required to make higher tempo sounds more distinguishable from one another.

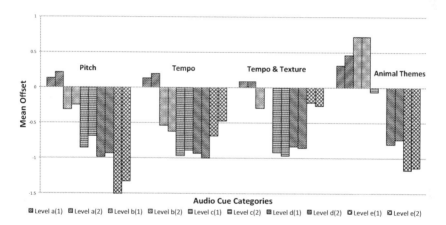

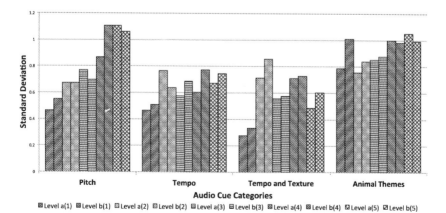

Fig. 3. The mean and standard deviation of the offset between actual and perceived level for second and third instance of each audio cue

The standard deviation and offset plots show that the tempo cues performed better than the pitch cues on both the bottom and top ends of the scale, especially the latter. This indicates that increasing urgency can be imparted via the use of higher tempos, and that they also perform well in the lower range. Given that all of the tones used in this test were of the same pitch, and thus could be reproduced with equal presence through all varieties of audio-speaker, it can be concluded that the use of tempo is likely considerably more effective for expressing lower urgency levels than pitch would be under good sonic conditions.

Tempo and Texture. The introduction of the texture parameter significantly improves the consistency at levels (c) and (e) by 10% and 15% respectively, at the expense of level (b), down by 25%. This suggests that five levels of urgency may not be practical for an audio interface of this nature. Rather, the use of a maximum of three notification levels would likely lead to better results, with users making the correct associations far more easily. This category is the most consistent for the extreme low and high levels. Levels (a) and (e) also show a small offset (<0.25) and a low standard deviation (<0.5). The offset and standard deviation of levels (c) and (d) remain unchanged when adding texture. This category is also the most accurate for the extreme low and high levels.

Animal Themes. This set of audio cues yielded the highest consistent results overall (>70%), indicating that respondents found it easy to make associations between the sounds and energy consumption levels. However, the mean and standard deviation of the offset are the worst of the four categories. These sounds contain significant meaning making them easy to distinguish, but results indicate that each user interprets the sound differently. If similarly complex sounds samples can be found that generate more universal associations within users, then the approach could yield far more accurate results.

6.2   Appropriate Response Timing

The third design criterion states that the feedback should provoke a response at the appropriate point in time. As this test was not conducted in a live setting, users where instead asked at which level they would consider taking action. The results are shown in Fig. 4.

The majority of respondents indicated that they would take physical action to reduce energy consumption around the audio cue level they had perceived to be associated with level (c) usage. Respondents may have interpreted this question to be an assessment of their own commitment to energy reduction, and may thus have chosen a moderate response level that they felt to be the appropriate response. However, the responses tail off in both the high and low directions, providing at least some basic indication that the overall range of urgency covered in the tests is centred around a level where an active user response may be triggered.

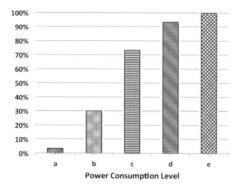

Fig. 4. Cumulative user perception of level at which action should be taken to reduce demand

6.3   User Perceptions

This fourth design criterion states that the feedback should be positively perceived the user. This was assessed by analysing the responses to the question "Please tell us which set of three tests you thought were the most effective and why". Results are shown in Fig.5. This data indicates the users perception of the efficacy of the different categories of audio cues.

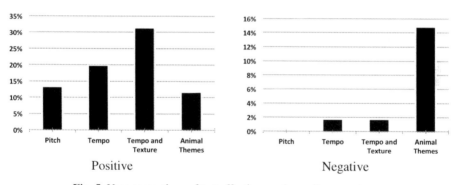

Fig. 5. User perceptions of test effectiveness by audio cue category

The combined tempo and texture category was perceived to be most effective (>30%). This result tallies with the analysis presented in Section 6.1. Respondents deemed the tempo cues to be the next most effective, although considerably less so, receiving 37% less positive feedback than the combined cues. The standalone pitch and animal sound variants of the test were found to be the least effective, receiving 58% and 63% less positive feedback respectively than the combined tempo and texture test.

The overwhelming majority of negative perceptions were aimed towards the animal themed audio cues, users finding them to be either high in annoyance factor or challenging to rank in terms of urgency (again backed up by the numerical analysis).

It should be noted that many respondents acknowledged the tempo element of the tempo and texture audio cues as being a significant contributor to that test's effectiveness. Thus, when considered in combination with the positive feedback recorded for the tempo and texture test, respondents can be considered to have found tempo to be the most effective parameter by a wide margin.

Whilst this study has tested for four specific audio traits, it would be of considerable interest to investigate a wider range of properties, such as rhythm, melody and harmony, as well as testing further cultural associations beyond animal themes. However, these would have to be applied in such a manner that they also featured low irritation indices for lower energy usage levels, perhaps via combined usage with tempo, volume or frequency of performance.

7   Conclusion

This paper addresses the issue of developing a design methodology for providing immediate and intuitive audio feedback about high power consumption, especially during periods when the power level is approaching the capacity of the main circuit breaker.

The four criteria used in this study for the assessment of the efficacy of the feedback mechanism are that: (1) it is appropriate to the specific context in which it is intended to be used; (2) it is interpreted consistently and accurately, (3) it provokes a response at the appropriate point in time, and (4) it is positively perceived by the user.

Due to the specific requirement for an immediate response that is independent of the location of the user, and that multiple levels of feedback are useful, a group of five audio cues were used. Four categories of cues were developed - three based on fundamental musical properties: pitch, tempo and tempo-with-texture, and one based on complex sounds (animal noises).

A survey of 61 respondents showed that the tempo-with-texture category best met the four requirements.

References

1. Paton, C.: Eskom Was 'On the Brink of a Power Shutdown'. Business Day Live (May 20, 2003), http://www.bdlive.co.za/business/energy/2013/05/20/eskom-was-on-the-brink-of-a-power-shutdown (retrieved February 1, 2014)
2. Zehir, M.A., Bagriyanik, M.: Demand Side Management by Controlling Refrigerators and its Effects on Consumers. Energy Conversion and Management 64(1), 238–244 (2012)
3. Van Blommestein, K.C., Daim, T.U.: Residential Energy Efficient Device Adoption in South Africa. Sustainable Energy Technologies and Assessments 1(1), 13–27 (2013)
4. Xia, X., Setlhaolo, D., Zhang, J.: Residential Demand Response Strategies for South Africa. In: IEEE Power and Energy Society Conference and Exposition in Africa (PowerAfrica), pp. 1–6. IEEE (2012)
5. Tewari, D., Shah, T.: An Assessment of South African Prepaid Electricity Experiment, Lessons Learned, and Their Policy Implications for Developing Countries. Energy Policy 31(9), 911–927 (2003)

6. CBi-electric Load Control Relay (2014), http://www.cbi-electric.co.za/products_select.php?p=13#245 (retrieved February 3, 2014)
7. He, H.A., Greenberg, S., Huang, E.M.: One Size Does Not Fit All: Applying the Transtheoretical Model to Energy Feedback Technology Design. In: Proc. CHI 2010, pp. 927–936. ACM Press (2010)
8. Allcott, H., Mullainathan, S.: Behavior and Energy Policy. Science 327(3), 1204–1205 (2010)
9. Ehrhardt-Martinez, K., Donnelly, K.A., Laitner, J.A.: Advanced Metering Initiatives and Residential Feedback Programs: a Meta-Review for Household Electricity-Saving Opportunities. American Council for an Energy-Efficient Economy, Washington (2010)
10. Froehlich, J., Findlater, L., Landay, J.: The Design of Eco-Feedback Technology. In: Proc. CHI 2010, pp. 1999–2008. ACM Press (2010)
11. Fitzpatrick, G., Smith, G.: Technology-Enabled Feedback on Domestic Energy Consumption: Articulating a set of design concerns. IEEE Pervasive Computing 8(1), 37–44 (2009)
12. Ford, R., Karlin, B.: Graphical Displays in Eco-Feedback: A Cognitive Approach. In: Marcus, A. (ed.) DUXU/HCII 2013, Part IV. LNCS, vol. 8015, pp. 486–495. Springer, Heidelberg (2013)
13. Util Labs Low Voltage Smart System (2011), http://www.utillabs.com/sites/default/files/news-events-downloads/lvss_brochure_final_web_2.pdf (retrieved February 4, 2014)
14. Walker, B.N.: Consistency of magnitude estimations with conceptual data dimensions used for sonification. Applied Cognitive Psychology 21(5), 579–599 (2007)
15. Fogg, B.J.: A Behavior Model for Persuasive Design. In: Proc. International Conf. on Persuasive Technology, pp. 40–46. ACM Press (2009)
16. Kallinen, K.: Emotional Responses to Single Voice Melodies: Implications for Mobile Ringtones. In: Human-Computer Interaction - Interact, pp. 797–800 (2003)

Personalized Energy Priorities:
A User-Centric Application for Energy Advice

Rebecca Ford[1], Ondrej Sumavsky[2], Auren Clarke[2], and Paul Thorsnes[2]

[1] Victoria University of Wellington, New Zealand
rebecca.ford@ecs.vuw.ac.nz
[2] University of Otago, Dunedin, New Zealand
paul.thorsnes@otago.ac.nz

Abstract. This research presents a new web-based application, called Personalised Energy Priorities (PEP), that provides households with personalised and tailored advice on practices or technologies they might adopt to improve the energy efficiency of their home. PEP proceeds in a manner similar to an online energy audit, but combines a user centric design approach with relatively new choice modelling software that allows recommendations to be tailored to individual preferences. The tool also provides links to further information about each energy recommendation, creating a more successful, one-stop-shop for persuasion.

Keywords: energy demand management, personalised advice, energy efficiency, choice modelling.

1 Introduction

This paper describes Personalized Energy Priorities (PEP), a user-centric web-based application that provides households with personalized advice to help tailor their practices and technologies to improve the energy efficiency of their home. The motivation for developing this tool is twofold: (1) the growing need for more efficient use of energy; and (2) the difficulty for households in obtaining personal advice that they both want and trust, to support and facilitate energy efficient behaviour.

The first motivation stems from resource consumption. On the basis of current trends, global demand for energy is expected to increase by more than 50% by 2030 [1]. Given our current dependency on fossil fuels for electricity, transport, and industry, this implies an increasing pollution of greenhouse gases into the atmosphere. Thus the need to use energy more efficiently is more pressing than ever, and will require consumers, as well as energy suppliers, to take action [2]. Households have potential to reduce their overall energy consumption significantly by implementing more energy efficient behaviour in the home and car [3]. Dietz et al. [4] report, for example, that energy savings of approximately 20% could be achieved in the U.S. through changes to 17 different typical household actions using readily available technology (e.g. stopping draughts, applying thermostat setbacks, making changes to

A. Marcus (Ed.): DUXU 2014, Part III, LNCS 8519, pp. 542–553, 2014.
© Springer International Publishing Switzerland 2014

driver behaviour, etc.). These relatively easy changes could improve energy efficiency relatively quickly, with most savings occurring within a 5-year timescale.

The second motivation for the development of this tool is due to the slow rate of uptake of energy efficiency improvements; opportunities like these have been available for decades, which raises the question of why these savings have not yet been realised. One explanation is that people typically have limited information about the energy savings potential of different actions [5]. They may express a desire to reduce expenditure on energy or improve environmental outcomes, but the cost of obtaining reliable information, that is specific to their own needs and that they can trust, prevents action. Gardner and Stern [3] conclude; "crucially households lack accurate, accessible, and actionable information on how best to achieve potential savings through their own steps." General information programmes are rarely effective, and better results are seen when the information is made personal to the user, that is, when it is based on the specific characteristics of their own circumstances [6]. This makes it more appealing to users, and helps to reduce information overload by removing anything not relevant.

A home energy audit provides a starting point for personalization. Energy is an input into a wide variety of services in the home, and while householders see the total energy bill for all of those services, they often have little idea of how much each service contributes to that total [5]. An energy audit provides that critical information. The process involves an in-depth assessment of household energy use and, given the services that householders currently demand, an auditor can recommend physical improvements that would deliver the same or similar services at lower energy cost, i.e., more energy efficiently.

Despite the practical approach taken during an energy audit, research findings are mixed regarding its effectiveness in helping consumers to make changes and reduce their energy bills [7]. We suggest that this is due to several shortcomings in the information provided during an energy audit, which are examined in the following section. The remainder of this paper then goes on to describe the design elements of PEP, outline the identification of energy efficiency actions and their characteristics that are used to develop a prototype, discuss findings from initial testing, and suggest and discuss options for further development.

2   Going Beyond Energy Audits

Although the approach taken by most energy audits is fairly systematic and inclusive of all physical elements of the dwelling, they tend not to incorporate either users' perspectives or user behaviour, potentially limiting the effectiveness of the information provided [8]. The following sections explore the elements of user behaviour, user preference, and communicating recommendations to users.

2.1   User Behaviour Matters

The way in which energy is consumed is the result of the users' house characteristics, the energy related technologies they own, and the way in which they use those technologies. However, conventional energy audits tend to focus only on energy efficiency improvements that can be made to the building envelope and appliances in the home, and ignore behavioural changes that may be implemented [9]. This may be problematic, as residential demand is affected by more than just dwelling form, technology, and climate; indeed patterns of occupancy and household behaviour may determine up to two-thirds of the energy demand in homes [10]. Furthermore, there are limits to the gains from retrofits. If done well, each additional increment of energy efficiency comes at a successively higher cost. At some point, it may make more sense to change the way in which we use energy technology than to keep buying more energy efficient technology.

In addition, the rebound effect [11] means that changes in how technology is used can counteract energy savings made by technology changes: more energy efficient appliances mean lower costs, which householders may take advantage of by demanding more services. In short, householder behaviour becomes a key determinant of energy consumption. And there are as a practical matter a large proportion of people, such as renters or those on low incomes, who are unable to make significant investments in energy-efficient appliances. Thus is it important to provide advice about changes in user behaviour that complements changes to the house and contents.

2.2   Preference Matters

There are usually multiple ways to tackle each problem identified in an audit, and each of these options typically varies along multiple dimensions (e.g. cost to implement, efficiency gains, skills level required to implement, impact on house value, etc.). The appropriateness of each of these options depends both on the characteristics of the house *and* household members, yet audits tend to account only for cost and efficiency impacts of each option as determined by the house characteristics. However, the additional dimensions of energy efficient retrofits and impact of these on household members is important to consider as this may affect the likelihood of a particular action being considered [12].

In an evaluation of home energy audits from a consumer perspective, Ingle et al. [8] found that the main driver for households making upgrades to their home was the extent to which the change addressed "specific aspects of their own experience in the house". Consumer preferences for the characteristics of the energy saving measures themselves, in addition to their cost-effectiveness, influenced choices. These findings have been mirrored in other research, which have shown that users express concern about different attributes of energy efficient products, e.g. risks associated with the reliability of heating systems [13], or express preference for different aspects of heating and hot water systems, e.g. the aesthetics of the technology or the level of independence from the national power grid it provided [14].

These studies illustrate the importance of consumer preferences for different characteristics of energy saving measures at an aggregated level, however, underlying this there is often a significant variation in people's individual preferences, which is also important to account for [12].

2.3   Communication Matters

Variations to the way in which energy related information is communicated to users can have an impact on subsequent behaviour change. Recommendations following an audit-based process are typically provided to users as a long list of actions, and simply changing the order of recommended actions can have a significant impact [15]. Actions are typically presented in order of net financial benefit, but non-financial preferences, such as ease of use, aesthetics or reliability, may outweigh financial implications for many households [16], and this should be customized to each user.

Although home energy audits do tend to result in positive savings for those who implement changes [7], not all households go on to make changes [8]. This may be because users have trouble finding information about the recommended changes or how to actually implement them, and thus information programs that provide users with a one-stop shop where they can access a full set of energy advice information tailored to their context, incentives for action (e.g., better energy efficiency means lower power bills, a better lifestyle and less damage to the environment) and links to information about implementing changes are relatively more successful [16, 17].

2.4   Personalised Energy Priorities (PEP)

In order to overcome the shortcomings of existing audit-based approaches, the design of PEP introduces three novel elements. Firstly, PEP provides advice for households in terms of changes to the way in which they use energy technologies, as well as the physical retrofits that could be implemented in their homes; advice about changes in user behaviour is designed to complement changes to the house and contents.

Secondly, PEP takes a user centric approach, putting householders, not their homes, in the centre of the decision making process. PEP enables the various characteristics of energy-efficiency actions to be accounted for through the use of an innovative choice-modelling platform. In this way householder preferences can be incorporated into the advice provided to the householder, and used to structure the order in which recommendations are provided.

Finally, PEP represents a significant step toward a one-stop on-line information shop customized for each user's context and motivations. For each of the actions recommended, web-links are provided to users to enable easy access to more detailed information about the recommendations most attractive to them, as well as any contacts needed to implement the actions.

3   Developing PEP

In developing PEP we identified the following key steps: (1) identify the set of energy efficiency actions to be used in the tool and the attributes that can be used to describe them, (2) elicit information from users so that their preferences toward different attributes can be determined, and (3) communicate information about energy efficiency actions to users in an appropriate manner.

3.1   Energy Efficiency Actions and Attributes

Data collection began by compiling a list of energy efficient or pro-environmental behaviours and their attributes mentioned in key known academic literature [3, 4, 5, 18, 19, 20]. Further actions and attributes were identified via forward citations from these articles and keyword searches in academic databases (e.g. Scopus), and non-academic databases (e.g. Google) using terms such as home energy efficiency, home energy behaviours, home energy savings, home energy audits, energy-saving measures, and so on.

Table 1. Alternative energy efficient actions available to householders

Actions to improve residential energy efficiency	
• Install more energy-efficient dishwasher	• Turn off lights in unused rooms
• Install more energy efficient refrigerator	• Install a more energy-efficient water heater
• Install more energy efficient clothes washer	• Install a heat recovery unit on shower system
• Install more energy-efficient clothes dryer	• Install a shower dome
• Duct clothes-dryer exhaust outside	• Install low-flow showerheads
• Install/upgrade ceiling insulation	• Cut shower time in half
• Install/upgrade under-floor insulation	• Set hot water cylinder to 60°C
• Install/upgrade wall insulation	• Shut off any unused hot water cylinders
• Fill the sink with hot water rather than leaving the hot water running	• Turn hot water cylinder off when you go away for more than a week
• Install secondary glazing to windows	• Wrap hot water cylinder and pipes
• Apply DIY window insulation film	• Fix leaky pipes and taps
• Install thermal-lined curtains and pelmets	• Install double-glazed windows
• Replace/upgrade windows	• Line-dry laundry outside
• Draught stop around doors and windows	• Use lower temperature settings on the washing machine
• Seal gaps around window frames, skirting boards and cornices with sealant	• Wait for a full load before you use the washing machine
• Seal wall, floor and ceiling penetrations for electrical and plumbing services	• Remove unused food from refrigerator and freezer
• Block unused open fireplaces	• Fill kettle appropriately
• Fit and draught-stop ceiling hatch	• De-ice the refrigerator
• Install more energy efficient space heating	• Cover pots with lids when cooking
• Avoid using unflued gas heaters	• Check under house for dampness issues
• Thermostat setbacks	• Install an on-ground vapour barrier

Contacts from industry and government (e.g. Building Research Association New Zealand, and the New Zealand Energy Efficiency and Conservation Authority) provided data on various energy efficiency actions that they had previously compiled, which we incorporated. Finally, we sent our compiled list of energy behaviours and their attributes to industry experts from Beacon Pathway and the Energy Efficiency and Conservation Authority for review.

In total 60 different actions including changes to the building envelope and technology as well as changes to energy practices (i.e. how users interact with those technologies) were identified. These are presented in Table 1.

Table 2. Attributes of energy efficiency actions

Attribute	Example 1: Efficient wood burner	Example 2: Shower time in half
Upfront monetary cost	Moderately high	No or low
Upfront time cost	Low	No or low
DIY installation?	No	NA
Structural alterations required	Moderate	None
Capitalisation into home value	Full	NA
Try before buying	Limited	Yes
Energy efficiency	Moderate	High
Ongoing $ maintenance costs	Moderate	Nil
Ongoing time costs	Low	Moderate
Ongoing energy savings	Moderate	Low
Reliability	High	High
Confident will work as advertised	High	High
Ease of use	Moderate	High
Skills required to operate	Moderate	Moderate
Requires changes in habits	Yes	Yes
Lifespan	Long	Long
Transferrable to another dwelling?	Limited	Yes
Effect on comfort	Positive	Negative
Effect on aesthetics	Positive	None
Effect on safety	Negative	None
Effect on damp/mould	Positive	Positive
Impact on the Environment	Neutral	Nil
Impact on household members	None	Positive
Impact on neighbours	Some	Nil
Provides independence from the grid	Yes	NA

Due to the nature of the data collection and our intended audience, there are some actions that are fairly specific to the New Zealand housing context. On the whole New Zealand houses have low levels of insulation, poor air-tightness, and persistent underheating, resulting in many homes failing to reach the World Health Organizations healthy indoor temperature range of 18-24°C [21], which often leads to dampness and mould growth. Thus there may be a higher proportion of actions focussing on improvements to insulation, heating and dampness than is necessary in other contexts.

Each action listed in Table 1 can be described in terms of its attributes, which were identified through an iterative process; the authors first reviewed the literature and developed an initial list of 31 attributes in an attempt to construct an exhaustive set of characteristics by which the energy efficiency actions could be described. The attributes were then tested to check for orthogonality (the final attributes must be mutually exclusive) and attributes found redundant were removed. Several additional attributes not found in the literature but of apparent relevance to local homeowners were added, resulting in the list of 25 attributes presented in Table 2 along with two examples of actions that have been rated on each attribute.

The first example provided in Table 2, "efficient wood burner", is a specific example of the action "Install an energy-efficient heating system" in Table 1. Installing a wood burner has what might be considered a moderately-high purchase cost, is only moderately energy efficient, but is reliable, generates comfort and aesthetic appeal, and provides users with some independence from the distribution (i.e., gas or electricity) grid. The second example provided "shower time in half" provides a contrast; this action has no upfront cost and is highly energy efficient, but has a negative impact on comfort and requires users to change their habits. The appeal of each of these actions (and of the other 58 actions identified and shown in Table 1) depends on the degree to which users value one attribute over another; for example, a householder may value comfort, aesthetics, and energy efficiency more highly than saving money from the installation of an energy-efficient space heating system. Thus preference for one action over another may be predicted for individual users by eliciting information about the degree to which they value one attribute over another.

3.2   Determining User Preferences

To determine user preferences for one energy-efficient action over another, PEP elicits householder preferences toward their attributes, and uses this to generate a personalised list of suggestions for change. This elicitation process can be carried out in a variety of ways. A simple and effective method is to ask the householder about their willingness to trade off each attribute against each of the others one at a time. For example, we could ask the householder to choose between a heating system that costs more upfront and is easy to operate and another that costs less but requires more effort day-to-day, assuming all else the same. The choice directly provides information about the householder's relative preference for these two attributes. The process carries on by presenting other pairs of alternatives, each of which requires a trade-off. This general method of 'paired comparison' has been used widely in various contexts to elicit preferences for multi-attribute goods [22].

The disadvantage of this approach is tedium. Working through all pairs takes time and may seem repetitive, and the time and concentrated effort needed increases with the number of levels each attribute is defined on. For example, the upfront cost of purchase and installation of an action alternative can vary considerably. The more levels of each attribute, the more potential paired comparisons to consider. With a large number of attributes, the number of comparisons can become unrealistic.

We deal with this problem in several ways. First, we use web-based decision software called 1000minds[1], which reduces the number of paired comparisons the householder must respond to by eliminating from consideration all pairs implied by each choice via transitivity [23]. This often reduces the number of choices by two-thirds without loss of information (assuming that the choices are accurate).

Though smaller, the number of choices can still be large. To reduce the burden further requires its own trade-offs. First, elimination of some of the levels of an at-

---

[1] www.1000minds.com

tribute reduces the number of choices, while interpolation provides estimates of the weights on intermediate levels. Second, we allow the householder to choose the subset of attributes that matter most to his or her household, eliminating consideration of attributes that have little value (by assuming they have no value). Finally, the software recalculates weights and updates the prioritised list of action alternatives immediately after each paired comparison so that the householder can skip to the personalised list of actions when boredom sets in (and he or she can go back to the choice survey if the ordering in the list seems to need more work).

3.3   Communicating Energy Advice

Having elicited user preference by evaluating the relative weights the householder places on each attribute, the energy-efficient actions can be sorted so that those with the most desirable combination of attributes to that user are presented first. The next major step in the PEP process is to provide information about the action alternatives that fit the householder's preferences. To access this information, the householder clicks on an action alternative that seems of interest (and is presumably high on the personalised list of actions), which takes them to a webpage with further information.

This page is designed to provide several types of information to users in one easy to access place. To compile this information we relied primarily on several sources widely regarded as independent and reliable in New Zealand: the NZ Energy Efficiency and Conservation Authority Energywise website[2]; the Beacon Homeowner Manual [24]; the Consumer NZ website[3], which reports the results of independent testing of a wide variety of products; the Smarter homes website[4]; and the Building Research Association New Zealand, an independent testing agency providing information for the building sector. We provided links to these sites where appropriate and occasionally to other trusted NZ and international sites.

The page starts with an explanation of how the action alternative treats the problem ('How does it work?'). While this explanation can be somewhat technical, the aim is provide the rationale for the action in an accessible way. Where appropriate, weblinks to helpful explanatory videos as well as to more advanced technical information are included.

The next section aims to help the householder evaluate whether the action alternative is suitable for his or her situation ('Is it right for you?'). Critical issues are how well the action will fit with the house and with the characteristics and behaviours of the householders. Continuing with the heat pump example, the section describes the climates in which a heat pump works well and its various advantages and disadvantages in installation and use. This information helps the householders' start to think about how to tailor actions to their context,

The next section describes how to implement the action ('How do I do it?'). In the case of installing a heat pump, the section identifies key issues to consider, such as size and placement. The section may list local installers or provide a link to a

---

[2] www.energywise.govt.nz

[3] www.consumer.org.nz

[4] www.smarterhomes.org.nz

directory of installers, as appropriate. The section may also either describe DIY installation or link to one or more good descriptions.

The page then describes complementary actions, such as other improvements or changes in behaviour ('What else should I consider?'). In the case of installing a heat pump, one could also consider improving insulation (in any of various ways) and developing habits to use the heat pump most efficiently. These suggestions link to other pages describing these actions. The web page concludes with links to other reliable and accessible sources of information, such as independent product reviews or sites that provide more detailed information. The goal is to make accessing reliable information as easy as possible.

4   Testing

A pilot version of PEP has been constructed and tested in Dunedin, New Zealand. The software proceeds in four stages, as illustrated in Fig. 1. Initially the list of energy efficient actions contains all those identified in Table 1 presented in a random order. As the user progresses through PEP, they first select 6 attributes of the 25 outlined in Table 2. The software uses this information to order the actions according to the limited information provided so far; that certain attributes are more important than others. The user is then guided through a choice survey, where they make trade-offs between pairs of attributes, such that the relative value of each attribute can be determined. This enables the list of actions to be prioritised according to the user's preferences, and presented back to them in this fashion. They are then able to click on each action on the list to access further information.

To test PEP we selected a random sample of 450 single-family, owner-occupied homes in three suburban areas of Dunedin, New Zealand with census demographic characteristics similar to those of New Zealand homeowners generally. An invitation to participate in our pilot survey was sent in the name of the householder listed in city council records. After follow-up telephone calls, 149 (33%) respondents completed the survey, which consisted of working through the trial version of PEP and then completing a more standard tick-the-box survey.

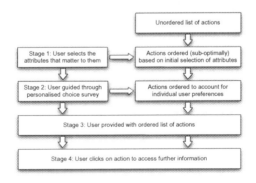

Fig. 1. The four stages of PEP

Of primary research interest in this pilot study was the variation across households in the attributes they care most about, i.e., in the heterogeneity in preferences for attributes. Each household was required to choose six attributes (in addition to upfront cost which was selected automatically). We conducted a cluster analysis designed to uncover clusters of households who chose similar sets of attributes. After experimentation, a six-cluster solution seemed the most informative.

A large majority in all clusters chose energy efficiency or 'value for money' as an important attribute. Over 80% of respondents in the three largest clusters, comprising 70% of respondents in total, also considered it important that the action be as energy efficient as advertised. A similar proportion considered it important that the action works reliably. These attributes are all sensibly seen as important, and it is not a surprise to see a large majority that consider them important.

The clusters are mainly distinguished by other attributes. About 30% value other practical aspects, including the lifespan of the improvement, the amount that the investment capitalises into house value, and that it needs only infrequent maintenance. About 22% care mostly about environmental benefits, 17% about dampness and ventilation, 16% about home safety, 9% want to avoid structural alterations and fiddly operation, and 7% prefer DIY installation and achieving independence from the grid. The characteristics of the respondents in each cluster correlate only weakly with the house and householder characteristics collected in the survey; preferences for attributes of action alternatives seem rather idiosyncratic.

Of interest is that 62% of respondents agreed or strongly agreed with the statement "making choices about energy efficiency in the home is complex", whilst only 25% disagreed. Most respondents also agreed with the statement "it's difficult to know what information about energy efficiency to trust", suggesting that there is a need for decision-making support tools such as this. In addition, 60% agreed that they "have the skills to make effective energy efficiency changes"; further suggesting that access to appropriate information is providing a barrier to action. Regarding the design of the online tool, 85% of respondents found the format of PEP easy to follow and 60% found it easy to answer the trade-off questions. Although only 5% found answering the trade-off questions very difficult, there is some room for improvement here.

5   Conclusions and Recommendations

Our pilot project provides useful information about the heterogeneity in consumer preferences for the attributes of energy-efficiency actions. The survey results indicate that most respondents find the format of the platform easy enough to understand and are also able to work through the decisions that elicit their personalised preference weightings. However, additional work that explores the extent to which users find the information provided by PEP to be beneficial, trustworthy, and engaging, and their likelihood to use that information to help make improvements and change behaviour would be useful to inform further development. In addition, the ability to track respondents over time and observe the extent to which their interaction with PEP encourages improvements to the house and coordinated changes in behaviour is recommended. That is, we would like to test user levels of engagement and interaction with PEP over time.

Engagement over time raises a key issue: home energy efficiency improvements, especially those to appliances or the building envelop, often happen incrementally over extended periods of time, usually years. For example, householders may choose to install a more energy efficient heating system one year, add some double-glazing a couple years later, and so on. With each incremental change, householders change how they interact with their altered environment, building new habits. Furthermore, once an incremental change has been made, it may have implications for choices in the future. It would be an advantage if householders could envisage and plan for the sequence of changes that might occur over perhaps the next decade.

This raises a challenge for the design of a tool such as PEP: How do users interact with it over potentially long periods of time? How does it take into account changes that a household has already made? Can it learn not only from the hypothetical decisions in the choice survey, but also from the actual decisions householders make? And can it help householders plan the sequence of improvements they would like to make over an extended period of time? Further work investigating these questions and the impact of such a tool on user interaction and subsequent behaviour change is recommended.

Acknowledgments. The authors would like to acknowledge Dr Paul Hansen, CEO and Director of 1000Minds Ltd., for his insight and advice during the development of PEP, and for his helpful comments on earlier versions of this paper. This research was conducted as part of the Energy Cultures project funded by the Ministry of Business, Innovation, and Employment in New Zealand.

References

1. International Energy Agency (IEA): World Energy Outlook 2006. OECD/IEA, Paris (2006)
2. International Energy Agency (IEA): World Energy Outlook 2009. OECD/IEA, Paris (2009)
3. Gardner, G.T., Stern, P.C.: The Short List: The Most Effective Actions U.S. Households Can Take to Curb Climate Change. Environment: Science and Policy for Sustainable Development 50(5), 12–25 (2008)
4. Dietz, T., Gardner, G.T., Gilligan, J., Stern, P.C., Vandenbergh, M.P.: Household actions can provide a behavioral wedge to rapidly reduce US carbon emissions. Proceedings of the National Academy of Sciences of the United States of America 106(44), 18452–18456 (2009)
5. Attari, S.Z., DeKay, M.L., Davidson, C.I., Bruine de Bruin, W.: Public perceptions of energy consumption and savings. Proceedings of the National Academy of Sciences of the United States of America 107(37), 16054–16059 (2010)
6. Benders, R.M., Kok, R., Moll, H.C., Wiersma, G., Noorman, K.J.: New approaches for household energy conservation: In search of personal household energy budgets and energy reduction options. Energy Policy 34(18), 3612–3622 (2006)

7. Abrahamse, W., Steg, L., Vlek, C., Rothengatter, T.: A review of intervention studies aimed at household energy conservation. Journal of Environmental Psychology 25(3), 273–291 (2005)
8. Ingle, A., Moezzi, M., Lutzenhiser, L., Diamond, R.: How Well Do Home Energy Audits Serve the Homeowner? In: ACEEE Summer Study on Energy Efficiency in Buildings, pp. 2-217–2-229. American Council for an Energy-Efficient Economy (2012)
9. Lutzenhiser, L.: Social and Behavioral Aspects of Energy Use. Annual Review of Energy and Environment 18, 247–289 (1993)
10. Lutzenhiser, L., Hu, H., Moezzi, M., Levenda, A., Woods, J.: Lifestyles, Buildings and Technologies: What Matters Most? In: ACEEE Summer Study on Energy Efficiency in Buildings, pp. 2-256–2-270. American Council for an Energy-Efficient Economy (2012)
11. Greening, L.A., Greene, D.L., Difiglio, C.: Energy efficiency and consumption — the rebound effect — a survey. Energy Policy 28, 389–401 (2000)
12. Desmedt, J., Vekemans, G., Maes, D.: Ensuring effectiveness of information to influence household behaviour. Journal of Cleaner Production 17(4), 455–462 (2009)
13. Farsi, M.: Risk aversion and willingness to pay for energy efficient systems in rental apartments. Energy Policy 38(6), 3078–3088 (2010)
14. Thorsnes, P., Barton, B., Carrington, G., Lawson, R., Stephenson, J.: Household preferences of characteristics of space and water heating systems. In: International Association for Energy Economics, Stockholm, Sweden (2011)
15. Magat, W.A., Payne, J.W., Brucato, P.F.: How Important Is Information Format? An Experimental Study of Home Energy Audit Programs. Journal of Policy Analysis and Management 6(1), 20–34 (1986)
16. Stern, P.C.: What psychology knows about energy conservation. American Psychologist 47(10), 1224–1232 (1992)
17. Stern, P., Black, J., Elworth, J.: Home energy conservation: programs and strategies for the 1980's. Institute for Consumer Policy Research, Consumers Union Foundation (1981)
18. Poortinga, W., Steg, L., Vlek, C., Wiersma, G.: Household preferences for energy-saving measures: A conjoint analysis. Journal of Economic Psychology 24, 49–64 (2003)
19. Karlin, B., Davis, N., Sanguinetti, A., Gamble, K., Kirkby, D., Stokols, D.: Dimensions of Conservation: Exploring Differences Among Energy Behaviors. Environment and Behavior (2012), doi:10.1177/0013916512467532
20. Flora, J., Boudet, H., Roumpani, M., Armel, C., Bhagat, S., Humphreys, E.: Attributes of energy reduction behaviors. Presented at Stanford University Energy Seminar on the ARPA-E Sensor and Behavior Initiative (December 2011)
21. Isaacs, N., Saville-Smith, K., Camilleria, M., Burrough, L.: Energy in New Zealand Houses: Comfort, Physics and Consumptions. Building Research and Information 38(5), 470–480 (2010)
22. Louviere, J.J., Hensher, D.A., Swait, J.D.: Stated choice methods: analysis and applications. Cambridge University Press, Cambridge (2000)
23. Hansen, P., Ombler, F.: A new method for scoring multi-attribute value models using pairwise rankings of alternatives. Journal of Multi-Criteria Decision Analysis 15, 87–107 (2008)
24. Easton, L., Blackmore, A.: Making Your Home HomeSmart: A Homeowner Manual. Report HR2420/14 for Beacon Pathway Limited

Experiencing CSR in Asia:
A Social Media Perspective from the Outside In

Constance Kampf

Business & Social Sciences, Aarhus University
Aarhus, Denmark
cka@asb.dk

Abstract. This paper focuses on Corporate Social Responsibility (CSR) as strongly linked to expectations for corporations in the cultural contexts in which they operate. Using an approach based in a macro-level for socio-technical design, it examines the interaction between digital activist efforts to (re)define CSR and corporate responses to these efforts. Two cases of interaction between stakeholders and corporations with activist interventions are examined. Findings demonstrate that this interaction around CSR is often indirect, and misses a critical interaction around contesting knowledge. This calls into question the viability of CSR practices mediated by policy and NGOs, because businesses appear to be simply adopting mediators' perspectives to avoid a crisis rather than building a strategy based on critical engagement with the issues.

Keywords: Socio-Technical Design, Culture, Knowledge.

1 Introduction

In Mumford's 2006 article on the past, present and future of socio-technical design, she focuses on core socio-technical values of prioritizing human needs and democracy as critical to future business models [1]. Human needs can be understood as part of CSR. Thus, we can understand her position in terms of the role of human needs in business models as socio-technical approach to CSR.

So why does CSR matter for our understanding of socio-technical design? Part of the answer lies in the expanding role and scope of technology use in daily life. Kampf [2,3] called for a re-framing of socio-technical design to include a macro-level of understanding beyond organizational contexts. This re-framing sets up macro social-technical design and CSR as both acting at the interfaces of business, technology and society. Adding a technology component to our social understanding of CSR offers us the chance to examine Internet supported communication processes in which stakeholders communicate with business about CSR, and businesses respond through adjustments to their strategy.

To examine these technology supported CSR communication processes, two cases documented on YouTube.com will be discussed. First, a 2013 case in which an activist organization influenced several clothing suppliers to stop using angora will be

A. Marcus (Ed.): DUXU 2014, Part III, LNCS 8519, pp. 554–561, 2014.

introduced. Then an earlier, ongoing case in which employee wages and working conditions in South East Asia were protested by both European Activists and the workers themselves will be compared and contrasted with the angora case. These two cases together show a range of results emerging from Internet activism, which can be argued to have effects on both short and longer-term business strategy choices. These effects can be seen as a form of socio-technical (re)design at the macro level.

2   Method

The method is a multiple case study. The two cases were selected because they offered recent examples of companies altering their business strategies in response to online activism. These two cases come from the fashion industry. The combination of these cases demonstrates a range of business responses to online activism from adopting activist demands for short term action to re-envisioning their business strategy by including benefits to society as a primary goal for their organization.

This primary data is approached through a multidisciplinary model for socio-technical design at the macro-level [2]. It uses a "multidisciplinary lens combing socio-technical design, organizational theory and sociological concepts." [2]   This model is knowledge focused, looking at knowledge in terms of 1) The cultural production of new forms of knowledge [4]; 2) epistemic or knowledge producing circuits which form the basis for a knowledge producing culture [5]; and 3) active, contested knowledge processes [6].

Treating knowledge as the focus for examining the intersection of business and society reveals the cultural pressures to which companies respond [7].   Understanding these cultural pressures in terms of their potential effects on both knowledge about an issue and business strategy adjustments in response reveals a part of the interface between business and society as socio-technical space of negotiation.

3   Two Cases of Digital Activism about CSR and Corporate Responses

Both CSR and macro socio-technical design can be understood as affecting and reflecting surrounding cultural contexts by addressing norms and values.   These cases demonstrate the effects of using knowledge underlying value choices to attempt to reframe norms for both consumer behavior and corporate strategy.

3.1   PETA Condemning Angora through a Viral Video, Blogs, and Media

In the first case, a non-profit organization called People for the Ethical Treatment of Animals (PETA) posts a viral video about the treatment of rabbits whose fur is used for angora sweaters.   The video went viral, and several companies in the clothing industry removed angora sweaters from their racks, and offered to refund any recently purchased angora sweaters.

PETA is a non-profit 501c(3) organization founded in 1980. PETA's mission is to support animal rights, and it targets factory farms, laboratories, the clothing trade and the entertainment industries. [8]. Since 1980, PETA has been legally engaging with corporations and research institutions around animal rights, and promotes a vegan diet and cruelty free consumer practices as cultural values.

The organization has expanded globally from a small US based activist group established in the 1980s, and currently claims to have over 3 million members worldwide, with sections in South America, Europe and Asia. [9].

The organization is funded by individual and corporate donations, and features logos of corporate donors on their website. On their donations page, PETA implies that association with them is a way to advertise your cruelty free corporate practices. Yet, on the page where donors are recognized, PETA posts a disclaimer stating that they are not responsible for the actions of their donors, and donations do not necessarily mean an organization has PETAs approval.

PETA engages in the cultural practice of presenting online videos of product production practices that PETA claims hurt animals. The videos are shown from a covert perspective, emphasizing the negative effects of these practices on animals. In addition to the video, PETA uses their website to advertise and organize protests that challenge conventional knowledge about clothing retailers.

One example was a protest by returning stuffed rabbits with red paint on them to the retailer, the GAP. These stuffed "bloody" rabbits are meant to represent rabbits treated cruelly in the production of angora [10].

PETA also uses discourse that challenges common knowledge about producing products from animals. This discourse is based on terms such as "cruelty-free" that highlight production processes, which are, in contrast to their label, not cruelty free. Examples are in this case, the production of angora, or in other cases the use of animals in cosmetic testing, and pharmaceutical science. PETA has been using this discourse since the 1980s to affect knowledge about the use of animals in products, which in turn attempts to reframe norms of consumer, producers and retailers related to animal rights. These norms include the use of animals for food as well, with PETA emphasizing a vegan lifestyle as part of their website.

The spreading of terms such as "cruelty-free" throughout the industries using animals in their products or production processes can be seen as a knowledge-producing circuit which brings awareness of industry practices to consumers. This awareness, in turn, encourages consumers to reconsider their norms and the connection between their norms and their purchasing habits. This encouragement is reinforced through the "Action" page on their website. The "Action" page offers several different issues related to animal rights, and names companies to which people can direct their protest action. One example of this is an "action –alert" on PETA's website naming Air France as an airline that carries monkeys for laboratory experiments as cargo. PETA calls for supporters to contact Air France and ask them to stop. [11]

PETA can be seen as trying to affect corporate strategy by telling both consumers and clothing producers which materials they should and should not use. In the case of "the angora rabbit cry heard round the world," PETA called for clothing manufacturers around the world to stop using angora by targeting retailers and asking them not to carry items containing angora.

Retailers responded in two ways—some of them announced they would stop using angora and refund angora products that were recently purchased, while others simply ignored PETA.

Consumers also made decisions about whether to ignore or engage in the practice of avoiding products with angora. But the media coverage ensured that regardless of reaction, their knowledge about how angora was produced was at least publically challenged, and possibly changed.

The PETA website is attached to several social media sites and an iPhone app, which viewers can use to further disseminate PETA's findings, stories of success and action campaigns. PETA USA has over 2 million "likes" on Facebook. [12], expanding the breadth of their knowledge producing circuit. They have 458 thousand followers on Twitter [13], and over 23,000 followers on Instagram [14]. These numbers show that social media can also be seen as part of the knowledge producing circuit.

In sum, PETA uses social media, their website, and traditional media to challenge knowledge about whether animals should be used in the production of products, and whether consumers should take animal cruelty into account when making purchasing decisions. In doing so, PETA has successfully affected the strategies of major clothing retailers who have chosen to stop selling products with angora in response to PETA's video and subsequent actions regarding the rights of angora rabbits. Thus, the combination of an activist group with an agenda that affects business practices—that of animal rights, is revealed through a viral YouTube video about angora rabbits with over 1 million views [15], and then discussed social media and consumer/retailer interaction reveal part of the interface between business and society. However, the retailer response to the issue is not to engage with it, but rather either ignore it or respond as PETA asks them too. This results in an interaction between PETA, corporations, and consumers that enables consumer engagement, but does not encourage corporate engagement around producing knowledge about the issue, but rather corporations that simply choose to comply or not with activists demands.

3.2   Southeast Asian Garment Worker Protests: Videos that Never Went Viral

In contrast to the PETA video and subsequent ability to change some industry practice at least at the retailer level, online protests both by activists and garment workers themselves have not resulted in viral videos or had enough media impact to change the practices. In this section, videos about garment workers that should also be emotionally moving and affect consumer perspectives are analyzed. So, why don't these videos go viral?

Frequently viewed videos are produced by independent media channels such as the Journeyman TV channel on YouTube [16]. Their videos include protests in Bangladesh, where the local police are using crowd control with nonviolent garment worker protests (over 8,800 views in the first day)[17]. This video has the potential to go viral because of the broader audience of the channel, which has about 240,000 subscribers. This video is also professionally produced and visually connects the global fashion industry with video footage of worker protests, in comparison with the amateur videos of protests and conditions posted by the workers or individual activists supporting the workers. However, it still is not to viral status. This begs the question of what kinds of cultural practices affect clothing consumers ability to hear and be interested in the worker's plights in Asia?

In the YouTube forum, the main activists for garment workers are the workers and unions themselves. They work with amateur videographers to produce videos that explain their situation. These videos are documentary style, and show the workers protesting, as well as describe the conditions in which these workers are living. They also directly address both companies and consumers as an active part of their context. This choice of addressing the videos directly to the global consumer audience reflects an effort to become a publicly and commonly acknowledged part of the global fashion industry for consumers and companies. It also reflects the workers efforts to establish their working conditions as a concern that could affect consumer's purchasing choices.

An example of this type of video is titled "Cambodian Garment Workers seek support from Walmart, H&M shoppers" and in the first year it has been available on YouTube, it has only achieved about 3,200 views [18]. This video depicts garment workers speaking directly towards consumers. In the video, workers explain that the people who hired them supplied Walmart and H&M. When Walmart and H&M change their CSR policies to distance themselves from garment worker abuse by setting a no tolerance policy for subcontractors who do not comply with their CSR perspectives on worker rights [19], the result portrayed in the video is that owners of the subcontractor companies picked up and left overnight, the factories are closed, the garment workers are left unpaid, and homeless. They protest both towards industry and consumers, holding signs that depict different amounts of unpaid wages, representing several months to over a year which subcontractors for H&M and Walmart have not paid them. The video is intended to get consumers thinking about why they are able to buy such cheap clothes, and who is actually paying the true price of production.

This is one of several videos explaining the workers' perspectives on the factories and their role in the global fashion industry. These videos reveal an interface between business and society that connects garment workers in Asia with clothing consumers in Europe and North America. They work to change the knowledge of the costs involved in producing cheap clothes, and get consumers to question whether they want to buy products that are cheap because of worker exploitation. Thus, the videos are working to change consumer knowledge about garment production, the reasons behind the prices they pay for clothing, and the effects of global companies enforcing CSR policies which have an effect that is different than the intention of the company itself. Ironically, the voices of the garment workers addressing clothing retailers are less visible than PETA's angora rabbit. The Journeyman video [16] ends with footage of a garment working crying as she is treated for wounds from rubber bullets. Why is it that the cries of an angora rabbit are more easily heard on social media than the cries of an injured person?

In this case, the efforts to change:

1. what consumers know about the production of cheap clothing, and
2. what companies know about the effects of their CSR policies

represent another form of the cultural practice of revealing the effects of production. They reveal the negative side of CSR policies intended to protect workers rights by demonstrating their experiences, which, least in the short term, show that enforcing CSR policies about the supply chain by eliminating suppliers who do not comply results in hurting the garment workers they are intended to protect However, these efforts trying to tell corporations how they are hurting garment workers in Asia appear to fall short. Not only are the companies not engaging with issue, but the media and social media are not able to support high level engagement yet either. It is possible that Journeyman's video will go viral in the coming months. At least YouTube is betting on it because it has added a requirement for the viewer to look at advertising before viewing the videos. But will this type of video and the questions it begs about the production of cheap clothing enable corporations, consumers, and garment workers in Asia to engage in building knowledge together at the interface of business and society?

4   Conclusions

These two cases—1) the PETA movement for animal rights to be considered in the production of products by corporations, and 2) the Garment workers in Asia— demonstrate social media as a virtual space that can reveal interfaces between business and society. In this space, traditional knowledge about products and considerations that consumers can make in their ethical choices related to purchasing productions is challenged. This space is contested, yet not used fully as a space for engagement about production issues that both affect and reflect the effectiveness and outcomes of company initiated CSR initiatives. In each case, activists work to redefine CSR. For PETA, CSR becomes focused on eliminating products whose production processes or materials involve any actions which can be understood as related to animal cruelty. In contrast, for the Asian garment workers, CSR emerges in a new form when they begin asking global companies to take responsibility to pay wages that their subcontractors have denied them due to the enforcement of CSR policies intended to protect garment workers in the first place. In both cases, industry appears to avoid engaging in the issue, only responding to social media and media pressures by either changing a visible practice, such as stopping the use of angora, or refusing to engage with the issue.

These cases call into question the viability of CSR practices mediated by policy and NGOs, because businesses appear to be simply adopting mediators' perspectives when the social media and media coverage appear to have the potential to affect their consumer base to avoid a crisis. As we apply the frame of socio-technical design to knowledge processes, such as the development of knowledge related to framing and defining CSR, the social issues inherent in CSR take on a new perspective through voices which are enabled and take on a new level reach with the technology of social media. However, the reach of social media is not only technical, but also social. Although any video has the potential to go viral, why do some videos, such as PETA's video about angora rabbits, go viral? Why do other videos with a case that is just as compelling, such as the garment industry worker documentary videos, stay relatively unheard and unseen? Is it because of the strategies used by the video producers? Or is it mainly because of the social networks that have been built up over time which allow people to be open to some issues more than others? What role does a history of activism play in the ability for a video to go viral? Are activists and business competing for cultural resources—each trying to present a framework for understanding consumption and lifestyle which foregrounds their concerns? And, if so, does social media provide more of a covert game of tactics played out between activist groups and businesses vying to shape cultural practices of consumption? Will social media spaces such as YouTube enable a socio-technical redesign of CSR, as the technology is used to reveal and encourage engagement at the interface of business and society? These questions raise key issues about the nature of social-technical design at the macro-level. What is the balance between the social and the technical aspects of social media? Do current technologies, such as social media, enable engagement because of the speed in which they allow people to exchange ideas and replicate them through interpersonal networks? Or is engagement a social characteristic, which needs to come from the intentions and actions of consumers and corporations in their approach to creating cultural practices in and through social media?

Questions for further inquiry related to understanding CSR as it is played out in online web presences and social media include: Whether, and how social media can play a role in building strategies for corporations, communities, and governments based on critical engagement with the issues? And how can this produce a common understanding of CSR with multiple perspectives that engages issues affecting societies from global perspectives rather than being used as a form of risk avoidance or a platform for ideology? And can perspectives on CSR from the outside in, from NGOs or garment workers towards corporations, be integrated into corporate strategy at a deeper level than risk management?

References

1. Mumford, E.: The story of socio-technical design: reflections on its successes, failures and potential. Information Systems Journal 16(4), 317–342 (2006)
2. Kampf, C.: Reconfiguring the corporate and commons: mobile and online activism as a form of socio-technical design. In: Kurosu, M. (ed.) Human-Computer Interaction, Part III, HCII 2013. LNCS, vol. 8006, pp. 388–395. Springer, Heidelberg (2013)
3. Kampf, C.: Revealing the Socio-technical Design of Global e-Businesses: a case of digital artists engaging in radical transparency. International Journal of Sociotechnology and Knowledge Development 4(4) (2012)
4. Suchman, L., Bloomberg, J., Orr, J.E., Trigg, R.: Reconstructing Technologies as Social Practice. American Behavioral Scientist 43, 392 (1999)
5. Knorr Cetina, K.: Culture in global knowledge societies: knowledge cultures and epistemic cultures. Interdisciplinary Science Reviews 32(4) (2007)
6. Blackler, F.: Knowledge, Knowledge Work and Organizations: An Overview and Interpretation. Organization Studies 16(6), 1021–1046 (1995)
7. Kampf, C.: Walmart, Mærsk and the Cultural Bounds of Representation. Corporate Communication: An International Journal 12(1), 41–57 (2007)

8. PETA, Learn About PETA (2013), http://www.peta.org/about-peta/learn-about-peta/ (accessed December 20, 2013)

9. PETA. About us (2013), http://www.peta.org/about-peta/ (accessed December 20, 2013)

10. PETA. Blog: "Update: Photos of the Day: Shoppers 'Return' 'Bloody Rabbits' to Gap" (2013), http://www.peta.org/blog/bloody-rabbits-gap/#ixzz2sa2OZQr3 (accessed December 31, 2013)

11. PETA. Action: "Ask Airlines to stop shipping monkeys to be tortured" (2013), http://www.peta.org/action/action-alerts/ask-airlines-stop-shipping-monkeys-tortured/ (accessed December 31, 2013)

12. PETA. Facebook Page (2014), https://www.facebook.com/officialpeta (accessed January 15, 2014)

13. PETA. Twitter Page (2014), https://twitter.com/peta (accessed January 15, 2014)

14. PETA. Instagram Page (2014), http://instagram.com/officialpeta (accessed January 15, 2014)

15. PETA. YouTube: "The Truth Behind Angora Fur" (2014), https://www.youtube.com/watch?v=PtAFHyXS31M (accessed December 31, 2013)

16. Journeyman Pictures. YouTube: Journeyman TV channel (2014), https://www.youtube.com/channel/UCM2YmsRUeIbRkqjgNm0eTGQ (accessed January 6, 2014)

17. Journeyman Pictures. The Abuse behind Cambodian Garment Worker Protests (January 6, 2014), https://www.youtube.com/watch?v=i8L_E2x5Aic (accessed January 6, 2014)

18. Stromberg, P.: (2013), http://www.youtube.com/watch?v=WD71SHK-X6E (accessed January 6, 2014)

19. H&M. About the Factory Collapse in Cambodia, http://about.hm.com/AboutSection/en/news/newsroom.html (accessed September 1, 2013)

Pumping Up the Citizen Muscle Bootcamp: Improving User Experience in Online Learning

Beth Karlin[1], Birgit Penzenstadler[2], and Allison Cook[3]

[1] School of Social Ecology, University of California,
Irvine, 300 Social Ecology I, Irvine, California, 92697-7075
bkarlin@uci.edu
[2] School of Information and Computer Sciences,
University of California, Irvine, 314 Donald Bren Hall, Irvine, California, 92697-7075
bpenzens@uci.edu
[3] Story of Stuff Project, 1442 A Walnut Street #272, Berkeley, CA, 94709
allison@storyofstuff.org

Abstract. This paper introduces and presents preliminary findings from the Citizen Muscle Bootcamp (CMB), an online learning program designed by The Story of Stuff Project for environmental activism. We first introduce the program and its potential to leverage online learning for citizenship training. Next, we report findings from two pilot studies in which we identify strengths and weaknesses of the current user experience. Finally, we present a revised course design that integrates insights from the fields of HCI, psychology, and requirements engineering to improve participant engagement and retention. Suggestions focus on variables related to recruitment, topic, process, and completion to identify key leverage points for improving user experience. It is our hope that this partnership represents the potential of research to inform practice to support best practices in HCI for sustainability.

Keywords: sustainability, citizenship, online learning, user experience.

1 Introduction

"I know of no safe depository of the ultimate powers of the society but the people themselves; and if we think them not enlightened enough to exercise their control with a wholesome discretion, the remedy is not to take it from them, but inform their discretion." Thomas Jefferson (1820)

Our democracy relies just as much upon the participation of its citizens today as it did when it was founded. We are facing tough issues as a nation and a planet that require the active participation of its citizens. Our democracy is based on an educated and empowered citizenry holding elected officials accountable for their actions and decisions. When the citizens do not take up this critical check in our system of checks and balances, we leave all of our decisions to the politicians and the lobbyists who inform and persuade them. As voter turnout continues to decline, many public and private institutions are looking for ways to increase civic knowledge, interest, and participation among the public.

A. Marcus (Ed.): DUXU 2014, Part III, LNCS 8519, pp. 562–573, 2014.

With the rise of time spent online across demographic groups, web content has become an increasingly common way of disseminating important information to people and engaging them in social causes. However, the sheer quantity of content online makes it vital that any program attempting to engage and retain an audience for longer than a few minutes focus on user experience. Human computer interaction (HCI) as a field addresses how to best approach the questions of how people interact with online content and how to maximize it for the best possible user experience and response.

This paper introduces and presents preliminary data on the Citizen Muscle Bootcamp (CMB), an online learning program designed by The Story of Stuff Project for environmental activism. The goal of the bootcamp is to train some of the 500,000 members of the Story of Stuff community into citizen activists to work toward social change on sustainability issues. After introducing the project, we analyze data from the first two pilot studies to identify key areas within the Citizen Muscle Bootcamp in which principles from HCI can be integrated to improve user experience. We then present a re-designed user experience of the course to leverage our insights from the fields of psychology and software engineering. These include variables related to recruitment, topic, process, and completion. As a result of this new design, we hope to improve the user experience so that interested participants in the Citizen Muscle Bootcamp will be better targeted to the right courses for them and provided with reinforcement and accountability throughout the course, leading to increased engagement, retention and subsequent civic engagement with the organization and its campaigns.

2   Theoretical Foundations

In this section, we will briefly point out the foundations for this work in the areas of sustainability and technology, online learning, user experience, and requirements engineering.

2.1   Sustainability and Technology

The term sustainability refers to the ability "to last or continue for a long time" [1] and the United Nations [2] has defined sustainable development as that which "meets the needs of the present without compromising the ability of future generations to meet their own needs". Scientists have shown that the behavior of humans has caused unprecedented changes to the earth's atmosphere; achieving a sustainable planet must involve changes in the habits and behaviors of individuals and communities, especially in the developed world.

While technological innovation (e.g., extraction and use of fossil fuels) has certainly enabled this growth, technology also has the potential to support solutions to key sustainability issues [3]. Technologies such as virtual reality, social media, and mobile technology enable humans to interact, not only with computers, but through computers with other people and with their natural and built environments. Thus, the potential of Human Computer Interaction (HCI) research is vital and important to the study of sustainability.

2.2   Online Learning

One way of leveraging technology to connect people and ideas is through online learning. The philosophy of freely sharing information and the pervasiveness of the Internet have created many new opportunities for teaching and learning [4]. People have to be confident and competent in using the different tools provided, and it takes time for people to feel comfortable to learn in an autonomous fashion. Collaboration, creativity, and a flexible mindset are vital for active learning in a changing and complex learning environment [5]. In a study on students' perceptions of characteristics of online courses [6], most agreed that course design, learner motivation, time management, and comfortableness with online technologies impact success. Elaborating on the advantages and drawbacks of online courses, Daphne Koller summarizes the success of Coursera: "Online course content has been available for a while. What made it different was that it was a real course experience, it started on a given day, and then the students would watch videos on a weekly basis and do homework assignments" [7].

2.3   Design and User Experience

A key function of HCI research is to assess the subjective user experience of computer systems, programs, and interfaces [8]. As such, HCI research has identified several key characteristics related to user experience. While a simple definition of usability refers to "ease of use", more comprehensive definitions take into account several characteristics [9].

One common definition of usability includes the following five key characteristics: effectiveness, efficiency, error tolerance, ease of use, and engagement [9]. The first three refer to the users' ability to complete program tasks. A program is effective if the user is able to complete the task, efficient if it can be done fairly quickly, and error tolerant if it can be completed with few to no errors. Ease of use and engagement refer to the users' experience within the program. A program is easy to use when the user feels relatively confident navigating it and engaging when the system or interface is pleasing and satisfying to use. These last two variables are particularly important in predicting the degree to which people accept, use, and are loyal to particular information technologies [10].

2.4   Requirements Engineering

Requirements engineering (RE) is the branch of software engineering concerned with the real-world goals for, functions of, and constraints on software systems [11]. Requirements engineering is concerned with interpreting and understanding stakeholder terminology, concepts, viewpoints and goals. Hence, RE must concern itself with an understanding of beliefs of stakeholders (epistemology), the question of what is observable in the world (phenomenology), and the question of what can be agreed on as objectively true (ontology). Such issues become important whenever one wishes to talk about validating requirements, especially where stakeholders may have divergent goals and incompatible belief systems [12]. RE facilitates the process of consolidating different stakeholders' concerns and agreeing on a system vision [13]. One method to transform the use cases of a system vision into more detailed descriptions of the interaction between user and system is to write user stories [14].

3   Project Background: Introducing the Bootcamp

One way of overcoming the cognitive complexity of climate science is through media and storytelling approaches. Dozens of films related to sustainability issues such as water, climate, food, and transportation have been released over the past decade. Research has shown that films such as An Inconvenient Truth and Food Inc. have the ability to impact viewers' knowledge and attitudes around sustainability issues [15,16]. Many issue-based films are working to extend their influence through transmedia social action campaigns. Such campaigns combine the film with new technologies such as streaming video, social media and network applications, allowing viewers to engage in the issues presented to learn more, connect with others, and get engaged to take action.

3.1   The Story of Stuff Project

One example of such a campaign is The Story of Stuff Project. Story of Stuff started as a film project in 2007 designed to tell the story of "stuff (i.e. consumer goods) from its creation, through its sale and use, and eventually to its disposal" in a catchy and engaging manner. The single film, with an initial viewership goal of 50,000 views, quickly exceeded this goal and sparked the launch of The Story of Stuff Project as a 501(c)3 nonprofit organization.

The Story of Stuff Project has since created 8 additional films and has also translated into other mediums, including television (interstitials for PBS), print (Story of Stuff book), online (website, social media), curricula (K-12 and religious groups), and a podcast. Their combined films have been translated into 39 languages and seen by over 40 million people and counting. This viewership has also translated into an active online community of nearly a half million people.

The initial goal of the project was to create and provide media resources to environmental activists and educators as well as to the general public. All Story of Stuff media have a Creative Commons license and are free to distribute for any non-commercial use. However, a community of potential activists formed around the organization, who started to want to become more actively engaged in the issues discussed in the films. They began communicating with staff via social channels and email that they were excited about the issues discussed in the film and wanted to do more. It became clear that educating people on the "story of stuff" was important but equally important was equipping and engaging them to act upon the knowledge they had gained through the films.

3.2   Citizen Muscle Bootcamp

To address this need, The Story of Stuff Project created a new program in 2013 called the Citizen Muscle Bootcamp. The Citizen Muscle Bootcamp is a six-week, online program designed to provide Story of Stuff Project community members with the skills, motivation and peer support they need to act on issues related to environmental sustainability. It was designed in response to inquiries and requests from the Story of Stuff community to help members learn, engage, connect, and act on the issues raised in their films.

Modeled on other successful multi-week online engagement programs—for weight loss [17] or financial literacy [18,19], for example—the Citizen Muscle Bootcamp guides participants through a series of weekly trainings aimed at strengthening their civic activism skills, or "citizen muscle". Each week of the program focuses on a unique skill:

1. Purpose: discovering your change making style and goal
2. Talk: learning how to communicate effectively about your issue
3. Grow: finding and developing a community of allies
4. Focus: getting strategic about how to accomplish your goals
5. Push: figuring out which tactics you'll need to employ to effect change
6. Practice: putting your learning into action.

Members of the Story of Stuff community were contacted via email and invited to register for the course free of charge. Those who registered were enrolled in the course as participants. Each week, participants received an email with a link to a 2-3 minute video lesson, accompanied by additional resources (e.g., framing, tips, readings) to get them practicing their change-making skills and a homework activity to put their new skills into practice. The program was designed so that each weekly module could be completed in 1-2 hours per week.

Even though the Story of Stuff Project was able to recruit participants to register, retention has been low and reported outcomes mixed. In the following sections, we will discuss the first two pilots of the Citizen Muscle Bootcamp and propose a revised design to improve user experience.

4   Learning from Pilot Studies: Testing the Bootcamp

Two rounds of pilot testing of the bootcamp were conducted in 2013. All participants were asked for feedback both before and after the bootcamp to assess strengths, weaknesses, and opportunities for improvement.

4.1   Measures

For the first pilot, participants received an initial intake survey at the beginning of the course and an exit survey at the end. The second pilot also had an intake survey; instead of an exit survey, they received a follow-up survey six months after the program.

The intake survey included questions about demographics (gender, age) as well as past experience (civic engagement, training, involvement with other organizations), current skills and abilities, community involvement, perspectives on the best way to make change, barriers to change, and motivation to take part in the bootcamp.

The exit survey for the first pilot asked about units they completed and which were most helpful as well as feedback on program length, level of interaction, interface, organizational support, and adaptations that would increase participation. They also repeated questions from the intake survey regarding current skills and abilities, perspectives on the best way to make change and barriers to change, community involvement, and motivation to participate.

The follow-up survey for the second pilot asked participants what they learned from the program, what specific actions they had taken as a result of their participation, their self-reported outcomes related to knowledge, skills, and leadership, and their most rewarding and challenges parts of the experience.

4.2   Participants

51 people participated in the first and 342 in the second pilot. The intake surveys revealed a diverse group of participants with a wide range of experiences and perspectives. Ages ranged from 18 to 74 with approximately 2/3 women and 1/3 men. About a quarter came with over a decade of "changemaker" experience and another quarter had less than a year of experience. Table 1 presents summary data on demographic variables for the two pilot samples compared to U.S. Census data (2010) as well as and average number of years as a changemaker.

Table 1. Characteristics of the pilot samples compared to US Census data

Variable	Pilot 1	Pilot 2 – General	Pilot 2 - Plastics	Census
Gender	32% Male	33% Male	32% Male	49% Male
Average age	41.3 Years	46.9 Years	44.8	36.8 Years
# of years as a changemaker	4.8	4.9	5.0	--

4.3   Importance of Citizen Muscle Bootcamp

The intake surveys provided insights that supported the need for citizenship training such as the Citizen Muscle Bootcamp. For example, 61% of participants reported that their skills and abilities as a changemaker were either "underdeveloped" or "very underdeveloped" and the most frequently reported motivation for participating in the course was to develop and/or refine existing "changemaker" skills (see Table 2). Over half (53%) said they had never received any formal or informal training on the being a changemaker.

Table 2. Motivation for participating in Citizen Muscle Bootcamp

Reason	Percentage
Develop changemaker skills	33%
Refine existing skills	30%
Learn to plug into action on issues	27%
Connect with other changemakers	11%

In addition, 50% felt that the best way they could make change was "through conscious lifestyle and shopping choices" as opposed to "voting" or "organizing in their community." This reaffirmed the significant opportunity (and need) to help people shift their primary change-making identity from consumer to citizen.

4.4   Outcomes of Citizen Muscle Bootcamp

Overall, the participants who completed the bootcamp reported positive outcomes. They reported increases in knowledge, skills, and likelihood to engage in work for a sustainable planet (see Table 3).

Table 3. Outcomes of Bootcamp on a scale of 1 (strongly disagree) to 5 (strongly agree)

Statement	Average
My knowledge about the skills needed to flex my Citizen Muscle have increased.	3.80
The information provided was useful	4.25
I developed leadership skills that I can use in my life.	3.65
I am more likely to engage in work for a healthy, sustainable, and just planet.	4.00

Participants reported learning about "how to try and influence people without just rattling off boring facts" and "what it takes to lead and to create change that is grounded, focused, and effective". Some reported that they already knew most of the material but that it was a nice refresher for them.

Most rewarding aspects reported by participants included "getting to do something new", "resources and learning new ideas on advocacy and activism", and "knowing that other people around the world were participating".

4.5   Challenges of Citizen Muscle Bootcamp

We identified three key challenges for participants based on survey results: project focus, interaction, and program length.

Focus. The first pilot featured a general curriculum for anybody interested in citizenship and activism training. While there are benefits to such an open approach, the lack of a clear issue focus created challenges for quite a few participants. For example, the first week of the Bootcamp focused on identifying the participant's core purpose as a changemaker. While participants clearly enjoyed the Purpose unit (it was one of the top rated weeks), a number of participants voiced concerns that either their purpose was too vague or that it was too difficult to select one or that they wanted to feel more connected to the work of the Story of Stuff Project. Ultimately, they wanted more direction as to what to work on.

In the second round of pilot testing, project organizers ran two bootcamps simultaneously. The first maintained the broader approach from the first round and the second focused specifically on one of the project's core campaign areas—plastic pollution—with a central goal of preparing participants to work on plastic bag bans in their communities.

Interaction. The bootcamps took place exclusively online with opportunities for interaction limited to the blog and Google Hangout. Several participants requested more interaction with the other people going through the bootcamp. They wanted to be part of a peer group going through the program and feel that sense of connection.

Program organizers attempted to increase the interaction of the bootcamp in the second pilot, with preliminary but limited success. Program organizers reached out via personal email to try and get people to organize in-person groups; two individuals responded positively but no groups were made. They also hosted a webinar in the middle of the seminar for participants to interact with Annie Leonard, the project director, and each other. They experienced technical difficulties and Annie was not able to join, but dozens of participants stayed online and chatted for a half hour with one another.

Time. The most commonly reported challenge by participants was that of limited time: Several reported that they "didn't always manage to complete the task on time" and that "keeping 100% on top of the activities week to week" was very difficult. The six-week length of the program also posed some participation challenges, given the hectic nature of most people's daily lives. The first pilot had 56 shared comments in Week 1; by Week 3 that number had dropped to 12. The significant drop-off in engagement was also reflected in participants' email click through rates. Although some attrition is normal and expected, it is hoped that an improved user experience will combat some of this.

5   Redesign: Pumping Up the Bootcamp

We identified the following key variables for re-design: recruitment, topic, process, and completion. Re-designing the user experience of the course leverages insights from the fields of psychology and software engineering to improve recruitment, retention, and outcomes.

5.1   Recruitment

The way in which participants are recruited and/or invited to participate has impacts on how they view and experience the subsequent course. Robert Cialdini [20] identified six key principles of influence that can be used to maximize compliance: scarcity, commitment, social proof, liking, authority, and reciprocity. Deploying these principles via message framing in the recruitment process can enhance participants' commitment to complete the course. A scarcity appeal, for example, emphasizes limited availability or the potential to lose an opportunity if not acted upon. We predict that recruitment messaging reminding participants that they are taking a limited spot in the bootcamp will enhance their desire to participate and subsequent commitment to complete the course (since they took what is seen as a limited spot). Following such an appeal with a commitment message, by formally asking participants to commit to complete the course before they agree to sign up, can further increase retention.

Additionally, engaging the principle of social proof by encouraging participants to share on their social media sites when they sign up, liking by creating personalized messages from Annie Leonard (founder and spokesperson for The Story of Stuff Project), authority by bringing on key figures in the environmental movement to promote the course, and reciprocity by emphasizing how the organization is providing this course and their other media resources free of charge will be tested for their ability to increase response in the form of email click through numbers, registrations, and subsequent course retention.

5.2   Topic

As mentioned above, several participants in the general bootcamp mentioned being unclear on how or where to utilize their newly acquired skills in their communities. Creating issue-specific bootcamps can provide such specific targets for action that participants can take individually and together as a community.

This variable was already tested in the second bootcamp pilot. The plastics-focused bootcamp had both higher participation numbers and improved outcomes over the general bootcamp. Since it had a goal of engaging participants to work on plastic bag ban initiatives, they had a clear direction to guide their engagement in the course. We plan to test this variable again in the next iteration of the program.

5.3   Process

The user experience in the initial pilot studies was a largely individual one. Participants engaged with the course material but had very little interaction with one another. Since many participants expressed an interest in meeting other changemakers, including an interactive element is hypothesized to increase engagement and subsequent retention.

To test this idea, we plan to test three different levels of "social experience" in the bootcamp: individual experience, online cohorts, and local cohorts. The three differ in the following ways:

1. **Individual experience:** Similar to pilots described above; anonymous; engage with content; doing exercises

2. **Online cohort:** Participants matched online by the program organizers; groups meet online and communicate throughout the course.
3. **Local community:** Participants asked to form place-based learning groups in their community; convening groups locally to participate together in person

5.4   Completion

Providing rewards for completion of a task can be a compelling motivational factor [21]. Although rewards can be tangible in the form of a certificate, ribbon, or t-shirt, non-monetary rewards such as a virtual badge or title may also be effective. As such, the next pilot will provide a formal recognition of completion in the form of an online certificate, virtual badge to display on social media, and an invitation to join a special group of advisors to the Story of Stuff Project which is limited to those who have completed the bootcamp.

Additionally, some participants found the time commitment of the course difficult to complete, suggesting a shorter duration may enhance completion. The next bootcamp will be broken into two parts, with the initial "Citizen Muscle Bootcamp" being four weeks long, with a follow-up "advanced" course for those who complete the initial program.

5.5   User Stories

User stories enable program staff and web developers to community about the desired user experience, which influences many programming decisions. We developed a set of user stories to describe the interaction of the user with the system. An overview of these stories is provided in Figure 1. A sample user story for the login process of a user in the online cohort is:

1. John Smith logs into the system and creates a profile
2. After completing the profile, he is directed to the homescreen of the bootcamp
3. On his dashboard, he sees:

- His profile
- All course units
- A marker representing "Start Here" or "You are here"
- A list of Group Members and links their profiles
- The dates/times for group Google Hangouts

After clicking around the different user profiles, John begins the first unit.

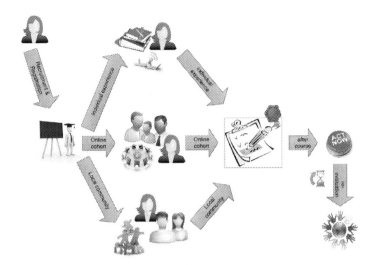

Fig. 1. Overview of the user stories and the redesign

6   Conclusion

The Citizen Muscle Bootcamp builds on insights from the fields of psychology and human computer interaction to create a online learning environment for citizenship. Through improved design, it is our hope that people will be better targeted to the right courses for them, complete the bootcamp program, and go on to use the knowledge gained to become active in their local and global communities.

This project was designed to have both practical and theoretical impacts. Practical impacts include a positive influence on civic engagement by teaching participants the skills that enable them to take action on important sustainability issues. Theoretical impacts include the testing of key usability variables related to influence, commitment, online social experience, and rewards that can be replicated in other programs in the future.

It is our hope that this project presents an example of the potential to be gained from action research partnerships between university researchers and non-profit organizations working together to promote individual and collective behavior for sustainability. In addition to improving the bootcamp for all subsequent participants, such analysis of user engagement with online learning systems for the purpose of sustainability education and pro-active engagement is a topic with much potential for other organizations as well. Future work will execute the study and report on results.

References

1. Merriam-Webster: Sustainable (2013),
   http://www.merriam-webster.com/dictionary/sustainable
2. United Nations, Our Common Future (1987),
   http://www.un-documents.net/ocf-02.htm#I

3. Karlin, B.: Technology and Psychology - Natural enemies or just plain natural? Ecopsychology 5(4), 217–218 (2013)
4. Martin, F.G.: Will massive open online courses change how we teach? Commun. ACM 56(8), 26–28 (2012)
5. Kop, R.: The challenges to connectivist learning on open online networks: Learning experiences during a massive open online course. The International Review of Research in Open and Distance Learning, Special Issue-Connectivism: Design and Delivery of Social Networked Learning 12(3) (2011)
6. Song, L., et al.: Improving online learning: Student perceptions of useful and challenging characteristics. The Internet and Higher Education 7(1), 59–70 (2004)
7. Kohler, D.: What we're learning from online education (2012),
   http://www.ted.com/talks/daphne_koller_what_we_re_learning_
   from_online_education.html
8. Card, S.K., Moran, T.P., Newell, A.: The Psychology of Human-Computer Interaction. Lawrence Erlbaum Associates (1983)
9. Quesenbery, W.: What Does Usability Mean: Looking Beyond 'Ease of Use'. In: Proceedings of the 48th Annual Conference, Society for Technical Communication (2001)
10. Davis, F.D.: Perceived usefulness, perceived ease of use, and user acceptance of information technology. MIS Quarterly, 319–340 (1989)
11. Zave, P.: Classification of research efforts in requirements engineering. ACM Computing Surveys 29(4), 315–321 (1997)
12. Nuseibeh, B., Easterbrook, S.: Requirements Engineering: A Roadmap. In: Proceedings of the Conference on the Future of Software Engineering, pp. 35–46. ACM, New York (2000)
13. Monk, A., Howard, S.: The Rich Picture: A Tool for Reasoning about Work Context. Interactions 5(2), 21–30 (1998)
14. Cohn, M.: User stories applied: For agile software development. Addison-Wesley, Pearson Education, Boston (2004)
15. Nolan, J.: "An Inconvenient Truth" Increases Knowledge, Concern, and Willingness to Reduce Greenhouse Gases. Environment and Behavior 42, 643–658 (2010)
16. Blakley, J.: Movies for a Change (2012),
   http://www.youtube.com/watch?v=Pb0FZPzzWuk
17. Glasgow, R., Nelson, C.C., Kearney, K.A., Reid, R., Ritzwoller, D.P., Strecher, V.J., Couper, M.P., Green, B., Wildenhaus, K.: Reach, Engagement, and Retention in an Internet-Based Weight Loss Program in a Multi-Site Randomized Controlled Trial. J. Med. Internet Res. 9(2), e11 (2007)
18. Siegel Bernard, T.: Finance Class on the Web, for Students of All Ages. New York Times (2013)
19. Federal Deposit Insurance Corporation: Money Smart: A Financial Education Program (2012), http://www.fdic.gov/consumers/consumer/moneysmart/
   mscbi/mscbi.html
20. Cialdini, R.: Influence: The Psychology of Persuasion. William Morrow and Company (1984)
21. Deci, E.L., Koestner, R., Ryan, R.: A Meta-Analytic Review of Experiments Examining the Effects of Extrinsic Rewards on Intrinsic Motivation. Psychological Bulletin 125(6), 627–668 (1999)

Enhancement of Usability for Farmers: User Interface for Rural Community

Muhammad Faraz Khokhar, Hassan Ejaz, Tayyab Asif Butt, Shahzaib Iftikhar,
Umar Muzaffer, Abbas Illyas, Faizan ul Mustafa,
Adeel Mushtaq, Usman Ahmad, and Usman Asghar

University of Gujrat, Pakistan
{10050656-021,10050656-091,10050656-115,10050656-068,
10050656-087,10050656-096}@uog.edu.pk,
faizan_ab@gmx.com, {ch.adeelmushtaq,
itprof.usman,usmanasghar.pk}@gmail.com

Abstract. This research covers how to empower or improve the role of technology and bridge rural digital divide via ICT solutions in the agriculture sector of rural belt of Pakistan and suggests some new ideas like interconnection of web communities with e-boards and mobile phones for sake of giving access to all latest agricultural updates and news. Farmers will be encouraged towards the use of technology for their betterment, ease and efficient output in simple way while using HCI techniques.

Keywords: Farmers, Rural area, Pakistan, E-board, Mobile Phones, linkage.

1 Introduction

World has become a global village, technology is spreading at great speed in the developing countries too and like other fields of life, its proliferation has also encouraged agriculture sector very efficiently. Importance of food growers cannot be ignore [30][37][38] because according to a survey, roughly agriculture is accounted for between 38-45 % of world's labor force whereas in the developing countries it is about 55% of the labor force in agriculture [12]. 45% of the population of Pakistan works in agriculture field [35]. Pakistan cultivates about 25% of its land and agriculture is the largest income and the employment-generating sector of Pakistan's economy. Being a dominant sector according to recent Pakistan economic survey 2012-13 it exhibited growth of 3.3 percent in agriculture related sub-sectors also contributes 21.4% to the gross domestic product (GDP) employs 45 percent of country's labor force [35] and also contributes in other growth of other domains in economy [10]. A lot of people who are linked with this field but still they rely on face to face communication [37].

In section 2 background of research is discussed to explore, problem statement and research question, than in section 3 research methodology along with proposed model, finely conclusion.

A. Marcus (Ed.): DUXU 2014, Part III, LNCS 8519, pp. 574–582, 2014.

2   Background

The digital rural divide in both developing and under developing countries that occur due to many reasons, among which major one is lack of timely and efficient information[6]. Mostly their work is focused on application based or web based job to facilitate the laymen in their rural areas for example some states of Africa and South Asia. Information today is shared using technology like [14] mobile, telephone [32], radio [36], voice messages [32] and internet etc. to get more and efficient output. All these technologies are increasing their users day by day [33]. In Australia multifunctional agriculture (MFA) is used to maximize the potential of the farms [29].

   HCI: It involves the study, planning and design of interaction between Human and Computers. Cultural factor has lot of impact on the design [31][46][47]. This paper focus on all the principles of HCI and Universal Usability challenges in our system [18][24][43][44].

   Rural community: Pakistani rural community old communication means, the traditional and interpersonal by default due to relevancy in content and the context [25][27]. An interesting research in East African state of Tanzania was done to assess the sources of the agricultural information used by farmers and the results showed that the major source was predominantly the Locals [28][45].

2.1   Internationally Available Solutions

Web based: ICT is helping agriculture market by creating decision support, web based agriculture information management software [9] like e-agriculture [7] Hartigyan.com, Krishiworld.com etc. have been also launched. Similarly Initiative [1] by SAARC Agrinet is launched, a website named www.saarcagri.net is launched also for this purpose so that efficient conveying of information would be made possible for different   stakeholders   like   farmers,   educationist,   researchers,   Agricultural entrepreneurs, NGO and business institution agencies etc.

   Short Messaging Services (SMS): Kenya Agricultural Commodity Exchange (KACE) [5] has developed a short messaging service as well. Any farmer anywhere in the country can access updated and reliable market information on prices and commodity offers at an affordable rate using their mobile phones. So far, the service is easy to use, reliable, convenient and affordable. Call Centers: Some of the Call centers are also established to facilitate the farmers with facilities of toll free or paid calls, and initiatives like video conferencing [2][10] [15] have been taken for rural uplift. Several smartphone apps have been launched [3][8][19]. The ratio in using technologies like mobiles, computer internet is almost same in both rural and urban areas in India [22][23]. Japanese agriculture industries are actively involved in facilitating an integrated knowledge creation and sharing initiatives within the organizations [39]. In Sri Lanka cellphone are the predominant mode for connecting community [26].

   Many of solutions described above are implementable internationally but nationally these solutions are difficult to implement in Pakistan due to illiteracy in rural areas.

2.2   Pakistan Perspectives

In foreign countries, there are many ways of getting information in the rural areas as they have internet facility, Smart Phones [4] etc. but rural areas of Pakistan are far behind due to illiteracy. They don't have much source of information. Even some of the villages don't have electricity and landlines. It is very difficult for them to get information and the knowledge which are the key component of an improved agricultural development [27]. Field offices are the most approachable place for laymen to get timely information about their domain, it is very clearly evident from the Fig. 1 that how they assess useful information/news.

Fig. 1. Field Issues

So the system we are going to design is especially for the illiterate people. Our main target is to provide information and updates to the illiterate farmers. We will make our messages and updates effective and attractive. If the one hand technology like mobile phone, websites have brought access to information and facilitate communication [6] than on the other hand there is an issue being faced in common in almost every developing country i-e being non-familiar with technology usage due to many reasons, among which illiteracy, poverty and usability are the major one [9]. Many of the farmers don't know much about their usage in agriculture. They remain unfamiliar with the market increasing and decreasing rates and other useful information just because of this rural-digital divide. So, technologies need to be enhanced more and more in their functionalities. Agriculture is a core sector of Pakistan just as any other agricultural state. In Pakistan the issues/problems and proposed solutions are not implementable exactly like other parts of developing and developed world. Pakistan as an agricultural state, the country is facing some other problems like poverty, illiteracy, inflation and even lack of awareness and access to the latest technologies and their usage due to non-user friendly interfaces and high costs as compared to their income [10]. One who can afford smartphone does not prefer to work in field here so the game need to be is played differently here. No matter how better the mobile based applications are the usability factor affects them badly so we have to encourage the rural belts via designing and developing some already known projects but in much efficient and user friendly way in accordance of usability, efficiency and ease of access to encourage the rural belt of Pakistan towards usage and acceptance of ICT in agriculture.

Education: Another big factor is education. It has the key role of development of any country. Pakistan has low literacy rate and there is a gap between rural and urban education system [21][25] [20].

2.3   Problem Statement

Pakistani Rural belt is facing many challenges among which most important one is the lack of updated/current information which like other domains/fields affects agriculture too. There are little or no proper channels of conveying message/sending information to the farmers about weather, diseases, seeds, soil and fertilizers etc. They are facing many problem of long journey for laboratory tests or to get information or some other purposes. They are illiterate and poverty people. They don't know about the market increasing and decreasing rates. No efficient bridging between farmers and latest updates/information.

2.4   Research Question

What are the effective and innovative approaches to bridge the gap between global knowledge and local knowledge?

3   Research Methodology

We will conduct/take interviews of different stakeholders, like farmers, agriculturist, field officers and other officers and staff members of agriculture offices at Tehsil and district level. We can also analyze via questionnaires and in the end we will do statistical analysis to generate our problem and its solution in an efficient way. Tool that we will use for statistical analysis is Excel.

3.1   Proposed Model

A community based website will be designed where daily based updates will be shared. These automatic updates will be sent to the e-boards at field office in the form of pictography and local language in the union council in the form of images/pictures and in form of text message on their cell phones to stay updated with current updates (Fig. 2 Proposed Model).

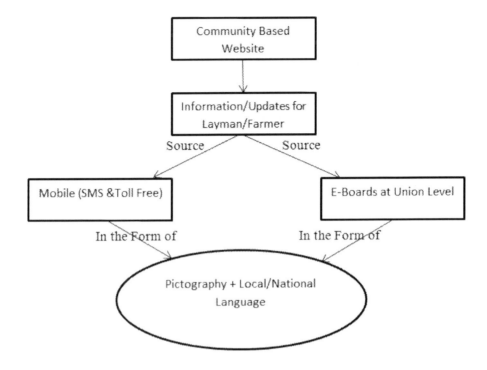

Fig. 2. Proposed Model

4   Expected Results

By implementing such a setup in a user friendly environment even an illiterate user can use/entertain technological services in the field of agriculture simply by signing in (himself or by assistance of officials) an online web community which will be updated with all useful data/information and that will be interconnected with the e-boards at union-council/field office and also by getting the information via cell phones in the form of picture messages and national/local/international languages (Fig. 3 Implementation).

This work (Fig. 3 Implementation) if done will be very innovative step in the rural sector and will not only solve the issues of ICT digital divide in the agriculture field but also this will motivate a layman towards the use of technology due to its ease or usability.

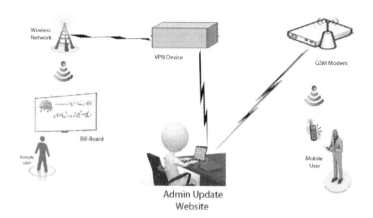

Fig. 3. Implementation

5   Conclusion

This research focuses on user perceive information to present in easy and understandable way [31][34] [41].We are going to provide information system to the Pakistani illustrate farmers. Information plays vital role in agriculture development and production and their effective communication will help in facilitating farmers and mutual understanding among them [40]. By providing updates/information with more usability and effectiveness to the farmers, we are going to increase the productivity of crops and bring rural community to the (standards of) international level.

References

1. Sohoo, S.: ICT Initiative of SAARC agriculture Center in the SAARC Region, 978-0-7695-3308-7/08 $25.00 © 2008 IEEE (2008), doi:10.1109/ICCSIT.2008.151
2. Vijayalakshmi, R., Preetha, J., Selvarajan, S.: Video Conferencing Streaming for the Rural Upliftment. In: 2010 International Conference on Innovative Computing Technologies (ICICT) (2010) ISBN: 978-1-4244-6488-3
3. Baumüller, H.: Mobile Technology Trends and their Potential for Agricultural Development. In: von Braun, J., Denich, M., Gerke, S., Hornidge, A.-K. (eds.). University of Bonn, Bonn (2013) ISSN 1864-6638
4. Myhr, J., Nordstrom, L.: "Livelihood changes enabled by mobile phones" -The case of Tanzanian fisherman Bachelor thesis, Department of Business Studies, Uppsala University (2006)
5. Muriithi, A.G., Bett, E., Ogaleh, S.A., et al.: Information Technology for Agriculture and Rural Development in Africa: Experiences from Kenya. In: Conference on International Researchon Food Security, Natural Resource Management and Rural Development, University of Hamburg, Tropentag (2009)

6. Meera, S.N., Jhamtani, A., Rao, D.U.M.: Information and communication technology in agricultural development: A comparative analysis of three projects from India. In: Agriculture Research and Extension Network, UK Department for International Development (DFID), UK, Paper No.135 (2004) ISBN 0 85003 705 0

7. Gupta, S., Priyadarshi, R., Singh, S.: Role of IT in Agricultural Marketing in India: A case study. In: 1st International Conference on Recent Advances in Information Technology (RAIT 2012) (2012) 978-1-4577-0697-4/12/$26.00 ©2012 IEEE

8. Carlisle, B., Wadsworth, J.: Technology and its contribution to pro-poor agricultural development, UK, London (2004)

9. Agarwal, V., et al.: Reaching the masses through a rural services platform. In: Annual Global Conference 2011 (2011) 978-0-7695-4371-0/11 $26.00 © 2011 IEEE, doi:10.1109/SRII.2011.96

10. Pakistan economic survey 2012-13 Ministry of finance, http://www.finance.gov.pk/survey_1213.html

11. Joseph, M.K., Andrew, T.N.: Information and Communication Technology policy imperatives for rural women empowerment: focus on South Africa. In: IEEE AFRICON 2009, Kenya (2009) 978-1-4244-3919-5/09/$25.00 ©2009 IEEE

12. Chandra, D.G., Malaya, D.B.: Role of e-Agriculture in Rural Development in Indian Context, 978-1-4577-0240-2/11/$26.00 ©2011 IEEE

13. Shibusawa, S.: A Role of Bio-Production Robots in Precision Farming Japan Model. In: International Conference on Advanced Intelligent Mechatronics (AIM 2003) (2003) 0-7803-7759-1/03/$17.OO 0 2003 IEEE

14. Duncombe, R.: Mobile Phones for Agricultural and Rural Development: A Literature Review and Future Research Directions, Paper No. 50. University of Manchester, Manchester (2012) ISBN: 978-1-905469-31-4

15. Noree, A., Nestor, S., Lawson, M.: IEEE transaction on computer based multimedia video conferencing system. IEEE Transactions on Consumer Electronics 39(3) (1997) ISSN: 0098-3063, INSPEC Accession Number: 4536826

16. Zahedi, S.R., Zahedi, S.M.: Role of Information and Communication Technologies in Modern Agriculture. Intl. J. Agri. Crop. Sci. 4(23), 1725–1728 (2012)

17. Maumbe, B.M., Okello, J.: Uses of Information and Communication technology (ICT) in agriculture and Rural Development in Sub-Saharan Africa: experiences from South Africa and Kenya. International Journal of ICT Research and Development in Africa 1(1), 1–22 (2010)

18. Shneiderman, B.: Universal Usability: Pushing Human-Computer Interaction Research to Empower Every Citizen. Communications of the ACM 43(5) (May 2000)

19. Dey, B.: Analysing appropriation and usability in social and occupational lives. Information Technology & People 24(1), 46–63 (2011) 0959-3845, doi:10.1108/09593841111109413

20. Memon, G.R.: Education in Pakistan: The Key Issues, Problems and The New Challenges. Journal of Management and Social Sciences 3(1), 47–55 (2007)

21. Tayyaba, S.: Rural-urban gaps in academic achievement, schooling conditions, student, and teachers'characteristics in Pakistan. International Journal of Educational Management 26(1), 6–26 (2012) 0951-354X, doi:10.1108/09513541211194356

22. Kumar, S.: Use of computer, internet, and library OPACs among rural and urban postgraduates in Indian universities 28(3), 144–163 (2012) 1065-075X, doi:10.1108/10650751211262137

23. Akoijam, S.L.S.: Rural credit: a source of sustainable livelihood of rural India. International Journal of Social, Economics 40(1), 83–97 (2013)

24. Nielsen, J.: Usability 101: Introduction to usability. Alertbox (2003), http://www.useit.com/alertbox/20030825.html

25. Mujahid, Y.H.: Digital opportunity initiative for Pakistan. Electronic Journal on Information Systems in Developing Countries, EJISDC (2002), http://www.ejisdc.org

26. Widyantha, N., et al.: Useful and easy to use interactive voice for emergency data exchange 15(5) (2013)

27. Elly, T., Silayo, E.E.: Agriculture information needs and sources of the rural farmers in Tanzania (June 2013), http://www.emeraldinsight.com/reprints

28. Mwalukasa, N.: Agricultural information sources used for climate change adaptation in Tanzania. Library Review 62(4/5), 266–292 (2013) 0024-2535, doi:10.1108/LR-12-2011-0096

29. Alonso, A.D., Northcote, J.: Investigating farmers' involvement in value-added activities. A preliminary study from Australia. British Food Journal 115(10), 1407–1427 (2013) 0007-070X, doi:10.1108/BFJ-04-2011-0104

30. Goel, K.: A complete agro-financial service framework for emerging economies. The Journal of Risk Finance 14(5), 490–497 (2013) 1526-5943, doi:10.1108/JRF-04-2012-0023

31. Huertas-Garcia, R., Casas-Romeo, A., Subira, E.: Cross-cultural differences in the content and presentation of web sites. Kybernetes 42(5), 766–784 (2013) 0368-492X, doi:10.1108/K-03-2013-0061

32. Waidyanatha, N., et al.: Useful and easy-to-use interactive voice for emergency data exchange 15(5), 82–98 (2013) ISSN 1463-6697, doi:10.1108/info-05-2013-0022

33. Stork, C., Calandro, E., Gillwald, A.: Internet going mobile: internet access anduse in 11 African countries 15(5), 34–51 (2013) ISSN 1463-6697, doi:10.1108/info-05-2013-0026

34. Dey, B.L., et al.: A qualitative enquiry into the appropriation of mobile telephony at the bottom of the pyramid. International Marketing Review 30(4), 297–322 (2013) 0265-1335, doi:10.1108/IMR-03-2012-0058

35. Shahbaz, M., Shabbir, M.S., Butt, M.S.: Effect of financial development on agricultural growth in Pakistan. International Journal of Social Economics 40(8), 707–728 (2013) 0306-8293, doi:10.1108/IJSE-01-2012-0002

36. Nyareza, S., Dick, A.L.: Use of community radio to communicate agricultural information to Zimbabwe's peasant farmers. In: Aslib Proceedings: New Information Perspectives, vol. 64(5), pp. 494–508 (2012) 0001-253X, doi:10.1108/00012531211263111

37. Lwoga, E.T., Stilwell, C., Ngulube, P.: Access and use of agricultural information and knowledge in Tanzania. Library Review 60(5), 383–395 (2011) 0024-2535, doi:10.1108/00242531111135263

38. Alonso, A.D.: Farmers' involvement in value-added produce: the case of Alabama growers. British Food Journal 113(2), 187–204 (2011) 0007-070X, doi:10.1108/00070701111105295

39. Zakaria, S., Nagata, H.: Knowledge creation and flow in agriculture. Library Manaagement 31(1/2), 27–35 (2010), doi:10.1108/01435121011013377

40. Oduwole, A.A., Okorie, C.N.: Access to agricultural information and millennium development goals. Library Hi Tech News (1), 10–12 (2010) 0741-9058

41. Duncker, E., Sheikh, J.A., Fields, B.: From Global Terminology to Local Terminology: A Review on Cross-Cultural Interface Design Solutions. In: Rau, P.L.P. (ed.) CCD/HCII 2013, Part I. LNCS, vol. 8023, pp. 197–207. Springer, Heidelberg (2013)

42. Sheikh, J.A., Fields, B., Duncker, E.: The Cultural Integration of Knowledge Management into Interactive Design. In: Smith, M.J., Salvendy, G. (eds.) Human Interface, Part I, HCII 2011. LNCS, vol. 6771, pp. 48–57. Springer, Heidelberg (2011)

43. Sheikh, J.A., Fields, B., Duncker, E.: Cultural representation by Card Sorting. Ergonomics for All: Celebrating PPCOE's 20 years of Excellence. Selected Papers of the Pan-Pacific Conference on Ergonomics, Kaohsiung, Taiwan, November 7-10, 2010, pp. 215–220. CRC Press (2011a)

44. Sheikh, J.A., Fields, B., Duncker, E.: Multi-Culture Interaction Design. Advances in Cross-Cultural Decision Making, pp. 406–415. CRC Press (2010b)

45. Sheikh, J.A., Fields, B., Duncker, E.: Cultural based e-Health information system. Presentation at the Health Libraries Group Conference 2010, July 19-20. CILIP, Salford Quays (2010a)

46. Sheikh, J.A., Fields, B., Duncker, E.: Cultural Representation for Interactive Information system. In: Proceedings of the 2009 International Conference on the Current Trends in Information Technology, Dubai (2009c)

47. Sheikh, J.A., Fields, B., Duncker, E.: Cultural Representation for Multi-culture Interaction Design. In: Aykin, N. (ed.) IDGD 2009. LNCS, vol. 5623, pp. 99–107. Springer, Heidelberg (2009b)

User-Experience for Personal Sustainability Software: Applying Design Philosophy and Principles

Aaron Marcus, Jennifer Dumpert, and Laurie Wigham

Aaron Marcus and Associates, Inc., 1196 Euclid Avenue, Suite 1F, Berkeley, CA, 94708 USA
{aaron.marcus,jenniferdumpert,laurie.wigham}@amanda.com

Abstract. Business developers worldwide seek to develop sustainability software with a user experience that provides usability, usefulness, and appeal. We describe using previously determined design principles on an application under development. The design and usability testing undertaken were intended to make a rewards program regarding sustainability more compelling and engaging. The approach sought to take advantage of people's interests, expertise, and experience with sustainability.

Keywords: business, design, development, enterprise software, management, rewards, sustainability, user experience, user interface.

1 Introduction

User-experience development (UXD) and sustainability are both of increasing concern to developers of business-oriented applications worldwide. This project describes the activities undertaken to apply a user-centered UX philosophy and set of design principles oriented to sustainability developed in a Phase 1 of a project, which were described in a separate paper (Marcus et al, 2011), to a software application then undergoing actual development.

In October 2010, the authors' firm and SAP embarked on Phase 2 of a project to embed personal sustainability functions into business software. The objective of Phase 2 was to apply research and design principles developed in Phase 1 to the redesign of an existing SAP application. The target software was the Rewards section of SAP's Carbon Impact suite. SAP asked AM+A to define the vision for a tool that would genuinely motivate people to change their behavior, initially as corporate citizens, eventually extending out into the community as citizens of the world.

2 Background on Carbon Impact Rewards

SAP's Carbon Impact applications suite was a set of Web-based software tools that enables a corporation accurately to measure and compare carbon intensity across its entire operations, as well as to execute an effective abatement strategy. The Rewards section is designed to encourage individual employees of a corporation to define and undertake their own sustainability initiatives and to involve their fellow employees in

A. Marcus (Ed.): DUXU 2014, Part III, LNCS 8519, pp. 583–593, 2014.
© Springer International Publishing Switzerland 2014

these projects. Involvement with initiatives is optional, but employees receive rewards points for participating.

3   Design Process

During Phase 1 of the personal sustainability project undertaken by AM+A for SAP, AM+A undertook user research to define several overall design principles for personal sustainability tools. Phase 2 of the project, the design of Carbon Impacts Rewards, began with a review of the existing application to prioritize these design principles for the specific tool. Though an early version of Carbon Impact Rewards existed previous to the project, SAP stressed that this initial model should not place constraints on design. In order to further explore the possibilities of the application, AM+A developed use scenarios that explored how users might approach the application. A mental map and process flow diagrams created showed the relationships between different parts of the application, with wire-frames showing basic content of key screens. See Fig. 1.

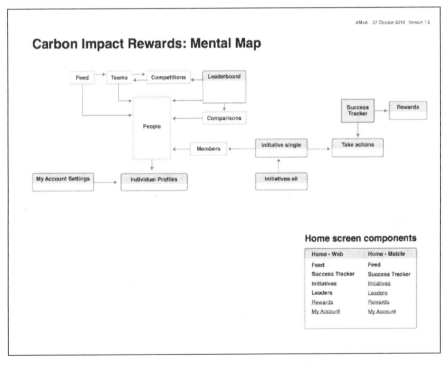

Fig. 1. Carbon Impact Rewards Mental Map

As part of re-conceiving Carbon Impoact Rewards, mobile usage was added, and a social/community component was enhanced. The team explored different approaches to adding fun, surprise, and interesting visual elements. AM+A designed a photo-based visual theme that reflected the sustainability objectives and look-and-feel of the application. AM+A also developed a prototype game, "Vampire Hunters," designed to introduce the "fun factor" into the tool. For the final presentation, AM+A designed a few detailed, "finished" screens to illustrate key Web and mobile interactions in the narrative AM+A wrote to describe the use of the application.

4   Applying Design Principles

Five of the design principles developed as part of Phase 1 of the project were prioritized as most relevant to Carbon Impact Rewards. The challenge of Phase 2 was to apply these principles to design an application that would make it easy for users to make significant changes in their behavior concerning sustainability. The following sections summarize those principles and show some of the ways they were incorporated into the new design for Carbon Impact Rewards.

4.1   Principle 1: Sustainability Actions Need to Fit into Users' Daily Lives

Users should not have to change their lifestyles to use the tool. Usage should occur during tasks users normally perform, fitting into natural ecosystems with minimal interruption of natural actions. Design needs to focus on what users do, not what they say they care about. In the user research AM+A conducted as part of Phase 1, people said they cared most about high-level concerns, such as environmental degradation, peak oil, wasteful consumer culture. However, the actions they reported actually taking occurred during daily life, including actions such as recycling, biking, taking public transit, and buying organic food.

How this Principle was Applied. AM+A added a mobile component to the application, making it possible for users to participate in an initiative whenever and wherever they would most naturally use the software. It was assumed that initial usage would occur over the course of the workday, but mobile components were designed to ultimately extend that usage into homes and communities as well. Mobile components also allow users to upload photos and videos on the go. In the iPhone sequence in Fig. 2, from left to right, the user selects an initiative from the Participate screen, looks

Fig. 2. iPhone sequence for Participate and Take Action functions

through the list of available actions, selecting "Bike Among Buildings", then posts the action. The sequence is streamlined and efficient, requiring very little time or effort.

The Success Tracker panel, available on most screens, is designed to allow users to quickly participate in initiatives, with minimal effort, by clicking on the "Take Action" link. This navigation brings users to a screen listing their favorite actions. Location and time filters help users participate in actions and events close to them both spatially and also temporally, in terms of schedule. See Fig. 3

Fig. 3. Example of location and time filters

Carbon Impact Rewards initiatives provide users with lists of "Actions:" discrete, easy-to-accomplish tasks that help users feel they are participating and contributing to a better future without requiring them to undertake major life change. Primary responsibility for starting Initiatives and creating Actions and Events lies with users. This causes the system to form around what users actually want to do, and activities in which other users want to participate. A rating system brings most popular Initiatives and Actions to the top, so users first see those activities that other users actually do. AM+A recommended seeding CI Rewards with ready-to-use packaged Initiatives and Actions around topics known to motivate users to act, such as recycling and biking.

4.2   Principle 2: Motivate Effectively

Research showed that users' key motivators are money and concern for future generations. Nagging, or making users feel guilty, tended to discourage people from taking action. The design team also focused on building elements of fun, beauty, and surprise into the application, to make it less like a workplace chore, and more like something users would enjoy for its own sake.

How this Principle was Applied

A reward system allows users to enjoy direct financial reward or benefit from their actions. The Success Tracker, visible on almost every page, allows users to constantly monitor their progress toward their chosen rewards. See Fig. 4.

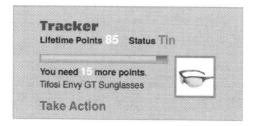

Fig. 4. Example of Success Tracker

Because this software is designed as a user-driven application, the concerns users feel about the next generation naturally rise to the surface. The system avoids nagging because, as a system with no central authority, there is no centralized, overarching moral stance, which avoids the sense of nagging. Furthermore, because users interact with whichever parts of the system they prefer, they can avoid interacting with any specific parts or people that are unappealing. To make the application more playful and interactive, AM+A added several new features. AM+A's design allows users to upload photos and videos to share, and the most popular ones appear on the Home page. AM+A also designed a prototype "Vampire Hunters" game that is also an office energy reduction project to use fun as a motivator. See Fig. 5.

Fig. 5. News Feed screen and Vamire Hunters screen

In order to encourage users to visit the Home page more frequently, AM+A de-signed a pop-up image section, in which users could click on colored squares to dis-cover different kinds of changing content. (The last-chosen category would persist as

the open window for the next time the user opened the application.) The design includes categories such as the Most Beautiful Picture or the Most Popular Tip, to be
chosen by user votes or ratings. This mini-contest approach motivates users to participate in the program by uploading their own images and other media. The application
also includes a "Random Surprise" as well as an easy way to track what's popular
among users: "Most Active Initiative." A "Featured Infographic" provides rich visual
information. Because good information graphics, or information visualizations, have a
strong potential to "go viral," the infographic holds the potential to spread sustainability information to their wider communities. See Fig. 6 and Fig. 7.

Fig. 6. Picture of the Week, Voted Most Beautiful, and Random Surprise images

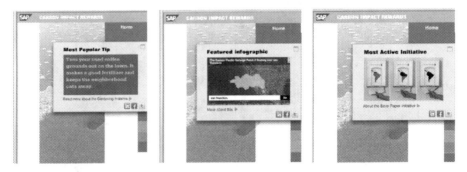

Fig. 7. Most Popular Tip, Featured InfoGraphic, and Most Active Initiative images

AM+A developed a new visual theme for the application that features a photo
showing footprints in a pristine sandy beach (see Fig. 8) to represent the goal of sustainability: to leave only a temporary trace of human activity on the earth. The footprint image also refers to the bare footprint used in association with most other carbon
footprint applications. The images of sand and water near the beach are associated
with ease, relaxation and freedom, counteracting the pressure, guilt, and "preachi-
ness" associated with many "green" activities and writings. The images also suggest
an escape from the constraints of the workplace environment, where the application is
most-commonly used.

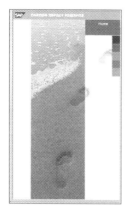

Fig. 8. Sandy beach image and previous CI screen of image with trees

Fig. 9. Sandy beach image and previous CI screen of image with trees

The previous version of Carbon Impact Rewards used a forest as the theme image (see Fig. 9), but AM+A's research into competitive products indicated that images with trees or leaves should be avoided, because they have been overused and may have negative associations.

4.3   Principle 3: Leverage Community Influence

Another goal for the project was to promote community building. Research showed that individuals are more likely to embrace sustainability goals and to take action if their friends, neighbors, and co-workers are active. A community can also coerce sustainable behavior, within limits, so it is effective, and appropriate, for companies to compel employees and members to take sustainable action, as part of the job. However, a company must avoid appearing too monolithically authoritative because users' distrust of business use of sustainability as a marketing ploy undermines centralized authority.

How this Principle was Applied. Community lies at the core of Carbon impact Rewards. Feeds exist on Home pages, Initiative screens, and Profiles. Initiative, Events, and Actions are created by the community. Popularity ratings let the community decide what rises to the top. The success rate of any specific user is visible to all users, creating a subtle community coercion. Also, companies can compel their employees to participate, in addition to rewarding them.

CI Rewards encourages and supports users in forming communities around specific ideas or concerns, by allowing users to set up Initiatives. Member photos are featured prominently on the Initiative Home page, encouraging people to join the initiative because they like the community, even if they have little knowledge of the goal of the initiative or the bigger picture (See Fig. 10) As a user-driven system, CI Rewards avoids appearing as a monolithic authority making overarching proclamations. Ideas come from a network of users, instead of being imposed from above.

Fig. 10. Initiative Home page screen layout showing Member photos

4.4   Principle 4: Build Trust

Research showed users are confused by and suspicious of much of the current media information about sustainability and are reluctant to act unless they feel they can trust the information. AM+A concluded the application must provide a means to get advice from already trusted sources and to encourage users to share their experience and expertise. Information sources must be transparent, so users can trace and review data sources.

How this Principle was Applied. User profiles allow others to review an individual's values and approaches to issues as well as their experience and expertise. Users can choose to follow the feed of any other user, and also can see the feeds of initiatives they join, allowing them to find their own trusted sources. Users are awarded points for participating, both for taking action and also for creating actions or events that allow them to share their experience and expertise. Users can see which other user provided a specific data source, such as information visualization tools and links uploaded to the Resource Library. See Fig. 12. Users can also see which user created a specific Initiative or Action. See Fig. 11.

Fig. 11. Initiative creator screen

Fig. 12. Information resource display

4.5   Principle 5: Leverage Persuasion Theory

AM+A's Carbon Impact Rewards application seeks to promote competition, reward success, and give clear, actionable recommendations. Research showed that users felt confusion about how to take action or what actions to take. The desire for clear guidance makes general recommendations, such as "avoid unnecessary packaging" impractical. Instead, the tool provides concrete goals and strategies, like "buy 50% of your produce loose instead of packaged". Users don't need obvious recommendations, such as "turn out the lights".

How this principle was applied. Users can create competitions for rewards or just for points that lead to rewards. Users establish and join teams, and they can review high-scoring users or teams, or compare themselves or their teams to any other user or team via the Leader Board. Rewarding success is one of the core features of the tool. Users can redeem points for tangible rewards. The community element also rewards success with bragging rights. Actions and Events provide clear, specific, actionable tasks. Users can conceive and post their own, or perform or attend those suggested by others.

4.6   Mapping the Interactions

AM+A developed a mental model and process flow diagrams (see Fig. 13) to show relationships among different parts, or modules, of the application.

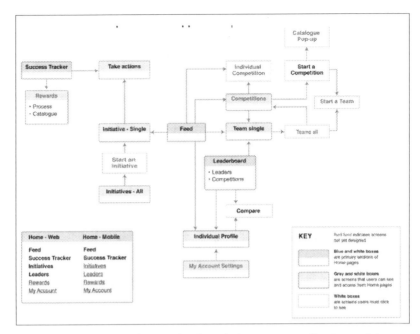

Fig. 13. Process flow diagram showing relations among application modules

5   Conclusions

The preceding sections describe the application of design principles of Phase 1 to a specific product design in Phase 2. While the instantiation was well received by the Client, future user testing in a Phase 3 was to determine what modifications are required in the user-experience design of a business software product that makes concrete, practical use of sustainability concepts directed to users needs, wants, and expectations.

Acknowledgment. The authors acknowledge Ms. Janaki Kumar, Mr. Garrett Miller, and Dr. Dan Rosenberg of SAP for their guidance and support in preparating this paper. The authors thank many SAP employees for their participation in discussions and survey responses.

References

1. Jean, J., Marcus, A.: The Green Machine: Going Green at Home. User Experience (UX) 8(4), 20–22 (2009)
2. Marcus, A.: User-Centered Design in the Enterprise, Fast Forward Column. Interactions 13(1), 18–23 (2005)

3. Marcus, A.: User Interface Design's Return on Investment: Examples and Statistics. In: Bias, R.G., Mayhew, D.J. (eds.) Cost-Justifying Usability, ch. 2, 2nd edn., pp. 17–39. Elsevier, San Francisco (2005)
4. Marcus, A., Dumpert, J., Wigham, L.: User-Experience for Personal Sustainability Software: Determining Design Philosophy and Principles. In: Marcus, A. (ed.) Design, User Experience, and Usability, Part I, HCII 2011. LNCS, vol. 6769, pp. 172–177. Springer, Heidelberg (2011)
5. Marcus, A., Jean, J.: Green Machine: Designing Mobile Information Displays to Encourage Energy Conservation. Information Design Journal 17(3), 233–243 (2010)

Energy Consumption Feedback: Engagement by Design

Ruth Rettie, Kevin Burchell, and Tim Harries

Kingston University, Kingston Hill, Surrey, KT2 7LB, UK
{r.rettie,k.burchell,t.harries}@kingston.ac.uk

Abstract. This paper reports two energy feedback studies and explores the role of design in increasing householder engagement with energy feedback. The paper discusses a range of design issues that arise when developing an energy feedback system. It argues 1) that it is important to provide feedback in terms of activities rather than energy units, which have little relevance to householders, and 2) that emphasising the avoidance of waste could help to make energy consumption visible and prompt changes in energy consuming behaviours.

Keywords: energy consumption feedback, social norms approach, feedback design, randomised control trial, community research.

1 Introduction

The provision of energy consumption feedback to householders has emerged as an important climate change mitigation strategy in a number of countries. In the UK, for instance, a nationwide roll-out of electricity and gas smart meters, and in-home displays (IHDs) is planned for some 30 million homes between 2015 and 2020. IHDs are included in the UK smart meter project on the grounds that the information they provide will 'help [householders] manage their energy use, save money and reduce emissions' [1, p1].

2 Theoretical Background

Electricity differs from most other consumer products in being abstract, invisible and intangible and in only being consumed as a by-product of other practices [2]. Its consumption has been compared to a situation where products don't have price labels and bills are only sent out at quarterly intervals [3]. Research shows that consumption feedback reduces domestic energy consumption by between 2% and 15% [4-8]. Recent ethnographic studies suggest that consumption feedback can increase the visibility and salience of energy consumption and of related behaviours, and can prompt re-evaluation, behaviour change and consumption reduction [9-16]. However, these studies also identify a number of factors that constrain the effectiveness of energy feedback: householder engagement with feedback tends to be relatively short-lived and may be limited to one person within the household; people find it hard to relate their feedback to their everyday activities around the home and when feedback prompts a desire to change this may be confounded by household conflict.

A. Marcus (Ed.): DUXU 2014, Part III, LNCS 8519, pp. 594–604, 2014.

Energy feedback can include normative comparisons with the energy use of others in what is known as the social norms approach (SNA) [17-18]. The SNA attempts to influence behaviour by changing perceptions of what is normal. The approach assumes that descriptions of what is normal behaviour can simplify decision-making by acting as a heuristic short-cut or 'nudge' [19]. The social norms approach has been applied to electricity consumption feedback by providing feedback about average consumption alongside individual household feedback [6, 20]. These two US studies examined the impact of a programme implemented by Opower that mailed reports containing social norms with households' bimonthly/quarterly electricity bills. With samples of 85,000 [20] and 600,000 [6] and intervention periods of one year and two years, respectively, these evaluations found reductions of 2% - 2.35%. However, these studies did not distinguish the impact of social norms feedback from that of feedback of a household's own consumption, because social norms feedback was always presented to participants alongside their own household's data (see Fig. 1).

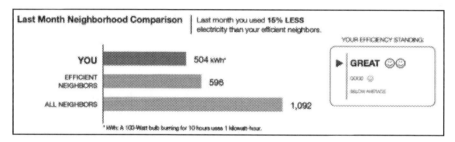

Fig. 1. Opower feedback evaluated by Allcott [6]

3   Methodology

The paper is based on two studies in which energy consumption and normative feedback about other households played a key role: the CHARM Home Energy Study, an 18-week randomised controlled trial involving 316 households (www.projectcharm.info) and Smart Communities, a 2 year community action project involving 400 participants (www.smartcommunities.org.uk).

3.1   The CHARM Home Energy Study

The CHARM Home Energy Study compared the effect of individual household feedback with that of social norms feedback. The randomised controlled trial therefore compared three experimental conditions: 1) feedback that included only data about an individual household's consumption; 2) feedback that also included a neighbourhood average, and 3) a control condition without feedback.

Fieldwork took place in Bristol, UK. Over 400 households were professionally recruited, door-to-door, from one poorer and one richer area of the city, using an £80 incentive. Three hundred and sixteen households (79% of those recruited) successfully completed the 18-week study and the pre- and post-study questionnaires. Technological collaborators at the University of the West of England built electricity consumption monitoring devices that automatically sent data to the study server via the mobile telephone network.

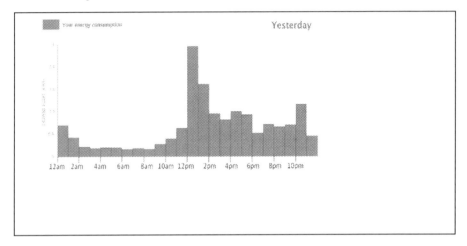

Fig. 2. An example of a graph for participants in the individual feedback condition

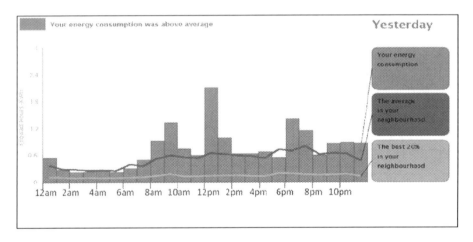

Fig. 3. An example of a graph for participants in the social norms feedback condition

After a two-week baseline period feedback was provided to those in the two intervention conditions using graphs showing usage for the current day, the previous day, the previous seven days and from the start of the study (for examples, see Fig. 2 and 3). For those in the social norms condition, this feedback included information on average consumption for other households in their locality (the higher of the two lines, in red) and the consumption of the lowest consuming 20% (the lower line, in orange). They also included statements that reflected the household's position relative to the average, with smiley emoticons if consumption was below average (see Table 1). Participants were able to access all four types of graph on personalized, password-protected websites and were each sent a weekly marketing email containing one recent graph and one energy-saving tip. The websites and emails also contained generic tips on household energy saving. Fortnightly mobile phone SMS reminded participants to read their emails and access their web pages - e.g. 'How has your electricity usage changed over the past two months? Login at homeenergystudy.org to find out'.

Table 1. Social norms messages used in graphs for the social norms condition

Condition	Descriptive norms	Injunctive norms
Consumption above average for those in the social norms condition	Your energy consumption was above average	None
Consumption 0-30% lower than average	Your energy consumption was just below average	☺ Well done, keep it up!
Consumption 31-59% lower than average	Your energy consumption was well below average	☺☺ Well done, keep it up!
Consumption lower than average by 60%+	Your energy consumption was among the best 20%	☺☺☺ Well done, keep it up!

The CHARM project monitored how much electricity participants used and recorded how often they looked at the feedback. In addition, analysis included pre- and post-trial questionnaires, 21 in-depth interviews and three focus groups.

The study was conducted at a time when increasingly long days and warmer weather were causing a reduction in electricity consumption for all the participants. However, linear regression analysis showed that average consumption levels reduced by 3% more for those who received feedback than for those who did not [12]. The sample was not large enough to test the statistical significance of this unexpectedly small effect, but comments by participants in the interviews suggest that the feedback did lead to changes in energy-consuming behaviours. For example, some participants reduced their use of tumble driers; some purchased low-energy white goods, and some reduced their use of standby. The interviews suggest that the main reason the feedback had this effect was that the graphs provided householders with benchmarks against which to compare their usage – i.e. their own consumption at different times of day or the consumption of other people. This made it easier for users to see when their usage was higher than usual, to relate this usage to particular practices, to see this usage as potentially wasteful, and to make changes to their behaviour. For further details of the findings from this study please see [12].

3.2 Smart Communities

Smart Communities was a two-year community project in Kingston-upon-Thames involving families of children attending a local primary school, together with other households in the area [21]. The project combined community action activities (such as workshops, bespoke guidance and demonstrations in people's homes and activities in the school) with electricity and gas consumption feedback, and weekly emails. Feedback followed the social norms approach, as shown in Fig. 4. Leaflets were distributed door-to-door to homes within the geographical area of the project, while parents at the school were invited to join through leaflets in school book bags.

Over 400 out of approximately 2000 eligible households (about 20%) joined Smart Communities by logging onto the project website. Smart Communities participants were sent a basic electricity in-home display (IHD) showing both real time and cumulative electricity consumption (see Fig. 5). They were sent weekly email reminders to read their cumulative energy consumption data from their household monitors and enter this data into a My Energy section on the project website. Participants' websites then showed their weekly consumption alongside the average energy consumption and the best 20% consumption for the community as a whole (see Fig. 4). They were also able to view their feedback relative to the number of people living in their house and the number of rooms in their homes.

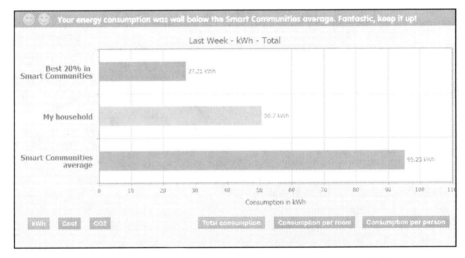

Fig. 4. An example of feedback on the Smart Communities website

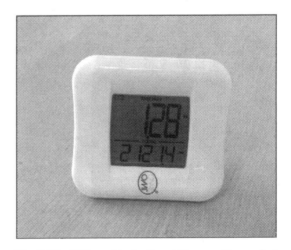

Fig. 5. The IHD used in the Smart Communities project

Project fieldwork included 50 in-depth interviews (37 with project participants, 5 with non-participating residents of the area, and 8 with project partners), five workshops, a focus group with school children and an end of study survey questionnaire (n=460). Analysis of the project data demonstrates long term engagement with feedback. After two years, about 50 participants were still entering their weekly energy consumption readings into the Smart Communities website, and 40% of survey respondents who had IHD's claimed they looked at them daily. Participants who had IHDs learned a lot about their energy consumption, and made some changes around their homes (for example, with respect to lighting, use of the kettle, showering and use of heating). However, participants found it easier to change some behaviours than others (e.g. switching off lights in unoccupied rooms) and many treated their everyday ways of doing things as fixed ('the washing is the washing!', as one project participant put it).

4   Design Issues in the Two Projects

There are many issues and alternatives to consider when designing an energy feedback system. The impact of the feedback is likely to depend on the manner in which it is communicated – e.g. the choice of medium, the choice of unit and the layout of any web-pages. Some of the issues and alternative identified in our work are shown in Table 2.

Table 2. Energy consumption feedback design alternatives

Design Element	Examples of options
Communication medium	website, email, post, SMS, mobile or tablet app
Design	
positioning	environmental, energy management, budgetary control
benefit	save money, save energy, avoid waste
style	modern, geeky, sophisticated, traditional
Information	
fuel	gas, water, oil
disaggregation	disaggregated by fuel type, appliance, room, practice, user
units	money, kWh, kg of carbon dioxide
period	hourly, daily, weekly, monthly, bill period
graphs	bar, line, pie
advice	personalisation, descriptive or injunctive
Social norms comparisons	
reference group	house size, occupancy, housing type
basis of comparison	Total, disaggregated by practice or appliance

4.1   Communication Medium

The CHARM study provided feedback via password protected websites and in weekly emails. In contrast, Smart Communities provided web-based feedback but used weekly emails to encourage participants to enter their energy readings on their websites. The research indicates that in both studies the weekly emails were accessed regularly and often appreciated. However, some users found it difficult to access password-protected websites, either because of low levels of web-literacy or because they forgot their passwords.

4.2   Design

Both projects avoided an overtly environmental positioning (though both used the colour green in the project logos and leaflets). The CHARM Home Energy Study was positioned as research on energy consumption and Smart Communities was positioned as a community project that would save participants energy and money. The surveys conducted in the two studies indicate that only a small percentage of our participants were environmentally conscious. The interviews in both studies suggest that users were generally more motivated by avoiding wasting energy than by either the money saved or the effect on the environment.

As shown in Fig. 2, 3 and 5, the design of feedback in both the CHARM and Smart Communities projects was simple and direct, using large blocks of easily distinguishable colours, sans serif fonts and bar charts.

4.3   Feedback

The CHARM study provided near real-time feedback charts (with about ½ hour lag) that showed hourly consumption (see Fig. 6). Participants were also able to access charts that showed daily usage for the previous week or since the start of the study. Usage data suggests that the charts showing hourly consumption were accessed most frequently. These made it easy for participants to identify and attribute consumption to particular appliances or practices – for example, in Fig. 6 the peak between 12 and 1pm suggests lunch-related energy consuming activities such as cooking. The interviews suggest that the charts had the effect of highlighting 'waste' because anything dramatically higher than usual was treated as a possible waste of energy.

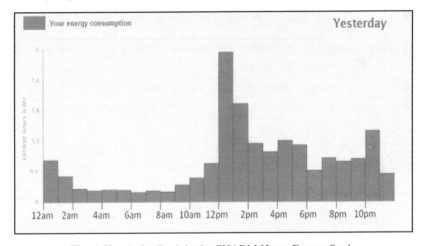

Fig. 6. Hourly feedback in the CHARM Home Energy Study

The time period used is important because if it is too long it is difficult to relate usage to behaviour. The CHARM Home Energy Study showed cumulative consumption for periods of an hour or a day. Our research suggests that hourly or half-hourly feedback makes it easier for participant to relate their usage to their behaviour.

Smart Communities participants received feedback both on personalised websites and on in-home displays (IHDs) that displayed current and cumulative usage (in a choice of kWh, £ or kg of CO_2). They were encouraged to enter the cumulative figures from the IHD into their personalised websites, which calculated weekly energy consumption for that household and displayed this alongside figures for the average and the 'best 20%' Smart Communities households for the same period. The Smart Communities interviews suggest that current usage figures, such as those shown on IHDs, can mislead users into thinking that an appliance that has high energy consumption for a short period of time, such as a kettle, uses a lot of energy overall.

Both projects used bar charts to represent energy consumption. The CHARM study also used lines to represent the average consumption of other users and the average consumption of 'the best 20% in your neighbourhood' (see Fig. 3). The interviews suggest that users found the charts easy to understand, even though energy consumption was shown in kWh, which they did not really understand. They have no sense of what a kWh is or of whether 1000 kWh is a lot or a little. The unit of kWh can also be confusing, because it can be interpreted as measuring the rate of energy used per hour (in the same way that mph is miles per hour) but is actually a measure of energy consumption (kW is a measure of the rate of use of energy - 1kW is 1000 joules of energy per second). However, the CHARM research suggests that the use of kWh did not matter, because participants focused on their relative use of energy rather than on the amount of energy used, for example comparing their usage at different times. The graphs in both projects were self-scaling. This meant that the size of the bars shown on the graphs changed when the scales changed, for instance, to accommodate a particularly high usage. Unfortunately, this meant that participants who focused on relative usage or on patterns of usage could misread their usage if they did not notice changes in the scale of the graphs.

Both the CHARM and Smart Communities projects provided overall rather than disaggregated consumption; the interviews suggest that users would welcome disaggregation in terms of appliances or practices.

The CHARM and Smart Communities projects both included energy reduction tips on their websites, but these were not personalised to the user or their energy consumption. Tips were also provided in weekly emails and in the case of CHARM, in SMS; these tips were seasonally appropriate, for instance advising on insulation in winter or advocating line drying in summer, but again were not personalised to the user. Advice that is tailored to the circumstances of a particular household (as in the personal energy advice provided by British Gas and other utilities in the UK) is likely to be more salient and therefore more motivating. Energy advice systems can also automatically provide advice linked to feedback and the user's profile, rather than expecting the user to search for advice (i.e. 'push' rather than 'pull' communication). Energy saving advice can either be descriptive, for example, describing the amount of energy that could be saved with insulation, or injunctive, exhorting householders to improve their insulation. Strengers [13] suggests that injunctions are more likely to challenge established practices.

4.4   Social Norms Feedback

The CHARM Home Energy Study and Smart Communities both used social norms feedback. In each case the studies followed the format used in the OPOWER research (see Fig. 1) by including both the average of all users, the average of the 'best 20%' and up to three 'smiley' emoticons (see Table 1) for those who were below average. The interviews indicate that the social norms feedback was well received and stimulated interest and a degree of competition between households. The CHARM analysis did not find any difference between the energy consumption of those households in the individual condition and those in the social norms condition. However, those receiving individual feedback opened an average of 14 emailed graphs (standard deviation 13.81) while those receiving the social norms feedback opened 20 (standard deviation 21.18); this difference is statistically significant, and suggests that users find feedback more engaging if it includes social norms data.

Use of the social norms approach in other domains shows that the impact of the approach on any individual is increased if comparisons are made with the most appropriate reference groups [22, 23]. In the CHARM study we were unable to target specific reference groups, and so the social norms feedback was the average total consumption of all households receiving social norms feedback. It is possible that feedback targeted at relevant reference groups (for instance, people living in similar houses or people with large families) might be more effective. Similarly, social norms feedback disaggregated for specific practices or appliances might be more effective than feedback of overall consumption.

4.5   Designing Consumption Feedback

The alternatives discussed above reflect some of the design issues that arise when developing an energy feedback system. Generally the research in the two projects suggests that it is important to provide feedback in terms of everyday activities rather than just in terms of energy units, and that even when social norms feedback is engaging it may not have an impact on consumption.

Although the research in the two projects suggests that the feedback had some impact on consumption, this effect was smaller than anticipated. The next section considers why energy consumption feedback appears to have only a small impact on consumption.

5   Motivating Behaviour Change

There is a tacit assumption among some researchers and suppliers of energy feedback that simply providing energy feedback will lead to significant reduction in energy consumption; this is belied by the research [4-7]. It is easy to assume when designing energy consumption feedback that householders have both a desire to reduce their energy consumption and a deficit of information, and therefore that providing information in the appropriate design format will lead to changes in behaviour and a reduction in consumption. However, as noted in the theoretical background above, energy consumption is indirect and often invisible, and measured in units that most householders do not understand. Ironically, this renders problematic the provision of energy consumption feedback. Strengers [14] argues that current forms of energy feedback are based on a mistaken assumption that most householders are the rational micro-resource managers imagined in the 'smart ontology' that underlies the design of most consumption feedback. Harries and Brightwell [24] suggest that control and management of electricity can also conflict with the caring ethos of home-making.

Ethnographic research [9-16] shows that feedback can make energy more visible, but also suggests that current forms of feedback do not challenge those energy-consuming practices that are taken-for-granted by householders. Strengers [14] calls for forms of feedback that challenge and disrupt these practices, and emphasises the inclusion of normative messages. One possible way of using established norms to challenge existing practices emerged from the two studies reported here. The research suggests that for some people the avoidance of waste is a moral imperative and more motivating than saving the environment, saving energy or saving money [12, 21, 24]. It is possible that a focus on wasteful usage might increase awareness of energy consumption and motivate behaviour change more effectively than consumption feedback. Such a focus could be achieved via the visualisation of wasteful usage (such as occurs in unoccupied heated bedrooms or poorly insulated homes), perhaps using interactive animated digital displays.

References

1. DECC: Smart Meter Roll-out (GB) Impact Assessment No: DECC0009 (2013)
2. Fischer, C.: Feedback on Household Electricity Consumption: a Tool for Saving Energy? Energy Efficiency 1, 79–104 (2008)
3. Kempton, W., Layne, L.L.: The Consumer's Energy Analysis Environment. Energy Policy 22(10), 857–866 (1994)
4. Darby, S.: The Effectiveness of Feedback on Energy Consumption: Review for Defra (2006)
5. Erhardt-Martinez, K., et al.: Advanced Monitoring Initiatives and Residential Feedback Programs: a Meta-Review for Household Electricity-Saving Opportunities. ACEEE Report E105 (2010)
6. Allcott, H.: Social Norms and Energy Conservation. Journal of Public Economics 95(9-10), 1082–1095 (2011)
7. Ofgem: Energy Demand Research Project: Final Analysis (2011)
8. Stromback, J., Dromacque, C., Yassin, M.H.: Empower Demand: The Potential of Smart Meter Enabled Programs to Increase Energy and Systems Efficiency: A Mass Pilot Comparison. Global Energy Think Tank. VaasaETT, Helsinki (2011)
9. Grønhøj, A., Thøgersen, J.: Feedback on Household Electricity Consumption: Learning and Social Influence Processes. International Journal of Consumer Studies 35, 138–145 (2011)

10. Hargreaves, T., Nye, M., Burgess, J.: Making Energy Visible: A Qualitative Field Study of How Householders Interact with Feedback from Smart Energy Monitors. Energy Policy 38, 6111–6119 (2010)

11. Hargreaves, T., Nye, M., Burgess, J.: Keeping Energy Visible? Exploring How Householders Interact with Feedback from Smart Energy Monitors in the Longer Term. Energy Policy 52, 126–134 (2013)

12. Harries, T., Rettie, R., Studley, M., Burchell, K., Chambers, S.: Is Social Norms Marketing Effective? A Case Study in Domestic Electricity Consumption. European Journal of Marketing 47(9), 1458–1475

13. Harries, T., Rettie, R., Studley, M.: Is Social Norms Marketing Effective? A Case Study in Domestic Electricity Consumption. In: Kubacki, K., Rundle-Thiele, S. (eds.) Contemporary Issues in Social Marketing, ch. 9, pp. 158–172. Cambridge Scholars Publishing, Newcastle Upon Tyne (2013)

14. Strengers, Y.: Smart Energy Technologies in Everyday Life: Smart Utopia? Palgrave Macmillan, London (2013)

15. Strengers, Y.: Negotiating everyday Life: The Role of Energy and Water Consumption Feedback. Journal of Consumer Culture 11(3), 319–338 (2011)

16. van Dam, S., Bakker, C., van Hal, J.: Home Energy Monitors: Impact Medium-Term. Building Research 38(5), 458–469 (2010)

17. Perkins, H.W.: The Social Norms Approach to Preventing School and College Age Substance Abuse. Jossey-Bass, San Francisco (2003)

18. Cialdini, R., Goldstein, N.J.: Social influence: compliance and conformity. Annual Review of Psychology 55, 59–621 (2004)

19. Thaler, R.H., Sunstein, C.R.: Nudge: Improving Decisions about Health, Wealth and Happiness. Yale University Press, London (2008)

20. Ayres, I., Raseman, S., Shih, A.: Evidence from Two Large Field-Experiments that Show that Peer Comparison Feedback can Reduce Residential Energy Usage. In: Annual Conference on Empirical Legal Studies. Yale University, New Haven (2009)

21. Burchell, K., Rettie, R., Roberts, T.: Final Report of the Smart Communities Project (June 11, 2014), http://www.smartcommunities.org.uk

22. McAlaney, J., Bewick, B., Bauerle, J.: Social Norms Guidebook: A Guide to Implementing the Social Norms Approach in the UK (2010)

23. Burchell, K., Rettie, R., Patel, K.: Marketing Social Norms: Social Marketing and the 'Social Norms Approach'. Journal of Consumer Behaviour 12, 1–9 (2013)

24. Harries, T., Brightwell, M.G.L.: Notions of 'House' and Notions of 'Home' – Their Importance for Interventions to Reduce Domestic Electricity Consumption. Working paper

The Design and Evaluation of Intelligent Energy Dashboard for Sustainability in the Workplace

Ray Yun[1], Azizan Aziz[2], Bertrand Lasternas[2], Chenlu Zhang[2], Vivian Loftness[2], Peter Scupelli[3], Yunjeong Mo[2], Jie Zhao[2], and Nana Wilberforce[4]

[1] Computational Design, School of Architecture
[2] Building Performance and Diagnostics, School of Architecture
[3] School of Design,
Carnegie Mellon University, Pittsburgh, PA, United States
{ryun,azizan,blastern,chenluz,loftness,
scupelli,yleahmo,jayzhao}@cmu.edu
[4] Realty Services, PNC Bank, Pittsburgh, PA, United States
nana.wilberforce@pnc.com

Abstract. Office workers typically don't know how much energy they consume at work. Since the workers don't pay the energy bills, they tend to waste energy. To support energy conservation and motivate workers, the Intelligent Dashboard for Occupants (ID-O) was developed using multiple intervention strategies – eco-feedback (self-monitoring, advice, and comparison), remote controls, and automated controls. The baseline data was collected for fourteen weeks from eighty office workers and ID-Os with different features were deployed for seven weeks. The results show that the group with all the features (eco-feedback, remote controls, automated controls) made the biggest energy savings at 35.4%, the group that had eco-feedback and the remote controls showed 20.2% energy savings, the feedback only group achieved 9% energy savings, and the last group (the control group) produced 3.6% energy savings. The automated control feature produced the biggest energy savings, and was most effective in energy management for lights and phones, but not for computers and monitors.

Keywords: energy dashboard, sustainability, workplace, behavior change, eco-feedback, remote and automated control, plug load management, organization.

1 Introduction

Commercial buildings consume about 20% of the electricity in the United States [1] and 30-40% of this electricity can be saved as a result of changes in the behavior of the building occupants [7, 8]. To motivate people towards pro-environmental behavior, Human-Computer Interaction (HCI) researchers have developed various display technologies such as energy dashboards [e.g., 10,11,12,24], eco-art [e.g., 14], computer games [e.g., 13,15,16], and ambient displays [e.g., 17,18]. However, most of the HCI studies have the following limitations. First, as Froehlich et al. [9] pointed

A. Marcus (Ed.): DUXU 2014, Part III, LNCS 8519, pp. 605–615, 2014.
© Springer International Publishing Switzerland 2014

out, most of the HCI studies are not evaluated in depth in terms of the methods, number of participants, and the length of the study. Second, many of the studies targeted residential users [19, 20] and few focus on the domain of the office environment. Finally, the "control" strategy has not been thoroughly evaluated in the field of HCI research, in terms of moving the behavioral change towards increasing attainment of sustainability goals. The control strategy is an approach that allows people to easily manage their energy usage, using web or mobile based tools [4]. The research team is interested particularly in the workplace domain because office workers typically do not know how much energy they consume at work [4]. Also, since they do not pay the utility bill, they lack an incentive to save energy at work [19, 20]. To promote sustainability in the workplace, we designed and developed the Intelligent Dashboard for Occupants (ID-O), using multiple strategies, and conducted field studies to evaluate the impact of this system.

2   Background

Our previous study reviewed the nine intervention techniques to promote sustainability in the workplace [4]. Among these techniques, this study focuses on the most commonly used informational techniques – self-monitoring, advice, and comparison - and a relatively new approach, control intervention strategy. There are several related studies, which do focus on the workplace domain. For example, Granderson et al. (2010) evaluated the use of energy dashboard in commercial buildings for two to three years. The web-based dashboard displays real-time electricity consumption for the whole building. An 18-35% reduction of energy consumption was measured. Carrico et al. [2] provided employees with electricity consumption feedback (self-monitoring) and monthly advice via email for eight months. This approach led to an 8% reduction of energy consumption. Lucid's building dashboard [3] displays a building's real-time energy consumption (self-monitoring) and compares the consumption with other buildings' (comparison). This technique reduced energy consumption by an estimated 30%. These documented energy savings indicate the importance of energy data display about the whole building.

Another strategy, control, has not been thoroughly studied but has potential benefits [4]. Mercier et al. provided power strips and timers (control) to office workers for two months and measured up to 55% energy savings [5]. This study shows the importance of the use of distributed monitoring hardware and controls. In the ID-O system, more advanced features, such as real-time individual user's consumption (instead of the whole building's energy consumption), and online remote controls to actuate devices (instead of using offline plug controllers), were developed to further reduce energy consumption.

3   Intelligent Dashboard for Occupants (ID-O)

As shown in Figure 1, the ID-O is equipped to provide self-monitoring, advice, comparison and control. The features are designed as follows:

Self-monitoring (Chart). The energy Chart is designed to display the energy consumption data item by item in real time with historical data. Many studies (e.g., [21, 22, 23]) suggest this mode of data presentation offers opportunities to save more energy. As shown in Figure 1, the system provides views of data usage in different time ranges (day, week, month) and chart types (area, bar, line) so that people can view their energy consumption from a variety of angles. By clicking specific items in the legend section, users can hide or display them in the chart, and by hovering over a data point they can view the numeric values and related statistics. The chart also projects past data, so that people can understand their previous consumption (e.g. a week ago) and predict their future performance.

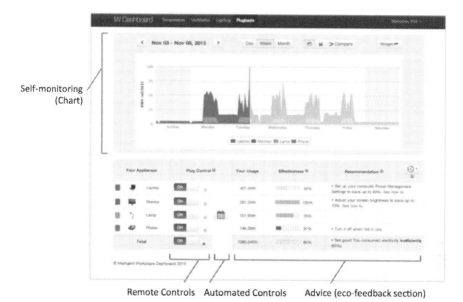

Fig. 1. User interface of Intelligent Dashboard for Occupants home page

Advice (Eco-feedback Section). The ID-O offers 1) tips users can follow immediately, 2) suggestions to replace their inefficient devices with energy-efficient products for a long-term savings, and 3) user behavior effectiveness towards energy savings per device. When the system detects energy waste (e.g. the task light had been left on during the night last week), the advice text is displayed in red in the Recommendations column to alert the users. In addition to the information about the individual user, organization scaled monetary impact can be viewed as well. This shows the cost or savings if all employees in the organization acted as the user has done.

Comparison (Chart). The system provides a line chart that displays the energy consumption of the user, the office average, and the best person (least energy consumption) in the office (Figure 2). The blue line represents the user's personal energy usage at work. To highlight the user's personal energy usage, the area under the line is shaded with light blue. The red line represents the average value of the employees' energy usage in the office. The green line represents the user in the office with the lowest energy consumption for the selected period. Users whose offices are unoccupied, due to vacations or business travel are excluded. This occupancy was estimated based on their computer monitor's consumption.

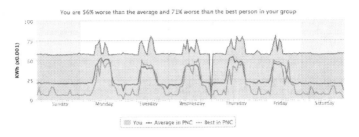

Fig. 2. Comparison chart example

Remote Controls. The dashboard also enables users to remotely control their connected devices individually or as a group. Users are able to switch off their devices by one-click action when they leave the office. Even if they forget to turn off the devices before leaving the office, users can still access the controls to the devices remotely by using this feature.

Automated Controls. Additionally, the automated control/scheduling feature is equipped to turn on and off devices automatically, based on the users' weekly schedule. Users set schedulers that can be dragged and dropped and place them on a timetable to set the day and time for this event to occur (see Figure 3).

Fig. 3. Weekly calendar for automated controls

The Plugwise (http://plugwise.com) plug-load smart meter is used to measure a user's disaggregated electricity consumption and allows remote control of the individual devices. As shown in Figure 4, electrical devices plugged into individual Plugwise meters (Circles) transmit data wirelessly to the Plugwise server. The python program in the server uploads this data to a web server or conveys the control commands to the main server as a mediator. PHP is used to retrieve energy data from the database.   For the chart representation, Highcharts (http://www.highcharts.com/), Javascript chart library is used. For styling the overall web components (e.g., buttons, forms, fonts, colors), Bootstrap (http://getbootstrap.com/) CSS library is used.

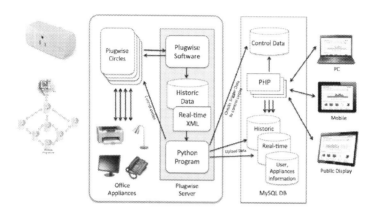

Fig. 4. The smart meter used for this study (*left*) and the ID-O's system structure (*right*)

4   Method

To investigate which strategies best contribute to energy savings, the research team is currently conducting a large-scale field study with eighty participants. The participants were recruited from one department (realty services) in a large company and all of them reported they are full-time workers and spend most of their time doing computer work. The participants were randomly assigned to four groups (twenty

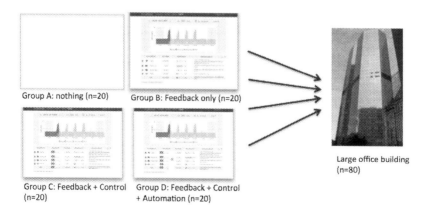

Fig. 5. Different energy dashboards were provided to four groups in a large office building

people per group) and their baseline data was collected for fourteen weeks. After the baseline data collection, the ID-O systems equipped with different features were introduced to the four groups as follows (Figure 5). The first group (Group A) was provided without any dashboard interface and served as a "control" group. The second group (Group B) was provided with feedback only (self-monitoring, advice, comparison), the third group (Group C) was provided with feedback and remote controls, and the last group (Group D) was provided with feedback, remote controls, and automated controls.

To introduce the systems to each group, group-training sessions were held at the company (Figure 6). The team demonstrated the system features, provided user names and passwords, and answered participants questions. After these training sessions, energy data was collected for seven weeks and each group's energy saving was measured.

Fig. 6. Group training session

Energy savings were calculated based on the difference between post-intervention energy usage compared to pre-intervention energy usage with similar occupancy patterns. Savings due to participants being away from the office, such as off-site work and being on vacation, are excluded from the energy savings calculation. Occupancy was estimated based on each participant's daily monitor usage. Our pilot study [24] revealed the need for a weekly reminder regarding use of the dashboard. To support engagement with the dashboard, participants received a reminder email every Monday morning. An example reminder email says "We encourage you to visit the energy dashboard site regularly and hope you're able to learn your energy performance and behave more pro-environmentally", with the dashboard URL and contact information included in case they have questions about the system. The reminder did not include any energy consumption information or other statistical data because the team wanted to measure the energy saving impact made by the dashboard intervention only.

5 Preliminary Results

The area charts (Figure 7) show each group's average energy consumption per person for a typical week before and after the systems were introduced. The groups equipped with the various ID-O interfaces (Group B, C, D) reduced more energy at night and during the weekends compared to Group A, where no intervention was provided.

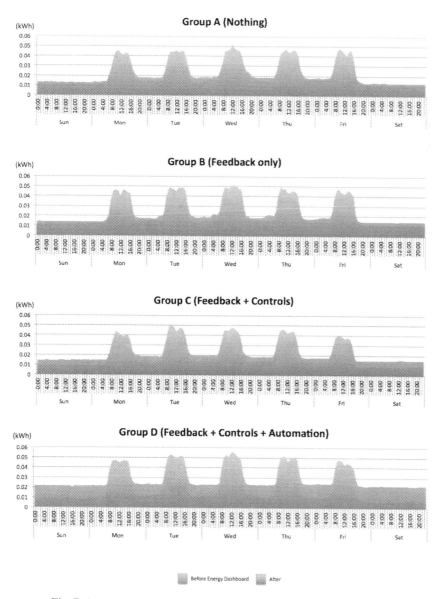

Fig. 7. Average energy usage before and after the dashboard intervention

The bar charts (Figure 8) show each group's typical week total energy savings, before and after the ID-O intervention. Group D, equipped with all the features including automated controls, achieved the biggest energy savings of 35.4%, followed by Group C with 20.2% energy savings. Group B reduced energy consumption by 9.0% and Group A, even without a dashboard, reduced consumption by 3.6%. Much of the savings were achieved during weekends (B: 18%, C: 39%, D: 64%) and at night (B: 19%, C: 23%, D: 47%).

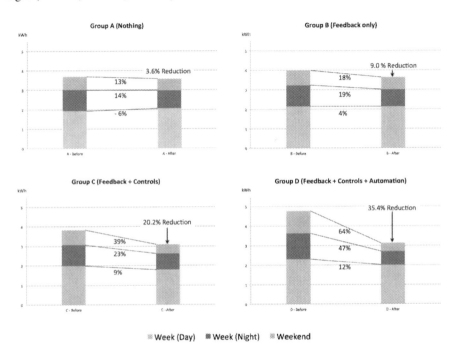

Fig. 8. Energy savings before and after the dashboard intervention

Figure 9 shows the average energy saving rates per device. Group C and Group D, equipped with the control features, showed relatively larger energy savings for lights (e.g., task lamps or under-bin light). Group D also showed relatively larger savings for phones. It was found that 70% and 65% of the participants in Group D set up the calendar for lights and phones respectively. However, only 12% of the participants set up the calendar for computers and monitors resulting in considerably lower savings. Only marginal savings were achieved from computer monitors throughout the groups since most of their monitors were already energy efficient and do not consume electricity when not in use.

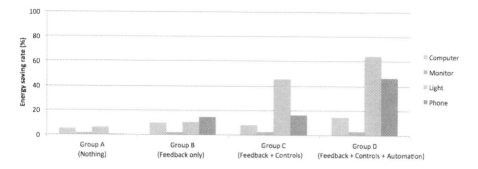

Fig. 9. Average energy saving rates achieved per device

6   Discussion

This section discusses the issues encountered during the implementation of the study.

6.1   Awareness and Discussion Frequency

This study measured not only the energy usage change but also the energy consumption awareness change before and after the interventions by conducting a survey [6]. Whereas Group D showed the biggest energy savings (35.4%), their awareness increase of 1.2% was relatively lower than Group B (6.5%) and Group C (10.4%). Each group's energy-related discussion frequency was also investigated. Group D's discussion frequency increase of 22.7% is also relatively lower than Group B's (77.5%) and C's (56.5%). The automation system may not support active learning of energy information from the system and energy-related discussions with coworkers.

6.2   Application Platforms

This study investigates the potential energy saving impact from the introduction of different user interface (UI) strategies aimed at changing user behavior regarding energy consumption in the workplace. To focus on the effectiveness of a "web-based" UI strategy, we did not include a mobile system in this study. However, mobile UI is expected to increase the energy saving potential significantly. The current dashboard system generates advice based on the last week's energy usage (if the week range is selected), but if the system can detect energy waste in real time and send advice messages with a control button to individual users, this will strengthen our current system resulting in increased energy conservation.

6.3   Control Group

The team assumes that Group A was not completely controlled because the participants were recruited from the same department and were located in close proximity to participants in other groups. As described earlier, Group A achieved an energy savings of 3.6% and their energy-related discussion frequency increased by 19.4% after the dashboard intervention [6], even though as the control group they did not receive a dashboard or any feedback directly. These numbers for Group A are relatively low compared to the other group's savings and discussion frequency, however, it indicates the control group might have been affected by the system users in other groups.

7 Summary

This study investigates the effectiveness of dashboard user interface strategies towards increasing energy conservation in the office environment. Three energy dashboards equipped with different strategies (eco-feedback, remote controls, and automations) were provided to the groups of participants. Over a seven-week period of dashboard system deployment, energy usage was measured and compared to the baseline data collected over a fourteen-week period. The group with the automation feature (Group D) showed the biggest energy savings (35.4%). The group equipped with the remote control feature but without the automation feature (Group C) produced the second biggest reduction (20.2%). The group that was given feedback only (Group B) showed the third biggest energy savings (9%). Finally the control group (Group A) showed a 3.6% energy savings. These are preliminary findings from an ongoing research study. The authors will continue this measurement for the additional seven weeks and then remove the systems from the users to study how persistently the savings will last with no intervention.

Acknowledgments. This study is supported by the Energy Efficient Buildings Hub Consortium (EEBHub.org, a U.S. DOE Innovation Hub, Subtask 6.4) under the U.S. Department of Energy Award Number EE0004261. We would like to thank all the participants who volunteered to take part in the study and Christopher Leininger who contributed to the editing of this paper.

References

1. EIA, U.: Annual energy review. Energy Information Administration, US Department of Energy, Washington, DC (2011), http://www.eia.doe.gov/emeu/aer
2. Carrico, A.R., Riemer, M.: Motivating energy conservation in the workplace: An evaluation of the use of group-level feedback and peer education. Journal of Environmental Psychology 31(1), 1–13 (2011)
3. Lucid Design. Elon University Strives to Meet Carbon Commitment Through Behavior Change (July 1, 2010), http://www.luciddesigngroup.com/download.php?id=20100701 (retrieved April 14, 2013)
4. Yun, R., Scupelli, P., Aziz, A., Loftness, V.: Sustainability in the Workplace: Nine Intervention Techniques for Behavior Change. In: Berkovsky, S., Freyne, J. (eds.) PERSUASIVE 2013. LNCS, vol. 7822, pp. 253–265. Springer, Heidelberg (2013)
5. Mercier, C., Moorefield, L.: Commercial office plug load savings and assessment: Final report. Produced by ECOVA and Supported Through the California Energy Commission's Public Interest Energy Research Program (2011)

6. Yun, R., Scupelli, P., Aziz, A., Lasternas, B., Loftness, V., Wilberforce, N.: Investigating Sustainability Stages in the Workplace. In: Marcus, A. (ed.) Proceedings, HCI International 2014. LNCS, vol. 8519, pp. 616–627. Springer, Heidelberg (2014)
7. Energy Star, Fast Facts on Energy Use (2009), http://www.energystar.gov/ia/business/challenge/learn_more/FastFacts.pdf
8. NBI, "Managing Your Office Equipment Plug Load" (2012), http://newbuildings.org/plug-load-best-practices-guide
9. Froehlich, J., Findlater, L., Landay, J.: The design of eco-feedback technology. In: CHI 2010, pp. 1999–2008. ACM, New York (2010), doi:10.1145/1753326.1753629
10. Granderson, J., Piette, M.A., Ghatikar, G.: Building energy information systems: user case studies. Energy Efficiency 4(1), 17–30 (2011)
11. Bartram, L., Rodgers, J., Woodbury, R.: Smart homes or smart occupants? Supporting aware living in the home. In: Campos, P., Graham, N., Jorge, J., Nunes, N., Palanque, P., Winckler, M. (eds.) INTERACT 2011, Part II. LNCS, vol. 6947, pp. 52–64. Springer, Heidelberg (2011)
12. Alrowaily, M.A.: Energy Monitoring through Social Networks (Doctoral dissertation, University of Waikato) (2012)
13. Gamberini, L., Spagnolli, A., Corradi, N., Jacucci, G., Tusa, G., Mikkola, T., Zamboni, L., Hoggan, E.: Tailoring Feedback to Users' Actions in a Persuasive Game for Household Electricity Conservation. In: Bang, M., Ragnemalm, E.L. (eds.) PERSUASIVE 2012. LNCS, vol. 7284, pp. 100–111. Springer, Heidelberg (2012)
14. Holmes, T.G.: Eco-visualization: combining art and technology to reduce energy consumption. In: C&C 2007, pp. 153–162. ACM, New York (2007)
15. Bang, M., Gustafsson, A., Katzeff, C.: Promoting New Patterns in Household Energy Consumption with Pervasive Learning Games. In: de Kort, Y.A.W., IJsselsteijn, W.A., Midden, C., Eggen, B., Fogg, B.J. (eds.) PERSUASIVE 2007. LNCS, vol. 4744, pp. 55–63. Springer, Heidelberg (2007)
16. Shiraishi, M., Washio, Y., Takayama, C., Lehdonvirta, V., Kimura, H., Nakajima, T.: Using individual, social and economic persuasion techniques to reduce CO2 emissions in a family setting. In: Persuasive, pp. 13:1–13:8. ACM, New York (2009)
17. Kuznetsov, S., Paulos, E.: UpStream: motivating water conservation with low-cost water flow sensing and persuasive displays. In: Proceedings of the 28th International Conference on Human Factors in Computing Systems, pp. 1851–1860. ACM (April 2010)
18. Kim, T., Hong, H., Magerko, B.: Designing for persuasion: Toward ambient eco-visualization for awareness. In: Ploug, T., Hasle, P., Oinas-Kukkonen, H. (eds.) PERSUASIVE 2010. LNCS, vol. 6137, pp. 106–116. Springer, Heidelberg (2010)
19. Lehrer, D., Vasudev, J.: Evaluating a social media application for sustainability in the workplace. In: CHI EA 2011, pp. 2161–2166. ACM, New York (2011)
20. Foster, D., Lawson, S., Wardman, J., Blythe, M., Linehan, C.: "Watts in it for me?": design implications for implementing effective energy interventions in organisations. In: CHI 2012, New York, NY, USA, pp. 2357–2366 (2012)
21. Fogg, B.J.: Persuasive technology: using computers to change what we think and do. Ubiquity (December 2002), doi:10.1145/763955.763957
22. Fischer, C.: Feedback on household electricity consumption: a tool for saving energy? Energy Efficiency 1(1), 79–104 (2008)
23. Fitzpatrick, G., Smith, G.: Technology-Enabled Feedback on Domestic Energy Consumption: Articulating a Set of Design Concerns. Pervasive Computing 8(1), 37–44 (2009)
24. Yun, R., Lasternas, B., Aziz, A., Loftness, V., Scupelli, P., Rowe, A., Kothari, R., Marion, F., Zhao, J.: Toward the Design of a Dashboard to Promote Environmentally Sustainable Behavior among Office Workers. In: Berkovsky, S., Freyne, J. (eds.) PERSUASIVE 2013. LNCS, vol. 7822, pp. 246–252. Springer, Heidelberg (2013)

Investigating Sustainability Stages in the Workplace

Ray Yun[1], Peter Scupelli[3], Azizan Aziz[2], Bertrand Lasternas[2],
Vivian Loftness[2], and Nana Wilberforce[4]

[1] Computational Design, School of Architecture
[2] Building Performance and Diagnostics, School of Architecture
[3] School of Design, Carnegie Mellon University, Pittsburgh, PA, United States
{ryun,scupelli,azizan,blastern,loftness}@cmu.edu
[4]Realty Services, PNC Bank, Pittsburgh, PA, United States
nana.wilberforce@pnc.com

Abstract. Prior research on stage-based, behavior-change models investigated intervention effectiveness for stress management, smoking cessation, weight management, adherence to lipid-lowering drugs and the like. Few sustainability centered studies identify people's stage-based levels for energy use reduction or sustainability. In this paper, we investigate sustainability stages with measured behavior and eco-awareness scores based on Geller's behavior change model. Eighty office employees were assigned to one of four experimental energy dashboard conditions: (a) no energy dashboard; (b) feedback only; (c) feedback and manual on/off controls; and (d) feedback, manual on/off controls, and on/off calendaring. We measured with pre-post surveys change in sustainability levels, energy efficiency discussions frequency, and organizational efforts to understand the work environment. We found that the dashboard with feedback, controls, and on/off calendaring were significantly associated with reported greater energy saving behavior compared to no energy dashboards, and dashboards with fewer features (i.e., feedback only; feedback and on/off control).

Keywords: behavior change, stages, sustainability, energy dashboard, persuasive system, workplace, organization.

1 Introduction

Behavior-change researchers develop strategies and investigate intervention effectiveness in terms of improving health, decreasing environmental degradation and other benefits. There are a number of theories and approaches that explain the causes, processes, methods and barriers that influence behavioral change [e.g., 1, 3, 4, 5]. Among other theories, stage-based, behavior-change models are widely employed to explain the process of behavior change. The main idea is that behavior change occurs by progressing through a series of stages. For example in healthcare, the Transtheoretical Model (TTM), also known as the Stages of Change Model, involves five stages (i.e., pre-contemplation, contemplation, planning, action, maintenance) [10]. In health related studies on stress management, smoking cessation, weight

A. Marcus (Ed.): DUXU 2014, Part III, LNCS 8519, pp. 616–627, 2014.
© Springer International Publishing Switzerland 2014

management, adherence to lipid-lowering drugs and the like, surveys were used to identify study participants' stage of change [e.g., 18, 19]. Unfortunately, there is limited research on stages of change for sustainability related behavior, notable exceptions include [6]. This study investigates the measurement of sustainability-level changes in combination with different experimental interventions. In the home environment, wasted energy usually bears financial costs for the energy consumers. Instead in the large office environments typically office energy consumers are unaffected financially by the energy they use. We target office workers in this study, to investigate whether lack of direct financial incentives limits pro-environmental behavior in work environments.

2   Behavior Change Models for Sustainability

Previous research [8] and Valente [14] review various behavior change models and five stage-based models were found – TTM [10], Diffusion of Innovations [16], Piotrow's Steps to Behavior change [9], Mcguire's Hierarchy of Effects [17] and Geller's model [11]. Table 1 illustrates the comparison of the stages of the behavior change models. TTM explains the process of health-behavior change in five stages (Precontemplation – Contemplation – Preparation – Action – Maintenance), Rogers Diffusion theory demonstrates five stages in the adoption process (Awareness – Persuasion – Decision – Implementation – Confirmation). Piotrow et al. and McGuire expanded the stages of behavior change into more specific hierarchy to health promotion evaluation as illustrated in Table 1. Geller's model demonstrates four performer behavior stages (unconscious incompetence, conscious incompetence, conscious competence, unconscious competence).

These models contain a similar behavior change process. For example, people do not perform the target behavior at first, because they do not know the value of it. If they realize the value, they move onto the next stage. Even if people know the value of the behavior change, they may not act on that knowledge immediately because they need time to process and assimilate the new information before making decisions. After they decide to change, people perform the target behavior and reach the next stage. The last stage is where people continuously perform the target behavior to the point where it has become habitual.

There are three distinctions among the models. First Diffusion theory [12] was initially derived from studies on knowledge adoption whereas others focus on behavior adaption. Second, TTM model was initially developed to understand the process of quitting bad habits (e.g., quitting smoking), however the rest rather focus on the process of adopting a new behavior [14]. Third, the first four models are associated with health behavior change whereas the last one focuses on environmental behavior change. The Geller's model clearly and simply explains the stages of behavior change and more importantly, it focuses on sustainability, therefore we employ his model for our study to investigate an individual's sustainability level. One of the limitations of Geller's model is that it focuses on the level of the individual, whereas in the office environment individual behavior is shaped by a larger context that includes at least the workgroup and organization. The Process-Person-Context-Time Model (PPCT) by Bronfenbrenner includes such dimensions [1].

Table 1. Comparison of Stages of Behavior Change (Adapted from Valente [14])

Diffusion of Innovations (Rogers, 1995)	Hierarchy of effects (Mcguire, 1989)	Steps to behavior change (Piotrow et al., 1997)	TTM (Prochaska et al. 1992)	Behavior Change for Sustainability Geller, 2002)
			1. Pre-contemplation	1. Unconscious incompetence
1. Knowledge	1. Recalling message 2. Liking message 3. Comprehending message 4. Knowledge of behavior	1.Recalls message 2.Understands topic 3.Can name source of supply	2. Contemplation	2. Conscious incompetence
2. Persuasion	5. Skill acquisition 6. Yielding to it 7. Memory storage of content	4. Responds favorably 5. Discusses with friends/family 6. Thinks others approve 7. Approves oneself 8. Recognizes that innovation meets need		
3. Decision	8. Information search and retrieval 9. Deciding on basis of retrieval	9. Intends to consult a provider 10. Intends to adopt 11. Go to provider	3. Preparation	
4. Trial	10. Behaving in accordance with decision	12. Initiates use 13. Continues use	4. Action	3. Conscious competence
5. Adoption	11. Reinforcement of desired acts 12. Post-behavior consolidation	14. Experiences benefits 15. Advocates that others practice behavior change 16. Supports practice in the community	5. Maintenance	4. Unconscious competence

3   Measurement of the Stages

As mentioned earlier, we found few studies that assess sustainability stages. Mair et al. [6] developed a survey that asks twenty-nine questions on how often they carry out certain sustainable practices such as commuting by bicycle, recycling and cold-water wash. The response options provided were: never – sometimes – often – regularly – always. Scores were calculated per person and classified to each TTM stage. When this approach was reviewed, three issues were found. First their survey covered a wide range of sustainable practices (transportation, energy, water use, waste management, etc.) and they were equally weighted. We contend that people may be committed to one aspect of sustainability but not others. Hence, TTM stages may vary by sustainability area practice. For example, one may be a committed recycler at home but commute by car to work. Second, the TTM model was applied to sustainability, whereas typically it is used for health behavior change. In other words, there may be a requirement for modifications in order for the model to apply to sustainable behavior change. Third, the stages were defined based on the level of practice (e.g., Pre-contemplation: 26-52,

Contemplation/preparation: 52-78, Action: 78-104, Maintenance: 104-130), despite the fact that this does not distinguish knowledge, awareness, planning, and behavior. In other words, one may be very informed about sustainability issues and do very little to put into action such knowledge.

Our study refined Mair et al.'s approach to complement the limits as follows. First, we narrowed the sustainability domain to plug-load management for desktop technology in the workplace, second, we employed Geller's model because it was developed specifically for sustainability, and third, instead of assigning each person to a specific stage, we mapped awareness and behavior scores in scatter plot to describe one's stage. The survey questions we developed are listed in Table 2.

Table 2. Survey question examples

Question examples	Option examples

Q1. How often do you turn off or unplug your:
  - Computer when not in use on nights and weekends?
  - Computer monitor when not in use on nights and weekends?
  - Task light (lamp, underbin light) when not in use?
  - Office phone on nights and weekends?
	a) Never (1)
	b) Rarely (2)
	c) Sometimes (3)
	d) Often (4)
	e) Always (5)
	f) Do not know (0)

Q2. Have you:
  - Adjusted power settings (e.g., to power saver mode) for the computer you are using at work?
  - Adjusted brightness settings for your computer monitor at work?
	a) Yes (5)
	b) No (1)
	c) Do not know (0)
	d) Not applicable

Q3. Put in order the actions you think will have the greatest impact on energy savings:
  - Turn the computer off when not in use (e.g., nights, weekends)?
  - Turn the computer monitor off when not in use (e.g., nights, weekends)?
  - Turn the task light (lamp, underbin light) off when not in use (e.g., nights, weekends)?
  - Turn the phone off or unplug it when not in use (e.g., nights, weekends)?
  - Adjust computer power settings (e.g., to power saver mode)?
  - Adjust computer monitor's brightness settings?
  - Buy energy star office equipment such as: computers, printers, lights, and so forth?	

Q4. Have you: - Discussed energy usage/saving in your work group?	a) Yes (5) b) No (1) c) Do not know (0) d) Not applicable

Q5. How often does your organization:
  - Provide workers with very energy efficient products (e.g., computers, displays, lights)?
  - Encourage workers to reduce energy use in the office?
	a) Never (1)
	b) Rarely (2)
	c) Sometimes (3)
	d) Often (4)
	e) Always (5)
	f) Do not know (0)

These questions were developed based on the PIER's report [12] which suggests the most effective methods of plug-load management for the office environment. Question one and two identify the frequency with which users select pro-environmental behavior in terms of the use of office appliances. Question three investigates user understanding of their own energy consumption at work. Questions four and five help understanding users' work environment and organizational culture [2].

4   Method

A field study has been designed and implemented at a large office building to investigate the proposed "sustainability stages" described above. Eighty employees in one department (realty services) were recruited. They were randomly assigned to four groups and the different interventions (different energy dashboards equipped with different features) were given to each group (Figure 1, [13]). The survey above was conducted twice - right before and one month after the interventions were given to each group.

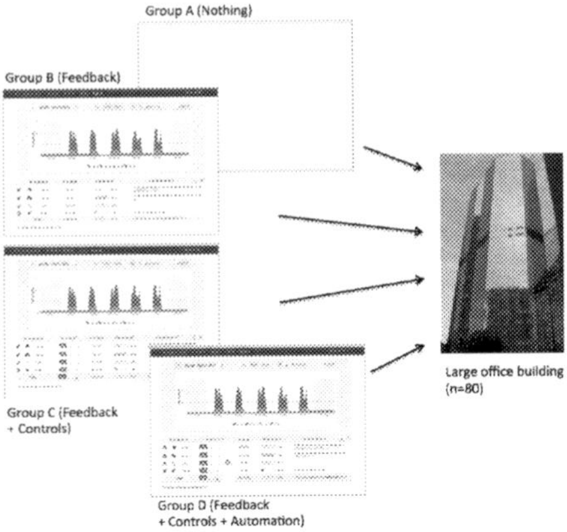

Fig. 1. Energy dashboard interventions: Nothing for Group A, feedback only for Group B, feedback and controls for Group C, and feedback, control and automated control for Group D. See [13] for more details on the dashboard system.

To quantify behavior change from the survey, a certain score number value has been assigned to each option in table 1. Those numbers are summed per group and averaged. To quantify the awareness change, correct answers from questions #3 were counted and averaged. The correctness of the answers was evaluated based on the energy usage data collected from the smart meters installed for individual users.

5   Preliminary Results

As noted above, eighty participants were recruited for this study. Sixty-three participated in the pre intervention survey (Group A:16, B:17, C:14, D:16) and fifty-one participated in the post intervention survey (Group A:13, B:17, C:10, D:11). Age and gender were not collected due to the company policy. To simply present the comparative data, all results have been converted to percentages.

Based on the survey responses, behavior change was measured as follows. (Figure 2) The y-axis is the average score percentage calculated from each group's response to questions one and two. For example, if a person answered to always (5) to all Q1 questions and yes (5) to all Q2 questions, his or her behavior score is 30 and is converted to 100. Seven weeks after the energy dashboard was given, Group A's behavior score was increased only 5.7% but in Group B, C and D score increased by 26.9%, 36.8%, and 51.9% respectively. The pre-post measures for Group D (feedback, on/off controls, automation) were significantly different [t(23)= 3.4, p<0.002]. For post intervention Group D (feedback, on/off controls, automation) was significantly different than Group A (no dashboard), B (feedback only), and C (feedback and on/off controls) [F(3, 46) = 4.99, p < 0.005]. Group A (no dashboard) and D (feedback, on/off controls, automation) were statistically different [t(21)= 3.93, p<0.001; Group B (feedback only) and D (feedback, on/off controls, automation) were significantly different [t(25)= 2.90, p<0.01]; Group C (feedback and on/off controls) and D (feedback, on/off controls, automation) trended towards statistical significance [t(18)= 1.82, p<0.08].

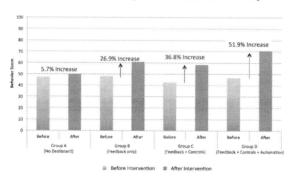

Fig. 2. Behavior change measured with survey responses for respondents' behavioral effort based on their answer to questions one and two (Pre N=63; Post N=51)

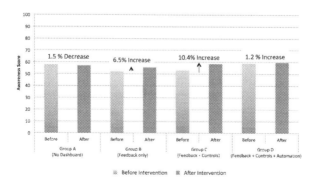

Fig. 3. Awareness changes measured with seven questions on the impact of energy savings (Pre N=63; Post N=51)

Awareness change between before and after the intervention was also measured using the survey. The y-axis in Figure 3 represents the average correctness of each group's response to the question three (impact on energy savings). For example, if a person answered correctly to all seven questions in Q3, his or her correctness represented as 100%. Awareness change from Group A and Group D was measured at less than 1.5%, but Group B and C showed a 6.5% and a 10.4% increase, respectively. We found no statistically significant differences of the groups pre-post or between groups.

The behavior and awareness was measured pre and post intervention for each experimental group. Figure 4 shows the average sustainability behavior and awareness. As mentioned earlier, behavior change stage-based models (e.g., Geller's model) mainly consist of two dimensions – awareness and behavior. People in the first stage who don't have knowledge and don't perform the pro-environmental behavior can be positioned at the lower left corner on the chart (unconscious incompetence, pink). Once they understand the knowledge but still think of changing their behavior, they are located at the upper left corner on the chart because their awareness increased (conscious incompetence, orange). If the pro-environmental behavior starts to be performed and its frequency increases, people on the chart start to move to right hand side. If this behavior is performed fluently, they are positioned close to the end of the right hand side. The last stage is Unconscious competence. This is when people conduct the behavior automatically without conscious effort. It is located not at the lower-right corner, but at the upper-right because Geller [8] argued once the knowledge is gained, it is not likely to be lost and go back to the beginning stage where there is no knowledge. Also, the last stage contains the word "unconscious" because the behavior already became a habit and performed "unconsciously". It is used differently from the first stage where people are "unconscious"(unaware) of the value of behavior change. The stages in the chart (Figure 4) are overlapped each other because based on Valente [14], behavior stages are not mutually exclusive.

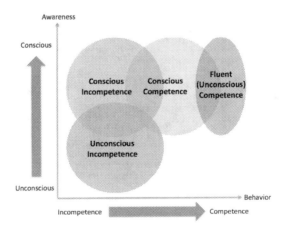

Fig. 4. Sustainability level based on the measured behavior and awareness

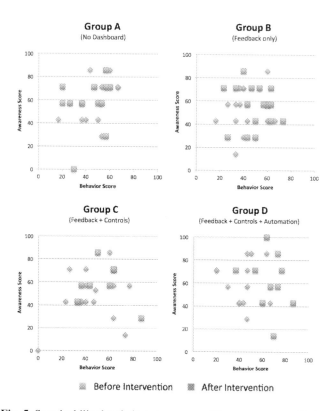

Fig. 5. Sustainability level changes measured for awareness and behavior

Using the behavior and awareness percentage measured from the survey, each group's sustainability level can be presented as follows. Based on the Figure 5, the majority of the results from our participants in four groups are positioned in the second stage (conscious incompetence) and the third stage (conscious competence) areas of the graph before the intervention is given (blue diamond in Figure 5). Seven weeks after the intervention, when the follow-up survey was given, the results show that Group A remained virtually unchanged, while Group B moved to right, Group C moved mostly to the upper-right with some in the lower right, and Group D moved to the right even further (but up-down direction was random).

In addition to behavior and awareness, questions focused on discussion frequency and the company's effort related to energy conservation were also asked on the survey. Figure 6 illustrates the discussion frequency with the Y-axis representing the average discussion frequency of each group. For example, if a person answered "yes" to the question 4, the frequency becomes 100 percent. All groups reported that their discussion frequency was increased after the intervention (A: 19.4%, B: 77.5%, C: 56.5%, D: 22.7%). It was found that Group A and D had relatively small frequency increases compared to Group B and C.

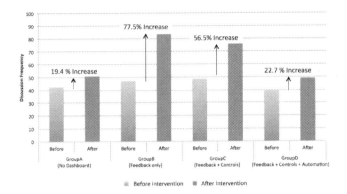

Fig. 6. Discussion of energy usage and savings in workgroup measured pre-post with one survey question (Pre N=63; Post N=51)

To investigate the organization's effort, at providing energy efficient products and increasing encouraging energy saving employee behavior, those two specific inquiries were included as part of question five. The first part of question five asked employees directly whether the company provides energy efficient products for their use. The second part of question five asked participants whether the company encourages them to save energy. Participants generally reported positively. Only 9% of people surveyed responded that their organization "never" or "rarely" provided energy efficient products and just 6% responded that their organization "never" or "rarely" encouraged them to save energy. After the dashboard intervention was given, results from the two questions were similar to each other (Figure 7 and 8). On both questions, Group D showed the biggest increase (Q5-1: 42%, Q5-2: 22.9%), Group C showed the second-biggest (Q5-1: 24%, Q5-2: 10.2%), and Group B showed the third-biggest (Q5-1: 13%, Q5-2: 3.1%). Participants might have thought that as more technologically advanced systems were given, the more effort was made by the organization.

The pre-post intervention survey responses to the survey question about discussion on energy usage and savings for Group B (feedback only) were significantly different [t(31)= 3.97, p<0.001]. The pre-post intervention survey responses to the same question for Group C (feedback and on/off controls) trended towards significant differences [t(22)= 1.69, p<0.10]. The post intervention survey responses to the survey question about discussion about energy usage and savings in the four groups were significantly different [F(3, 45) = 3.84, p < 0.02]. Group A (no dashboard) and B (feedback only) were statistically different [t(27)= 3.54, p<0.001; Group B (feedback only) and D (feedback, on/off controls, automation) were significantly different [t(24)= 2.76, p<0.01.

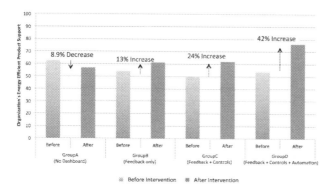

Fig. 7. Company's effort on providing energy efficient product from Group A to Group D (Pre N=63; Post N=51)

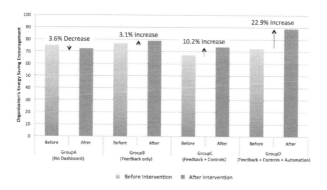

Fig. 8. Company's effort on encouraging office workers from Group A to Group D (Pre N=63; Post N=51)

6   Discussion

This section discusses the issues the team had during the implementation of our study.

First, in Figure 2, the result from each group showed that their average behavior score was increased as follows: Group A 5.7%, Group B 26.9%, Group C 36.8%, and Group D 51.9%. These results indicate the feedback that as more advanced features were equipped as part of the user dashboard, the greater the positive percentage change to the behavior score. The behavior score was measured from each users voluntary report to the survey, not from using any sensors. To supplement the survey result, smart electricity meters were used to measure each individual participant's energy consumption. In this field study, using the smart meters for verification, these quantitative measurements showed the following results in terms of energy savings: Group A 3.6%, Group B 9.0%, Group C 20.2%, and Group D 35.4%. These results support our survey results.

Second, we demonstrated that the scatter plots show the individual groups sustainability level change based on their behavior and awareness. The stage based behavior change models define the stages in term of whether a person knows the value of the behavior change, whether a person performs the target behavior, and whether the changed behavior is fluently performed. To assess a person's stage, those questions should be answered as yes or no, but in reality it is not simple to answer that way. Instead of showing how many people in the group change their stages, our approach is to display each users status in the scatter plots. The movement of dots overall indicates each group's of users sustainability level change before and after the intervention. Thus, overall performance of the company toward increasing sustainability attainment can be better understood.

Third, we created Group A as a control group. As shown in Figures 2, 5 and 6, this group may be influenced by talking to other dashboard users because all the participants were recruited from one department. To deduct the change led by the Hawthorn effect and the seasonal effect from each group, the difference value made in Group A, in terms of percent change, can be subtracted from each group.

Finally, due to the limited sample size, there may have not been enough statistical power to show all significant relationships. Limited responses in the second post survey further may have reduced the sample. Another limitation regards the accuracy and reliability of survey measures. The corporate sponsor limited the total number of questions we could include in the survey. More questions would have allowed us to explore a broader range of scales seeking to demonstrate and document a more reliable measure of behavior and awareness change.

7   Summary

This paper discusses investigating sustainability stages on plug-load management in the office environment. The authors developed a survey based on Geller's behavior change model, measured participants behavior and awareness scores, and displayed their sustainability level on the scatter plots. It was found that as more advanced systems were provided, more energy savings (behavior change) were realized and the more vigorous movement towards the last stage (unconscious incompetence) was indicated in the scatter plot. In two months the research team will remove the interventions (energy dashboards) from the participant's work environment and conduct the survey again to investigate if their sustainability change can last persistently without the interventions. If that result is displayed in the scatter plots together with the current findings, it will show a good overview of the sustainability stages in operation before intervention, after intervention, and after the intervention is removed.

Acknowledgments. This study is supported by the Energy Efficient Buildings Hub Consortium (EEBHub.org, a U.S. DOE Innovation Hub, Subtask 6.4) under the U.S. Department of Energy Award Number EE0004261. We would like to thank all the participants who volunteered to take part in this study and Christopher Leininger who contributed to the editing of this paper.

References

1. Fogg, B.J.: Persuasive technology: using computers to change what we think and do. Ubiquity (December 2002), doi:10.1145/763955.763957
2. Bronfenbrenner, U.: Making human beings human: Bioecological perspectives on human development. Sage Publications, Thousand Oaks (2005)
3. Pajares, F.: Overview of social cognitive theory and of self-efficacy (2002)
4. Stern, P.C., Oskamp, S.: Managing scarce environmental resources. In: Stokols, D., Altman, I. (eds.) Handbook of Environmental Psychology, New York, pp. 1043–1088 (1987)
5. Skinner, B.F.: Science and Human Behavior. Simon and Schuster (1965)
6. Mair, J., Laing, J.H.: Encouraging pro-environmental behaviour: the role of sustainability-focused events. . Journal of Sustainable Tourism 21(8), 1113–1128 (2013)
7. Riemsma, R.P., Pattenden, J., Bridle, C., Sowden, A.J., Mather, L., Watt, I., Walker, A.: A systematic review of the effectiveness of interventions based on a stages-of-change approach to promote individual behaviour change in health care settings. Health Technology Assessment 6(24), 1–242 (2002)
8. Yun, R., Scupelli, P., Aziz, A., Loftness, V.: Sustainability in the Workplace: Nine Intervention Techniques for Behavior Change. In: Berkovsky, S., Freyne, J. (eds.) PERSUASIVE 2013. LNCS, vol. 7822, pp. 253–265. Springer, Heidelberg (2013)
9. Piotrow, P.T., Kincaid, D.L., Rimon II, J.G., Rinehart, W.: Health communication: lessons from family planning and reproductive health (1997)
10. Prochaska, J.O., Velicer, W.F.: The transtheoretical model of health behavior change. American Journal of Health Promotion 12(1), 38–48 (1997)
11. Geller, E.S.: The challenge of increasing proenvironmental behavior. In: Betchel, R.B., Churchman, A. (eds.) Handbook of Environmental Psychology, New York, pp. 525–540 (2002)
12. Mercier, C., Moorefield, L.: Commercial office plug load savings and assessment: Final report. Produced by ECOVA and Supported Through the California Energy Commission's Public Interest Energy Research Program (2011)
13. Yun, R., Aziz, A., Lasternas, B., Zhang, C., Loftness, V., Scupelli, P., Mo, Y., Zhao, J., Wilberforce, N.: The Design and Evaluation of Intelligent Energy Dashboard for Sustainability in the Workplace. In: Marcus, A. (ed.) Proceedings, HCI International 2014. LNCS, vol. 8519, pp. 605–615. Springer, Heidelberg (2014)
14. Valente, T.W.: Evaluating health promotion programs. Oxford University Press, Oxford (2002)
15. Riemsma, R.P., Pattenden, J., Bridle, C., Sowden, A.J., Mather, L., Watt, I., Walker, A.: A systematic review of the effectiveness of interventions based on a stages-of-change approach to promote individual behaviour change in health care settings. Health Technology Assessment 6(24), 1–242 (2002)
16. Rogers, E.: Diffusion of innovations, 4th edn. The Free Press, New York (1995)
17. McGuire, W.J.: Theoretical foundations of campaigns. In: Rice, R.E., Atkins, C.K. (eds.) Public Communication Campaigns, pp. 39–42. Sage Publications, Newbury Park (1989)
18. Prochaska, J.O., Velicer, W.F., DiClemente, C.C., Fava, J.L.: Measuring the processes of change: Applications to the cessation of smoking. Journal of Consulting and Clinical Psychology 56, 520–528 (1988)
19. O'Connell, D., Velicer, W.F.: A decisional balance measure for weight loss. The International Journal of Addictions 23, 729–750 (1988)

Public Perception and Acceptance of Electric Vehicles: Exploring Users' Perceived Benefits and Drawbacks

Martina Ziefle[1], Shirley Beul-Leusmann[1], Kai Kasugai[1], and Maximilian Schwalm[2]

[1] Human-Computer-Interaction Center, RWTH Aachen University, Germany
{ziefle,beul,kasugai}@comm.rwth-aachen.de
[2] Institute for Automotive Engineering, RWTH Aachen University, Germany
schwalm@ika.rwth-aachen.de

Abstract. In this research, we describe an empirical study, which aimed at identifying influencing factors on acceptance of electric vehicles. Understanding individual arguments and to reach a high usage rate of these vehicles in the public and a broad acceptance, the identification of possible pro-using motives as well as perceived drawbacks is essential, which would allow a sensitive and individually-tailored communication and information policy. Using an exploratory approach, a questionnaire study was carried out in which participants were requested to indicate the level of acceptance and the intention to use electric cars. The questionnaire items were taken from several focus groups, which had been carried out prior to the questionnaire study. Outcomes show that the traditional car is perceived still as much more comfortable, and receives a high trustfulness in comparison to electric cars. In addition, user diversity in terms of age and gender was found to considerably the perceived benefits and barriers. Female users but also aged persons show a higher level of acceptance, which might be due to their higher environmental consciousness in contrast to male persons and younger participants. Interestingly, the self-reported level of domain knowledge (significantly higher in men) did not show a large influence on the level of acceptance.

Keywords: Electro-Mobility, electric vehicles, technology acceptance, user diversity, adoption behavior of novel technologies.

1 Motivation and Related Work

Facing the increasing threat through climate change, CO_2-emissions and the thereby caused air pollution, the area-wide roll-out of electric vehicles might be an adequate escape from shortcomings of fossil oil resources [1]. From a technical point of view, alternative vehicles, such as plug-in hybrid electric vehicles, are –technologically– quite mature and thus might serve as valuable alternatives to traditional car technology [2] [3]. The potential of electric mobility has been studied in recent research from a technical [4] [5] [6], economic [7], logistic [8], environmental [9] and inner-urban [10][11] [12] point of view. However, research showed also that there is considerable struggle for electric vehicles to create appropriate markets [13], at least

A. Marcus (Ed.): DUXU 2014, Part III, LNCS 8519, pp. 628–639, 2014.

in Germany. A high consumer acceptance for alternative fuel vehicles is an important prerequisite to determine the practicality of a successful implementation [14]. Still, however, there is a far-reaching reluctance to accept a novel mobility concept in urban environments [15]. Speculating, the reluctance of citizens towards electric mobility and novel developments in the automotive sector might have very different reasons.

First, traditional experiences with cars could be an influential factor. For a long time, citizens value the huge potential of having a car, connected to the feeling of independence (in time and space) and universal access, which has a profound tradition in history [16]. Car consumption has always been much more than mere rational choice [17]. Car consumption represents a behavior that is naturally linked to emotional attitudes, social esteem and branding [18] [19] [20]. A second factor to adopt novel instead of an old, traditional and highly conversant technology is related to the willingness of citizens to tolerate risks as well as uncertainties in how far the novel technology bring more than the traditional technology does [21] [22] [23]. In this context, technology acceptance and social reasons of technology adopting behavior comes into fore [24] [25] [26]. A third factor for the reluctance to adopt novel technology is the user diversity and the increasing diffusion of modern technology with a diversely skilled user group [27] [28] [29] [30]. Especially age and gender are crucial factors, which might influence substantially the adoption behavior of novel technology [31] [32] [33]. A forth point regards the usability, the ease of using the technical system and its perceived usefulness [34] [35] [36]. Also the way information presentation is delivered [37] [38] [39] is a key factor that determines the technology acceptance and the readiness of users to adopt a novel technology [40] [41].

While those human factors are sufficiently examined in information and communication technology [42], still, for electric mobility there is yet not sufficient knowledge about perceived benefits and barriers.

2   Questions Addressed and Logic of the Exploratory Approach

In this study we focus on user opinions regarding the use of traditional car technology in comparison to electric cars. Understanding the individual motives and barriers in the context of novel car technology is a highly relevant topic for modern societies. In order to learn which using motives militate in favor of using these technologies and which kind of using barriers are prevalent, we take user diversity in terms of age and gender as a specific focus.

There is a considerable need to explore and to understand the components contributing to users' acceptance of electronic car technologies. Regarding the specific information needs and the requirements for a sensitive communication strategy it is important to learn which of the reported pro-using motives and barriers are more decisive than others and which of both, using arguments or barriers is prominently influencing the intention to use electric car technology. Outcomes are expected to allow insights into the major public opinion drivers for and against electric mobility. This is not only be useful for taking acceptance issues into account, but may also elucidate the public awareness of a diligent information politics and communication rationale in this field.

3   Method

3.1   Variables and Procedure

As independent variable the type of vehicle (car vs. E-car), gender and age (young: 20-40 years, middle-aged: 41-60 years, older: 61-75 years) were examined. Dependent variable was the level of acceptance (benefits) and non-acceptance (barriers). As both, benefits and barriers might be based on different arguments, we examined environmental-related, cost-related, comfort-related, trust-related and technology-related argumentations for both, benefits and barriers, when using cars and electric cars. All participants evaluated the benefits and barriers for both vehicle types in succession. Avoiding sequence effects, the order of items related to cars (benefits/barriers) and E-cars (benefits/barriers) was altered across participants.

3.2   Questionnaire

In order to collect comprehensive opinions and to reflect them across a broader sample of women and men of different ages, we chose the questionnaire-method. The items and sections used in the questionnaire were based on previous empirical work in our workgroup, in which we collected argumentation patterns and user experience (focus groups) of female and male persons of a wide age range [36] [37] [38]. The questionnaire was delivered online (filling in took about 40 minutes). The questionnaire was arranged in five main sections (Figure 2).

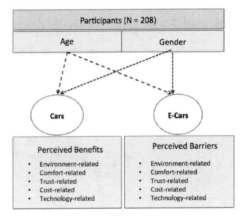

Fig. 1. Structure of the questionnaire

Demographic Data: The first part included demographic data.

Benefits /Barriers of cars: The second part focused on pro-using and con-using arguments regarding the use of cars. The motives and barriers were conceptualized along five dimensions (identified on the base of user argumentations in the focus groups which had been carried out prior to the questionnaire study: environment-related arguments, cost-related arguments, comfort-related arguments, trust-related arguments as well as technology-related arguments. Items had to be answered on a Likert Scale (1 = I do not agree at all, 4 = I completely agree). Per dimension, we used three items and summarized the answers to an overall score (due to analysing purposes).

Benefits /Barriers of E-cars: The third focused on pro-using and con-using arguments regarding the use of E-cars. Again, the motives and barriers were conceptualized along the five dimensions (environment, comfort, costs, trust and technology). Note that these dimensions were used for benefits and barriers likewise. In Table 1, exemplary items are given.

Table 1. Item examples for the evaluations of benefits and barriers of cars and E-cars. Items had to be answered on a Likert Scale (1 = I do not agree at all, 4 = I completely agree).

Car: Benefits	I use/would use a car, because
Environment	... filters reduce the pollution of the environment
Costs	... taxes and insurances have reasonable costs
Comfort	... driving experience is fine
Trust	... my car has never run out on me
Technology	... care technology has a long tradition
Car: Barriers	**I do not use/would not use a car, because**
Environment	... fossil resources are scarce
Costs	... purchase of a car is too expensive
Comfort	... long trips with the car are bothersome
Trust	... there are too many accidents
Technology	... I do not understand current car electronics any more
E-car: Benefits	**I use/would use an e- car, because**
Environment	... electric mobility safes the environment
Costs	... it is affordable on the long run
Comfort	... driving noise is reduced
Trust	... novel technology is up-to-date
Technology	...electric mobility is the future
E-car: Barriers	**I do not use/would not use an e-car, because**
Environment	... it still consumes electricity produced by nuclear power
Costs	... accessory charges are high
Comfort	... I do not want to plan the refueling exactly
Trust	... electricity is not trustworthy for me
Technology	... technology is not yet mature enough

3.3   Participants

Overall, 208 persons in an age range of 18-75 years of age took part (51% were mal, 49% female). All of them were experienced drivers and had a high education. Participants were reached through the social networks of younger and older adults and reacted to advertisements in the local newspaper. Participants were not gratified for their efforts. In order to learn about the level of domain knowledge about electric mobility participants had to indicate their self-reported knowledge (Likert scale, 1= very low, 4 = very high). Figure 1 shows the descriptive outcomes. While age groups had a comparable knowledge, women reported a significantly lower domain knowledge than men (F1,207) = 61.2, p<0.00).

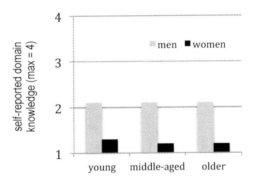

Fig. 2. Descriptive outcomes regarding the self-reported knowledge in electric mobility

4   Results

The data was analyzed by using multivariate analyses of variance (MANOVA) and variance analyses for repeated measurements, if applicable. The significance level was set at 5%. Significance outcomes within the less restrictive 10% level were referred to as marginally significant.

4.1   Evaluation of Benefits, Contrasting Cars and E-cars

A first analysis regards the evaluation of benefits for cars and E-cars, respectively. In order to get insights into the main argumentation line, items were summed up for each of the five categories.

The MANOVA yielded a significant effect of the vehicle type regarding environmental-related benefits (F(1,202)=105.9; p<0.000), for cost-related benefits (F(1,202)=27.7 p<0.00, also for comfort-related benefits (F(1,202)=37.9 p<0.00 and for trust-related arguments (F(1,202)=31.6 p<0.00. Interestingly, technology related benefit perceptions did not differ between car and e-car (n.s.). In Figure 2, descriptive results are given evaluations (Cars: gray bars; E-cars: black bars).

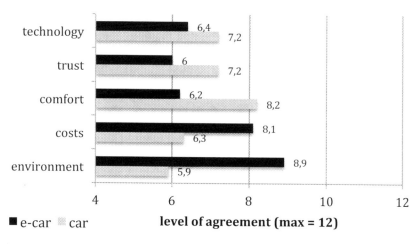

Fig. 3. Level of agreement (means) for the total group regarding perceived benefits on different argumentation dimensions for cars and e-cars (4 = not at all, 12 = completely agree)

Both vehicle types differ distinctly in all categories. Apparently, the perceived benefits of using a car are diametrically opposite to the benefits, which militate in favor of the E-car. User diversity is a critical factor that significantly influenced the perception of the benefits. In Table 2, the outcomes regarding the impact of user diversity on perceived benefits is presented (age and gender as well as interacting effects).

Table 2. Perceived benefits: User diversity (age, gender) as well as 2 and 3-way interactions

Dimension	Age	Gender	2-way interaction	3-way interaction
Environment	--	F (1,202)=16.9; p<0.03	vehicle x gender (F(1,202)=4.5; p<0.04	vehicle x gender x age F(1,202)=2.4; p<0.09
Costs	--	--	vehicle x gender F(1,202)=4.9; p<0.04 vehicle x age F(1,202)=7.7; p<0.01	--
Comfort	--	--	vehicle x age F(1,202)=3.5; p<0.03	--
Trust	--	--	--	--
Technology	--	--	vehicle x age F(1,202)=7.7; p<0.01	--

Regarding environmental benefits, women report stronger environmental benefits in the E-car, especially with increasing age (three fold interaction, Figure 3). When focusing on costs, 2-way interactions of vehicle type x gender (F(1,202)=4.9; p<0.04) and vehicle type x age (F(1,202)=7.7; p<0.01) were found. The benefit was perceived more strongly in women and with increasing age (Figure 4).

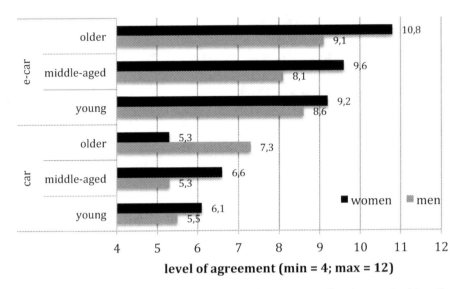

Fig. 4. 3-way interacting effect of age x gender x vehicle type regarding the perceived benefits in terms of environment protection (4 = not at all, 12 = completely agree)

It is highly insightful that one and the same argument – cost saving – is used for both vehicle types as a benefit, though with different connotations ("E-cars are more cost saving on the long run" vs." tax and assurance is less costly in cars"). Another interesting finding regards the interaction between vehicle type x age for the perceived comfort (Figure 5).

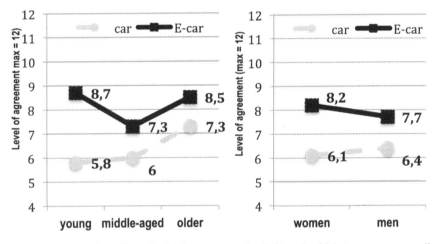

Fig. 5. 2-way interacting effect of vehicle type x gender (left) and vehicle type x age regarding the perceived benefits in terms of costs (4 = not at all, 12 = completely agree)

The comfort perception is related to age: With increasing age, the perceived comfort is rated as more advantageous, especially in the traditional car.

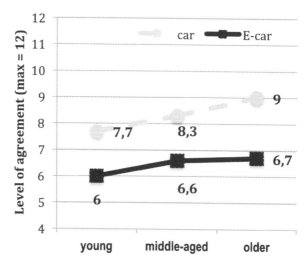

Fig. 6. 2-way interaction of vehicle type x age regarding the perceived comfort (4 = not at all, 12 = completely agree)

4.2   Evaluation of Barriers, Contrasting Cars and E-cars

A next analysis regarded the perceived barriers of using cars and E-cars, respectively. Again, first the descriptive outcomes with respect to the nature of the seen disadvantages are depicted (along the five dimensions, Figure 4).

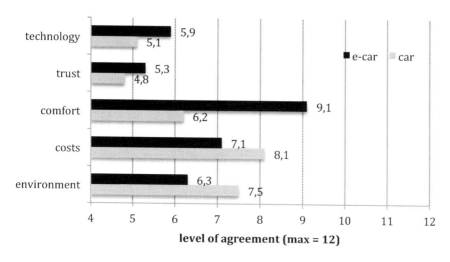

Fig. 7. Level of agreement (means) for the total group regarding perceived barriers for cars (gray bars) and e-cars (black bars) (4 = not at all, 12 = completely agree)

As can bee taken from Figure 4, perceptions of barriers using a traditional car in comparison to the E-car differ distinctly from each other, in nearly all argumentation lines.

Significant differences between both vehicle types regard environmental-related barriers ($F(1,202)=156.2$; $p<0.000$), cost-related barriers ($F(1,202)=5.5$ $p<0.02$, also comfort-related barriers ($F(1,202)=168.1$ $p<0.00$ and technology-related disadvantages ($F(1,202)=9.3$ $p<0.03$. Trust did not impact the perceived disadvantages for neither vehicle technology. For the perceptions of barriers, user diversity did not play a major role neither when using a car noir an E-car. (Table 3).

Only age impacted the perceptions of negative costs (the younger participants, the higher were the perceived costs in both vehicle types).

Table 3. Perceived barriers: User diversity (age, gender) as well as 2 and 3-way interactions

Dimension	Age	Gender	2-way interaction	3-way interaction
Environment	--	--	--	--
Costs	$F(1,202)=23.9$; $p<0.01$	--	--	--
Comfort	--	--	--	--
Trust	--	--	--	--
Technology	--	--	--	--

4.3   Effects of Domain Knowledge on Perceived Benefits and Barriers

A final analysis regarded the question if the self-reported knowledge about electric mobility does impact the acceptance. One could have expected that persons with a high information level in the context of electric mobility ground their attitudes for or against a novel technology on a deeper understanding in comparison to persons, which rely predominately on a quite superficial public knowledge. Correlation analyses (Spearman Rho) revealed only marginal relations between domain knowledge and acceptance. Interestingly though, domain knowledge did not impact any of the perceived benefit arguments (in neither dimension), but impacted mainly the perceived barriers (in both vehicle types).

Car: With increasing knowledge, the more negative are the perceived environmental consequences($r = -1.6$; $p<0.05$), the less negative are the perceived costs ($r =-1.7$ $p<0.05$) and the less negative are the perceptions of the car technology ($r =-1.4$ $p<0.05$). E-car: The more participants reported to have high domain knowledge of electric mobility, the lower are perceived costs ($r =-1.6$ $p<0.05$), perceived risks ($r=-3.2$ $p<y.0.05$) and potential technology barriers ($r =-1.6$ $p<y.0.05$).

5   Discussion and Future Research

Overall, this study yielded insights into users' attitudes towards electric cars (in comparison to traditional car technology). Main arguments against electric cars are the low comfort and technological barriers (in terms of availability of charging stations). In contrast, the comfort perception (including design, feel and looks as well as optics) in traditional care technology is still perceived as much higher compared to the electric car, especially with increasing age.

Gender and age were significant drivers of acceptance, especially in women, which have a higher environmental consciousness in comparison to men. User diversity though did not play a major role in the explanation of barriers. Apparently, the arguments militating against the use of both vehicles types are not modulated by age and gender but represent a quite generic view, what has implications for public information and communication strategies.

However even if the findings here represent a valuable insight into users' attitudes, there is also a cautionary note. Respecting the validity of empirical findings it is of crucial importance, whether the acceptance towards a novel technology is examined in persons, already using electric cars and having practical experience with the technology. Critically, one could argue that novices cannot "feel" the potential of electric mobility as long as they do not rely on real operating experience. Even if this argument cannot be dismissed, there is still a knowledge gap about the public discourse and potential ambivalent attitudes to electric mobility, in combination with individual beliefs, uncertainty as well as perceptions of potential benefits and risks. The understanding of individual beliefs and general attitudes are of crucial impact as the public opinion also considerably impacts on the cognitive mind setting of future users. Therefore, we selected a quite uninformed sample of a wide age range, to get a broad insight into attitudes. In future studies though we will examine expert users and explore also attitudes towards electric mobility in the context of public transport.

Acknowledgements: This research was funded by the German Ministry of Economics and Technology (reference no. 01 ME 12052). Authors thank Firat Alagöz, Barbara Zaunbrecher, Julia van Heek and Julian Hildebrandt for research support.

References

1. Neumann, I., Cocron, P., Franke, T., Krems, J.F.: Electric Vehicles as a Solution for Green Driving in the Future? A Field Study Examining the User Acceptance of Electric Vehicles. In: Proceedings of European Conference on Human Centred Design for Intelligent Transport Systems, pp. 445–453 (2010)
2. Claas, B., Marker, S., Bickert, S., Linssen, J., Strunz, K.: Integration of Plug-In Hybrid and Electric Vehicles: Experience from Germany. In: 2010 IEEE Power and Energy Society General Meeting, pp. 1–3. IEEE (2011)
3. Winter, M., Kunze, M., Lex-Balducci, A.: Into a Future of Electromobility. German Research 32, 20–24 (2010)

4. Werther, B., Hoch, N.: E-Mobility as a Challenge for New ICT Solutions in the Car Industry. In: Bruni, R., Sassone, V. (eds.) TGC 2011. LNCS, vol. 7173, pp. 46–57. Springer, Heidelberg (2012)

5. Frischknecht, R., Flury, K.: Life Cycle Assessment of Electric Mobility: Answers and Challenges. International Journal of Life Cycle Assessment 16, 691–695 (2011)

6. Labeye, E., Adrian, J., Hugot, M., Regan, M.A., Brusque, C.: Daily Use of an Electric Vehicle: Behavioural Changes and Potential for ITS Support. IET Intelligent Transport Systems 7, 210–214 (2013)

7. Kley, F., Lerch, C., Dallinger, D.: New Business Models for Electric Cars: A Holistic Approach. Energy Policy 39, 3392–3403 (2011)

8. Ehrler, V., Hebes, P.: Electromobility for City Logistics: The Solution to Urban Transport Collapse? Procedia-Social and Behavioral Sciences 48, 786–795 (2012)

9. Sourkounis, C., Ni, B., Broy, A.: Pollution of High Power Charging Electric Vehicles in Urban Distribution Grids. In: 2011 7th International Conference-Workshop on Compatibility and Power Electronics (CPE), pp. 34–39. IEEE (2011)

10. Schaumann, H.: Development of a Concept for Inner-City Delivery & Supply Utilising Electromobility. In: Efficiency and Logistics, pp. 121–127. Springer, Berlin (2013)

11. von Radecki, A.: Transition Management Towards Urban Electro Mobility in the Stuttgart Region. In: Evolutionary Paths Towards the Mobility Patterns of the Future, pp. 203–223. Springer, Heidelberg (2014)

12. Solar, A., Bolovinou, A., Heijenk, G., Lasgouttes, J.M., Giménez, R.: Mobility 2.0: Co-Operative ITS Systems for Enhanced Personal Electromobility. In: 27th International Electrical Vehicle Symposium & Exhibition, EVS27 (2013)

13. Yu, A.S.O., Silva, L.L.C., Chu, C.L., Nascimento, P.T.S., Camargo, A.S.: Electric Vehicles: Struggles in Creating a Market. In: 2011 Proceedings of PICMET 2011, Technology Management in the Energy Smart World (PICMET), pp. 1–13. IEEE (2011)

14. Steinhilber, S., Wells, P., Thankappan, S.: Socio-Technical Inertia: Understanding the Barriers to Electric Vehicles. Energy Policy (2013)

15. Hoffmann, C., Hinkeldein, D., Graff, A., Kramer, S.: What Do Potential Users Think About Electric Mobility? In: Evolutionary Paths Towards the Mobility Patterns of the Future, pp. 85–99. Springer, Heidelberg (2014)

16. Kirsch, D.A.: The electric vehicle and the burden of history (2000)

17. Motavalli, J.: Forward Drive: The Race to Build the Clean Car of the Future. Routledge (2012)

18. Scheller, M.: Automotive Emotion: Sensual Velocities and the Ethics of Car Consumption. Department of Sociology, Lancaster University (2002) (under review)

19. Sheller, M.: Automotive emotions feeling the car. Theory, Culture & Society 21(4-5), 221–242 (2004)

20. Dohle, S., Keller, C., Siegrist, M.: Conjoint Measurement of Base Station Siting Preferences. Hum. Ecol. Risk Assess. Int. J. 16, 825–836 (2010)

21. Joffe, H.: Risk: From perception to social representation. Br. J. Soc. Psychol. 42, 55–73 (2003)

22. Kasperson, R.E., Renn, O., Slovic, P.: The social amplification of risk: A conceptual framework. Risk Anal. 8, 177–187 (1988)

23. Arning, K., Kowalewski, S., Ziefle, M.: Health Concerns vs. Mobile Data Needs: Conjoint Measurement of Preferences for Mobile Communication Network Scenarios. Hum. Ecol. Risk Assess. Int. J. (2013), doi:10.1080/10807039.2013.838127

24. Bühler, F., Franke, T., Krems, J.F.: Usage patterns of electric vehicles as a reliable indicator for acceptance? Findings from a German field study. Transportation Research Board 90th Annual Meeting No. 11-0227 (2011)

25. Callon, M.: The sociology of an actor network: the case of the electric vehicle. In: Callon, M., Law, J., Rip, A. (eds.) Mapping the Dynamics of Science and Technology, pp. 19–34. MacMillan, London (1986)

26. Davis, F.D.: Perceived Usefulness, Perceived Ease of Use, and User Acceptance of Information Technology. MIS Q. 13, 319–340 (1989)

27. Venkatesh, V., Davis, F.D.: A Model of the Antecedents of Perceived Ease of Use: Development and Test. Decis. Sci. 27, 451–481 (1996)

28. Melenhorst, A.-S., Rogers, W.A., Bouwhuis, D.G.: Older Adults' Motivated Choice for Technological Innovation: Evidence for Benefit-Driven Selectivity. Psychol. Aging 21, 190–195 (2006)

29. Gaul, S., Ziefle, M.: Smart Home Technologies: Insights into Generation-Specific Acceptance Motives. In: Holzinger, A., Miesenberger, K. (eds.) USAB 2009. LNCS, vol. 5889, pp. 312–332. Springer, Heidelberg (2009)

30. Arning, K., Ziefle, M.: Different Perspectives on Technology Acceptance: The Role of Technology Type and Age. In: Holzinger, A., Miesenberger, K. (eds.) USAB 2009. LNCS, vol. 5889, pp. 20–41. Springer, Heidelberg (2009)

31. Arning, K., Ziefle, M.: Understanding age differences in PDA acceptance and performance. Comput. Hum. Behav. 23, 2904–2927 (2007)

32. Wilkowska, W., Ziefle, M.: Which Factors Form Older Adults' Acceptance of Mobile Information and Communication Technologies? In: Holzinger, A., Miesenberger, K. (eds.) USAB 2009. LNCS, vol. 5889, pp. 81–101. Springer, Heidelberg (2009)

33. Wilkowska, W., Ziefle, M.: User diversity as a challenge for the integration of medical technology into future home environments. In: Human-Centred Design of eHealth Technologies, pp. 95–126. IGI Global, Hershey (2011)

34. Carp, F.M.: Significance of mobility for the well-being of the elderly. In: Transportation in an Aging Society: Improving Mobility and Safety of Older Persons, pp. 1–20 (1988)

35. Wilkowska, W., Farrokhikhiavi, R., Ziefle, M., Vallée, D.: Mobility Requirements for the Use of Carpooling Among Different User Groups. In: 1st International Symposium on Human Factors, Software & Systems Engineering. CRC Press, Boca Raton (2014)

36. Beul-Leusmann, S., Samsel, C., Wiederhold, M., Krempels, K.-H., Jakobs, E.-M., Ziefle, M.: Usability evaluation of mobile passenger information systems. In: Marcus, A. (ed.) DUXU 2014, Part I. LNCS, vol. 8517, pp. 217–228. Springer, Heidelberg (2014)

37. Peischl, B., Ziefle, M., Holzinger, A.: A Mobile Information System for Improved Navigation in Public Transport. In: DCNET/ICE-B/OPTICS, pp. 217–221 (2012)

38. Schaar, A.K., Ziefle, M.: Potential of eTravel Assistants to Increase Older Adults' Mobility. In: Leitner, G., Hitz, M., Holzinger, A. (eds.) USAB 2010. LNCS, vol. 6389, pp. 138–155. Springer, Heidelberg (2010)

39. Samsel, C., Beul, S., Wiederhold, M., Krempels, K.-.H., Ziefle, M., Jakobs, E.-.M.: Cascading Information for Public transport. In: IEEE, WEBIST 2013, pp. 1–12 (2014)

40. Ziefle, M., Pappachan, P., Jakobs, E.-M., Wallentowitz, H.: Visual and Auditory Interfaces of Advanced Driver Assistant Systems for Older Drivers. In: Miesenberger, K., Klaus, J., Zagler, W.L., Karshmer, A.I. (eds.) ICCHP 2008. LNCS, vol. 5105, pp. 62–69. Springer, Heidelberg (2008)

41. Ziefle, M.: Modelling Mobile Devices for the Elderly. In: Khalid, H., Hedge, A., Ahram, T.Z. (eds.) Advances in Ergonomics Modeling and Usability Evaluation, pp. 280–290. CRC Press, Boca Raton (2010)

42. Arning, K., Gaul, S., Ziefle, M.: "Same Same but Different". How Service Contexts of Mobile Technologies Shape Usage Motives and Barriers. In: Leitner, G., Hitz, M., Holzinger, A. (eds.) USAB 2010. LNCS, vol. 6389, pp. 34–54. Springer, Heidelberg (2010)

Design for Human-Computer Symbiosis

FX e-Makeup for Muscle Based Interaction

Katia Vega[1], Abel Arrieta[2], Felipe Esteves[3], and Hugo Fuks[1]

[1] Department of Informatics, PUC-Rio, Rio de Janeiro, Brazil
{kvega,hugo}@inf.puc-rio.br
[2] Department of Mechanical Engineering, PUC-Rio, Rio de Janeiro, Brazil
abel.arrieta@aluno.puc-rio.br
[3] Department of Administration, PUC-Rio, Rio de Janeiro, Brazil
felipeesteves@aluno.puc-rio.br

Abstract. Our aim with Beauty Technology is to transform our body in an interactive platform by hiding technology into beauty products for creating muscle based interfaces that don't give the wearer a cyborg look. FX e-makeup is a Beauty Technology prototype that applies FX makeup materials embedded with electronics for sensing the face's muscles. This work presents Winkymote and Kinisi as proof of concept of the FX e-makeup.

Keywords: Wearable Computers, Beauty Technology, Electronic Makeup, Muscle Based Interface.

1 Introduction

Beauty Technology transforms our body in an interactive platform by making use of makeup that stealthily integrates technology on the body. FX e-makeup is a new Beauty Technology prototype that makes use of special effects makeup that hides electronic components and is applied to the face for sensing its muscles, acting as a second skin. Two applications will be presented, namely, Winkymote, an infrared remote control for individuals with quadriplegic disability and Kinisi, an artistic makeup that acts as an empowered second skin for triggering multiple devices.

In previous studies [1, 2, 3], Beauty Technology prototypes were developed using conductive makeup (for connecting sensors and actuators on the face) and black fake eyelashes that were chemically metalized for acting as blinking switches. In order to prove the feasibility of the Conductive Makeup Prototype as a conductive component, some applications were developed. Blinklifier uses blinking for switching LEDs on and off on an artistic head dress. Arcana uses blinking for changing music tracks and images visualizations. Superhero is another artistic application that makes use of Conductive Makeup for triggering a remote control to levitate an object.

In this work, we propose FX e-makeup, another prototype that is focused on the human agency for controlling devices by sensing voluntary movements of face's muscles. It differs from: Vision Computing that provides methods for facial expression analysis by automatically recognizing facial motions and facial feature changes from visual information [4]; Biopotential sensors such as Electroencephalogram (EEG),

A. Marcus (Ed.): DUXU 2014, Part III, LNCS 8519, pp. 643–652, 2014.
© Springer International Publishing Switzerland 2014

Electromyogram (EMG), and Electrooculogram (EOG) that have been used as inputs for several healthcare devices [5]; and Brain- Computer Interfaces that links the computer to the human nervous and muscular system for recognizing user's gestures in several hands free interfaces [6-8].

Section 2 identifies previous works on recognition of facial muscle movements. Section 3 describes our approach of creating a second skin a combination of FX makeup and sensors for sensing facial movements where a muscle movement is interpreted as commands to devices. Section 4 shows Winkymote a proof of concept of this technology that is geared for individuals with quadriplegic disabilities. Section 5 presents Kinisi, an artistic FX e-makeup application that tries to answer the question: "Could your skin act as an interface?" Section 6 reviews the lessons learned from prototyping and using FX e-makeup. Conclusion and future work are shown in the last section.

2   Related Work

In past decades, significant effort has been done in developing techniques for sensing facial expressions [9]. A facial expression originates from the motion of the muscles beneath the skin of the face. Involuntary movements convey the emotional state of an individual to observers in a non verbal communication.

Micro-movements involve facial muscles actions which are triggered by the nerve impulses generated by emotions. Maximally Discriminative Facial Movement Coding System (MAX) [10] and Facial Action Coding System (FACS) [11] are observational coding systems to identify micro-movements thought to be associated with emotion. All possible facial displays are coded in 44 action units that represent a set or an individual muscle movement [11]. Traditionally, FACS' measurements are done by experts' observation [12]. However, thanks to the advances of technology, there are other techniques that support the action units' recognition like Computational Vision techniques that senses movements and gestures, and reproduce them in a 3D environment [13]. Unfortunately, they present some issues like occlusion and lighting limiting their sensing opportunities [14]. Bartlett et al. [15] uses a neural network approach to detect six individual action units combining holistic spatial analysis and optical flow with local feature analysis. Cohn et al. [16] uses facial feature point tracking and discriminant function analysis. Pantic et al. [17] uses face-profile-contour tracking and rule-based reasoning to recognize 20 action units.

For the purpose of this work we are interested in sensing voluntary movements. When humans initiate a voluntary action, the brain sends an electrochemical signal that traverses our nervous system through the spinal cord and eventually reaches the motor neurons. They stimulate specific muscles causing movement or force [18]. Non-vision techniques for identifying voluntary actions include Electromyogram (EMG) that is based on electrical measurement of the potential difference between two muscles. There are some known issues about using EMG [12] such as the placement of the leads on the face inhibits the subject movement, ambiguities on the measure due to the proximity of the muscles and no specific place for putting the electrodes. Figure 1.a show a head-mounted measurement device that senses the intensity of facial activity [19]. The muscles responsible for raising the eyebrows, lowering the eyebrows, raising the mouth corners, and pulling down the mouth corners are measured simultaneously with a capacitive method and EMG. Figure 1.b shows Manabe using electric sensors to stimulate muscles in his face in synchronization with music [20]. Another example is a Tongue Computer Interface that was developed for patients with paralyzing injuries or medical conditions. Infrared optical sensors are embedded within a dental retainer in order to sense explicit tongue movements [21].

Fig. 1. a) Measuring upper face movements with a Head-Mounted Measurement Device [19]. b) Music created by face muscle movements [20].

A Beauty Technology prototype that senses blinking using a non-vision technique approach is the Conductive Makeup [22]. It is an aesthetic interface that detects voluntary blinking by embedded electronics into conductive eyeliner and eyelashes. Conductive eyeliner connects sensors and actuators by using conductive materials that stick to the skin. Conductive fake eyelashes are plastic eyelashes that are chemically metalized. FX e-makeup hides the conductive makeup inside a latex material that matches skin colour. The following session describes the design of this technology.

3   FX e-makeup

The senses of agency and of body ownership are two aspects in the bodily self which must be distinguished to identify different effects in body awareness [23]. A person has the capacity to act in the world through his sense of agency. Thus, intending and executing actions include the feeling of controlling one's own body movements, and, through them, events in the external environment [24]. Only voluntary actions produce a sense of agency and it is originated in neural processes responsible for the motor aspects of action [25]. On the other hand, the sense of body ownership refers to the understanding that the person's own body is the source of her movements or sensations, whether it was voluntary or not [24]. During a voluntary action, sensor mechanisms generate a sense of body ownership; however, only action provides a coherent sense of the whole body. Thus, the unity of bodily self-consciousness comes from action and not from sensation [26]. In this work, we propose an interface that makes use of sense of agency inherent in humans to augment their capacities through voluntary muscle movements.

The muscles of the face are divided into two groups according to the function they serve: mastication muscles (four muscles attached to the bone and ligament that are mainly used for chewing and have a minor effect on expression) and expressive or "mimitic" muscles [26]. Facial expressions are caused by the movement of the mimitic muscles that are attached to the skin and fascia in the face, unlike other skeletal muscles that are attached to the bones. This group of muscles move the skin, creating lines, folds and wrinkles, causing the movement of facial features, such as mouth and eyebrows. [26]. FX e-makeup sensors act as switches when strategically placed on these muscles.

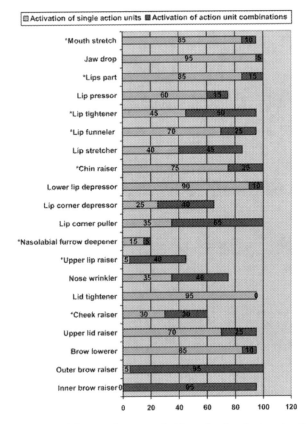

Fig. 2. Percentage of participants who succeeded in activating the target action units [29]

Duchenne de Boulogne [27] found that some muscles that are activated by emotions are difficult to activate voluntarily. Ekman et. al. [28] also addresses the same difficulty in voluntary movements but got different results when children were asked to voluntarily activate muscular actions by imitating a model presented on a video monitor. Gosselin et. al. [29] report is based on FACS to determine the extent to which adults are able to voluntarily produce facial muscular actions and also to discover the muscles that could be activated without the co-activation of other unwanted muscles. Twenty participants were asked to produce 20 facial action units, reproducing five times each action. Figure 2 indicates the percentage of participants who were able to activate the target action units at least once [29].

Based on this report, we identified the action units that will be used in our study. FACS' action units plus combinations that achieved more than 95% of success (except for the lip pressor that achieved roughly 75% of success) and have fewer associations with other movements were the ones that were considered in this work: jaw drop, lips part, lip corner puller, lid tightener, outer low brow raiser and lip pressor. Jaw drop and lips part action units had no associated movements. The lip corner puller action unit is associated with the check raiser action unit and the outer brow raiser is associated with the inner brow raiser one: in both cases, the associated movement is not constantly repeated. The chin raiser was the action unit most associated with other movements (5 times). The lower lip depressor has the chin raiser action unit as an associated movement. Both action units were discarded. The lid tightener action unit achieved 95% of success and got the lowest percent of associated movements. Figure 3.a shows the sensors on these muscles.

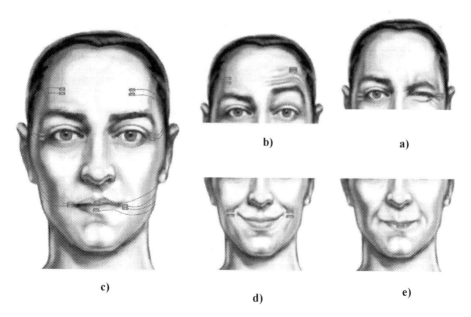

Fig. 3. FX e-makeup interface

Figure 3.b shows the sensor located on the brow, associated with the outer low brow raiser action unit, and it is activated when the user raises his eyebrow and both contacts of the sensors are touched. Figure 3.c shows the eyelid sensor (associate with the lid tightener action unit) that senses blinking when the lid is tightener and both contacts are touched. Figure 3.d shows the sensor associated with the Jaw drop, lips part, lip corner puller action units. It senses a smile when there is no contact, in an opposite way of the other sensors. Finally, the sensor on Figure 3.e is associated with the lip pressor action unit and it activates when both lips are pressed together. Wires are hidden with FX makeup materials like ink and latex.

4   Kinisi

Figure 4 presents Kinisi, a FX e-makeup application. It tries to answer the question: "Could your skin act as an interface?" with an artistic video [30] that exposes the use of FX e-makeup for activating different light patterns with smiles, winks, raised eyebrows and lips [30]. The voluntary movements approximate the points closing circuits. According to one's face, action units are identified and marked as it is show in Figures 4.a and 4.b. A first layer of latex is applied to isolate the skin from the electronics. Sensors are precisely glued to the latex mask on the chosen points. LEDs are placed on the mask and between braids. Finally, face paint was used for colouring the user's face black.

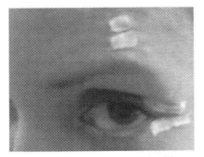

a) Eyebrow in a neutral position.

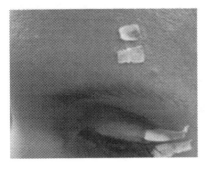

b) Eyebrow up closing the circuit.

c) Kinisi wearing FX e-makeup.

Fig. 4. Kinisi

5   Winkymote

Numerous approaches have been tried to develop technological solutions to facilitate independent communication and mobility for individuals with disabilities, among these the mouth stick, sensors activated by blinking, respiration and head movement [31, 32]. A communication interface controlled by voluntary blinking that activates infrared controlled devices simulating a remote control is being developed for individuals with quadriplegic disability.

Winkymote is inspired by Felipe, a 33-year-old master student in Administration. He hurt himself playing jujitsu and now has quadriplegic disability for 13 years. Felipe uses a speech recognition system keyboard replacement for controlling his computer but, unfortunately, depends on others to do common activities such as changing TV channels.

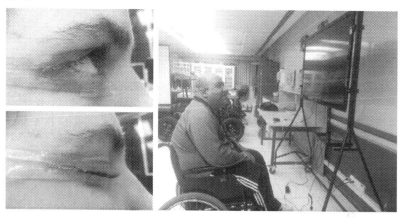

Fig. 5. Winkymote, an infrared-controlled interface for individuals with quadriplegic disability

Winkymote (Figure 5) is an infrared-controlled interface that uses FX e-makeup sensors connected to an infrared-transmitting module mounted on the user's necklace. These sensors are placed close to the outer end of each eye, i.e., close to the lid tightener action unit. They are connected through wires to the infrared-transmitting module mounted placed on his chest. Whenever he winks tightly, the switch closes sending a digital signal to the microcontroller that activates a sound feedback informing that an infrared LED is sending the appropriate sequences for triggering the TV. Blinking with his left or right or both eyes turns the TV on, off or change the channels up and down.

6   Discussion

The first FX e-makeup prototype comprised gelatine powder without flavour, distilled water and glycerine. This kind of FX makeup is often used for creating prosthetics such as wounds, scars, burns and blisters. Finding the proper makeup consistence of the makeup depends on its preparation given that it requires heating the ingredients. Our initial results were too thick and had the tendency to fell off depending on the skin properties and the user's movements. Three participants worn the makeup for 6 hours but it didn't work on Felipe, whose makeup fell off after 1 hour, because of his oily skin. After deciding to use hydrogel, which help to fix the electronics, we had to give up for the same reason: his oily skin. Finally, we decided for using liquid latex. It was applied to the skin using a disposable sponge taking about five minutes to dry. As it dries it turns to a rubbery consistency getting moulded to the user's skin. Then, more layers were applied to the skin for embedding and isolating the electronic components.

The face has over 40 anatomically independent muscles referred as specific action units that could be coactivated. The corrugator muscle group, for instance, which brings the brows down and together, is comprised of three muscles that are normally activated together. Although, the sensors on the FX e-makeup action units could operate independently, not combinations are possible like concurrently raising the left eyebrow and tighten the left eyelid, and raising each eyebrow independently.

Action units' activation differs in duration and intensity. Differently from previous works [1, 2, 3] where a preset time interval for sensing voluntary movements was defined, given that FX e-makeup sensors are precisely located, they are only activated when the intensity of the movement reaches a high level.

FX e-makeup may be used to control multiple devices. Sensors could be connected to a variety of devices providing user feedback and communication with other devices. For example, a device for changing slides (closing the right eye the presentation moves forward to the next slide) was prototyped for working with Winkymote.

7   Conclusion and Future Works

This work proposes FX e-makeup as a Beauty Technology prototype for sensing voluntary face's movements for triggering multiple devices. FX e-makeup is moulded as a second skin on the user's face for embedding electronics.

Action Units were selected based on a previous study that identifies the success rate to activate an action unit and the other muscle's movements associated with it. Jaw drop, lips part, lip corner puller, lid tightener, outer low brow raiser and lip pressor were the action units chosen as inputs for FX e-makeup. The FX e-makeup sensors acts as switches that are activated with the folding of the skin.

Two applications showed the feasibility of this technology. Kinisi is an artistic application that uses muscle movements for activating light patterns on the face and hairdo. Winkymote is an application for individuals with quadriplegic disability that controls infrared devices like TV sets.

Future work will include new Beauty Technology prototypes for sensing other facial action units via FX e-makeup. Sensors and their duration/intensity level combinations connected to other action units will be incorporated to FX e-makeup applications. We also intend to expand FX e-makeup sensors to explore neck movements for controlling different devices like air conditioning and hospital beds. Other future potential uses of this technology will explore novel hands free interfaces like dealing with amplifying or unnoticed gestures, keeping people awake, and decoding blinking gestures for physical and physiological analysis.

As seen above, there are several possibilities to turn FX e-makeup prototypes into products. Firstly, there are market challenges that should be overcome in order to deliver value to their potential customers. How to segment the market? Who are the potential targets? How to position the new products? These are decisions to be taken by the holders of this promising Muscle Based Interface technology in the future.

Acknowledgments. Katia Vega (grant 140859/2010-1) and Hugo Fuks (Project 302230/2008-4) are recipients of grants awarded by the National Research Council (CNPq). This work was partially financed by Research Support Foundation of the State of Rio de Janeiro-FAPERJ/INCT (E-26/170028/2008) and CNPq/INCT (557.128/2009-9).

References

1. Vega, K.F.C., Fuks, H.: Empowering electronic divas through beauty technology. In: Marcus, A. (ed.) DUXU/HCII 2013, Part III. LNCS, vol. 8014, pp. 237–245. Springer, Heidelberg (2013)
2. Vega, K.: Exploring the power of feedback loops in wearables computers. In: Proceedings of the 7th International Conference on Tangible, Embedded and Embodied Interaction, TEI 2013, pp. 371–372. ACM, New York (2013)
3. Vega, K., Fuks, H.: Beauty technology as an interactive computing platform. In: Proceedings of the 2013 ACM International Conference on Interactive Tabletops and Surfaces, ITS 2013, pp. 357–360. ACM, New York (2013)
4. Jain, A.K., Li, S.Z.: Handbook of Face Recognition. Springer-Verlag New York, Inc., Secaucus (2005)
5. Lin, M., Li, B.: A wireless EOG-based human computer interface. Biomedical Engineering and Informatics (BMEI) 5, 1794–1796 (2010)
6. Curran, E., Sykacek, P., Stokes, M., Roberts, S., Penny, W., Johnsrude, I., Owen, A.: Cognitive tasks for driving a brain-computer interfacing system: a pilot study. IEEE Transactions on Neural Systems and Rehabilitation Engineering 12(1), 48–54 (2004)
7. Tanaka, K., Matsunaga, K., Kanamori, N., Hori, S., Wang, H.: Electroencephalogram-based control of a mobile robot. In: IEEE International Symposium on Computational Intelligence in Robotics and Automation, vol. 2, pp. 688–693 (2003)
8. Fabiani, G., McFarland, D., Wolpaw, J., Pfurtscheller, G.: Conversion of eeg activity into cursor movement by a brain-computer interface (bci). IEEE Transactions on Neural Systems and Rehabilitation Engineering 12(3), 331–338 (2004)
9. Kanade, T., Cohn, J., Tian, Y.: Comprehensive database for facial expression analysis. In: Proceedings of the Fourth IEEE International Conference on Automatic Face and Gesture Recognition, pp. 46–53 (2000)
10. Izard, C.E.: The maximally discriminative facial movement coding system. University of Delaware (1979)
11. Ekman, P., Friesen, W.: Facial Action Coding System: A Technique for the Measurement of Facial Movement. Consulting Psychologists Press, Palo Alto (1978)

12. Scherer, K., Ekman, P.: Handbook of methods in nonverbal behavior research, pp. 45–135. Cambridge University Press, New York (1982)
13. Chambayil, B., Singla, R., Jha, R.: Virtual keyboard BCI using eye blinks in EEG. In: 2010 IEEE 6th International Conference on Wireless and Mobile Computing, Networking and Communications (WiMob), pp. 466–470 (2010)
14. Królak, A., Strumiłło, P.: Eye-blink detection system for human-computer interaction. Universal Access in the Information Society 11(4), 409–419 (2012)
15. Bartlett, M.S., Hager, J.C., Ekman, P., Sejnowski, T.J.: Measuring facial expressions by computer image analysis. Psychophysiology 36, 253–263 (1999)
16. Cohn, J.F., Zlochower, A.J., Lien, J., Kanade, T.: Automated face analysis by feature point tracking has high concurrent validity with manual facs coding. Psychophysiology 36, 35–43 (1999)
17. Pantic, M., Patras, I., Rothkruntz, L.: Facial action recognition in face profile image sequences. In: IEEE International Conference on Multimedia and Expo, vol. 1, pp. 37–40 (2002)
18. Singla, R., Chambayil, B., Khosla, A., Santosh, J.: Comparison of SVM and ANN for classification of eye events in EEG. Journal of Biomedical Science and Engineering 4, 62–69 (2011)
19. Rantanen, V., Venesvirta, H., Spakov, O., Verho, J., Vetek, A., Surakka, V., Lekkala, J.: Capacitive measurement of facial activity intensity. IEEE Sensors Journal 13(11), 4329–4338 (2013)
20. Manabe, D.: Daito manabe, http://www.daito.ws/ (accessed April 4, 2010)
21. Saponas, T.S., Kelly, D., Parviz, B.A., Tan, D.S.: Optically sensing tongue gestures for computer input. In: Proceedings of the 22nd Annual ACM Symposium on User Interface Software and Technology, UIST 2009, pp. 177–180. ACM, New York (2009)
22. Vega, K.: Conductive makeup, http://katiavega.com (accessed April 4, 2010)
23. Gallagher, S.: Self-reference and schizophrenia: A cognitive model of immunity to error through misidentification. In: Exploring the Self: Philosophical and Psychopathological Perspectives on Self-Experience, pp. 203–239. John Benjamins (2000)
24. Tsakiris, M., Prabhu, G., Haggard, P.: Having a body versus moving your body: How agency structures body-ownership. Consciousness and Cognition 15(2), 423–432 (2006)
25. Tsakiris, M., Schutz-Bosbach, S., Gallagher, S.: On agency and body-ownership: Phenomenological and neurocognitive reflections. Consciousness and Cognition 16(3), 645–660 (2007)
26. William, E.R.: The neuropsychology of facial expression: A review of the neurological and psychological mechanisms for producing facial expressions. Psychological Bulletin 95, 52–77 (1984)
27. Duchenne de Boulogne, G.B.: The Mechanism of Human Facial Expression. Cambridge University Press (1990)
28. Paul Ekman, G.R., Hager, J.C.: Deliberate facial movement. Child Development 51, 886–891 (1980)
29. Gosselin, P., Perron, M., Beaupr, M.: The voluntary control of facial action units in adults. Emotion 10, 266–271 (2010)
30. Vega, K.: Kinisi, http://katiavega.com (accessed January 20, 2014)
31. Lathem, P.A., Gregorio, T.L., Garber, S.L.: High-level quadriplegia: an occupational therapy challenge. The American Journal of Occupational Therapy 39, 705–714 (2008)
32. Sipski, M.L., Richards, J.S.: Spinal cord injury rehabilitation, state of the science. American Journal of Physical Medicine & Rehabilitation 95, 310–342 (2006)

The HARSim Application to the Task
of Carrying School Supplies

Ricardo Dagge[1] and Ernesto Filgueiras Vilar[2,3]

[1] Faculty of Engineering of the University of Porto (FEUP)
[2] Laboratory of Online Communication of University of Beira Interior (LabCom)
[3] Centre for Architecture, Urban Planning and Design (CIAUD)
{ricardodagge,ernestovf}@gmail.com

Abstract. This paper presents the use of a software called Humanoid Articulation Reaction Simulation (HARSim) to a field study with the intended purpose of understanding which is the approximate intensity of the loads applied to the spine of children attending middle school while carrying their school supplies on their way to and from school, using a common backpack. HARSim proved to be an efficient and effective way of further understanding this task. Its results allowed to demonstrate that in most of the cases of forces applied to the spine of the simulated models, the use of both carrying handles, that compose the common backpack, proved to be better than the use of only one of these handles. Furthermore it was found that scientific software allows designers and development teams to create more efficient, safe and effective products ultimately resulting in better ergo design ones, allowing them to change some paradigms that surrounds product design discipline.

Keywords: Humanoid simulation, Backpack and back pain, Product design, User behaviors, Spine efforts.

1 Introduction

Due to market demands the design and research made around the products responsible for carrying school supplies tend mostly to the aesthetical aspect of these kind of product. This demand results in the arise of products in the market which are not fully explored in all of their aspects, namely considering its functionality.

Therefore, backpack use has been pointed out as a determinant aspect that tends to contribute to the appearance of back pain and musculoskeletal disorders in growth stage children, approaching its value to the ones observed in adults [1, 2]. Goodgold et al. [2] claim that this happens because an individual's center of gravity is displaced to the direction of the load, and therefore to compensate, the individual tends to lean his body into the opposite direction, which can generate fatigue of the soft tissues and ultimately can lead to postural deformities.

While developing this type of product, designers and development teams struggle to gather, manage and understand the broad range of work and knowledge available, regarding the problems caused by the use of the common backpack. This is where

A. Marcus (Ed.): DUXU 2014, Part III, LNCS 8519, pp. 653–661, 2014.
© Springer International Publishing Switzerland 2014

software has the ability to intervene, helping to reduce the existing gap, while providing designers and development teams technical solutions based on a Human-Computer interactional language capable to be understood and explored.

The efforts evaluation performed on the spine of subjects tended to be done by analogue methods in controlled environments (i.e. laboratories) [3] and mainly involved the insertion of a needle directly in their intervertebral discs. However, with the dissemination of computerized technologies, through a whole new way of dealing with these, through more complex and therefore capable computer interfaces, the analogue method can be considered outdated. Consequently, Rebelo et al. [4] present us with a software called Humanoid Articulation Reaction Simulation that can be used to evaluate approximate efforts on the spine of a simulated user, without putting at risk the user himself with any invasive procedure.

This way Humanoid Articulation Reaction Simulation provides the designer and development teams, responsible for the development of a product capable of carrying school supplies, a noninvasive method that gives them the ability to study the reaction of the human body to a small change made on the product.

1.1   Humanoid Articulation Reaction Simulation

This paper presents the use of the Humanoid Articulation Reaction Simulation (HARSim) to a field study, with the intended purpose of understanding which, and how much is the intensity, of the approximate loads applied on the spine of children attending middle school while carrying their school supplies. HARSim is presented as an efficient and effective way of further understanding this task, without the possibility presented by the use of invasive procedures that can be harmful to the studied subjects.

HARSim incorporates ergonomic and biomechanical knowledge that allow the evaluation of human interaction with products and services, which are still in an early stage of development. This software was developed with the purpose of optimizing users' safety and well-being through the minimization of musculoskeletal stress and strain, while, at the same time, improving the overall efficiency of the system. [4]

Providing a humanoid computer representation with 38 segments, a full spine with 24 vertebrae, and upper and lower limbs with 8 and 6 segments, respectively, HARSim model was developed with a total amount of 100 degrees of freedom, 72 of which are for the spine, 12 for the lower limbs and 16 for the upper limbs. HARSim calculates each of its joint articulations based on three reaction forces (one axial and two shear) and three bending moments around each axis of the orthonormal reference frame, and the maximal compression force in the intervertebral space. [4]

This software provides to its user the ability to: generate anthropometrical profiles based on population percentiles, for different age groups and genders; simulate numerous postures and movements through a fully articulated spine; create geometrical objects to simulate the physical surroundings of the simulated task; and finally, calculate forces, strain and stress in each articulation joint. [4]

Regarding the interface presented to the user of this software, HARSim besides providing a graphic representation of the simulated model and forces applied, as shown on Fig. 1, also provides efforts representation applied to the vertebral column of the simulated model through a bar graph, sectioned in three parts each representing an area of the spine, as seen on Fig. 2.

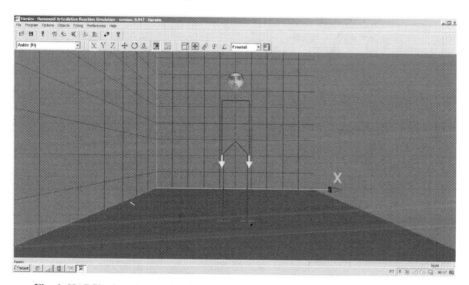

Fig. 1. HARSim interface and default representation model and force applied on these

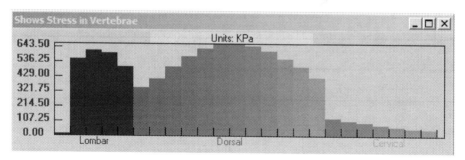

Fig. 2. HARSim default bar graph representing the Intervertebral Force, sectioned in three parts each representing an area of the spine

1.2   Carrying School Supplies

Some authors [1] consider the backpack as a not fully appropriated way of load carriage on the spine although this product tends to be the elected one, by students, to carry their own school supplies.

In the beginning of each new school year parents, guardians, teachers and health care professionals, tend to demonstrate their concern for the weight carried by middle school children in their backpacks every day. They claim that the weight carried by these tend to overcome the internationally recommended safe limit of 10% and 15% of the user's body weight. [2]

Goodgold et al. [2] observed that there are common behaviors adopted by back-pack's users, which involve:

— A heavy backpack worn low over the sacrum, typically tends the individual to move his head and trunk forward;
— Lumbar hyperextension accompanied by hand support on the shoulder straps;
— Finally, wearing a backpack over one shoulder can lead to muscle spasms; neck, shoulder and back pain; and postural deformities.

Based on above problems it is noted that common backpack does not perform the task to which was developed in an efficient and effective way, since it tends to originate musculoskeletal disorders to its users.

2   Method

Following is presented the HARSim application method, without using any invasive procedure, to a field study to realize if it is possible to understand the approximate efforts, performed on the spine of a backpack user while carrying his own school supplies.

2.1   Sample

Conducted in public educational system in Portugal, from March to June of 2013, this field study was attended by 110 students, 56% of which were female, with ages between 12 and 15 years old (M=13.1; SD=0.92) from 7th to 9th regular school grades.

2.2   Study Procedures

Based upon in-loco observations, the above mentioned field study was carried out with the intent of gathering information regarding physical aspects of children attending middle school, while registering the adopted postures to carry their own school supplies and the typologies of products used to perform this task.

Based upon the overall height of 163 cm, achieved in this field study, the HARSim human model was configured according to Julius Panero and Martin Zelnik [5] anthropometric book, while the Rotation Limits parameter was left by HARSim default, resulting, for each of the body segments measures, in:

• Lower Limbs:
    — Feet: 40 mm;
    — Lower Limb: 353.8 mm;
    — Upper leg: 388.5 mm;
    — Hip: 144.4 mm.

- Spine:
  - L5 to L1 (each): 36.3 mm;
  - T12 to T1 (each): 26.2 mm;
  - C7 to C1 (each): 15.6 mm.
- Upper Limbs:
  - Clavicle: 167.8 mm;
  - Upper Limbs: 328.5 mm;
  - Forearm: 251.2 mm;
  - Hand: 52.5 mm;
  - Externoclavicular: 40 mm.

This field study also allowed to achieve the average weight carried by Portuguese students, of 5.06 Kg, in their everyday backpacks. This weight calculated by the difference between student's weight with and without the product used for carrying their own school supplies, to and from school, led to the configuration of the effort practiced on the spine of children.

The collected information allowed the configuration of HARSim human model based upon the studied subjects and the different adopted postures by those in interaction with the ordinary backpack. This inputs resulted in the calculations that led to the approximate efforts applied to the spine of children attending middle school.

This paper presents the inputs given to this software for the configuration of the simulated situation when middle school children use an ordinary backpack with one and two of their carrying handles.

Situation 1. Regarding the simulated carrying of an ordinary backpack using both of its handles located between the neck and the shoulder of its user, the HARSim human model was set up with a 2 degrees inclination of his torso, according to the photographic registry made during the field study performed, which is presented on the left side of Fig. 3. Then the effort made by the weight of the backpack, on the spine of the simulated model, was achieved through the multiplication of 5.06 Kg by 9.81 resulting in the total amount of effort practiced by both carrying handles, of 49.6386 N. This allowed to conclude that each of the carrying handles of the ordinary backpack used, applied 24.8193 N in this simulated situation.

The orientation and application of the force practiced by each of the carrying handles, were deducted from both of the images placed on the left side of Fig. 3, resulting in an inclination similar to the diagonal of a cube, based on its back and lateral visualization. This allowed to conclude that each of the force vectors, practiced by one of the carrying handles, has a magnitude of 14.329 N.

Fig. 3. Adopted posture for carrying an ordinary backpack using both of its handles and the resulting HARSim simulated model (left and right side respectively)

Situation 2. Regarding the simulated carrying of an ordinary backpack using only one of its handles, between the neck and the shoulder of its user, the HARSim human model besides being set up with a 2 degrees inclination of its torso also had an inclination of 1 degree of his lumbar area, according to the photographic registry made during the field study performed, which is presented on the left side of Fig. 4. In this case, the effort applied by the weight of the backpack to the spine of the simulated model was achieved through the multiplication of 5.06 Kg by 9.81 resulting in 49.6386 N, applied to only one side of the user's body.

The orientation and application of the force practiced by the carrying handle were deducted from both images placed on the left side of Fig. 4, resulting in an inclination similar to the diagonal of a parallelepiped, based on its back and lateral visualization. This allowed to conclude that each of the force vectors, practiced by the carrying handle used, has different magnitudes according to the values shown: 46.645 N, on the down force vector and 12.005 N on the lateral and frontal vectors.

Fig. 4. Adopted posture for carrying an ordinary backpack using one of its handles and the resulting HARSim simulated model (left and right side respectively)

3   Results

The outputs given by the HARSim software, based upon the inputs presented before, consist of a chart indicating the approximate efforts applied to the spine of the simulated model when subjected to a load resulting from the use of the ordinary backpack. Concerning the approximate efforts applied to the spine of the simulated model, this paper highlights the Intervertebral Pressure, the Bending Moments of flexion and hyper flexion, the Shear Force and the Axial Force for the two simulated situations presented before.

Table 1. Maximum Intervertebral Pressure for each zone of the spine of the middle school user of the common backpack

Intervertebral Pressure (kPa)			
Simulated situation	Lumbar area	Thoracic area	Cervical area
1 Carrying handle	246.1	287.71	128.61
2 Carrying handles	222.68	226.2	129.26

Table 2. Maximum Bending Moments for each zone of the spine of the middle school user of the common backpack

Bending Moments (N m)			
Simulated situation	Lumbar area	Thoracic area	Cervical area
1 Carrying handle	4,33	10,996	3,49
2 Carrying handles	4.199	8,189	3,56

Table 3. Maximum Shear Forces for each zone of the spine of the middle school user of the common backpack

Shear Forces (N)			
Simulated situation	Lumbar area	Thoracic area	Cervical area
1 Carrying handle	159,86	130,39	54,18
2 Carrying handles	149,07	155,21	55,27

Table 4. Maximum Axial Forces for each zone of the spine of the middle school user of the common backpack

Axial Forces (N)			
Simulated situation	Lumbar area	Thoracic area	Cervical area
1 Carrying handle	356,34	286,71	111,54
2 Carrying handles	344,27	255,18	111

According to Tables 1, 2, 3 and 4 it is demonstrated that in most of the cases of forces applied to the spine of the simulated models the use of both carrying handles, that compose the common backpack, proved to be better than the use of only one of these handles.

Major findings, regarding the most observed typologies of products and carrying methods used, revealed that a common backpack used with both of its carrying handles, located between the neck and shoulder of its middle school user, practice: a maximum Intervertebral Pressure, located on the thoracic area of his spine, of 226.2 kPa; 8.189 N m of maximum Bending Moment, also located on the thoracic area; 155.21 N of maximum Shear Force, also practiced on the thoracic area of the spine; and finally, 344.27 N of Axial Force, located on the lumbar area, of the spine of its user.

It was also found that a common backpack used with only one of its carrying handles tends to practice: 287.71 kPa of maximum Intervertebral Pressure, located on the thoracic area, of the spine; 10.996 N m of maximum Bending Momen,t also located on the same area, of the spine; and finally, 356.34 N of Axial Force, located on the lumbar area, of the spine of its user.

Although this different might seem minimal, it is highly important to highlight that the simulated model concerning the use of only one carrying handle was configured according to the position of the body adopted by the case subject, that demonstrate a compensation due to the use of the asymmetrical weight which can lead, according Goodgold et al. [2] to future postural deformities.

4 Conclusions

Major findings achieved, proved that HARSim is a capable software that allows designers and development teams to understand the efforts performed on the spine of middle school children while carrying their school supplies, without having to harm real users with any invasive procedures.

It was also found that product design has a lot to benefit from the use of computer scientific software with well-conceived and constructed interfaces, since it allows designers and development teams to quickly understand and work with a complex set of knowledge.

This kind of software allows designers and development teams to create more efficient, safe and effective products ultimately resulting in better ergo design ones, allowing them to change some paradigms that surrounds product design discipline.

Despite HARSim capabilities and proven results, it was difficult to interact with it. Some features required the restart of the software in order to work properly and some program controls took a considerable amount of time to act, not providing feedback to the user when they started processing.

Furthermore, it is important to highlight that the interface of this kind of software is an issue that should be considered high priority, within the software development process, once is through this that the user interacts with its technical aspects.

Acknowledgments. The authors would like to thank to Escola Secundária Quinta do Marquês and in particular its students, which volunteered to the field study developed.

References

1. Ramprasad, M., Alias, J., Raghuveer, A.K.: Effect of Backpack Weight on Postural Angles in Preadolescent Children. Indian Pediatrics 47(7), 575–580 (2010)
2. Goodgold, S., Corcoran, M., Gamache, D., Gillis, J., Guerin, J., Quinn, C.J.: Backpack Use in Children. Pediatric Physical Therapy 14, 122–131 (2002)
3. Chaffin, D.B., Anderson, G.B.J., Martin, B.J.: Occupational Biomechanics. Editora Ergo, Brazil (2001) (Portuguese)
4. Rebelo, F., Correia da Silva, K., Karwowski, W.: A Whole Body Postural Loading Simulation and Assessment Model for Workplace Analysis and Design. International Journal of Occupational Safety and Ergonomics 18(4), 509–519 (2012)
5. Panero, J., Zelnik, M.: Dimensionamento Humano para Espaços Interiores. Editorial Gustavo Gili, Barcelona (2001)

Human-Bed Interaction: A Methodology and Tool to Measure Postural Behavior during Sleep of the Air Force Military

Gustavo Desouzart[1], Ernesto Filgueiras Vilar[2], Filipe Melo[1,3], and Rui Matos[4]

[1] Motor Behavior Laboratory, Faculty of Human Kinetics, University of Lisbon
Rua 25 Abril, 72-C, Gândara dos Olivais 2415-600 Leiria, Portugal
[2] LabCom - University of Beira Interior
[3] Faculty of Human Kinetics, the Technical University of Lisbon
[4] School of Education and Social Sciences, Polytechnic Institute of Leiria
gustavodesouzart@gmail.com

Abstract. The behavioral and postural habits and sleep rhythm of air force military change depending on the specialty work at the airbase or other types of events but we did not find anything in the literature to analyze and evaluate this behavior through sleep disorders. Perhaps this is related to the fact that the evaluation of this behavior is complex and the observation of these postural behaviors in the environmental context is needed. However the observation methodology based on ISEE software [9] allows the classification and registration of postural behaviors for long periods of time and can be applied in this context. This paper presents a study whose objective was to research the human interaction with postural behaviors during sleep in the residences' bedrooms of male air force military during the periods in which the subjects were asleep, awake, out of bed, doing activities, using a pillow in different time periods and with ecological validation with observation method and Visual Analogical Scale (VAS). A sample of 8666 observations, which corresponds to 240 sleep-hours of 12 air force military, was classified into six (6) Interaction Categories (IC). The results show that 50,2% of the participants presented the Lateral position (25,38% on the left and 24,86% on the right) as the most common postural behavior during sleep and 94,1% used only one pillow under their head. In the IC´s, the most common interactions were sleep period using the pillow with 66,47%, followed by category Out of bed with 25,32% and followed the category the activities and using the pillow with 6,95%. Findings of this study allow suggesting what graphical interface designers must seek as new strategies and solutions for behavior change in posture in bed, exploring other peripheral equipment for sleep position; or, at least, to improve the posture of the participants when using the number and the placement of the pillow in bed and if these Ergonomic changes can influence the reduction in back pain indications.

Keywords: sleeping position, air force military product interaction, health care professionals procedures, back pain, ISEE.

A. Marcus (Ed.): DUXU 2014, Part III, LNCS 8519, pp. 662–674, 2014.

1   Introduction

Video analysis has been used in many areas, especially in the sociology field that traditionally uses observation theory techniques ([15]; [21]; [26]; [19]). Posture, according to Silva et al. [20], is considered to be the biomechanical alignment and the spatial arrangement of body parts in relation to their segments. The risk of back pain is due to a multi-factorial nature, being that poor posture is one of these factors ([20]; [27]; [11]). Many young adults have occasional sleep disorders and the pain may be one of the factors that cause them. However, in some cases, these problems can become chronic, causing serious consequences in their behavior and their quality of life [18]. The risk of back pain is due to a multi-factorial nature, being that poor posture is one of these factors ([20]; [27]; [11]). Posture, according Silva et al. [20], is considered to be the biomechanical alignment and the spatial arrangement of body parts in relation to their segments.

Back pain (BP) is one of the most common forms of chronic pain and is a significant cause of disability and cost in society ([17]; [1]; [28]). Chronic BP substantially influences the capacity to work and has been associated with the inability to obtain or maintain employment and lost productivity ([22]; [24]).

Musculoskeletal back pain, are the most common reasons for medical evacuation in military with return to occupation being uncertain. BP is also a common reason for long-term Soldier disability ([4]; [3]; [16]).

The behavioral and postural habits and sleep rhythm of air force military change depending on the specialty work at the airbase or other types of events but we did not find anything in the literature to analyze and evaluate this behavior through sleep disorders. Perhaps this is related to the fact that the evaluation of this behavior is complex and the observation of these postural behaviors in the environmental context is needed. However the observation methodology based on ISEE software [9] allows the classification and registration of postural behaviors for long periods of time and can be applied in this context.

The complexity of some newer product interactions in complex context systems demands a higher level of user performance and involves risk that may possibly negatively impact the user's safety and health. For this reason, the evaluation or design of new products used in complex systems requires extensive knowledge of human interaction, including the operation and vulnerabilities of the whole system. Therefore, taking this into consideration, the use of video analysis increases the capability to collect more detailed information on human activity during the interaction of the user with a product-environment system. With this data comes increased understanding of user strategies and awareness of possible safety and health issues as well as system dysfunctions [19].

Video analysis has been used in many areas; especially in the sociology field that traditionally uses observation theory techniques ([15]; [21]; [26]; [19]).

In a general way, the data regarding the sleep analysis is collected in simulated laboratory conditions. Although these kinds of studies interfere with the tasks and with the natural behaviors in the sleep period, they have some advantage such as: an accurate control of variables, a high potential to collect physiological measures and the accuracy of data collected, mainly the quantitative data ([5]; [7]; [10]).

Handrick & Kleiner [13] argue that the main element for a good ergonomic analysis of the activity is to adopt a systemic approach of activity through the analysis of all possibilities of interactions in a real context.

The complexity of some newer product interactions in complex context systems demand a higher level of user performance and involves risk that may possibly negatively impact the user's safety and health. For this reason, the evaluation or design of new products used in complex systems requires extensive knowledge of human interaction, including the operation and vulnerabilities of the whole system. Therefore, taking this into consideration, the use of video analysis increases the capability to collect more detailed information of human activity during the interaction of the user with a product-environment system. With this data comes increased understanding of user strategies and awareness of possible safety and health issues as well as system dysfunctions [19].

Recently, with the technological advances of digital video equipment and computers, associated with low costs, video analysis is being routinely used in human behavior research. Video analysis usage makes multiple revisions possible, thereby allowing the collection of detailed information that would be impossible to collect in field studies involving only the researcher's visual memory. In this case, the use of a single source of observation (visual memory) may cause losses due to memory lapses and potential interpretation difficulties. It is, however, important to point out that for the ergonomist, the exclusive use of video analysis is not a substitute for traditional tool usage in ergonomic analysis. In addition, some aspects, such as user interpersonal relations, environmental issues, and macro-ergonomic data, are also important in analyzing product quality [19]. In order to minimize the difficulty in applying these experimental methods in real context, researchers combine some objective with subjective techniques, which generally are qualitative such as questionnaires, interviews and direct/indirect activity observation. Usually, this approach is also related to the interpretation and evaluation of the comfort or discomfort that is experienced through users testimony and the understanding of the real activity through self-report ([9]; [2]; [8]; [25]). In this context, the main objective of this study is apply systematic observations of the motor behaviors with the equipment of residence bedrooms in the Portuguese air force through digital video recording using a methodology proposed by Rebelo, Filgueiras & Soares [19], to understand the human interaction with postural behaviors during sleep of male air force military during the periods in which the subjects were asleep, awake, out of bed, doing activities, using a pillow, in different time periods and with ecological validity.

This knowledge will allow to: a) understand the possible origin of incidence of back pain referred in the day-by-day activities; and, b) elaborate more specific recommendations to the changes in postural behaviors and products' development. However, for this paper we will only present the results for interaction patterns during the use of a set of specific Interaction Category - IC [19].

2   Methodology

This paper presents a part of a larger study which aims to analyze the relationship between the perception of Back Pain and the sleeping position and is based on the observation of the human interaction (with Visual Display Terminals [VDTs]) with postural behaviors in bed during the night period (10 hours/night) in the residences' bedrooms of male air force military. We used the same group of equipment and the same model of bed, in order to analyze if there are similar patterns of interaction between users. This study started on the 2nd of September 2013 and finished on the 3rd of October 2013.

Study Site and Residence Bedrooms' Properties. Data was collected from the Portuguese air force military. Twelve soldiers aged between 18 and 25 years, of different categories (1st Corporal, 2nd Corporal or Soldier), residing in dormitories of the air base were selected. The bedrooms were in dormitories with 2 beds in each bedroom with the same type of bed, mattress and pillow.

The Subjects and Night Activities. 134 soldiers (112 male and 22 female), aged between 18 and 25 years, belonged to the air base n°5 of the Portuguese air force when the research began . These, 66 soldiers answered a questionnaire about the perception of pain in the spine according to the Visual Analogue Scale (VAS) and, 12 male (mean=22.17 years old+ 1.749) were volunteers in this study. The soldiers worked in the area of: mechanical aviation material (n = 6), hospitality services and sustenance (n = 2), car driver (n = 1), mechanical, electrical and flight instrument work (n = 1), weaponry and equipment mechanics (n = 1), health service (n = 1). Participants were informed about the study's objective through a group meeting and an individual approach on the day before each video recording. All video collection was authorized by the participants through a consent form. Finally, participants were instructed to perform their tasks as usual and to not change their schedule due to the presence of the cameras.

Recording Procedure and Features. The participants' interactions with the bedroom equipment were video recorded on a normal rest period day and were assessed using: a) one infrared digital camera (Wireless AEE Weather-proof -
2,5 GHz – color); b) one multiplexer video recorder (ACH MPEG-4 Realtime DVR) and c) DVD recorder HD (LG recorder). All devices' lights were turned off or hidden and participants were informed about the placement of all cameras. However, they did not know the real video recording time.
The digital video cameras turned on automatically from 11:00 p.m. to 9:00 a.m. and during the periods in which the subjects were asleep, awake, out of bed, doing activities, using a pillow, they were filmed using one plan (frontal superior) considering the best visualization of the participant and activity (Fig. 1).
In order to ensure similar interaction times in the bedroom and to not interfere in the evening activity and sleep period, all volunteers were filmed during three days during ten hours continuously (starting at 11:00 p.m.). After the filming period for each participant, a quick analysis of the video was done in order to select the best two days, according to the following criteria:

- Longer stay of soldiers in the bed (preferred > 6 hours);
- More than 60% of the video had a good visualization of the postural behaviors during sleep times.

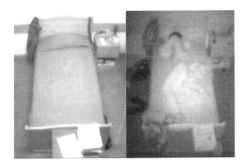

Fig. 1. Images of the first plan (Frontal superior) of the bed Observations

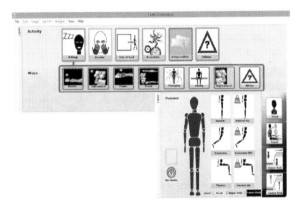

Fig. 2. Functional areas of the ISEE software interface

Categories of behaviors					
Base categories			Interaction´s categories		Others
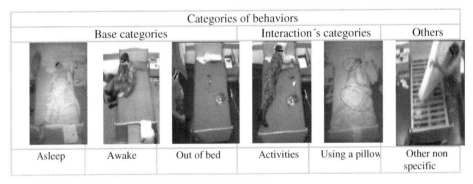					
Asleep	Awake	Out of bed	Activities	Using a pillow	Other non specific

Fig. 3. Level 1 - Six categories of behaviors

The data, collected through video using a methodology proposed by Rebelo, Filgueiras & Soares [19], analyzed the postural behavior in real situations in bed and was done using software developed for this purpose (Fig. 2). The fundamental aspect of this analysis was the definition of interaction categories of behavior that will be quantified later. Following of the analysis of the results of the previous phases and of the observation of the collected videos, the categories were defined.

Six (6) categories of behaviors were defined, that represent the night activity or posture behaviors in this residences' bedrooms, divided into three base categories, two interaction categories and one other non specific category (Fig. 2, 3 and 4).

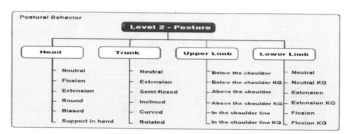

Fig. 4. Level 2 - Postural Behaviors

Table 1 to 6 show the codes and description for ICs "asleep", "awake", "out of bed", "activities", "using a pillow" and "others" groups.

Table 1. Categories, ways and description for asleep group

Category	Ways	Description
Asleep		Period of time when the participant did not have any activity associated to the bed.
	Supine	They were in the supine sleep position with their back in contact with the mattress.
	Prone	They were in the prone sleep position with their frontal trunk in contact with the mattress.
	Left lateral decubitus	They were in the left lateral sleep position with their trunk and hip left side in contact at mattress.
	Right lateral decubitus	They were in the right lateral sleep position with their trunk and hip right side in contact at mattress.
	Mixed position	They were at least two different sleep position at same time with their trunk, hip and shoulder in different contact at mattress.
	Position change	They were a change at sleep position.
	Sitting	They were in the sitting sleep position with their back in contact at pillow and your hip in contact at mattress.
	Other	Any posture activity that represent some kind of specific Category which was not anticipated.

Table 2. Categories, ways and description for awake group

Category	Ways	Description
Awake		Period of time when the participant had activity associated to the bed.
	Supine	They were in the supine sleep position with their back in contact with the mattress.
	Prone	They were in the prone sleep position with their frontal trunk in contact with the mattress.
	Left lateral decubitus	They were in the left lateral sleep position with their trunk and left side hip in contact with the mattress.
	Right lateral decubitus	They were in the right lateral sleep position with their trunk and right side hip in contact with the mattress.
	Mixed position	They were in at least two different sleep position at the same time with their trunk, hip and shoulder in different contact with the mattress.
	Position change	There was a change in sleep position.
	Sitting	They were in the sitting sleep position with their back in contact with the pillow and their hip in contact with the mattress.
	Other	Any posture activity that represents some kind of specific Category which was not anticipated.

Table 3. Categories, ways and description for out of bed group

Category	Ways	Description
Out of bed		Period of time in which the participants are not in bed.
	Standing	They are standing.
	Getting out of bed	They are getting out of bed.
	walking	They are walking.
	out of the picture	They are absent from the picture.
	Other	Any activity that represents some kind of specific Category which was not anticipated.

Table 4. Categories, ways and description for activity group

Category	Ways	Description
Activity		It includes all the activity/action behaviors of a specific task, which interacts with other categories.
	Personal communication	The category "Personal communication" must be activated whenever the participant observes a facial articulation characteristic of an oral or gestural communication, for a period of time greater than or equal to 2 seconds.
	Using the computer	The category "using the computer" should be considerd whenever there is contact of the participant with a computer system.
	Reading	The category "reading" where the position of the participant's head is facing a readable medium (eg., paper, book), for a period of time greater than or equal to two seconds.

Table 4. (*continued*)

Eating / Drinking		The category " eating / drinking " records all behavior related to eating or handling liquids (drink) or solids (food) for a period of time greater than or equal to 2 seconds.
Using mobile devices (phone or tablet)		The category "using mobile devices" must be activated whenever the participant observes a set of actions relating to the handling of equipment (eg., tablet, mobile phone), for a period of time greater than or equal to 2 seconds.
In housekeeping		The category of "housekeeping" aims to identify all the situations in which the participant was engaged in activities for the organization, cleaning or adjusting their bed or bedroom (eg., organizing or reposition equipment, making the bed), for a period of time greater than or equal to 2 seconds.
Watching TV		The category "watching tv" where the position of the participant's head is turned to the television screen, for a period of time greater than or equal to 2 seconds.
Other		Any activity that means some kind of specific Category which was not anticipated.

Table 5. Categories, ways and description for using a pillow group

Category	Ways	Description
Using a pillow	Under the head	The category "Under the head" must be activated whenever the participant used one pillow under the head.
	Between the legs	The category "between the legs" must be activated whenever the participant uses one pillow between the legs.
	Between the arms	The category "between the arms" must be activated whenever the participant used one pillow between the arms.
	Mixed	The category "mixed" must be activated whenever the participant used two or more pillows at the same time in some place of the body (head, leg, arm, feet and/or trunk).
	On the trunk	The category "on the trunk" must be activated whenever the participant used one pillow under the trunk.
	Between the feet	The category "between the feet" must be activated whenever the participant used one pillow between the feet.
	Without support	The category "without support" must be activated whenever the participant did not use any pillow.
	Other	Any activity that means some kind of specific Categorys which was not anticipated.

Table 6. Categories, ways and description for others group

Category	Ways	Description
Others	Other	Any posture activity that represent some kind of specific Category which was not anticipated.

As mentioned, the analysis was done using software developed for this purpose. It allows classifying the IC (through video analysis) in levels. According to Filgueiras, Rebelo & Moreira da Silva [9], although the system allows the observation and register of categories in a continuous time, the high number of categories for this analysis represents a cognitive overload to the observer and may contribute to a significant increase in classification errors.

Thus, the classification of systematic activity sequences was done using samples controlled by the software (10 seconds of analysis for each 100 seconds of activity). Each one of these activity sequences represents an "event" which remained in looping (10 seconds) until all ICs were registered (Fig. 5).

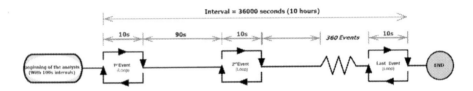

Fig. 5. Flowchart with the systematic observation stages used by the software

3   Results

A sample of 8666 observations, which corresponds to 240 sleep-hours of 12 air force military participants, was classified into six (6) ICs. The results can be seen in Fig. 6, 7 and 8.

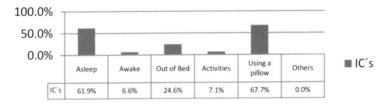

Fig. 6. Results for ICs groups

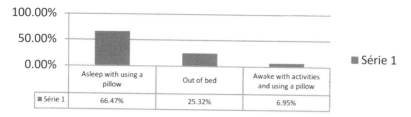

Fig. 7. Results for IC and their interactions

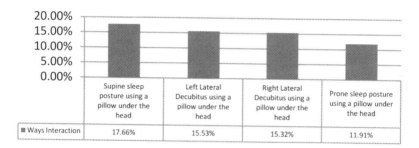

Fig. 8. Results for ways interaction

The results show that 50,2% of the participants presented the Lateral position (25,38% on the left and 24,86% on the right) as the most common postural behavior during sleep and 94,1% used only one pillow under their head.

In the IC´s, the most common interactions were sleep period using the pillow with 66,47%, followed by category Out of bed with 25,32% and followed the category the activities and using the pillow with 6,95%.

The category Asleep and Using a pillow are the most common IC´s with 60.42% of all classifications. In the ICs of most interaction, Supine using a pillow under the head occurs 17,66%, Left Lateral Decubitus using a pillow under the head corresponds to 15,53%, Right Lateral Decubitus using a pillow under the head occurs 15,32% and Prone using a pillow under the head occurs 11,91%.

4   Conclusion

The ICs of Asleep and Awake are the largest periods of the postural behaviors in bed during rest period. The influence of the sleep position on the physiological damage in the rest of the period with or without activities in bed is not very known [6]. The results obtained with this method of analysis of postural behaviors for long periods of continuous time are important to understand their influence on musculoskeletal conditions. This data can be associated to the increase of the musculoskeletal problems, which can be found among young adults of the Portuguese air force when these remain in bad postures for long periods of time in bed.

While held image capture, participants answered a questionnaire about the perception of pain in the spine according Visual Analogue Scale (VAS). The questionnaire´s result presented: 100% of air force military answered complaints back pain; 33.3% referred to the evening and wake up whose the pain was more intense; 50% of participants reported that pain disrupts sleep and; The bigger indication of median of pain was in the Lumbar region (3,25+ 2.094).

Finally, this ISEE methodology was considered efficient for the proposed objectives and the findings suggest new challenges for future research. Findings of this study allow suggesting what graphical interface designers must seek as new strategies and solutions for behavior change in posture in bed, exploring other peripheral equipment for sleep position; or, at least, to improve the posture of the participants when using the number and the ideal placement of pillows in the bed and if these Ergonomic changes can influence the reduction in back pain indications.

This data is essential for health care professionals, in particular the rehabilitation professionals, who can use this information to enable a reduction factor of complaints of back pain and obtain tools to measure postural Behavior. However, the ISEE software methodology defines the categories of observation, called categories of interactions, and the software to quantify them [9]. This software is essential to analyze the data. Without it, it would be necessary to directly observe the video with notes on paper or a computer record of every change without the application of categories for the purpose and with a loss of important information.

Acknowledgments. The authors would like to thank the Portuguese Air Force and in particular its Air Base n.5 as well as the General Staff of the Portuguese Air Force. The authors also thank the commander of the air base for assisting in the sample collection process and the research assistants, particularly Aspiring Officer Carvalho and Lieutenant Colonel Damásio, for their help during the data collection phase. The authors want to thank the in English Company workers, for their excellent contribution to the article literature review. We would also like to thank the air force military participants for their contribution of time and effort to the research, without them, this study would not be possible.

References

1. Andersson, H., Ejlertsson, G., Leden, I., Rosenberg, C.: Chronic pain in a geographically defined general population: studies of differences in age, gender, social class, and pain localization. Clin. J. Pain 9, 174–182 (1993)
2. Bergqvist, U.: Visual display terminal work-a perspective on long-term changes and discomforts. International Journal of Industrial Ergonomics 16(3), 201–209 (1995)
3. Cohen, S., Nguyen, C., Kapoor, S., Anderson-Barnes, V., Foster, L., Shields, C., Mclean, B., Wichman, T., Plunkett, A.: Back pain during war: an analysis of factors affecting outcome. Arch. Intern. Med. 169, 1916–1923 (2009)
4. Cohen, S., Brown, C., Kurihara, C., Plunkett, A., Nguyen, C., Strassels, S.: Diagnoses and factors associated with medical evacuation and return to duty for service members participating in Operation Iraqi Freedom or Operation Enduring Freedom: a prospective cohort study. Lancet 375, 301–309 (2010)
5. De Bruijn, I., Engels, J., Van Der Gulden, J.: A simple method to evaluate the reliability of OWAS observations. Applied Ergonomics (1998)

6. Desouzart, G., Matos, R., Melo, F., Filgueiras, E.: Effects of Sleeping Position on the Back Pain in Physically Active Seniors: A controlled pilot study. Work: A Journal of Prevention, Assessment and Rehabilitation (in press)

7. Engström, T., Medbo, P.: Data collection and analysis of manual work using video recording and personal computer techniques. International Journal of Industrial Ergonomics 19(4), 291–298 (1997)

8. Fenety, A., Walker, J.: Short-Term Effects of Workstation Exercises on Musculoskeletal Discomfort and Postural Changes in Seated Video Display Unit Workers. Physical Therapy (2002)

9. Filgueiras, E., Rebelo, F., Moreira Da Silva, F.: Support of the upper limbs of office workers during a daily work. WORK: A Journal of Prevention, Assessment & Rehabilitation (2012)

10. Forsman, M., Hansson, G., Medbo, L., Asterland, P., Engström, T.: A method for evaluation of manual work using synchronised video recordings and physiological measurements. Applied Ergonomics 33(6), 533–540 (2002)

11. Geldhof, E., Clercq, D., Bourdeaudhuij, I., Cardon, G.: Classroom postures of 8–12 year old children. Ergonomics 50(10), 1571–1581 (2007)

12. Haex, B.: Back and Bed: Ergonomic Aspects of Sleeping. CRC Press, Boca Raton (2005)

13. Hendrick, H., Kleiner, B.: Macroergonomics: An Introduction to Work System Design. Human Factors & Ergonomics Society, Santa Monica (2001)

14. Huang, A., Hsia, K.: Multimodal Sleeping Posture Classification. In: International Conference on Pattern Recognition, pp. 4336–4339. IEEE (2010)

15. Kazmierczak, K., Mathiassen, S., Neumann, P., Winkel, J.: Observer reliability of industrial activity analysis based on video recordings. International Journal of Industrial Ergonomics 36(3), 275–282 (2006)

16. Lincoln, A., Smith, G., Amoroso, P., Bell, N.: The natural history and risk factors of musculoskeletal conditions resulting in disability among US Army personnel. Work 18, 99–113 (2002)

17. Mantyselka, P., Kumpusalo, E., Ahonen, R., Kumpusalo, A., Kauhanen, J., Viinamaki, H., Halonen, P., Takala, J.: Pain as a reason to visit the doctor: a study in Finnish primary health care. Pain 89, 175–180 (2001)

18. Pter, J.: Sleep Apnea and Cardiovascular diseases. In: Guilleminaut, C., Partinen, M. (eds.) Obstructive Sleep Apnea Syndrome: Clinical no Treatment. Ravem Press, Nova York (1990)

19. Rebelo, F., Filgueiras, E., Soares, M.: Behavior Video: A Methodology and Tool to Measure the Human Behavior: Examples in Product Evaluation. In: Handbook of Human Factors and Ergonomics in Consumer Product Design: Methods and Techniques. CRC Press, Taylor & Francis Group (2011)

20. Silva, A., Punt, T., Sharples, P., Vilas-Boas, J., Johnson, M.: Head posture assessment for patients with neck pain: Is it useful? International Journal of Therapy and Rehabilitation 16(1) (2009)

21. Spielholz, P., Silverstein, B., Morgan, M., Checkoway, H., Kaufman, J.: Comparison of self-report, video observation and direct measurement methods for upper extremity musculoskeletal disorder physical risk factors. Ergonomics 44(6), 588–613 (2001)

22. Stang, P., Von Korff, M., Galer, B.: Reduced labor force participation among primary care patients with headache. J. Gen. Intern. Med. 13, 296–302 (1998)

23. Sternbach, R.: Pain and 'hassles' in the United States: findings of the Nuprin pain report. Pain 27, 69–80 (1986)

24. Stewart, W., Ricci, J., Chee, E., Morganstein, D., Lipton, R.: Lost productive time and cost due to common pain conditions in the US workforce. JAMA 290, 2443–2454 (2003)
25. Straker, L., Pollock, C., Mangharam, J.: The effect of shoulder posture on performance, discomfort and muscle fatigue whilst working on a visual display unit. International Journal of Industrial Ergonomics 20(1), 1–10 (1997)
26. Strauss, A., Corbin, J.: Basics of Qualitative Research: Grounded Theory, Procedures, and Techniques. Sage, Newbury Park (1990)
27. Vieira, E., Kumar, S.: Working Postures: A Literature Review. Journal of Occupational Rehabilitation 14(2) (2004)
28. Walker, B., Muller, R., Grant, W.: Low back pain in Australian adults: prevalence and associated disability. J. Manipulative Physiol. Ther. 27, 238–244 (2004)

A Vibrant Evolution: From Wearable Devices to Objects as Mediators of Experience

Patricia J. Flanagan

Academy of Visual Arts, Hong Kong Baptist University
Communication and Visual Arts Building
5 Hereford Road, Kowloon Tong
Hong Kong SAR
Peoples Republic of China
flanagan@hkbu.edu.hk, triciaflanagan.com

Abstract. This article envisages objects and materials in terms of actants (entities that have the ability to modify other entities). Things are temporary assemblages of vibrant matter in emergent systems. In the context of human computer interaction, a flat ontology enables a discussion of 'counter-consciousness' where a traditional interface 'user' is better described as a 'co-producer' and, further, materials and objects are crafted with an appreciation of their life beyond the conscious realm of the human perspective. Proposing tactics that engage with physical and electronic realms, this article promulgates vibrant matter as artistic media to sculpt creative experiences. We are glimpsing the periphery of a paradigm shift in our understanding of the world, in ways that are no longer static but dynamic, where change is ubiquitous but never predetermined. Wearable tangible interfaces are central to the shift that will profoundly affect the way we interact in societies of the future.

Keywords: Wearables, Haptic interface, Object, Onticology, Art, Design, Vibrant matter, Flat ontology, Actants, Reciprocity, Feedback loops, Entropy, Reverse predictive practices, Blinklifier, Snoothood, Wearables Lab, Systems thinking, Embodied knowledge, Human technogenesis, Critical design.

1   Introduction

This research contributes to the growing canon of academic literature that contends dominant epistemological modes of history, through an awareness of the inherent hierarchy of objects, which reinforce the dominance of a human-centric perspective. As our methods and media evolve, our perspectives are expanding, enabling us to visualise and appreciate the world in terms that have been invisible until recently. This article is written with a toolbox methodology, as if by a bricoleur, drawing freely from a diverse range of ideas and disciplines. The author is an artist and academic with a conviction that creativity is fundamental to research. With this comes an awareness that the content of this article draws on science as well as science fiction in order to promulgate new ideas; how these futures play out in reality will become clear in due course.

A. Marcus (Ed.): DUXU 2014, Part III, LNCS 8519, pp. 675–686, 2014.
© Springer International Publishing Switzerland 2014

2   Inter-linking Information

Machines, like organisms, are devices 'which locally and temporarily seem to resist the general tendency for the increase of entropy. The ability of a device to make decisions produces a local zone of organization around it in a world whose general tendency is to run down' [1]. If we consider organisms or mechanisms equally as constellation of matter, their abilities to make decisions run in parallel with each other. Analogous in both are sense organs, which stimulate actuators as the basis of decisions. Local zones of organisation come about through entanglements of interactions and collectives of various actors. Communication between actants are the basis of the 'theory of the message among men, machines, and in society as a sequence of events in time which, though it itself has a certain contingency, strives to hold back nature's tendency toward disorder by adjusting its parts to various purposive ends' [2]. A theory of communication underlay the way in which Norbert Wiener articulated cybernetic principles. His analogy between machines and living organisms is simple – the synapse between nerves in biological organisms corresponds to switching devices in machines. The 'certain contingency' Wiener proposes can be otherwise described as equilibrium. In thermodynamics, constellations of matter in the temporary form of objects can be viewed as a measure of disorder; the entropy of these isolated systems is always towards decomposition, deterioration and disintegration into constituent elements or energy, evolving towards thermodynamic equilibrium. Leibnitz's concepts of 'characteristica universalis', a universal scientific language, and 'calculus ratiocinator', the calculus of logic, influenced Wiener's ideas [3]. There is no denying the second law of thermodynamics, but in addition to Wiener's entropic philosophy, Doyne Farmer posits a contrapuntal process he calls 'the second law of organisation' as an adaptive complex system where the overall tendency is towards self-organisation. Through computer simulations, he has observed that simple forms of self-organisation are evident which suggest the existence of some form of complex adaptive systems. 'A weak system gives rise to simpler forms of self-organisation; a strong one gives rise to more complex forms, like life' [4]. Both views are evidence of systems thinking and complexity as a general theory that explains dynamics in terms of emergent systems and non-equilibrium flows of inter-linking information.Wiener's thoughts on cybernetics are still relevant in consideration of the contemporary machine – the computer – and the inter-linking of these machines through digital networks that augment individual human thoughts in the noosphere. Teilhard de Chardin's 'Hominization' is fundamental to the origins of the notion of the noosphere as a global network [5]. Our techno genesis could be described as a growing awareness of our perception of ourselves in terms of our integration into this network, as 'the nerve cells of an awakened global brain' [6]. This metaphor is useful to help visualise the evolution that we are now witnessing with cloud computing. Finding equilibrium between the noosphere and the biosphere on organism earth embraces environmental concerns and one world thinking, and we see them forming in the structures around us. Noospheric institutions are already in place representing a new world order in terms of ideological, economic and political structures. In the dystopian vision of

'Empire' depicted by Negri and Hardt the future is one in which capitalism expands 'to subsume all aspects of social production and reproduction, the entire realm of life' [7]. In 'Empire' monarchy, aristocracy and democracy converge to form a new type of government represented by global institutions: the International Monetary Fund (IMF), the World Bank, the World Trade Organization (WTO), NATO (monarchy); transnational capital (aristocracy); and nation states and non-governmental organisations (NGOs) (democracy) [8].

3   Universality of Information

In an inter-linked world of information people's experience with technology is swiftly changing in the areas of voice and visual interaction, reflecting the diversity of languages and cultures of those engaging with the media. Claiming 99% accurate voice interpretation, voice interaction is mashing-up with other technologies. For wearable technologies the small-scale input sensor, as opposed to a keypad device, enables portability in design and leaves the body free to do other things. Fundamental to wearable technologies is the evolution, from software that runs on flat hardware fields housed in individual computers, to data centres connected around the world hosting software. The future offers access to seemingly unlimited computing power. The challenge for design is to translate the constant flood of information into clear interpretations. Affirmative design is too often governed by software applications and market analysis; design starts with the tools and then packages information into the given framework. Critical design on the other hand, is mode neutral and uses whatever tools are necessary to present information in the best way possible; the information mediates experience. 'Images are cosmopolitan and forever, [whereas] words are local and parochial' [9]. Images and words become separated when language is foreign. In a global context, visual design should convey information without relying on text. Artists and designers should be conscious of 'the universality of images and the stupefying locality of languages,' to use Edward Tufte's phrase [10]. Data visualisation and voice recognition are evolving quickly and have profound implications when thinking about human computer interaction. Research at Future Lab provides evidence of the effects contemporary interfaces are having on the body. 'Curious rituals' analyses ways our bodies are adapting to technologies and documents strange behaviours and movements, for example, mythical gestures linked to old technologies such as raising an arm in an effort to get better mobile phone reception, or swinging a hip, or handbag to swipe radio frequency identification (RFID) chipped transport or security gate cards [11]. Not only have we developed body language around technologies but the way we use space has altered. People cluster together, not necessarily where the urban space was designed to accommodate them, on urban furniture for example, but where the wi-fi signal is strongest. In the airport we often find people tethered to power outlets, sitting in passageways or on the floor, rather than seated in the designated waiting area. Wearables mediate experience; they merge with the body and interface with the city. Design is not only thinking in terms of smart cities but smart citizens that inhabit them, encouraging intelligent participants in the design, rather than users; everybody is potentially a co-designer. Edward Tufte, invented many visual tools and advocates that the primary goal of his work is to provide information to educate the public. To educate implies a hierarchy of sorts, but a closer look at his design philosophy reveals a respect for the intelligence of humanity. Principles include showing comparisons, causality mechanisms, multi variable data (more than two dimensions), and the integrity of the content (by documenting and revealing sources). His research into ninth century manuscripts supports his philosophy. Maps of star constellations charted three-dimensional sky-scapes, visible to the human eye, as two-dimensional surfaces, and embellished these maps with imagined figures and mythologies, which served as memory aids to locate the position of the stars. With the invention of the telescope cartographer's maps became evidence of the truth, 'visible certainty replacing wordy authority' [12]. The telescope augmented the eye and new ways of perceiving the world based on scientific fact were adopted into our epistemology. Aristotle believed science could be understood in different ways – theoretical, practical and poetical. He viewed creativity as a kind of poetry. It is an attempt to portray actions rather than objects, 'to describe, not the thing that has happened, but a kind of thing that might happen' [13]. Critical design practice looks forward and plays a part in creating the future by imagining it; affirmative design looks backward to facts and evidence to justify design. If we acknowledge the hierarchal dominance of scientific facts in our Cartesian phase of epistemology, Aristotle's three categories are worth reconsidering with equal weighting, embracing creativity by focussing as much consideration to the poetics of design, as we do to its functional and theoretical attributes. New technologies are presenting new perspectives that challenge the way we understand physical reality, time and space. We will come back to a discussion about future visions driven by new perspectives after a brief analysis of current and near future wearable technologies. A model that is worth considering when thinking about designing interfaces is a 'casual drawing that organises the feedback between environment, stimuli from the environment, the artist's person, the artistic processing of the external stimuli, and the impact of the artistic intervention on the environment' drawn by Stephen Willats circa 1959 [14] (See Fig. 1.) Feedback loops and their wider reciprocity are inherent in Willats's approach to creativity. Bruno Latour's Actor Network Theory also provides a model that is useful to interaction designers: the idea of entelechy systems that exist because people act in a particular way within a network, and the perpetuation of that activity keeps the network alive. Individuals' behaviour effects and is affected by the characteristics of the network in a kind of dynamic equilibrium [15]. Combining art and science involves stepping away from thinking about them as different disciplines; 'if there is a third domain, to which scientists and artists are willing to go – what [Latour] call[s] the new aesthetics of reason, because of a long linkage between rationality and visual display – then it can work' [16].

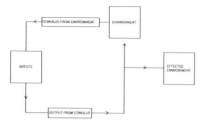

Fig. 1. Vector Diagram adapted from Stephen Willats's 'Art Society Feedback' circa 1959

4   Current Directions

Within the field of wearables, the author aims to open up new questions that can be inspirational for the design of new technological artefacts and interactions. The author's research projects have been heralded as 'On-Board Interface Technologies [that] are leveraging gestures and other natural inputs to enable new forms of intuitive computing and control' [17]. By exploring new ways of sensing, interacting and communicating emotions in ways where the mechanics of the interface dissolve into the surfaces and materials of the objects and environment, it is not the author's intention to disguise or hide technology but embed it into the integral structure of things in meaningful ways. This is in line with Dunne and Raby's position that critical design makes people think. 'Critical Design uses speculative design proposals to challenge narrow assumptions, preconceptions and givens about the role products play in everyday life. It is more of an attitude than anything else, a position rather than a method' [18]. PSFK's independent research report predicts that the evolution of wearable technology will be fully embedded into materials and objects (human and non-human) in the future to not only support, nudge and augment, but to record, control, verify, restore and align systems. The report describes three areas of innovation: connected intimacy, tailored eco-systems and co-evolved possibilities [19]. Using the key terms of reference in this report, the following paragraphs are examples of their application in prototypes developed at the Wearables Lab at the Academy of Visual Arts in Hong Kong.

4.1   Human to Human

'Connected intimacy' describes the sensation two people feel when they experience each other's heartbeat. 'Pulse Swarm' is a wearable set of white leather gauntlets that is an experiment in near field interaction and explores how such awareness modifies the behaviour of participants. The sensation is felt as a haptic vibration on the wrist and visualised as pulsating pink light emanating from beneath a row of white plumes of ostrich feathers on the outer arm of each gauntlet[1]. 'Connected intimacy' also describes data streamed care, where 'body sensor networks are embedded into

---

[1] By Priscilla Bracks, Dean Brough and Gavin Sade 2012 http://kuuki.com.au

garments and track bodily data in order to sustain healthier lives' [20]. Many examples of human to human devices are already on the market including a recent proliferation of wristbands that monitor health and provide instant personal information often combined with connected medical advice or care. Another trend coined by PSFK is 'emotional mirroring' where data is reflected back to the participant. 'Psychological well-being, such as stress control and emotional regulation, has become an important issue. By stimulating different sensorial channels, emotions can be induced or regulated in the body' [21]. For example, 'Snoothoods' is a device to self-monitor snoring. It is a wearable felt sculpture that contains a vibration sensor located over the throat. Inside its padded hood activation of the sensor by snoring alerts the wearer, through silent haptic feedback against the temple, to change position whilst not disturbing other sleepers. The sculpture was designed as a humorous, aesthetic pun to address one of the co-designer's professed relationship problems – snoring. But the result revealed just the kind of emotional mirroring that Ugur describes. In order to first get to sleep in the 'Snoothood', one must enter a conscious meditative state to avoid inadvertently setting off the buzzer. The fact that the felt hood encapsulates the head entirely, with only the nose, mouth and chin exposed, further heightens the self-reflective experience[2] [22]. Think of these experiences as artistic tactics for the creative designer who models a stage or a social space that becomes the participant's reality for the time of the staging, and creates a second level of reality that is the mirror, commentary and invitation to self-empowering practice in the participant as well as in us, the observers. The design of new technological artefacts enables us to break through physical and emotional barriers such as distance. Long distance togetherness is the effect of designs such as a set of prototype pairs of shoes that communicate with each other across the globe enabling each wearer to feel the footsteps of the other. Sensors on the soles track footsteps and actuators on the top of the partner pair of shoes pulse the same rhythm[3]. This leads to an odd experience of an intimate understanding of the mobility of the other person and an overlaying of that information onto personal biorhythms. The experience is further estranged by the global time zones of the participants.

4.2   Person to Computer

The availability of personal data (statistics and real time data) enables eco-systems in both the production and the design of artefacts to be tailored to individual measurements, tastes, fitness levels, moods, etc. In addition to personal data, the incorporation of environmental data such as location, weather and temperature, and last of all, small-scale rapid manufacture or the potential for self-manufacture, such as 3D printing, has fostered bespoke biotechnology. In projects being prototyped in the Wearables Lab at the time of writing, participants' brain waves during sleep and activity levels during waking hours are tracked. The real time bio-data drives servos in dying machines that control the colour depth of a filament thread that is then used

---

[2] By Tricia Flanagan, Katia Vega and Hugo Fuks as part of Haptic InterFace 2012.
[3] By Daniel Gilgen and Jarad Donovan as part of Haptic InterFace 2012.

to weave a blanket (from the sleeping data) and create a series of non-loom constructed garments (from the activity data). The number of stitches and their pattern, as well as their depth of colour, are translated from bio-data to create unique body coverings.

4.3   Person as Computer

The co-evolved possibilities of the person as computer are also known as humanistic intelligence [23] and viewed as part of our natural evolution. We have a long history of augmenting our bodies with prosthetic materials. Evidence of wound dressings used to aid healing has been dated back to 1500 BC. Plates from 1597 by Gaspare Tagliocozzi, a surgeon from Bologna, illustrate Autograft procedures for replacing a nose. 'Materials used in reconstruction of the nose bridge alone have historically included rubber, celluloid, iron, copper, platinum, ivory and gold' [24]. The future will include on-board interfaces, augmented sensory perception, authentic self, and cloud memory. Launched in 2012 at the Asia Pacific Conference on Computer Human Interaction (APCHI), 'Blinklifier' incorporated an on-board interface and conductive eyelashes and eye-liner to augment the eye movements of blinking into an exaggerated expression in the form of an LED light array in a head dress. The research explored a new method of interface with the computer that subverts consciousness and is directly connected to signals produced by the body [25]. The opportunities afforded through augmented perception and cloud computing will be explored later; first a short discussion about objects.

5   Flat Ontology

Traditionally we view the object as stable and fixed, the opposite to events and processes that are active. But do we really know what objects are? This is not an epistemological question about how we 'know' the object. Our knowledge of objects is different to the being of objects [26]. This sounds like a circular argument but what is in question here is our fundamental separation of culture and nature into distinct realms; a bifurcated model makes impossible any intermingling of their distinct properties. Freedom is implicit in the culture/subject realm, whereas nature/object, on the other hand, is tied to matter and mechanistic causality [27]. From the epistemological standpoint, the separation of subject/object has historically resulted in a primary focus on propositions and representations with a total disregard for the role that non-human actors play in knowledge production. The shift from the 'nature/culture split to collectives, onticology and object-oriented philosophy place[s] all entities on equal ontological footing. [...] There are collectives that involve humans and other collectives of objects that have nothing to do with humans' [28] Pioneers of object-oriented onticology that have influenced this article are Bruno Latour, Jane Bennett, Manuel De Landa, Marshall McLuhan, Deleuze and Guattari. The relationship between micro and macro objects, their autonomy and coalescence into forms recognised as other objects, for example in parasitic existence, or within co-evolved bio-spheres needs to become more acute in our perception of the world. We must acknowledge as part of our own existence our interdependence on non-human objects and equally the interdependence of non-human to non-human objects and their affects in terms of actants[4] on one another. Just as the internet is enabling us to think about the notion of a connected realm of thought – 'gaiga' – the same is true of biological and physical worlds. The fungibility of digital media and the speed that it is transmuted effortlessly into different formats, from painting, to video, to photographic prints, or 3D printouts 'points to the loss of "stickiness" that once cemented a medium to a given material substrate, guaranteed its particularity, and the limited way in which it could be received and used' [29]. This apparent slipperiness of matter gives cause for consideration of the democracy of objects themselves. The world is not constructed of active vibrant subjects and passive dormant objects. We must acknowledge objects themselves as actants. If we think in terms of entropy, objects are rarely in a solid state but always changing and evolving. The time and scale of that change may not be geared to the scale of human perception, but none the less they are still active. Collectives of actants create an ecology of human and non-human elements. Latour locates political agency, not in the acting out of our choices, but in the call and response between prepositions within these collectives where the tug and tussle eventually results in a tipping point towards one trajectory of action or another [30]. Latour uses the word 'conatus' to describe this 'active impulsion' or tendency to persist [31]. 'Theories of democracy that assume a world of active subjects and passive objects begin to appear as thin descriptions at a time when the interactions between human, viral, animal and technological bodies are becoming more and more intense. [...] We need not only to invent or re-invoke concepts like conatus, actant, assemblage, small agency, operator, disruption, and the like but also to devise new procedures, technologies, and regimes of perception that enable us to consult non-humans more closely, or to listen and respond more carefully to their outbreaks, objections, testimonies, and propositions' [32]. The technologies that will enable us to listen and respond more carefully are with us already; the integration of these technologies into wearable interfaces will enable them to be submerged into the activities of our daily lives and become part of our general perception of the world.

6   New Scales of Perspectives

A flat ontology enables us to think about the autonomy of different entities while exploring the ways they influence one another. The collective is an entanglement of objects: it is an open system, always evolving, influenced by and influencing other entanglements. Our propensity to visualise the world is amplified more than ever before in our history, enabling an expanded horizon in both micro and macro directions. An example of micro sculpture is the iconic building 'Lloyd's' of London,

---

[4] An actant is a term Bruno Latour used to describe the source of an action. It is 'an entity that modifies another entity in a trial', has efficacy and can do things. It can be human or non-human. Latour, B., Politics of Nature: How to bring the sciences into Democracy. Trans. Catherine Porter, p. 237. Harvard University Press, Cambridge.

sculpted on the head of a pin by Willard Wigan. Using a two-photon photo polymerization process, Satoshi Kawata laser moulded a 7 micrometre tall bull [33]. Micro-sculptors are working at the intersection and periphery of artistic and scientific exploration, using nanotechnology to create works of art, but it is indicative of what will be possible and available in the future. Super computers generate massive data sets that can be ordered or sorted, and visualised into a fungible variety of outputs. Data that was once beyond the human mind's capacity to comprehend can become digestible through modelling. It is as if we can now rise high enough above the information to see it clearly, like looking back at the earth from the moon for the first time. The profound impact those images had on humanity is the kind of new perspective evoked here. The data imaging work of Lewis Lancaster [34] into computational analytics and reverse predictive practices is exemplary here and illustrates the point made earlier – the need for better aesthetic interpretation of information. In his research he took a volume of canonical Asian literature and digitally converted every written character into a dot, each a different shade of blue. The pages of the books now appear as digital pages of blue dots, stacked in a virtual three-dimensional pile, with the paper itself rendered transparent. The resulting block of blue dots can be viewed as a whole object in a way that the original text never could. In this case an example of an insight drawn from the modelling process involved a strange anomaly found in the patterning of the dots. On further investigation into the cause of the pattern, it was discovered that when male individuals in the narrative spoke of places they were often far from where they lived, whilst females discussed neighbouring towns and communities. This insight reveals information about the role of the sexes in that society. Lancaster calls this methodology 'reverse predictive practices'. This method, employed by the artist or designer, is an example of a tactic that can be used to sculpt vibrant matter. Reverse predictive practice is the conceptual basis for the creation of the bio-data body coverings described earlier. The blankets and garments can be viewed as aesthetic expressions of the body, generated from the body; they evidence the life of the wearer. Just as in the production of skin, where the epidermis is a 'strata of cells that migrate toward the surface where they compact into a layer of dead material' [35] the evolution of the bio-data body coverings starts within the body and ends up as an outer surface.

Reverse predictive analysis can be self-reflective (as the participant considers their bio data depicted in the patterning of one or a series of bespoke garments) or comparative to other participants' bio-data body coverings. The installation and exposition of a series of these experiments is a conscious framing of the content in order to reflect on a social affliction of contemporary society, that is its dislocation from natural body rhythms and the health and social problems that result. The development of the telescope augmented our ability to see far into space and the later development of the portable camera altered the eyes' normal perspective. Photographing the earth from outer space profoundly influenced our ability to think of the world as one ecological organism with finite resources that are shared. The latest technologies further augment our senses and our perception. We are becoming acclimatised to living between virtual and physical time and space. The next threshold is one of scales, when the nano-immediacy of real time information stored in 'clouds' of data and software enables smart materials and objects to embody nano-scales and macro information (vast boundless content) and make it visible, like zooming in and zooming out at any given moment.

7   New Media for Artists and Designers

The notion of 'vibrant matter' is a term borrowed from Jane Bennett (Bennett 2010). She promulgates the need for an expanded vocabulary and syntax to describe and discern the active powers issuing from non-subjects as a way to reinforce a flat ontology. In advocating material agency or the efficacy of things, Bennett challenges our position as consumer and subjugator. The categorical positioning of 'us' as alive and vibrant and 'objects' as dead and dormant prevents us 'from detecting (seeing, hearing, smelling, tasting, feeling) a fuller range of the nonhuman powers circulating around and within human bodies' [36].This article advocates that artists and designers take up this challenge and think of vibrant matter as a new sculptural medium. Levine articulates a similar idea 'Electronic media capable of transmitting real-time could be new material for art production' [37]. In the classic text 'The Work of Art in the Age of Mechanical Reproduction' Walter Benjamin describes the way we relate to the montage of film as 'tactile' and describes the filmmaker as a surgeon [38]. It is easy to imagine this 'new art material' in terms of electronic media, but why not extend the notion beyond the digital and into the haptic, physical, tactile world of stuff where the line between machine and human is already becoming indistinct.

8   The Reciprocity of Interfaces

An important notion to consider when taking up the challenge to sculpt vibrant matter is one that Wiener describes in his discussion of the world in terms of systems governed by entropic tendencies, namely feedback loops and systems of reciprocity. Like dropping a stone into water and creating ripples, think about creation in terms of effects and interconnected agency. Integral to interface design's capacity for flexibility, change or mutation is the integration of feedback loops, systems governed by tolerances that have tipping points, or oscillation switches seeking equilibrium rather than on/off switches. The tipping point is a decision, and produces an action. [39] 'Feedback may be as simple as that of the common reflex, or it may be a higher order feedback, in which past experience is used not only to regulate specific movements, but also whole policies of behaviour. Such a policy-feedback may, [...], appear to be what we know under one aspect as a conditioned reflex, and under another as learning' [40]. As our technology merges with our biology, not only will the synapse in organisms 'be analogous' to the switching apparatus in the machine, they will be conjoined. The evolution of our tools away from the traditional computer screen and keyboard interface, back into our hands and onto our bodies means we can look to the crafts in a new way, not with nostalgia for techniques lost but for lessons in how to develop tools that augment our capacity and sensitivity to these thresholds.

We need to foster highly skilled artisans to carry into the future the embodied knowledge inherent in the relationship between body, tools and materials and embrace 'more ecological and materially sustainable modes of production and consumption' [41] to craft our future societies.

9   Conclusion

Throughout this article the evolution of human perception is evident in the stories of the augmented eye from telescope to microscope, through to nano perspectives. In contemporary times the power of super-computing, the rapid growth in data storage capacity, and the hyper-immediacy of capture and retrieval mechanisms, leaves us with the estranged feeling that we are defying the laws of nature, of time and space, when actually what we are facing is a period of adjustment to these new ways of perceiving the world. Once we accept the inter-linked world as part of us, we can be responsible for our role within these assemblages. 'Decoding of an electronic signal or software can be just as real, touching or effective as an encounter with a work of art situated in physical space' [42]. The power resides no longer within the objects of desire, nor between them, but in the persistence of ideas in the collective consciousness of the media itself (its efficacy). The aesthetics that emerge from the new machine/human interfaces are a combination of virtual and actual media in new kinds of haptic interfaces; the emotional experience of these encounters creates residual memory and objects are the mediators of these experiences in our vibrant evolution.

Acknowledgements. Haptic InterFace (HIF) prototypes were supported by Seeed Studios and The Woolmark Company. Flanagan received support for HIF from Hong Kong Baptist University RC-start up grant for new academics 38-40-006.

References

1. Wiener, N.: The human use of human beings, p. 34. Free Association, London (1989)
2. Abid, p. 27
3. Abid, p. 19
4. Farmer, J.D.: The second Law of Organisation. In: Brockman, J. (ed.) The Third Culture Beyond the Scientific Revolution, pp. 359–376. Simon & Shuster, New York (1995)
5. de Chardin, T.: Hominization. In: de Chardin, T. (ed.) The Vision of the Past, p. 63. Harper and Row, New York (1966)
6. Russell, P.: The global brain awakens: Our next evolutionary leap. In: Samson, P., Pitt, D. (eds.) The Biosphere and Noosphere Reader..., p. 179. Routledge, New York (1999)
7. Hardt, M., Negri, A.: Empire, p. 248. Harvard University Press, Cambridge (2000)
8. Abid, p. 247
9. Tufte, E.R.: Pen and parchment, The Metropolitan museum on modern art, http://www.youtube.com/watch?v=HfXSltlDfDw (accessed January 26, 2014)
10. Abid
11. Nova, N.: Curious Rituals, http://curiousrituals.wordpress.com/ (accessed Febraury 6, 2014)
12. Tufte, E.R.: Pen and parchment (accessed January 26, 2014)

13. Aristotle, Bywater, I.: On the art of poetry, pp. 8–12. Clarendon Press, Oxford (1920)
14. Wege, A.: In the black box: Stephen Willats. In: Wappler, F. (ed.) New Relations in Art and Society (Christoph Keller Editions), pp. 196–208. JRP/Ringier, Zurich (2012)
15. Flanagan, T., Gibson, R.: Interview with Gibson at Conversations II. Biennali of Sydney, Sydney (2008)
16. Katti, C.S.G.: Mediating political "things", and the forked tongue of modern culture: A conversation with Bruno Latour. Art Journal 65(1), 112 (2006)
17. Fawkes, http://www.psfk.com/publishing/future-of-wearable-tech (accessed January 29, 2014)
18. Dunne and Raby, http://www.dunneandraby.co.uk (accessed February 4, 2014)
19. Fawkes, Abid
20. Ugur, S.: Wearing embodied emotions: A practice based design research on wearable technology, p. 1. Springer, Milan (2013), doi:10.1007/978-88-470-5247-5
21. Abid, p. 1
22. Flanagan, P.J., Vega, K.F.C.: Future fashion – at the interface. In: Marcus, A. (ed.) DUXU/HCII 2013, Part I. LNCS, vol. 8012, pp. 48–57. Springer, Heidelberg (2013)
23. Mann, S.: Wearable computing: Toward humanistic intelligence. IEEE Intelligent Systems 16(3), 10–15 (2001), doi:10.1109/5254.940020
24. Tobias, J.: Artifical skin: Ingrown and outsourced. In: Lupton, E., Tobias, J. (eds.) Skin: Surface, Substance + Design, p. 47. Princeton Architectural Press, New York (2002)
25. Flanagan, P., Vega, K.: Blinklifier: The power of feedback loops... In: 10th Asia Pacific Conference on Computer Human Interaction (APCHI 2012), Matsue, Japan (August 2012)
26. Bryant, L.: The democracy of objects, p. 18. Open Humanities Press, Michigan (2011)
27. Abid, p. 23
28. Abid, pp. 24–25
29. Schnapp, J.T., Shanks, M.: Artereality (rethinking craft in a knowledge economy). In: Madoff, S.H. (ed.) Art School, p. 148. MIT Press, Cambridge (2009)
30. Latour, B.: Pandora's hope: essays on the reality of science studies, p. 288. Harvard University Press, Cambridge (1999)
31. Latour, B.: Politics of Nature: How to bring the sciences into democracy. Trans. Catherine Porter, p. 237. Harvard University Press, Cambridge (2004)
32. Bennett, J.: p. 108
33. Seo, M.: Microsculptures: 10 of the World's Smallest Works of Art, PopularMechanics.com, http://www.popularmechanics.com (accessed February 7, 2014)
34. Lancaster, Nodem - Future Culture Symposium, Hong Kong City Uni., December 3-5 (2012)
35. Lupton, E., Tobias, J.: Skin: Surface, substance + design, p. 31. Princeton Architectural Press, New York (2002)
36. Bennett, J.: p. ix
37. Thomsen, B.M.S.: The haptic interface - on signal transmission and events. In: Andersen, C.U., Pold, S. (eds.) Interface Criticism: Aesthetics Beyond the Buttons, p. 45. Aarhus University Press, Aarhus (2010)
38. Benjamin, W.: The work of art in the age of mechanical reproduction. In: Arendt, H. (ed.) Illuminations, Zolm, H. (trans.), pp. 217–251. Schocken, New York (1969)
39. Wiener, p. 33 (1954)
40. Abid, p. 33
41. Bennett, p. ix (2010)
42. Thomsen, B.M.S.: p. 47

Extended Senses in Responsive Environments

An Artistic Research Project on Atmosphere

Christiane Heibach, Andreas Simon, and Jan-Lewe Torpus

Institute of Research in Art and Design, Academy of Art and Design FHNW Basel, Switzerland
{christiane.heibach,andreas.simon,jan.torpus}@fhnw.ch

Abstract. Mobile, networked, multi-sensory systems and technologies with open and modular interfaces are about to change our established concept of technical extensions for humans. It will not be on the level of prosthesis or implants that humans are connected with machines, but rather on the level of wearable sensors and intelligent environments, which make interfaces disappear and allow "unmediated" contact between the human user and the technological systems. Departing from a notion of holistic bodily experience and media developed in current phenomenological approaches [1-3], we want to examine the affective human perception in a mediated responsive environment. By this, we aim to explore the connecting area between the human body and a sensitive environment that feels like it connects to the body as a "second skin".

Keywords: Extended Human Senses, Embodied Interaction, Responsive / Sensitive Environment, Holistic Experience, Atmosphere, Affective Computing, Media Art, Artistic/Design Research, Adaptive Architecture.

1 The Modelling of Human and Non-Human Systems

The history of computer technology is accompanied and influenced by theoretical reflections on the relation between humans and machines, or – to put it more generally – between humans and their non-human environment. Most prominently, this relation has been reflected by a movement of interdisciplinary relevance: cybernetics. As Norbert Wiener underpinned in his foreword to the second edition of his groundbreaking book *Cybernetics or Control and Communication in the Animal and the Machine,* which first appeared in 1948, cybernetics has proven to be relevant for engineering, physiology, psychology and sociology alike [4, p. 9]. The core idea of cybernetics is an epistemological rather than an ontological one: Cybernetics, and derived from it, systems theory rely on the modelling of organisms as well as machines as autopoietic systems, which are characterized by operational closure. According to the sociologist Niklas Luhmann (who adapts cybernetics to societies), systems are inherently defined by their separation from the environment: Therefore, the initial process that gives birth to a system is the recognition of differences [5, p. 45]. This means that the existence of systems is not ontologically defined by certain never-changing characteristics (*substantia*), but rather by epistemological processes,

A. Marcus (Ed.): DUXU 2014, Part III, LNCS 8519, pp. 687–698, 2014.

which construct the system's "self" through acts of separation. Consequently, it is characterized primarily by its operations: "Cybernetics marks a shift away from the building blocks of phenomena (...) to the form of behaviors, what things do and how they are observed." [6, p. 3]

Thus, the epistemological model of cybernetics views the system as an inherently self-referential and operationally closed mechanism that aims at gaining and maintaining stability. This is mainly guaranteed by feedback processes, which adapt external influences to the system's condition.

From a technical point of view, feedback loops describe how information about the current or past state of a system can dynamically influence the system in the future. They consist of a feedback signal – a measurement of the level of a parameter of interest in a system – and a feedback mechanism – a means to control or influence this parameter. Feedback loops specify how information flows through a control system, typically in the form of block diagrams.

In control theory the reference or system set point is an external input to a control loop, with the corresponding system output as the controlled variable. A sensor detects the system output to produce a measured output value that is compared to the reference to determine the measured error. This difference between the reference and the measured output is "fed back" into the controller to generate a system input that produces a desired change in the system. A controlled system is assumed to be dynamic, and inherent changes that produce variations of the system output are described as load disturbances. An objective of control theory is to calculate solutions for the proper corrective action from the controller on the system that result in overall system stability, the ability to follow changes in the reference and the attenuation of dynamic load disturbances [7].

Important but often conflicting design goals for control systems are low complexity, small deviations and quick reaction to changes in the reference signal as well as robustness – the ability to maintain stability under a variety of conditions. Unreliable sensors, long delays, nonlinear system behaviour and volatile external inputs can make real systems difficult to control.

Common examples of the technical application of closed-loop feedback systems are to constrain engine rotation speed as a servomechanism, to control heating and cooling systems with the help of thermostats, and for the implementation of cruise control in automobiles. In biology, examples of feedback loops are found in processes maintaining homeostasis. Temperature regulation in endothermic animals, the regulation of the blood pH-level, as well as the maintenance of glucose levels and the control of carbon-dioxide concentration are controlled by feedback mechanisms. Certain imbalances, such as a high core temperature, a high concentration of salt or a low concentration of oxygen in the blood, produce "homeostatic emotions", such as the sensation of warmth, thirst, or breathlessness that motivate high-level behaviour to restore homeostasis.

This concept of the cybernetic control feedback loop has been enormously influential, not only for the (isomorphic) modelling of machines and organisms, but also for the question of how human and non-human systems interact. For Wiener, machines – like humans – are connected to their environment by data exchange and interactive processes, which can be grasped statistically [4, p. 80]. Neither cybernetics nor systems theory have a notion of semantic communication. Instead, Luhmann adopts the concept of "structural coupling" to explain interactive processes between the social system and its environment – a quite complicated procedure of adaptation, the main aim of which is to guarantee the system's stability [5].

The dualistic division of system and environment elaborated by cybernetics and systems theory has recently been challenged by alternative concepts of the human-environment relation. In contrast to Niklas Luhmann's theory of self-referential social systems, theorists like Bruno Latour propose a different approach to the formation of societies: For Latour, it is the association (in its original sense of assembly) that stands for a concept of society based on flexible relations rather than on differentiations, which emphasize processes of exclusion. Latour aims to dissolve systems and concentrates on actors, that are defined mainly through their specific actions in certain constellations. Therefore, the focus is on their activity-based relations to other actors. While systems theory defines systems through processes within systems criteria, the ANT emphasizes agency beyond systems – agencies that constitute flexible networks, where actors change their roles according to the frame in which they act [8].[1]

The influence of cybernetics on our concepts of human-computer interfaces is not to be underestimated and manifests itself in our understanding of interactivity as the core notion of the human-machine relationship. Interactivity is mostly understood as the structure that allows two ontologically different types of systems to interact with each other. While cybernetics quantifies information and thus reduces it to a pure technical transmission problem, Luhmann's system theory has no detailed concept of interactivity between different systems. On the contrary, for Luhmann communication is implausible, because we can never know what the other (system) means [9, p. 78]. Of course, there is interactivity between systems, but *how* it works has never been the main interest – neither of cybernetics nor of systems theory.

In interactive media art the problem of human-machine communication has been approached from an experimental, partly playful perspective, which adds relevant insights to the outlined question of the human-machine and the human-environment interrelation: Generally spoken, interactive installation art mainly generates meaning by entering into a dialogue with a participating visitor and therefore produces a unique expression with each human-artwork encounter. "Meaning occurs through the process of exchange, and interactivity itself is the very medium of the work" [10, p. 147]. Of course, interactive art works differ from each other according to the applied types of interaction. In the context of interactive art works Heibach distinguishes initial interactivity (the user initiates a process, which she can then no longer influence) from reactive interactivity (the user reacts to impulses from the system) and creative interactivity, which means that the user is enabled to create an output that

---

[1] Although Clarke and Hansen see Latour in the tradition of cybernetics and label his theory as "neocybernetic" [6, p. 7] this seems to be too optimistic in terms of theoretical continuity: There is a decisive shift from systems to networks that is performed by ANT and which needs to be analyzed thoroughly in relation to cybernetics.

is only partly determined by the technological system or might even change it [11, pp. 71-74]. Creative or "mutual" [12] interactivity requires a more complex system that does not only react to human input, but learns, adapts and makes unpredictable proposals to the human. This seems to be a contradiction to the established function of the feedback loop: Normally, for interactive systems, the model of feedback loops is applied to the ability of users to control the behaviour of a system and to reach an interaction goal or objective. A user acts in an environment to provide an input to the system and measures the effect of her action by evaluating the output from the system, comparing the result with the objective. But in responsive environments the feedback loop might fundamentally change its character: The system becomes unpredictable, irreproducible and atmospherically inspiring because of the human-in-the-loop, but also because of the intelligent-machine-in-the-loop reversing the direction of control.

2 From Systems Theory to Atmospheric Experience

Interactive art installations do not only focus on interactivity as a specific form of human-machine interaction and – to use the terms of systems theory – the coupling of two different systems. Instead, they emphasize another perspective on the human-machine relationship, which lies beyond the concepts of cybernetics: the (anthropocentric) processes of multisensory perception and bodily experience. For now, the design of human-computer interaction in interactive art installations mainly focuses on the human-machine relationship and therefore on the problem of communication between different systems: Works like Luc Courchesne's *Portrait No. One* (1991)[2] or Daniela Alina Plewe's artificial intelligence installation *Ultima Ratio* (1998)[3] confront the user with seemingly intelligent machines that challenge her standardized communication habits, although they simulate human behaviour.

Furthermore, interactive art works reflect the changes that computer technologies cause in human perception and proprioception. Marshall McLuhan has pointed out the inherent oscillation between media and epistemological structures when linking the culture of the printing press to the implementation of linear, causal and analytical (in the sense of thinking in discrete elements and not in synthesizing relations) patterns of thinking [13], [14].

While McLuhan emphasizes the co-evolution between media and the social standards of perception, recently the focus on bodily experience has intensified considerably in media theory [2], [15], [16]. Terms like "embodiment" and "atmosphere" are introduced into the discussion, thereby adopting elements of phenomenological thinking. Philosophers like Maurice Merleau-Ponty [17] and the contemporary German founder of "New Phenomenology", Herman Schmitz, develop a holistic notion of bodily experience, which lies beyond rationality and conscience. This approach neglects not only the traditional difference between body and mind, but

---

[2] http://www.fondation-langlois.org/html/e/page.php?NumPage=157 (last accessed on 06.02.2014)

[3] See the documentation on http://www.sabonjo.de/ (last accessed on 06.02.2014).

also between human bodily experience and environment. Hermann Schmitz introduces a detailed description of processes that he calls "bodily communication" which rely on a continuous exchange of the human somatic apparatus with the environment [18], [19]. This concept is inherently linked to a phenomenon which has long been excluded from scientific approaches: atmosphere. For Schmitz and some other philosophers [20-22], bodily affection and atmosphere are inherently bound together, because atmospheres are sensed in a primordial, multisensory and pre-conscious process, which precedes any kind of reflection. According to Schmitz, atmospheres are feelings that are not bound to a subject, but are perceivable within a spatial area, be it a room, an apartment, a public building etc. Consequently, Schmitz concentrates on the process of sensing atmospheres, which he describes as a primordial synaesthetic process that involves the whole body and the mind and cannot be distinguished according to our traditional division of the sense organs. He speaks of "affective involvement" ("affektive Betroffenheit", [18, p. 94]), which is situated between physical instinctive re/action and pre- and subconscious feelings. Media theorists, like the Canadian philosopher Brian Massumi, pick up such concepts of unspecific feeling and classify the latter as "pure experience" that precedes any kind of mediated perception [23].

It is an interesting development that in current media-philosophical reflections these concepts of primordial, "unmediated" experiences are linked to recent developments in computer technology. This tendency seems to be another expression of the desire to transcend dualistic thinking and epistemological models that emphasize analytic differences instead of synthetic relations. New technological devices support the latter approach: "With the advent of cyberware and cyber-implants, virtual reality simulators, and mirror boxes (...) our capacity to distinguish the mental from the physical, and our perception of the real from our perception of the illusory or virtual has been made increasingly problematic." [24, p. 255] This diagnosis can also be transferred from the ontological to the epistemological level: bodily experience inherently transcends the subject-object differentiation and probably also the system-environment or even the system-system differentiation.

Nevertheless the question remains, in which way such dense and diffuse processes like "sensing" something (e.g. atmosphere) work. Without re-establishing the subject-object differentiation (or – to put it in the terms of systems theory – subject-environment differentiation) there seems to be a never-ending feedback loop between the sensing human and the space in which she experiences herself and her surrounding. This non-dualistic perspective also has a decisive impact on art and design, as the dualism of the real world and virtual reality is increasingly abandoned in favour of "a fluid interpretation of realms" [16, p. 2], supported by recent technological developments: With the miniaturization and the decline in prices of sensors and actuators, and the open source development of popular physical computing platforms, such as Arduino or Raspberry Pi, networked sensor-actor systems, that until recently were confined to development in technical institutions, can now be used for new forms of installations that turn away from the simulation on the screen and begin to experiment with interaction and experience in physical space. This development brings new dynamics into the phenomenological concept of bodily experience and the related discussion on atmosphere: Primordial sensing and atmospheric spaces seem to be the paradigm for media art that works with these new interface technologies.

3   Atmospheric Interactive Art – Some Examples

Within the philosophy of atmosphere developed by the above-mentioned thinkers, the question of media is mostly neglected. Experiencing atmospheres is a process that is inherently bound to physical presence and to an immediate exchange between the subject and her environment (which, of course, can be a complex combination of spatial arrangement, social interaction and further elements, like e.g. weather, light and temperature conditions). The impact of animated physical presence is also intriguing for interactive arts, since it breathes life into a technical installation and gives it the opportunity to leave the *black box*, which is needed for audiovisual presentations, to enter the *white cube* or even public space and everyday life. Artistic, physically responsive spaces can be set up in different contexts.

If we look for examples of interactive art that sense spatial user behaviour, we find inspiring works like *One Hundred and Eight*[4] by Nils Völker or *Rain Room*[5] developed by Random International. Both use poetically staged physical displays to represent the responsiveness of the environment, the first with the help of pixel-like arranged in- and deflatable plastic bags on a wall, the second with an immersive rainfall climate fake. They are presented in interior exhibition spaces. In contrast, *Dune*[6] by Studio Roosegaarde is an outdoor installation, though with a similar approach regarding interaction. *Dune* invites visitors to a walk of light in the black of the night in a hybrid of nature and technology at the border of the Maas River in Rotterdam. Large amounts of fibres react to the sounds and motions of passersby or flâneurs. Another example regarding the diverse applicability of interactive art concepts is the "pulse" series of Raphael Lonzano-Hemmer, in which he employs heart rate biofeedback signals for human-machine interaction. He stages the individual heartbeat of exhibition visitors with the help of the reactive hanging light bulb sculpture *Pulse Spiral* and in the form of water reflections with the installation *Pulse Tank. Pulse Park*[7] is the visualization of heart rates with light beams, adapted to the outdoor space in nocturnal Madison Square Park in New York.

The step from poetic expression in an interactive artwork – as briefly described with reference to *Pulse Park* and *Dune* – to an applied setting of urban planning research that focuses on energy efficiency for the illumination of a town square, is small. The Department of Architecture, Design, and Media Technology at Aalborg University Denmark carried out a full-scale research experiment to investigate the possibility of controlling urban lighting by human motion patterns [25]. Monitoring passersby's activities on a square with thermal cameras made it possible to test different lighting concepts and to examine the public's reactions to them.

---

[4] http://www.nilsvoelker.com/content/onehundredandeight/
(last accessed 06.02.2014).
[5] http://random-international.com/work/rainroom/ (last accessed 06.02.2014).
[6] http://www.studioroosegaarde.net/project/dune-4-2/
(last accessed 06.02.2014).
[7] http://www.lozano-hemmer.com/projects.php (last accessed 06.02.2014).

Furthermore, the technical accomplishments in the context of sensor-actor systems have also given the concepts of ubiquitous computing [26] and "The Internet of Things" [27] a new boost. The well-known example of the intelligent refrigerator that autonomously manages its contents and proposes menus according to the health condition of the users still serves as an example of ubiquitous computing. Accordingly, most publications in the field of architecture and ubiquitous computing still refer to building performance: comfort and energy efficiency, optimized services in buildings and urban infrastructures as well as production workflow efficiency. What seems to have been neglected so far is the human psychophysical experience within the respective space, which can only be achieved by taking into consideration her perceptual perspective. More recently established terms like adaptive architecture or responsive environment stand for an emerging field of practice and research in architecture with the aim of creating buildings that are intelligent and reconfigurable according to environmental conditions and the behavioural patterns of the residents in question. Publications like the *Situated Technologies Pamphlet Series*[8] explore the implications of ubiquitous computing for architecture and urban planning with a more human experience-centred approach. Pamphlet 4: *Responsive Architecture/Performing Instruments* by Philip Beesley and Omar Khan [28] proposes to develop "more mutually enriching relationships between people, the space they inhabit, and the environment" and discuss "key qualities of responsive architecture as a performing instrument that is both mutable and contestable." [28,] With his immersive, interactive installation *Hylozoic Ground*, Beesley creates an environment that moves and breathes around its viewers, creating an environment that can feel and care [see 28, p. 27]. He expects next-generation artificial intelligence, synthetic biology, and interactive technology to create an environment that is alive in almost every sense of the word.

4   Research Questions

The discussion on unmediated, primordial experience in media philosophy, which has a strong relation to interactive art, emphasizes the complexity of the human-environment and of course also the human-machine relationship: In contrast to the cybernetic view, the dualistic separation of system and environment is transcended in atmospheric thinking, as the subject is part of atmosphere (and also creates it) and, vice versa, the atmosphere influences the subjects in their perception, affection and, of course, also in their strategies of agency. Considering an environment of responsive technologies, which reacts to the user's feelings and actions, we suddenly face the problem that a feedback-driven technological system creates an atmosphere of immediate experience. Two very different epistemological concepts seem to meet here. With technologies of ubiquitous computing, the existing environment, which is normally controlled by the user, is 'computerized' [29, p. 77 ff.]: everyday objects become "intelligent" and gain the ability to interact with the user. The passive object becomes active, which also means that new forms of interactivity and new ranges of

---

[8] http://www.situatedtechnologies.net (last accessed 06.02.2014).

agencies emerge. While in "traditional" interactive art the user is involved in an existing feedback loop and is allowed to interact with the system in specific ways, ubiquitous computing concentrates on the needs of the user and tries to make her feel comfortable. The aim is to make the media and the mediated experience disappear: The user should have no experience of irritation and alienation.

This leads to the core idea of our artistic research project: Can a mediated physical entourage be perceived as an extended part of oneself, as an extended skin, if the parameters of design are dynamically connected and adaptable to the perception and affective response of the human? The approach is not focused on usability matters in the classic human-machine interaction context, but on the examination of the space between the self and a responsive entourage. Of course, this approach can also be critically reversed, when the environment causes irritations through a "misfunctioning" or through the development of a manipulative "behaviour".

This twofold perspective corresponds to the concepts of negative and positive feedback: In the technical definition, positive feedback increases the gain along a control loop, while negative feedback reduces it. Negative feedback tends to make a system self-regulating, it can produce stability and reduce the effect of fluctuations. Positive feedback is a process in which the effects of a small disturbance on a system produce an increase in the magnitude of the perturbation. In this situation, the feedback is in phase with the input, making an input larger. A key feature of positive feedback is that it works as an amplifier, making small differences of disturbances get bigger, thereby typically triggering a system to accelerate towards extreme output values and catastrophic system states. Positive feedback tends to cause system instability and is therefore usually avoided in technical systems.

This main research question of examining processes concerning technical adaptation (in the sense of a "second-skin-effect") and alienation (in the sense of perturbations coming from the responsive environment) needs to be subdivided into concrete research questions. We will examine the topic with a modular feedback system consisting of three component groups: sensor inputs, data processing and parametric mapping, and output media. The underlying research questions will not be examined in depth, but are expected to provide insights for the assignment of the components within the artificial setting. There will be questions that are more closely related to the anthropocentric perspective of proprioception and atmospheric sensing, and others that are more bound to technological conditions, but both perspectives will be treated as complementary. Thus, initial and rather basic questions regarding the use of biofeedback sensors already point to the creation of a specific atmosphere and the way the user may feel: What sensor data can represent which human affects? What are the characteristics of the different sensor inputs: stability, number of extractable parameters, interval, long-term progression, etc.? Which combinations of sensor data can proportion synergies or improve the notion of environmental responsiveness? How can the sensors be staged in the setting and attached to the human being?

Secondly, there is the question of agency and interaction emerging from processing and mapping, which makes it necessary to consider the following aspects: To which extend should the media response be causally linked to the human affect in order to be recognizable? Do the participants recognize long-term changes? How do the participants interpret their interaction with the reactive entourage? How many sensor input/media output channels can be combined or synchronized to create a richer experience without creating the impression of random noise? How artificially intelligent should the system be to create mutual interaction and to generate unforeseeable input, similar to human input?

Thirdly output media selection and parameters are closely related to the generation of an emotionally immersive, responsive environment: What media types or combinations of media are appropriate, and how multi-layered and complex can the dramaturgy be in order to create a strong immersive impact?

These examinations are expected to lead to a rich artistically staged research setting providing insights into atmospheric design conditions and paving the way for critical questions regarding the interrelation of pervasive technologies and human bodily experience: What are the potential applications of the examined topic, and which possibly negative social implications are to be expected? Is it possible to draw a clear line between the prosperous, functionally and culturally extended human and one that is controlled and manipulated by the media? Does the amalgamation of the self and the environment have negative impacts on human identity?

5   Artistic Experimental Setting

In order to be able to investigate all these aspects we intend to create an artistic research setting for experiments with participants and for their evaluation. Instead of analyzing the approach and impact of existing art works, which might reveal valuable findings regarding the perception of atmosphere, we intend to build a modular networked laboratory of media and measuring components, adaptable to the methodological examinations of the proposed research questions. The Institute for Research in Art and Design HGK FHNW is equipped with a new media lab, with sufficient space for a generous research installation. In order to gain insights regarding the perception of atmosphere we will make heuristic presumptions and selections based on artistic experience. The objective of this artistic setting is to create an emotionally immersive environment; artistic authorship of a final composition is not the goal. The installation will therefore not be based on a predefining artistic script, but on conclusions gained from a series of small-scale empirical experiments on affective reactions to staged stimuli.

The setting is artistic in the sense that it does not aim to have an applicable outcome as expected in a design or architectural context. Another reason why it can be considered as artistic is that despite being inspired by research fields like perceptual psychology, neurosciences, phenomenology, media theory, human-computer-interaction, artificial intelligence and others, it is not based on scientifically documented test assemblies.

To investigate human perception on dramaturgically composed atmosphere and the resulting experience we will develop a biofeedback-actor-network laboratory. The measurement of psycho-physiological response, such as heart rate, breathing, body temperature, or skin conductance allow the real-time recording of the affective reaction of a human subject to sensory experience generated by changes in the artistically staged environment. The environment is spatiotemporally composed of different media implementations, such as light and colour, sound, temperature, airflow and vibration, and it allows the involved participant to touch different materials, choose positions in space or to alter shapes. Since the parameters of these media implementations are connected to the processed biofeedback data of the participant, they close a (positive or negative) bidirectional feedback loops between the human and her environment: the human controls or is controlled by the surrounding system.

By isolating the participants from their routine context and audiovisual sensations the predominance of seeing (and hearing) will be equalized to other intero- and exteroceptive senses. The environment will be artistically abstract to reduce intellectual contemplation. It is not only expected to be a direct extension and representation of the subject's affect, but also a poetically stimulating and surprising part of the self. It will be immersive and beyond human scale to strengthen the spatial aspect. Movements should be smooth and non-mechanic, which is why pneumatics (e.g. inflation and deflation) will be one of the starting points.

6   Evaluation Programme and Methods

We will accomplish the evaluation with different participants that were not involved in the development process of the setting, but will be introduced to the basic research questions of the project to focus their attention. This can be achieved by means of a text, a conversation, a demo or even a short walk-through of the system. All participants will follow a sequence of comparable presets, which are timed and triggered by the system, the operators or by the participants themselves. In order to find a calibrating baseline the initial preset will work with random processing and consist of a noisy environmental output, followed by a series of presets with increasing in- and output complexity. To examine the border between the controlling and the system-controlled human, some settings will react to the feedback input and adapt the environment to the participants psycho-physiological input, and others will work the other way round, subtly compelling the human to attune herself to the system.

The evaluation will be based on a combination of various established approaches from usability evaluation and methods of qualitative ethnographic research. During some sequences the participants will be accompanied and invited to describe their experiences during the process (think-aloud protocols), during other sequences they will communicate with the system on their own. The setting will allow permanent field observation and the recording of biofeedback and audiovisual data. In some sequences the test persons might be given little tasks to complete, and after the evaluation a short (narrative) interview will be made and recorded, looking back and reflecting on the experience, either based on immediate memories or with the help of recorded audiovisual documents (retrospective testing). In the course of the project it might become necessary to apply additional methods or to modify the existing ones in a way that cannot yet be foreseen. Generally we aim to establish a fruitful combination of qualitative and quantitative data to combine the analysis *and* interpretation of the technological applications and the anthropocentric perspective of bodily experience.

7   Outlook

The objective of our artistic research project is to build bridges between different perspectives: On the theoretical level it aims to bring together the different approaches to models of the human-machine/human-environment relationship represented by cybernetics and systems theory on the one hand, and by phenomenological approaches to bodily experience and atmosphere on the other. While cybernetics and systems theory ignore the individual cognitive system, phenomenological approaches do not consider factors of social and medial preformation and cultural standardization. In our opinion, these two perspectives are far more likely to be complementary than contradictory, which might point to concepts of networks, as formulated in theories of ecology. Therefore, our artistic experimental setting departs from and critically extends the classic human-machine-paradigm and the model of the interactive feedback loop. But in building a responsive environment and applying biofeedback technologies, the feedback loop becomes much more complex, because it loses its main purpose of control and moves towards surprising, unpredictable reactions, triggered by the technological system and the human being alike. The core question from the phenomenological perspective will be, whether and in which way such technologies change the user's perception of the self in relation to the environment (epistemological level), as well as her exchange with the environment (level of agency). From a technological point of view it will be of interest, how the medial settings are able to generate certain atmospheres and how the biofeedback data influence the responsiveness of the environment. This finally leads us to the meta-level of cultural critique and the relation between responsiveness and manipulation.

The interdisciplinary approach of this project involves a combination of methods – both qualitative and quantitative– that challenge the scientific tradition. In addition, the abstract but nevertheless immersive environment created by the artistic setting will open new perspectives and provide valuable insights. This combination of different approaches and new perspectives – so we believe – can be regarded as an essential characteristic of "artistic research".

References

1. Hansen, M.B.N.: Ubiquitous Sensation: Toward an Atmospheric, Collective, and Microtemporal Model of Media. In: Ekman, U. (ed.) Throughout. Art and Culture Emerging with Ubiquitous Computing, pp. 63–88. MIT Press, Cambridge (2013)
2. Massumi, B.: Semblance and Event. Activist Philosophy and the Occurrent Arts. MIT Press, Cambridge (2011)
3. Manning, E.: Relationscapes: Movement, Art, Philosophy. MIT Press, Cambridge (2006)
4. Wiener, N.: Kybernetik. Regelung und Nachrichtenübertragung im Lebewesen und in der Maschine. Econ, Düsseldorf (1963)

5. Luhmann, N.: Die Gesellschaft der Gesellschaft, vol. 1. Suhrkamp, Frankfurt (2001)
6. Clarke, B., Hansen, M.B.N.: Introduction. In: Clarke, B., Hansen, M.B.N. (eds.) Emergence and Embodiment. New Essays on Second-Order Systems Theory, pp. 1–25. Duke University Press, Durham (2009)
7. Åström, K.J., Murray, R.M.: Feedback Systems: An Introduction for Scientists and Engineers. Princeton University Press, Princeton (2008)
8. Latour, B.: Reassembling the Social. An Introduction to Actor-Network-Theory. Oxford University Press, Oxford (2005)
9. Luhmann, N.: Aufsätze und Reden. Reclam, Stuttgart (2001)
10. Muller, L., Edmonds, E.: Living Laboratories: Making and Curating Interactive Art (Article No. 160). In: ACM SIGGRAPH, Electronic Art and Animation Catalog, New York, pp. 147–150 (2006)
11. Heibach, C.: Literatur im elektronischen Raum. Suhrkamp, Frankfurt (2003)
12. Schwier, R.A.: A Taxonomy of Interaction for Instructional Multimedia. In: Annual Conference of the Association for Media and Technology in Education in Canada, Vancouver (1992)
13. McLuhan, M.: The Gutenberg-Galaxy. The Making of Typographic Man. Toronto University Press, Toronto (1962)
14. McLuhan, M.: Understanding Media: The Extensions of Man. McGraw/Hill, New York (1964)
15. Hansen, M.B.N.: New Philosophy for New Media. MIT Press, Cambridge (2004)
16. Hansen, M.B.N.: Bodies in Code. Interfaces with Digital Media. Routledge, New York (2006)
17. Merleau-Ponty, M.: Phenomenology of Perception. Humanities Press, New York (1962)
18. Schmitz, H.: Der Leib, der Raum und die Gefühle. edition tertium, Ostfildern (1998)
19. Schmitz, H.: Kurze Einführung in die Neue Phänomenologie. Alber, Freiburg (2009)
20. Tellenbach, H.: Geschmack und Atmosphäre. Medien menschlichen Elementarkontaktes. O. Müller, Salzburg (1968)
21. Böhme, G.: Aisthetik. Vorlesungen über Ästhetik als allgemeine Wahrnehmungslehre. Fink, München (2001)
22. Böhme, G.: Atmosphäre. Essays zur neuen Ästhetik. Suhrkamp, Frankfurt (2013)
23. McKim, J.: Of Microperception and Micropolitics. An Interview with Brian Massumi (August 15, 2008). In: Inflexions (3), 1–20 (2009), http://www.senselab.ca/inflexions/volume_3/node_i3/massumi_en_inflexions_vol03.html#1 (last accessed Febraury 6, 2014)
24. Stuart, S.A.J.: From Agency to Apperception: Through Kinaesthesia to Cognition and Creation. Ethics and Information Technology 10, 255–264 (2008)
25. Poulsen, E.S., Andersen, H.J., Jensen, O.B., Gade, R., Thyrrestrup, T., Moeslund, T.B.: Controlling urban lighting by human motion patterns results from a full scale experiment. In: Proceedings of the 20th ACM International Conference on Multimedia, New York, pp. 339–348 (2012)
26. Weiser, M.: The computer for the 21st century. Scientific American, New York (1991)
27. Ashton, K.: Internet things ± MIT, Embedded Technology and the Next Internet Revolution. Tag 2000. Baltic Conventions, London (2000)
28. Beesley, P., Khan, O.: Situated Technologies Pamphlets 4: Responsive Architecture, Performing Instruments. The Architectural League of New York (2009)
29. Wiegerling, K.: Philosophie intelligenter Welten. Fink, München (2011)

Ultralight Backpack System for Heavy Loaded Users

Michal Pelczarski

Wroclaw University of Technology, Wroclaw, Poland
michal.pelczarski@pwr.wroc.pl

Abstract. It is known that because of the vertical position of the human body, there are few serious imperfections in the human musculoskeletal structure. These critical defects, results in the uncomfortableness of heavy loaded backpack users. Proposed in the article system, can greatly reduce that imperfections. That can be done, by considering the right "flow of forces", "running" through the ultralight structure, supporting the safe way of transmission of the loadings through the body. The ultralight exoskeleton walking system combines of two subsystems: pneumatic cushion system, and attached, to the backpack ultralight structural system. Pneumatic one, saves the human spine structures and the second one gives the right way of force transmission. Both systems, are made, to reduce the muscles fatigue, and the uncomfortableness during long the loading periods.

Keywords: backpack, heavy loadings, spine, flow of forces, musculoskeletal disorders, musculoskeletal strain reduce.

1 Introduction

Typical loading of the fully equipped soldier, chemically-biological rescue team member or professional mountain climber, range from 25 to 50 kG. Fully equipped, school backpacks, are also critical for the young body's systems.

Spine column, and elastically supported shoulders, are highly vulnerable for all kinds of a long lasting loadings. The human spine is a multimodular structure, with limited stability, decreased additionally by the high location of the center of gravity and very small cross section area [1,2,3,4,5,6,7,8].

To reduce that disadvantages, designers are trying to find more proper ways of force transmitting, from the backpack, through flexible hip belt, legs and foots.

This article shows the new backpack generation, which hopefully, will reduce, the most known disadvantages in existing systems.

Generally all existing backpacks systems, can be divided on a few types :

— backpacks with stiff structure,
— backpacks with semi stiff structure,
— flexible backpacks,
— backpacks with "belly belt",
— backpacks without "belly belt",
— others.

A. Marcus (Ed.): DUXU 2014, Part III, LNCS 8519, pp. 699–709, 2014.
© Springer International Publishing Switzerland 2014

2   Human Musculoskeletal and Backpack Systems Mechanics

Generally there are two kinds of backpack systems: equipped with the typical belt and without it.

In the backpacks with no belt, forces from the backpack loadings are transmitted through the shoulder straps, than spine column, legs and foots. That solution has two critical paths: vulnerable shoulders and curved spine structure[1,2,3,4,5,6,7,8].

Interestingly, shoulders are connected to the spine just through the one bone – collarbone and the rest is built of muscles and ligaments. What is important, is that this tape of connection, do not have a grate stiffness in "x" direction (Fig.1.) so it should not be over forced. These features are the relic of our evolution path, when the human hands were used as front limbs, and their elastic characteristics, were important for minimizing the shock, acting on the brain, during the movements.

The consequences of that, are that the almost everyone, feel the pain in these groups of the shoulder muscles. To reduce that pain, many of us unconsciously, keeps their hands insight their pockets. These muscles are permanently tensioned, because of the arms self-weight, asymmetrical loading- during hand bag carrying, or symmetrical loading from backpack straps. Additionally, the long lasting, asymmetrical loading, often causes, the permanent lowering of the loaded shoulder, and that leads to all chain of compensations at the spine column and changes in its proper geometry. Presented here new backpack system, reduces totally shoulder loadings on "x" direction (Fig.1.) and creates just horizontal forces, transmitted by the tendon no. 10 at (Fig. 3. to 6.). The great advantage of that solution, is that the shoulders are pulled out in horizontal direction "y" (Fig.1.). That action prevents of the negative lowering of the shoulders, pushing them slightly up, reducing their self-weight, minimizing the shoulder muscles tension and make easier, the blood and lymph flow(Fig. 3.).

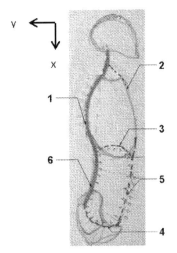

Fig. 1. The scheme drawing of the human musculoskeletal supporting system. Internal pressure chamber is visible. It extends from top muscular membrane (3) to bottom muscular membrane (4) and from left lumbar spine section (6) to right stomach muscles (5). (1)- spine, (2)- ribs, (author).

Analyzing the spine structure (Fig.1.), during its evolution, it has changed from the arched structure with internal organs hanged to it uniformly, to compressed curved column. And again, the spine curvatures, exists mainly because of the need, for shock absorption. So finally, spine column, with the stabilizing muscles, create the spring system with a grate amortization abilities.

Although, examining spine structure internally, we will find that the price of its amortization abilities, leads to a bending during compressing, called also the eccentric compressing. Bending during compression, causes rotation of the bones between the joints, and that lids to overstressing the joints edges, and increase of its internal pressure. During the long time exploitation, with many similar loading cycles, it leads to local joint damages, elastic properties losses and ruptures.

To avoid these extremely important disadvantages, we need to reduce all factors, which increase the natural spine curvatures.

It means that, we should minimize the axial forces, acting on the spine column and support it dynamically during amortization and deflection processes. Dynamic stabilization means that the system actively resists, when the natural spine curvature is rising. Because of the pneumatic cushions no. 11 and 12 (Fig. 7.) the spine deformation increases the internal ear pressure, and that make the cushion stiffer, and more resistant for further deflection.

The natural dynamic human spine support, comes from the internal pressure chamber (Fig.1 and Fig. 2.) and surrounding ligaments, muscles and joints with movement restrictions.

In case the there is a poor quality of the stomach muscles and core muscles new backpack system will have ability, to increase the level of dynamic support, by using "belly belt" no. 3 (Fig. 3.), localized at the navel level. The "belly belt" will reduce the tension forces at the stomach muscles, what will help to achieve the high pressure level in the chamber.

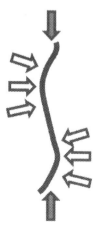

Fig. 2. The scheme drawing of the human spine system during axial loading. Such loading leads to a bending, during compression and causes increase of the chest and lumbar spine part curvatures. White arrows shows the stabilizing forces acting radially on the spine curvatures. Bottom part comes from the internal pressure chamber (Fig. 1.), top one naturally comes from the ligament and core muscles, (author).

To realize dynamic support of the chest spine section, system will have additional, orthogonal spine support, realized by the upper pneumatic cushions, shown at the drawing (Fig. 7.). User will be able to pressurize them, by blowing them himself, to achieve needed pressure level, or using other pressurizes method.

3   Existing Backpack Systems Disadvantages

Existing, backpacks, equipped with the belts, facing generally three problems:

a) first one is that the, belt often is too flexible;

b) second one is that the, belt often works mainly as the hip belt with greatly reduced "belly" belt function;

c) third one is responsible for the main drawbacks. The forces form the backpack, are transmitted to the body, by the hip belt and it is positioned at the distance "e", measuring from its main body axis "Z"(Fig. 7, 8, 11, 12.).

In the case a) belt shape is deforming as shown at (Fig. 10.) and causes negative action at the stomach muscles. In case b) the problem comes from the lack of support for the internal pressure chamber. The one narrow belt, cannot do two things in one time.

As it is seen at the drawing (Fig. 4.) the "belly" belt lays at different level than the hip belt. In case c) the distance "e" causes eccentric compression and that generates compression with the bending "Mb" or "Mc" (Fig. 9.,10., 12., 13.). That bending moment causes forces (Mb/h) acting on the vulnerable stomach area (Fig. 10). During long time period, these forces makes uncomfortable perception and causes users energy loses.

4   Model of Equilibrium for the Backpack User

There are two types of equilibrium, of the backpack user: external and internal.

The first one, helps to analyze, what is happening with whole externally loaded body, and the second one analyzes what is happening internally insight the user's body.

When checking the external equilibrium, engineer compares the overturning moment "Mo" caused by the load "Q" with resisting moment "Mr", caused by the user's self-weight. In case that "Mo" is stronger than "Mr", the user naturally tilts forward, reducing the lever arm of force "Q", what finally reduces the overturning moment. Tilted position is analyzed at (Fig. 11. and Fig. 12.). In that case, the only things which designers can do are: minimizing the "Q" load, minimizing the distance between "Q" and axis "Z" (Fig. 3.) or adding the extra load at the front of the user.

In case checking of the internal equilibrium, external forces must be balanced by an internal forces.

Designing the new backpack supporting system was subjected to minimize the internal forces, as far as possible, to minimize the musculoskeletal disorders and fatigues.

5   New Backpack System Drawings and Schemes

A drawing (Fig. 3. to Fig. 7.) explains the new idea of structural backpack system. Searching for the new generation of the backpacks system, was constantly checked from both sides: static and esthetic. Most of the structures, which follows the flow of forces rules, have finally positive and elegant form, and there is a great chance that form will be attractive to any layman and future user.

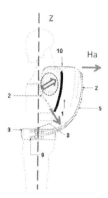

Fig. 3. Backpack system, left side view. A dashed line, shows a typical backpack, existing at the market. Main axis "Z" is visible. Loads from the backpack system, are transmitted exactly to the meeting point with the axis "Z". (1)- backpack, (2)- tube duct, (3)- hip belt, (4)- "belly" belt, (5)- supporting tube system, (8)- force transmitter, (9)- regulation sockets for the force transmitter location,(10)- horizontal tendon. The arrows, shows the forces in the shoulder and the top straps. Elastic tubes (5) acting as a spring, creates the tension forces in the tie (10). White arrow, can be seen at the louvered shoulder, shows the direction of positive lifting up, and pulling out action. Fat curved lines, shows ear bags, located at the back of the backpack, (author, graphic made by Pavlo Prokoptsiv).

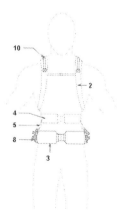

Fig. 4. The drawing shows the front view of the backpack system. A dashed line shows a typical backpack, existing at the market. (2)- shoulder strap, (3)- hip belt, (4)- "belly" belt, (5)- supporting tube system, (8)- force transmitter, (10)- horizontal tendon, (author, graphic made by Pavlo Prokoptsiv).

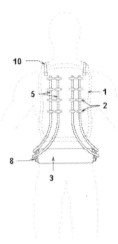

Fig. 5. The drawing shows the back view of the backpack user. A dashed line shows a typical backpack, existing at the market. (1)- backpack, (2)- tube duct, (3)- hip belt, (5)- supporting tube system, (8)- force transmitter, (10)- horizontal tendon, (author, graphic made by Pavlo Prokoptsiv).

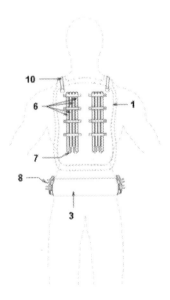

Fig. 6. The drawing shows the back of the backpack system, during folded stage. A dashed line shows a typical backpack, existing at the market. (1)- backpack, (3)- hip belt, (6)- supporting system tubes in the folded stage, (7)- spring connectors ,(8)-force transmitter (10)- horizontal tendon, (author, graphic made by Pavlo Prokoptsiv).

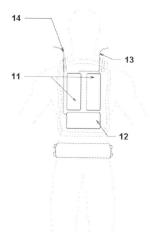

Fig. 7. The scheme drawing shows the cushion system, build in the back of the backpack. (11)-chest pneumatic cushions, built in to the back of the backpack, (12)- lumbar cushion, gives the support for high loaded spine area, (13)- blowing tubes for the chest cushions, (14)- blowing tubes for the lumbar cushion. Cushions will create, elastic buffer, between the backpack and the user. They will help to reduce all possible movements, between them, (author, graphic made by Pavlo Prokoptsiv).

6 Graphical Static Analysis of the New and the Traditional Backpack Structural System

Below drawings (Fig. 8 to Fig. 14.) analyzes the four types of idealistic models, of backpacks and users body configurations. It is idealistically assumed that the backpack is like a stiff block, connected to the body by a straps and the belts. Last scheme (Fig. 14.) shows the new concept static model. Note that there is a distance "e" between the users back and axis "Z".

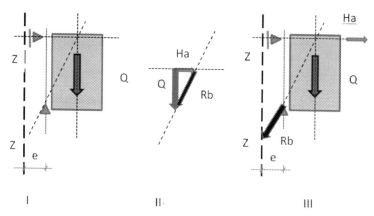

Fig. 8. The above scheme drawings "I-III", shows the idealistic static model of a typical backpack system. The schemes show the graphic method of reaction calculations. Note that the main axis "Z-Z" running through the main body, is based on the scheme from (Fig. 3), (author).

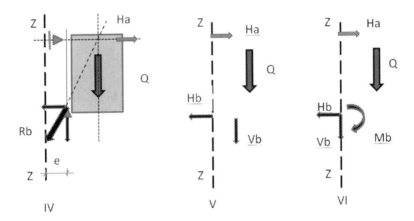

Fig. 9. Scheme drawings "IV-VI" shows the further to(Fig. 8.)graphic method of reaction calculations. Resultant reaction "Rb" is shown by horizontal "Hb" and vertical "Vb" components. Because of the eccentricity "e", the bending moment "Mb" is occurring, (author).

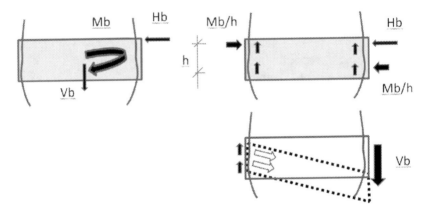

Fig. 10. The top scheme drawings, shows the way of backpack loadings transmission, running from the "hip belt" in to the users body. The bottom scheme, shows the deformations, which occurs in the typical flexible belt. Action "Vb" is balanced by the friction forces, occurring between the body and the belt. The resultant bending moment "Mb" is balanced by the pare of the horizontal forces "Mb/h"("h" is around the 80% height of the belt). The white arrows, shows the forces acting on the stomach muscles, which are caused by the "hanging backpack effect". Obviously, during long time period, these forces may cause pain, and users discomfort, because of constant pressure action, which disturbs the blood flow and breathing action, (author).

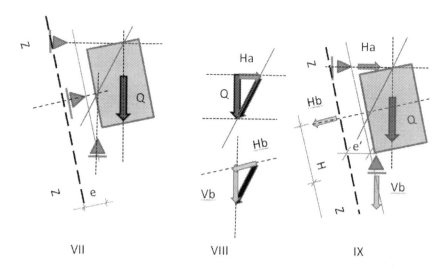

Fig. 11. The scheme drawings "VII-IX", shows the force distributions when the user is tilted. Force "Hb" is taken by the users back, but it causes bending moment "Md" (Fig. 12.) which must be taken by the spine and spine protractor muscles, (author).

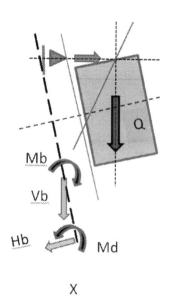

Fig. 12. The scheme drawing "X" shows the resultant bending moments "Md" and "Mb" made by the forces from scheme "XI" (Fig. 11.) acting on the users body in a tilted position. Again in that case bending moment "Mb" will cause negative effects on a hip belt shown at (Fig. 10.), (author).

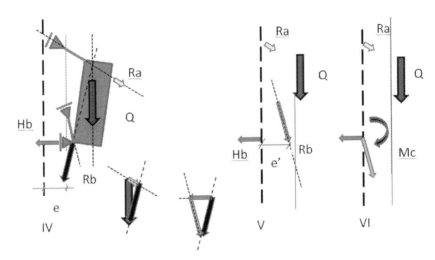

Fig. 13. The scheme drawings "IV-VI" shows the reactions appearing when the backpack is hanged to the flexible hip belt as it is shown at (Fig. 10). It happens after long time of walking when the hip belt is deforming and the backpack bottom is rotating and lowering to the fundament level. Note that in this case horizontal force "Hb" is transmitted at the buttock level. Note also that in this configuration fore Ra is inclined and gives some axial action at the spine direction, (author).

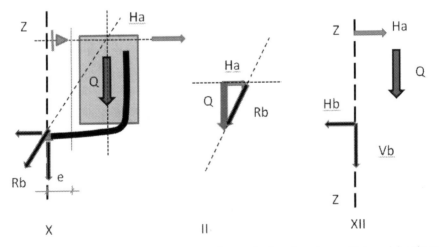

Fig. 14. The scheme drawing "X-XII" shows the new backpack system, which explains the way of force distribution and shows the main idea of explained above new backpack concept. Action "Rb" is transmitted exactly to the main axis "Z", New system of supporting tubes shown at scheme "X" weights less than 1 kG and allows more proper way of force transmission, according to the rules of flow of forces theory, (author).

7   Elastic Type of the Supporting Systems

Elastic tubes no. 5 (Fig. 3. to 6.) works as the elastic force transmitter's, from the backpack to the users hip belt. These tubes may be made of several materials, but because of folding abilities it is preferred to use elastic materials, which after deformation will get beck to straight geometry. The main supporting elements, can have several types of cross section, but because of the static properties, circular hollow sections are the best.

Elastic tubes are specially dedicated to elastic backpacks, because during walking or running the gives relatively comfortable swinging effect, which can increase the level of ventilation of the user's beck. The level of swinging may be controlled by changing the tube number from 2, 4 or 6 tubes, depending of the backpack dead load Additionally, it can be moderate by changing the air pressure in the cushions located at the back of the backpack (Fig. 7.). The grate advantage of the elastic tube system is that the forces "Ha" (Fig. 3.) are horizontal, and do not load the shoulders in "Z" direction. Additionally 4 or 6 tubes give lateral stability during walking or running.

System may be also folded, if needed, according to the (Fig. 6).

8   Conclusions

Recapitulating above article, it is visible, that the new solution does not reduce the backpack weight "Q", but transmit it to the stiff, and strong part of the human body, very close to the main human axis "Z", without creating the unfavorable bending moment "Mb" or "Mc".

Resultant action "Rb" may be splited on the horizontal force "Hb", and vertical "Vb". The bending moment absence gives height comfort, and proper ergonomic conditions, for the heavy loaded backpack user.

The prototype of the ultralight backpack system is being tested now. At that moment it is visible that the system gives extremely high advantages for all kind heavy loaded backpacks and that type of loadings. Further researching will be done in the near future.

References

1. Ackermann, W.P.: Chiropraktyka ukierunkowana, diagnoza i techniki. Ackermann Institutet
2. Bochenek, A., Reicher, M.: Anatomia człowieka, Wydawnictwo Lekarskie PZWL, T.1
3. Hansen, A.: Ergonomia, na co dzień, Instytut Wydawniczy Związków Zawodowych, Warszawa (1987)
4. Horst, W.: Obciążenia układu ruchu, przyczyny i skutki, Oficyna Wydaw PWr, Wrocław (2006)
5. Marcinkowski, J.I., Horst, W.: Aktualne problemy bezpieczeństwa pracy i ergonomii
6. Paluch, R., Kuliński, M., Michalski, R.: Obciążenia układu ruchu, przyczyny i skutki, PAN, Komitet Ergonomii, p. 45. Wrocław (2005)
7. Poplewski, R.: Anatomia ssaków, Spółdzielnia Wydawnicza Czytelnik, T2 (1947)

Human Interactive Wearable Devices: Applications of Artificial Electronic Skins and Smart Bandages

Kuniharu Takei

Department of Physics and Electronics, Osaka Prefecture University, Osaka, Japan
takei@pe.osakafu-u.ac.jp

Abstract. Wearable devices have high potentials for a wide range of applications for future electronics. One of the possible applications is human interactive devices for health monitoring system. In this study, we present high performance flexible and stretchable devices for artificial electronic skins and health monitoring system utilizing inorganic nanomaterial films patterned by printing methods as a proof of concepts. Inorganic-based flexible devices realize a low voltage operation <5 V compared to other flexible devices using organic materials. Mechanical flexibility and stretchability are experimentally characterized, and different types of applications are demonstrated. This inorganic-based printing method may lead the field in high performance flexible electronics and open new fields in human interactive wearable devices.

Keywords: electronic skin, smart bandage, interactive device, nanomaterials.

1 Introduction

Wearable devices interacted with humans would be the next class of electronics in the future. In fact, some wearable products as the first proof-of-concept have been recently available to purchase. However, those wearable devices were usually built up with bulk sensor and transistor components. To realize the truly human interactive wearable devices, the electronic components should also be flexible, so that people can wear the devices like clothes without feeling anything from the devices. In the research level, there have been a variety of reports to demonstrate flexible devices by fabricating the sensors and transistors on flexible substrates [1-12]. Conventional approaches to realize the flexible devices were to use printable organic materials for transistors, showing promising results for the integrated circuits and sensors [2-4]. However, organic material-based devices have not been realized high electron mobility for low voltage and high performance operations due to fundamental problems. To address the problems, we here proposed to use inorganic nanomaterials with the reasons of that (1) inorganic materials usually have high electron/hole mobility like silicon, which is used for the present electronics, (2) nanomaterials can be mechanically flexible even though the inorganic bulk wafer is not flexible. By combining the inorganic and nano structures, that would be possible to address the bottleneck of organic and inorganic materials for the flexible electronic applications. However, there is still

A. Marcus (Ed.): DUXU 2014, Part III, LNCS 8519, pp. 710–718, 2014.

a big challenge to use nanomaterials for macro-scale flexible devices that is a uniform patterning over the entire substrates. In this report, we propose and demonstrate inorganic nanomaterial patterning over the large flexible substrates and its device application of the artificial electronic skin (e-skin) and the smart bandage by integrating nanomaterial transistors and sensors.

2   Device Fabrication

2.1   Nanomaterial Printing

For the transistor and sensor materials, inorganic nanomaterial printing techniques were developed. For transistor materials, inorganic nanowires (Ge/Si, InAs etc.) and carbon nanotubes (CNTs) were used to pattern uniformly over the macroscale flexible substrates by controlling the surface chemistry. As an example for CNTs (Fig.1), first the surface of flexible substrates was chemically treated with poly-L-lysine by dipping the substrate into the solution for 5 min. Subsequently, 99 % semiconductor-riched CNT solution (Nanointegris) was dropped over the treated surface. Due to the surface interaction between CNT and flexible substrates, random CNT network film was formed. Atomic force microscope (AFM) image depicts that the CNT network was uniformly patterned over the macroscale substrates (Fig. 2a). The density of CNT network can be controlled by the exposed time of CNT solution. Although here CNT network printing is only explained, another nanomaterial systems such as the nanowires can be also printed with the similar mechanism [9].

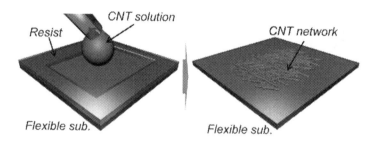

Fig. 1. 99 % semiconductor-riched CNT printing process on a flexible substrate

2.2   Inorganic-Based Nanomaterial Flexible Transistors

High performance, flexible transistor is a very important component to realize truly flexible devices without taking a large battery. By using the developed inorganic nanomaterial film (Fig. 1) for a transistor channel, it can be possible to operate the devices at low voltage like conventional Si devices. Figure 2 indicates the flexible and stretchable thin-film transistor (TFT) printed on a polyimide substrate. In this study, we fabricated TFTs using the conventional photolithography method to pattern electrodes and dielectric layers except for nanomaterial patterning as a proof-of-concept for high performance flexible devices. Figure 2b shows the TFT integration as an active matrix circuitry, which selects a pixel to read out the output signal. Pressure sensitive rubber (PSR) was laminated over the active matrix circuitry that allows monitoring pressure distribution like a human skin. By patterning the polyimide substrate with hexagonal structures as shown in Fig. 2c, the device can be stretchable although the polyimide film itself is not stretchable, and conformally covered a three dimensional object such as a baseball.

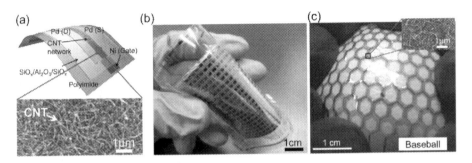

Fig. 2. (a) Schematic of CNT network TFT on the polyimide substrate and AFM image of CNT network, which was used in the channel of TFT. (b) Photo of the e-skin integrated with nano-material film active matrix circuitry and pressure sensor array. Reproduced with permission from ref. [5] (Copyright 2010 Nature Publishing Group). (c) Photo of the stretchable e-skin. Reproduced with permission from ref. [7] (Copyright 2011 American Chemical Society).

3   Device Characteristics

3.1   Electrical Properties

Electrical characteristics of TFTs are the most important factor to achieve wearable electronics. Figure 3 describes I_{DS}-V_{GS} switch properties of CNT-TFTs with CNT deposition time of 5 min, showing high on-current >1 µA/µm and on/off ratio >10^5 at V_{DS}=-5 V. Based on the gate capacitance ~2.45×10^{-8} F/cm^2 and average transconductance ~0.4 µS/µm, the field-effect mobility of CNT-TFTs on flexible substrates was ~18 cm^2/Vs. By increasing the CNT deposition time, the mobility can be improved up to ~30 cm^2/Vs due to high CNT density as shown in Fig. 4a. The density of CNTs was 6, 8, 10 CNTs/µm for the deposition time of 5, 30, 90 mins, respectively. By modifying the gate dielectric materials, we have also observed the highest mobility >50 cm^2/Vs [12]. Figure 4b-d shows the properties of CNT-TFT for each CNT deposition time as well as uniformity of CNT-TFTs. Although the CNT films were deposited out of a Cleanroom environment in this study, the uniformity of CNT-TFT is relatively good, and standard deviation of fluctuation is ~15 %. In the practical application, this uniformity may not be enough. To improve this, the uses of higher purity of the semiconductor CNT solution (99 % used in this study) and a better fabrication environment like a cleanroom may realize better uniformity of CNT-TFTs.

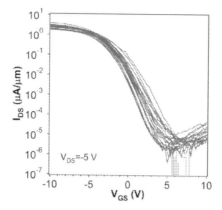

Fig. 3. CNT-TFT (5 min CNT deposition) characteristics at V_{DS}=-5 V. Reproduced with permission from ref. [7] (Copyright 2011 American Chemical Society).

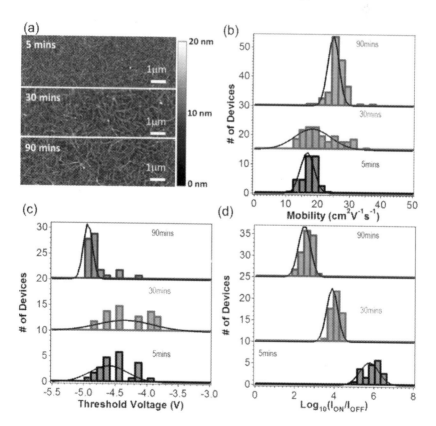

Fig. 4. (a) AFM images of 5, 30, 90 mins CNT deposition on the polyimide substrates. The uniformities of CNT-TFT characteristics: (b) Peak field-effect mobility, (c) Threshold voltage, and (d) I_{on}/I_{off} ratio for 5, 30, 90 mins CNT depositions. Reproduced with permission from ref. [7] (Copyright 2011 American Chemical Society).

3.2   Mechanical Properties

Mechanical flexibility and stretchability were investigated by measuring the CNT-TFT characteristics while the substrates were bent or stretched. The normalized conductance change of CNT-TFT, $\Delta G(=G-G_o)/G_o$, was compared as functions of curvature radius up to 2 mm and stretchability (tensile strain) up to 9 %, where G is the conductance while bending or stretching the substrates and G_o is the conductance before bending or stretch. The CNT-TFT conductance was measured at $V_{GS}=V_{DS}=-5$ V that is on-state of CNT-TFTs. Figure 5 depicts that the CNT-TFTs are mechanically flexible and stretchable since the normalized conductance change shows only small difference. The reason of small conductance change was because the CNT-TFT was designed to place at the neutral region of strain against the bending and stretch by considering the strain distribution confirmed by the finite-element method simulation (Comsol Multiphysics 3.3). For the stretchability test, we could only conduct <8% stretchability because the polyimide substrate with honeycomb structure as shown in Fig. 5b inset was broken when the substrate was stretched >9%. By considering the size of honeycomb structure, that can be possible to make more stretchability.

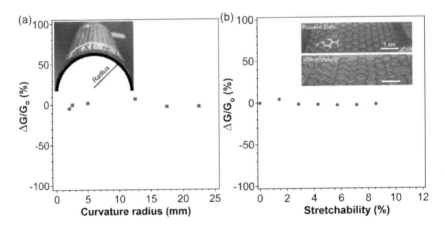

Fig. 5. Mechanical properties of CNT-TFT when the substrates were (a) bent and (b) stretched. Reproduced with permission from ref. [7] (Copyright 2011 American Chemical Society).

4   Artificial Electronic Skin (e-skin)

4.1   Pressure Sensor Integrated with CNT-TFTs

For e-skin application, a pressure sensor is integrated with CNT-TFT to detect applied pressure like human skin. For the pressure sensor, a PSR was laminated over the CNT-TFT array on a flexible substrate. This PSR consists of carbon nanoparticles in polymer, and the tunneling current between carbon nanoparticles changes as a function of applied pressure. This PSR resistance was connected to a source electrode of the CNT-TFT to read out the resistance difference of PSR. CNT-TFT works as a switching for the active matrix circuitry for mapping of pressure distribution. Figure 6a inset shows the circuit diagram of one pixel of e-skin, and Fig. 6a exhibits the output characteristics as a function of applied pressure ranging from 0 kPa to 9.8 kPa at V_{DS}=-5 V. The compiled output conductance at V_{DD}=-5 V (Fig. 6b) depicts that the pressure sensitivity of CNT-TFT-PSR is ~30 µS/kPa below 4 kPa that enables to detect a gentle human touch.

Response time of applied and released pressure on the e-skin was also characterized as shown in Fig. 7. To characterize the response time, the system to apply force onto the e-skin was controlled by a stepping motor and a computer, and applied force as well as output current was recorded. The output conductance increased when the pressure was added onto the e-skin. Based on this measurement, operating speed is more than 10 Hz, which is good enough for the application of e-skin. Due to the measurement system problem at >10 Hz, the maximum operating speed could not be confirmed. However, the maximum operating speed is most likely a few tens Heltz. This is because here elastomer rubber was used for the pressure sensor. If the high operating speed is required, it is needed to develop new type of flexible pressure sensor.

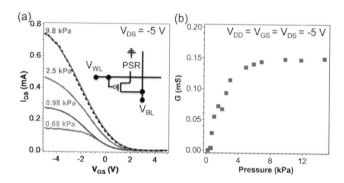

Fig. 6. (a) Output characteristics of CNT-TFT and PSR device as a function of applied pressure at V_{DS}=-5 V. (b) Output conductance at V_{DD}=$V_{GS (WL)}$=$V_{DS (BL)}$=-5 V. Reproduced with permission from ref. [7] (Copyright 2011 American Chemical Society).

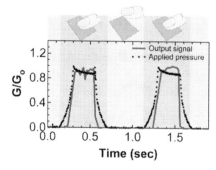

Fig. 7. Pressure response of integrated CNT-TFT and PSR on a flexible substrate at V_{DS}=3 V and V_{GS}=-5 V. Reproduced with permission from ref. [5] (Copyright 2010 Nature Publishing Group).

4.2   CNT-TFT Integration for e-Skin Application

As a proof-of-concept of printed nanomaterial-integrated devices, a stretchable e-skin was demonstrated. The pressure sensor array on the active matrix circuitry was integrated with 8 × 12 pixels. The polyimide substrate was patterned with hexagonal holes using a laser cutter as shown in Fig. 8a. "L" shape object was placed onto the e-skin and applied the pressure ~20 kPa. By scanning V_{WL} and V_{BL}, pressure distribution was mapped by reading the output current through TFT and PSR. Figure 8b exhibited the two-dimensional pressure distribution. As explained above, this flexible nanomaterial-based integrated device was operated at low voltage <5 V compared to other material system on flexible substrates.

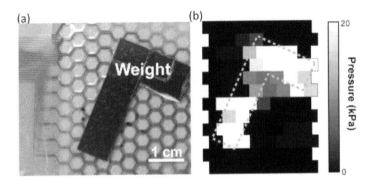

Fig. 8. (a) Photo of the fabricated 12×8 array stretchable e-skin with CNT-TFT active matrix circuitry and PSR pressure sensor. (b) Two-dimensional pressure distribution at V_{WL}=-5 V and V_{BL}=-1 V when a "L" shape object was placed onto the e-skin. Reproduced with permission from ref. [7] (Copyright 2011 American Chemical Society).

5   Human Interactive Health Monitoring System

For future wearable electronics, one of the target applications is health monitoring systems. In this study, we proposed human interactive smart bandage as the health monitoring and curing systems on flexible substrates [11]. As the first proof-of-concept of the smart bandage, temperature and touch sensors with a wireless coil were integrated on a Kapton substrate. For the curing system, drug delivery pump fabricated by using soft-lithography method was also integrated. Although the devices were fabricated by printing techniques, the sensitivity of temperature sensor was similar or slightly better than other type of temperature sensors on flexible substrates. By integrating the wireless coil, human touch could be detected wirelessly. For the flexible drug delivery pump, the ejection rate was easily controlled by an applied pressure. In addition to these operations, fundamental properties of temperature sensor, wireless coil, and drug delivery pump were also characterized [11]. Finally the smart bandage was placed onto a human skin and successfully monitored real-time skin surface temperature during activities.

6   Summary

To realize future wearable electronics, flexible devices such as e-skin and health monitoring system were demonstrated by developing nanomaterial printing methods. Since inorganic materials were used for TFT materials, high mobility TFTs were successfully realized on the flexible substrates, resulting in low voltage operation <5 V for the active matrix circuitry. In addition to the TFTs, sensor materials were also printed and demonstrated relatively high sensitivity. By developing the materials and techniques of integration of each component using printing methods, it can be possible to realize truly wearable, low-cost, and low voltage-drive multi-functional wearable electronics in the future.

Acknowledgements. The author would like to thank Professor Ali Javey, Professor Ronald S. Fearing, Dr. Toshitake Takahashi, and Dr. Chuan Wang at UC Berkeley and Professor Seiji Akita, Professor Takayuki Arie, Mr. Shingo Harada, Mr. Wataru Honda at Osaka Prefecture University for fruitful discussions and works. This work was partially supported by the Mazda Foundation, the Foundation Advanced Technology Institute, and JSPS KAKENHI Grant (#25889048).

References

1. Webb, R.C., et al.: Ultrathin conformal devices for precise and continuous thermal characterization of human skin. Nature Mater. 12, 938–944 (2013)
2. Kaltenbrunner, M., et al.: An ultra-lightweight design for imperceptible plastic electronics. Nature 498, 458–463 (2013)
3. Someya, T., Kato, Y., Sekitani, T., Iba, S., Noguchi, Y., Murase, Y., Kawaguchi, H., Sakurai, T.: Conformable, flexible, large-area networks of pressure and thermal sensors with organic transistor active matrixes. Proc. Natl. Acad. Sci. (PNAS) 102, 12321–12325 (2005)
4. Mannsfeld, S.C.B., Tee, B.C.-K., Stoltenberg, R.M., Chen, C.V.H.-H., Barman, S., Muir, B.V.O., Sokolov, A.N., Reese, C., Bao, Z.: Highly sensitive flexible pressure sensors with microstructured rubber dielectric layers. Nature Mater. 9, 859–864 (2010)
5. Takei, K., Takahashi, T., Ho, J.C., Ko, H., Gillies, A.G., Leu, P.W., Fearing, R.S., Javey, A.: Nanowire active matrix circuitry for low-voltage macro-scale artificial skin. Nature Mater. 9, 821–826 (2010)
6. Takahashi, T., Takei, K., Adabi, E., Fan, Z., Niknejad, A., Javey, A.: Parallel array InAs nanowire transistors for mechanically bendable, ultra high frequency electronics. ACS Nano 4, 5855–5860 (2010)
7. Takahashi, T., Takei, K., Gillies, A.G., Fearing, R.S., Javey, A.: Carbon nanotube active-matrix backplanes for conformal electronics and sensors. Nano Lett. 11, 5408–5413 (2011)
8. Wang, C., Hwang, D., Yu, Z., Takei, K., Park, J., Chen, T., Ma, B., Javey, A.: User-interactive electronic-skin for instantaneous pressure visualization. Nature Mater. 12, 899–904 (2013)
9. Fan, Z., Ho, J.C., Takahashi, T., Yerushalmi, R., Takei, K., Ford, A.C., Chueh, Y.-L., Javey, A.: Toward the development of printable nanowire electronics and sensors. Adv. Mater. 21, 3730–3743 (2009)

10. Takei, K., Yu, Z., Zheng, M., Ota, H., Takahashi, T., Javey, A.: Highly sensitive electronic whiskers based on patterned carbon nanotube and silver nanoparticle composite films. Proc. Natl. Acad. Sci., PNAS (2014), doi:10.1073/pnas.1317920111
11. Honda, W., Harada, S., Arie, T., Akita, S., Takei, K.: Wearable human-interactive health-monitoring wireless devices fabricated by macroscale printing techniques. Adv. Func. Mater. (in press, 2014)
12. Wang, C., Chien, J.-C., Takei, K., Takahashi, T., Nah, J., Niknejad, A.M., Javey, A.: Extremely bendable, high-performance integrated circuits using semiconducting carbon nanotube networks for digital, analog, and radio-frequency applications. Nano Lett. 12, 1527–1533 (2012)

Aesthetically Enhanced RFID Inkjet Antenna Logos on Skin (AERIALS)

James Tribe[1], Will Whittow[1], and John Batchelor[2]

[1] Loughborough University, Loughborough, UK
w.g.whittow@lboro.ac.uk
[2] University of Kent, Canterbury, UK
j.c.batchelor@kent.ac.uk

Abstract. This paper will present antenna designs for RFID tags which can be tattooed directly onto the skin's surface. The antennas presented will be functional wearable technology with aesthetic principles which will contribute to the emerging area of Beauty Technology. These tags are suitable for the monitoring of people for a wide variety of applications. The antennas with an equivalent impedance of an RFID chip are simulated on a layered human body cubic model. Results indicated that the slot determined the operational frequency (915MHz) while the shape had only a secondary effect on the performance of the antenna. This paper shows that any shape could function as an RFID tag.

Keywords: aesthetic design, body centric communication, conducting ink, RFID.

1 Introduction

RFID technology can be used for tracking people and creating a database of their location and behaviour. Applications include patients; elderly people with dementia; firefighters; elite and recreational athletes; military and ticketing for sports and music fans attending an event. Using a tattoo that can be directly printed onto the skin has many advantages. These include the improved security and convenience to the user as a tattoo cannot be lost or stolen. Also this method is a fast process that can be carried out onsite. As the tag would be placed directly on the skin it is desirable for the tattoo to look appealing to the user. There are many possible shapes that could be considered for example a smiley face or the logo of a sports team. It is important with wearable technology and particularly beauty technology that the aesthetics are considered for the product to be accepted by the user.

Previously, the authors have considered logo antennas and tattoo RFID tags. This paper will combine the two elements together to consider aesthetic tattoo RFID tags. By using a slot as the main radiating element of the antenna there is a degree of flexibility in the overall shape. The efficiency and radiation patterns can be determined through the use of electromagnetic simulations with the antennas on generic human body models. A range of shapes are considered and the performance of each will be analysed and compared.

A. Marcus (Ed.): DUXU 2014, Part III, LNCS 8519, pp. 719–730, 2014.
© Springer International Publishing Switzerland 2014

2   Logo Antennas

Using a logo as an antenna has been looked at in [1] where the Loughborough University shield was designed as a patch antenna. The design could be scaled to the required frequency and the optimal feed point should be chosen based on the geometry. There are different challenges for different designs that would have to be addressed such as disconnected shapes or concave and angular sections.

A wearable logo textile antenna was designed in [2] which is of the authors university name. It was shown that the bending of the antenna did not affect the radiation however it did affect the impedance matching. The antenna had an Omni-directional radiation pattern that was deformed at higher frequencies but overall it showed good performance. Using a patch antenna for the City University of Hong Kong logo was carried out in [3]. By carefully designing slots it was possible to broaden the band of the patch antenna. This worked by effectively having two antennas with low Q so there is little reactance cancellation between them resulting in wideband.

3   Transfer Tattoo Tags

3.1   Tattoo Design

The usual approach for body tagging is to produce a tag on a printed circuit board substrate and often to include a metal ground plan between the body and the radiating tag [4].   Additionally, the tag is often mounted on clothing, or some object such as a wrist band, rather than directly on the skin [5].   In this paper we describe a different idea, whereby the tag is mounted directly on the skin, with a vanishingly thin insulating layer between the tag antenna and the body itself [6].   Creating such tags means they can be much more intimately interfaced to the skin for sensing functions, and also there is physical security that the transfer cannot be taken from one individual and passed to another.

The process for creating and mounting the tag uses digital fabrication (Inkjet) to deposit a layer of conducting ink on a proprietary transfer paper for creating bespoke transfer tattoos (marketed by Crafty Computer Paper: www.craftycomputerpaper.co.uk).   The processing steps are as follows: (i) the conducting tag design is Inkjet printed direct to the transfer surface of the tattoo paper.   The ink must be sintered to render the printed shape conducting; this is usually achieved by heat, but more innovative and lower temperature techniques such as plasma, chemical or photonic treatments can also be used to save energy and reduce damage to the transfer material; (ii)   a small RFID transponder chip is mounted on the printed structure, for instance using a small amount of conducting epoxy resin;   (iii)   a thin adhesive polymer layer is applied over the conducting surface as per the standard transfer process;   (iv) the transfer is inverted and attached to the skin using the adhesive;   (v) water is applied to remove the paper backing from the transfer.

The application process leaves the conducting tag sandwiched between two polymer layers. This both fixes the delicate conducting structure and isolates the ink materials from direct contact with the skin. A certain amount of optimization is required at the sintering stage to obtain usefully high conductivity values in the ink without burning the transfer paper or making the ink to brittle. The former issue degrades the ink surface and breaks the circuit, while the later makes the tattoo susceptible to failure while mounted on the flexing skin surface [7].

While mounting RFID tags directly onto the skin brings advantages for personalized sensing and interfacing, there is a significant challenge to the wireless performance owing to the very high capacitance and electrical loss associated with human tissues. Although the wireless energy associated with RFID tags is very low and does not prevent a health hazard, there is a challenge due to the effect of the losses reducing the useful transmitted power. This is alleviated by using the designs described in this paper and published elsewhere [5, 8] where the use of a slot to connect the transponder chip significantly reduces the detuning and losses experienced by other single layer designs.

The tag fields that give rise to the wireless channel exist largely in the slot and do not impinge greatly into the skin tissues underneath the tag.

The slotted loop structure dimensions are critical and dominate the tag performance as an antenna. This brings the benefit that the outer shape of the structure is of much lesser importance in the tag functionality, and there is a design freedom to profile them aesthetically. A suitable design is illustrated in Fig. 1 [8] (dimensions in Table 1) was produced to minimize the overall surface area, however, where real estate is not critical, more artistic solutions can be explored.

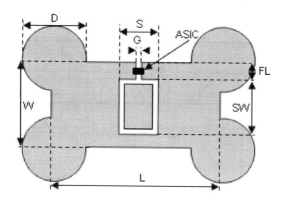

Fig. 1. Design of first prototype RFID tattoo tag [8]

Table 1. Principal dimensions of first tattoo tag design

Dimension	L	W	D	SL	SW	FL
mm	65	25	18	10	16	5.5

3.2   Simulated Results

Fig. 2 shows the distribution of the currents on the conducting tag that give rise to the radiated wireless signal.   It can be seen that the most intense currents are associated with the slot, while the current magnitude is almost zero at the outer profile.

The fabrication of the transfers has been improved via optimisation of the inkjet deposition and sintering processes, while Fig. 3 shows an early prototype sprayed onto skin via a stencil mask. In this case the skin was first protected by a thin polymer layer created by a commercial first aid spray bandage.   The edge profiling was relatively poorly defined in the stencil process and this did not compromise the tag performance.   This gave further confidence that the overall shape of the tag did not strongly influence wireless performance.

To create a proper transfer tattoo, the design was inkjet printed onto tattoo transfer paper and the conducting tag transferred to the skin.

The durability of the prototype tag was tested over a working day on a volunteer's forearm with the reading functionality regularly checked during normal office activities. The functionality did not degrade during this period.

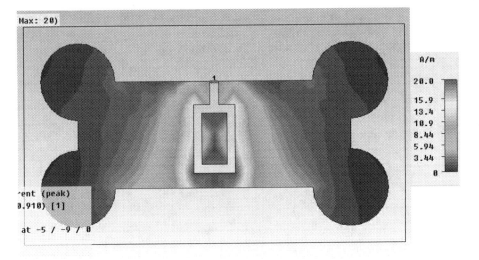

Fig. 2. Simulated surface currents of first tattoo tag design [8]

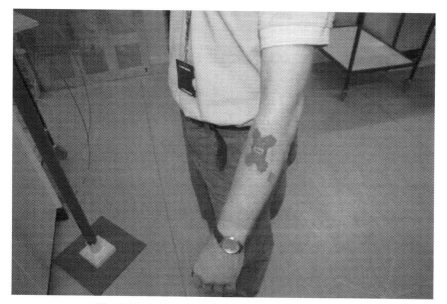

Fig. 3. First tattoo tag design during read process [8]

4   Read Range and Impedance Matching

The tags used in RFID systems can be passive which means it requires no internal energy source but instead it is powered by radiated or coupled electromagnetic waves from the reader. Due to the RF power rectifying behaviour of the chip its input impedance has a capacitive element and therefore it is not purely real [9]. For an RFID tag design to work effectively it is essential to maximise the read range which can be calculated for free space by the Friis equation [10]

$$D_{Friss} = k_{Friis} \sqrt{\tau}, \text{ where } k_{Friis} = (\lambda/4\pi) * \sqrt{((P_r G_r G_t)/P_t)} \tag{1}$$

where D_{Friis} is the predicted maximum read range, τ is the power transmission coefficient, λ is the wavelength, P_r is the power of the reader, G_r is the gain of the reader antenna, G_t is the gain of the tag antenna and P_t is the sensitivity of the RFID chip. The power transmission coefficient τ is also known as the impedance-matching coefficient and is given by [11]

$$\tau = (4R_c R_a)/ |Z_c + Z_a|^2 \tag{2}$$

where $Z_a = R_a + jX_a$ is the complex impedance of the antenna and $Z_c = R_c + jX_c$ is the complex impedance of the chip. From this equation it can be seen that the maximum transmission coefficient will occur when the impedance of the antenna is the complex conjugate of the impedance of the chip. Having the maximum transmission coefficient will result in a greater read range showing that the match between the antenna and the chip of the tag is of vast importance.

5   RFID Antenna Design

The antenna designs were based on nested slotline antennas [12] that produce a surface current on a rectangular conductive patch and radiate at the RFID UHF band.
This design can be seen in Fig. 4 and shows that the slot is halfway down the patch
and a distance t from the edge. At the centre of the slot at the edge of the patch is the
gap G between two coplanar lines which is where the ASIC RFID chip is connected.
As the ASIC has a negative reactance an inductance is required to cancel it out. This
inductance is produced by a current loop flowing around the slot which is caused by
an electric field induced inside the slot. The size of the antenna effective aperture is
large enough to provide improved efficiency through the current not being confined to
the edge of the slot and free to spread out over the patch, and the width of the slot is
small compared to the wavelength [13].

Tags have been designed using different shapes but have kept the same slot parameters as the tag for mounting on the human body that was in [6]. This tag was
designed to work at 915 MHz with the NXP G2XL flip chip strap package which had
a quoted typical port impedance of 14.8-j125 Ω. The parameters used for this tag
where L = 65 mm, W = 20 mm, l = 14.5 mm, w = 3 mm and t = 0.5 mm which were
chosen to match the impedance of the tag to the chip while optimising the gain, power
transfer and bandwidth. The different tag dimensions can be seen in Fig. 5 where the
slot for each has the same parameters as mentioned above.

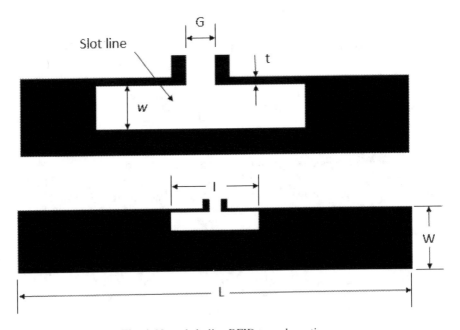

Fig. 4. Nested slotline RFID tag schematic

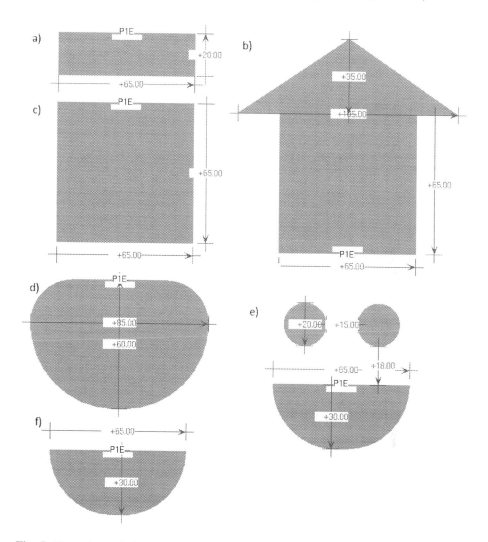

Fig. 5. Dimensions of six patches: a) rectangular, b) house, c) square, d) circular, e) smiley face, and f) semi-circle (units are in mm)

6   Antenna Simulations

To represent the tags being placed on skin a multilayer model of human tissue was used within EMPIRE based on the data in Table 2 [14]. The tag on the 4 layer human model can be seen in Fig. 6. To represent the chip on the tag a port was place in series with a capacitor across the gap between the two coplanar lines to get the appropriate complex impedance. The values chosen were a source impedance of 14.8 Ω and a capacitor value of 1.39 pF calculated from equation (3).

$$C = 1/(2\pi f X_c) \tag{3}$$

where C is capacitance, f is frequency and X_c is the reactance of the chip. The six different shapes for the patches were simulated on the 4 layer model with the port set up as mentioned above.

The gain and radiation efficiency results from these simulations can be seen in Table 3. The gain values varied by approximately 2 dB depending on the shape of the patch. This will affect the read range of tag according to the Friis equation (1). The radiation efficiency values are very low and have small variations which would account for the changes in the gain of the tags. The S11 for all the tags was around -12 dB as it is shown in Fig. 7. There are also very small changes in the shape of the graphs showing that the impedance match to the tags is mainly down to the slot and not the overall shape of the antenna. The surface currents for the patches can be seen in Fig. 8 which shows that for all the patches there are strong currents close to the slot which spread out on the surface of the tag. Fig. 9 shows polar plots of the gain for each of the tags on the human model. These plots show that the direction of the maximum gain changes depending on the shape of the patch but the value of the maximum does not change significantly.

Table 1. Human model: electrical parameters at 900 MHz from [14]

Layer	ε_r	σ (S/m)	Layer thickness (mm)
Skin and fat	14.5	0.25	5
Muscle	55	0.94	10
Bone	12.6	3.85	5
Internal organs	52	0.91	20

Table 2. Gain and radiation efficiency from simulations of the six patches

Patch Shape	Gain (dBi)	Radiation efficiency (%)
Rectangular	-18.11	0.60
House	-20.18	0.33
Square	-18.61	0.51
Circular	-18.96	0.48
Smiley face	-19.05	0.43
Semi-circle	-19.62	0.44

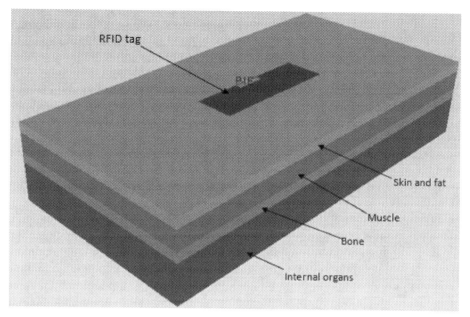

Fig. 6. RFID tag on multilayer human model

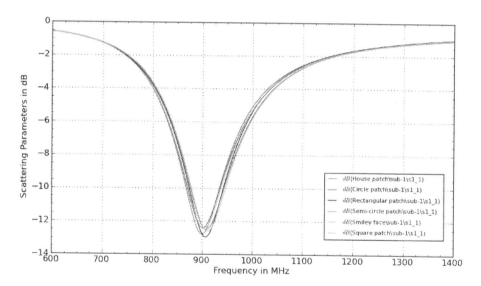

Fig. 7. S11 for the six patches

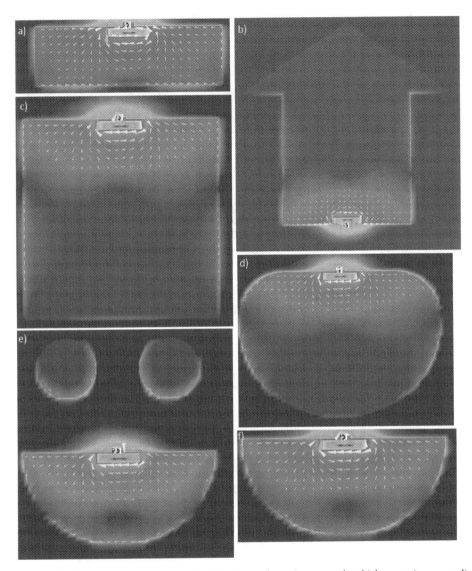

Fig. 8. Surface currents at 915 MHz for the six patches: a) rectangular, b) house, c) square, d) circular, e) smiley face, and f) semi-circle

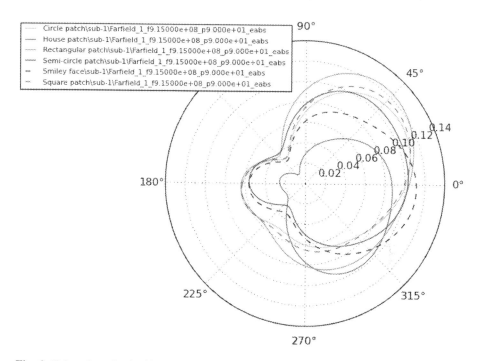

Fig. 9. Polar plot of gain Abs (phi=90) for 6 patches: a) rectangular, b) house, c) square, d) circular, e) smiley face, and f) semi-circle

7   Conclusions

This paper has introduced the concept of using aesthetic shapes for RFID tags that are tattooed directly onto the skin's surface. By using a slot as the main radiating element for the tags there is a variety of shapes that can be used for the antenna. Simulations showed that using different shaped patches but with the same slot does not have a substantial effect on the performance of the tag. The use of aesthetic shapes opens up using tattoo tags for many applications as they will enhance the user experience. Inkjet printing using conducting ink could make this a cheap and convenient process [15].

References

1. Whittow, W.: Antenna Emblems Reshaped as Icons and Esthetic Logos (Aerial). Microw. Opt. Technol. Lett. 55, 1711–1714 (2013)
2. Mahmud, M.S., Dey, S.: Design, performance and implementation of UWB wearable logo textile antenna. In: 2012 15 Int. Symp. Antenna Technol. Appl. Electromagn., pp. 1–4 (2012)
3. Chow, Y., Fung, C.: The city university logo patch antenna. In: Asia Pacific Microwave Conference, pp. 4–7 (1997)

4. Manzari, S., Occhiuzzi, C., Marrocco, G.: Feasibility of Body-Centric Systems Using Passive Textile RFID Tags. IEEE Antennas Propag. Mag. 54, 49–62 (2012)
5. Moradi, E., Koski, K., Ukkonen, L., Rahmat-samii, Y., Björninen, T.: Embroidered RFID Tags in Body-Centric Communication, pp. 367–370 (2013)
6. Ziai, M., Batchelor, J.: Temporary on-skin passive UHF RFID transfer tag. IEEE Trans. Antennas Propag. 59, 3565–3571 (2011)
7. Sanchez-Romaguera, V., Ziai, M.A., Oyeka, D., Barbosa, S., Wheeler, J.S.R., Batchelor, J.C., Parker, E.A., Yeates, S.G.: Towards inkjet-printed low cost passive UHF RFID skin mounted tattoo paper tags based on silver nanoparticle inks. J. Mater. Chem. C. 1, 6395 (2013)
8. Ziai, M., Batchelor, J.: RFID TAGs as transfer tattoos. In: 2011 Loughborough Antennas and Propagation Conference (LAPC), pp. 1–4 (2011)
9. Ghiotto, A., Vuong, T.P., Wu, K.: Chip and Antenna Impedance Measurement for the Design of Passive UHF RFID Tag. In: 2010 European Microwave Conference (EuMC), Paris, pp. 1086–1089 (2010)
10. Chen, S., Lin, K., Mittra, R.: A Measurement Technique for Verifying the Match Condition of Assembled RFID Tags. IEEE Trans. Instrum. Meas. 59, 2123–2133 (2010)
11. Nikitin, P., Rao, K.: Sensitivity and impedance measurements of UHF RFID chips. IEEE Trans. Microw. Theory Tech. 57, 1297–1302 (2009)
12. Marrocco, G.: RFID Antennas for the UHF Remote Monitoring of Human Subjects. IEEE Trans. Antennas Propag. 55, 1862–1870 (2007)
13. Kraus, J., Marhefka, R.: Antennas. McGraw-Hill, New York (1988)
14. Gabriel, C., Gabriel, S., Corthout, E.: The dielectric properties of biological tissues: I. Literature survey. Phys. Med. Biol. 41, 2231–2249 (1996)
15. Batchelor, J., Parker, E.: Inkjet printing of frequency selective surfaces. Electron. Lett. 45, 1–2 (2009)

ReFlexLab: Designing Transitive Wearable Technologies towards Poetic Aesthetics

Clemens Winkler[1] and Soomi Park[2]

[1] Zurich University of the Arts, Interaction Design, Ausstellungsstr,
60, 8031 Zurich, Switzerland
`clemens.winkler@zhdk.ch`
[2] Royal College of Art, Design Interactions, Kensington Gore,
SW7 2EU, London, United Kingdom
`soomi.park@network.rca.ac.uk`

Abstract. This paper investigates new ways of expressing emotions and desires through adaptable and wearable devices. Therefore a conceptual framework is being developed to clarify questions on new upcoming interfaces and their relation to body expression. What kind of aesthetic practices do we have for novel wearable interfaces to guide social interactions? The platform ReFlexLab is proposed, being situated in the academic and market research field, to design wearable interfaces that are changing in response to gestures, both affecting our physical and intellectual selves. Focusing on combining human expressions and emotional design with the responsiveness of new material and computational technologies, this research aims to bring up a new understanding for wearable technologies. These investigations will push novel ways to further express the complex methods of communication – methods that linger behind every bodily expression.

Keywords: Smart Material Interface, Body Interface, Transitive Materials, Transient Electronics, Adaptive Environments, Ubiquitous Computing, Clothing Physiology, Information Experience, Ecological and Environmental Concerns, Emotional Design.

1 Introduction

1.1 Background

Taking an aesthetic approach towards new wearable technologies in order to mediate between technologies and the human body, and in turn effectively facilitate interaction between human beings. Combined with our abilities in engineering, and research into technical solutions, brings a uniqueness into the work of ReFlexLab.

Compared to existing wearable technologies on the market, for example heart-rate devices, blood pressure sensors, or movement sensors, the focus of our wearable devices lies in the curiosity of new technologies, but also keeping aware of how this may affect the human body, along with potential cultural implications and consequences for natural behaviours.

A. Marcus (Ed.): DUXU 2014, Part III, LNCS 8519, pp. 731–738, 2014.

Today, there seems to be a lack of expressing emotions and desires through wearable technologies. The discrepancy between various human movements, intentions, expressions and the more static containers defined as wearable devices can often be criticized as dead extensions. So, as the human body in its responsive nature can be seen as an expressive layer, a tangible wearable interface itself could have a more mutable and responsive behaviour[1]. Influenced through nano- and bio-technologies, taking the responsive approach of nature for artificially-made systems, and cognitive sciences, investigating in dynamic behavioural patterns, brings up a route towards wearable wetware[2] rather than hardware. By converging those technologies, we can experiment in multi-facetted ways altering human intentions and body expressions. For this, it is useful to consider that new upcoming physical interfaces may fully implement the represented information using new responsive materials. By bringing in new visions such as Hiroshi Ishii´s 'Radical Atoms'[3], using reactive materials as carriers of information, it seems more related to bringing Graphical User Interfaces (GUI) and Tangible User Interfaces (TUI) into physical real-time adaptations towards 'Smart Material Interfaces' (SMI)[3]. It underlines the way we can see our whole material environment much more reactive – even seeing matter itself becoming alive. The architect Philip Beesley has claimed once in his work 'Hylozoic Ground', in a responsive installation out of many interwoven life-like objects, "we are working with subtle materials, electricity and chemistry, weaving together interactions that at first create an architecture that simulates life but increasingly these interactions are starting to act like life, like some of the ingredients of life"[4]. While his environment breathes, shifts and moves in relationship to people walking through it, touching it, and sensing it, microprocessors bring in a swarm-like intelligence. This design perspective in creative practice is adaptable to wearable animated body interfaces, which can treat or can be treated by humans.

1.2   ReFlexLab – A Creative Research Platform

Building on such effort, ReFlexLab as a creative research platform explores the combination of mutable materials and interfacing expressions of the body, its reactions and reflexes to external signals from the environment. Applications for these new wearable mutable interfaces range from health and well-being to the dialogue with the human body for posing fact and fiction of one´s own body. Materials as literally embodied interfaces in different states[5] become associated with individual needs, physical and mental conditions. The wearable material interface, nearly indistinguishable from the material human body itself, entangles with the emotional state of a person, rather than just being purely attached to the human body. How would anger, fear, excitement or attraction look like expressed by a wearable interface?

Analysing emotions, the discipline of emotional design[6], contains many complex aspects, because it is now spreading over to various fields of study and life and continuously evolving to find new meanings. One of the most important aspects of emotional design is that it can be an element for catching new demands and/or needs of users and consumers.

In the context of our current obsession with beauty and physical perfection in modern society, wearable technologies based on emotional design can find its niche. Although fashion and cosmetics have allowed people to alter or even transform their appearances by utilizing all the accessible tools of style, people often have realized the disposable nature of such efforts. Within emotional design wearable technologies can suggest an alternative solution.

1.3   Related Work

More abstractly capturing emotional states, numerous wearable electronic devices in healthcare and well-being, such as the iWatch, Google glass and the Nike Fuelband came out recently. These devices are capturing moments; people can use to act more flexible and creative in specific situations, in social relations and certain environments. In parallel, a survey at rackspace[7] showed public reaction to wearable technology has been positive, with people feeling more intelligent and better informed with equivalent devices. Additionally, through the industries of jewellery and textiles in particular, wearables have caused huge cultural implications by embedding human desires or even pure functionalities, like heat and sun protection, forcing us to embed those views into new responsive wearable technologies.

A more immersive approach comes with the body-worn devices that display information by augmenting parts of the human body. This shows the tendency to support mobile and ubiquitous interaction with information around the human body. Especially through design, here the discussion appears between the desires to implement new technologies into subtle interfaces on the human body by utilising the body. Some examples for using biological signals in computing through hand- and forearm-devices shows Skinput[8] of the Microsoft Research Group & Carnegie Mellon University. Here the skin surface interaction stays in focus. It uses the acoustic conduction properties of human skin as input system for display application. "The acoustic sensor is used to calculate the exact tissue density and other biometric data's, to determine the type of command you have given."[9] Another approach towards shifting electronics back into material related topics is the e-skin[10] project by the University of Tokyo. Through a thin stretchable film with tiny printable transistors precise control and sensing can be enabled through it. The devices can be built to be degradable for certain steps of development, f.e. in therapy.

Dattoos[11], or Data Tattoos, are printed onto the user's skin, and would identify the user via their DNA. Medical Sensor Tattoos like the Dattoos of Frog Design allow a non-invasive monitoring of real-time pH levels in a patient. Dattoos show how we are gearing to the smart self, questioning ourselves how to collect even more data. Those examples of Human-Computer-Interfaces are transferring in wearable applications in on-the-body technology - User Interfaces showing body health state.

2   Application Scenario

On the potential incorporation of new technologies on and in the human body, for example through signals induced through muscle movements, we were elaborating two practical 'wearable' devices for ReFlexLab. Our practice challenges the balance between the visible (the embodied technologies) and the graspable, tangible (outside/ inside the human body). We are studying also how interfacing the human expressions can force or reduce social interactions. In this young stage of our practice-led research platform ReFlexLab, we are offering two prototypes – 'LED Eyelash' and an electrified textile called 'Tensed up'. Rather than purely applying electronic devices on the human body, we thought about extending unconscious twinkling of the eyes into an obsession with beauty through light on eyelashes or applying electro-sensitive fabrics to measure the excitement level of a person´s behaviour and emotional state.

The first project, the LED Eyelash, explores how certain human emotions can facilitate the development of interactive design and predict why they lead people to choose particular products.

(a)   (b)

Fig. 1. (a) A wearer performed with the LED Eyelash in public space; (b) LED Eyelash

This project examines the effects of our obsession with beauty; that is, in order to calm anxiety about their appearances, people go as far as distorting their looks through plastic surgery. Asian people tend to show desires for big eyes. Sometimes the technique of makeup helps Asian women to have bigger-looking eyes. Certain types of jewellery may help as well. Asian women's desire for bigger eyes may be understood as a kind of fetish, a fetish for big eyes, which may be explicable with the plastic surgery obsession.

LED Eyelash may be a very clever product that has an inclination sensor with mercury to turn on and/or off. The sensor can perceive movements of the pupil in the eyes and eyelids. If someone wears it and moves her head, the LED will flicker following the movement. It is as simple to use as wearing a false eyelashes and as easy to remove as taking off a piece of jewellery.

The second project, 'Tensed Up'[12], shows how novel material structures with traditional crafting can suggest new shapes of wearable technology that expresses and delivers human emotion. A wearable sensor, lace-made out of conductive, nonconductive threads, enables electrical charges from excited behaviour of a person.

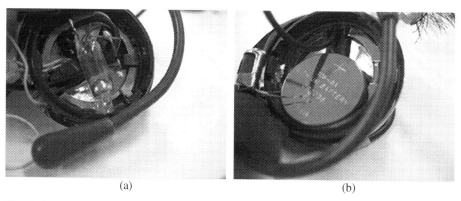

(a)   (b)

Fig. 2. (a) An inclination sensor that installed in the earpiece part of LED Eyelash; (b) a 5V battery for producing power to LEDs and sensor

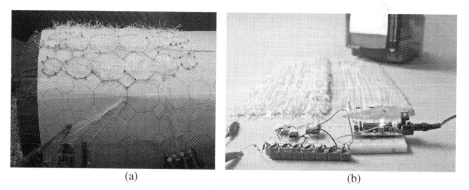

(a)   (b)

Fig. 3. (a) Tradionally lace making nonconductive and conductive threads; (b) First tests of charging and sensing the electric current stored in the fabric

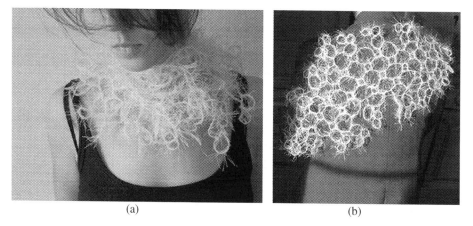

(a)   (b)

Fig. 4. (a)+(b) The finished electro-sensitive material

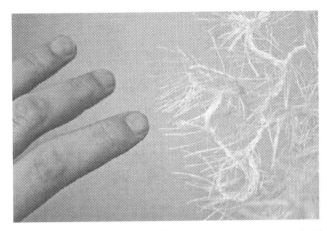

Fig. 5. A hand gesture forces the shape shifting effect through electrostatically attraction

On the shoulder of the participant the electrical charge causes exposed yarns, which represent hairs standing high related to the excitement level of the person. It gets more and more inflexible until it will discharge in its environment or to the wearer itself to interrupt and consequently remind the wearer of the energy collected over time. It can be applied anywhere onto the body.

A new responsive material has been developed to express naturally an emotional state, raising awareness without bringing the electronic or smartness of technology on the forefront. The possibility to enhance and sensitise materials was investigated to explore a change in perception. The material probe describes electric current as something natural, which has different manifestations. Inconvenient electric charges penetrate the skin and technical devices in our closer surroundings. This fabric can ask questions about cultural trends that will emerge from our constantly growing need for energy. Beside the technical aspects of textile technologies and electronics, here it is more important to focus on our (dis-)like of certain common electric/ material technologies.

2.1   ReFlexLab – A Subtle Technological Approach

ReFlexLab serves as a platform for creating and testing technologies and interweaving them on a human level, applying them to the human body, where sensations and expressions are physiologically housed and generated. By shifting new digital technologies towards the human body, specific technological logics like recognition systems for tracking gestures need to be rethought by a transitive material approach and human capacities.

How can we imagine interaction with invisible technologies, like pre-programmed crèmes, pills, liquids are reacting with the human body to guide movements and support body expressions? The example of incorporating biological signals from the human skin in multi-touch displays or applying temporarily transient electronics in pills to swallow makes new wearable technologies much more attractive for applications as it includes the human body and its aesthetics into account. Sensing the movement of the eyelids, like for capturing micro gestures concerning emotional states, can be made in a few years much more integrative over measuring electric impulses and further developed EMG, EEG devices and that is what we are aiming to integrate in our design practice.

Furthermore hypothetical systems for wearable alterations, such as the intersection of the human self, its physical environment and new technologies can be investigated. What are the social issues on immersive technologies on or inside the body and how can we emphasize in it? The surrounding issues of big data sharing or transferring via the fast growing digital technologies can be a good area to experiment the potential development of wearable technologies. By observing closely the changing human behaviours that follow the technological-cultural phenomenon of the revolution in communicative technologies could result in an implantable design output, Audio Tooth Implant[13] by Auger-Loizeau, 2001. As technology can also enter the body, this allows new proposals for the possible future of wearable concepts that adopt the social issues around human life as well as leading to human enhancement.

3   Conclusion

This paper presents ReFlexLab as a platform for designing new forms wearable technologies. It explores wearable interfaces and the human body as elements of designing new interfaces expressing and altering the human self. Methods are described through the authors' own projects or other related projects in the field. We are aiming to push new technologies further in a sense to integrate those into expressions of the human body and its aesthetics. Wearable devices as representative body extensions might be a truly material-induced approach in the field of HCI. Spreading personalized wearable expression devices could widen the scope for democratic participation in the future of social interactions. We hope to achieve surfaces, potentially less stable, therefore offering fertile involvement that requires mutual relationships and negotiation with the wearable products and surrounding environments.

"If my clothing floats and ripples outwards, and if fluxing heat and cold cloaks me, then it might not be necessary to say that the boundaries of my body lie at my skin [...] more towards the expanded physiology and dynamic form of a metabolism."[14]

References

1. Jones, R.: Soft machines – Nanotechnology and Life. Oxford University Press (2006)
2. Clark, A.: Where brain, body, and world collide. Journal of Cognitive Systems Research 1 (1999)
3. Ishii, H.: Radical Atoms: Beyond Tangible Bits, Toward Transformable Materials, MIT Media Lab. Interactions Journal (2012)
4. Beesley, P.: Hylozoic Ground: Liminal Responsive Architecture (2010)

5. Coelho, M., Sadi, S., Maes, P., Oxman, N., Berzowska, J.: Transitive Materials: Towards an Integrated Approach to Material Technology, Ubicomp (2007)
6. Norman, D.A.: Emotional Design: Why We Love (or Hate) Everyday Things. Basic Books (2005)
7. The CAST research team.: Cloud-powered wearable tech improves intelligence and self-confidence, says new in-depth study (2013), http://www.rackspace.co.uk/press-releases/cloud-powered-wearable-tech-improves-intelligence-and-self-confidence-says-new-depth (last accessed July 31, 2013)
8. Harrison, C., Tan, D., Morris, D.: Skinput: Appropriating the Body as an Input Surface. In: Proceedings of the 28th Annual SIGCHI Conference on Human Factors in Computing Systems, CHI 2010, Atlanta, Georgia, April 10-15, pp. 453–462. ACM, New York (2010)
9. John. Human Skin as a Touch-Screen Interface (2011), http://www.circuitstoday.com/human-skin-as-a-touch-screen-interface (last accessed February 18, 2014)
10. Someya, T.: Biomedical Bionics Cover Bionic Skin for a Cyborg You (2013), http://spectrum.ieee.org/biomedical/bionics/bionic-skin-for-a-cyborg-you (last accessed February 18, 2014)
11. Coxworth, B.: Dattoos would be the ultimate user/machine interface (2010), http://www.gizmag.com/datto-concept-from-frog-design/15944/ (last accessed Febraury 17, 2014)
12. Winkler, C.: Tensed Up - About the Connection of Electric Charges and Human Behaviour. In: Ambience 2011 Proceedings (2011)
13. Auger, J.: Speculative design: crafting the speculation. Digital Creativity 24(1) (2013)
14. Beesley, P.: Diffusive, thermal architecture – New work from the hylozoic series. Architectural Design. Wiley and Sons Publ. (2014)

Author Index